# SAGE PUBLISHING: OUR STORY

We believe in creating fresh, cutting-edge content to help you prepare your students to thrive in today's business world and be tomorrow's transformational leaders. Founded in 1965 by 24-year-old entrepreneur Sara Miller McCune, SAGE continues its legacy of making research accessible and fostering creative thinking.

- Our **authors** draw upon their remarkable teaching, research, and real-world experience to provide you with the most current and applied content.

- As a student-friendly publisher, we offer **affordable** choices so students can choose the option that works best for them.

- Being permanently **independent** means we are fiercely committed to publishing the highest-quality resources.

# Praise for *The Nature of Leadership*

Curated by two prominent leadership experts of our time, John Antonakis on leader charisma and David V. Day on leadership development, this handbook is a gold mine for students of leadership. Whether coming to the topic for the first time or going back to review various specific areas, readers are sure to find value. This handbook pulls together the top authors in the field writing on their explicit specialties in chapters that combine both research findings and practical cases. The chapters provide an easy way to catch up on the research in that area and to see its practical import.

**Susan Ashford**
*University of Michigan*

In this volume two of the world's pre-eminent leadership scholars have assembled a stellar cast of researchers to explore the broad range of perspectives that inform contemporary understanding of this immensely important topic. The result is a volume that explores the rich landscape of leadership with unrivalled breadth and penetrating depth. This will be an outstanding resource for readers of any disciplinary and professional background who want to journey to the heart of this fascinating field and to have to have a 360-degree appreciation of what it is all about.

**S. Alexander Haslam**
*University of Queensland*

Many leadership books are written up in a rather scholastic and dry way as an exhaustive review of the literature. The Third Edition of *The Nature of Leadership* is different. Providing both conceptual and empirical findings written by leading scholars in the field, as well as mini case studies, practical examples and TED-style talks, this book gives students the opportunity to gain valuable and up-to-date academic knowledge and insights on leadership, while making students discover a passion for leadership.

**Ronit Kark**
*Bar Ilan University*

Antonakis and Day join forces once again to shepherd a stellar group of scholars in crafting a comprehensive guidebook for the student of leadership. *The Nature of Leadership* first educates the reader about major leadership paradigms—groundwork for then exploring current leadership issues. The result is a rich and authoritative examination of what leadership is, how it happens, and why it matters.

**Cindy McCauley**
*The Center for Creative Leadership*

Antonakis and Day create another outstanding volume of their comprehensive leadership textbook, *The Nature of Leadership*. In addition to providing updated classic content that forms the basis of our current understanding of leadership study and practice, the volume addresses topics important for today and tomorrow's leaders in diverse organizations to promote innovation and purpose. The book covers crucial issues such as shared leadership, corporate social responsibility, and relational leadership between diverse leaders and followers. Readers will find both the extensive scientific evidence and practical examples important in understanding what leaders need to "do," how leaders develop the skills and abilities to "do what they must do", and also for identifying ways to assess the effectiveness of that "doing." This third edition covers all the bases!

**Susan E. Murphy**
*University of Edinburgh*

*The Nature of Leadership* by Antonakis and Day provides a comprehensive review of important substantive, philosophical, and methodological issues in the field of leadership. It is a must read for every serious student of leadership.

**Philip Podsakoff**
*University of Florida*

*The Nature of Leadership* has managed to improve substantially on the highly successful first and second editions. Besides updating the coverage, the editors and contributors have added new features to make the product far more useful as either textbook or handbook. I know of no book better suited for its target audience—those who seek an accessible and complete introduction to what we know about leadership.

**Dean K. Simonton**
*University of California*

This is a great book for anyone who wants to understand the nature of leadership! It provides an excellent overview of the fascinating field's primary theories and topics, and reveals the new and upcoming issues and questions. The inclusion of concrete study materials (e.g., cases, suggestions for further reading, discussion topics, and links to videos) also make this an ideal textbook for students.

**Barbara Wisse**
*University of Gronignen*

*The Nature of Leadership* is both unique and a tour de force. Unique, because no other book wonderfully serves three distinct audiences as a leadership textbook for undergraduate and master's students, a compendium of leadership research for doctoral students, and a state-of-the-science review on leadership for the novice and veteran researcher. Tour de force, because the topics covered—everything of importance in leadership—and the authors included—a who's who of established and rising leadership scholars—make this book a must-have for your bookshelf/e-files and courses. Enjoy!

**Francis J. Yammarino**
*Binghamton University*

# The Nature of Leadership

Third Edition

*To our first leaders, our parents:*
*Irene Bardi-Antonaki and Paul Antonakis*
*Evelyn Day and Donald Day*

Sara Miller McCune founded SAGE Publishing in 1965 to support the dissemination of usable knowledge and educate a global community. SAGE publishes more than 1000 journals and over 800 new books each year, spanning a wide range of subject areas. Our growing selection of library products includes archives, data, case studies and video. SAGE remains majority owned by our founder and after her lifetime will become owned by a charitable trust that secures the company's continued independence.

Los Angeles | London | New Delhi | Singapore | Washington DC | Melbourne

# The Nature of Leadership

## Third Edition

EDITORS

**John Antonakis**

*University of Lausanne, Switzerland*

**David V. Day**

*Claremont McKenna College*

Los Angeles | London | New Delhi
Singapore | Washington DC | Melbourne

FOR INFORMATION:

SAGE Publications, Inc.
2455 Teller Road
Thousand Oaks, California 91320
E-mail: order@sagepub.com

SAGE Publications Ltd.
1 Oliver's Yard
55 City Road
London EC1Y 1SP
United Kingdom

SAGE Publications India Pvt. Ltd.
B 1/I 1 Mohan Cooperative Industrial Area
Mathura Road, New Delhi 110 044
India

SAGE Publications Asia-Pacific Pte. Ltd.
3 Church Street
#10–04 Samsung Hub
Singapore 049483

Acquisitions Editor:   Maggie Stanley
Editorial Assistant:   Alissa Nance
Production Editor:   Bennie Clark Allen
Copy Editor:   Talia Greenberg
Typesetter:   C&M Digitals (P) Ltd.
Proofreader:   Sarah J. Duffy
Indexer:   Jeanne Busemeyer
Cover Designer:   Janet Kiesel
Marketing Manager:   Amy Lammers

Printed in the United States of America

*Library of Congress Cataloging-in-Publication Data*

Names: Antonakis, John, editor. | Day, David V., 1956- editor.

Title: The nature of leadership / [edited by] John Antonakis, University of Lausanne, Switzerland, David V. Day, Claremont McKenna College.

Description: Third Edition. | Thousand Oaks : SAGE Publications, Inc., [2018] | Revised edition of The nature of leadership, c2012. | Includes index.

Identifiers: LCCN 2017020063 | ISBN 9781483359274 (pbk. : alk. paper)

Subjects:  LCSH: Leadership.

Classification: LCC HD57.7.N377 2017 | DDC 658.4/092—dc23
LC record available at https://lccn.loc.gov/2017020063

This book is printed on acid-free paper.

17 18 19 20 21 10 9 8 7 6 5 4 3 2 1

# Brief Contents

# Detailed Contents

# Preface

## *Why* The Nature of Leadership, Third Edition?

*"If you think that anything is more important than a student, then think again!"*

The above sentence was our *leitmotif,* guiding our efforts in the third edition of this book. How can a student of leadership understand the key topics of leadership at a time when the pace of published research is increasing exponentially? The scientific record is overflowing with findings. Some of these findings are informative; others are not. How should one separate the wheat from the chaff? Where has leadership research been, and where is it heading?

For students studying leadership, trying to figure out what leadership is can be rather daunting because the topic is complex and diverse. We distinguish our book from three different types of books:

1. Encyclopedic research handbooks of leadership, which can be very long and scholastic.

2. Single-authored textbooks, which are limited by their authors' perspective and knowledge.

3. Edited books, which are usually a slap-bang collection of contributions.

Most students simply do not have the time to master a voluminous body of knowledge. Reading complex handbooks makes it hard for the uninitiated to join the dots and fully grasp the core of leadership research. Authors of single-authored textbooks simply cannot keep up with the pace of knowledge creation today, and such books invariably are slow to catch up to the current literature and might not cover all important topics. Chapters in edited books often do not flow together.

We thus worked closely with expert contributors in the key areas of leadership to provide them with a strategic overview of our volume and asked them to write on their topic, ensuring that it complemented what is in the rest of the book. We reviewed every chapter to ensure that it fits seamlessly. The book is the culmination of distinguished contributions from more than 30 contributors, including the eminent, the rising superstars, and the up and coming, but the reader will get the distinct impression that the book was single or dual authored.

What we do is evident in the title: *The Nature of Leadership*. By *nature* we mean the essence or defining characteristics of leadership; however, we also cover the term literally by looking at the evolutionary and biological bases of leadership. This book will help readers to fully understand and appreciate what leadership is by providing some background knowledge of the history of leadership research, the various theoretical streams that have evolved over the years, and current topics that are pushing the boundaries of the leadership frontier, as well as philosophical and methodological issues.

This edition of the book has changed rather substantially from the second edition. We received extensive comments from reviewers and adopters of the previous book and from our publisher at Sage. Because the book is finding a niche as a textbook to be used in upper bachelor and master-level classes on leadership, we have now ensured to pitch the level appropriately to students. We thus removed some chapters that we judged to be too complex or advanced, and added new chapters in fast-growing and important new areas of leadership; most important, we included more pedagogical material to make the book easier to learn from. We want students of leadership to love our book!

Each chapter now opens with a mini-case, "A day in the life of a leader." This mini-case covers the major topics of discussion of the chapter and includes some suggested questions to guide class discussion. All chapters include at least one table and one figure to summarize the key concepts covered; these materials are available on Sage's website so that teachers can download them and incorporate them in presentation materials in class, thus making the book easier to teach from. Each chapter also includes general discussion questions, supplementary readings, and recommended case studies. Moreover, we also suggest a publicly available video from the TED or TEDx talks (or something similar) that link to the chapter content.

We trust that our volume will continue to create interest in leadership, which is arguably one of the most important functions of society. As John Gardner (1965), the eminent leadership scholar and politician, who was instrumental in launching Medicare—and who also resigned his position because he could support neither the war in Vietnam nor Lyndon Johnson's reelection—had this to say about the importance of leadership:

Leaders have a significant role in creating the state of mind that is the society. They can serve as symbols of the moral unity of the society. They can express the values that hold the society together. Most important, they can conceive and articulate goals that lift people out of their petty preoccupations, carry them above the conflicts that tear a society apart, and unite them in the pursuit of objectives worthy of their best efforts. (p. 12)

Gardner's ideas are still valid, even more so today. Finally, as Warren Bennis eloquently elaborates in this book's conclusion, in our time, we still witness scandals, bankruptcies, war, misery, and suffering, mostly because of corrupt and immoral leadership. Yet who gave the impetus to put men on the moon? Why was South Africa able to transition out of apartheid peacefully? How does the unimaginable become concrete, whether in business, politics, or other spheres? Whether bad or good, what our leaders do matters. Between here and Bennis's concluding chapter, readers will learn to bring to light the many facets of *The Nature of Leadership*.

—*JA and DVD*

## Reference

Gardner, J. (1965). The antileadership vaccine. In *1965 Annual Report, Carnegie Corporation of New York* (pp. 3–12). New York, NY: Carnegie Corporation of New York.

# Acknowledgments

We are grateful to the world-class chapter authors who made outstanding contributions to this book. We thank you for your cooperation and for cogently distilling the most important aspects of leadership into a readable and teacher-friendly textbook and research handbook.

We are very grateful to the staff at Sage Publications for making this volume possible. In particular, we thank our acquisitions editor, Maggie Stanley, for encouraging us to edit a third edition of the book and for helping us to rethink its structure and target market. Particular thanks go to the editorial staff, especially Ashley Mixson, Alissa Nance, and Neda Dallal, as well as our production editor, Bennie Clark Allen, for keeping the project on track. We thank, too, our copy editor, Talia Greenberg, who ensured the prose was perfect. We also appreciate the reviewers and adopters of the previous edition of the book, who provided us with invaluable feedback on what to include and exclude in the third edition and how to make the book more pedagogical and useful for teaching. Finally, we thank the countless leaders who have shared their time and experiences with leadership researchers over the decades. Without them, we would have no leadership science; their world is our lab.

John Antonakis appreciates most profoundly the guidance and companionship of Saskia through the journey of life so far; the two highlights of this voyage—which have made it most interesting and gratifying—are without doubt Athena and Artemis. You have all taught me so much, and I am a more complete person for you. Baerli and Muscat, our trusty friends, need mention too, as does Roesti, who we miss much.

David Day owes a deep debt of gratitude to Bob Lord, who has been a wise and caring mentor for more than 30 years. His life is profoundly enriched by the love and support of Meghan and Emerson, who, ultimately, make it all worthwhile.

We would also like to thank the following reviewers for their invaluable feedback: Dr. Ahmed Al-Asfour, Oglala Lakota College; Theodore Brown Sr., Oakwood University; Charles B. Daniels, Old Dominion University; Osarumwense Iguisi, University of Benin, Nigeria; Dave Lees, University of Derby; Jeanette Lemmergaard, University of Southern Denmark; Oliver Mallett, Durham University Business School; Veronica Manlow, Brooklyn College; and Margaret F. Sloan, James Madison University.

—JA and DVD

# PART I

# Introduction

# CHAPTER 1

# Leadership: Past, Present, and Future

*John Antonakis*

*David V. Day*

> *There are few problems of interest to behavioral scientists with as much apparent relevance to the problems of society as the study of leadership. The effective functioning of social systems [to countries] is assumed to be dependent on the quality of their leadership. This assumption is reflected in our tendency to blame a football coach for a losing season or to credit a general for a military victory. . . . [T]he critical importance of executive functions and of those who carry them out to the survival and effectiveness of the organization cannot be denied.*
>
> —Vroom (1976, p. 1527)

The epigraph above captures three important themes in the study of leadership. First, Victor Vroom suggests that leadership objectively matters; who is at the helm determines to a large extent what will happen to the vessel, whether it is a team, an institution, or even a country. Second, Vroom demonstrates that most laypeople believe leadership matters and that the "buck stops" with leaders. In other words, leaders are ultimately responsible for what happens to the entities they lead. It is the leaders who are in the limelight and it is they who reap the rewards or are pilloried. Third, the above suggests an interesting cognitive phenom-enon that occurs in the minds of observers. Independent of what the leader does, those who observe leaders tend to "fill in the blanks." If things go well (or poorly) they will tend to evaluate the leader, whether on leadership behaviors or other vari-ables, in very favorable (or unfavorable) terms independent from what the leader might have actually done (Lord, Binning, Rush, & Thomas, 1978; Rush, Thomas, & Lord, 1977). That is, the outcomes "make" the leader, whether or not responsibility for the outcome is traceable to the leader or whether it was due to some exogenous event beyond the leader's control (Weber, Camerer, Rottenstreich, & Knez, 2001).

The above three themes seem contradictory. The first two themes say that leaders matter. The third theme suggests that leaders may not matter, in that leadership may well be a social construction (Gemmill & Oakley, 1992; Meindl, 1995). As leadership scholars, we obviously believe that leadership matters; however, both the realist and the social constructionist perspectives contribute to explaining what happens in that alchemy called "leadership." But what is leadership, exactly? That question turns out to be challenging to answer, and it is a guiding question of the book.

More than 100 years of leadership research have led to several paradigm shifts, as well as zeniths and nadirs, and much confusion. On several occasions, scholars of leadership became quite frustrated by the large amounts of false starts, incre-mental theoretical advances, and contradictory findings. As stated almost six decades ago by Warren Bennis (1959, pp. 259–260), "Of all the hazy and con-founding areas in social psychology, leadership theory undoubtedly contends for top nomination. . . . Probably more has been written and less is known about leadership than about any other topic in the behavioral sciences." In a similar vein, Richard Hackman and Ruth Wageman (2007) more recently concluded that the leadership field is "curiously unformed" (p. 43). How could such big names make such belittling statements about leadership?

For those who are not aware of the various crises leadership researchers have faced, imagine taking pieces of several sets of jigsaw puzzles, mixing them, and then asking someone to put the pieces together into one cohesive picture. Relatedly, leadership researchers have struggled for most of the last century to put together an integrated, theoretically cohesive view of the nature of leadership, invariably lead-ing to disappointment in those who attempted it. Also, the puzzle itself is changing and leadership is an evolving construct (Day, 2012). For all these reasons, there has been much dissatisfaction and pessimism in the leadership field (Greene, 1977; Schriesheim & Kerr, 1977)—even calls for a moratorium on leadership research (Miner, 1975).

Fortunately, a clearer picture is beginning to emerge. Leadership scholars have been re-energized by new directions in the field, and research efforts have revitalized areas previously abandoned for apparent lack of consistency in findings (e.g., leader-ship trait theory). Our accumulated knowledge now allows us to explain—with a high degree of confidence—what leadership is, whether its antecedents, contextual constraints, or consequences. This accumulated knowledge is reflected in our vol-ume, which will provide readers with a thorough overview of leadership that is suf-ficiently broad in scope to cover the most important topics, but sufficiently succinct so that it is not overwhelming. The book is divided into four major parts:

Part I begins with this introductory chapter, where we define leadership, provide a brief history of leadership research and where it is currently heading, and then summarize the book's contents.

Part II covers the seven major schools of leadership: individual differences; charisma and the new leadership; cognitive perspectives; relational leadership; shared leadership; and finally evolutionary, biological, and neuroscience perspectives of leadership.

Part III includes current topics in leadership: social cognition, gender, power, identity, culture, leadership development, and entrepreneurial leadership.

Part IV provides an understanding of philosophical and methodological issues: how to study leadership, ethics and effectiveness, and corporate social responsibility. It concludes with some insights from Warren Bennis, along with commentary by us.

# What Is Leadership?

Leadership is one of social science's most examined phenomena. The scrutiny afforded to leadership is not surprising, given that it is a universal activity evident in humankind and in animal species (Bass & Bass, 2008). Reference to leadership is apparent throughout classical Western (e.g., Aristotle, Plato) and Eastern writings (Rindova & Starbuck, 1997), with a widespread belief that leadership is vital for effective organizational and societal functioning.

Although leadership is often easy to identify in practice, it is difficult to define precisely. Given the complex nature of leadership, a specific and widely accepted definition of leadership currently does not exist. Moreover, our knowledge in social sciences is not yet unified, and the paradigm from which we as leadership researchers work is weak (Antonakis, 2017; Pfeffer, 1993). It would thus be difficult to get leadership scholars ever to agree on a definition. Fred Fiedler (1971), for example, noted: "There are almost as many definitions of leadership as there are leadership theories—and there are almost as many theories of leadership as there are psychologists working in the field" (p. 1).

Even in this absence of universal agreement, broad definitions of leadership and the science of leadership are required before introducing the construct as a domain of scholarly inquiry. For the purposes of this book we use the following definitions:

*Leadership is a formal or informal contextually rooted and goal-influencing process that occurs between a leader and a follower, groups of followers, or institutions. The science of leadership is the systematic study of this process and its outcomes, as well as how this process depends on the leader's traits and behaviors, observer inferences about the leader's characteristics, and observer attributions made regarding the outcomes of the entity led.*

We recognize that we are rather "leader centric" by largely describing one-way effects associated with the personal characteristics of a leader; however, we also recognize the importance of followers (in terms of their perceptions and attributions) in studying leadership. It is largely because of followers that leaders are legitimized.[1] We mention, too, that leadership is ultimately concerned with achieving a particular goal—that is, the point of leadership is to federate human and organizational resources and to coordinate these resources toward a particular outcome and hence solve complex problems. We acknowledge that leadership is rooted in a context, which may affect the type of leadership that emerges and whether it will be effective (Liden & Antonakis, 2009). We thus incorporate important definitional features to understand this phenomenon, including formal and informal leadership, the leader as person, leader behavior, the effects of a leader, the interaction process between leader(s) and follower(s), and the importance of social cognition as well as context (Bass & Bass, 2008; Day, 2012; Lord & Maher, 1991).

## What Leadership Is Not

In setting forth any definition of leadership, it is also important that we differentiate it conceptually from power and management, because these two concepts are often confused with leadership. Power refers to the means leaders potentially have to influence others, and can be defined as "having the discretion and the means to asymmetrically enforce one's will over entities" (Sturm & Antonakis, 2015, p. 139). Examples include referent power (i.e., followers' identification with the leader), expertise, the ability to reward or punish performance, and the formal power that is accorded legitimately based on one's role (Etzioni, 1964; French & Raven, 1968). Thus, the ability to lead others toward some goal, and get them to exert costly effort toward concretizing the goal, requires that one has power; whether one has formal authority or not does not matter, though by having formal authority one obtains power *ex officio*.

Regarding its distinction from management, leadership, particularly as seen from the "new" perspective (Bryman, 1992), is purpose-driven based on values, ideals, vision, symbols, and emotional exchanges. Management is task-driven, resulting in stability grounded in rationality, bureaucratic means, and the fulfillment of contractual obligations (i.e., transactions). Although some view leaders and managers as different sorts of individuals (Zaleznik, 1977), others argue that successful leadership also requires successful management, that leadership and management are complementary, but that leadership goes beyond management and that leadership is necessary for outcomes that exceed expectations (Bass, 1985, 1998; Bass & Riggio, 2006).

## The Need for Leadership

At its essence, leadership is functional and necessary for a variety of reasons (Lord, 1977). On a supervisory level, leadership is required to complement organizational

---

1. A great example of the importance of followers is discussed in the short TED talk by Derek Sivers: How to Start a Movement: https://www.ted.com/talks/derek_sivers_how_to_start_a_movement

systems (Katz & Kahn, 1978) and resolve complex task and social problems (Fleishman et al., 1991; Morgeson, 2005; Morgeson, DeRue, & Karam, 2010). On a strategic level, leadership is required to direct and guide organizational and human resources toward the strategic objectives of the organization and ensure that organizational functions are aligned with the external environment (Zaccaro, 2001); it is necessary to ensure the coordinated functioning of the organization as it interacts with a dynamic external environment (Katz & Kahn, 1978). Thus, from a functional perspective, a leader is a "completer" who does or gets done whatever is not being adequately handled by a group (McGrath, 1962).

For the organization to adapt to its context, leaders must monitor the external and internal environments, formulate a strategy based on the strengths and weakness of the organizations and the opportunities presented by the environment, communicate a vision that is inspiring, provide socio-emotional support, put in place rewards and sanctions, and then monitor outcomes so that its strategic goals are met (Antonakis & House, 2014). Some of the elements of leadership are oftentimes equated to management making the lines between leadership and management rather blurry to some; after all, leadership is not about just leading *in* organizations, but leading *of* organizations (Hooijberg, Hunt, Antonakis, Boal, & Lane, 2007; Hunt, 1991). Of course, some aspects of task-oriented influence have motivational elements and can be called leadership; also, having task-oriented expertise must precede vision communication to ensure that the right vision is chosen. Thus, leadership and management are two sides of a coin—and this currency can only have value if the leader has power.

# The Study of Leadership

In this section, we discuss how the study of leadership has evolved. Our description is succinct because many of the details relating to the different theoretical perspectives of leadership are discussed in various chapters that follow. Our intention is to provide readers with a general understanding of how leadership theory evolved into the major schools and current themes presented in this book. We then discuss two important emerging issues: how best to inform policy from robustly done research and how to integrate disparate leadership models into cohesive frameworks.

# A Brief History of Leadership Research

We have divided leadership research into nine major schools (see Figure 1.1) and classified the schools on two dimensions: temporal (i.e., the time period in which the school emerged) and productivity (i.e., the indicative degree to which the school attracted research interest in a *specific* period of time). The derivation of the schools and the research productivity of the schools are based on our professional judgment; however, we have also been guided by recent reviews of the literature that have appeared in *The Leadership Quarterly* (Antonakis, Bastardoz, Liu, & Schriesheim,

2014; Dinh et al., 2014; Gardner, Lowe, Moss, Mahoney, & Cogliser, 2010). We have also relied on several historical reviews (Bass & Bass, 2008; Day, 2012; House & Aditya, 1997; Lowe & Gardner, 2000; Van Seters & Field, 1990) to which readers can refer for more complete accounts of the history and development of leadership research. We also project how leadership research will evolve in the 2020s!

## Trait School of Leadership

The scientific study of leadership began at the turn of the 20th century with the "great man" or trait-based perspective, which saw the shaping of history through the lens of exceptional individuals. This school of thought suggested that certain dispositional characteristics (i.e., stable personality attributes or traits) differentiated leaders from nonleaders. Thus, leadership researchers focused on identifying robust individual differences in personality traits that were thought to be associated with effective leadership. In two influential reviews (Mann, 1959; Stogdill, 1948), traits such as intelligence and dominance were identified as being predictive of leadership. However, trait research, for most intents and purposes, was shut down following the rather pessimistic interpretations of these findings by many leadership scholars (see also Day & Zaccaro, 2007; Zaccaro, 2012). This crisis was the first major one faced by leadership researchers, and it took almost 30 years for this line of research to reemerge.

The impetus for the re-emergence of leadership trait theory came from a reanalysis of Mann's (1959) data examining the relationship between traits and leadership

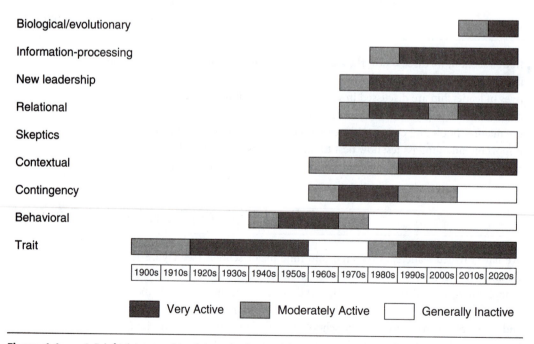

**Figure 1.1**    A Brief History and Look Into the Future of Leadership Research

using a relatively new and innovative analytic procedure at the time—meta-analysis (Lord, De Vader, & Alliger, 1986). The meta-analytic results offered by Lord et al. (1986) suggested that the trait of intelligence was strongly correlated with *perceptions* of leadership and that this effect was robust across studies included in Mann's data as well as studies published subsequent to Mann. More recent meta-analyses confirmed that objectively measured intelligence correlates with leadership effectiveness as well (Judge, Colbert, & Ilies, 2004). Studies by Kenny and Zaccaro (1983) and Zaccaro, Foti, and Kenny (1991) were also instrumental in demonstrating stable leader characteristics, such as traits related to leader emergence. There have been some high-profile reviews of the trait perspective on leadership and particularly the moderately strong relationship of the big-five personality factors with leader emergence and effectiveness (Judge, Bono, Ilies, & Gerhardt, 2002; Zaccaro, 2007).

In terms of quantity of articles published, research in leader traits is currently on the uptake (Antonakis, Bastardoz, et al., 2014; Dinh et al., 2014) and is being considered at the cusp of a renaissance (Antonakis, Day, & Schyns, 2012; Zaccaro, 2012). Moreover, inroads are being made to look at traits from a too-much-of-a-good-thing perspective (Judge, Piccolo, & Kosalka, 2009; Pierce & Aguinis, 2013); doing so shows that relations of personality (Ames & Flynn, 2007) or intelligence (Antonakis, House, & Simonton, 2017) to leadership are not linear but more likely nonlinear (i.e., inverted-U shaped for traits that are "good"), which suggests that much of the research done before on traits did not correctly model the functional form of the relation and thus potentially underrepresented the true relationships between traits and leadership.

## Behavioral School of Leadership

Given the early pessimistic reviews of the trait literature, leadership researchers began in the 1950s to focus on the behavioral styles of leaders. Similar to the Lewin and Lippitt (1938) exposition of democratic versus autocratic leaders, this line of research focused on the behaviors that leaders enacted and how they treated followers. The influential Ohio State (Stogdill & Coons, 1957) and University of Michigan (Katz, Maccoby, Gurin, & Floor, 1951) studies identified two overarching leadership factors generally referred to as *consideration* (i.e., supportive, person-oriented leadership) and *initiating structure* (i.e., directive, task-oriented leadership). Others extended this research to organization-level effects (e.g., Blake & Mouton, 1964). Leadership research, though, found itself again in crisis because of contradictory findings relating behavioral "styles" of leadership to relevant outcomes. That is, there was no consistent evidence of a universally preferred leadership style across tasks or situations. From these inconsistent findings, researchers suggested that the success of the leader's behavioral style must be contingent on the situation. As a result, leadership theory in the 1960s began to focus on leadership contingencies.

Research on behavioral theories of leadership is waning (Antonakis, Bastardoz, et al., 2014; Dinh et al., 2014; Gardner et al., 2010); however, many of the ideas of the behavioral movement have been incorporated into other perspectives of leadership (e.g., contingency theories, transformational leadership). In addition, recent meta-analytic results suggest that there is perhaps more consistent support for consideration and initiating structure in predicting leadership outcomes than has been generally acknowledged (Judge, Piccolo, & Ilies, 2004). Consequently, interest in an initiating structure (or what is also called "instrumental leadership") is again on the increase (Antonakis & House, 2014; Rowold, 2014).

## Contingency School of Leadership

The leadership contingency theory movement is credited in large part to Fiedler (1967, 1971), who stated that leader–member relations, task structure, and the position power of the leader determine the effectiveness of the type of leadership exercised. Another well-known contingency approach was proposed by House (1971), who focused on the leader's role in clarifying paths to follower goals. Kerr and Jermier (1978) extended this line of research into the "substitutes-for-leadership" theory by focusing on the conditions where leadership is unnecessary as a result of factors such as follower capabilities, clear organizational systems, and routinized procedures. Other lines of research, presenting theories of leader decision-making style and various contingencies, include the work of Vroom and associates (Vroom, 1976; Vroom & Jago, 1988; Vroom & Yetton, 1973). Whereas there is some ongoing interest in revised versions of contingency theories (Fiedler, 1993, 1995), the overall influence of the approach appears to have tapered off dramatically (Antonakis, Bastardoz, et al., 2014; Dinh et al., 2014; Gardner et al., 2010). Aspects of the contingent school now included in contextual approaches to leadership are discussed next.

## Contextual School of Leadership

Related to the contingency movement is the contextual school of leadership, which is currently enjoying growing interest (Antonakis, Bastardoz, et al., 2014; Dinh et al., 2014). This perspective has its roots, initially, in cross-cultural psychology (Hall, 1976; Hofstede, 1980, 1983, 1993, 1997; Kluckhohn & Strodtbeck, 1961; Meade, 1967; Triandis, 1995). Today, this perspective covers a broader range of issues regarding how contextual factors, like leader hierarchical level, national culture, leader–follower gender, organizational characteristics, and crises, among other factors, give rise to or inhibit certain leadership behaviors or their dispositional antecedents, or moderate what kind of leadership is seen as effective (Antonakis, Avolio, & Sivasubramaniam, 2003; Bligh, Kohles, & Meindl, 2004; Liden & Antonakis, 2009; Lord, Brown, Harvey, & Hall, 2001; Osborn, Hunt, & Jauch, 2002; Porter & McLaughlin, 2006; Shamir & Howell, 1999). Understanding the contextual factors in which leadership is embedded is necessary for advancing a more general understanding of leadership. Simply put, leadership does not occur in a vacuum (House & Aditya, 1997). Leadership is always rooted contextually, and its boundaries must be made explicit so that its nature is better understood; doing so is what makes theories more powerful and useful (Bacharach, 1989).

## Relational School of Leadership

Soon after the contingency movement became popular, another line of research focusing on relationships between leaders and followers began generating substantial attention. This movement was based on what originally was termed vertical dyad linkage theory (Dansereau, Graen, & Haga, 1975), which evolved into leader–member exchange (LMX) theory (Graen & Uhl-bien, 1995). LMX theory describes the nature of the relations between leaders and their followers. High-quality relations between a leader and his or her followers (i.e., the "in-group") are based on trust and mutual respect, whereas low-quality relations between a leader and his or her followers (i.e., the "out-group") are based on the fulfillment of contractual obligations.

Important to note is that the quality of leader–follower relations refers to affective and attitudinal outcomes. Thus, LMX is not a style of leadership but a dependent variable that is driven by some process at multiple levels of analysis, whether due to the leader, the followers, organizational level, or the context (Antonakis, Bendahan, Jacquart, & Lalive, 2014; House & Aditya, 1997); these aspects of leadership are important to study in their own right. LMX theory suggests that high-quality relations generate more positive leader outcomes than do lower-quality relations, which has been supported empirically (Gerstner & Day, 1997; Ilies, Nahrgang, & Morgeson, 2007). This line of research continues to find new directions, and overall interest in relational approaches to leadership appears to be relatively strong (Antonakis, Bastardoz, et al., 2014; Dinh et al., 2014; Gardner et al., 2010).

## Skeptics-of-Leadership School

Leadership research faced yet other series of challenges in the 1970s and 1980s. The validity of questionnaire ratings of leadership was criticized as likely biased by the implicit leadership theories of those providing the ratings (Eden & Leviathan, 1975; Rush et al., 1977). This position suggests that what leaders do (i.e., leadership) is largely attributed to performance outcomes and may also reflect the implicit leadership theories that individuals carry "in their heads" (Eden & Leviathan, 1975, p. 740). To some extent, observers attribute leadership as a way of explaining observed results, even if those results were due to factors outside of the leader's control (Weber et al., 2001). Scholars argued that these evaluations were made by observers in the process of understanding and assigning causes to organizational outcomes (Calder, 1977; Meindl & Ehrlich, 1987; Meindl, Ehrlich, & Dukerich, 1985). Thus, what leaders do might be largely irrelevant given that performance outcomes of the leader's group or organization affect how leaders are rated (Lord et al., 1978). In short, leadership was an attribution made to an individual based on how well their respective unit performed. Another related line of research doubted whether leadership existed at all or was even needed, thus questioning whether it made any difference to organizational performance (Gemmill & Oakley, 1992; Meindl & Ehrlich, 1987; Pfeffer, 1977).

Many of the above arguments have been addressed by leadership scholars who might be classified as realists rather than skeptics (Barrick, Day, Lord, & Alexander, 1991; Day & Lord, 1988; Smith, Carson, & Alexander, 1984), and there is an interest to reconcile the two perspectives into one theory (Jacquart & Antonakis, 2015). Interest in the skeptics' perspective has diminished, although there is increasing research in followers' roles in leadership processes (Gardner et al., 2010). In addressing many of the questions posed by the skeptics' school, the study of leadership has benefited from (a) using more rigorous methodologies, (b) differentiating top-level leadership from supervisory leadership, and (c) focusing on followers and how they perceive reality. Furthermore, the study of followership and the resultant information-processing perspective of leadership have generated many theoretical advances that have strengthened the leadership field immensely.

## Information-Processing School of Leadership

The major impetus for the information-processing perspective is based on the work of Lord and colleagues (Lord, Foti, & De Vader, 1984). The focus of the work has mostly been on understanding how and why a leader is legitimized (i.e., accorded influence) through the process of matching his or her personal characteristics (i.e., personality traits) with the prototypical expectations that followers have of a leader. The information-processing perspective has also been extended to better understand how cognition is related to the enactment of various behaviors (e.g., Balkundi & Kilduff, 2006; Wofford, Goodwin, & Whittington, 1998). Also notable are the links that have been made to other areas of leadership, for example, prototypes and their relation to various contextual factors (Epitropaki & Martin, 2004; Lord et al., 2001; Lord & Emrich, 2001; Lord & Maher, 1991).

Information-processing perspectives of leadership have generated much attention, and the interest in leader/follower cognitions among contributors to *The Leadership Quarterly* continues to grow (Antonakis, Bastardoz, et al., 2014; Dinh et al., 2014; Gardner et al., 2010). As a result, research in the areas of cognition, information processing—and emotions—should continue to provide us with novel understandings of leadership.

## The New Leadership School
## (Charismatic, Visionary, Transformational)

At a time when leadership research was beginning to appear especially dull and lacking in any theoretical advances or insights, the work of Bass and his associates (Bass, 1985a, 1985b, 1990; Bass & Avolio, 1994; Bass, Waldman, Avolio, & Bebb, 1987; Hater & Bass, 1988; Seltzer & Bass, 1990) and others promoting visionary and charismatic leadership theories (Bennis & Nanus, 1985; Conger & Kanungo, 1998, 1988) reignited interest in leadership research in general (Bryman, 1992; Hunt, 1999) and in related schools of leadership (e.g., trait school). The impetus for this movement was House's (1977) theory of charismatic leadership, which inspired the work of Bass (1985a); he, and previously Burns (1978) and Downton (1973), argued that the then-paradigms of leadership were mainly transactional; that is, they were focused on the mutual satisfaction of transactional (i.e., social exchange) obligations. Bass believed that a different form of leadership was required to account for follower outcomes centered on a sense of purpose and an idealized mission. He referred to this type of leadership as *transformational leadership,* in which idealized and inspiring leader behaviors induced followers to transcend their interests for that of the greater good. Transformational and charismatic leadership, and other models categorized under the heading of "neo-charismatic" approaches, currently make up the single most dominant leadership paradigm and also hold the top spot in terms of published articles in all the premier journals (Antonakis, Bastardoz, et al., 2014; Dinh et al., 2014).

## Biological and Evolutionary School

Ironically, one of the oldest branches of science—biology and evolution—is the new kid on the block in leadership studies. As with the previous edition of the book, we confirm that this new research stream—which is related somewhat to the trait perspective of leadership in terms of measuring individual differences—has come of age in leadership studies. This perspective is rooted in the hard sciences by directly measuring observable individual differences (e.g., biological variables or processes); it also considers the "ultimate" (as opposed to proximal) causes of adaptive behaviors via evolutionary processes.

This research stream is novel and is currently producing interesting findings including, for instance, the heritability of leadership emergence (Ilies, Gerhardt, & Le, 2004) and leadership role occupancy (Arvey, Rotundo, Johnson, Zhang, & McGue, 2006; Ilies et al., 2004), as well as identifying specific genes associated with leader emergence (De Neve, Mikhaylov, Dawes, Christakis, & Fowler, 2013). Other interesting avenues include studying the effect of hormones on correlates of leadership and leader outcomes (Bendahan, Zehnder, Pralong, & Antonakis, 2015; Diebig, Bormann, & Rowold, 2016; Grant & France, 2001; Gray & Campbell, 2009; Sellers, Mehl, & Josephs, 2007), neuroscientific perspectives of leadership (Balthazard, Waldman, Thatcher, & Hannah, 2012; Lee, Senior, & Butler, 2012; Waldman, Balthazard, & Peterson, 2011a, 2011b), and general evolutionary points of view on leadership (Van Vugt & Grabo, 2015; Van Vugt, Hogan, & Kaiser, 2008; Van Vugt & Schaller, 2008; Von Rueden & Van Vugt, 2015). Another trendy topic concerns the effects of physical appearance on leader outcomes (Antonakis & Dalgas, 2009; Antonakis & Eubanks, 2017; Bøggild & Laustsen, 2016; Olivola, Eubanks, & Lovelace, 2014; Spisak, Dekker, Kruger, & van Vugt, 2012; Spisak, Grabo, Arvey, & van Vugt, 2014; Spisak, Homan, Grabo, & Van Vugt, 2011; Trichas & Schyns, 2012).

We are quite sure that this school will be making major contributions in understanding the sociobiology of leadership. Interest in the area is growing rapidly. A recent special issue of *The Leadership Quarterly* was published on this topic (Lee et al., 2012), and a new call was just made in the journal on the "Evolution and Biology of Leadership."

# Emerging Issues

Researchers in leadership have put together a big part of the leadership puzzle, but there are still many pieces missing. We discuss two areas of research on which leadership researchers need to focus so that they can better inform practice. The first concerns doing more informative research, that is, focusing on estimating correctly identified causal models, which is a precondition for informing policy and practice. The second area concerns how future leadership research might be consolidated and integrated.

## Informing Policy From Properly Identified Causal Models

In all areas of science, the culmination of research efforts should be to produce theory (Kerlinger, 1986)—a theory explains a naturally occurring phenomenon by identifying how variables are causally related in some contextual conditions (Bacharach, 1989; Dubin, 1976). Research in leadership is currently facing a big challenge in this regard—we still do not have well-specified theories built on properly identified variables having proper definitions and tested causally (Day & Antonakis, 2013).

A theory, if properly specified, is able to inform, and then guide, practice. Even in the absence of a plausible theoretical explanation, scientists can still inform practice if they have precisely identified a causal relation between, say, $x$ and $y$ (Antonakis, 2017). Research must therefore be rigorously done so that it can adequately inform practice (Vermeulen, 2005), and our jobs as researchers is to ultimately identify causal relations so that we can inform policy. Whether we can provide a theoretical explanation or not is a secondary matter, though in the long run having a theoretical explanation is ideal. For instance, arguably one of the greatest discoveries in modern medicine is anesthetic. We know that, causally speaking, a patient who has been anesthetized with the correct dosage ($x$) of an anesthetic (e.g., Propofol) will not wake up ($y$) during surgery. Yet science is currently unable to provide a full explanation as to how anesthetic works, which does not preclude informing policy in an evidence-based, causal manner about the effect of the anesthetic (Antonakis, 2017).

The social sciences, in all its branches including the organizational sciences, has only recently come to terms with the fact that much of the previous research that has been done has not been causally identified (e.g., Angrist & Krueger, 2001; Bascle, 2008; Bollen, 2012; Duncan, Magnusson, & Ludwig, 2004; Foster & McLanahan, 1996; Gennetian, Magnuson, & Morris, 2008; Halaby, 2004; Hamilton & Nickerson, 2003; Larcker & Rusticus, 2010; Semadeni, Withers, & Certo, 2014; Shaver, 1998). In other words, much of the research done has been simply correlational; observing a correlation between two variables, $x$ and $y$, does not necessarily mean that $x$ causes $y$. Science, and hence practice, can only progress when the scientist is reasonably sure that this correlation is not explained by the fact that both variables are outcomes of an unmodeled cause or causes, $z$ for short. Models that have not properly accounted for omitted causes are said to be *endogeneity* plagued (Antonakis, Bendahan, Jacquart, & Lalive, 2010).

Recent surveys conducted to assess the state of the art in leadership studies shows that, because of endogeneity issues, much of the research in leadership is not causally identified and thus cannot inform policy (Antonakis, Bastardoz, et al., 2014; Antonakis et al., 2010; Fischer, Dietz, & Antonakis, 2016). It is ironic that leadership research is challenged in this way, given that one of the founding disciplines of leadership is psychology and it is psychology that has led the way in the social sciences by using the gold standard in causal design: the randomized experiment. Even though it is oftentimes not possible to randomize units—whether individual leaders, work groups, even organizations—to treatments there are many ways in which causal relations can be established without resorting to randomization (Cook, Shadish, & Wong, 2008; Shadish, Cook, & Campbell, 2002). It is therefore important for researchers to consider these issues when conducting research or evaluating research findings. Explicit links to the leadership literature have been made regarding how to use these quasi-experimental procedures (Adams, 2016; Antonakis et al., 2010; Antonakis, Bendahan, et al., 2014; Li, 2013) and readers will find ample discussion of these issues in the chapters of this volume as well (especially Chapter 16).

## Integration and Consolidation

Our field, like many others in the social sciences, does not have a strong paradigm to guide it. Consequently, it suffers from *disjunctivitis*, a proclivity to produce disjointed, redundant, salami-sliced works that are not cohesively and paradigmatically produced (Antonakis, 2017). The time is right to start putting the pieces of the puzzle together, to throw out redundant pieces, and to begin to unify what we do with other branches of the sciences.

Given how much is currently known about the nature of leadership, researchers must begin to integrate overlapping and complementary conceptualizations of leadership. Van Seters and Field (1990) argued that the new era of leadership research will be one of converging evidence and integration. In a similar vein— and almost 20 years later—Avolio (2007) urged the promotion of more integrative strategies for leadership theory building. Constructing hybrid theories of leadership, or even hybrid-integrative perspectives (i.e., integrating diverse perspectives), including not only psychological and contextual variables but biological ones as well, is indeed possible, particularly process-type models (Antonakis, 2011; Antonakis et al., 2012). An example of an integrative perspective includes the work of House and Shamir (1993), who integrated various "new" leadership theories. Zaccaro's (2001) hybrid framework of executive leadership links cognitive, behavioral, strategic, and visionary leadership theory perspectives. Zaccaro's work is also a good example of a hybrid-integrative perspective, given that he also integrated overlapping perspectives of leadership. Another recent example of a hybrid-integrative framework is the integrative approach to leader development proposed by Day, Harrison, and Halpin (2009, 2012) that seeks to connect the relatively disparate fields of expertise and expert performance, identity and self-regulation, and adult development.

There are many other ways in which hybrid approaches could be developed. For example, LMX theory—included under the "Relational School of Leadership"—has been criticized for not specifying behavioral antecedents of high- or low-quality relations (House & Aditya, 1997). LMX could potentially be integrated into behavioral or traits theories (as antecedents), as long as the modeled variables are exogenous (i.e., like leader intelligence or other traits, which cannot change as function of other variables in the model). Doing so, and when modeled using what is termed "instrumental-variable estimation," also brings an advantage by causally locking in the effect of endogenous leadership construct on outcomes and thus doing away with the endogeneity problem that bedevils most leadership models (Antonakis, 2017; Antonakis, Bendahan, et al., 2014).[2]

It is only through efforts to consolidate findings that leadership research will go to the next level, where we may finally be able to construct and test more general theories of leadership. Previous research has laid the foundations for such theories. Now, leadership researchers need to begin to conceptualize ways in which many of the diverse findings can be united, theories trimmed, and then synthesized and integrated both within and between disciplines (Antonakis, 2017). In fact, hybrid models of leadership are currently on the uptake (Antonakis, Bastardoz, et al., 2014) and we hope to see more evidence of such research when we update this book a few years from now.

# Organization and Summary of the Book

We have introduced readers to the major paradigms and current issues relating to leadership. In the remainder of this chapter, we provide a brief summary of the chapters that compose the third edition of *The Nature of Leadership*.

## Part II. The Major Schools of Leadership

**Chapter 2:** Zaccaro, Dubrow, and Kolze ("Leader Traits and Attributes") discuss the traits that are useful for predicting leader emergence and effectiveness. Beyond looking at the utility of individual traits in predictive models, they argue for more sophisticated approaches to modeling groups of traits in process models, bearing in mind too contextual conditions.

**Chapter 3:** Antonakis ("Charisma and the 'New Leadership'") reviews how leadership research shifted from models looking at task or relation focus to potent forms of leadership that are symbolic-, value-, and emotion-based. Most of these models

---

2. Many leadership behaviors or styles, $x$, are endogenous in that they are caused by other variables or simultaneously caused by the dependent variable, $y$ (e.g., a leader may be more considerate with more agreeable and better-performing subordinates). Solving the endogeneity problem is not as simple as reversing the causal arrow from $y$ to $x$. One has to model appropriate "instrumental variables" (exogenous variables) and estimate the model using an instrumental-variable estimator.

are spinoffs of charismatic leadership; this literature is critically assessed and the importance of understanding these forms of leadership for practice is highlighted.

**Chapter 4:** Brown ("In the Minds of Followers: Follower-Centric Approaches to Leadership") considers key foundations regarding followers and follower cognition. If we are to understand why followers legitimize leadership, we must first understand the inferential and attributional processes that affect how they see the leader and how these cognitive processes are also driven by context-triggered prototypes.

**Chapter 5:** Epitropaki, Martin, and Thomas ("Relational Leadership") discuss the nature of relationship leadership from a dyadic and collective point of view. Key in their chapter is discussing interactive processes between a leader and followers. They cover correlates of LMX, how relationships are maintained, as well as social-constructionist perspectives, and they discuss future directions of these research streams.

**Chapter 6:** Ayman and Lauritsen ("Contingencies, Context, Situation, and Leadership") focus on how context, broadly defined, and leadership are inextricably bound. They compare and contrast the major theories that defined this aspect of leadership research and then look at contextual variables that have been linked to leader-related outcomes so as to ultimately explain what makes the leader-situation fit optimally.

**Chapter 7:** Wassenaar and Pearce ("Shared Leadership") present the shared leadership perspective, where the focus is not on the leader but on how individuals can harness the experience and talent of all the team to collectively lead to the given goal. This perspective, which complements the leader-centric points of view, is reviewed to understand its antecedents and consequences, and well as its practical implications.

**Chapter 8:** Van Vugt ("Evolutionary, Biological, and Neuroscience Perspectives") uses evolutionary theory to provide ultimate explanations of behavior. He reviews broad-based evidence to show how selection pressures explain the psychology of leaders and followers, and also why some of our evolved behaviors may be mismatched to today's technological and cultural milieu.

## Part III. Current Topics in Leadership

**Chapter 9:** Tskhay and Rule ("Social Cognition, Social Perception, and Leadership") use a social psychological perspective of leadership to focus on the intuitive and quick judgments individuals make about leaders, often using only slivers of information to make large inferences. They link this literature to literature on prototypes and implicit leadership theories to explain emergence and effectiveness.

**Chapter 10:** Carli and Eagly ("Leadership and Gender") discuss that although few differences exist between males and females regarding leadership potential, there is underrepresentation of females in leadership roles. From the various theoretical explanations proposed, they find it is prejudice and discrimination as well as corporate cultures and male networks that impede women's progression to consequential power.

**Chapter 11:** Sturm and Monzani ("Power and Leadership") examine a key lever of leadership, power. They review various literatures, from philosophical to psychological, to show what power entails, how power is gained, and its consequences on the leader, in terms of cognition, affect, and behavior; they also discuss the impact of leader power on outcomes. whether pro- or antisocial.

**Chapter 12:** van Knippenberg ("Leadership and Identity") shows that the shared group context in which leadership occurs is critical to understanding leadership. He provides an overview of the identity approach to leadership, showing that identity shapes perceptions, attitudes, and behavior, of both self and others, and how they develop over time. Thus, the identity perspective is key to better understanding leadership.

**Chapter 13:** Den Hartog and Dickson ("Leadership, Culture, and Globalization") take a contextual approach to show that in a globalized world, we must not forget that leadership is rooted in culture. A leadership style effective in one culture may be ineffective in another. They discuss different frameworks used to describe culture and how these frameworks predict what kind of leadership is considered to be prototypical.

**Chapter 14:** Day and Thornton ("Leadership Development") distinguish individual leader development from a broader and more complete leadership development perspective that includes individual leaders, teams, and organizations. They survey the available literature on leadership development and also discuss key methodological issues that should be brought to the fore to ensure evidence-based leadership interventions.

**Chapter 15:** Renko ("Entrepreneurial Leadership") focuses on how leadership can be seen in situations involving the recognition and exploitation of entrepreneurial opportunities; such opportunities are vital for economic growth, especially in developing countries. Renko covers the measurement of entrepreneurial leadership and also identifies its causes and consequences.

## Part IV: Philosophical and Methodological Issues in Leadership

**Chapter 16:** Jacquart, Cole, Gabriel, Koopman, and Rosen ("Studying Leadership: Research Design and Methods") introduce the design conditions needed to study leadership scientifically. They introduce an overlooked threat to the validity of research—endogeneity—along with the conditions that engender it, and how it can be avoided using the experimental method as well as quasi-experimental analogs.

**Chapter 17:** Ciulla ("Ethics and Effectiveness: The Nature of Good Leadership") writes from the perspective of a philosopher to discuss what leadership is but also what technically and morally good leadership should be. Ciulla highlights ethical dilemmas of leaders, the importance of judging the ethics of leader outcomes in the short and long run, and the implications for leader–follower relations.

**Chapter 18:** Palazzo ("Corporate Social Responsibility and Leadership") argues that a key pillar of corporate legitimacy is corporate social responsibility. He makes explicit the importance of leadership for the social and environmental outcomes of organizations, particularly in current times where organizations operate in regulatory voids and where there is much scrutiny of corporations by various stakeholders.

**Chapter 19:** Bennis ("The Chronicles of Leadership") takes the reader on an odyssey of leadership and captivates the reader with his engaging writing style. The importance of leadership for the functioning of organizations is amply made clear by Bennis, who brings to light key leadership issues in political and economic contexts. His wise words and counsel are timeless; they are also priceless for future leaders.

# Enjoy the Book

In the last century, the often-misunderstood phenomenon of leadership has been tossed and battered while social scientists tried to make sense of a force they knew was important, but which seemed beyond the reach of scientific inquiry. Remarking about the difficulties leadership researchers have faced, Bennis (1959, p. 260) noted: "Always, it seems, the concept of leadership eludes us or turns up in another form to taunt us again with its slipperiness and complexity." Not anymore!

Our book will introduce you to what is a fascinating body of research on a consequential topic. As you read the chapters that follow, the complexity and mystique that may have surrounded the leadership concept before you picked up this book will turn into understanding. Perhaps this understanding may turn into passion to learn more about leadership as you see how critical the need for effective leadership is in our lifetimes.

Science has confirmed what humans intuitively knew through the ages: Leadership matters. But we know a whole lot more than that as well, including how to better select leaders, how to train them, along with many other important topics discussed in this book. Although we all have much to learn about leadership, we are guided by a spirit of optimism emanating from the findings of those researchers before us who went through their own "crucibles"—trying events. Pummeled but unbowed, they continued to study leadership and to inspire succeeding generations of scientists to continue their exploration.

All the while, leaders influenced followers and will continue to do so, regardless of the fads, follies, and folderol that have distracted leadership researchers in the past.

## References

Adams, R. B. (2016). Women on boards: The superheroes of tomorrow? *The Leadership Quarterly, 27*(3), 371–386.

Ames, D. R., & Flynn, F. J. (2007). What breaks a leader: The curvilinear relation between assertiveness and leadership. *Journal of Personality and Social Psychology, 92*(2), 307–324.

Angrist, J. D., & Krueger, A. B. (2001). Instrumental variables and the search for identification: From supply and demand to natural experiments. *Journal of Economic Perspectives, 15*(4), 69–85.

Antonakis, J. (2011). Predictors of leadership: The usual suspects and the suspect traits. In A. Bryman, D. Collinson, K. Grint, B. Jackson, & M. Uhl-Bien (Eds.), *Sage handbook of leadership* (pp. 269–285). Thousand Oaks, CA: Sage.

Antonakis, J. (2017). On doing better science: From thrill of discovery to policy implications. *The Leadership Quarterly, 28*(1), 5–21.

Antonakis, J., Avolio, B. J., & Sivasubramaniam, N. (2003). Context and leadership: An examination of the nine-factor full-range leadership theory using the Multifactor Leadership Questionnaire. *The Leadership Quarterly, 14*, 261–295.

Antonakis, J., Bastardoz, N., Liu, Y., & Schriesheim, C. A. (2014). What makes articles highly cited? *The Leadership Quarterly, 25*(1), 152–179.

Antonakis, J., Bendahan, S., Jacquart, P., & Lalive, R. (2010). On making causal claims: A review and recommendations. *The Leadership Quarterly, 21*, 1086–1120.

Antonakis, J., Bendahan, S., Jacquart, P., & Lalive, R. (2014). Causality and endogeneity: Problems and solutions. In D. V. Day (Ed.), *The Oxford handbook of leadership and organizations* (pp. 93–117). New York, NY: Oxford University Press.

Antonakis, J., & Dalgas, O. (2009). Predicting elections: Child's play! *Science, 323*(5918), 1183.

Antonakis, J., Day, D. V., & Schyns, B. (2012). Leadership and individual differences: At the cusp of a renaissance. *The Leadership Quarterly, 23*(4), 643–650.

Antonakis, J., & Eubanks, D. L. (2017). Looking leadership in the face. *Current Directions in Psychological Science, 26*(3), 270–275.

Antonakis, J., & House, R. J. (2014). Instrumental leadership: Measurement and extension of transformational-transactional leadership theory. *The Leadership Quarterly, 25*, 746–771.

Antonakis, J., House, R. J., & Simonton, D. K. (2017). Can super smart leaders suffer from too much of a good thing? The curvilinear effect of intelligence on perceived leadership behavior. *Journal of Applied Psychology*. Advance online publication. doi:10.1037/apl0000221

Aristotle. (1954). *Rhetoric* (1st Modern Library ed.). (W. Rhys Roberts, Trans.). New York, NY: Modern Library.

Arvey, R. D., Rotundo, M., Johnson, W., Zhang, Z., & McGue, M. (2006). The determinants of leadership role occupancy: Genetic and personality factors. *The Leadership Quarterly, 17*(1), 1–20.

Avolio, B. J. (2007). Promoting more integrative strategies for leadership theory-building. *American Psychologist, 62*(1), 25.

Bacharach, S. B. (1989). Organizational theories: Some criteria for evaluation. *Academy of Management Review, 14*(4), 496–515.

Balkundi, P., & Kilduff, M. (2006). The ties that lead: A social network approach to leadership. *The Leadership Quarterly, 17*(4), 419–439.

Balthazard, P. A., Waldman, D. A., Thatcher, R. W., & Hannah, S. T. (2012). Differentiating transformational and non-transformational leaders on the basis of neurological imaging. *Leadership Quarterly, 23*(2), 244–258.

Barrick, M. R., Day, D. V., Lord, R. G., & Alexander, R. A. (1991). Assessing the utility of executive leadership. *The Leadership Quarterly, 2*(1), 9–22.

Bascle, G. (2008). Controlling for endogeneity with instrumental variables in strategic management research. *Strategic Organization, 6*(3), 285–327.

Bass, B. M. (1985a). *Leadership and performance beyond expectations*. New York, NY: Free Press.

Bass, B. M. (1985b). Leadership: Good, better, best. *Organizational Dynamics, 13*(3), 26–40.

Bass, B. M. (1990). From transactional to transformational leadership: Learning to share the vision. *Organizational Dynamics, 19*(3), 19–31.

Bass, B. M., & Avolio, B. J. (Eds.). (1994). *Improving organizational effectiveness through transformational leadership*. Thousand Oaks, CA: Sage.

Bass, B. M., & Bass, R. (2008). *The Bass handbook of leadership: Theory, research, and managerial applications* (4th ed.). New York, NY: Free Press.

Bass, B. M., Waldman, D. A., Avolio, B. J., & Bebb, M. (1987). Transformational leadership and the falling dominoes effect. *Group and Organization Studies, 12*(1), 73–87.

Bendahan, S., Zehnder, C., Pralong, F. P., & Antonakis, J. (2015). Leader corruption depends on power and testosterone. *The Leadership Quarterly, 26*, 101–122.

Bennis, W. G. (1959). Leadership theory and administrative beahvior: The problem of authority. *Administrative Science Quarterly, 4*(3), 259–301.

Bennis, W. G., & Nanus, B. (1985). *Leaders: The strategies for taking charge*. New York, NY: Harper & Row.

Blake, R. R., & Mouton, J. S. (1964). *The managerial grid*. Houston, TX: Gulf.

Bligh, M. C., Kohles, J. C., & Meindl, J. R. (2004). Charisma under crisis: Presidential leadership, rhetoric, and media responses before and after the September 11th terrorist attacks. *The Leadership Quarterly, 2*(15), 211–239.

Bøggild, T., & Laustsen, L. (2016). An intra-group perspective on leader preferences: Different risks of exploitation shape preferences for leader facial dominance. *The Leadership Quarterly, 27*(6), 820–837.

Bollen, K. A. (2012). Instrumental variables in sociology and the social sciences. *Annual Review of Sociology, 38*(1), 37–72.

Bryman, A. (1992). *Charisma and leadership in organizations*. London, UK: Sage.

Burns, J. M. (1978). *Leadership*. New York, NY: Harper & Row.

Calder, B. J. (1977). An attribution theory of leadership. In B. M. Straw & G. R. Salancik (Eds.), *New directions in organizational behavior* (pp. 179–204). Chicago, IL: St Clair.

Conger, J. A., & Kanungo, R. N. (Eds.). (1988). *Charismatic leadership: The elusive factor in organizational effectiveness*. San Francisco, CA: Jossey-Bass.

Conger, J. A., & Kanungo, R. N. (1998). *Charismatic leadership in organizations*. Thousand Oaks, CA: Sage.

Cook, T. D., Shadish, W. R., & Wong, V. C. (2008). Three conditions under which experiments and observational studies produce comparable causal estimates: New findings from within-study comparisons. *Journal of Policy Analysis and Management, 27*(4), 724–750.

Dansereau, F., Graen, G. B., & Haga, W. J. (1975). A vertical dyad linkage approach to leadership within formal organizations: A longitudinal investigation of the role making process. *Organizational Behavior and Human Performance, 13*, 46–78.

Day, D. V. (2012). Leadership. In S. W. J. Kozlowski (Ed.), *The Oxford handbook of organizational psychology* (pp. 696–729). New York, NY: Oxford University Press.

Day, D. V., & Antonakis, J. (2013). The future of leadership. In H. S. Leonard, R. Lewis, A. M. Freedman, & J. Passmore (Eds.), *The Wiley-Blackwell handbook of the psychology of leadership, change and organizational development* (pp. 221–235). Oxford, UK: John Wiley & Sons.

Day, D. V., Harrison, M. M., & Halpin, S. M. (2012). *An integrative approach to leader development: Connecting adult development, identity, and expertise*: New York, NY: Psychology Press.

Day, D. V., & Lord, R. G. (1988). Executive leadership and organizational performance: Suggestions for a new theory and methodology. *Journal of Management, 14*(3), 453–464.

Day, D. V., & Zaccaro, S. J. (2007). Leadership: A critical historical analysis of the influence of leader traits. In L. L. Koppes (Ed.), *Historical perspectives in industrial and organizational psychology* (pp. 383–405). Mahwah, NJ: Lawrence Erlbaum.

De Neve, J.-E., Mikhaylov, S., Dawes, C. T., Christakis, N. A., & Fowler, J. H. (2013). Born to lead? A twin design and genetic association study of leadership role occupancy. *The Leadership Quarterly, 24*(1), 45–60.

Diebig, M., Bormann, K. C., & Rowold, J. (2016). A double-edged sword: Relationship between full-range leadership behaviors and followers' hair cortisol level. *The Leadership Quarterly, 27*(6), 684–696.

Dinh, J. E., Lord, R. G., Gardner, W. L., Meuser, J. D., Liden, R. C., & Hu, J. (2014). Leadership theory and research in the new millennium: Current theoretical trends and changing perspectives. *The Leadership Quarterly, 25*(1), 36–62.

Downton, J. V. (1973). *Rebel leadership: Commitment and charisma in the revolutionary process.* New York, NY: Free Press.

Dubin, R. (1976). Theory building in applied areas. In M. D. Dunnette (Ed.), *Handbook of industrial and organizational psychology* (pp. 17–40). Chicago, IL: Rand McNally.

Duncan, G. J., Magnusson, K. A., & Ludwig, J. (2004). The endogeneity problem in developmental studies. *Research in Human Development, 1*, 59–80.

Eden, D., & Leviathan, U. (1975). Implicit leadership theory as a determinant of the factor structure underlying supervisory behavior scales. *Journal of Applied Psychology, 60*(6), 736–741.

Epitropaki, O., & Martin, R. (2004). Implicit leadership theories in applied settings: Factor structure, generalizability, and stability over time. *Journal of Applied Psychology, 89*(2), 293–310.

Etzioni, A. (1964). *Modern organizations.* Englewood Cliffs, NJ: Prentice-Hall.

Fiedler, F. E. (1967). *A theory of leadership effectiveness.* New York, NY: McGraw-Hill.

Fiedler, F. E. (1971). *Leadership.* New York, NY: General Learning Press.

Fiedler, F. E. (1993). The leadership situation and the black box in contingency theories. In M. M. Chemers & R. Ayman (Eds.), *Leadership theory and research: Perspectives and directions* (pp. 1–28). San Diego, CA: Academic Press.

Fiedler, F. E. (1995). Cognitive resources and leadership performance. *Applied Psychology, 44*(1), 5–28.

Fischer, T., Dietz, J., & Antonakis, J. (2016). Leadership process model: A review and synthesis. *Journal of Management.* Advance online publication. doi:10.1177/0149206316682830

Fleishman, E. A., Mumford, M. D., Zaccaro, S. J., Levin, K. Y., Korotkin, A. L., & Hein, M. B. (1991). Taxonomic efforts in the description of leader behavior: A synthesis and functional interpretation. *The Leadership Quarterly, 2*(4), 245–287.

Foster, E. M., & McLanahan, S. (1996). An illustration of the use of instrumental variables: Do neighborhood conditions affect a young person's change of finishing high school? *Psychological Methods, 1*(3), 249–260.

French, J. R. P., & Raven, B. H. (1968). The bases of social power. In D. Cartwright & A. F. Zander (Eds.), *Group dynamics: Research and theory* (3rd ed., pp. 259–269). New York, NY: Harper & Row.

Gardner, W. L., Lowe, K. B., Moss, T. W., Mahoney, K. T., & Cogliser, C. C. (2010). Scholarly leadership of the study of leadership: A review of *The Leadership Quarterly*'s second decade, 2000–2009. *The Leadership Quarterly, 12*(6), 922–958.

Gemmill, G., & Oakley, J. (1992). Leadership: An alienating social myth? *Human Relations, 45*(2), 113–129.

Gennetian, L. A., Magnuson, K., & Morris, P. A. (2008). From statistical associations to causation: What developmentalists can learn from instrumental variables techniques coupled with experimental data. *Developmental Psychology, 44*(2); 381–394.

Gerstner, C. R., & Day, D. V. (1997). Meta-analytic review of leader–member exchange theory: Correlates and construct issues. *Journal of Applied Psychology, 82*(6), 827–844.

Graen, G. B., & Uhl-bien, M. (1995). Relationship-based approach to leadership: Development of leader–member exchange (LMX) theory of leadership over 25 years: Applying a multi-level multi-domain perspective. *Leadership Quarterly, 6*(2), 219–247.

Grant, V. J., & France, J. T. (2001). Dominance and testosterone in women. *Biological Psychology, 58*(1), 41–47.

Gray, P. B., & Campbell, B., C. (2009). Human male testosterone, pair-bonding, and fatherhood. In P. T. Ellison & P. B. Gray (Eds.), *Endocrinology of social relationships* (pp. 270–293). Cambridge, MA: Harvard University Press.

Greene, C. N. (1977). Disenchantment with leadership research: Some causes, recommendations, and alternative directions. In J. G. Hunt & L. L. Larson (Eds.), *Leadership: The cutting edge* (pp. 57–67). Carbondale: Southern Illinois University Press.

Hackman, J. R., & Wageman, R. (2007). Asking the right questions about leadership. *American Psychologist, 62*, 43–47.

Halaby, C. N. (2004). Panel models in sociological research: Theory into practice. *Annual Review of Sociology, 30,* 507–544.

Hall, E. T. (1976). *Beyond culture.* Garden City, NY: Anchor Press/Doubleday.

Hamilton, B. H., & Nickerson, J. A. (2003). Correcting for endogeneity in strategic management research. *Strategic Organization, 1*(1), 51–78.

Hater, J. J., & Bass, B. M. (1988). Superiors' evaluations and subordinates' perceptions of transformational and transactional leadership. *Journal of Applied Psychology, 73*(4), 695–702.

Hofstede, G. H. (1980). Motivation, leadership, and organization: Do American theories apply abroad? *Organizational Dynamics,* 42–63.

Hofstede, G. H. (1983). The cultural relativity of organizational practices and theories. *Journal of International Business Studies,* 75–89.

Hofstede, G. H. (1993). Cultural constraints in management theories. *Academy of Management Executive, 7*(1), 81–94.

Hofstede, G. H. (1997). *Cultures and organizations: Software of the mind* (Rev. ed.). New York, NY: McGraw-Hill.

Hooijberg, R., Hunt, J. G., Antonakis, J., Boal, K. B., & Lane, N. (Eds.). (2007). *Being there even when you are not: Leading through strategy, structures, and systems.* Amsterdam, Netherlands: Elsevier Science.

House, R. J. (1971). Path-goal theory of leadership effectiveness. *Administrative Science Quarterly, 16*(3), 321–339.

House, R. J. (1977). A 1976 theory of charismatic leadership. In J. G. Hunt & L. L. Larson (Eds.), *The cutting edge* (pp. 189–207). Carbondale: Southern Illinois University Press.

House, R. J., & Aditya, R. N. (1997). The social scientific study of leadership: Quo vadis? *Journal of Management, 23*(3), 409–473.

House, R. J., & Shamir, B. (1993). Toward the integration of transformational, charismatic, and visionary theories. In M. M. Chemers & R. Ayman (Eds.), *Leadership theory and research: Perspectives and directions* (pp. 167–188). San Diego, CA: Academic Press.

Hunt, J. G. (1991). *Leadership: A new synthesis.* Newbury Park, CA: Sage.

Hunt, J. G. (1999). Tranformational/charismatic leadership's transformation of the field: An historical essay. *The Leadership Quarterly, 10*(2), 129–144.

Ilies, R., Gerhardt, M. W., & Le, H. (2004). Individual differences in leadership emergence: Integrating meta-analytic findings and behavioral genetics estimates. *International Journal of Selection and Assessment, 12*(3), 207–219.

Ilies, R., Nahrgang, J. D., & Morgeson, F. P. (2007). Leader–member exchange and citizenship behaviors: A meta-analysis. *Journal of Applied Psychology, 92*(1), 269–277.

Jacquart, P., & Antonakis, J. (2015). When does charisma matter for top-level leaders? Effect of attributional ambiguity. *Academy of Management Journal, 58,* 1051–1074.

Judge, T. A., Bono, J. E., Ilies, R., & Gerhardt, M. W. (2002). Personality and leadership: A qualitative and quantitative review. *Journal of Applied Psychology, 87,* 765–780.

Judge, T. A., Colbert, A. E., & Ilies, R. (2004). Intelligence and leadership: A quantitative review and test of theoretical propositions. *Journal of Applied Psychology, 89,* 542–552.

Judge, T. A., Piccolo, R. F., & Ilies, R. (2004). The forgotten ones? The validity of consideration and initiating structure in leadership research. *Journal of Applied Psychology, 89*(1), 36–51.

Judge, T. A., Piccolo, R. F., & Kosalka, T. (2009). The bright and dark sides of leader traits: A review and theoretical extension of the leader trait paradigm. *The Leadership Quarterly, 20,* 855–875.

Katz, D., & Kahn, R. L. (1978). *The social psychology of organizations.* New York, NY: John Wiley & Sons.

Katz, D., Maccoby, N., Gurin, G., & Floor, L. G. (1951). *Productivity, supervision and morale among railroad workers.* Ann Arbor: Survey Research Center, Institute for Social Research, University of Michigan.

Kenny, D. A., & Zaccaro, S. J. (1983). An estimate of variance due to traits in leadership. *Journal of Applied Psychology, 68*(4), 678–685.

Kerlinger, F. N. (1986). *Foundations of behavioral research* (3rd ed.). New York, NY: Holt, Rinehart and Winston.

Kerr, S., & Jermier, J. M. (1978). Substitutes for leadership: Their meaning and measurement. *Organizational Behavior and Human Performance, 22,* 375–403.

Kluckhohn, F. R., & Strodtbeck, F. L. (1961). *Variations in value orientations.* Evanston, IL: Row, Peterson, and Company.

Larcker, D. F., & Rusticus, T. O. (2010). On the use of instrumental variables in accounting research. *Journal of Accounting and Economics, 49*(3), 186–205.

Lee, N., Senior, C., & Butler, M. (2012). Leadership research and cognitive neuroscience: The state of this union. *The Leadership Quarterly, 23*(2), 213–218.

Lewin, K., & Lippitt, R. (1938). An experimental approach to the study of autocracy and democracy: A preliminary note. *Sociometry, 1*(3/4), 292–300.

Li, M. (2013). Social network and social capital in leadership and management research: A review of causal methods. *The Leadership Quarterly, 24*(5), 638–665.

Liden, R. C., & Antonakis, J. (2009). Considering context in psychological leadership research. *Human Relations, 62*(11), 1587–1605.

Lord, R. G. (1977). Functional leadership behavior: Measurement and relation to social power and leadership perceptions. *Administrative Science Quarterly, 22*, 114–133.

Lord, R. G., Binning, J. F., Rush, M. C., & Thomas, J. C. (1978). The effect of performance cues and leader behavior on questionnaire ratings of leadership behavior. *Organizational Behavior and Human Performance, 21*(1), 27–39.

Lord, R. G., Brown, D. J., Harvey, J. L., & Hall, R. J. (2001). Contextual constraints on prototype generation and their multilevel consequences for leadership perceptions. *The Leadership Quarterly, 12*, 311–338.

Lord, R. G., De Vader, C. L., & Alliger, G. M. (1986). A meta-analysis of the relation between personality traits and leadership perceptions: An application of validity generalization procedures. *Journal of Applied Psychology, 71*, 402–410.

Lord, R. G., & Emrich, C. G. (2001). Thinking outside the box by looking inside the box: Extending the cognitive revolution in leadership research. *The Leadership Quarterly, 11*(4), 551–579.

Lord, R. G., Foti, R. J., & De Vader, C. L. (1984). A test of leadership categorization theory: Internal structure, information processing, and leadership perceptions. *Organizational Behavior and Human Performance, 34*, 343–378.

Lord, R. G., & Maher, K. J. (1991). *Leadership and information processing: Linking perceptions and performance.* Boston, MA: Unwin Hyman.

Lowe, K. B., & Gardner, W. L. (2000). Ten years of the *Leadership Quarterly*: Contributions and challenges for the future. *The Leadership Quarterly, 11*(4), 459–514.

Mann, R. D. (1959). A review of the relationship between personality and performance in small groups. *Psychological Bulletin, 56*(4), 241–270.

McGrath, J. E. (1962). *Leadership behavior: Some requirements for leadership training.* Washington, DC: U.S. Civil Service Commission, Office of Career Development.

Meade, R. D. (1967). An experimental study of leadership in India. *The Journal of Social Psychology, 72*, 35–43.

Meindl, J. R. (1995). The romance of leadership as a follower-centric theory: A social constructionist approach. *The Leadership Quarterly, 6*(3), 329–341.

Meindl, J. R., & Ehrlich, S. B. (1987). The romance of leadership and the evaluation of organizational performance. *Academy of Management Journal, 30*(1), 91–109.

Meindl, J. R., Ehrlich, S. B., & Dukerich, J. M. (1985). The romance of leadership. *Administrative Science Quarterly, 30*(1), 78–102.

Miner, J. B. (1975). The uncertain future of the leadership concept. An overview. In J. G. Hunt & L. L. Larson (Eds.), *Leadership frontiers* (pp. 197–208). Kent, OH: Kent State University.

Morgeson, F. P. (2005). The external leadership of self-managing teams: Intervening in the context of novel and disruptive events. *Journal of Applied Psychology, 90*(3), 497–508.

Morgeson, F. P., DeRue, D. S., & Karam, E. P. (2010). Leadership in teams: A functional approach to understanding leadership structures and processes. *Journal of Management, 36*(1), 5–39.

Olivola, C. Y., Eubanks, D. L., & Lovelace, J. B. (2014). The many (distinctive) faces of leadership: Inferring leadership domain from facial appearance. *The Leadership Quarterly, 25*(5), 817–834.

Osborn, R. N., Hunt, J. G., & Jauch, L. R. (2002). Toward a contextual theory of leadership. *The Leadership Quarterly, 13*(6), 797–837.

Pfeffer, J. (1977). The ambiguity of leadership. *Academy of Management Review, 1,* 104–112.

Pfeffer, J. (1993). Barriers to the advance of organizational science: Paradigm development as a dependent variable. *The Academy of Management Review, 18*(4), 599–620.

Pierce, J. R., & Aguinis, H. (2013). The too-much-of-a-good-thing effect in management. *Journal of Management, 39,* 313–338.

Plato. (1901). *The republic of Plato; an ideal commonwealth* (Rev. ed.). (B. Jowett, Trans.). New York, NY: Colonial Press.

Porter, L. W., & McLaughlin, G. B. (2006). Leadership and the organizational context: Like the weather? *The Leadership Quarterly, 17*(6), 559–576.

Rindova, V. P., & Starbuck, W. H. (1997). Ancient Chinese theories of control. *Journal of Management Inquiry, 6*(2), 144–159.

Rowold, J. (2014). Instrumental leadership: Extending the transformational-transactional leadership paradigm. *German Journal of Human Resource Management, 28*(3), 367–390.

Rush, M. C., Thomas, J. C., & Lord, R. G. (1977). Implicit leadership theory: A potential threat to the internal validity of leader behavior questionnaires. *Organizational Behavior and Human Performance, 20,* 93–110.

Schriesheim, C. A., & Kerr, S. (1977). Theories and measures of leadership: A critical appraisal of current and future directions. In J. G. Hunt & L. L. Larson (Eds.), *Leadership: The cutting edge* (pp. 9–45). Carbondale: Southern Illinois University Press.

Sellers, J. G., Mehl, M. R., & Josephs, R. A. (2007). Hormones and personality: Testosterone as a marker of individual differences. *Journal of Research in Personality, 41*(1), 126–138.

Seltzer, J., & Bass, B. M. (1990). Transformational leadership: Beyond initiation and consideration. *Journal of Management, 16*(4), 693–703.

Semadeni, M., Withers, M. C., & Certo, S. T. (2014). The perils of endogeneity and instrumental variables in strategy research: Understanding through simulations. *Strategic Management Journal, 35*(7), 1070–1079.

Shadish, W. R., Cook, T. D., & Campbell, D. T. (2002). *Experimental and quasi-experimental designs for generalized causal inference.* Boston, MA: Houghton Mifflin.

Shamir, B., & Howell, J. M. (1999). Organizational and contextual influences on the emergence and effectiveness of charismatic leadership. *The Leadership Quarterly, 10*(2), 257–283.

Shaver, J. M. (1998). Accounting for endogeneity when assessing strategy performance: Does entry mode choice affect FDI survival? *Management Science, 44*(4), 571–585.

Smith, J. E., Carson, K. P., & Alexander, R. A. (1984). Leadership: It can make a difference. *Academy of Management Journal, 27*(4), 765–776.

Spisak, B. R., Dekker, P. H., Kruger, M., & van Vugt, M. (2012). Warriors and peacekeepers: Testing a biosocial implicit leadership hypothesis of intergroup relations using masculine and feminine faces. *PLoS ONE, 7*(1).

Spisak, B. R., Grabo, A. E., Arvey, R. D., & van Vugt, M. (2014). The age of exploration and exploitation: Younger-looking leaders endorsed for change and older-looking leaders endorsed for stability. *The Leadership Quarterly, 25*(5), 805–816.

Spisak, B. R., Homan, A. C., Grabo, A., & Van Vugt, M. (2011). Facing the situation: Testing a biosocial contingency model of leadership in intergroup relations using masculine and feminine faces. *The Leadership Quarterly, 23*(2), 273–280.

Stogdill, R. M. (1948). Personal factors associated with leadership: A survey of the literature. *Journal of Psychology, 25*(1), 35–71.

Stogdill, R. M., & Coons, A. E. (1957). *Leader behavior: Its description and measurement* (Research Monograph Number 88). Columbus: Ohio State University Bureau of Business Research.

Sturm, R. E., & Antonakis, J. (2015). Interpersonal power: A review, critique, and research agenda. *Journal of Management, 41*(1), 136–163.

Triandis, H. C. (1995). *Individualism and collectivism.* Boulder, CO: Westview Press.

Trichas, S., & Schyns, B. (2012). The face of leadership: Perceiving leaders from facial expression. *The Leadership Quarterly, 23*(3), 545–566.

Van Seters, D. A., & Field, R. H. G. (1990). The evolution of leadership theory. *Journal of Organizational Change Management, 3*(3), 29–45.

Van Vugt, M., & Grabo, A. E. (2015). The many faces of leadership: An evolutionary-psychology approach. *Current Directions in Psychological Science, 24*(6), 484–489.

Van Vugt, M., Hogan, R., & Kaiser, R. B. (2008). Leadership, followership, and evolution—Some lessons from the past. *American Psychologist, 63*(3), 182–196.

Van Vugt, M., & Schaller, M. (2008). Evolutionary approaches to group dynamics: An introduction. *Group Dynamics-Theory Research and Practice, 12*(1), 1–6.

Vermeulen, F. (2005). On rigor and relevance: Fostering dialectic progress in management research. *Academy of Management Journal, 48*(6), 978–982.

Von Rueden, C., & Van Vugt, M. (2015). Leadership in small-scale societies: Some implications for theory, research, and practice. *The Leadership Quarterly, 26*(6), 978–990.

Vroom, V. H. (1976). Leadership. In M. D. Dunnette (Ed.), *Handbook of industrial and organizational psychology* (pp. 1527–1551). Chicago, IL: Rand McNally.

Vroom, V. H., & Jago, A. G. (1988). *The new leadership: Managing participation in organizations.* Englewood Cliffs, NJ: Prentice Hall.

Vroom, V. H., & Yetton, P. W. (1973). *Leadership and decision making.* Pittsburgh, PA: University of Pittsburgh Press.

Waldman, D. A., Balthazard, P. A., & Peterson, S. J. (2011a). Leadership and neuroscience: Can we revolutionize the way that inspirational leaders are identified and developed? *Academy of Management Perspectives, 25*(1), 60–74.

Waldman, D. A., Balthazard, P. A., & Peterson, S. J. (2011b). Social cognitive neuroscience and leadership. *Leadership Quarterly, 22*(6), 1092–1106.

Weber, R., Camerer, C., Rottenstreich, Y., & Knez, M. (2001). The illusion of leadership: Misattribution of cause in coordination games. *Organization Science, 12*(5), 582–598.

Wofford, J., Goodwin, V. L., & Whittington, J. L. (1998). A field study of a cognitive approach to understanding transformational and transactional leadership. *The Leadership Quarterly, 9*(1), 55–84.

Zaccaro, S. J. (2001). *The nature of executive leadership: A conceptual and empirical analysis of success.* Washington, DC: American Psychological Association.

Zaccaro, S. J. (2007). Trait-based perspectives of leadership. *American Psychologist, 62*(1), 6.

Zaccaro, S. J. (2012). Individual differences and leadership: Contributions to a third tipping point. *The Leadership Quarterly, 23*, 718–728.

Zaccaro, S. J., Foti, R. J., & Kenny, D. A. (1991). Self-monitoring and trait-based variance in leadership: An investigation of leader flexibility across multiple group situations. *Journal of Applied Psychology, 76*(2), 308–315.

Zaleznik, A. (1977). Managers and leaders: Are they different? *Harvard Business Review, 55*(3), 67–78.

# PART II

# The Major Schools of Leadership

# CHAPTER 2

# Leader Traits and Attributes

*Stephen J. Zaccaro*

*Samantha Dubrow*

*MaryJo Kolze*

---

## Opening Case: A Day in the Life of a Leader

Tom had a busy week ahead of him. As CEO and president of one of the top 10 community banks in the United States he had some critical decisions to make. His bank was leaning toward acquiring another bank that would make his the largest bank in the region. However, he needed to consider how much the acquisition and consolidation of the new bank would alter his bank's brand, one that he had cultivated very carefully and that he believed had contributed to the extraordinary growth of the bank over the last 5 years. Also, he was concerned that nearly doubling the size of his bank would create a number of strains for the existing management structure and workforce. He pondered how exactly the acquisition would advance his 10-year plan for the bank.

The acquisition would mean a need to hire additional executives, essentially rebuilding his top management team. What would he want as key qualities in these new executives? He knew that they had to be trustworthy and smart—and not just "book-smart," but also "street-smart." Also, the demands of the job, especially after the acquisition, required an executive willing to work very hard, putting in long work hours. Finally, as one of the public faces of the expanded bank, the new executive had to have good communication and networking skills, along with an ability to connect well with customers. A great hire should also have that "executive presence." How would he integrate these new people into his team to continue its strong sense of shared leadership and commitment to the bank?

Tom put aside his thoughts about the acquisition. He had a series of meetings to attend: He needed to first meet with bank officers to discuss some large loan requests, and then attend another meeting to review loan delinquencies. Following that meeting, he would be conferring with top officers to consider marketing strategies and opportunities, and then getting together with HR to go over some personnel problems and potential opportunities. They were ready to implement the executive succession program he had long championed, and they wanted some last-minute input. Later that afternoon, he had to speak at a large gathering of major bank customers to discuss the possible merger. He knew there were some concerns on that front.

Tom had other leadership roles in his life that would take up some of his time that evening and this upcoming weekend. He was chair of his state's infrastructure development commission, and it had some community projects that were up for consideration. He strongly favored these projects, but knew he had a tough challenge to convince and persuade other committee members to agree with going forward with them.

He also chaired his district's Republican Committee, and it was an election year. This coming weekend, he had a meeting with donors for his candidate. Some of these donors were quite annoying, but he would have to keep his composure as the meeting would eventually get heated. He knew some questions would come up about campaign strategy. There were some potential political minefields that he and his candidate would need to detect and negotiate without losing supporters.

Sunday, he was looking forward to doing something different. He was a scoutmaster, and that weekend he was meeting with a group of new recruits for his unit; he looked forward to being able to teach these teenagers about leadership, survival skills, and being responsible citizens. He thought about the motivation speech he would give them and how he would tweak his usual one to talk more about the environmental challenges facing our planet. Although he found great joy and energy in all of his leadership roles, this was the one that satisfied him the most.

### Discussion Questions

1.  What are the different performance requirements in each of Tom's leadership roles?

2.  What key attributes would Tom need to succeed in each leadership role? What attributes are common across all of the roles? What attributes are unique to each role?

3.  What personal qualities does Tom possess that help him display different behaviors in each role and lead successfully in the different roles?

## Chapter Overview

Leadership scientists have struggled long and hard to understand the role of individual differences and personal attributes in explaining leader role occupancy and leadership effectiveness. The earliest scientific approaches date back to the "great man" perspectives from the 19th century. These perspectives sought to identify the unique qualities possessed by heroes (Carlyle, 1841/1907) or geniuses (Galton, 1869), arguing that these qualities denoted leadership and were innate properties of people. Terman (1904) initiated more focused scientific study of the individual differences between leaders and nonleaders. Over the first half of the 20th century, such research flourished in number, until midcentury reviews could point to over 75 attributes shown to distinguish leaders from followers and successful leaders from failures (Bird, 1940; Stogdill, 1948). However, several major reviews also noted that observed relationships were often quite small and inconsistent in their magnitude (Mann, 1959; Stogdill, 1948). They argued that the search for significant leader traits was not likely to be fruitful and that researchers should turn to other avenues to explain leader role occupancy and effectiveness.

This turn lasted for almost 40 years, until several researchers used more sophisticated statistical procedures to show that indeed leader individual differences did have significant and consistent associations with leadership outcomes (Kenny & Zaccaro, 1983; Lord, De Vader, & Alliger, 1986). These studies were followed by other meta-analyses that affirmed their central conclusions (e.g., Judge, Bono, Ilies, & Gerhart, 2002; Judge, Colbert, & Ilies, 2004). Other researchers argued anew for unique attributes possessed by inspirational leaders who motivated and empowered followers (House & Howell, 1992). These contributions led to a revival of leader trait explanations for leadership effectiveness. However, to advance understanding about the role of leader traits and attributes, such explanations should not reflect prior, rather simplistic approaches. Instead, more sophisticated models of trait combinations, situational parameters, and trait-behavior processes are necessary to further understand the role of leader traits in leadership outcomes (Zaccaro, Kemp, & Bader, 2004; Zaccaro, LaPort, & Jose, 2013). Accordingly, researchers have begun to offer more complex models describing the influences of leader attributes. These efforts have led to what Antonakis, Day, and Schyns (2012) labeled a renaissance in leader trait research and established the basis for what Zaccaro (2012) termed the third tipping point in such research.

This chapter builds on several prior reviews of this revitalized literature (e.g., Chen & Zaccaro, 2013; Judge & Long, 2012; Zaccaro et al., 2004; Zaccaro et al., 2013). In particular, Zaccaro et al. (2013) summarized research published up to 2011 that focused on multivariate, pattern, and multiphase models of leader attributes. Recently, there has been an exponential increase in studies of leaders' individual differences. For example, Xu et al. (2014) counted 44 articles on leader traits published in *The Leadership Quarterly* over a 20-year span between 1991 and 2010. They noted that over the subsequent 4-year span of 2011–2014, some 45 additional articles on this topic had been published in this journal. In this chapter, we review this recent literature and examine evidence for various models of leader attributes, including multivariate, pattern, nonlinear, and collective leadership models. Our intent is to provide further impetus to the renaissance in this research noted by Antonakis et al. (2012).

Our focus in this chapter is on psychological traits and attributes, including cognitive abilities, social capacities, personality, motives, and other mental characteristics of leaders. We note that physical attributes have also long been linked to leadership outcomes. For example, Stogdill (1948) summarized studies linking leadership to differences in height, age, weight, physique, and physical appearance. Recent studies have provided additional support for some of these linkages (e.g., Elgar, 2016; Little, 2014). Also, many studies have associated gender with leadership outcomes (see meta-analyses by Eagly, Karau, & Makhijani, 1995; Eagly, Makhijani, & Klonsky, 1992). While leader physical characteristics have been demonstrated as important correlates of leadership, because of space limitations, we have chosen to limit our attention to psychological characteristics. We refer readers to other chapters in this volume, including Chapter 8 ("Evolutionary, Biological, and Neuroscience Perspectives"), Chapter 9 ("Social Cognition and Leadership"), and Chapter 10 ("Leadership and Gender"), for discussions of leadership and biological/physical characteristics.

# An Empirical Summary of Recent Research on Leader Attributes

Several major reviews of leadership traits and attributes have been published over the last 25 years, including Bass (1990, 1998); Kirkpatrick and Locke (1991); Hogan, Curphy, and Hogan (1994); Zaccaro et al. (2004); Day and Zaccaro (2007); Judge and Long (2012); and Zaccaro et al. (2013). The current review covers primarily research published over the last 5 years or so. We begin by identifying individual qualities that have been found to have consistent relationships with leader role occupancy and leadership effectiveness.

# Categories of Leader Attributes

Over the years, many personal attributes have been linked to different leadership outcomes. Zaccaro et al. (2013) listed 49 attributes that were mentioned in 25 conceptual and empirical reviews of the leadership literature between 1924 and 2011. These attributes were grouped into sets of *cognitive, social, personality, motives, self-beliefs,* and *knowledge and skills.* They justified these attribute categories by linking them to functional performance requirements that are part of most if not all leadership positions. For example, setting direction for followers and units is a fundamental leadership performance requirement (Morgeson, DeRue, & Karam, 2010; Zaccaro, 2001). This function entails scanning operational environments, detecting and making sense of emergent problems, generating and evaluating potential solutions, and planning for solution implementation (Mumford et al., 2000). At a broader scale, leaders take a longer-term perspective to develop a vision and strategy that provides the basis for task and operational direction setting (Zaccaro, 2001). These leadership functions require a range of cognitive abilities, including reasoning skills, problem-solving skills, divergent thinking skills, metacognitive thinking skills, cognitive complexity, and cognitive flexibility (Zaccaro et al., 2013). Zaccaro et al.

also noted that several personality traits contribute to the accomplishment of cognitive performance functions in complex and demanding operational environments, including tolerance for ambiguity, openness, emotional stability, and conscientiousness. These latter traits provide a foundation for leaders to apply cognitive abilities and skills in complex and demanding operational environments and to persist through the development of solutions to ill-defined problems (Mumford et al., 2000).

Managing followers and units in accordance with set direction represents another key leader performance requirement (Zaccaro, 2001). This function includes activities such as hiring and training subordinates, staffing teams, matching subordinate skills to task requirements, motivating others, resolving conflicts, negotiating with and persuading others, and representing units and organizations to external stakeholders (Zaccaro et al., 2013). The accomplishments of these functions are facilitated by social capacities such as social intelligence, self-monitoring, and skills in perspective-taking, communication, persuasion, negotiation, and conflict management (Zaccaro et al., 2004; Zaccaro et al., 2013). Personality traits such as extraversion, sociability, and agreeableness help orient the leader toward engaging in social interactions and navigating them successfully (Judge et al., 2002).

Leadership work is often tough and demanding, especially at higher organizational levels (Hambrick, Finkelstein, & Mooney, 2005). It often requires attendance to many demands, an unrelenting pace, and the exertion of power. Accordingly, Zaccaro et al. (2013) argued that a number of self-motivational or self-management attributes such as motivation to lead, dominance, need for power, achievement motivation, and high energy are necessary to accomplish leader performance requirements. The trait pattern called core self-evaluation by Judge, Locke, and Durham (1997) also contributes to leadership engagement (Zaccaro et al., 2013). It includes self-esteem, locus of control, generalized self-efficacy, and emotional stability. These core self-beliefs reflect high personal confidence; they also promote persistence and resilience though personal challenge.

Leadership performance requirements, then, establish the basis for specification of different leader attributes grouped into categories of cognitive abilities, personality orientations, motives and values, social capacities, and core self-beliefs. To these sets we would add knowledge and expertise, particularly tacit knowledge and business acumen (Zaccaro et al., 2013). Table 2.1 summarizes leader attributes subsumed under each category that have been shown in meta-analyses to be linked to leader emergence and leadership effectiveness.

Cognitive leader attributes supported by meta-analyses include intelligence, divergent or creative thinking capacities, problem-solving skills, and judgment and decision-making skills. For example, corrected correlations between intelligence and leader emergence ranged from .25 to .52; those between intelligence and leadership effectiveness ranged from .15 to .17 (e.g., Judge, Colbert, & Ilies, 2004; Lord et al., 1986). Likewise, Ensari et al. (2011) reported a corrected correlation of .35 for divergent thinking skills with indices of leadership emergence. Hoffman et al. (2011) found a corrected correlation of .31 of this capacity with leadership effectiveness.

Personality has been the focus of multiple meta-analyses (e.g., Hoffman et al., 2011; Judge et al., 2002). All five facets of the Big Five model (McCrae & Costa, 1987), extraversion, conscientiousness, openness, agreeableness, and emotional

**Table 2.1**    Key Leader Attributes Identified Across Meta-Analyses

| Attributes | Range of Correlations From Meta-Analyses | |
| --- | --- | --- |
| | Leader Emergence | Leader Effectiveness |
| Cognitive Capacities and Skills | | |
| • General intelligence | • .25–.52 | • .15–.17 |
| • Creative/divergent thinking capacities | • .35 | • .31 |
| • Problem-solving skills | | • .39 |
| • Decision-making skills | | • .52 |
| Personality | | |
| • Extraversion | • .15–.32 | • .12–.31 |
| • Consciousness | • .19–.33 | • .16–.28 |
| • Openness | • .17–.24 | • .09–.24 |
| • Agreeableness | • .01–.05 | • .03–.21 |
| • Neuroticism | • −.08–−.24 | • −.22–.24 |
| • Positive affectivity | • .28 | • .33 |
| • Narcissism | • .16 | • .03 |
| • Integrity | | • .29 |
| Motives | | |
| • Dominance | • .17–.37 | • .35 |
| • Achievement orientation | | • .28 |
| • Energy | | • .29 |
| • Need for power | | • .16 |
| • Proactivity | | • .19 |
| • Ambition | | • .05 |
| Social Skills | | |
| • Self-monitoring | • .14 | • .19–.21 |
| • Social acuity | | • .30 |
| • Communications | | • .24–.25 |
| • Emotional regulation | | • .14–.37 |
| Task Skills | | |
| • Administrative skills | | • .17 |
| Self-beliefs | | |
| • Self-efficacy/Self-esteem | • .17 | • .24 |
| Knowledge | | |
| • Technical knowledge | | • .19 |

NOTE: These corrected correlations come from the following meta-analyses: Day et al. (2002); Deinert et al. (2015); DeRue et al. (2011); Ensari et al. (2011); Gaddi & Foster (2013); Grijalva (2013); Harms & Crede (2010); Hoffman et al. (2011); Joseph et al. (2015); Judge et al. (2002); Judge, Colbert, & Ilies (2004); Lord, DeVader, & Alliger (1986); Woo et al. (2014).

stability, have displayed corrected correlations higher than .20 in at least one meta-analysis examining either leader emergence or leadership effectiveness (see Table 2.1 note for list of meta-analyses). Extraversion and conscientiousness have generally yielded the highest corrected correlations with leadership outcomes. Agreeableness has generally displayed lower corrected correlations with leader emergence and effectiveness than the other facets.

Key leader motives include dominance, achievement orientation, need for power, and proactivity or initiative. The strongest corrected correlations have generally been with dominance. Ensari et al. (2011) indicated a corrected correlation of .37 for this attribute and leader emergence. For leadership effectiveness, Hoffman et al. (2011) reported a corrected correlation of .35 for dominance.

Social capacities and skills that have been supported by meta-analyses include self-monitoring, social acuity, communication skills, and emotional intelligence or emotion regulation skills. For example, Day et al. (2002) reported a corrected correlation of .21 for self-monitoring and leadership effectiveness. Hoffman et al.'s (2011) meta-analysis contained an attribute described as "interpersonal skills." They defined these to "include a broad range of skills associated with an understanding of human behaviour and the dynamics of groups" (p. 352), which reflects the attribute of social acuity. They reported a corrected *r* for this attribute of .30.

Harms and Crede (2010) completed a meta-analysis of emotional intelligence and leadership effectiveness, separating same-source ratings from different-source ratings. Their results indicated a source bias: The corrected *r* from same-source ratings was .37; the corrected correlation from different-source ratings was .14. They reported similar differences in corrected correlations between emotional intelligence and ratings of transformational and transactional leadership. Corrected correlations ranged from .35 to .45 for same-source ratings and .10 to .14 for different-source ratings.

## Summary

Meta-analyses have provided considerable evidence for the validity of a wide range of leader attributes being linked to leadership outcomes. Table 2.1 indicates those grouped into four major categories of attributes, as well as some others. A caveat to note: This list is still not a full representation of leader attributes that have been connected to leadership; it only contains a portion of those supported by meta-analyses. For example, attributes such as cognitive flexibility, metacognitive skills, learning agility, behavioral flexibility, negotiation and persuasion skills, and conflict management skills have been linked to leadership outcomes in prior conceptual and qualitative reviews (Zaccaro et al., 2013) but have not been subjects of particular meta-analyses. Thus, the list in Table 2.1 should be regarded as the attributes most consistently supported by multiple studies in the empirical literature.

A second caveat to note: The attributes examined in prior meta-analyses generally display small- to moderate-sized corrected correlations. This observation speaks to the futility noted by Zaccaro et al. (2004) in trying to explain meaningful amounts of variance in leadership with only one or even a small number of leader traits and attributes. Instead, understanding the role of leader attributes in leadership outcomes requires more complex models. We turn now to a discussion and review of such models.

# More Complex Models of Leader Attributes and Leadership Outcomes

In light of the modest relationships between individual leader characteristics and leadership outcomes, researchers have argued the need for more multivariate and complex models of leader traits, attributes, and outcomes (Lord & Hall, 1992; Zaccaro, 2007). Accordingly, several recent studies have offered more sophisticated approaches to how the range of individual differences noted in Table 2.1 may combine to influence leadership processes, leader performance, and leader role occupancy. Table 2.2 defines these approaches. In this section, we review the evidence from these studies for several leader attribute-outcome frameworks, including variable, pattern, multistage, shared leadership, and curvilinear models.

**Table 2.2**    Multivariate and Nonlinear Models of Leader Attributes

| Model | Description |
| --- | --- |
| 1.  Variable | The effects of single or linear combinations of multiple variables with leadership behaviors and outcomes |
| 2.  Multistage | Distal sets of attributes act as predictors of more proximal sets of attributes, which in turn mediate the effects of distal attributes on leader and follower behaviors, and leadership outcomes |
| 3.  Pattern | *Minimal pattern model*: The interaction of two or more leader attributes predicts leader behaviors and leadership outcomes |
|  | *More complex pattern model*: Three or more attributes are combined into a leader profile predicting leader behaviors and leadership effectiveness |
| 4.  Collective leadership | The attributes of multiple leaders combine to predict shared leadership processes and outcomes |
| 5.  Nonlinear | Leader attributes exhibit a nonlinear relationship with leadership, such that too little or too much of the attribute is detrimental to leader behaviors and outcomes. |

## Multi-Attribute Models

Foti and Hauenstein (2007) defined *variable* models of leader attributes as those that focus on how individual variables explain unique variance in leader emergence and leadership effectiveness. They noted that such an approach "conceptualizes the person as a summation of variables" (p. 347). Zaccaro et al. (2013) argued that the specification of multivariate or multi-attribute models should be grounded in the leader performance requirements in which leadership outcomes are a collective function of cognitive, personality, motivational, skill-based, and knowledge sets of attributes.

A number of recent studies have supported this argument. For example, Bakker-Pieper and de Vries (2013) found that sets of social and personality leader attributes yield a multiple correlation of .77 with leader performance. Serban et al. (2015) explained a significant amount of variance in leader emergence with cognitive ability, personality attributes, and self-efficacy. Troth and Gyetvey (2014) found a multiple correlation of .74 between social, motivational, and cognitive ability with ratings of leadership potential. Finally, Zaccaro et al. (2015) reported a strong association between sets of social, motivational, cognitive, and personality attributes with leader continuance in an organization. Taken together, these studies indicate moderate to robust multiple correlations between multiple sets of leader attributes and various leadership outcomes. They point to the efficacy of considering a multiple attribute approach to modeling the effects of leader traits and attributes on such outcomes.

## Multistage Models

Zaccaro et al. (2013) defined several process models, also called multistage models (Chen & Zaccaro, 2013; Zaccaro, 2012), of leader attributes, mediators, and outcomes. The first and simplest model specifies follower behaviors as mediators of leader attributes on leadership outcomes. For example, Nadkarni and Hermann (2010) found that an organization's strategic flexibility mediated the influence on CEO personality on organizational performance. More recently, Luria and Berson (2013) provided supportive evidence for the role of teamwork behaviors as mediating the joint influence of leader cognitive ability and motivation to lead on leader emergence scores. A second set of multistage models posited by Zaccaro et al. (2013) specifies that leadership behaviors mediate the effects of leader attributes on leadership outcomes. For example, DeRue et al.'s (2011) meta-analysis examined how various leadership behaviors mediated the effects of sets of interpersonal and task-related traits. They found that initiating structure, transformational leadership, and contingent reward behaviors mediated the effects of intelligence on leadership effectiveness. Likewise, two of these leadership behaviors (initiating structure and transformational leadership) mediated the effects of consciousness on this outcome. They reported several similar mediated relationships for other leader attributes and behaviors.

Hur, van den Berg, and Wilderom (2011) examined transformational leadership as a mediator of the relationship between emotional intelligence and three leadership outcomes—leader effectiveness, team effectiveness, and service climate. The latter was defined as "employee perceptions of the practices, procedures, and behaviors that get rewarded, supported and expected with regard to customer service and customer service quality" (Schneider, White, & Paul, 1998, p. 151). They found that transformational leadership mediated the effects of emotional intelligence and leader effectiveness and service climate.

Cavazotte, Moreno, and Hickman (2012) assessed the meditating role of transformational leadership in the relationship between emotional intelligence and managerial performance. This study is particularly noteworthy because it also examined intelligence and personality as predictive leader attributes. Thus, they included attributes from three of the attribute sets described earlier in the paper. They found that transformational leadership mediated the effects of conscientiousness and intelligence, but not emotional intelligence, on managerial performance. Walter et al. (2012) examined one aspect of emotional intelligence, emotion recognition, testing whether task coordination behavior (i.e., initiating structure) mediated its joint effects on leader emergence scores. This study is also noteworthy because it posits a trait interaction as a predictor (see attribute pattern models below) within a multistage attribute model. They found support for the proposed mediated effects in two samples, one from student project groups in the Netherlands and the other from a student assessment center. Blickle et al. (2013) examined how leader initialing structure and consideration mediated the joint influences of political skill and position power on follower job satisfaction. They found that for leaders with high position power, leadership behaviors mediated the effects on political skills on such satisfaction; low position power leaders showed such effects of political skill. Taken together, these studies provide considerable support for models that propose leadership behaviors as mediators of leader attributes on leader outcomes.

A third set of multistage models refers to those that differentiate leader attributes into distal and proximal sets (Zaccaro et al., 2004). Distal attributes refer to those that are relatively stable and resistant to short-term developmental change. Proximal attributes are more mutable and will change as a function of training and experience. Distal attributes are presumed to be predictors of proximal attributes, with the relationship likely moderated by the quality of developmental experiences incurred by the leaders. Proximal predictors should be stronger predictors of leadership outcomes. A simple version of this model posits two stages of attributes directly predicting leadership outcomes. For example, Hong, Catano, and Liao (2011) examined motivation to lead as a mediator of the relationship between emotional intelligence and leader emergence. They found that different aspects of motivation to lead led to different emergence outcomes: The affective-identity component was associated with leader emergence in leaderless group discussions, while the social-normative component was associated with longer-term project leadership. Affective-identity motivation to lead mediated the effects of the emotion use aspect of emotional intelligence on leader emergence.

Guerin et al. (2011) examined social skills as a mediator of extraversion and intelligence effects on leadership potential, measured as reported leadership work duties and transformational leadership. A noteworthy aspect of this study was that the distal attributes were assessed in 17-year-old adolescents, while social skills and leadership potential were measured 12 years later when they were adults. Their results showed that social skills mediated the effects of extraversion but not intelligence on both reported work duties and transformational leadership. Attesting to the stable quality of distal traits, Guerin et al. also found that approach/withdrawal to novel stimuli dimension of temperament, defined as a key precursor to extraversion, exhibit high intercorrelations across assessments over 14 years (ages 2–16) and in turn were significantly corrected with extraversion scores assessed at age 17.

Two other recent studies also tested versions of the multistage attribute-to-outcome model. Gentry et al. (2013) examined personality as a distal predictor and political skill as a proximal predictor of rated leader decisiveness. Their personality attributes included predispositions toward (a) creating good impressions and (b) displaying tolerance and acceptance. They also examined the social astuteness dimension of political skill (Ferris et al., 2007) as a mediator, which refers to skill in accurately perceiving social situations. They found that aspects of political skills significantly mediated the effects of personality on leader decisiveness. Allen et al. (2014) investigated the effects of motivation to lead and leadership self-efficacy as mediators of the effect of personality and cognitive ability on both leadership potential and leadership performance. They found that interest in leadership (similar to the affective-identity component of motivation to lead) and leadership self-efficacy fully mediated the effects of hostility to authority on both leadership outcomes; the effects of equity sensitivity on these outcomes were partially mediated by the two mediators.

Van Iddekinge, Ferris, and Heffner (2009) examined a more elaborated version of this multistage attribute-to-outcome model. They posited three stages of leader attributes, with cognitive ability, personality, and motives at stage 1; leadership experience and motivation to lead at stage 2; and leader knowledge and skills as stage 3. Leader performance was the targeted outcome. They found that variables at stage 3 partially mediated the effects of attributes at earlier stages on leader performance.

The studies reviewed thus far that examined multistage attribute models had only leadership outcomes as criteria. However, more elaborated multistage models could include either or both leadership behaviors and follower behaviors as mediators of two or more sequenced attribute sets on leadership outcomes. One study by Hinrichs (2011) measured personality motivation to lead; leadership behaviors; team processes; and two leadership outcomes, leadership potential and satisfaction with the leader. While he did not test a full multistage mediated model, some of his findings are suggestive. He found that personality was associated with motivation to lead, leadership behaviors, and team processes; leadership behaviors were predictive of both team processes and outcomes; some team processes were predictive of leadership outcomes. However, motivation to lead was only marginally related to one team process: According to Hinrichs, being motivated to lead without calculating the costs of such effort expenditure exhibited a slight negative effect on some team processes. This study is a good example of research examining complex relationships among multiple stages of leader attributes, leadership processes, and leadership outcomes.

LaPort (2012) also tested a complex multistage model that included distal and proximal leader attributes, leadership processes, and leadership outcomes. She measured cognitive abilities, personality (emotional stability, extraversion), and achievement motivation as distal traits; motivation to lead and social intelligence as proximal attributes; army leadership behaviors; and subordinate ratings of leadership effectiveness. This study is particularly noteworthy because (a) it included stable traits from three attribute categories; (b) it included mutable proximal traits; and (c) it tested the fit of a multistage mediated model. LaPort found that the distal attributes were associated with both social intelligence and motivation to lead. Social intelligence was predicted by cognitive ability, emotional stability, and extraversion, while motivation to lead was predicted by extraversion and achievement motivation. Motivation to lead also predicted social intelligence. The effects of distal traits on leadership behaviors were mediated by motivation to lead, but not social intelligence; leadership behaviors mediated the effects of motivation to lead on ratings of leadership effectiveness.

## Attribute Pattern Models

Pattern models of leader attributes argue that multiplicative combinations of attributes will explain unique variance in leadership outcomes beyond that explained by single attributes or additive combinations of multiple attributes (Foti & Hauenstein, 2007; Zaccaro et al., 2004). The simplest forms of such models specify the joint or interactive effects of two leader attributes on leader behaviors and outcomes. More complex forms will specify patterns or profiles of three or more attributes. As Foti and Hauenstein (2007) noted, in the latter, "the person is considered as an integrated totality rather than a summation of variables" (p. 347). The specific premise of these approaches is that one attribute, or multiple attributes from the same attribute set, are necessary but not sufficient to explain leadership behavior and outcomes. For example, one may be predisposed toward leadership roles but lack the social or cognitive skills to effectively engage the leadership activities required of such roles. Likewise, an individual may possess cognitive and social skills but lack the motivation to strive for leadership positions. Thus, leadership outcomes are defined as an integrated function of multiple variables from cognitive, personality, motive, social, and skills/knowledge attribute sets.

Several recent studies have examined simple attribute models—those that specify the joint or interactive effects of two leader attributes. Mencl, Wefald, and van Ittersum (2016) found that political skills interacted with dimensions of emotional regulation skills to predict transformational leadership. They found that the association between emotion control skills and leadership was indeed stronger under conditions of higher political skills. Owens, Wallace, and Waldman (2015) also examined the interaction of two attributes, leader narcissism and humility, on leadership outcomes. This study is interesting because it connects seemingly opposite personality traits. Narcissism refers to "an excessively self-centered perspective, self-absorption, extreme confidence or superiority, exploitiveness/entitlement, and a strong desire to lead" (Owens et al., 2015, p. 1203). Humility "is manifested by admitting mistakes and limitations, spotlighting the strengths and contributions of others, and modeling teachability" (Owens et al., p. 1204). The researchers offered several models to show how leaders can possess both the self-centeredness characteristic of narcissism and the other-centeredness associated with humility. In support of these models, they found that narcissism was more strongly related to both perceived leader effectiveness and follower job engagement under conditions of higher leader humility.

Both of these studies provide support for attribute patterns models by confirming proposed effects on leadership outcomes of two variables from within the same attribute set. They do not address, however, the research question of patterns composed of attributes from different sets, including personality, cognitive abilities and skills, social capacities, and motives. One study that examined such across-set patterns, Bickle et al. (2014), tested the joint effects of the personality trait of leader inquisitiveness, a facet of openness to experience, and the social capacity of political skill on charisma and leadership effectiveness. As expected, leader political skills moderated the effects of leader inquisitiveness on attributed charisma, such that the relationship was stronger under conditions of higher skills. Leader charisma was in turn related to leadership effectiveness. Walter et al. (2012) also investigated the effects of a personality attribute, extraversion, and a social capacity, emotion recognition skills, on leader task coordination behavior. They found that, as expected, emotion recognition skills were positively related to task coordination under conditions of higher extraversion; the effect was reversed under conditions of lower extraversion. Task coordination was in turn related to leader emergence. Finally, Luria and Berson (2013) examined the joint effects of a cognitive set attribute, cognitive ability, and a motivational variable, motivation to lead, on teamwork behaviors and leader emergence. As with the previous two studies, the two attributes exhibited a positive interaction on teamwork behaviors, which in turn were related to leader emergence.

These studies shared a common feature in that they tested and found support for more complex models of leader attributes, leader or follower/team behaviors, and leadership outcomes. This approach supports in part a feature of the model suggested by Zaccaro et al. (2004), where the effects of patterns of distal attributes on leader/follower processes and outcomes are mediated by more proximal attributes. However, each paper actually examined an interaction between a distal trait and a proximal trait on a proposed mediator. Thus, while they support the proposition that interactive patterns of traits would influence leadership outcomes through their effects on leadership behaviors and follower processes, the compositions of these patterns are different from those proposed by Zaccaro et al. in the original framework. However, as we noted earlier, a number of studies have also supported the role of distal traits as exogenous to proximal attributes in models of leadership outcomes. Thus, we suspect future studies will need to uncover the mechanisms to integrate these different strands of research. Nonetheless, all of these studies illustrate the greater complexity that has recently infused research on leader traits and attributes.

The studies described thus far examined the joint influences of two leader attributes on leadership outcomes. Other studies have examined the combination of three or more leader attributes into leader patterns or profiles. For example, Foti and Hauenstein (2007) found that a pattern of high intelligence, dominance, general self-efficacy, and self-monitoring was more strongly associated with measures of leader emergence, leader promotion, and ratings of leadership effectiveness than patterns that were mixed or low on the four attributes. Their pattern included variables from the cognitive ability, motives, and social capacities attribute sets. Lisak and Erez (2015) examined a narrower pattern including cultural intelligence, global identity, and openness to cultural diversity. The first two attributes reflect social capacities while the latter can be construed in terms of the more general personality attribute of openness. As with the Foti and Hauenstein study, Lisak and Erez found that the high/high/high pattern was more strongly related to leadership emergence than the mixed patterns or one that included low scores on all of the attributes.

LaPort (2012) attempted a test of the two-stage pattern model suggested by Zaccaro et al. (2004). She created a distal attribute pattern from cognitive ability, extraversion, and achievement motivation and a proximal pattern from motivation to lead and social intelligence (high on all attributes, mix of high and low on attributes, low on all attributes). The distal pattern was significantly correlated with the proximal pattern and leadership behaviors; the proximal pattern was significantly correlated with both leadership behaviors and leadership effectiveness. However, LaPort did not find support for the specific mean differences in distal attributes suggested by the pattern approach, which was that the high attribute group would differ significantly from the other patterns, but that the remaining patterns would not differ significantly from one another.

LaPort (2012) also used cluster analysis to derive three leader profiles. One profile was composed of individuals high on all leader attributes and labeled "intelligent extraverts." The second profile consisted of individuals with moderate scores on most of the attributes, but high scores on achievement motivation and lower scores in intelligence. This profile was labeled "motivated lower intelligence." The last profile included individuals slightly lower on most attributes, but much lower on achievement motivation and higher on intelligence. This profile was labeled "disengaged introverts." Analyses by LaPort showed significant differences between intelligent extraverts and disengaged introverts in displayed leadership behaviors and leadership effectiveness. However, the clusters did not add significant overall variance to the additive combination of all of the attributes.

Taken as a whole, LaPort's (2012) study provides some support for the pattern models of leader attributes, while also demonstrating the complexity of this research when patterns combine more than two or three attributes. A priori distal attribute patterns were linked to a priori proximal patterns, but only the latter related to any leader outcomes. The empirically derived patterns showed greater promise, but they did not demonstrative incremental validity over linear attribute combinations. LaPort does point to several sample issues that limited the construction of her patterns. Research on leader attribute patterns will need to provide a strong justification for the designation of traits to be combined and their expected relationships with different leadership outcomes.

In line with leader categorization theories (e.g., Lord, Foti, & De Vader, 1984), leaders may vary in the trait combinations they use in their self-leadership perceptions. Foti and colleagues have examined the correspondence between perceptions of self-leader attribute profiles and those of ideal leaders. For some perceived leader profiles, self and ideal leader perceptions were congruent, while for others, leaders diverged in their self and ideal leader perceptions (Foti, Bray, Thompson, & Allgood, 2012). Bray, Foti, Thompson, and Wills (2015) found that combinations of leader attributes into perceived self leader profiles were related to perceived ideal leader profiles; the latter were in turn associated with profiles of leaders judged to be effective. Leader attribute perceptions by leaders and followers play a significant role in predicting leadership behaviors and leader effectiveness (Lord & Maher, 1991; Shondrick, Dinh, & Lord, 2010). In line with the conceptual framework described by Dinh and Lord (2012), Foti and colleagues provide evidence of how such perceptions encode holistic profiles of self and ideal leaders and how these holistic profiles can influence key leadership outcomes.

## Collective Leadership and Leader Attributes

Over the last decade leadership researchers have intensified their examination of collective or shared leadership (Contractor et al., 2012; Day, Gronn, & Salas, 2004; Pearce & Conger, 2003). Shared leadership has been defined as "a dynamic, interactive influence process among individuals in groups for which the objective is to lead one another to the achievement of group or organizational goals or both. . . . [In such groups], leadership is broadly distributed among a set of individuals instead of centralized in [the] hands of a single individual who acts in the role of a superior" (Pearce & Conger, 2003, p. 1). Because shared leadership derives from team members' interactions, it is an emergent property of the team (Carson, Tesluk, & Marrone, 2007; Day et al., 2004). Such leadership includes team situations in which (a) all leadership functions are shared among all team members; (b) different members have responsibility for different leadership functions; or (c) members rotated into and out of the leader role and, when in that role, have primary responsibility for leadership functions (Contractor et al., 2012).

Collective leadership offers a different perspective of leader attributes. Such leadership should emerge from the composition of attributes possessed by individuals sharing leadership functions. This composition can reflect either attribute similarity or attribute complementarity. In the former case, individuals sharing leadership possess similar higher levels of particular leader attributes. For example, Friedrich et al. (2009) argued that effective collective leadership derives from team members all possessing a range of leadership skills. Attribute complementarity refers to individual members possessing different skills that complement the leadership skills of other members. For example, some members may be skilled in formation of team strategy, while others may be more skilled in implementation of such strategies.

Despite the increased interest in shared leadership, there has been little research on the attribute composition of the team and indices of shared leadership. Research by Colbert, Barrick, and Bradley (2013) examined the influences of top management team (TMT) personality composition on organizational performance and collective organizational commitment. They also examined CEO personality to determine the unique contribution of the TMT to leadership outcomes.

Finally, they examined the average level of transformational leadership in the team as a mediator of the effects of team personality on organizational effectiveness. Thus, their model reflected a multistage model. Results suggested that TMT mean extraversion was associated with higher collective organizational commitment, while TMT mean conscientiousness was positively associated with organizational performance. These effects were independent of the effects of CEO personality, but were not mediated by transformational leadership. While this was not directly a study of shared leadership, the TMT does set the direction and policies of the organization as a whole (Hambrick & Mason, 1984), and presumably engages in collective interaction at least some of the time to accomplish these functions (Hambrick, 1994).

Chen (2014) examined particular team attribute patterns and the emergence of shared leadership in teams. She argued that shared leadership required first a shared commitment to the team, including a willingness to work on behalf of the team, as well as an orientation toward getting along with others. Thus, she proposed that both mean psychological collectiveness and agreeableness in the team should be related to shared leadership emergence. However, she also argued that team members must be willing to engage in the leadership role; accordingly, she also proposed that extraversion or motivation to lead should interact with psychological collectiveness or agreeableness to influence shared leadership. Motivation to lead was included to isolate the ambition or striving elements of extraversion. Her results indicated support for some of these proposals: The effects of psychological collectiveness on the emergence of shared leadership was indeed moderated by both mean levels of extraversion and motivation to lead, such that shared leadership occurred when team members possessed both drive for the leader role and a willingness to work on behalf of their team. This study is noteworthy not only because it examined team attribute composition and shared leadership, but also because it focused on a simple pattern model as an antecedent of such leadership.

The studies by Colbert et al. (2013) and Chen (2014) provide some promising insights into shared leader attributes and collective leadership. They represent an important extension of research on leader individual differences. However, these studies also signal a need for additional future research. A key question is whether different attribute compositions are necessary for different forms of shared leadership. For example, complementary team composition may be better for distributed and intensive forms of shared leadership, but not for rotated leadership. Also, shared leadership may derive from high mean levels of some attributes, but from complementary or diverse levels of other attributes. Thus, high levels of certain personality variables, but diversity in particular leadership skills, may be a stronger predictor of shared leadership than other combinations. We urge further investigation into these types of questions.

## Curvilinear Models of Leader Attributes

The various models we have discussed in this chapter have in common the premise of a linear relationship between individual or multiple attributes and leadership outcomes, such that more (or less) of certain traits and attributes will result in better or worse outcomes. However, some researchers have applied the "too-much-of-a-good-thing" phenomenon (Pierce & Aguinis, 2013) to leadership, pressing the argument that not only low but also high levels of certain attributes are more deleterious for leadership than moderate levels of these attributes. That is, they advance a curvilinear relationship between leader attributes and leadership outcomes.

The research on bright and dark traits represents one example of such relationships. Judge and Long (2012) described how bright traits such as the Big Five personality factors could have both beneficial and deleterious effects on leadership. For example, openness to experience, which displays some of the higher corrected correlations in meta-analyses of leadership (see Table 2.1), can lead to greater innovation and adaptation; however, it may also result in accepting less direction from senior leadership in organizations. Likewise, extraversion can lead to perceptions of greater charisma, but also to more impulsiveness and less persistence according to these researchers.

Judge and Long (2012) also point out that dark traits such as narcissism and Machiavellianism can yield leadership benefits and costs. Narcissism can lead to greater leader role-taking and perceptions of charisma, but also exploitive leadership. Machiavellianism can result in more politically savvy leaders but also less consideration for others. The bright/dark framework of leader attributes, then, argued for a curvilinear relationship between personal attributes and leadership outcomes, where moderate levels are better than having too much or too little of the trait.

Kaiser and colleagues have provided empirical support for the too-much-of-a-good-thing phenomenon in leader personality. For example, Kaiser and Hogan (2011) investigated a range of seven personality attributes from the Hogan Personality Inventory that can be grouped within the Big Five Factor model (Hogan & Hogan, 2007). They examined the effects of these attributes on four leadership behaviors—being forceful, enabling, strategic, and operational. Some of these behaviors, particularly forcefulness, have been found to exhibit a curvilinear relationship with leader effectiveness (Hereford, 2011). They found support for the pattern whereby personality scores one standard deviation above and below the mean were associated with too much of particular leadership behaviors.

Kaiser, LeBreton, and Hogan (2015) extended this work by exploring the degree to which dark side traits would be associated with either too much or too little of the four aforementioned leadership behaviors. They examined 12 dark traits measured with the Hogan Development Survey (Hogan & Hogan, 2009) and found that four of them were associated with too much of one or more behaviors; four of them were also associated with too little of one or more of the leadership behaviors. However, they also found that higher scores on emotional stability moderated some of these effects, such as leaders with higher emotional stability were more able to control or manage the tendencies sparked by their dark side traits.

These studies provide some affirmation for a curvilinear relationship between both bright and dark traits and leadership outcomes. However, of particular interest is the notion suggested by Kaiser et al. (2015) that other attributes may reduce this curvilinear effect, reflecting a pattern approach to this research question. This work supports the importance of leader traits for leadership, while illustrating the complexity of this relationship.

## Summary and Conclusions

Researchers have argued that advancing research on traits or personal attributes and their effects on leadership required more complex models and approaches (Bass, 1990; Lord & Hall, 1992; Zaccaro et al., 2013). This review indicates validity for that argument. Over the last decade, and particularly in the last 5 years, there has been an exponential increase in the number of studies that specified and validated multi-attribute, multistage, and pattern models of leader attributes. Moreover, we have seen the beginnings of a research stream on combined leader attributes in team and shared leadership, and we have seen advancement of research on curvilinear associations between leader traits and leadership outcomes. This body of work provides support for Antonakis et al.'s (2012) suggestion that we are entering a renaissance period of research on leader traits and attributes.

In the first edition of this book, Zaccaro et al. (2004) proposed a model of leader attributes and performance that incorporated several propositions about the role of such attributes. Figure 2.1 presents a revision of this model based on research since then, some of which has been summarized in this chapter. As in the earlier model, we define a multistage framework, where distal or more immutable characteristics are predictors of the subsequent emergence of more state-like or malleable skills, capacities, and knowledge. However, we argue that this emergence is dependent upon—that is, moderated by—nascent leaders engaging in critical developmental activities and experiences (Mumford et al., 2000).

As with the earlier model offered by Zaccaro et al. (2004), we argue that the effects of proximal attributes on leadership outcomes are mediated by their influence of leadership processes and behaviors. Leadership behaviors are also influenced by situation-based performance requirements, as effective leadership requires alignment between what leaders are expected to accomplish and what behaviors they display (Zaccaro, Gilbert, Thor, & Mumford, 1991). However, such an alignment is not a given based on stable distal traits and the repertoire of capacities leaders bring to the situation. Researchers have argued that leaders need to exhibit considerable flexibility in how well they adjust their behavioral tendencies to particular situational contingencies (Dinh & Lord, 2012; Zaccaro, 2007; Zaccaro et al., 1991). Accordingly, we include in the set of proximal attributes such capacities as social acuity, political savvy, and emotion regulation skills. Several recent studies have provided evidence for such moderation (Blickle et al., 2014; Lisek & Erez, 2015; Walter et al., 2012).

### Future Research

This review has highlighted a number of advancements in research on leader attributes and individual differences. Nonetheless, the model in Figure 2.1 suggests several avenues for future research. First, the multistage feature of the model points to the need for longitudinal research tracking the influence of distal traits on proximal skills and capacities. Studies that have examined this influence have

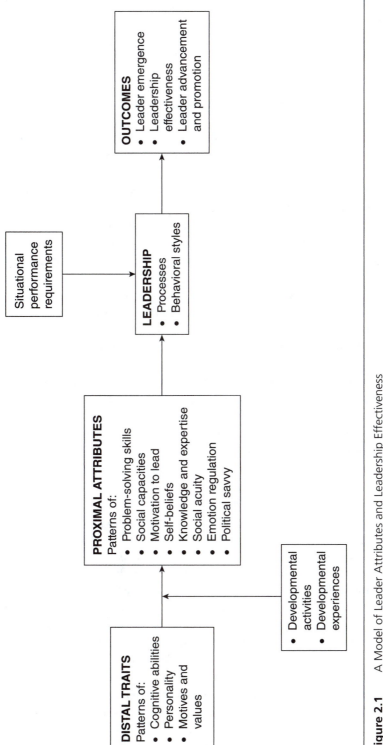

**Figure 2.1**  A Model of Leader Attributes and Leadership Effectiveness

gathered static or cross-sectional assessments of both types of attributes (e.g., Allen et al., 2014; LaPort, 2012; Van Iddekinge et al., 2009). However, the proposition specified in our model is that of a developmental process in which distal traits condition the emergence of proximal attributes (Mumford et al., 2000). Accordingly, researchers should engage in more longitudinal studies that explore growth models of proximal capacities from stable traits. Recent examples of such work include Daly, Egan, and O'Reilly (2015); Reichard et al. (2011); and Guerin et al. (2011). Future studies along this line of research should integrate variable and pattern approaches within a longitudinal perspective (e.g., Guerin et al., 2011).

The model in Figure 2.1 suggests that developmental experiences moderate the influence of distal traits on the emergence of proximal attributes. Accordingly, we urge that researchers investigate the particular developmental experiences most likely to expedite the evolution of proximal capacities from distal traits. Recent studies have postulated about the effects of age-related changes on leader attributes from life span perspective (Zacher, Clark, Anderson, & Ayoko, 2015). Olivares (2011) examined the role of momentous events on leadership development. However, there is still a need for systematic research that identifies key experiences that contribute to the development of proximal attributes and, more specifically, help explain the conditions under which distal traits drive the emergence of these attributes. Moreover, such research should also consider the leader attributes that facilitate gains from such learning experiences (Avolio & Hannah, 2008; Day & Sin, 2011; Hannah & Avolio, 2010).

Finally, future research needs to consider more thoroughly the role of the situation as an influence on leaders' behavioral expressions of their attributes. Research has verified that while traits remain relatively stable, leader behaviors do vary across situations (Dinh & Lord, 2012; Zaccaro et al., 1991). Xu et al. (2014) also noted how leader traits can evolve over time, and they defined separate categories of traits depending upon their variance in expression across situations. However, there is insufficient understanding of how (and what) situational parameters condition and shape the expression of leadership behaviors. Accordingly, Zaccaro (2012) called for taxonomy development of situation-leadership effects to advance research in this area. We echo that call here.

In our model, we suggest that certain attributes that promote behavioral flexibility increase the leaders' capacity to adapt or align their activities to contextual contingencies. Alternatively, some researchers have argued for the construct of personality strength, or the tendency of some individuals to display less behavioral variability across different situations (Dalal et al., 2015). We have already noted the need for research demonstrating how our proposed flexibility profile moderates the influence of certain proximal and distal leader attributes on leadership behaviors. However, the work of Dalal et al. (2015) suggests an alternate pattern of attributes that mitigate functional variability of leaders' behavioral expressions in response to shifting contexts. Integrating these various themes of situational variance and invariance with leader attributes that promote both variable behavioral expression and consistent effectiveness across diverse leadership situations represents a critical direction for future research on leadership and individual differences. Such integration can help resolve the controversies and misgivings that have bedeviled this research domain over the last 70 years.

## Discussion Questions

1. What combinations or patterns of traits are likely to be most predictive of leadership outcomes at different levels of an organization (low, middle, and upper)?
2. What developmental experiences are powerful in shaping the emergence of proximal leadership skills and capacities?
3. How would you define the role of the situation in the model in Figure 2.1? What situational parameters are likely to cause the most variation in leadership behaviors?
4. We have suggested a set of social capacities that facilitate situational flexibility in leadership behavior. What other nonsocial attributes (i.e., cognitive, personality, motives) would you argue promote such flexibility?
5. In this chapter, we describe research on personality attributes that exhibit curvilinear effects on leadership outcomes. Build an argument for curvilinear effects of a cognitive, social, personality, and motivational attribute on such outcomes. Ground your argument in existing theories, models, and research.

## Recommended Readings

- DeRue, D. S., Nahrgang, J. D., Wellman, N., & Humphrey, S. E. (2011). Trait and behavioral theories of leadership: An integration and meta-analytic test of their relative validity. *Personnel Psychology, 64,* 7–52.
- Judge, T. A., Bono, J. E., Ilies, R., & Gerhardt, M. W. (2002). Personality and leadership: A qualitative and quantitative review. *Journal of Applied Psychology, 87,* 765–780.
- Judge, T. A., Piccolo, R. F., & Kosalka, T. (2009). The bright and dark sides of leader traits: A review and theoretical extension of the leader trait paradigm. *The Leadership Quarterly, 20,* 855–875.
- Kirkpatrick, S. A., & Locke, E. A. (1991, May). Leadership: Do traits matter? *Academy of Management Executive, 5,* 48–60.

## Recommended Case Studies

- **Film Case:** *Invictus*
  - *Paired readings for the film*:
    - Seijts, G., Gandz, J., & Crossan, M. (2014). *Invictus:* Introducing leadership competencies, character, and commitment. Ivy Publishing, Case W14042.
    - Wraith, D. (2014). Three leadership characteristics that made Mandela a legend. http://www.movieleadership.com/2014/01/27/three-leadership-characteristics-that-made-mandela-a-legend/
- **Case:** Isaacson, W. (2012). The real leadership lessons of Steve Jobs. *Harvard Business Review, 90*(4), 92–102.
- **Case:** Tim Cook's leadership and management style: Building his own legacy at Apple. ICMR: IBS Center for Management Research, Case LDEN101.

## Recommended Video

- McChrystal, S. (2011). Stanley McChrystal: Listen, learn . . . then lead. https://www.ted.com/talks/stanley_mcchrystal

## References

Allen, M. T., Bynum, B. H., Oliver, J. T., Russell, T. L., Young, M. C., & Babin, N. E. (2014). Predicting leadership performance and potential in the U.S. Army Officer Candidate School (OCS). *Military Psychology, 26*(4), 310–326.

Antonakis, J., Day, D. V., & Schyns, B. (2012). Leadership and individual differences: At the cusp of a renaissance. *The Leadership Quarterly, 23*, 643–650.

Avolio, B. J., & Hannah, S. T. (2008). Developmental readiness: Accelerating leader development. *Consulting Psychology Journal: Practice and Research, 60*, 331–347.

Bakker-Pieper, A., & de Vries, R. E. (2013). The incremental validity of communication styles over personality traits for leader outcomes. *Human Performance, 26*, 1–19.

Bass, B. M. (1990). *Bass & Stogdill's handbook of leadership: Theory, research and managerial applications* (3rd ed.). New York, NY: Free Press.

Bass, B. M. (2008). *The Bass handbook of leadership: Theory, research, and managerial applications* (4th ed.). New York, NY: Free Press.

Bird, C. (1940). *Social psychology.* New York, NY: Appleton-Century.

Blickle, G., Kane-Frieder, R. E., Oerder, K., Wihler, A., von Below, A., Schütte, N., . . . Ferris, G. R. (2013). Leader behaviors as mediators of the leader characteristics—Follower satisfaction relationship. *Group and Organization Management, 38*, 601–629.

Blickle, G., Meurs, J. A., Wihler, A., Ewen, C., & Peiseler, A. K. (2014). Leader inquisitiveness, political skills, and follower attributions of leader charisma and effectiveness: Test of a moderated mediation model. *International Journal of Selection and Assessment, 22*, 272–285.

Boyatzis, R. E., Good, D., & Massa, R. (2012). Emotional, social, and cognitive intelligence and personality as predictors of sales leadership performance. *Journal of Leadership and Organizational Studies, 19*, 191–201.

Bray, B. C., Foti, R. J., Thompson, N. J., & Wills, S. F. (2014). Disentangling the effects of self leader perceptions and ideal leader prototypes in leader judgments using loglinear modeling with latent variables. *Human Performance, 27*, 393–415.

Butler, A. M., Kwantes, C. T., & Boglarsky, C. A. (2014). The effects of self-awareness on perceptions of leadership effectiveness in the hospitality industry: A cross-cultural investigation. *International Journal of Intercultural Relations, 40*, 87–98.

Carlyle, T. (1841/1907). *Heroes and hero worship.* Boston, MA: Adams.

Carson, J. B., Tesluk, P. E., & Marrone, J. A. (2007). Shared leadership in teams: An investigation of antecedent conditions and performance. *Academy of Management Journal, 50*, 1217–1234.

Caruso, D. R., Mayer, J. D., & Salovey, P. (2002). Emotional intelligence and emotional leadership. In R. Riggio (Ed.), *Multiple intelligences and leadership* (pp. 55–73). Mahwah, NJ: Lawrence Erlbaum.

Cattell, R. B. (1965). *The scientific analysis of personality.* Baltimore, MD: Penguin.

Cavazotte, F., Moreno, V., & Hickmann, M. (2012). Effects of leader intelligence, personality and emotional intelligence on transformational leadership and managerial performance. *The Leadership Quarterly, 23*, 443–455.

Chen, T. (2014). *Team composition, emergent states and shared leadership emergence on project teams.* (Unpublished doctoral dissertation). George Mason University, Fairfax, VA.

Chen, T. R., & Zaccaro, S. J. (2013). The personality of leaders: From vertical to shared leadership. In R. Tett & N. Christiansen (Eds.), *Handbook of personality at work* (pp. 772–795). New York, NY: Routledge.

Church, A. T., Katigbak, M. S., Ching, C. M., Zhang, H., Shen, J., Arias, R. M., . . . Alvarez, J. M. (2013). Within-individual variability in self-concepts and personality states: Applying density distribution and situation-behavior approaches across cultures. *Journal of Research in Personality, 47*, 922–935.

Colbert, A. E., Barrick, M. R., & Bradley, B. H. (2013). Personality and leadership composition in top management teams: Implications for organizational effectiveness. *Personnel Psychology, 67*, 351–387.

Contractor, N. S., DeChurch, L. A., Carson, J., Carter, D. R., & Keegan, B. (2012). The topology of collective leadership. *The Leadership Quarterly, 23*, 994–1011.

Dalal, R. S., Meter, R. D., Bradshaw, R. P., Green, J. P., Kelly, E. D., & Zhu, M. (2015). Personality strength and situational influences on behavior: A conceptual review and research agenda. *Journal of Management, 41,* 561–587.

Daly, M., Egan, M., & O'Reilly, F. (2015). Childhood general cognitive ability predicts leadership role occupancy across life: Evidence from 17,000 cohort study participants. *The Leadership Quarterly, 26,* 323–341.

Day, D. V., Gronn, P., & Salas, E. (2004). Leadership capacity in teams. *The Leadership Quarterly, 15,* 857–880.

Day, D. V., Schleicher, D. J., Unckless, A. L., & Hiller, N. J. (2002). Self monitoring personality at work: A meta-analytic investigation of construct validity. *Journal of Applied Psychology, 87,* 390–401.

Day, D. V., & Sin, H. P. (2011). Longitudinal tests of an integrative model of leader development: Charting and understanding developmental trajectories. *The Leadership Quarterly, 22,* 545–560.

Day, D. V., & Zaccaro, S. J. (2007). Leadership: A critical historical analysis of the influence of leader traits. In L. L. Koppes (Ed.), *Historical perspectives in industrial and organizational psychology* (pp. 383–405). Mahwah, NJ: Lawrence Erlbaum.

Deinert, A., Homan, A. C., Boer, D., Voelpel, S. C., & Gutermann, D. (2015). Transformational leadership sub-dimensions and their link to leaders' personality and performance. *The Leadership Quarterly, 26,* 1095–1120.

DeRue, D. S., & Ashford, S. J. (2010). Who will lead and who will follow? A social process of leadership identity construction in organizations. *The Academy of Management Review, 35,* 627–647.

DeRue, D. S., Nahrgang, J. D., Wellman, N., & Humphrey, S. E. (2011). Trait and behavioral theories of leadership: An integration and meta-analytic test of their relative validity. *Personnel Psychology, 64,* 7–52.

Dinh, J. E., & Lord, R. G. (2012). Implications of dispositional and process views of traits for individual difference research in leadership. *The Leadership Quarterly, 23,* 651–669.

Dragoni, L., Oh, I., Vankatwyk, P., & Tesluk, P. (2011). Developing executive leaders: The relative contribution of cognitive ability, personality, and the accumulations of work experience in predicting strategic competency. *Personnel Psychology, 64,* 829–864.

Eagly, A. H., Karau, S. J., & Makhijani, M. G. (1995). Gender and the effectiveness of leaders: A meta-analysis. *Psychological Bulletin, 117,* 125–145.

Eagly, A. H., Makhijani, M. G., & Klonsky, B. G. (1992). Gender and the evaluation of leaders: A meta-analysis. *Psychological Bulletin, 111,* 3–22.

Ensari, N., Riggio, R. E., Christian, J., Carslaw, G. (2011). Who emerges as a leader? Meta-analyses of individual differences as predictors of leadership emergence. *Personality and Individual Differences, 51,* 532–536.

Ferris, G. R., Treadway, D. C., Kolodinsky, R. W., Hochwarter, W. A., Kacmar, C. J., Douglas, C., & Frink, D. D. (2005). Development and validation of the Political Skill Inventory. *Journal of Management, 31,* 126–152.

Fleishman, E. A., Mumford, M. D., Zaccaro, S. J., Levin, K. Y., Korotkin, A. L., & Hein, M. B. (1991). Taxonomic efforts in the description of leader behavior: A synthesis and functional interpretation. *The Leadership Quarterly, 2,* 245–287.

Foster, C., & Roche, F. (2014). Integrating trait and ability EI in predicting transformational leadership. *Leadership & Organization Development Journal, 35,* 316–334.

Foti, R. J., Bray, B. C., Thompson, N. J., & Allgood, S. F. 2012. Know thy self, know thy leader: Contributions of a pattern-oriented approach to examining leader perceptions. *The Leadership Quarterly, 23*(4): 702–717.

Foti, R. J., & Hauenstein, N. M. A. (2007). Pattern and variable approaches in leadership emergence and effectiveness. *Journal of Applied Psychology, 92,* 347–355.

Friedrich, T. L., Vessey, W. B., Schuelke, M. J., Ruark, G. A., & Mumford, M. D. (2009). A framework for understanding collective leadership: The selective utilization of leader and team expertise within networks. *The Leadership Quarterly, 20,* 933–958.

Gaddis, B. H., & Foster, J. L. (2015). Meta-analysis of dark side personality characteristics and critical work behaviors among leaders across the globe: Findings and implications for leadership development and executive coaching. *Applied Psychology: An International Review, 64,* 25–54.

Galton, F. (1869). *Hereditary genius.* New York, NY: Appleton.

Gentry, W. A., Leslie, J. B., Gilmore, D. C., Ellen, B. P., III, Ferris, G. R., & Treadway, D. C. (2013). Personality and political skill as distal and proximal predictors of leadership evaluations. *Career Development International, 18*, 569–588.

Grijalva, E. J. (2013). Narcissism and leadership: A meta-analysis of linear and nonlinear relationships (Unpublished doctoral dissertation). University of Illinois at Urbana-Champaign, Urbana, IL.

Groves, K. S., & Feyerherm, A. E. (2011). Leader cultural intelligence in context: Testing the moderating effects of team cultural diversity on leader and team performance. *Group & Organization Management, 36*, 535–566.

Guerin, D. W., Oliver, P. H., Gottfried, A. W., Gottfried, A. E., Reichard, R. J., & Riggio, R. E. (2011). Childhood adolescent antecedents of social skills and leadership potential in adulthood: Temperamental approach/ withdrawal and extraversion. *The Leadership Quarterly, 22*, 482–494.

Guilford, J. P. (1975). Factors and factors of personality. *Psychological Bulletin, 82*, 802–814.

Hambrick, D. C. (1994). Top management groups: A conceptual integration and reconsideration of the "team" label. *Research in Organizational Behavior, 16*, 171–213.

Hambrick, D. C., Finkelstein, S., & Mooney, A. C. (2005). Executive job demands: New insights for explaining strategic decisions and leader behaviors. *Academy of Management Review, 30*, 472–491.

Hambrick, D. C., & Mason, P. A. (1984). Upper echelons: The organization as a reflection of its top managers. *Academy of Management Review, 9*, 195–206.

Hannah, S. T., & Avolio, B. J. (2010). Ready or not: How do we accelerate the developmental readiness of leaders? *Journal of Organizational Behavior, 31*, 1181–1187.

Harms, P. D., & Crede, M. (2010). Emotional intelligence and transformational and transactional leadership: A meta-analysis. *Journal of Leadership and Organizational Studies, 17*, 5–17.

Hereford, J. M. (2012). *Enough is enough: The curvilinear relationship between personality and leadership* (Unpublished doctoral dissertation). Seattle Pacific University, Seattle, WA.

Hinrichs, A. W. T. (2011). *Motivation to lead: Examining its antecedents and consequences in a team context* (Unpublished doctoral dissertation). Texas A&M University, College Station, TX.

Hoffmann, B. J., Woehr, D. J., Maldagen-Youngjohn, R., & Lyons, B. D. (2011). Great man or great myth? A quantitative review of the relationship between individual differences and leader effectiveness. *Journal of Occupational and Organizational Psychology, 84*, 347–381.

Hogan, R., Curphy, G. J., & Hogan, J. (1994). What we know about leadership: Effectiveness and personality. *American Psychologist, 49*, 493–504.

Hogan, R., & Hogan, J. (2007). *Hogan Personality Inventory manual*. Tulsa, OK: Hogan Press.

Hogan, R., & Hogan, J. (2009). *Hogan Development Survey manual*. Tulsa, OK: Hogan Press.

Holland, S. J. (2015). *Perceptual disconnects in leadership emergence: An integrated examination of the role of trait configurations, dyadic relationships, and social influence* (Unpublished doctoral dissertation). George Mason University, Fairfax, VA.

Hong, Y., Catano, V. M., & Liao, H. (2011). Leader emergence: The role of emotional intelligence and motivation to lead. *Leadership & Organization Development Journal, 32*, 320–343.

House, R. J., & Howell, J. M. (1992). Personality and charismatic leadership. *The Leadership Quarterly, 3*, 81–108.

Hur, Y., van der Berg, P. T., & Wilderman, C. P. M. (2011). Transformational leadership as a mediator between emotional intelligence and team outcomes. *The Leadership Quarterly, 22*, 591–603.

Joseph, D. L., Dhanani, L. Y., Shen, W., McHugh, B. C., & McCord, M. A. (2015). Is a happy leader a good leader? A meta-analytic investigation of leader trait affect and leadership. *The Leadership Quarterly, 26*, 558–577.

Judge, T. A., Bono, J. E., Ilies, R., & Gerhardt, M. W. (2002). Personality and leadership: A qualitative and quantitative review. *Journal of Applied Psychology, 87*, 765–780.

Judge, T., Colbert, A., & Ilies, R. (2004). Intelligence and leadership: A quantitative review and test of theoretical propositions. *Journal of Applied Psychology, 89*, 542–552.

Judge, T. A., Locke, E. A., & Durham, C. C. (1997). The dispositional causes of job satisfaction: The role of core evaluations. *Journal of Applied Psychology, 83*, 17–34.

Judge, T. A., & Long, D. M. (2012). Individual differences in leadership. In D. V. Day & J. Antonakis (Eds.), *The nature of leadership* (2nd ed., pp. 179–217). Thousand Oaks, CA: Sage.

Judge, T. A., Piccolo, R. F., & Kosalka, T. (2009). The bright and dark sides of leader traits: A review and theoretical extension of the leader trait paradigm. *The Leadership Quarterly, 20,* 855–875.

Kaiser, R. B., & Hogan, J. (2011). Personality, leader behavior, and overdoing it. *Consulting Psychology Journal: Practice and Research, 63,* 219–242.

Kaiser, R. B., LeBreton, J. M., & Hogan, J. (2015). The dark side of personality and extreme leader behavior. *Applied Psychology: An International Review, 64,* 55–92.

Kant, L., Skogstad, A., Torsheim, T., & Einarsen, S. (2013). Beware the angry leader: Trait anger and trait anxiety of predictors of petty tyranny. *The Leadership Quarterly, 24,* 106–124.

Kenny, D. A., & Zaccaro, S. J. (1983). An estimate of variance due to traits in leadership. *Journal of Applied Psychology, 68,* 678–685.

Kim, Y. J., & Van Dyne, L. (2012). Cultural intelligence and international leadership potential: The importance of contact for members of the majority. *Applied Psychology: An International Review, 61,* 272–294.

Kirkpatrick, S. A., & Locke, E. A. (1991, May). Leadership: Do traits matter? *Academy of Management Executive, 5,* 48–60.

Kristoff-Brown, A. L., Zimmerman, R. D., & Johnson, E. C. (2005). Consequences of individuals' fit at work: A meta-analysis of person-job, person-organization, person-group, and person-supervisor fit. *Personnel Psychology, 58,* 281–342.

LaPort, K. A. (2012). *A multistage model of leader effectiveness: Uncovering the relationships between leader traits and leader behaviors* (Unpublished doctoral dissertation). George Mason University, Fairfax, VA.

Livi, S., Kenny, D. A., Albright, L., & Pierro, A. (2008). A social relations analysis of leadership. *The Leadership Quarterly, 19,* 235–248.

Lisak, A., & Erez, M. (2015). Leadership emergence in multicultural teams: The power of global characteristics. *Journal of World Business, 50,* 3–14.

Lord, R. G., De Vader, C. L., & Alliger, G. M. (1986). A meta-analysis of the relation between personality traits and leadership perceptions: An application of validity generalization procedures. *Journal of Applied Psychology, 71,* 402–410.

Lord, R. G., Foti, R. J., & De Vader, C. L. (1984). A test of leadership categorization theory: Internal structure, information processing, and leadership perceptions. *Organizational Behavior and Human Performance, 34,* 343–378.

Lord, R. G., & Hall, R. (1992). Contemporary views of leadership and individual differences. *The Leadership Quarterly, 3,* 137–157.

Lord, R. G., & Maher, K. J. (1991). *Leadership and information processing: Linking perceptions and performance.* London, UK: Routledge.

Luria, G., & Berson, Y. (2012). How do leadership motives affect informal and formal leadership emergence? *Journal of Organizational Behavior, 34,* 995–1015.

Mann, R. D. (1959). A review of the relationship between personality and performance in small groups. *Psychological Bulletin, 56,* 241–270.

McCrae, R. R., & Costa, P. T. (1987). Validation of the five-factor model of personality across instruments and observers. *Journal of Personality and Social Psychology, 52,* 81–90.

Melwani, S., Mueller, J. S., & Overbeck, J. R. (2012). Looking down: The influence of contempt and compassion on emergent leadership categorizations. *Journal of Applied Psychology, 97,* 1171–1185.

Mencl, J., Wefald, A. J., & van Ittersum, K. W. (2016). Transformational leader attributes: Interpersonal skills, engagement, and well-being. *Leadership and Organization Development Journal, 37,* 635–657.

Morgeson, F. P., DeRue, D. S., & Karam, E. P. (2009). Leadership in teams: A functional approach to understanding leadership structures and processes. *Journal of Management, 36,* 5–39.

Mumford, M. D., Zaccaro, S. J., Harding, F. D., Jacobs, T. O., & Fleishman, E. A. (2000). Leadership skills for a changing world: Solving complex social problems. *The Leadership Quarterly, 11,* 11–35.

Nadkarni, S., & Hermann, P. (2010). CEO personality, strategic flexibility, and firm performance: The case of the Indian business process outsourcing industry. *Academy of Management Journal, 53,* 1050–1073.

Olivares, O. J. (2011). The formative capacity of momentous events and leadership development. *Leadership and Organizational Development Journal, 32,* 837–853.

Owens, B. P., Wallace, A. S., & Waldman, D. A. (2015). Leader narcissism and follower outcomes: The counterbalancing effect of leader humility. *Journal of Applied Psychology, 100,* 1203–1213.

Pearce, C. L., & Conger, J. A. (2003). All those years ago: The historical underpinnings of shared leadership. In C. L. Pearce & J. A. Conger (Eds.), *Shared leadership: Reframing the hows and whys of leadership* (pp. 1–18). Thousand Oaks, CA: Sage.

Pervin, L. A. (1994). A critical analysis of current trait theory. *Psychological Inquiry, 5,* 103–113.

Pierce, J. R., & Aguinis, H. (2013). The too-much-of-a-good-thing effect in management. *Journal of Management, 39,* 313–338.

Reichard, R. J., Riggio, R. E., Guerin, D. W., Oliver, P. H., Gottfried, A. W., & Gottfried, A. E. (2011). A longitudinal analysis of relationships between adolescent personality and intelligence with adult leader emergence and transformational leadership. *The Leadership Quarterly, 22,* 471–481.

Richards, D. A., & Hackett, R. D. (2012). Attachment and emotion regulation: Compensatory interactions and leader–member exchange. *The Leadership Quarterly, 23,* 686–701.

Rus, D., van Knippenberg, D., & Wisse, B. (2012). Leader power and self-serving behavior: The moderating role of accountability. *The Leadership Quarterly, 23,* 13–26.

Schaumberg, R. L., & Flynn, F. J. (2012). Uneasy lies the head that wears the crown: The link between guilt proneness and leadership. *Journal of Personality and Social Psychology, 103,* 327–342.

Schneider, B., Ehrhart, M. G., Mayer, D. M., Saltz, J. L., & Niles-Jolly, K. (2005). Understanding organization-customer links in service settings. *Academy of Management Journal, 48,* 1017–1032.

Schneider, B., White, S. S., & Paul, M. C. 1998. Linking service climate and customer perceptions of service quality: Tests of a causal model. *Journal of Applied Psychology, 83*(2): 150–163.

Serban, A., Yammarino, F. J., Dionne, S. D., Kahai, S. S., Hao, C., McHugh, K. A., . . . Peterson, D. R. (2015). Leadership emergence in face-to-face and virtual teams: A multi-level model with agent-based simulations, quasi-experimental and experimental tests. *The Leadership Quarterly, 26,* 402–418.

Shondrick, S. J., Dinh, J. E., & Lord, R. G. (2010). Developments in implicit leadership theory and cognitive science: Applications to improving measurement and understanding alternatives to hierarchical leadership. *The Leadership Quarterly, 21,* 959–978.

Smith, J. A., & Foti, R. J. (1998). A pattern approach to the study of leader emergence. *The Leadership Quarterly, 9,* 147–160.

Sosik, J. J., Gentry, W. A., & Chon, J. (2012). The value of virtue in the upper echelons: A multisource examination of executive character strengths and performance. *The Leadership Quarterly, 23,* 367–382.

Stogdill, R. M. (1948). Personal factors associated with leadership: A survey of the literature. *Journal of Psychology, 25,* 35–71.

Stogdill, R. M. (1974). *Handbook of leadership: A survey of the literature.* New York, NY: Free Press.

Terman, L. M. (1904). A preliminary study of the psychology and pedagogy of leadership. *Pedagogical Seminary, 11,* 413–451.

Troth, A. C., & Gyetvey, C. (2014). Identifying leadership potential in an Australian context: Identifying leadership potential in an Australian context. *Asia Pacific Journal of Human Resources, 52,* 333–350.

Van Iddekinge, C. H., Ferris, G. R., & Heffner, T. S. (2009). Test of a multistage model of distal and proximal antecedents of leader performance. *Personnel Psychology, 62,* 463–495.

Waasdorp, T. E., Baker, C. N., Paskewich, B. S., & Leff, S. S. (2013). The association between forms of aggression, leadership, and social status among urban youth. *Journal of Youth and Adolescence, 42,* 263–274.

Walter, F., Humphrey, R. H., & Cole, M. S. (2012). Unleashing leadership potential. *Organizational Dynamics, 41*(3), 212–219.

Woo, S. E., Chernyshenko, O. S., Stark, S. E., & Conz, G. (2014). Validity of six openness facets in predicting work behaviors: A meta-analysis. *Journal of Personality Assessment, 96,* 76–86.

Xu, L., Fu, P., Xi, Y., Zhang, L., Zhao, X., Liao, Y., . . . Ge, J. (2014). Adding dynamics to a static theory: How traits evolve and how they are expressed. *The Leadership Quarterly, 25,* 1095–1119.

Zaccaro, S. J. (2001). *The nature of executive leadership: A conceptual and empirical analysis of success.* Washington, DC: American Psychological Association.

Zaccaro, S. J. (2007). Trait-based perspectives in leadership. *American Psychologist, 62,* 6–16.

Zaccaro, S. J. (2012). Individual differences and leadership: Contributions to a third tipping point. *The Leadership Quarterly, 23,* 718–728.

Zaccaro, S. J., Connelly, S., Repchick, K. M., Daza, A. I., Young, M. C., Kilcullen, R. N., . . . Bartholomew, L. N. (2015). The influence of higher order cognitive capacities on leader organizational continuance and retention: The mediating role of developmental experiences. *The Leadership Quarterly, 26,* 342–358.

Zaccaro, S. J., Foti, R. J., & Kenny, D. A. (1991). Self-monitoring and trait-based variance in leadership: An investigation of leader flexibility across multiple group situations. *Journal of Applied Psychology, 76,* 308–315.

Zaccaro, S. J., Gilbert, J. A., Thor, K. K., & Mumford, M. (1991). Leadership and social intelligence: Linking social perspectives and behavioral flexibility to leader effectiveness. *The Leadership Quarterly, 2,* 317–342.

Zaccaro, S. J., Gilrane, V. L., Robbins, J. M., Bartholomew, L. N., Young, M. C., Kilcullen, R. N., . . . Young, W. (2015). *Officer individual differences: Predicting long-term continuance and performance in the U.S. Army* (Technical Report 1324). Ft. Belvoir, VA: U.S. Army Research Institute for the Behavioral and Social Sciences.

Zaccaro, S. J., Kemp, C., & Bader, P. (2004). Leader traits and attributes. In J. Antonakis, A. Ciancola, & R. Sternberg (Eds.), *The nature of leadership* (pp. 101–124). Thousand Oaks, CA: Sage.

Zaccaro, S. J., LaPort, K., & Jose, I. (2013). Attributes of successful leaders: A performance requirements approach. In M. Rumsey (Ed.), *The Oxford handbook of leadership* (pp. 11–36). New York, NY: Oxford University Press.

Zacher, H., Clark, M., Anderson, E. C., & Ayoko, O. B. (2015). A lifespan perspective on leadership. In P. M. Bal, D. T. A. M. Kooij, & D. M. Rousseau (Eds.), *Aging workers and the employee–employer relationship* (pp. 87–104). New York, NY: Springer International.

Zacher, H., Pearce, L. K., Rooney, D., & McKenna, B. (2014). Leaders' personal wisdom and leader–member exchange quality: The role of individualized consideration. *Journal of Business Ethics, 121,* 171–187.

# CHAPTER 3

# Charisma and the "New Leadership"

*John Antonakis*

---

### Opening Case: A Day in the Life of a Leader

Timo just heard the news that he was going to be promoted to general manager of the new five-star hotel and also have corporate-level responsibilities. This new resort hotel was the flagship of the company. He had a few things to do that were urgent in his current post as general manager: announce the news to his current staff, make a presentation to the board about his vision for the new hotel, and develop a plan to recruit new staff. He had to send a few e-mails as well.

Although he was thrilled about the move, the announcement would be difficult to make—his current staff knew that something major was happening, and there had been rumors about his impending transfer. They did not want to lose "their manager"; whether line employees working in the rooms, the restaurants, or the front desk, whether gardeners, security, or health-spa staff, they and their supervisors all agreed on one thing: Timo was the best manager they had ever had and they did not want to lose him. They simply loved him.

From a young age, Timo appreciated the value of work; he helped his parents manage their shops. He learned much from watching his mother expertly use her charm to manage her staff and customers. He also learned from his father, a gifted orator and community leader who knew how to rouse the crowds. After studying hotel management and business, he started his career in the hotel industry, working up from assistant food and beverage manager to general manager; he was only 36 years old when he achieved what seems, to many, unachievable. He was a very visible manager; he did frequent rounds, knew all his staff personally, made clear what he expected from them, gave feedback, and coached. Yet he was firm, and he also laid down the law when needed. His staff, particularly the younger ones, saw Timo as a "rock-star manager." He had a quality, a mystical property that made him likeable and authoritative. There was always a "buzz" and excitement when he was around.

As he sat at his desk, he thought of how he would structure his speech; he'd probably start with a story—his story—of how he had started at the company and how he had grown within it. He had to inspire but also reassure his staff that all would be fine with the new manager. As he jotted down some points, his eye glanced at *The Economist* magazine on his desk. Greece was on the front cover again. "Darn the uncertainty that the debt crises are causing," he thought. "Plus the looming elections won't help." He had to build these uncertainties into his strategic plan and then make sure that his marketing and sales team had appropriate targets to shoot for.

## Discussion Questions

1. Why does Timo inspire such loyalty from his staff?

2. Why is Timo so successful?

3. Are the skills and behaviors that Timo has learnable?

# Chapter Overview

*But all this will avail us little unless we achieve our prime economic objective—the defeat of inflation. Inflation destroys nations and societies as surely as invading armies do. Inflation is the parent of unemployment. It is the unseen robber of those who have saved.*

*If our people feel that they are part of a great nation and they are prepared to will the means to keep it great, a great nation we shall be, and shall remain. So, what can stop us from achieving this? What then stands in our way? The prospect of another winter of discontent? I suppose it might. But I prefer to believe that certain lessons have been learnt from experience, that we are coming, slowly, painfully, to an autumn of understanding. And I hope that it will be followed by a winter of common sense. If it is not, we shall not be diverted from our course.*

*To those waiting with bated breath for that favourite media catchphrase, the "U" turn, I have only one thing to say. "You turn if you want to. The lady's not for turning." I say that not only to you but to our friends overseas and also to those who are not our friends.*

—Margaret Thatcher
Prime Minister of the United Kingdom
Speech to the Conservative Party
10 October 1980

Most people have heard of Margaret "Maggie" Thatcher—a towering figure of British politics. Why did she carry so much clout? Most would agree that she had that "something"—a special gift to communicate in very vivid ways, to get people excited and then committed to her course of action. She had *charisma*. She was adored by her supporters and loathed by her detractors.

Charisma and spinoff perspectives, which I call "neocharismatic" for simplicity, have been intensely studied by researchers. These constructs, though, have been hard to define and operationalize. Research aside, we know in practice that history has been marked by many men and women who have epitomized a potent messianic force capable of doing great deeds; this very force has also brought about destruction on a grand scale. Such is the assumed impact of charismatic leaders on individuals, organizations, and societies that philosophers, historians, psychologists, and other social scientists have taken turns to address what I think is probably one of the most interesting pieces of the leadership puzzle.

Charismatic leadership theory has had a massive impact on leadership as a scientific domain. This leadership approach was characterized by Bryman (1992) as the "new leadership," such was its break with existing leadership models. In a way, when charismatic leadership theory came along it was, ironically, a savior to leadership research just like charismatic leaders are to their collective (cf. Hunt, 1999). In other words, research on charisma delivered leadership researchers from their plight at a time when there was pessimism and no direction in leadership research, even with calls made to abandon leadership as a research topic (Greene, 1977; Miner, 1975). It is almost surreal to imagine that leadership, as a discipline, was not taken seriously a few decades ago; so when House (1977) first proposed a psychological theory of charismatic leadership, organizational scholars embraced it in full earnest.

Charismatic leadership and its closest cousin, transformational leadership, have been the focus of a great many research inquiries (Yukl, 1999); these approaches have helped shift the leadership paradigm to where it is today (Antonakis, Cianciolo, & Sternberg, 2004; Day & Antonakis, 2012; Hunt, 1999; Lowe & Gardner, 2000). This research stream dominates the leadership landscape—whether deservingly or not—at least in terms of published papers in the premier academic leadership journal, *The Leadership Quarterly* (Antonakis, Bastardoz, Liu, & Schriesheim, 2014; Gardner, Lowe, Moss, Mahoney, & Cogliser, 2010; Lowe & Gardner, 2000).

How did charismatic leadership and related approaches (e.g., transformational, visionary) develop? What gives charismatic leaders so much power? Where is charismatic leadership theory heading? I will try to answer these questions and others in this chapter. To do so, I will review some of the major historical works that provided the scaffolding for current theories of charisma as well as related forms of leadership. In terms of the contemporary theories, I will focus on the most dominant forms, charisma and transformational leadership. Although my initial work was focused on transformational leadership (Antonakis, 2001; Antonakis, Avolio, & Sivasubramaniam, 2003), I will draw on some of my more recent work to critically review these theoretical streams and explain why I am going back to the root construct, charisma (Antonakis, Bastardoz, Jacquart, & Shamir, 2016; Antonakis, Fenley, & Liechti, 2011; Jacquart & Antonakis, 2015). I realize, too, that I would be considered a part of the charisma "mafia," as Gemmill and Oakley (1992) would say. However, being part of the *famiglia* gives some credibility to my arguments, on which, as you will see, I do not hold back. I briefly discuss competing "new leadership" theories, and conclude with where this research is heading and what remains to be studied still.

## Charisma: A Brief History

Most writers credit Weber (1947) with having coined the term *charisma* and having provided the first modern theoretical explanation for the impact of charismatic leadership on followers. Evidence of the roots of the word *charisma*, however, predate Weber and are found in Greek mythology—the graces, or *Charites*—and the goddess *Charis* (see Antonakis et al., 2016, for details). Moreover, theoretical explanations of a phenomenon akin to charismatic leadership and the ways in which leaders should go about influencing followers using potent persuasive means are also found in the writings of Aristotle (trans., 1954), appearing in the fourth century BCE. Aristotle first laid the foundations to rhetoric, which is key to inducing the charismatic effect (Antonakis et al., 2011; Antonakis et al., 2016; Jacquart & Antonakis, 2015).

In *Rhetoric*, Aristotle argued that a leader must gain the confidence of his followers by using creative rhetorical means, which include providing a moral perspective via his personal character (*ethos*), rousing follower emotions (*pathos*), and then using reasoned argument (*logos*)—see Figure 3.1. It will become evident that these three dimensions, or what Aristotle termed the artistic means, as well as other means—including contracts, laws, tortures, witnesses, and oaths—can be seen as a parsimonious version of some contemporary leadership theories. These theories typically contrast (a) charisma and related approaches (e.g., transformational leadership) versus what can be termed (b) transactional leadership (Bass, 1985; Burns, 1978; Downton, 1973). To better understand the startling insights of Aristotle, which touch not only on charismatic leadership but also on affect and cognitive psychology, as well as other areas of science, I quote from Book I, Chapter II, where he refers to the three kinds of rhetorical influencing:

> Persuasion is achieved by the speaker's personal character when the speech is so spoken as to make us think him credible. We believe good men more fully and more readily than others: this is true generally whatever the question is, and absolutely true where exact certainty is impossible and opinions are divided. This kind of persuasion, like the others, should be achieved by what

the speaker says, not by what people think of his character before he begins to speak. It is not true, as some writers assume in their treatises on rhetoric, that the personal goodness revealed by the speaker contributes nothing to his power of persuasion; on the contrary, his character may almost be called the most effective means of persuasion he possesses. Secondly, persuasion may come through the hearers, when the speech stirs their emotions. Our judgments when we are pleased and friendly are not the same as when we are pained and hostile. It is towards producing these effects, as we maintain, that present-day writers on rhetoric direct the whole of their efforts. This subject shall be treated in detail when we come to speak of the emotions. Thirdly, persuasion is effected through the speech itself when we have proved a truth or an apparent truth by means of the persuasive arguments suitable to the case in question. (p. 7)

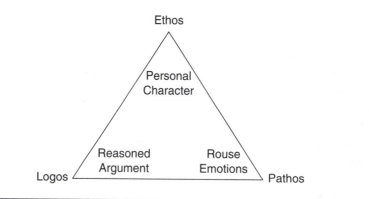

**Figure 3.1**    Leader Persuasion Using the Aristotelian Triad

NOTE: According to Aristotle (trans., 1954, p. 7): "The first kind [of persuasion, the ethos] depends on the personal character of the speaker; the second [the pathos] on putting the audience into a certain frame of mind; the third [the logos] on the proof, or apparent proof, provided by the words of the speech itself."

It is a real eye-opener to read classics such as *Rhetoric* and Plato's *Republic* (trans. 1901); these works provided important foundations for Western thought on topics concerning leadership, ethics, and good government. Yet what I also find troubling by reading these works is why humanity is not more sophisticated and responsible than it currently is, when so much was known so long ago. Why do institutions have trouble selecting the best leaders? Why is leader corruption still rife? Why are people so easily duped by slick sales pitches of leaders?

In essence, many of these problems are problems of leadership. These are big questions, which I find fascinating; for this reason, I have been looking at which traits predict effective leadership (Antonakis, House, & Simonton, 2017), how power corrupts (Bendahan, Zehnder, Pralong, & Antonakis, 2015), how leaders are elected (Antonakis & Dalgas, 2009; Antonakis & Eubanks, 2017; Jacquart & Antonakis, 2015), and other interesting questions. Yet it is only recently that these problems of humanity have been scrutinized scientifically, and the importance of leadership isolated and studied in a causal way (Bertrand & Schoar, 2003; Jones & Olken, 2005). Warren Bennis (this volume), who over the decades has demonstrated remarkable perspicacity about the problems of leadership, reminds us that leaders wield power and that it is important to put more science into understanding how better to manage the leadership production process.

Indeed, the most potent of leaders, charismatic ones, can bring about needed social change; these types of leaders have been capable of dreadful deeds, too, which explains Bennis's concerns. Of course, my chapter does not provide a treatise on issues concerning the selection, development, and outcomes of leadership and related topics; this is the job of the entire volume. I focus on charismatic and neo-charismatic leadership approaches, though I will touch on some of these important issues where relevant. Next, I discuss the most important contributions to this research stream, chronologically, using Weber as the point of departure. For a thorough historical overview, refer to a recent review I undertook with my colleagues (Antonakis et al., 2016).

## The Weberian Perspective

Weber (1947) used the term *charismatic* to describe a type of leader who could bring about social change. These leaders arose "in times of psychic, physical, economic, ethical, religious, [or] political distress" (Weber, 1968). For Weber (1968), charisma in leaders referred to "specific gifts of the body and spirit not accessible to everybody" (p. 19). These leaders were attributed "with supernatural, superhuman, or at least specifically exceptional powers or qualities" (Weber, 1947, p. 358) and could undertake great feats. Obviously, such vague descriptions and appeals to the supernatural do not allow charisma to be scientifically studied (Antonakis et al., 2016). Still, what Weber argued paved the way for other researchers to better see the outcomes of charismatic leadership.

Weber (1968) believed that followers of a charismatic leader willingly place their destiny in their leader's hands and support the leader's mission that may have arisen out of "enthusiasm, or of despair and hope" (p. 49). Weber argued that charismatic authority is different from bureaucratic authority and that at the core of charisma is an emotional appeal whose "attitude is revolutionary and transvalues everything; it makes a sovereign break with all traditional or rational norms" (p. 24). Finally, Weber stated that the charismatic effect and legacy of the leader may continue as artifacts of the organizational or societal culture, but then wane as the organization or society is enveloped in the rational and methodical processes of the bureaucracy.

What is interesting in the Weberian idea of the charismatic leader is the importance of context and the apparent salvationary effects of the charismatic leader. Also important is the notion of charismatic authority as being distinct from other sources of authority. Weber was not very clear on what, specifically, charismatic leaders do, and he was more concerned with ends than with means. Other sociologists continued in this vein (e.g., Shils, 1965). Etzioni's (1964) structuralist perspective, for instance, focuses on the effect that formal leadership has on individuals and the source of power that is used to exert influence over followers. Symbolic power is what Etzioni (1961) referred to as "charisma" (p. 203). According to Etzioni (1964), greater commitment and less alienation will be displayed in followers when their leaders are using symbolic over material or physical power, and material over physical power. Other sociologists extended Weber's ideas and tried to make the mystical concept more concrete (Friedland, 1964). Political scientists also became interested in charisma and tried expressly to pin it down (Davies, 1954; Friedrich, 1961; Tucker, 1968). I focus on Downton next, whose theory quietly upstaged some of the most dominant contemporary models of leadership, particularly the transformational-transactional leadership model.

## Downton's Theory of Charisma

In line with the Weberian notion of charisma, Downton (1973) proposed a theory of leadership in the context of the rebel political leader. This theory consisted of three factors: charismatic, inspirational, and transactional leadership. After Aristotle's work, this was the second theory to pit contractual (transactional) principal-agent type influence processes against charismatic authority. This work predates that of Bass (1985) by more than a decade, and it was not mentioned by Bass in his most famous work, though he does refer to it later (Hater & Bass, 1988). In discussing the transforming versus transactional leader, Burns (1978), a historian and political scientist, did refer to Downton's work indirectly and mostly in passing (regarding revolutionary leadership).

For Downton (1973) transactional leadership meant "a process of exchange that is analogous to contractual relations in economic life [and] contingent on the good faith of the participants" (p. 75). Downton believed that the fulfillment of transactional commitments forms the basis of trust among leaders and their followers, strengthens their relationship, and results in a mutually beneficial climate for further transactions to occur. Downton distinguished between positive and negative transactions. Positive transactions occur when followers receive rewards contingent on achieving desired outcomes, whereas negative transactions refer to followers' noncompliance, resulting in punishment (as discussed later, this precise notion of positive and negative transactional leadership is how Bass [1985] theorized contingent rewards and management-by-exception leader behavior).

Downton argued that charismatic leaders have potent effects on followers because of their transcendental ideals and authority that facilitate the followers' identification with the leader. In those conditions, trust is solidified as psychological exchanges occur. This commitment and trust is further augmented by inspirational leadership. The inspirational leader is persuasive, and he or she encourages followers to invest in and make sacrifices toward the identified ideals, gives followers a sense of purpose, and creates meaning for actions distinct from the charismatic appeal. Followers relate to these types of leaders, but they do not necessarily revere them. Thus, inspirational leadership is, apparently, independent of charismatic leadership; according to Downton (1973), inspirational leadership does not foster follower dependence in the leader. Rather, "inspirational commitment is always contingent on the leader's continuing symbolic presentation of the follower's world view" (p. 80). Downton argued further that although charismatic relations between leaders and followers will ultimately lead to inspirational relations, not all inspirational relations lead to charismatic relations. Finally, Downton proposed that all sources of leadership, whether transactional, inspirational, or charismatic, should be used in varying degrees (which is in line with the ideas of Bass, 1985). Although Downton set what were the foundations for transformational and charismatic leadership theory, the impact he had on the field was minimal—probably because his work was not picked up by psychologists studying leadership in the 1980s, by which time Bass's theory was firmly entrenched.

## House's Psychological Theory of Charismatic Theory

House (1977) was the first to present an integrated theoretical framework and testable propositions to explain the behavior of charismatic leaders; he also focused on the psychological impact of charismatic leaders on followers. Also important was that House provided a theoretical explanation regarding the means charismatic leaders use to influence followers (and thus manage the perceptions of followers); importantly, he referred to charismatic leaders as having the necessary persuasive skills to influence others. He also described the personal characteristics of charismatic leaders and suggested that individual-difference predictors of charismatic leaders might be measurable. This theory was perhaps the most important in setting the foundations for how charisma is studied today; although it was "undersold" in being published as a book chapter and not a journal article (thus limiting its impact), this work has been enormously influential and highly cited.

House (1977) proposed that the basis for the charismatic appeal is the emotional interaction that occurs between followers and their leader. Depending on mission requirements, charismatic leaders arouse followers' motives to accomplish the leader's ideals and values. Followers in turn display affection and admiration for the leader, and internalize a sense of identification with the leader. House believed that charismatic leaders are those "who by force of their personal abilities are capable of having profound and extra-ordinary effects on followers" (p. 189). According to House, these leaders display confidence in their own abilities and in their followers, set high expectations for themselves and their followers, and show confidence that these expectations can be achieved. As a result of these behaviors, House argued that these leaders become role models and objects of identification of followers, who in turn emulate their leader's ideals and values and are enthusiastically inspired and motivated to reach outstanding accomplishments. These types of leaders are seen as courageous, because they challenge a status quo that is seen as undesirable. Furthermore, "because of other 'gifts' attributed to the leader, such as extraordinary competence, the followers believe that the leader will bring about social change and will thus deliver them from their plight" (p. 204).

House (1977) stated that "In actuality, the 'gift' is likely to be a complex interaction of personal characteristics, the behavior the leader employs, characteristics of followers, and certain situational factors prevailing at the time of the assumption of the leadership style" (p. 193). Finally, in focusing on the personal characteristics of charismatic leaders, House argued that they display a high degree of self-confidence, pro-social assertiveness (dominance), and moral conviction. These leaders model what they expect their followers to do, exemplify the struggle by self-sacrifice, and engage in image-building and self-promotion actions to come across as powerful and competent.

The insights of House (1977) were prescient. His theory was beautifully and clearly expressed and shook leadership scholars out of their current ideas of how leadership should be conceived at a time when leadership was not being taken very seriously (Antonakis et al., 2004; Day & Antonakis, 2012). Although House missed some details—for instance, regarding a proper definition of charisma and specific pointers on how to model it—his ideas were the catalyst for a new leadership movement (Antonakis et al., 2016).

## Conger and Kanungo's Attribution (i.e., Inferential) Theory of Charisma

Conger and Kanungo (1998, 1988) proposed a theory of charismatic leadership whereby a leader is legitimized through an attributional process based on the perceptions that followers have of the leader's behaviors. Although this theory uses the term *attribution* with respect to ascriptions that followers make about the leader, to be more precise, the psychological processes that are occurring are actually *inferential* (Jacquart & Antonakis, 2015)—attributions concern understanding causes of effects (Calder, 1977) and inferences pertain to person perception (Erickson & Krull, 1999).

Conger and Kanungo (1998) proposed that individuals are validated as leaders by their followers through a three-stage behavioral process. This process is not necessarily linear, and the stages can occur in any order and may exist concomitantly. First, effective charismatic leaders assess the status quo to determine the needs of followers, evaluate the resources that are available within the constituency, and articulate a compelling argument to arouse follower interest. Second, leaders articulate a vision of the future that will inspire follower action to achieve objectives that are instrumental in fulfilling the vision. The idealized vision creates follower identification and affection for the leader, because the vision embodies a future state of affairs that is valued by followers. Third, leaders create an aura of confidence and competence by demonstrating conviction that the mission is achievable. Leaders use unconventional means and expertise to inspire action and display how objectives can be achieved. In this way, they serve as powerful role models to promote follower action. This three-stage process is hypothesized to engender high trust in the leader and follower performance that enables the organization to reach its goals. This theory has been operationalized via the CKS—the Conger Kanungo Scale (Conger & Kanungo, 1998)—and resulted in a fair amount of empirical work; however, the global factor of the CKS correlates very highly with transformational leadership, $r = .88$, uncorrected for measurement error (Rowold & Heinitz, 2007).

## Shamir and Colleagues on Charisma

In a refreshing and novel integration of charisma and theories of identity, House and Shamir (1993) proposed an integrative framework to explain how leaders engage the self-concepts of follower (see also Shamir, House, & Arthur, 1993). In this way, leaders have exceptional effects on followers, who are motivated by increased levels of self-esteem, self-worth, self-efficacy, collective efficacy, identification with the leader, social identification, and value internalization. Shamir et al. (1993) stated that these leaders affect followers as a result of motivational mechanisms that are induced by the leader's behaviors. These behaviors include providing an ideological explanation for action, emphasizing a collective purpose, referring to historical accounts related to ideals, referring to the self-worth and efficacy of followers, and expressing confidence in followers that they are capable of fulfilling the mission (see also Shamir, Arthur, & House, 1994). As a result of the leader's behavior, the motivational mechanisms trigger the self-concept effects that lead to personal commitment to the leader's mission, self-sacrificial behavior, organizational citizenship, and task meaningfulness. These effects are further enhanced by the generation of self-expression and consistency on the part of the followers. As an example of the intricateness of these effects, Shamir et al. (1993) stated that "charismatic leaders . . . increase followers' self-worth through emphasizing the relationships between efforts and important values. A general sense of self-worth increases general self-efficacy; a sense of moral correctness is a source of strength and confidence. Having complete faith in the moral correctness of one's convictions gives one the strength and confidence to behave accordingly" (p. 582).

# Transformational Leadership

I include here influential models that expressly contrast neocharismatic and transformational leadership with transactional forms of leadership. Those theories that have been operationalized using questionnaires have been enormously influential and have triggered much empirical work.

## Burns's Transforming-Transactional Leadership

Burns (1978), a Pulitzer Prize winner, published his magnum opus on leadership in political settings. His work laid the foundations for Bass (1985), particularly with respect to transformative effects of leaders on followers. Burns defined leadership as "inducing followers to act for certain goals that represent the values and the motivations—the wants and needs, the aspirations and expectations—*of both leaders and followers*" (p. 19). Although leaders are intricately connected to goals with followers, they act as an independent force in steering followers toward those goals. The leader–follower interaction that could occur was defined as either (a) transactional leadership, which entailed a relationship based on the exchange of valued items, whether political, economic, or emotional, or (b) transforming leadership, where the motivation, morality, and ethical aspirations of both the leader and followers are raised.

According to Burns (1978), transforming leadership—focused on transcendent and far-reaching goals and ideals—has a greater effect on followers and collectives as compared to transactional leadership, which is focused on promoting self-interest and is thus limited in scope and impact. Transforming leaders raise the consciousness of followers for what is important, especially with regard to moral and ethical implications, and make them transcend their self-interest for that of the greater good. Although both transactional and transforming leadership can contribute to human purpose, Burns saw them as opposing ends of a spectrum. As stated by Burns, "The chief monitors of transactional leadership are modal values, that is, values of means. . . . Transformational leadership is more concerned with end-values" (p. 426). Burns saw these two leadership styles as a trade-off, a zero-sum game.

Bass (1985) directly built on Burns's (1978) theory. Bass extended the model to include subdimensions of what he termed *transformational* (instead of transforming) leadership. Also, although in Bass's original conceptualization of transformational leadership he was not concerned with moral and ethical overtones, he eventually came around to agreeing with Burns that the likes of Hitler were pseudotransformational and that at the core of veritable transformational leadership were "good" values (see Bass & Steidlmeier, 1999).

## Bass's Transformational-Transactional Leadership Model

Bass's (1985) transformational-transactional theory, also called the "full-range" leadership theory, includes both elements of the "new leadership" (i.e., charisma, vision, and the like) and elements of the "old leadership" (i.e., transactional leadership behavior focused on role and task requirements). I mention some elements here because the idea of this theory was to go beyond the behavioral two-factor theories of leadership (see Seltzer & Bass, 1990). These theories (see Fleishman, 1953, 1957; Halpin, 1954; Stogdill & Coons, 1957) conceptualized leadership as being focused on tasks (initiating structure) or people (consideration) and were the dominant leadership paradigm in the 1950s and 1960s. The Bass model misses out, however, on task-related leader behavior, although Bass had suggested otherwise. Antonakis and House (2002) came to this conclusion by comparing and contrasting the Bass theory with other "new" theories. Their suggestion was recently tested, and there is strong evidence showing that the full-range theory is not as full as first purported (Antonakis & House, 2014; Rowold, 2014), particularly with respect to strategic as well as work-facilitation aspects (Hunt, 2004; Yukl, 1999)—what can be termed *instrumental leadership* (Antonakis & House, 2014).

The Bass theory is probably the best known and most influential contemporary theory—it has a long history of research emanating from the work of Bass, Avolio, and colleagues (Avolio & Bass, 1995; Avolio, Bass, & Jung, 1999; Bass & Avolio, 1993, 1994; Bass, Avolio, & Atwater, 1996; Bass, Waldman, Avolio, & Bebb, 1987; Hater & Bass, 1988; Waldman, Bass, & Yammarino, 1990; Yammarino & Bass,

1990). This theory has been operationalized and measured by the Multifactor Leadership Questionnaire, or MLQ (Antonakis et al., 2003; Antonakis & House, 2014). Although there has been much debate about the factor structure of the MLQ model, there is little or no controversy about the predictive (concurrent) validity of the MLQ factors, which has been supported by numerous meta-analyses (Banks, Engemann, Williams, & Gooty, 2016; DeGroot, Kiker, & Cross, 2000; Dumdum, Lowe, & Avolio, 2002; Fuller, Patterson, Hester, & Stringer, 1996; Gasper, 1992; Judge & Piccolo, 2004; Lowe, Kroeck, & Sivasubramaniam, 1996; Wang, Oh, Courtright, & Colbert, 2011). In its current form, the MLQ measures nine leadership factors. Five factors measure transformational leadership (i.e., idealized influence attributes, idealized influence behaviors, inspirational motivation, intellectual stimulation, and individualized consideration); the next three measure transactional leadership (i.e., contingent rewards, management-by-exception active, and management-by-exception passive); and the last factor is concerned with nonleadership (i.e., laissez-faire leadership). This questionnaire measure is the most popular measure of transformational leadership and charisma (Antonakis et al., 2016). Although Bass considered charisma to be a subcomponent of transformational leadership, his position has been strongly challenged (Yukl, 1999); my colleagues and I agree with Yukl that charisma and transformational leadership are two rather different constructs and that charisma should be untethered from transformational leadership (Antonakis et al., 2016).

## Podsakoff's Transformational-Transactional Leadership Model

This model is conceptually similar to the original Bass (1985) model. After the Bass model, the Podsakoff model is the most widely used transformational-transactional leadership model (Bass & Riggio, 2006). The model that Podsakoff and colleagues proposed (Podsakoff, MacKenzie, & Bommer, 1996; Podsakoff, MacKenzie, Moorman, & Fetter, 1990) includes both transformational and transactional leadership factors. The transformational factors include identifying and articulating a vision, providing an appropriate model, fostering the acceptance of group goals, communicating high performance expectations, providing individualized support, and being intellectually stimulating. The Podsakoff model also includes a transactional leader factor, contingent reward leadership. These factors essentially map on the Bass transformational-transactional model, except for the fact that the Podsakoff model does not include management-by-exception active and passive as well as laissez-faire leadership. For those wishing to include similar factors to these omitted styles, contingent and noncontingent punishment scales, also developed by Podsakoff and colleagues, could be useful (see Podsakoff, Todor, Grover, & Huber, 1984; Podsakoff, Todor, & Skov, 1982); these constructs have shown relatively good validities (Podsakoff, Bommer, Podsakoff, & MacKenzie, 2006). Although the Podsakoff questionnaire measure, the Transformational Leadership Inventory, has not been as closely scrutinized as the MLQ, it is particularly well appreciated by the research community because it is not a proprietary instrument (as is the MLQ).

### Other Transformational Leadership Models

Beyond the models that I have reviewed, there are other lesser-known models that are being used. Rafferty and Griffin (2004) proposed a five-factor model of transformational leadership, which looks like it might have had some potential; however, this instrument has not been extensively studied by independent research groups, and it omits important correlates of leader outcomes. Another measure, the Transformational Leadership Questionnaire (TLQ), has been proposed as an alternative to the United States–centered MLQ-type models (Alimo-Metcalfe & Alban-Metcalfe, 2001); however, there is not much evidence for the validity of the TLQ, and it has not triggered much research. Other measures have been proposed as well (e.g., De Hoogh, Den Hartog, & Koopman, 2004), but they have not gathered much traction in applied research. One measure, which seems to have had an important impact on practice, is the Leadership Practices Inventory (LPI), by Kouzes and Posner (1987). Although intuitively appealing and driven by the popularity of their book *The Leadership Challenge*, the validation results reported on the LPI are not impressive and there has been very little research on the psychometric properties of this model.

# Spinoffs of the New Leadership: Old Wine in New Bottles?

Recently there have been several spinoff theories that at the outset claim to be quite different from transformational and neocharismatic perspectives: Of these, authentic, ethical, and servant leadership are the best known (Hoch, Bommer, Dulebohn, & Wu, 2016). These theories have something in common: They are all "loaded" in terms of how they have been defined; that is, they include the outcome in their definitions, and the very term used to name the theory is positively and morally valenced. Transformational leadership suffers from the same problem. Terms like *transformational, authentic, ethical,* and the like suggest an outcome—that is, that the leader transforms or is morally good. Doing so is problematic from a scientific point of view (van Knippenberg & Sitkin, 2013) for three reasons: Constructs should not be defined by their outcomes, because doing so leads to tautologies and circular theorizing (MacKenzie, 2003); the nature of what is measured should be exogenous with respect to the outcomes it is supposed to cause (Antonakis et al., 2016); and scientists should separate ideological agendas from accurately describing how the world works (Antonakis, 2017; Eagly, 2016).

Let me be clear about the latter point. Of course, the vast majority of scientists want to ensure that leaders use their power to do good. But doing so depends on institutional constraints and the moral foundations of the leader, which, of course, are important to examine along with leader outcomes in empirical work (Bendahan et al., 2015). However, a leadership definition should be independent of contextual constraints and moral orientations so that its pure form, its defining conceptual bedrock, is identified. The very motivational mechanisms used by leaders to do good can also be used to do bad (Antonakis et al., 2016); thus, one should not develop a theoretical proposition (good leadership is authentic) to re-describe a particular outcome (authentic leaders do good) and hence reify a particular moral agenda. Moreover, as scientists, it is critical to separate our expectations—what outcomes we hope to find—from reporting what actually occurs. This separation is important because if ideology guides what we do, we will construct theories that might not be counterfactually challenged (Durand & Vaara, 2009; Gerring & McDermott, 2007); we will also create questionnaire measures that will find what we seek given that ratings of leadership are prone to many biases including using outcomes of leadership to fill in the blanks in an intuitive and cognitively consistent way (Lord, Binning, Rush, & Thomas, 1978; Rush, Thomas, & Lord, 1977). The rating of leadership thus becomes an outcome and this outcome is used to predict other outcomes, leading to circular testing and theorizing (Antonakis, 2017; Antonakis et al., 2016; van Knippenberg & Sitkin, 2013).

As for the three spinoffs, authentic leadership, as defined by Avolio and Gardner and colleagues (Avolio & Gardner, 2005; Avolio, Gardner, Walumbwa, Luthans, & May, 2004), has attracted much attention. A sufficient amount of research has been undertaken to now examine whether this form of leadership is different from established forms. Recent meta-analyses have shown that transformational and authentic leadership are very highly correlated (i.e., $r = .74$ to $.75$) and do not explain much in outcomes beyond each other (Banks, McCauley, Gardner, & Guler, 2016); in particular, when assessing the incremental validity of authentic leadership over transformational leadership, nothing much is gained (Hoch et al., 2016). There have also been some strong challenges with respect to the notion that the Authentic Leadership Questionnaire actually measures a high-order factor (Credé & Harms, 2015).

Ethical leadership has been another theory that has triggered much attention (Brown & Treviño, 2006; Brown, Treviño, & Harrison, 2005). However, similar to the above results, ethical leadership does not add much in terms of incremental validity and is highly correlated with transformational leadership at $r = .70$ (Hoch et al., 2016). Only servant leadership has a much lower correlation with transformational leadership (Hoch et al., 2016). However, it is still problematic, given what I mentioned above; being a servant leader is still an outcome of some process and should be modeled as such.

# Future Research

Research on the new leadership has been described as being in a mature stage, and this almost two decades ago (cf. Hunt, 1999). We are discovering more about its mediators and moderators, but we are not doing enough about rethinking and trimming the models (Antonakis, 2017). At least work in this area continues at a brisk pace, not only in the traditional spheres of management, applied psychology, business, and general and social psychology, but also in other disciplines—including, nursing, education, political science, public health, public administration, sociology, ethics, operations research, computer sciences, industrial engineering, and others. Still, there remains much to be done with respect to identifying the conceptual cores of theories, refining the theories, measuring and modeling constructs correctly, and developing process theories of leadership (Antonakis, 2017; Fischer, Dietz, & Antonakis, 2016). Also, more needs to be done on understanding how charismatic leadership can be developed, as well as its causal impact on outcomes. Apart from knowing that personality and intelligence—which are genetically determined, stable, and hence exogenous—matter for charisma (Antonakis, House, et al., 2017; Banks, Engemann, et al., 2016), we also know that charisma can be manipulated in the laboratory, whether with actors or normal folk (Frese, Beimel, & Schoenborn, 2003; Howell & Frost, 1989; Towler, 2003), and this in field experiments as well (Antonakis, d'Adda, Weber, & Zehnder, 2015; Antonakis et al., 2011).

## Correctly Modeling Leadership Style

Questionnaire measures of leadership can be safely modeled as endogenous variables (i.e., dependent variables). However, if used as predictors they have to be modeled correctly or manipulated, or else the causal effect of the variable on other variables cannot be correctly estimated. Unfortunately, this is an area that is not well understood in our field, and reviews of published outcomes show that much of what is published cannot inform policy (Antonakis, Bastardoz, et al., 2014; Antonakis, Bendahan, Jacquart, & Lalive, 2010; Fischer et al., 2016).

The discussion here is not only leveled to transformational and charismatic leadership models; it is relevant to all models of leadership, particularly the leader-member exchange construct, which is more of an outcome of leadership than it is a leadership style (House & Aditya, 1997). Briefly, the problem that researchers have when undertaking observational studies, whether cross-sectional or longitudinal research, is that the modeled independent variable—say, transformational leadership ($x$)—is not manipulated; that is, it is not exogenous with respect to what it is modeled to predict. In experimental research, the experimenter is assured that the effect of $x$ on $y$ is due to the manipulation and nothing else. By randomly assigning the treatment, the error term in the regression model captures no systematic variation that is correlated with the treatment—refer to Chapter 16 of this volume for a basic introduction to this issue (for a more detailed exposé refer to Antonakis et al., 2010; Antonakis, Bendahan, Jacquart, & Lalive, 2014). However, with nonexperimental research, the modeler has a problem: that $x$ may correlate with unobserved variation affecting $y$, or that $y$ might simultaneously cause $x$ (this problem is referred to as one of endogeneity). Thus, if $x$ is modeled as an independent variable when it is in fact endogenous, the effect of $x$ on $y$ is biased and uninterpretable.

For instance, if individuals rating a leadership style know of leader outcomes (e.g., how well the leader's unit has performed), they will be biased when rating the leader due to attribution processes (Lord et al., 1978; Rush et al., 1977). That is, good performance will be associated with prototypically good leadership, and thus raters will "see" the leader being better on aspects of leadership that are implicitly associated with good (or bad) outcomes. Thus, leadership is de facto operationalized in terms of follower perceptions and attributions, which may have little to do with how the leader actually acts and independent of whether the leader is the cause of the outcomes; thus, we cannot know anything about how leadership affects outcomes and cannot make any suggestions for policy! Such findings make for a sorry state of affairs in leadership research.

Of course, leaders can affect leader outcomes, too. Yet failure to correctly "lockin" the causal direction, as is usually done by applied researchers, will render estimates suspect. I cannot stress enough the importance of understanding the limitations of using leadership questionnaire measures (like the MLQ and others). Researchers must use the correct design conditions and statistical methods to overcome these limitations. When doing this correctly, for instance, we see that the effects of transformational leadership on outcomes, as usually tested, have been vastly exaggerated (Antonakis & House, 2014). To correctly estimate a model where $x$, the intended regressor, is potentially endogenous (as in the case of any questionnaire measure of leadership), in the following model $x \rightarrow y$, an exogenous source of variance must be used to "purge" $x$ of endogeneity bias. Thus, in this case, the model that must be estimated is $z \rightarrow x \rightarrow y$ (where $z$ in this case is referred to as an instrumental variable). The instrumental variable must be exogenous and vary independently of the disturbance of $y$. Examples of instrumental variables could be individual differences that can be reliably and ideally objectively measured (e.g., IQ, personality), fixed-effects of leaders (i.e., obtaining repeated measures over time or from many raters), contextual factors (e.g., country, industry, firm), or exogenous shocks (for ideas, see Antonakis et al., 2010). Although some research has been undertaken in this area of individual differences (Bono & Judge, 2004; Judge & Bono, 2000), not enough has been done to predict the factors of the full-range model. This is the case considering the full gamut of individual difference predictors, including general intelligence (Antonakis, House, et al., 2017).

Another problem that I often see, which follows from above, is models being estimated in a piecemeal way, having obvious omitted variables. For example, regressing $y$ only on charismatic leadership (e.g., Keller, 1992; Koene, Vogelaar, & Soeters, 2002) and failing to control for other leadership styles too. If variables are omitted from the regression equation that correlate with $y$ as well as with other predictors in the regression equation, then omitting them will produce biased estimates (Antonakis et al., 2010; Cameron & Trivedi, 2005). Thus, it is important to control for all theoretical causes of $y$ (e.g., instrumental leadership, transactional leadership) that may correlate with the modeled independent variables (Antonakis & House, 2014). The full-range leadership theory that is estimated must be truly a full one, though not to the point of bringing in redundant factors.

Thus, to fully understand the leadership phenomenon, it is important to model the full leadership process that produces leadership outcomes (Fischer et al., 2016; Lim & Ployhart, 2004; Zaccaro, Kemp, & Bader, 2004). That is, we must link together leader individual differences, leader styles, and leader outcomes, while also considering level-of-analysis and contextual issues (Antonakis & Atwater, 2002; Antonakis & House, 2014; Waldman & Yammarino, 1999), as both moderators and predictors (Liden & Antonakis, 2009). Doing so will not only ensure correct estimation of endogenous variables, but also provide us with a better understanding concerning the importance of leadership. More research should move in this direction to provide truly new and important discoveries. If it is too difficult to model the full process, then more work needs to be done to manipulate the independent variable. As Kurt Lewin has been credited to have said: "The best way to understand something is to try to change it." Although there have been some experiments done showing charisma can be manipulated, there is a dearth of studies showing that transformational leadership can be trained (for exceptions, see Barling, Weber, & Kelloway, 1996; Dvir, Eden, Avolio, & Shamir, 2002); there are no studies that I am aware of showing that authentic, ethical, or servant leadership can be directly manipulated in realistic and consequential settings (i.e., not "paper people" or hypothetical settings). Much more research needs to be conducted, particularly using field experiments (Eden, 2017), which are very useful for establishing causal relations and in making reliable policy implications.

## What Makes Leaders Charismatic?

As mentioned, MLQ-type instruments have not been developed to capture why leaders are charismatic, which means that the variables measured by the questionnaire can only be used as outcomes (else if used as predictors they should be corrected for endogeneity bias). However, much work has been done in understanding why some leaders are able to induce the charismatic effect. Isolating these causes thus makes it useful to study charisma unobtrusively or to manipulate it.

Charismatic leaders use specific communication and image-building strategies to project power and confidence (House, 1977). Researchers have identified some of these strategies with respect to the content of the speech, its framing, and the delivery mode (Den Hartog & Verburg, 1997; Shamir et al., 1993). Essentially, charismatic leaders use a number of tactics, which have been studied both experimentally and in the field, and which show that these tactics are strongly predictive of leader outcomes (Antonakis et al., 2011; Awamleh & Gardner, 1999; Frese et al., 2003; Howell & Frost, 1989; Jacquart & Antonakis, 2015; Towler, 2003). These charismatic leadership tactics, or signals, render the elusive charisma factor more tangible and can be used as a basis to measure a more pure and objective form of charisma from speeches of leaders (Antonakis, Tur, & Jacquart, 2017), independent of attributions and inferences of raters. For this reason, my colleagues and I have defined charisma as "values-based, symbolic, and emotion-laden leader signaling" (Antonakis et al., 2016, p. 304); doing so avoids tautologies and helps identify antecedents to the charismatic effect.

With respect to the use of charismatic signaling, my colleagues and I have conceptualized that these tactics fall into three major categories that can be reliably coded (for details and theoretical explanations, see Antonakis et al., 2011; Antonakis, Fenley, & Liechti, 2012; Antonakis, Tur, et al., 2017; Jacquart & Antonakis, 2015). Briefly, charismatic leaders frame to get attention and focus on the key issues, provide the substance to justify the vision and strategic goals, and then deliver the message in a lively way. Framing can be achieved by using (a) stories, to make the message easy to visualize and the moral salient; (b) metaphors, to trigger an image, simplify the message, and make it easy to remember; (c) rhetorical questions, to create a puzzle, an intrigue, where the answer is obvious or will be divulged later; (d) contrasts, to sharply define the leader's position from an undesirable position;

and (e) three-part lists, to show completeness of argumentation, to boil down the complex matters in fewer key issues, and to aid in recall. The substance is all about justifying the mission by (a) using moral conviction, to communicate important values and what is right to do; (b) expressing the sentiments of the collective, to close the psychological gap between the leader and followers and put into words what followers are thinking and feeling; (c) setting high and ambitious goals, to provide focus and align effort to a target; and (d) communicating confidence that goals can be achieved, which raises self-efficacy belief. Finally, delivery has to do with demonstrating passion and conviction by accurately signaling emotional states, and displaying confidence by use of voice, facial expressions, and body gestures. Note that the verbal aspects of signaling (framing and substance) correlated quite strongly with the nonverbal delivery (Antonakis et al., 2011), presumably because more vivid imagery requires, and more easily goes with, nonverbal signaling (Jacquart & Antonakis, 2015; Towler, 2003).

To the extent that the leader correctly signals, he or she will be seen as charismatic by those who are aligned with the leader's values; thus, charismatic signaling is necessary but insufficient for the charismatic effect (i.e., the emotional connection) to occur (Antonakis et al., 2016). Of course, charismatic signaling of this sort in no way suggests the leader is effective or good in any way. Thus, such an operationalization of charisma avoids the issues I identified previously with respect to using loaded terms and defining the construct by the outcomes. To better see how to extract these tactics from leader speeches, let us go back to the quotations of Thatcher to see just why she was charismatic (see Table 3.1).

**Table 3.1**   Analysis of Margaret Thatcher's Use of the Charismatic Leadership Tactics

| No. | Sentence | CLT 1 | CLT 2 | CLT 3 | CLT 4 | CLT 5 | CLT 6 | CLT 7 | CLT 8 | CLT 9 |
|-----|----------|-------|-------|-------|-------|-------|-------|-------|-------|-------|
| 1. | But all this will avail us little unless we achieve our prime economic objective—the defeat of inflation. | 1 | | | | | | | 1 | |
| 2. | Inflation destroys nations and societies as surely as invading armies do. | 1 | | | | | | | | |
| 3. | Inflation is the parent of unemployment. | 1 | | | | | | | | |
| 4. | It is the unseen robber of those who have saved. | 1 | | | | | | | | |
| 5. | If our people feel that they are part of a great nation and they are prepared to will the means to keep it great, a great nation we shall be, and shall remain. | | | | | | | | 1 | 1 |
| 6. | So, what can stop us from achieving this? | | 1 | | | 1[a] | | | | |
| 7. | What then stands in our way? | | 1 | | | | | | | |
| 8. | The prospect of another winter of discontent? | | 1 | | | | | | | |

*(Continued)*

**Table 3.1**     (Continued)

| No. | Sentence | CLT 1 | CLT 2 | CLT 3 | CLT 4 | CLT 5 | CLT 6 | CLT 7 | CLT 8 | CLT 9 |
|---|---|---|---|---|---|---|---|---|---|---|
| 9. | I suppose it might. | | | | 1[b] | | | | | |
| 10. | But I prefer to believe that certain lessons have been learnt from experience, that we are coming, slowly, painfully, to an autumn of understanding. | 1 | | | | | | | | |
| 11. | And I hope that it will be followed by a winter of common sense. | 1 | | | | | | | | |
| 12. | If it is not, we shall not be diverted from our course. | | | | | | | | | 1 |
| 13. | To those waiting with bated breath for that favourite media catchphrase, the "U" turn, I have only one thing to say. | | | | | | | 1 | | |
| 14. | "You turn if you want to. | | | | 1[b] | | | | | |
| 15. | The lady's not for turning." | | | | | | | | | |
| 16. | I say that not only to you but to our friends overseas and also to those who are not our friends. | | | | 1[c] | 1[d] | | | | |
| | **Total** | 6 | 3 | 0 | 3 | 2 | 0 | 1 | 2 | 2 |

NOTES: CLT1 = metaphor; CLT2 = rhetorical question; CLT3 = story; CLT4 = contrast; CLT5 = list; CLT6 = moral conviction; CLT7 = sentiment of the collective; CLT8 = ambitious goal; CLT9 = goal can be achieved.

[a]List begins and runs over sentences 6 to 8.

[b]Contrast begins and runs to next sentence.

[c] The list is composed of "you," "friends overseas," and "not our friends."

[d]"You" is contrasted with the latter two clauses in the list.

Total tactics used is 19 or 1.19 tactics per sentence (which is very high); of course, I selected this text for its density in the tactics. (For comparison, refer to speeches of candidates for the U.S. presidency [see Jacquart & Antonakis, 2015]).

# Conclusion

It is clear from this review that charismatic and other neocharismatic forms of leadership have become an integral part of leadership theory and are here to stay. However, I must admit that the field has been a bit carried away by these approaches, particularly regarding the heroic connotations and unrealistic expectations they create for leaders in practice, and the fact that many assume that such leaders do bring about needed change. Some sobering commentaries have been made recently with respect to these issues (Antonakis et al., 2016; Antonakis & House, 2014; Hunt, 2004; Judge, Piccolo, & Ilies, 2004; van Knippenberg & Sitkin, 2013; Yukl, 1999). For instance, House and I threw out a challenge to "new" leadership scholars about a decade ago, and we still have not had any takers. After paying tribute to

Bernard Bass for his contributions to the field—and this in an edited book emanating from his Festschrift—we noted the following in our conclusions (Antonakis & House, 2002):

> We hope to see [causally done] research that establishes that transformational leaders have the ability to actually transform individuals and organizations. This notion implicitly pervades the theories and assumptions of leadership scholars of the new paradigm (Beyer, 1999; House, 1999). We have evidence that behaviors of transformational leaders are associated with improved organizational effectiveness, follower satisfaction, and follower motive arousal, but this evidence does not imply that transformational leaders caused transformations in organizations and followers. Although causal links could be theorized, up to this point, we have seen no empirical evidence to make that deduction. (p. 27)

We continued to wait (Antonakis & House, 2013), and I am still waiting now. To conclude, I trust that my final thoughts do not give readers the impression that I am disillusioned by the state of research in this aspect of the leadership field. I am not. In fact, I am very impressed by how much research has been done and how much our understanding of the phenomenon has improved through the efforts of hundreds of researchers. I am also optimistic that we will learn much more about this research stream in the future. What is clear from my review is that even though research in charismatic leadership and related streams is maturing, there is still much to be done; just like in the medical sciences, where researchers constantly update treatments for diseases, so too must we find better measures and better interventions.

Leadership, particularly its charismatic form, is simply too important to leave to random processes or to weak institutions. Once societies, companies, or teams appoint leaders who have charismatic influence, they might be stuck with them for some time, so it is best to get this appointment right. We must better understand the processes that produce these leaders because history will, again and again, toss up leaders who will wield charismatic power.

## Discussion Questions

1. Who is more charismatic, President Barack Obama or President Donald Trump? Who is more transactional? Discuss.
2. Is it morally good for people to fall in behind a leader who is charismatic? Discuss.
3. To be able to produce the charismatic leadership signals, both verbal and nonverbal, what abilities and personality traits do you think leaders should have? Explain.

## Recommended Readings

- Antonakis, J., Fenley, M., & Liechti, S. (2012, June). Learning charisma: Transform yourself into someone people want to follow. *Harvard Business Review*, 127–130.
- Antonakis, J., & Hooijberg, R. (2008). Cascading a new vision: Three steps for real commitment. *Perspectives for Managers, 157*, 1–4.

- Bass, B. M. (1990). From transactional to transformational leadership: Learning to share the vision. *Organizational Dynamics, 18*(3), 19–31.
- Berlew, D. E. (1974). Leadership and organizational excitement. *California Management Review, 17*(2), 21–30.

## Recommended Case Studies

- **Film Case:** *Twelve angry men.* (1957). Starring Henry Fonda.
- **Case:** Gavetti, G., & Canato, A. (2008). Universita' Bocconi: Transformation in the New Millennium. Harvard Business School Case 709406-PDF-ENG.
- **Case:** Podsakoff, N. P., Podsakoff, P. M., & Valentina Kuskova. (2010). Dispelling misconceptions and providing guidelines for leader reward and punishment behavior. Harvard Business School Case BH388-PDF-ENG.

## Recommended Video

- Antonakis, J. (2015). Let's face it: Charisma matters. https://youtu.be/SEDvD1IICfE

## References

Alimo-Metcalfe, B., & Alban-Metcalfe, R. J. (2001). The development of a new transformational leadership questionnaire. *Journal of Occupational & Organizational Psychology, 79*, 1–27.

Antonakis, J. (2001). The validity of the transformational, transactional, and laissez-faire leadership model as measured by the Multifactor Leadership Questionnaire (MLQ5X). *Dissertation Abstracts International, 62*(01), 233 (UMI No. 3000380).

Antonakis, J. (2017). On doing better science: From thrill of discovery to policy implications. *The Leadership Quarterly, 28*(1), 5–21.

Antonakis, J., & Atwater, L. E. (2002). Leader distance: A review and a proposed theory. *The Leadership Quarterly, 13*, 673–704.

Antonakis, J., Avolio, B. J., & Sivasubramaniam, N. (2003). Context and leadership: An examination of the nine-factor full-range leadership theory using the Multifactor Leadership Questionnaire. *The Leadership Quarterly, 14*, 261–295.

Antonakis, J., Bastardoz, N., Jacquart, P., & Shamir, B. (2016). Charisma: An ill-defined and ill-measured gift. *Annual Review of Organizational Psychology and Organizational Behavior, 3*(1), 293–319.

Antonakis, J., Bastardoz, N., Liu, Y., & Schriesheim, C. A. (2014). What makes articles highly cited? *The Leadership Quarterly, 25*(1), 152–179.

Antonakis, J., Bendahan, S., Jacquart, P., & Lalive, R. (2010). On making causal claims: A review and recommendations. *The Leadership Quarterly, 21*, 1086–1120.

Antonakis, J., Bendahan, S., Jacquart, P., & Lalive, R. (2014). Causality and endogeneity: Problems and solutions. In D. V. Day (Ed.), *The Oxford handbook of leadership and organizations* (pp. 93–117). New York, NY: Oxford University Press.

Antonakis, J., Cianciolo, A. T., & Sternberg, R. J. (2004). Leadership: Past, present, future. In J. Antonakis, A. T. Cianciolo, & R. J. Sternberg (Eds.), *The nature of leadership* (pp. 3–15). Thousand Oaks, CA: Sage.

Antonakis, J., d'Adda, G., Weber, R. A., & Zehnder, C. (2015). Just words? Just speeches? On the economic value of charismatic leadership. *NBER Reporter, 4.*

Antonakis, J., & Dalgas, O. (2009). Predicting elections: Child's play! *Science, 323*(5918), 1183.

Antonakis, J., Eubanks, D. L. (2017). Looking leadership in the face. *Current Directions in Psychological Science, 26*(3), 270–275.

Antonakis, J., Fenley, M., & Liechti, S. (2011). Can charisma be taught? Tests of two interventions. *The Academy of Management Learning and Education, 10*(3), 374–396.

Antonakis, J., Fenley, M., & Liechti, S. (2012, June). Learning charisma: Transform yourself into someone people want to follow. *Harvard Business Review,* 127–130.

Antonakis, J., & House, R. J. (2002). An analysis of the full-range leadership theory: The way forward. In B. J. Avolio & F. J. Yammarino (Eds.), *Transformational and charismatic leadership: The road ahead* (pp. 3–34). Amsterdam, Netherlands: JAI Press.

Antonakis, J., & House, R. J. (2013). A re-analysis of the full-range leadership theory: The way forward. In B. J. Avolio & F. J. Yammarino (Eds.), *Transformational and charismatic leadership: The road ahead* (pp. 35–37). Amsterdam, Netherlands: JAI Press.

Antonakis, J., & House, R. J. (2014). Instrumental leadership: Measurement and extension of transformational-transactional leadership theory. *The Leadership Quarterly, 25,* 746–771.

Antonakis, J., House, R. J., & Simonton, D. K. (2017). Can super smart leaders suffer from too much of a good thing? The curvilinear effect of intelligence on perceived leadership behavior. *Journal of Applied Psychology.* Advance online publication. doi:10.1037/apl0000221

Antonakis, J., Tur, B., & Jacquart, P. (2017). *Scoring charismatic signaling for research and training* (Working paper). Department of Organizational Behavior, University of Lausanne.

Aristotle. (1954). *Rhetoric* (1st Modern Library ed.). (W. Rhys Roberts, Trans.). New York, NY: Modern Library.

Avolio, B. J., & Bass, B. M. (1995). Individual consideration viewed at multiple levels of analysis: A multi-level framework for examining the diffusion of transformational leadership. *The Leadership Quarterly, 6*(2), 199–218.

Avolio, B. J., Bass, B. M., & Jung, D. I. (1999). Re-examining the components of transformational and transactional leadership using the MLQ. *Journal of Occupational and Organizational Psychology, 72,* 441–462.

Avolio, B. J., & Gardner, W. L. (2005). Authentic leadership development: Getting to the root of positive forms of leadership. *The Leadership Quarterly, 16*(3), 315–338.

Avolio, B. J., Gardner, W. L., Walumbwa, F. O., Luthans, F., & May, D. R. (2004). Unlocking the mask: A look at the process by which authentic leaders impact follower attitudes and behaviors. *The Leadership Quarterly, 15*(6), 801–823.

Awamleh, R., & Gardner, W. L. (1999). Perceptions of leader charisma and effectiveness: The effects of vision content, delivery, and organizational performance. *The Leadership Quarterly, 10*(3), 345–373.

Banks, G. C., Engemann, K. N., Williams, C. E., & Gooty, J. (2016). A meta-analytic review and future research agenda of charismatic leadership. *The Leadership Quarterly.* Advance online publication. doi:10.1016/j.leaqua.2016.12.003

Banks, G. C., McCauley, K. D., Gardner, W. L., & Guler, C. E. (2016). A meta-analytic review of authentic and transformational leadership: A test for redundancy. *The Leadership Quarterly, 27*(4), 634–652.

Barling, J., Weber, T., & Kelloway, E. K. (1996). Effects of transformational leadership training on attitudinal and financial outcomes: A field experiment. *Journal of Applied Psychology, 81*(6), 827–832.

Bass, B. M. (1985). *Leadership and performance beyond expectations.* New York, NY: Free Press.

Bass, B. M., & Avolio, B. J. (1993). Transformational leadership: A response to critiques. In M. M. Chemers & R. Ayman (Eds.), *Leadership theory and research: Perspectives and directions* (pp. 49–80). San Diego, CA: Academic Press.

Bass, B. M., & Avolio, B. J. (1994). Transformational leadership and organizational culture. *International Journal of Public Administration, 17*(3&4), 541–554.

Bass, B. M., Avolio, B. J., & Atwater, L. (1996). The transformational and transactional leadership of men and women. *Applied Psychology: An International Review, 45*(1), 5–34.

Bass, B. M., & Riggio, R. E. (2006). *Transformational leadership* (2nd ed.). Mahwah, NJ: Lawrence Erlbaum.

Bass, B. M., & Steidlmeier, P. (1999). Ethics, character, and authentic transformational leadership behavior. *The Leadership Quarterly, 10*(2), 181–217.

Bass, B. M., Waldman, D. A., Avolio, B. J., & Bebb, M. (1987). Transformational leadership and the falling dominoes effect. *Group and Organization Studies, 12*(1), 73–87.

Bendahan, S., Zehnder, C., Pralong, F. P., & Antonakis, J. (2015). Leader corruption depends on power and testosterone. *The Leadership Quarterly, 26,* 101–122.

Bertrand, M., & Schoar, A. (2003). Managing with style: The effect of managers on firm policies. *Quarterly Journal of Economics, 118*(4), 1169–1208.

Beyer, J. M. (1999). Taming and promoting charisma to change organziations. *The Leadership Quarterly, 10*(2), 307–330.

Bono, J. E., & Judge, T. A. (2004). Personality and transformational and transactional leadership: A meta-analysis. *Journal of Applied Psychology, 89,* 901–910.

Brown, M. E., & Treviño, L. K. (2006). Ethical leadership: A review and future directions. *The Leadership Quarterly, 17*(6), 595–616.

Brown, M. E., Treviño, L. K., & Harrison, D. A. (2005). Ethical leadership: A social learning perspective for construct development and testing. *Organizational Behavior and Human Decision Processes, 97*(2), 117–134.

Bryman, A. (1992). *Charisma and leadership in organizations.* London, UK: Sage.

Burns, J. M. (1978). *Leadership.* New York, NY: Harper & Row.

Calder, B. J. (1977). An attribution theory of leadership. In B. M. Straw & G. R. Salancik (Eds.), *New directions in organizational behavior* (pp. 179–204). Chicago, IL: St Clair.

Cameron, A. C., & Trivedi, P. K. (2005). *Microeconometrics: Methods and applications.* New York, NY: Cambridge University Press.

Conger, J. A., & Kanungo, R. N. (Eds.). (1988). *Charismatic leadership: The elusive factor in organizational effectiveness.* San Francisco, CA: Jossey-Bass.

Conger, J. A., & Kanungo, R. N. (1998). *Charismatic leadership in organizations.* Thousand Oaks, CA: Sage.

Credé, M., & Harms, P. D. (2015). 25 years of higher-order confirmatory factor analysis in the organizational sciences: A critical review and development of reporting recommendations. *Journal of Organizational Behavior, 36*(6), 845–872.

Davies, J. C. (1954). Charisma in the 1952 campaign. *American Political Science Review, 48*(4), 1083–1102.

Day, D. V., & Antonakis, J. (2012). Leadership: Past, present, and future. In D. V. Day & J. Antonakis (Eds.), *The nature of leadership* (2nd ed., pp. 3–25). Thousand Oaks, CA: Sage.

De Hoogh, A., Den Hartog, D., & Koopman, P. (2004). De ontwikkeling van de CLIO: Een vragenlijst voor charismatisch leiderschap in organisaties. *Gedrag en Organisatie, 17*(5), 354–381.

DeGroot, T., Kiker, D. S., & Cross, T. C. (2000). A meta-analysis to review organizational outcomes related to charismatic leadership. *Canadian Journal of Administrative Sciences, 17*(4), 356–372.

Den Hartog, D. N., & Verburg, R. M. (1997). Charisma and rhetoric: Communicative techniques of international business leaders. *The Leadership Quarterly, 8*(4), 355–391.

Downton, J. V. (1973). *Rebel leadership: Commitment and charisma in the revolutionary process.* New York, NY: Free Press.

Dumdum, U. R., Lowe, K. B., & Avolio, B. J. (2002). A meta-analysis of transformational and transactional leadership correlates of effectiveness and satisfaction: An update and extension. In B. J. Avolio & F. J. Yammarino (Eds.), *Transformational and charismatic leadership: The road ahead* (pp. 35–66). Amsterdam, Netherlands: JAI.

Durand, R., & Vaara, E. (2009). Causation, counterfactuals, and competitive advantage. *Strategic Management Journal, 30*(12), 1245–1264.

Dvir, T., Eden, D., Avolio, B. J., & Shamir, B. (2002). Impact of transformational leadership on follower development and performance: A field experiment. *Academy of Management Journal, 45*(4), 735–744.

Eagly, A. H. (2016). When passionate advocates meet research on diversity: Does the honest broker stand a chance? *Journal of Social Issues, 72*(1), 199–222.

Eden, D. (2017). Field experiments in organizations. *Annual Review of Organizational Psychology and Organizational Behavior.* Advance online publication. doi:10.1146/annurev-orgpsych-041015-062400

Erickson, D. J., & Krull, D. S. (1999). Distinguishing judgments about what from judgments about why: Effects of behavior extremity on correspondent inferences and causal attributions. *Basic and Applied Social Psychology, 21*(1), 1–11.

Etzioni, A. (1961). *A comparative analysis of complex organizations.* New York, NY: Free Press.

Etzioni, A. (1964). *Modern organizations.* Englewood Cliffs, NJ: Prentice-Hall.

Fischer, T., Dietz, J., & Antonakis, J. (2016). Leadership process model: A review and synthesis. *Journal of Management*. Advance online publication. doi:10.1177/0149206316682830

Fleishman, E. A. (1953). The description of supervisory behavior. *Journal of Applied Psychology, 37*(1), 1–6.

Fleishman, E. A. (1957). A leader behavior description for industry. In R. M. Stogdill & A. E. Coons (Eds.), *Leader behavior: Its description and measurement* (Research Monograph Number 88, pp. 103–119). Columbus: Ohio State University, Bureau of Business Research.

Frese, M., Beimel, S., & Schoenborn, S. (2003). Action training for charismatic leadership: Two evaluations of studies of a commercial training module on inspirational communication of a vision. *Personnel Psychology, 56*, 671–697.

Friedland, W. H. (1964). For a sociological concept of charisma. *Social Forces, 43*(1), 18–26.

Friedrich, C. J. (1961). Political leadership and the problem of the charismatic power. *Journal of Politics, 23*(1), 3–24.

Fuller, J. B., Patterson, C. E. P., Hester, K., & Stringer, D. Y. (1996). A quantitative review of research on charismatic leadership. *Psychological Reports, 78*, 271–287.

Gardner, W. L., Lowe, K. B., Moss, T. W., Mahoney, K. T., & Cogliser, C. C. (2010). Scholarly leadership of the study of leadership: A review of *The Leadership Quarterly*'s second decade, 2000–2009. *The Leadership Quarterly, 12*(6), 922–958.

Gasper, J. M. (1992). *Transformational leadership: An integrative review of the literature.* Kalamazoo: Western Michigan University.

Gemmill, G., & Oakley, J. (1992). Leadership: An alienating social myth? *Human Relations, 45*(2), 113–129.

Gerring, J., & McDermott, R. (2007). An experimental template for case study research. *American Journal of Political Science, 51*(3), 688–701.

Greene, C. N. (1977). Disenchantment with leadership research: Some causes, recommendations, and alternative directions. In J. G. Hunt & L. L. Larson (Eds.), *Leadership: The cutting edge* (pp. 57–67). Carbondale: Southern Illinois University Press.

Halpin, A. W. (1954). The leadership behavior and combat performance of airplane commanders. *Journal of Abnormal and Social Psychology, 49*(1), 19–22.

Hater, J. J., & Bass, B. M. (1988). Superiors' evaluations and subordinate's perceptions of transformational and transactional leadership. *Journal of Applied Psychology, 73*(4), 695–702.

Hoch, J. E., Bommer, W. H., Dulebohn, J. H., & Wu, D. (2016). Do ethical, authentic, and servant leadership explain variance above and beyond transformational leadership? A meta-analysis. *Journal of Management*. Advance online publication. doi:10.1177/0149206316665461

House, R. J. (1977). A 1976 theory of charismatic leadership. In J. G. Hunt & L. L. Larson (Eds.), *The cutting edge* (pp. 189–207). Carbondale: Southern Illinois University Press.

House, R. J. (1999). Weber and the neo-charismatic leadership paradigm: A response to Beyer. *The Leadership Quarterly, 10*(4), 563–574.

House, R. J., & Aditya, R. N. (1997). The social scientific study of leadership: Quo vadis? *Journal of Management, 23*(3), 409–473.

House, R. J., & Shamir, B. (1993). Toward the integration of transformational, charismatic, and visionary theories. In M. M. Chemers & R. Ayman (Eds.), *Leadership theory and research: Perspectives and directions* (pp. 167–188). San Diego, CA: Academic Press.

Howell, J. M., & Frost, P. J. (1989). A laboratory study of charismatic leadership. *Organizational Behavior and Human Decision Processes, 43*(2), 243–269.

Hunt, J. G. (1999). Tranformational/charismatic leadership's transformation of the field: An historical essay. *The Leadership Quarterly, 10*(2), 129–144.

Hunt, J. G. (2004). Task leadership. In G. R. Goethels, G. J. Sorensen, & J. M. Burns (Eds.), *Encyclopedia of leadership* (Vol. IV, pp. 1524–1529). Thousand Oaks, CA: Sage.

Jacquart, P., & Antonakis, J. (2015). When does charisma matter for top-level leaders? Effect of attributional ambiguity. *Academy of Management Journal, 58*, 1051–1074.

Jones, B. F., & Olken, B. A. (2005). Do leaders matter? National leadership and growth since World War II. *Quarterly Journal of Economics, 120*(3), 835–864.

Judge, T. A., & Bono, J. E. (2000). Five-factor model of personality and transformational leadership. *Journal of Applied Psychology, 5*(85), 751–765.

Judge, T. A., & Piccolo, R. F. (2004). Transformational and transactional leadership: A meta-analytic test of their relative validity. *Journal of Applied Psychology, 89*(5), 755–768.

Judge, T. A., Piccolo, R. F., & Ilies, R. (2004). The forgotten ones? The validity of consideration and initiating structure in leadership research. *Journal of Applied Psychology, 89*(1), 36–51.

Keller, R. T. (1992). Transformational leadership and the performance of research-and-development project groups. *Journal of Management, 18*(3), 489–501.

Koene, B. A. S., Vogelaar, A. L. W., & Soeters, J. L. (2002). Leadership effects on organizational climate and financial performance: Local leadership effect in chain organizations. *The Leadership Quarterly, 13*(3), 193–215.

Kouzes, J. M., & Posner, B. Z. (1987). *The leadership challenge: How to get extraordinary things done in organizations.* San Francisco, CA: Jossey-Bass.

Liden, R. C., & Antonakis, J. (2009). Considering context in psychological leadership research. *Human Relations, 62*(11), 1587–1605.

Lim, B. C., & Ployhart, R. E. (2004). Transformational leadership: Relations to the five-factor model and team performance in typical and maximum contexts. *Journal of Applied Psychology, 89*(4), 610–621.

Lord, R. G., Binning, J. F., Rush, M. C., & Thomas, J. C. (1978). The effect of performance cues and leader behavior on questionnaire ratings of leadership behavior. *Organizational Behavior and Human Performance, 21*(1), 27–39.

Lowe, K. B., & Gardner, W. L. (2000). Ten years of *The Leadership Quarterly:* Contributions and challenges for the future. *The Leadership Quarterly, 11*(4), 459–514.

Lowe, K. B., Kroeck, K. G., & Sivasubramaniam, N. (1996). Effectiveness correlates of transformational and transactional leadership: A meta-analytic review of the MLQ literature. *The Leadership Quarterly, 7*(3), 385–425.

MacKenzie, S. B. (2003). The dangers of poor construct conceptualization. *Journal of the Academy of Marketing Science, 31,* 323–326.

Miner, J. B. (1975). The uncertain future of the leadership concept. An overview. In J. G. Hunt & L. L. Larson (Eds.), *Leadership frontiers* (pp. 197–208). Kent, OH: Kent State University.

Plato. (1901). *The republic of Plato; an ideal commonwealth* (Rev. ed.). (B. Jowett, Trans.). New York, NY: Colonial Press.

Podsakoff, P. M., Bommer, W. H., Podsakoff, N. P., & MacKenzie, S. B. (2006). Relationships between leader reward and punishment behavior and subordinate attitudes, perceptions, and behaviors: A meta-analytic review of existing and new research. *Organizational Behavior and Human Decision Processes, 99*(2), 113–142.

Podsakoff, P. M., MacKenzie, S. B., & Bommer, W. H. (1996). Transformational leader behaviors and substitutes for leadership as determinants of employee satisfaction, commitment, trust, and organizational citizenship behaviors. *Journal of Management, 22*(2), 259–298.

Podsakoff, P. M., MacKenzie, S. B., Moorman, R. H., & Fetter, R. (1990). Transformational leader behaviors and their effects on follower's trust in leader, satisfaction, and organizational citizenship behaviors. *The Leadership Quarterly, 1*(2), 107–142.

Podsakoff, P. M., Todor, W. D., Grover, R. A., & Huber, V. L. (1984). Situational moderators of leader reward and punishment behaviors: Fact or fiction? *Organizational Behavior and Human Performance, 34*(1), 21–63.

Podsakoff, P. M., Todor, W. D., & Skov, R. (1982). Effects of leader contingent and noncontingent reward and punishment behaviors on subordinate performance and satisfaction. *Academy of Management Journal, 25*(4), 810–821.

Rafferty, A. E., & Griffin, M. A. (2004). Dimensions of transformational leadership: Conceptual and empirical extensions. *The Leadership Quarterly, 15*(3), 329–354.

Rowold, J. (2014). Instrumental leadership: Extending the transformational-transactional leadership paradigm. *German Journal of Human Resource Management, 28*(3), 367–390.

Rowold, J., & Heinitz, K. (2007). Transformational and charismatic leadership: Assessing the convergent, divergent and criterion validity of the MLQ and the CKS. *The Leadership Quarterly, 18*(2), 121–133.

Rush, M. C., Thomas, J. C., & Lord, R. G. (1977). Implicit leadership theory: A potential threat to the internal validity of leader behavior questionnaires. *Organizational Behavior and Human Performance, 20,* 93–110.

Seltzer, J., & Bass, B. M. (1990). Transformational leadership: Beyond initiation and consideration. *Journal of Management, 16*(4), 693–703.

Shamir, B., Arthur, M. B., & House, R. J. (1994). The rhetoric of charismatic leadership: A theoretical extension, a case study, and implications for research. *The Leadership Quarterly, 5*(1), 25–42.

Shamir, B., House, R. J., & Arthur, M. B. (1993). The motivational effects of charismatic leadership: A self-concept based theory. *Organization Science, 4*(4), 577–594.

Shils, E. (1965). Charisma, order, and status. *American Sociological Review, 30*(2), 199–213.

Stogdill, R. M., & Coons, A. E. (1957). *Leader behavior: Its description and measurement* (Research Monograph Number 88). Columbus: Ohio State University, Bureau of Business Research.

Towler, A. J. (2003). Effects of charismatic influence training on attitudes, behavior, and performance. *Personnel Psychology, 56*(2), 363–381.

Tucker, R. C. (1968). The theory of charismatic leadership. *Daedalus, 97*(3), 731–756.

van Knippenberg, D., & Sitkin, S. B. (2013). A critical assessment of charismatic-transformational leadership research: Back to the drawing board? *The Academy of Management Annals, 7*(1), 1–60.

Waldman, D. A., Bass, B. M., & Yammarino, F. J. (1990). Adding to contingent-reward behavior—The augmenting effect of charismatic leadership. *Group & Organization Studies, 15*(4), 381–394.

Waldman, D. A., & Yammarino, F. J. (1999). CEO charismatic leadership: Levels-of-management and levels-of-analysis effects. *Academy of Management Review, 24*(2), 266–285.

Wang, G., Oh, I.-S., Courtright, S. H., & Colbert, A. E. (2011). Transformational leadership and performance across criteria and levels: A meta-analytic review of 25 years of research. *Group & Organization Management, 36*(2), 223–270.

Weber, M. (1947). *The theory of social and economic organization* (T. Parsons, Trans.). New York, NY: Free Press.

Weber, M. (1968). *On charisma and institutional building.* Chicago, IL: University of Chicago Press.

Yammarino, F. J., & Bass, B. M. (1990). Transformational leadership and multiple levels of analysis. *Human Relations, 43*(10), 975–995.

Yukl, G. A. (1999). An evaluation of conceptual weaknesses in transformational and charismatic leadership theories. *The Leadership Quarterly, 10*(2), 285–305.

Zaccaro, S. J., Kemp, C., & Bader, P. (2004). Leader traits and attributes. In J. Antonakis, A. T. Cianciolo, & R. J. Sternberg (Eds.), *The nature of leadership* (pp. 101–124). Thousand Oaks, CA: Sage.

# CHAPTER 4

# In the Minds of Followers

*Follower-Centric Approaches to Leadership*

*Douglas J. Brown*

---

### Opening Case: A Day in the Life of a Leader

Constantine sat slouched in the mall food court picking absently at his lunch and listening to his coworkers talk about the meeting they had just attended. They all worked for the largest technology company in the region and had just come from hearing from the new CEO who had been hired to resuscitate the company. Constantine could not help but be amazed at how quickly the company's fortunes had turned to bring about this event. When he had started, its product had been cool, the founders had been among the most influential people in the world, expansion had been exponential, and renowned musical acts had played at employee parties. Since then the company had failed at everything it tried. Within a 3-year period a major competitor had emerged and significantly diminished market share, the company's valuation had plummeted, and worse yet, its new products had been universally criticized. Constantine began to feel a bit sick thinking about it.

As Constantine reoriented himself to the conversation, he listened intently to the debate that was raging about the new CEO. "Did you see him?" Peter stated emphatically, wagging his finger at Mark. "He talks like someone you can trust, there's no hesitation in his voice, and he's got a lot of confidence and passion." "Not only that," Susan chimed in, "but he is smart; he attended one of the most prestigious MBA programs in the world." "Based on what I saw and know," Peter declared, "that guy is a leader and it's just a matter of time before he fixes what has been ailing us for years." Peter and Susan continued to harangue Mark for much of the lunch, but made little headway, as Mark's gut told him that it was not possible for someone who had failed elsewhere to be a particularly effective leader.

As Constantine walked back to his car reflecting on the debate, he could not help but think how strange it was that his friends were so adamant. After all, they knew very little about the new CEO, yet from a few snippets of information available and brief glimpses they had made up their minds. Really, what were they expecting? The CEO was not going to design the new products himself, and he had little control over what their competitors did or what consumers wanted. How could Peter and Susan think that the new CEO would have such a dramatic effect? He wondered whether the uncertainty of the past few years had made them overly optimistic. Regardless, they seemed comforted, even if Mark was not, and ready to roll up their sleeves and work for the new CEO. It did strike him as unusual, however, that based on the same information, his friends could hold such starkly different beliefs. He searched his memory of what he had learned about leadership in school. As he recalled, he had practiced using charismatic language in a memorable class and had learned that great leaders do great things. Nothing he thought of seemed useful in reconciling the differences of opinion between his friends.

## Discussion Questions

1. What role do perceivers, such as Peter, Susan, and Mark, play in creating leadership?

2. How important is the concept of leader to people such as Peter, Susan, and Mark in navigating the world?

3. What is the nature of the information that people draw upon to label someone, such as the new CEO, a leader?

# Chapter Overview

Despite the disproportional predominance of leader-centric leadership research, which emphasizes the systematic variance in the influence process due to leader characteristics, far less attention has been devoted to followers. The significance of this oversight seems readily apparent when contemplating the causes of consequential events. For instance, readers might consider that despite widespread belief that Hitler was personally responsible for the genocide of 6 million Jews during World War II, not a single individual died at his hands (Goldhagen, 2009). Similarly, despite little evidence of direct involvement, it is commonly understood that Pol Pot exterminated 1.7 million Cambodians; Jean Kambanda was responsible for butchering 800,000 Tutsis in Rwanda; Saddam Hussein was responsible for the deaths of an estimated 600,000 Kurds; and Slobodan Milošević was responsible for the ethnic cleansing of tens of thousands of Bosnians (Goldhagen, 2009). Although each of these examples certainly speaks to the depravity of individual leaders, each instance simultaneously highlights the limits of a strict leader-centric model and highlights the relevance of followers. Without the obedience, fanaticism, fervor, or support of followers, each of these genocidal directives would have been ineffectual. Ultimately, it is followers who legitimize leaders, empower them, and provide them with the means to attain their visions and goals. In addition, outstanding leadership depends on good followers—individuals who are proactive, competent, self-managing, high in integrity, and who willingly contribute to the success of their groups and organizations (Bass, 2008). Good followers help drive outstanding outcomes by pushing their leaders to be better, whereas bad followers do the opposite. In sum, there is no leadership without followers and followership (Hollander, 1993).

Given the centrality of followers for understanding leadership, historical scholarly indifference to the topic is rather curious (Bennis, 2008). In recent years, however, there seemingly has been a shift in thinking that has brought followers and followership into the foreground and has generated several relevant tomes (e.g., Kellerman, 2008; Riggio, Chaleff, & Lipman-Blumen, 2008). Despite the position advanced in these books that followers matter and that researchers have been largely silent on the topic, in actuality there is a rich history of follower-centric research that has been ignored, gone unnoticed, or been altogether forgotten by many commentators (Lord, 2008). This is not to say that the leadership field is not largely leader-centric (Meindl, 1995) or that followers do not "remain an underexplored source of variance" in leadership models (Lord, Brown, & Freiberg, 1999, p. 167), but rather that something is known about followers and followership and that the state of our understanding is not as bleak as we might be led to believe.

In this chapter, I begin with broad brush strokes, considering key assumptions about followers and the role that followers have played in previous leadership literature. Next, I focus on the dominant follower-centric perspective. Although recent discussions of followership have attempted to develop behavioral typologies, understand how followers influence leaders, and highlight the characteristics that make for good, bad, and indifferent followers, follower-centric theory and research itself have primarily dealt with the likely precursor to these activities—information processing. If we are to understand why followers behave as they do, a necessary first step is understanding their thought processes. Hence, my emphasis herein lies in examining two issues surrounding follower thought. First, why is it that we understand the world through leaders? Second, what is the nature of our mental category of leader, and how does it influence our perceptions of leaders? To assist readers in understanding the chapter, a summary of key ideas is provided in Table 4.1.

## What Is Followership?

The suggestion that followers are a relevant consideration in leadership models is not novel, as many leader-centric frameworks do account for followers (Howell & Shamir, 2005). For the most part, however, prior leader-centric work has characterized followers as passive elements of the context that necessarily should be considered when investigating the effectiveness of various leader styles (Avolio,

**Table 4.1**     A Summary of Key Concepts and Their Significance

| Concept | Definition | Significance or Importance |
| --- | --- | --- |
| Leader-centric | • A term for models that emphasize systematic variance due to the leader. | • The historically dominant approach to leadership, which largely emphasizes leaders. |
| Follower-centric | • A term for models that emphasize systematic variance due to followers. | • An approach that considers followers' role in the creation of leadership. |
| Romance of leadership | • A widely held implicit theory regarding the importance of leaders and leadership. | • Leadership may simply be a social construction. |
| Leader category | • A knowledge structure consisting of properties deemed to characterize leaders. | • The foundation of observers' leadership impressions. |
| Group prototype | • A knowledge structure composed of properties associated with the group. | • An alternative category that perceivers draw upon to form leadership impressions. |
| Social identity leadership model | • A model that depicts how the group prototype is utilized to form leadership impressions. | • Leadership impressions are dependent on how closely a target fits with the group. |
| Connectionist leader category | • A model that proposes how a context-specific leader category is generated. | • Argues that the leader category is fluid rather than fixed. |
| Categorization theory | • A model that outlines how observers determine a target's fit with the leader category. | • Depicts the underlying psychological process through which leadership impressions form. |
| Recognition versus attributional processes | • Psychological processes by which individuals assign the leader label to a target. | • Suggests that there are multiple routes to being deemed leader-like by perceivers. |

2007). The passivity of followers in such works is not surprising, as the primary underlying motivation guiding this literature has been leader-centric. For instance, contingency frameworks, such as Fiedler's (1967) leader-match theory, have suggested that the alignment of a leader's behavioral style and the context, which includes aspects of followers such as their loyalty and cooperation, are important precursors to effectiveness. Situational leadership models, such as Hersey and Blanchard's (1977) model, propose that the appropriate leadership style depends in part on the developmental level of subordinates. House's (1971) path-goal theory indicates that the skills and experience of followers are important antecedents of which leadership style will be most motivating. Kerr and Jermier (1978) argue in their leadership substitutes theory that characteristics of followers can both make leadership unnecessary (i.e., act as a substitute) and nullify a leader's actions (i.e., neutralize). Finally, thinking in the areas of charismatic leadership has likened followers to flammable material who are set ablaze by leaders (Klein & House, 1995).

The assumption of passivity that characterizes prior leader-centric work is at odds with our common understanding of human nature. Followers are not simply a passive part of the environment to be acted on by leaders, but rather act in a self-determining fashion (Grant & Ashford, 2008). Although it is certainly true that, at times, followers choose to behave as passive bystanders, neither participating nor objecting to their leaders' actions and directives, it is also true that in other instances, they are diehard zealots who are deeply devoted or opposed to their leaders and their leaders' causes (Kellerman, 2008). In organizations, employees range from those who narrowly define their roles in terms of their formal job requirements and who will simply do their jobs, to others who will choose to enthusiastically embrace their leader's vision and goals, oftentimes at a significant personal cost to their future freedom, health, family life, values, and well-being. In the end, our understanding of followers must be premised on the assumption that they are agentic, intelligent beings who actively attempt to understand and shape their environments (Bandura, 1986).

Research also demonstrates that different followers, as well as followers and leaders, differ considerably in terms of their views of how much leadership an individual has exhibited. For instance, behavioral ratings of transformational leadership indicate that there is such profound individual variability in ratings that rather than reflecting the leader, transformational leadership may exist solely in the "eye of the beholder" (Yammarino & Dubinsky, 1994, p. 792). Re-analyses of archival data suggest that roughly 20% of the variance in leadership ratings is idiosyncratic and, hence, is dependent on who is rating whom (Livi, Kenny, Albright, & Pierro, 2008). Such individual variability in perceptions is important, insofar as characteristics of the world are not given to observers and social actors but, rather, are constructed (Salancik & Pfeffer, 1978), and it is those constructions that are most relevant for understanding human activity (Fiske, 1998). Therefore, the influence afforded to an individual leader does not reside solely in his or her behavioral repertoire, but rather in part in the mind's eye of observers (Hollander, 1958). As such, it should not surprise us that perceived intelligence predicts leader emergence (Judge, Colbert, & Ilies, 2004) or that it is perceived competence and not actual competence that predicts who is and is not influential in a group (Anderson & Kilduff, 2009). Such findings should not be taken as evidence that actual intelligence or competence are necessarily unimportant, but rather that they are mediated through the perceptions of observers.

Building upon these ideas, follower-centric researchers have busied themselves for decades trying to comprehend follower sensemaking activities. The emphasis of followership research has been on understanding how followers make sense out of the vast quantities of information that flow unceasingly each day. Human information-processing capacity is finite, and the information-processing demands confronted each day exceed our capabilities. To circumvent this information-processing bottleneck, humans lean heavily on stable internal mental representations that allow us to "comprehend, understand, explain, attribute, extrapolate, and predict" (Starbuck & Milliken, 1988, p. 51). The mental categories that we use guide what we pay attention to, what we encode, and how we form judgments. Thus, rather than simply conceptualize followers as passive recipients of leader behaviors, follower-centric researchers instead propose that followers are active agents who construct leadership.

Although it is implicit in the preceding text, it is important to emphasize that follower sensemaking activities are not the consequence of the random firing of neurons, nor are followers dispassionate recorders of leadership information. Human information processing is a goal-directed activity. Effectively, followers are compelled to understand the world in terms of leadership because it serves some overarching purpose such as alleviating negative emotional states. Furthermore, as motivated thinkers, followers are guided by preexisting conclusions, goals, or expectations (Kunda, 1990). Hence, we should not be particularly surprised to learn that party identification colors perceptions of political leaders (Pillai, Kohles, & Bligh, 2007) or that the extent to which we like our leaders colors our judgments of their behavior (D. J. Brown & Keeping, 2005).

Follower-centric researchers further contend that these sensemaking activities are significant. Subordinate information processing serves as the most proximal determinant of who will emerge as a leader, how much leeway subordinates provide them, and how enthusiastically they will be followed. Effectively, leadership depends on the information processing of subordinates (Lord & Emrich, 2000). How subordinates make sense of the leadership context is important, insofar as this symbolic activity defines one's role in the social context and serves as a proximal antecedent to how one defines the self and the self-in-relation to significant others (Howell & Shamir, 2005; Lord & Brown, 2004). To define our role as that of a follower or subordinate should automatically trigger relevant behavioral norms and scripts in observers (Baumeister & Newman, 1995). Research, for instance, suggests that humans typically behave submissively when confronted with a dominant partner (Tiedens, Unzueta, & Young, 2007). Although there are, no doubt, universally shared followership scripts that exist and that need to be better understood, it is also likely that researchers need to uncover systematic idiosyncratic and dyadic script variability. For some individuals, to define one member of the group as a leader suggests that one is dependent, obedient, and powerless, whereas for others, the adopted identity might be that of the courageous follower who voices opinions and questions authority (Uhl-Bien & Pillai, 2007). Finally, as shown in the context of the charismatic leadership literature, the nature of the relationship form that results from followers' sensemaking efforts reverberates, influencing one's overall sense of self (Kark, Shamir, & Chen, 2003).

Beyond the fact that follower sensemaking mediates leadership influence, from a practical standpoint, it is pivotal to the discipline. The preponderance of the leadership literature depends on behavioral surveys in which subordinates are asked to report how frequently supervisors engage in various acts (Hunter, Bedell-Avers, &

Mumford, 2007). To operationalize leadership in such a manner makes the disentanglement of leader behavior and follower sensemaking difficult, if not impossible. It also raises serious questions regarding the construct validity of our most cherished behavioral taxonomies and, ultimately, what it is we have accumulated with our mountains of data. As follower-centric researchers repeatedly have documented, follower conceptualizations of leadership play a pivotal role in terms of how subordinates respond to behavioral questionnaires (Lord, Foti, & De Vader, 1984). As such, one might reasonably ask whether the dominant behavioral paradigm and methodology have actually addressed what it is leaders do or how followers encode, store, retrieve, and integrate information to render judgments (e.g., Rush, Thomas, & Lord, 1977). Ultimately, if as a discipline we are going to continue to lean on subordinate reports, it seems only reasonable that we should fully understand how those ratings are generated.

To summarize, followers are proactive sensemakers and their sensemaking is pivotal to our understanding of leadership. Below, I delve deeper into the cognitively oriented follower-centric literature, which I have bifurcated. In the first section, I address the overarching question of why humans are leader-centric thinkers and examine those factors that influence our inclination to comprehend the world through leaders. Building from this literature, I next dig deeper and address how it is we come to understand and label particular individuals as leaders. Here, I probe the content of the leader category and address the underlying social-cognitive processes that dictate our use of this category.

# Why and When Are We Leader-Centric Thinkers?

An enigma that has beguiled observers for some time is the tendency for humans to construe the world through the prism of leaders and leadership. A key to unlocking this mystery lies in developing an appreciation for the human tendency to romanticize leadership. The *romance of leadership* perspective suggests that "as observers of and as participants in organizations, we have developed highly romanticized, heroic views of leadership, what leaders do, what they are able to accomplish, and the general effects that they have on our lives" (Meindl, Ehrlich, & Dukerich, 1985, p. 79). At its core, the romance of leadership is an implicit theory that observers hold and utilize when they are attempting to comprehend the "causes, nature, and consequences of organizational activities" (Meindl & Ehrlich, 1987).

Building from the radical perspective advanced by several authors who have argued that leadership is simply an explanatory category (Calder, 1977; Pfeffer, 1977), Meindl proposed that the leader category has "achieved a heroic, larger-than-life value." Social actors have immense faith in the efficacy of leaders who are perceived to be the "premier force" underlying all organizational events, regardless of whether they are positive or negative (Meindl et al., 1985, p. 79). As naive scientists, perceivers utilize the leader category to organize, understand, and predict the world. Functionally, the leader category reduces our uncertainty and anxiety and allows us to "come to grips with the cognitive and moral complexities of understanding the myriad interactions among the causal forces that create and maintain organized activity" (Meindl & Ehrlich, 1987, p. 92).

In their initial work, Meindl and his colleagues (1985) sought evidence for the romance of leadership through a series of archival and experimental investigations. In two initial archival studies, Meindl et al. found that during times of extreme performance, interest in leadership soared—as indexed by the number of articles written in *The Wall Street Journal* about leadership and dissertations completed on the topic. Seemingly, in extreme situations, people turn to leadership. To directly test this idea, Meindl et al. completed a series of vignette studies in which participants read about companies that had performed positively or negatively to varying degrees (e.g., high, medium, low). After reading the vignettes, participants were asked to account for company performance by evaluating the causal significance of several factors. Relative to the alternative explanations (e.g., economy), extreme performance, regardless of valence, led individuals to accentuate leadership. Such findings underscore the romanticized view held by observers who see leaders as capable of controlling and influencing the fate of organizations and people.

Subsequently, Meindl and Ehrlich (1987) tested whether an individual's reactions to organizational performance might depend on whether outcomes are attributable to other factors (e.g., workforce) or leadership. To these ends, they completed a series of vignette studies in which they had their participants read descriptions of an organization that included a general organizational description, a summary of operating strengths, and a summary of selected performance indicators. Importantly, they manipulated the operating strengths paragraph to emphasize either leadership or other factors (e.g., regulatory policies). In line with the romance of leadership perspective, when outcomes were attributable to leadership, participants were generally more optimistic about the profitability of the organization and perceived it to be less risky. Such findings suggest that we are comforted when performance is linked to leadership.

Further work has refined our knowledge by examining the contexts that increase our propensity to generate heroic, charismatic leadership images. Perhaps most notably, researchers have explored the role of crises. Seemingly, crises propel even the most charismatically challenged individuals to act charismatically (Bligh, Kohles, & Meindl, 2004), can serve to whet perceivers' appetites for charisma (Bass, 2008), increase susceptibility to charismatic influence (Shamir & Howell, 1999), and unconsciously activate our search for leadership (Emrich, 1999). In a study of U.S. presidents, House, Spangler, and Woycke (1991) found a correlation between crisis measures and measures of presidential charisma. McCann (1997) found that threatening times were associated with the appeal of charismatic presidents. Pillai (1996) found that in student work groups, crisis situations fostered the emergence of charismatic leadership perceptions but, interestingly, not transactional leadership perceptions. These findings unambiguously suggest that charismatic perceptions and crises are related.

Why crises intensify perceivers' thirst for leadership can be understood by the reactions they elicit. Crises generate unpleasant feelings of ambiguity and uncertainty (Pearson & Clair, 1998), a state that conflicts with powerful motives to view the world as predictable (Pittman, 1998). Because direct control is oftentimes impossible during crises, individuals attempt to reassert control indirectly through secondary means, such as projecting charismatic qualities onto their leaders, who are viewed as a source of meaning, salvation, and distress relief (Shamir & Howell, 1999). In line with this motivational explanation, findings reveal that crisis-induced charismatic leadership perceptions fade rapidly once a crisis has passed (Hunt, Boal, & Dodge, 1999).

Although such research suggests that crises are unique, in actuality, any situation that heightens a perceiver's psycho-physiological state propels us to romanticize leaders (Meindl, 1995). For instance, Pastor, Mayo, and Shamir (2007) heightened arousal by having participants ride a stationary bike, whereas others have manipulated psycho-physiological states by reminding participants of their own mortality (Gordijn & Stapel, 2008; Landau, Greenberg, & Sullivan, 2009). Regardless of the manipulation utilized, heightened arousal accentuated charismatic leadership perceptions, and the perceptions were stronger when the target already possessed some semblance of charisma. Moving beyond simple perception, research further documents that heightened arousal increases support for incumbents (Landau et al., 2009), compliance (Landau et al., 2009), and receptivity to counterattitudinal visions (Gordijn & Stapel, 2008). Why cycling, thoughts of death, and experiencing a crisis function similarly requires further consideration from scholars.

Beyond crises, researchers have also demonstrated a link between charismatic leadership images and perceived distance to a target. Although perceptions of charisma are distributed across all organizational levels, it is widely recognized that there is a fundamental difference between proximal and distal leadership (Shamir, 1995). As distance increases between leaders and the led, observers are more prone to base their leadership impressions on simplified heuristics, such as the performance of the organization or their general stereotyped impression of leaders (Antonakis & Atwater, 2002). Better understanding of this perceptual bias may lie in a better appreciation of the principles of construal level theory (CLT; see Trope & Liberman, 2003), which suggests that with increasing distance, regardless of type, our conceptualizations of events and objects become simpler and more abstract. Seemingly, CLT may provide us with a promising overarching framework and important insights into the characteristics of leadership judgments that predispose perceivers to generate overly ideal, prototypic, and charismatic leadership evaluations.

A further contextual consideration that has received some attention is the social environment within which observers find themselves. Individual perceivers are interconnected into larger social networks, which raise the possibility that leadership perceptions are susceptible to social contagion (Meindl, 1990). Rather than simply resulting from individual sensemaking, leadership perceptions can spread like a common cold throughout a social network (Mayo & Pastor, 2007; Pastor, Meindl, & Mayo, 2002). Such findings undermine a common misperception regarding the wisdom of crowds and proposals that group-level analyses reflect the actual behavior of the target (Mount & Scullen, 2001). Instead, contagion research suggests that the social construction of leadership can, and does, span all levels of analysis (i.e., individual, dyadic, group).

Interestingly, communication along social pathways need not be explicit, but rather, it can spread subtly through seemingly irrelevant derogatory remarks (Goodman, Schell, Alexander, & Eidelman, 2008) or nonverbal displays. Nonverbal facial expressions represent a particularly intriguing investigative angle, not only because they are widely recognized to serve as clues to a fellow social actor's attitudes and behavioral intentions (Ekman & Oster, 1979) but also because their spread can be insidious and, therefore, unpreventable. Functionally, the nonverbal displays of fellow social actors assist us in making sense of a leader's activities. Once perceived, nonverbal information is spontaneously mimicked by observers, and the afferent feedback that results generates corresponding emotions, which can color subsequent information processing. Coinciding with this thinking, research shows that observers judge leaders to be more effective when they are surrounded by positive, versus negative, nonverbal displays from group members (V. Brown & Geis, 1984) and that negative attitudes toward a female leader may stem in part from the nonverbal disapproval on the faces of fellow subordinates (Butler & Geis, 1990). Interestingly, susceptibility to nonverbal leadership influences may depend on individual differences, such as one's interest in affiliating with others (Lakin & Chartrand, 2003), self-monitoring (Cheng & Chartrand, 2003), or information-processing style (van Baaren, Horgan, Chartrand, & Dijkmans, 2004).

To summarize, research indicates that humans are leader-centric thinkers who use the leader category to explain their worlds. What remains unclear is the very concept of leadership itself—what it looks like, how it develops, and the information processing that lies behind its application. I turn to these questions next.

# The Social-Cognitive Approach

To delve deeper into how followers generate leadership perceptions, it is necessary to underscore the fact that human cognition is premised on symbolic structures that are stored in long-term memory and that serve as a stable, internal, mental model. Instead of processing each instance of an object, event, person, or animal as novel, people transform their "transient experiences into internal models" (Bandura, 1986, p. 18). In categorizing instances, social actors are able to bring to bear enormous quantities of stored conceptual knowledge, which in turn allows them to know what to anticipate and how to behave (Murphy, 2002). Furthermore, concepts and categories are the bedrock of efficient, effective communication, which is premised on a common mental map of the world. In the end, the application of the leader category to a target allows us to infer a tremendous amount of information, to understand the actions of a target, to coordinate our actions in relation to the target, and to comprehend the activities of our fellow perceivers.

Given the centrality of categories for information processing, the content, creation, and deployment of the leader category are central to the follower-centric approach. In the sections that follow, I address these issues. First, I consider what is known about the content of the leader category. Second, I address issues surrounding the variability and stability of the category. Third, I consider the development of the category. Fourth, I address how the category influences information processing and comes to be applied. Finally, I briefly discuss how the application of relevant leader categories can free or constrain a leader's behavior.

## The Content and Nature of the Leader Category

As with other elements of the world, perceivers hold in memory a well-elaborated category that includes the features that distinguish leaders from non-leaders (Lord et al., 1984). Following the probabilistic view (Rosch, 1978), the leader category is conceptualized as a fuzzy and ill-defined knowledge structure composed of properties that, individually, are neither necessary nor sufficient to warrant inclusion in the category. As with other concepts, the application of the leader category follows the family resemblance principle, whereby potential category members vary along a prototypic fit gradient. As one example, consider that although "birds" typically fly, the fact that a particular animal does not fly (e.g., a chicken) does not preclude it from membership as a "bird," but rather simply suggests that the target is less bird-like than other exemplars (e.g., a robin). Ultimately, the higher the proportion of attributes a target shares with other category members, the more prototypical it is deemed to be.

Based on previous work (Cantor & Mischel, 1979), Lord and his colleagues have suggested that the leader category is structured around traits (Lord, De Vader, & Alliger, 1986). Such an approach is not surprising, given that traits are central to human thinking and memory processes and are automatically and spontaneously applied when perceivers are confronted with others' behavior (Uleman, Newman, & Moskowitz, 1996). In fact, traits are so hardwired into our thinking that we perceive much of the inanimate and animal world in trait terms (Epley, Waytz, & Cacioppo, 2007). In an initial investigation utilizing a free recall methodology, Lord et al. (1984) found that 59 leadership traits were uniquely generated by their participants and that these traits varied in terms of their prototypicality. Subsequent investigations have replicated this initial work, shortened the measure, and identified the second-order factor structure (Epitopaki & Martin, 2004; Offerman et al., 1994).

In the end, individuals do not extract a single leader category from the world, but rather a nested three-level structure: superordinate, basic, and subordinate (Rosch, 1978). At the most inclusive level, referred to as superordinate, the broadest and most abstract representation of the category exists. This level of representation contains those features that are generally common to most leaders and that overlap very little with contrasting categories (e.g., nonleaders). Immediately embedded beneath this level is the basic level, which incorporates context. Lord et al. (1984) have argued that individuals distinguish 11 different basic level leaders: business, finance, minority, education, religion, sports, national politics, world politics, labor, media, and military. Although Lord et al.'s work is seminal, it is worth noting that this structure is based on a single study and that alternative basic level categories may exist (Den Hartog & Koopman, 2005). Finally, at the subordinate level, leader categories are further differentiated, providing a highly nuanced understanding of leadership. As but one example, some research indicates that the leader category may differ for male and female leaders (Johnson, Murphy, Zewdie, & Reichard, 2008).

Before continuing, it is worth mentioning that in recent years, there has been growing interest in the role that group categories play in terms of our information processing about leadership (D. van Knippenberg, van Knippenberg, & Giessner, 2007). In everyday situations, leadership is enacted in group settings, and fit with a group is germane to understanding how followers react to potential leaders (D. van Knippenberg & Hogg, 2003). On the basis of social identity theory, Hogg and his colleagues have proposed that in addition to our general leader stereotype, discussed above, the group prototype that encapsulates the prototypical values, attitudes, and norms of a group also serves as a relevant yardstick against which potential leaders can be evaluated. As with the general leader category, potential leader targets vary along a group prototypicality gradient, and followers' endorsement of leaders depends on the target's fit with the shared social identity of a group. Fit with a group's shared identity is relevant to leadership perceptions because it serves to reassure followers that a leader is trustworthy and that he or she will behave in a manner that is consistent with the collective interest (D. van Knippenberg et al., 2007). Coinciding with this thinking, a substantial and ever-growing body of work indicates that leader fit to a group category relates to perceived leader effectiveness (Hains, Hogg, & Duck, 1997; Platow & van Knippenberg, 2001) and charisma (B. van Knippenberg & van Knippenberg, 2005). At this point, I simply acknowledge the relevance of the group category; subsequently, I discuss how perceivers reconcile and integrate information about a given target's fit with the general leader category and the group category.

## Variability and Stability of the Leader Category

Despite attempts to demonstrate otherwise, research findings indicate that the cumulative lifetime leadership observations and experiences of groups within a society are largely shared. Sensibly, just as most groups within a society share a common conceptual understanding of other concepts, they also share a common understanding of leadership. Findings indicate that university students and employees possess similar mental models of leadership, as do employees who differ in terms of age, organizational tenure, organizational position (Epitropaki & Martin, 2004; Offermann et al., 1994), and organizational identification (Martin & Epitropaki, 2001). If we are to find group-level differences, it seems likely that we will need to find groups who may have had significant, early, repeated exposure to different role models, group structures, and leadership experiences. Consistent with this idea, some evidence suggests that males and females exhibit slight differences in their leader categories (Deal & Stevenson, 1998; Den Hartog & Koopman, 2005). In this regard, some findings suggest that males, relative to females, may hold ideal leader categories that are more forgiving of antiprototypical characteristics, such as domineering and pushy, whereas females' ideal prototypes emphasize interpersonal sensitivity (Deal & Stevenson, 1998). Thus, despite some limited evidence for gender differences, the leader category appears to be highly robust, at least within a culture.

Increased globalization has motivated numerous scholars to investigate how culture can taint the leader category. Cultural differences exist in what individuals expect from, and how they perceive and react to, different leader behaviors (Ensari & Murphy, 2003; for a review, see Tsui, Nifadkar, & Ou, 2007). For instance, research suggests that individuals vary cross-culturally in how they react to abusive leaders (Bond, Wan, Leung, & Giacalone, 1985) or violations of justice principles (Tsui et al., 2007). Such findings underscore the possibility that Western leadership conceptualizations may not be universally endorsed (Den Hartog, House, Hanges, Ruiz-Quintanilla, & Dorfman, 1999; Gerstner & Day, 1994; Javidan, Dorfman, de Luque, & House, 2006).

To assess cross-cultural variability in the leader category, Robert House and his colleagues (Javidan et al., 2006) questioned 15,022 middle managers from 62 different societies (average per society $n = 250$), who were organized into 10 cultural clusters of nations. They asked the managers to rate 112 leadership items, which composed 21 primary and six underlying dimensions, in terms of each item's ability to impede or facilitate effective leadership. Research from this herculean effort has provided us with an initial glimpse into the cultural universality and divergence of the leader category. In terms of the second-order factors, significant differences emerged between the 10 cultural clusters along all six dimensions. For instance, results at this level of analysis suggest that the 10 clusters of nations differ significantly in terms of the extent to which they emphasize charismatic/value-based leadership, a form of leadership that focuses on motivating and expecting high outcomes from individuals. Thus, whereas Anglo countries, such as the United States, score high on the charismatic/value-based dimension, Middle Eastern countries, such as Egypt, place less emphasis on this dimension; countries in the Confucian Asia cluster (e.g., China) fall between these two extremes (Javidan et al., 2006).

Although results along the six dimensions suggest that cultures differ profoundly in terms of their understanding of what it means to be a leader, item-level analyses suggest that such conclusions should be tempered and that a significant, universally shared understanding of leadership exists. On this front, 22 attributes investigated by the GLOBE researchers emerged as universally desirable (e.g., honest, decisive, dynamic), whereas eight were widely regarded as undesirable (e.g., irritable, egocentric, ruthless). Such similarity suggests that there may be a common universal leadership experience. In this regard, evolutionary thinkers propose that leadership is a group adaptation and that ideal leaders fulfill common group functions, such as initiating group activity, maintaining cohesion, and planning for the future (Van Vugt, Hogan, & Kaiser, 2008).

Moving beyond group differences, our understanding of the leader category has also been enhanced by work that has assessed individual stability (Epitropaki & Martin, 2004). In one such examination, Epitropaki and Martin (2004) asked respondents to indicate how descriptive a series of traits were of a business leader in general, assessed on two occasions, 1 year apart. Overall, they concluded that the business leader category is not particularly ephemeral. To understand why stability emerged in their research, it is necessary that readers first recognize that although humans are capable of careful, conscious, serial thought, more often than not the world is experienced through a nonconscious system (Macrae & Bodenhausen, 2000). Knowledge in this system includes our generic beliefs about the world, which are gradually accumulated through repeated associations. Beginning early in childhood, we are repeatedly exposed to leaders who possess particular traits, such as dedicated, intelligent, and sensitive. These repeated associations become interconnected, forming a generic leader knowledge structure (i.e., a leader category). Once formed, this generic category is highly resistant to change and provides us with a stable backdrop on which to experience the world. Devoid of context, Epitropaki and Martin's procedures likely resulted in participants simply recovering and utilizing their generic, static, stable mental representation. Their findings show us that the generic leader category possesses the same stability as other generic concepts, such as chair, bird, car, and cat, which we would anticipate to remain highly stable over a 1-year period.

Notwithstanding these findings, cognitive research does unequivocally suggest that categories can be quite dynamic and can be generated *in the moment*. The cognitive architecture of the nonconscious system is generally regarded to be connectionist. It is a system that is subsymbolic, meaning that knowledge is represented by patterns of activation of neuron-like units (Smith & DeCoster, 2000). As information is input into this system, connectionist architectures settle into (i.e., recognize) the best interpretation through a process of parallel constraint satisfaction, finding the pattern of activation that maximally accommodates the stored associations and the momentary pattern of external (e.g., gender, behavior) and internal (e.g., motives) constraints. Thus, for instance, whereas our generic concept of a bird might remain highly stable over time, our image of the category *bird* might shift slightly when standing on a ship gazing out over the vast expanse of Antarctica (see Barsalou, 1982).

Based on connectionist principles, Lord and his colleagues have laid out in very general terms how such a system might operate to generate dynamic, *momentary*, leader categories (Hanges, Lord, & Dickson, 2000; Lord, Brown, & Harvey, 2001). In one of the few studies to directly test their ideas, Foti, Knee, and Backert (2008) found evidence that suggested that the leader category shifted depending on the internal goals of an observer. Despite such encouraging findings, empirical data into the dynamic generation of the leader category remain limited, and this area remains ripe for research. It is worth noting that to effectively proceed with such investigations, it is likely that applied leadership researchers will need to forsake their preference for field data and conduct laboratory studies that allow them to momentarily manipulate constraints, such as observer goals, in a controlled manner.

## The Development of the Leader Category

As noted above, beginning early in life, the leader category is unconsciously and slowly acquired as individuals soak up co-occurring leadership features. For instance, as children, we begin to associate business leaders with such characteristics as intelligent, competent, male, and White, and we mindlessly tether these together and lock them away in memory (Rosette, Leonardelli, & Phillips, 2008). Given that the bedrock of most leadership perception is the category stored in the slow-learning, slow-changing neocortical system, one may wonder whether there is a discernable developmental trajectory and age at which our generic leader category solidifies in memory. Simply put, leadership scholars largely have ignored this important basic scientific question. In one of the few studies to directly address this topic, Matthews, Lord, and Walker (1990) examined the development of the leader category among 159 children in the 1st, 3rd, 6th, 9th, and 12th grades. Coinciding with our understanding of the neocortical system, they found, relative to older children (i.e., 6th, 9th, and 12th grades), younger children (1st and 3rd grades) felt leadership was exemplified by specific actions, outcomes, and exemplars (e.g., parents), whereas older children based their judgments on a highly elaborated leader category. More recent work by Antonakis and Dalgas (2009) found that young children and naive adults were similarly capable, and quite successful, at predicting election results on the basis of photographs. Seemingly, their findings suggest that very early on, children associate facial features with personality characteristics (i.e., competent), which are used to make leadership decisions similar to those generated by adults. Together, these two studies indicate that the standards utilized to form leadership perceptions consolidate at a very early age. An important practical implication of this work is that it suggests that interventions intended to undermine biased leadership categories (e.g., emphasis on masculine characteristics) may be most efficacious at a very early age.

If the leader category takes shape early in our development, one might anticipate that the world as seen through the eyes of children would play a pivotal role in the nature of the leader category. As one obvious example, because children are generally shorter than leadership figures in their lives, height (Judge & Cable, 2004) and the vertical dimension of space (Schubert, 2005) should be tightly coupled to leadership, which they are. Beyond such universal childhood experiences, idiosyncratic childhood experiences with leadership figures should also be pivotal antecedents of category content. In one investigation, Keller (1999) asked participants to rate the extent to which a series of characteristics were descriptive of their mother, their father, and an ideal leader. Overall, her findings indicate that maternal and paternal characteristics influenced the ideal leader image. Although linkages between childhood experiences and the leader category are sensible, the topic remains poorly understood. This is unfortunate, as associations with early childhood experience are provocative and may possibly underlie cultural variability or gender bias in the category.

## Category Use and Application

Prior research indicates that categories, such as stereotypes, are an important determinant of the impressions that are formed about a target. When confronted with ambiguous or incomplete data, perceivers utilize categories in a top-down manner, filling in gaps and generating stereotypic judgments. Perhaps most famously, research shows that the factor structure of behavioral questionnaires can be extracted, even when raters are asked to rate imaginary leaders (Rush et al., 1977). In line with these findings, research also indicates that subordinate evaluations on behavioral leadership questionnaires are strongly related to the leader category (Avolio & Bass, 1989) and that raters who share a common leader category generate similar behavioral ratings, even when they are rating different targets (Rush & Russell, 1988). Categorical thinking also leads individuals to misremember what it is an observed target has done. For instance, several studies have documented that perceivers confuse unobserved category-consistent behavior with behaviors that were actually observed (Binning, Zaba, & Whattam, 1986; Phillips & Lord, 1982). Practically, these findings have important implications for leadership practice and, in particular, the amount of faith we should place in behavioral questionnaires. Although behavioral leadership instruments are presumed to capture the behavior of the target being scrutinized, categorical thinking processes can color memory, encoding, and the retrieval of behavior (Shondrick, Dinh, & Lord, 2010). Hence, what may be extracted from behavioral assessments may say more about the information processing of observers than the actual behavior of leaders.

One question that remains is how it is that perceivers decide to apply the label *leader* to a given target. In their categorization theory of leadership perceptions, Lord and his colleagues have argued that the assignment of the leader label to a target is contingent on the degree to which a target's features overlap with a perceiver's leadership category (Lord et al., 1984). In effect, one pathway to being perceived as a leader is recognition-based, whereby the perceiver draws upon the characteristics of the target to make a leadership judgment (Lord & Maher, 1993). The greater the overlap that exists between a target's perceived features and the category held in long-term memory, the more strongly the category label *leader* will be applied to a target. In their seminal work, Lord and his associates (1984; Study 3) randomly assigned 95 undergraduate participants to read one of three vignettes that described a target, John Perry, as displaying either prototypical, antiprototypical, or neutral leadership behaviors. Their results indicated that this manipulation accounted for significant variation in perceivers' expectations that John Perry would engage in prototypical, antiprototypical, and neutral behaviors, as well as in his perceived accountability and responsibility for the success of a new product. Overall, these findings provided strong causal evidence for the operation of the recognition system and suggested that the application of the leader label also generated expectations for a target's future behavior.

Since this initial investigation, further refinements have documented that leader categorization mediates the relationship between observable target behaviors and leadership ratings (Fraser & Lord, 1988), biases memory retrieval (Rush & Russell, 1988), and is not dependent on the availability of a perceiver's cognitive resources (Maurer & Lord, 1991). Although relatively underinvestigated, some research has also documented the applicability of categorization theory to real-world settings, thus documenting the theory's external validity and applied utility. Such fieldwork has demonstrated that fit to the leader category not only influences leadership perceptions but also serves as an antecedent of relevant employee outcomes (Engle & Lord, 1997; Epitropaki & Martin, 2005). On this latter point, in a longitudinal survey investigation, Epitropaki and Martin (2005) demonstrated that perceived supervisory fit to the leader category impacted the quality of the leader–member exchange (LMX) and, indirectly through LMX, influenced employee organizational commitment, job satisfaction, and well-being. Beyond demonstrating the applicability of the categorization approach, this research also highlights a way in which interested researchers might operationalize leader categorization. Although Lord's categorization theory has been highly regarded and cited, there has been little effort to understand how categorization mediates the impact of leader behavior, despite previous literature that has directly linked common behavioral measures with the leader category (Avolio & Bass, 1989).

Research also shows that seemingly irrelevant characteristics may lead to the recognition that a target is leader-like. For instance, data indicate that leadership is ascribed to targets based on their talkativeness (Stein & Heller, 1979), attractiveness (Cherulnik, Turns, & Wilderman, 1990), masculine appearance (Sczesny & Kühnen, 2004), or perceptual salience (Phillips & Lord, 1981). Recently, it has been suggested that thinking does not simply occur in the head and that our conceptual knowledge is grounded in our sensory and motor systems (Barsalou, Simmons, Barbey, & Wilson, 2003). Our conceptual representations are not simply stored as abstract symbols in memory but are also known through the way in which we directly experience the phenomenon in question. Motivational systems are intertwined with specific motor movements, emotions are linked to facial expressions, loneliness is linked to coldness (Zhong & Leonardelli, 2008), virtue is tied to clean smells (Liljenquist, Zhong, & Galinsky, 2010), and leadership is related to height (Judge & Cable, 2004). Dominant individuals lord over us, we look up to them, they are high in the food chain, they are at the top of the organizational chart, and they look down on us from high upon their thrones. The bodily experience of looking up, versus down, relates to leadership, power, and dominance and, hence, data indicate that we are more fluent in processing status information when it is presented in the appropriate spatial location (Schubert, 2005) and that vertical information conveyed through an organizational chart colors our leadership perceptions (Giessner & Schubert, 2007). Unraveling the links between bottom-up perceptual processes, embodied cognition, and the leader category promises to be an exciting research opportunity moving forward (see Lord & Shondrick, 2011).

Although the recognition of leadership based on a match to the leader category deepens our understanding, it draws back the curtain only partway. Followers defer to leaders, not simply because they fit leadership images or because they occupy the appropriate spatial location, but also because they are relevant for meeting our goals. As Barsalou (1985) noted many years ago, target categorization depends not only on fit to the central tendency of a category, but also on the end-state or goal toward which a perceiver is striving. Although there is some speculation regarding the focal functions of leaders for groups and their members, it seems clear that we do forgo our freedom in part because leaders promote group survival and success (Van Vugt et al., 2008). In fact, findings stretching back more than 40 years unequivocally support a link between leadership and group outcomes. This research has shown that the attribution of group performance to leaders is robust and is not contingent on when the performance information is delivered (Larson, 1982) or whether or not a perceiver has any personal experience with a leader (Binning & Lord, 1980). Such work highlights a second critical pathway to leadership perceptions, which have traditionally been labeled as inference-based (Lord & Maher, 1993). Interestingly, direct comparisons of the recognition pathway and inferential pathway indicate that they additively impact leadership judgment (Lord, Binning, Rush, & Thomas, 1978), but that the relative weighting of each may depend on national culture (Ensari & Murphy, 2003). Contemporary work conducted within the context of CEO selection further suggests that perceivers may be predisposed to the inferential pathway and only default to recognition-based processes when confronted with ambiguity regarding performance (Jacquart & Antonakis, 2015).

As many readers may already have deduced, targets elicit the activation of numerous, sometimes competing, categories. At a minimum, followers can think about targets in terms of their compatibility with the leader category (Lord & Maher, 1993), the group category (B. van Knippenberg & van Knippenberg, 2005), racial categories (Rosette et al., 2008), previous leaders (Ritter & Lord, 2007), group performance (Phillips & Lord, 1981), and gender categories (Scott & Brown, 2006). The competition and interaction among these sources of information ricochet throughout the observer's mind, marking information processing in a multitude of ways. For example, Scott and Brown (2006) demonstrated that gender categories interacted with the processing of prototypical leadership behavior to impact behavioral encoding. Other research has shown that the sources of information interact to influence our evaluations of leaders. In this regard, prototypical leaders are viewed more favorably than nonprototypical leaders following success (Ensari & Murphy, 2003)—an effect that is particularly pronounced for Whites, as opposed to ethnic minorities (Rosette et al., 2008). Finally, some research has shown that the relative influence of various pieces of information may depend on characteristics of the perceiver. Here, a growing body of work has demonstrated that whereas fit to the leader category is generally important, it diminishes in importance, relative to the group category, as a function of individual identification with the group (Hains et al., 1997). Clearly, the sensemaking of observers is complex and dependent on multiple pieces of data.

## Follower Perceptions and Leader Action

To this point, I have highlighted some of the nuances that underlie leadership perceptions. Ultimately, leadership is about bidirectional influence, and the nature of followers' categorizations can serve as an important constraint on leader actions. For instance, although their perceived ability to deliver success is critical and failure is typically not an option for leaders, not all failures are equal and, at times, leaders may be granted a license to fail by subordinates (Giessner & van Knippenberg, 2008; Giessner, van Knippenberg, & Sleebos, 2009). In two recent articles, Giessner and his colleagues manipulated a leader's fit to a group category, which was discussed previously, and the nature of the type of goal that the leader failed to achieve. Findings from this research indicated that although failure to meet minimal goals dampened the positive perceptions that subordinates had of leaders who fit a group category, the same was not true when leaders failed to reach maximal goals. In maximal goal contexts, group prototypical leaders were seemingly given the benefit of the doubt, and their failure did not undermine the benefits that they incurred from fitting the group category. Such findings reflect the wider literature that highlights the fact that performance and leadership inferences are not direct; rather, they are sensitive to the nature of the causal accounts offered for performance (Phillips & Lord, 1981) as well as to the processing schema utilized by observers (Foti & Lord, 1987).

The research mentioned above suggests that follower leadership standards are potentially flexible and that, at times, followers will free up leaders to behave in an idiosyncratic and nonnormative fashion (Hollander, 1992). For instance, research has demonstrated that self-sacrificial behavior, relative to self-beneficial behavior, is related to follower perceptions of a leader's legitimacy (Choi & Mai-Dalton, 1999; B. van Knippenberg & van Knippenberg, 2005; Yorges, Weiss, & Stickland, 1999). Although generally true, the relationship between leader self-sacrificial behavior and leader endorsement is contingent on whether or not a leader is categorized by observers to be a typical group member (B. van Knippenberg & van Knippenberg, 2005). Individuals categorized as typical of a group seemingly are not held to the same self-sacrificial standards as their less typical counterparts. Similarly, procedural fairness (Ullrich, Christ, & van Dick, 2009) and distributive justice (Platow & van Knippenberg, 2001) appear to be standards that are less important for leaders who are typical of the group than for those who are atypical. Finally, Platow Knippenberg, Haslam, van Knippenberg, and Spears (2006) found that whereas leaders who were prototypical of the group could flexibly employ either transactional or group-oriented rhetoric, leaders who were atypical were seemingly tolerated only when they utilized group-oriented rhetoric. According to Hollander's (1958) idiosyncrasy credit model, leaders accumulate subordinate trust from their contributions to groups. Findings such as those discussed above indicate that credit and leadership need not be hard fought, but instead can flow simply from followers' categorizations.

## Summary of the Literature

In this chapter I have discussed literature that highlights the role of followers in the generation of leadership. Figure 4.1 serves as a heuristic summary of many of the key themes that I have touched upon. As highlighted in the figure, the leader category is a critical perceptual schema that social actors draw upon to understand their world (i.e., the Romance of Leadership). As discussed, although this category is frequently used, it is particularly salient to observers under certain conditions, such as when they are uncertain or have a need to exert control. Turning to perceptions of specific leaders and the content of the leader category itself, it is largely composed of traits, develops at a young age, and can be altered by features of the context, such as one's culture. As well, more recent work (i.e., connectionist approaches) has emphasized the potential dynamic nature of the category, highlighting how the content of the category can be generated on the fly by social actors to accommodate immediate situational constraints. Figure 4.1 also highlights that the application of the leader label depends upon the overlap between the perceptions of the target and

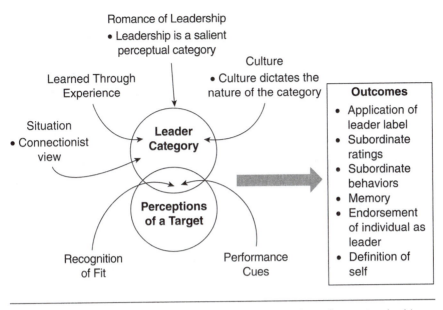

**Figure 4.1**    Heuristic Model Detailing the Key Factors That Influence Leadership Perceptions

the expected prototype. Finally, as highlighted in the figure, the application of the leader label has numerous consequences, such as altering memory and increasing susceptibility to a leader's influence attempts.

# Conclusion

This chapter began with a scenario depicting employees discussing their new CEO. Despite witnessing the same actions and behaviors, the employees arrived at different conclusions regarding the CEO's leadership ability. In this chapter, I have presented literature, data, theory, and thoughts that I hope serve the reader well should he or she ever be similarly befuddled by how variance in leadership perceptions arise. As well, I have attempted to highlight how critical these perceptions are to being an effective leader. Although traditionally leadership has been approached as a leader-centric phenomenon, the past 40 years of follower-centric research have demonstrated that leadership is highly dependent on followers. To wit, coaches, politicians, managers, and CEOs fail as leaders not simply because of behavioral shortcomings, but also because they are no longer categorized as being leader-like.

## Discussion Questions

1.  Is there one characteristic above all others that is essential to being seen as a leader? Why is it critical? Are there any circumstances under which it might not be critical?
2.  Does it matter whether a leader actually possesses prototypical leadership traits or simply manages the impression in an audience that he or she possesses these traits?

3. What elements of the context are most significant in altering the leader prototype?
4. Why might it be, or not be, important for leaders to understand how leadership impressions are formed by observers?
5. Research discussed in this chapter indicates that the business leader category is associated with being white (see Rosette, Leonardelli, & Phillips, 2008). What steps can society take to remedy this bias?

## Recommended Readings

- Javidan, M., Dorfman, P. W., de Luque, M. S., & House, R. J. (2006). In the eye of the beholder: Cross cultural lessons in leadership from project GLOBE. *Academy of Management Perspectives, 20,* 67–90.
- Kellerman, B. (2007, December). What every leader needs to know about followers. *Harvard Business Review, 85,* 84–91.
- Schyns, B., Kiefer, T., Kerschreiter, R., & Tymon, A. (2011). Teaching implicit leadership theories to develop leaders and leadership—How and why it can make a difference. *Academy of Management Learning & Education, 10,* 397–408.

## Recommended Case Studies

- **Case:** Ely, R. J., & Vargas, I. (2006). Managing a public image: Cheri Mack. Harvard Business School Case 406096- PDF-ENG.
- **Case:** Khoo, H. S., Chia, A., & Lim, V. K. G. (2010). Good intentions gone awry at the National Kidney Foundation. Harvard Business School Case 910M17-PDF-ENG.
- **Case:** Munyon, T. P., & Cleavenger, D. J. (2013). It's how you frame it: Transformational leadership and the meaning of work. Ivey Publishing BH535.

## Recommended Video

- Monk, P. (2011). Leaders and followers: What tango teaches. http://ed.ted.com/featured/ypFEhSjj

## References

Anderson, C., & Kilduff, G. J. (2009). Why do dominant personalities attain influence in face-to-face groups? The competence-signaling effects of trait dominance. *Journal of Personality and Social Psychology, 96,* 491–503.

Antonakis, J., & Atwater, L. (2002). Leader distance: A review and a proposed theory. *The Leadership Quarterly, 13,* 673–704.

Antonakis, J., & Dalgas, O. (2009). Predicting elections: Child's play! *Science, 323*(5918), 1183.

Avolio, B. J. (2007). Promoting more integrative strategies for leadership theory-building. *American Psychologist, 62,* 25–33.

Avolio, B. J., & Bass, B. M. (1989). Transformational leadership, charisma, and beyond. In J. G. Hunt, B. R. Baliga, H. P. Dachler, & C. A. Schreisheim (Eds.), *Emerging leadership vistas. International leadership symposia series* (pp. 29–49). Lexington, MA: Lexington Books.

Bandura, A. (1986). *Social foundations of thought and action: A social cognitive theory.* Englewood Cliffs, NJ: Prentice-Hall.

Barsalou, L. W. (1982). Context-independent and context-dependent information in concepts. *Memory & Cognition, 10*, 82–93.

Barsalou, L. W. (1985). Ideals, central tendency, and frequency of instantiation as determinants of graded structure in categories. *Journal of Experimental Psychology: Learning, Memory, and Cognition, 11*, 629–654.

Barsalou, L. W., Simmons, W. K., Barbey, A., & Wilson, C. D. (2003). Grounding conceptual knowledge in modality-specific systems. *Trends in Cognitive Sciences, 7*, 84–91.

Bass, B. M. (2008). *The Bass handbook of leadership: Theory, research, and managerial applications* (4th ed.). New York, NY: Free Press.

Baumeister, R. F., & Newman, L. S. (1995). The primacy of stories, the primacy of roles, and the polarizing effects of interpretive motives: Some propositions about narratives. In R. S. Wyer (Ed.), *Advances in social cognition* (Vol. 8, pp. 97–108). Hillsdale, NJ: Lawrence Erlbaum.

Bennis, W. (2008). Introduction. In R. E. Riggio, I. Chaleff, & J. Lipman-Blumen (Eds.), *The art of followership: How great followers create great leaders and organizations* (pp. xxiii–xxvii). San Francisco, CA: Jossey-Bass.

Binning, J. F., & Lord, R. G. (1980). Boundary conditions for performance cue effects on group process ratings: Familiarity versus type of feedback. *Organizational Behavior and Human Decision Processes, 26*, 115–130.

Binning, J. F., Zaba, A. J., & Whattam, J. C. (1986). Explaining the biasing effects of performance cues in terms of cognitive categorization. *Academy of Management Journal, 29*, 521–535.

Bligh, M. C., Kohles, J. C., & Meindl, J. R. (2004). Charisma under crisis: Presidential leadership, rhetoric, and media responses before and after the September 11th terrorist attacks. *The Leadership Quarterly, 15*, 211–239.

Bond, M. H., Wan, W. C., Leung, K., & Giacalone, R. (1985). How are responses to verbal insult related to cultural collectivism and power distance? *Journal of Cross-Cultural Psychology, 16*, 111–127.

Brown, D. J., & Keeping, L. M. (2005). Elaborating the construct of transformational leadership: The role of affect. *The Leadership Quarterly, 16*, 245–272.

Brown, V., & Geis, F. L. (1984). Turning lead into gold. Evaluations of men and women leaders and the alchemy of social consensus. *Journal of Personality and Social Psychology, 46*, 811–824.

Butler, D., & Geis, F. L. (1990). Nonverbal affect responses to male and female leaders: Implications for leadership evaluations. *Journal of Personality and Social Psychology, 58*, 48–59.

Calder, B. J. (1977). An attribution theory of leadership. In B. M. Staw & G. R. Salancik (Eds.), *New directions in organizational behavior* (pp. 179–204). Chicago, IL: St. Clair.

Cantor, N. W., & Mischel, W. (1979). Prototypes in person perception. In L. Berkowitz (Ed.), *Advances in experimental social psychology* (Vol. 12, pp. 3–52). New York, NY: Academic Press.

Cheng, C. M., & Chartrand, T. L. (2003). Self-monitoring without awareness: Using mimicry as a nonconscious affiliation strategy. *Journal of Personality and Social Psychology, 85*, 1170–1179.

Cherulnik, P. D., Turns, L. C., & Wilderman, S. K. (1990). Physical appearance and leadership: Exploring the role of appearance-based attribution in leader emergence. *Journal of Applied Social Psychology, 20*, 1530–1539.

Choi, Y., & Mai-Dalton, R. R. (1999). The model of followers' responses to self-sacrificial leadership: An empirical test. *The Leadership Quarterly, 10*, 397–421.

Deal, J. J., & Stevenson, M. A. (1998). Perceptions of female and male managers in the 1990s: Plus ça change. *Sex Roles, 38*, 287–300.

Den Hartog, D. N., House, R. J., Hanges, P. J., Ruiz-Quintanilla, S. A., & Dorfman, P. W. (1999). Culture specific and cross-culturally generalizable implicit leadership theories: Are attributes of charismatic/transformational leadership universally endorsed? *The Leadership Quarterly, 10*, 219–256.

Den Hartog, D. N., & Koopman, P. L. (2005). Implicit theories of leadership at different hierarchical levels. In B. Schyns & J. R. Meindl (Eds.), *Implicit leadership theories: Essays and explorations* (pp. 135–148). Greenwich, CT: Information Age.

Ekman, P., & Oster, H. (1979). Facial expressions of emotion. *Annual Review of Psychology, 20*, 527–554.

Emrich, C. D. (1999). Context effects in leadership perception. *Personality and Social Psychology Bulletin, 25*, 991–1006.

Engle, E. M., & Lord, R. G. (1997). Implicit theories, self-schemas, and leader–member exchange. *Academy of Management Journal, 40*, 988–1010.

Ensari, N., & Murphy, S. E. (2003). Cross-cultural variations in leadership perceptions and attribution of charisma to the leader. *Organizational Behavior and Human Decision Processes, 92,* 52–66.

Epitropaki, O., & Martin, R. (2004). Implicit leadership theories in applied settings: Factor structure, generalizability and stability over time. *Journal of Applied Psychology, 89,* 293–310.

Epitropaki, O., & Martin, R. (2005). The moderating role of individual differences in the relation between transformational/transactional leadership perceptions and organizational identification. *The Leadership Quarterly, 16,* 569–589.

Epley, N., Waytz, A., & Cacioppo, J. T. (2007). On seeing human: A three-factor theory of anthropomorphism. *Psychological Review, 114,* 864–886.

Fiedler, F. E. (1967). *A theory of leadership effectiveness.* New York, NY: McGraw-Hill.

Fiske, S. T. (1998). Stereotyping, prejudice, and discrimination. In D. T. Gilbert, S. T. Fiske, & G. Lindzey (Eds.), *Handbook of social psychology* (4th ed., Vol. 2, pp. 357–411). Boston, MA: McGraw-Hill.

Foti, R. J., Knee, R. E., & Backert, S. G. (2008). Multi-level implications of framing leadership perceptions as a dynamic process. *The Leadership Quarterly, 19,* 178–194.

Foti, R. J., & Lord, R. G. (1987). Prototypes and scripts: The effects of alternative methods of processing information on rating accuracy. *Organizational Behavior and Human Decision Processes, 39,* 318–340.

Fraser, S. L., & Lord, R. G. (1988). Stimulus prototypicality and general leadership impressions: Their role in leadership and behavioral ratings. *Journal of Psychology, 122,* 291–303.

Gerstner, C. R., & Day, D. V. (1994). Cross-cultural comparison of leadership prototypes. *The Leadership Quarterly, 5,* 121–134.

Giessner, S. R., & Schubert, T. (2007). High in the hierarchy: How vertical location and judgments of leaders' power are interrelated. *Organizational Behavior and Human Decision Processes, 104,* 30–44.

Giessner, S. R., & van Knippenberg, D. (2008). "License to fail": Goal definition, leader group prototypicality, and perceptions of leadership effectiveness after leader failure. *Organizational Behavior and Human Decision Processes, 105,* 14–35.

Giessner, S. R., van Knippenberg, D., & Sleebos, E. (2009). License to fail? How leader group prototypicality moderates the effects of leader performance on perceptions of leadership effectiveness. *The Leadership Quarterly, 45,* 434–451.

Goldhagen, D. J. (2009). *Worse than war: Genocide, eliminationism, and the ongoing assault on humanity.* New York, NY: PublicAffairs.

Goodman, J. A., Schell, J., Alexander, M. G., & Eidelman, S. (2008). The impact of a derogatory remark on prejudice toward a gay male leader. *Journal of Applied Social Psychology, 38,* 542–555.

Gordijn, E. H., & Stapel, D. A. (2008). When controversial leaders with charisma are effective: The influence of terror on the need for vision and impact of mixed attitudinal messages. *European Journal of Social Psychology, 38,* 389–411.

Grant, A. M., & Ashford, S. J. (2008). The dynamics of proactivity at work. *Research in Organizational Behavior, 28,* 3–34.

Hains, S. C., Hogg, M. A., & Duck, J. M. (1997). Self-categorization and leadership: Effects of group prototypicality and leader stereotypicality. *Personality and Social Psychology Bulletin, 23,* 1087–1100.

Hanges, P., Lord, R. G., & Dickson, M. W. (2000). An information-processing perspective on leadership and culture: A case for a connectionist architecture. *Applied Psychology: An International Review, 49,* 133–161.

Hersey, P., & Blanchard, K. H. (1977). *The management of organizational behavior* (3rd ed.). Upper Saddle River, NJ: Prentice Hall.

Hogg, M. A., Hains, S. C., & Mason, I. (1998). Identification and leadership in small groups: Salience, frame of reference, and leader stereotypicality effects on leader evaluations. *Journal of Personality and Social Psychology, 75,* 1248–1263.

Hollander, E. P. (1958). Conformity, status, and idiosyncrasy credit. *Psychological Review, 65,* 117–127.

Hollander, E. P. (1992). Leadership, followership, self, and others. *The Leadership Quarterly, 3,* 43–54.

Hollander, E. P. (1993). Legitimacy, power and influence: A perspective on relational features of leadership. In M. M. Chemers & R. Ayman (Eds.), *Leadership theory and research: Perspectives and directions* (pp. 29–47). San Diego, CA: Academic Press.

House, R. J. (1971). A path-goal theory of leader effectiveness. *Administrative Science Quarterly, 16,* 321–339.

House, R. J., Spangler, W. D., & Woycke, J. (1991). Personality and charisma in the U.S. presidency: A psychological theory of leader effectiveness. *Administrative Science Quarterly, 36,* 364–396.

Howell, J. M., & Shamir, B. (2005). The role of followers in the charismatic leadership process: Relationships and their consequences. *Academy of Management Review, 30,* 96–112.

Hunt, J. G., Boal, K. B., & Dodge, G. E. (1999). The effects of visionary and crisis-responsive charisma on followers: An experimental examination of two kinds of charismatic leadership. *The Leadership Quarterly, 10,* 423–448.

Hunter, S. T., Bedell-Avers, K. E., & Mumford, M. D. (2007). The typical leadership study: Assumptions, implications, and potential remedies. *The Leadership Quarterly, 18,* 435–446.

Jacquart, P., & Antonakis, J. (2015). When does charisma matter for top-level leaders? Effects of attributional ambiguity. *Academy of Management Journal, 58,* 1051–1074.

Johnson, S. J., Murphy, S. E, Zewdie, S., & Reichard, R. J. (2008). The strong, sensitive type: Effects of gender stereotypes and leadership prototypes on the evaluation of male and female leaders. *Organizational Behavior and Human Decision Processes, 106,* 39–60.

Judge, T. A., & Cable, D. M. (2004). The effect of physical height on workplace success and income: Preliminary test of a theoretical model. *Journal of Applied Psychology, 89,* 428–441.

Judge, T. A., Colbert, A. E., & Ilies, R. (2004). Intelligence and leadership: A quantitative review and test of theoretical propositions. *Journal of Applied Psychology, 89,* 542–552.

Kark, R., Shamir, B., & Chen, G. (2003). The two faces of transformational leadership: Empowerment and dependency. *Journal of Applied Psychology, 88,* 246–255.

Keller, T. (1999). Images of the familiar: Individual differences and implicit leadership theories. *The Leadership Quarterly, 10,* 589–607.

Kellerman, B. (2008). *Followership: How followers are creating change and changing leaders.* Boston, MA: Harvard Business School Publishing.

Kerr, S., & Jermier, J. M. (1978). Substitutes for leadership: Their meaning and measurement. *Organizational Behavior and Human Performance, 22,* 375–403.

Klein, K. J., & House, R. J. (1995). On fire: Charismatic leadership and levels of analysis. *The Leadership Quarterly, 6,* 183–198.

Kunda, Z. (1990). The case for motivated reasoning. *Psychological Bulletin, 108,* 480–498.

Lakin, J. L., & Chartrand, T. L. (2003). Using nonconcious behavioral mimicry to create affiliation and rapport. *Psychological Science, 14,* 334–339.

Landau, M. J., Greenberg, J., & Sullivan, D. (2009). Managing terror when self-worth and worldviews collide: Evidence that mortality salience increases reluctance to self-enhance beyond authorities. *Journal of Experimental Social Psychology, 45,* 68–79.

Larson, J. R. (1982). Cognitive mechanisms mediating the impact of implicit theories of leader behavior on leader behavior ratings. *Organizational Behavior and Human Decision Processes, 29,* 129–140.

Liljenquist, K., Zhong, C. B., & Galinsky, A. D. (2010). The smell of virtue: Clean scents promote reciprocity and charity. *Psychological Science, 21,* 381–383.

Livi, S., Kenny, D. A., Albright, L., & Pierro, A. (2008). A social relations analysis of leadership. *The Leadership Quarterly, 19,* 235–248.

Lord, R. G. (2008). Followers' cognitive and affective structures and leadership processes. In R. E. Riggio, I. Chaleff, & J. Lipman-Blumen (Eds.), *The art of followership: How great followers create great leaders and organizations* (pp. 255–266). San Francisco, CA: Jossey-Bass.

Lord, R. G., Binning, J. F., Rush, M. C., & Thomas, J. C. (1978). The effect of performance cues and leader behavior on questionnaire ratings of leadership behavior. *Organizational Behavior and Human Decision Processes, 21,* 27–39.

Lord, R. G., & Brown, D. J. (2004). *Leadership processes and follower self-identity.* Mahwah, NJ: Lawrence Erlbaum.

Lord, R. G., Brown, D. J., & Freiberg, S. J. (1999). Understanding the dynamics of leadership: The role of follower self-concepts in the leader/follower relationship. *Organizational Behavior and Human Decision Processes, 78,* 167–203.

Lord, R. G., Brown, D. J., & Harvey, J. L. (2001). System constraints on leadership perceptions, behavior, and influence: An example of connectionist level processes. In M. A. Hogg & R. S. Tindale (Eds.), *Blackwell handbook of social psychology: Vol. 3. Group processes* (pp. 283–310). Oxford, UK: Blackwell.

Lord, R. G., De Vader, C. L., & Alliger, G. M. (1986). A meta-analysis of the relation between personality traits and leadership perceptions: An application of validity generalization procedures. *Journal of Applied Psychology, 71,* 402–410.

Lord, R. G., & Emrich, C. G. (2000). Thinking outside the box by looking inside the box: Extending the cognitive revolution in leadership research. *The Leadership Quarterly, 11,* 551–579.

Lord, R. G., Foti, R. J., & De Vader, C. L. (1984). A test of leadership categorization theory: Internal structure, information processing, and leadership perceptions. *Organizational Behavior and Human Performance, 34,* 343–378.

Lord, R. G., Foti, R. J., & Philips, J. S. (1982). A theory of leadership categorization. In J. G. Hunt, U. Sekaran, & C. Schriesheim (Eds.), *Leadership: Beyond establishment views* (pp. 104–121). Carbondale: Southern Illinois University Press.

Lord, R. G., & Maher, K. J. (1993). *Leadership and information processing: Linking perceptions and performance.* New York, NY: Routledge.

Lord, R. G., & Shondrick, S. J. (2011). Leadership and knowledge: Symbolic, connectionist, and embodied perspectives. *The Leadership Quarterly, 22,* 207–222.

Macrae, C. N., & Bodenhausen, G. V. (2000). Social cognition: Thinking categorically about others. *Annual Review of Psychology, 51,* 93–120.

Martin, R., & Epitropaki, O. (2001). Role of organizational identification on implicit leadership theories (ILTs), transformational leadership and work attitudes. *Group Processes and Intergroup Relations, 4,* 247–262.

Matthews, A. M., Lord, R. G., & Walker, J. B. (1990). *The development of leadership perceptions in children.* Unpublished manuscript, University of Akron.

Maurer, T. J., & Lord, R. G. (1991). An exploration of cognitive demands in group interaction as a moderator of information processing variables in perception of leadership. *Journal of Applied Social Psychology, 21,* 821–840.

Mayo, M., & Pastor, J. C. (2007). Leadership embedded in social networks: Looking at inter-follower processes. In B. Shamir, R. Pillai, M. C. Bligh, & M. Uhl-Bien (Eds.), *Follower-centered perspectives on leadership: A tribute to the memory of James R. Meindl* (pp. 93–114). Greenwich, CT: Information Age.

McCann, S. J. H. (1997). Threatening times and the election of charismatic U.S. presidents: With and without FDR. *The Journal of Psychology, 131,* 393–400.

Meindl, J. R. (1990). On leadership: An alternative to the conventional wisdom. In B. A. Staw (Ed.), *Research in organizational behavior* (Vol. 12, pp. 159–203). New York, NY: JAI.

Meindl, J. R. (1995). The romance of leadership as a follower-centric theory: A social constructionist approach. *The Leadership Quarterly, 6,* 329–341.

Meindl, J. R., & Ehrlich, S. B. (1987). The romance of leadership and the evaluation of organizational performance. *Academy of Management Journal, 30,* 91–109.

Meindl, J. R., Ehrlich, S. B., & Dukerich, J. M. (1985). The romance of leadership. *Administrative Science Quarterly, 30,* 78–102.

Mount, M. K., & Scullen, S. E. (2001). Multisource feedback ratings: What do they really measure? In M. London (Ed.), *How people evaluate others in organizations* (pp. 155–176). Mahwah, NJ: Lawrence Erlbaum.

Murphy, G. L. (2002). *The big book of concepts.* Cambridge, MA: MIT Press.

Offerman, L. R., Kennedy, J. K., & Wirtz, P. W. (1994). Implicit leadership theories: Content, structure and generalizability. *The Leadership Quarterly, 5,* 43–58.

Pastor, J. C., Mayo, M., & Shamir, B. (2007). Adding fuel to fire: The impact of followers' arousal on ratings of charisma. *Journal of Applied Psychology, 92,* 1584–1596.

Pastor, J. C., Meindl, J. R., & Mayo, M. C. (2002). A network effects model of charisma attributes. *Academy of Management Journal, 2,* 410–420.

Pearson, C. M., & Clair, J. A. (1998). Reframing crisis management. *The Academy of Management Review, 23,* 59–76.

Pfeffer, J. (1977). The ambiguity of leadership. *The Academy of Management Review, 2,* 104–112.

Phillips, J. S., & Lord, R. G. (1981). Causal attributions and perceptions of leadership. *Organizational Behavior and Human Performance, 28,* 143–163.

Phillips, J. S., & Lord, R. G. (1982). Schematic information processing and perceptions of leadership in problem-solving groups. *Journal of Applied Psychology, 67,* 486–492.

Pillai, R. (1996). Crisis and the emergence of charismatic leadership in groups: An experimental investigation. *Journal of Applied Social Psychology, 26,* 543–562.

Pillai, R., Kohles, J. C., & Bligh, M. C. (2007). Through thick and thin? Follower constructions of presidential leadership amidst crisis, 2001–2005. In B. Shamir, R. Pillai, M. C. Bligh, & M. Uhl-Bien, M. (Eds.), *Follower-centered perspectives on leadership: A tribute to the memory of James R. Meindl* (pp. 135–166). Greenwich, CT: Information Age.

Pittman, T. S. (1998). Motivation. In D. Gilbert, S. Fiske, & G. Lindsay (Eds.), *Handbook of social psychology* (4th ed., pp. 549–590). Boston, MA: McGraw-Hill.

Platow, M. J., & van Knippenberg, D. (2001). A social identity analysis of leadership endorsement: The effects of leader ingroup prototypicality and distributive intergroup fairness. *Personality and Social Psychology Bulletin, 27,* 1508–1519.

Platow, M. J., van Knippenberg, D., Haslam, S. A., van Knippenberg, B., & Spears, R. (2006). A special gift we bestow on you for being representative of us: Considering leader charisma from a self-categorization perspective. *British Journal of Social Psychology, 45,* 303–320.

Riggio, R. E., Chaleff, I., & Lipman-Blumen, J. (2008) *The art of followership: How great followers create great leaders and organizations.* San Francisco, CA: Jossey-Bass.

Ritter, B. A., & Lord, R. G. (2007). The impact of previous leaders on the evaluation of new leaders: An alternative to prototype matching. *Journal of Applied Psychology, 92,* 1683–1695.

Rosch, E. (1978). Principles of categorization. In E. Rosch & B. B. Lloyd (Eds.), *Cognition and categorization* (pp. 27–48). Hillsdale, NJ: Lawrence Erlbaum.

Rosette, A., Leonardelli, G. J., & Phillips, K. W. (2008). The White standard: Racial bias in leader categorization. *Journal of Applied Psychology, 93,* 758–777.

Rush, M. C., & Russell, J. E. (1988). Leader prototypes and prototype-contingent consensus in leader behavior descriptions. *Journal of Experimental Social Psychology, 24,* 88–104.

Rush, M. C., Thomas, J. C., & Lord, R. G. (1977). Implicit leadership theory: A potential threat to the internal validity of leader behavior questionnaires. *Organizational Behavior and Human Performance, 20,* 93–110.

Salancik, G. R., & Pfeffer, J. (1978). A social information processing approach to job attitudes and task design. *Administrative Science Quarterly, 23,* 224–253.

Schubert, T. W. (2005). Your highness: Vertical positions as perceptual symbols of power. *Journal of Personality and Social Psychology, 89,* 1–21.

Scott, K. A., & Brown, D. J. (2006). Female first, leader second? Gender bias in the encoding of leadership behavior. *Organizational Behavior and Human Decision Processes, 101,* 230–242.

Sczesny, S., & Kühnen, U. (2004). Meta-cognition about biological sex and gender-stereotypic physical appearance: Consequences for the assessment of leadership competence. *Personality and Social Psychology Bulletin, 30,* 13–21.

Shamir, B. (1995). Social distance and charisma: Theoretical notes and an exploratory study. *The Leadership Quarterly, 6,* 19–47.

Shamir, B., & Howell, J. M. (1999). Organizational and contextual influences on the emergence and effectiveness of charismatic leadership. *The Leadership Quarterly, 10,* 257–283.

Shondrick, S. J., Dinh, J. E., & Lord, R. G. (2010). Developments in implicit leadership theory and cognitive science: Applications to improving measurement and understanding alternatives to hierarchical leadership. *The Leadership Quarterly, 21,* 959–978.

Smith, E. R., & DeCoster, J. (2000). Dual-process models in social and cognitive psychology: Conceptual integration and links to underlying memory systems. *Personality and Social Psychology Review, 4,* 108–131.

Srull, T. K., & Wyer, R. S. (1989). Person memory and judgment. *Psychological Review, 96,* 58–83.

Starbuck, W. H., & Milliken, F. J. (1988). Executive perceptual filters: What they notice and how they make sense. In D. Hambrick (Ed.), *The executive effect: Concepts and methods for studying top managers* (pp. 35–65). Greenwich, CT: JAI.

Stein, R. T., & Heller, T. (1979). An empirical analysis of the correlation between leadership status and participation rates reported in the literature. *Journal of Personality and Social Psychology, 37,* 1993–2002.

Tiedens, L. Z., Unzueta, M. M., & Young, M. J. (2007). The desire for hierarchy? The motivated perception of dominance complementarity in task partners. *Journal of Personality and Social Psychology, 93,* 402–414.

Trope, Y., & Liberman, N. (2003). Temporal construal. *Psychological Review, 110,* 403–421.

Tsui, A. S., Nifadkar, S. S., & Ou, A. Y. (2007). Cross-national, cross-cultural organizational behavior research: Advances, gaps, and recommendations, *Journal of Management, 33,* 426–478.

Uhl-Bien, M., & Pillai, R. (2007). The romance of leadership and the social construction of followership. In B. Shamir, R. Pillai, M. Bligh, & M. Uhl-Bien (Eds.), *Follower-centered perspectives on leadership: A tribute to the memory of James R. Meindl* (pp. 187–209). Greenwich, CT: Information Age.

Uleman, J. S., Newman, L. S., & Moskowitz, G. B. (1996). People as flexible interpreters: Evidence and issues form spontaneous trait inference. In M. P. Zanna (Ed.), *Advances in experimental social psychology* (Vol. 28, pp. 211–279). New York, NY: Academic Press.

Ullrich, J., Christ, O., & van Dick, R. (2009). Substitutes for procedural fairness: Prototypical leaders are endorsed whether they are fair or not. *Journal of Applied Psychology, 94,* 235–244.

van Baaren, R., Horgan, T., Chartrand, T. L., & Dijkmans, M. (2004). The forest, the trees, and the chameleon: Context dependency and nonconscious mimicry. *Journal of Personality and Social Psychology, 86,* 453–459.

van Knippenberg, B., & van Knippenberg, D. (2005). Leader self-sacrifice and leadership effectiveness: The moderating role of leader prototypicality. *Journal of Applied Psychology, 90,* 25–37.

van Knippenberg, D., & Hogg, M. A. (2003). A social identity model of leadership effectiveness in organizations. *Research in Organizational Behavior, 25,* 243–295.

van Knippenberg, D., van Knippenberg, B., & Giessner, S. R. (2007). Extending the follower-centered perspective on leadership: Leadership as an outcome of shared social identity. In B. Shamir, R. Pillai, M. Bligh, & M. Uhl-Bien (Eds.), *Follower-centered perspectives on leadership: A tribute to the memory of James R. Meindl* (pp. 51–70). Greenwich, CT: Information Age.

Van Vugt, M., Hogan, R., & Kaiser, R. B. (2008). Leadership, followership, and evolution: Some lessons from the past. *American Psychologist, 63,* 182–196.

Yammarino, F., & Dubinsky, A. (1994). Transformational leadership theory: Using levels of analysis to determine boundary conditions. *Personnel Psychology, 47,* 787–811.

Yorges, S. L., Weiss, H. M., & Strickland, O. J. (1999). The effect of leader outcomes on influence, attributions, and perceptions of charisma. *Journal of Applied Psychology, 84,* 428–436.

Zhong, C. B., & Leonardelli, G. J. (2008). Cold and lonely: Does social exclusion literally feel cold? *Psychological Science, 19,* 838–842.

# CHAPTER 5

# Relational Leadership

*Olga Epitropaki*

*Robin Martin*

*Geoff Thomas*

---

## Opening Case: A Day in the Life of a Leader

Alex is finance director of a consumer goods company. She supervises a team of 12 people with whom she believes she has built very good relationships during the 5 years of her tenure. Nevertheless, not all of them pull their weight as she would expect them to do and exceed performance targets. She is puzzled by this, as they are all highly skilled and competent. She also believes that she has invested the appropriate amount of time with every member of her team, offered them her support when needed, coached them, and given them many opportunities to develop and deliver high results.

Martha is one of Alex's direct reports. In performance evaluations, Alex praises Martha and tells her that she is dependable, competent, and raises the bar high for the team. Alex always makes time for Martha when she needs help, listens carefully to her concerns, and empathizes with her. She provides direction and all necessary resources to achieve the task but also emotional support and opportunities for growth. Martha is really happy to work for Alex. She feels motivated, energized, and able to achieve almost anything. Alex trusts Martha to make decisions on important issues and assigns to her very interesting and challenging tasks. She has recently begun to include Martha in work-related social functions and introduce her to influential senior managers. Martha knows that she will soon be receiving a salary raise and be a candidate for promotion. It appears that Martha is in Alex's "in-group" of direct reports.

Cathy is also one of Alex's direct reports. In performance evaluations, Alex tells Cathy that she expects more from her and that it is vital that employees fulfill the requirements of their job description. Alex is always busy when Cathy needs her, and in the few times they have met face to face Alex did not pay any attention to Cathy's concerns. Cathy cannot rely on Alex for either task guidance or emotional support and is not given access to important resources and key senior manager networks. Most of the tasks Alex assigns to her are boring and underutilize her skills. Even when she completes her projects satisfactorily Alex never praises her or says "thank you." Cathy feels stagnant, frustrated, demotivated, and has even considered leaving the organization. Unlike Martha, Cathy seems to be in Alex's "out-group" of direct reports.

### Discussion Questions

1. How important is the quality of the relationship that Martha and Cathy have with their manager, Alex, in determining how satisfied they are at work and how well they perform?

2. How can we explain the discrepancy of perceptions between Alex and Cathy regarding the quality of their relationship?

3. Can Alex's relationships with Martha and Cathy change over time? What can Cathy do to improve her relationship with her manager?

4. Do you think that Alex has differentiated relationships with the remaining 10 members of her team?

5. Why do leaders categorize followers—implicitly or explicitly—into in-groups and out-groups? Is that fair?

# Chapter Overview

*It was worthy that we existed to meet.*

*(Ἄξιζε να υπάρξουμε για να συναντηθούμε).*

—*Yiannis Ritsos, Vernal Symphony*

*Each friend represents a world in us, a world possibly not born until they arrive, and it is only by this meeting that a new world is born.*

—*Anaïs Nin, Diary*

*riendship* is not typically a word associated with workplace leadership. But if we substitute the word *friend* with *relationship,* Anaïs Nin's quote suddenly becomes relevant to the study of leadership. Relationships are the foundation of the human condition: "We are born into relationships, we live our lives in relationships and when we die, the effects of our relationships survive in the lives of the living" (Berscheid, 1999, p. 261). Leadership is also a relational concept. As Pearce, Conger, and Locke (2007) indicate, "Leadership is a concept of relationship; it assumes the existence of some people who follow one or more others. . . . There can be no leadership if there is just one person" (p. 287). Leadership involves at a minimum two people, the leader and the follower, who are enmeshed in a relational process of influence (Carter, DeChurch, Braun, & Contractor, 2015). This basic "nucleus of two" can then grow exponentially into complex relationships in extended social networks and collective systems.

Relationship-based approaches to leadership, such as leader–member exchange (LMX) theory, represent one of the dominant approaches to understanding organizational leadership. As Dihn et al. (2014) point out, LMX is "the archetypal social exchange leader–follower dyadic approach" (p. 39) that emphasizes the leader–follower relationship rather than individual leader or follower traits, styles, or behaviors as other leadership theories. From this perspective, leadership has mainly been viewed as a two-way influence relationship between a leader and a follower aimed primarily at attaining mutual goals (e.g., Graen & Uhl-Bien, 1995). Prior relationship-based research has also examined relationships between a leader and a group (Hollander, 1964), among team members such as TMX (e.g., Seers, 1989), or relationships within extended networks (e.g., Balkundi & Kilduff, 2005).

Recently, we have also seen a "relationality movement" in leadership drawing from social constructionist perspectives. Scholars have coined the term *relational leadership* (e.g., Brower, Schoorman, & Tan, 2000; Uhl-Bien, 2006) in an attempt to move beyond static exchanges and address dynamic leadership relationships within organizational contexts. As Uhl-Bien (2006) points out, "a 'relational' orientation starts with *processes* and not persons, and views persons, leadership and other relational realities as *made in* processes" (p. 655).

Based on the epistemological perspective, we can classify relational leadership research into positivist/post-positivist/entity and social constructionist perspectives. We can also distinguish between relational leadership research that focuses on dyadic relations versus social networks and collective systems. Table 5.1 presents this taxonomy of relational leadership research. This is the structure that we will follow in this chapter. We will start with positivist/post-positivist/entity work on the dyadic and group/network/collective level and then present social constructionist conceptualizations of relational leadership at both levels. We will conclude the chapter with a discussion of exciting new paths of relational leadership research for both epistemological camps and their intersection.

**Table 5.1**   A Taxonomy of Relational Leadership Perspectives

| | Epistemological Paradigm | |
|---|---|---|
| | *Positivist/Post-Positivist/Entity* | *Social Constructionist* |
| **Dyad** | ✓ LMX (e.g., Bauer & Erdogan, 2015; Dulebohn et al., 2012; Gerstner & Day, 1997; Graen & Uhl-Bien, 2005; Martin et al., 2016) <br> ✓ Perceived LMX differentiation (e.g., Hooper & Martin, 2008) <br> ✓ LMX development (Liden et al., 1993; Nahrgang & Seo, 2015; Thomas et al., 2013) <br> ✓ Relational leadership schemas (e.g., Huang et al., 2008) <br> ✓ Relational identity and leadership (Chang & Johnson, 2010) | ✓ Relational leadership as dialogue and discourse (e.g., Cunliffe & Eriksen, 2011; Fairhurst & Uhl-Bien, 2012) <br> ✓ Leadership as a *space of action* and *identity space* (Carroll & Levy, 2010) <br> ✓ Leadership as an identity negotiation process (DeRue & Ashford, 2010) |
| **Collective** | ✓ Relative LMX (Anand et al., 2015; Henderson et al., 2008; Hu & Liden, 2013) <br> ✓ Group-level LMX differentiation (e.g., Epitropaki et al., 2016; Erdogan & Bauer, 2010; Gooty & Yammarino, 2016) <br> ✓ Leadership in and as social networks (e.g., Carter et al., 2015) | ✓ Leadership as communication and collective discourse (e.g., Alvesson & Sveningsson, 2003; Clifton, 2012, 2014; Koivunen, 2007) <br> ✓ Leadership as collaborative practices (Fayerherm, 1994) <br> ✓ Relational leadership as a form of reciprocal control (Gittell & Douglass, 2012) |

*Level of analysis* (row label spanning Dyad and Collective)

# Leadership as a Dyadic Relationship

## Leader-Member Exchange

LMX remains the dominant relationship-based research area with an overwhelming amount of interest in the past four decades (1,824 articles) and an exponential growth of articles published in the last 5 years (1,010 articles; see Bauer & Erdogan, 2015). The basic premise of LMX is that leaders develop different types of exchange relationships with their followers and that the quality of these relationships affects important leader and member attitudes and behaviors (e.g., Gerstner & Day, 1997). Higher-quality leader–member exchanges are characterized by high trust, interaction, support, and rewards. In contrast, lower-quality exchanges are limited to exchanges that take place according to the formal employment contract (e.g., Dienesch & Liden, 1986; Graen & Uhl-Bien, 1995). Meta-analytic results (e.g., Dulebohn, Bommer, Liden, Brouer, & Ferris, 2012; Gerstner & Day, 1997) consistently indicate that high-quality LMX relationships are positively related to employee outcomes such as job performance and work attitudes.

Three main theories have been utilized in the context of LMX research, namely, social exchange theory (Blau, 1964), the resource theory of social exchange (Foa & Foa, 1974), and relative deprivation theory (Crosby, 1976). At the heart of social exchange theory are the concepts of equity and reciprocity. Individuals strive for fair exchanges in which they receive benefits from the relationship equal to what they are putting into the relationship. They are also motivated to gain rewards or avoid costs, return help received, and avoid hurting the ones who have helped them.

Foa and Foa's (1974) resource theory proposed that six types of resources are exchanged in relationships: money, goods, services, status, information, and love (affiliation/socio-emotional resources). In the LMX context, leaders and members are expected to frequently exchange resources within and across these categories (Wilson, Sin, & Conlon, 2010). Also, depending on members' status in the work group, they will perceive their environment as resource-munificent (in-group) or resource-constrained (out-group) with implications for behavioral outcomes, such as upward influence (Epitropaki & Martin, 2013). Finally, based on the premises of relative deprivation theory (Crosby, 1976), employees in low-quality exchanges are expected to experience deprivation in comparison to their coworkers. They can then resort to a series of possible responses to deprivation, both positive (e.g., engaging in self-improvement) and negative (e.g., counterproductive work behaviors; see Bolino & Turnley, 2009).

There have been several LMX reviews (e.g., Erdogan & Bauer, 2014; Martin, Epitropaki, Thomas, & Topakas, 2010); meta-analyses (Dulebohn et al., 2012; Martin, Thomas, Guillaume, Lee, & Epitropaki, 2016); as well as an *Oxford Handbook of LMX* (Bauer & Erdogan, 2015), recently published. Thus, our review will focus on some of the key themes and/or underdeveloped areas of leader–follower relationship dynamics. The interested reader is advised to consult the aforementioned resources for a broader coverage of the LMX literature.

### Traditional LMX Research: Antecedents and Outcomes

**Antecedents of LMX.** A wide range of factors have been examined as potential antecedents of LMX relationship quality (see Dulebohn et al., 2012), and these can be grouped into follower characteristics, leader characteristics, interactional variables, and contextual variables. We describe each of these below.

**Follower Characteristics.** One of the most common follower antecedents examined in relation to LMX quality is *personality*, and most studies focus on the Big Five model of personality (Costa & McRae, 1992). Research has shown that followers high in agreeableness, extraversion, and conscientiousness and lower in neuroticism tend to report higher LMX quality (see meta-analysis by Dulebohn et al.,

2012). The one personality factor from the Big Five that does not show a reliable effect on LMX quality is openness to experience. Indeed, some studies (e.g., Bernerth, Armenakis, Field, Giles, & Walker, 2007) have found a negative relationship between openness to experience and LMX quality. It is not known why this occurs, but one might speculate that people high in openness to experience are creative in orientation and derive more satisfaction from their work through task-related activities than from relationships with others.

Research has also proposed that followers who display *competence* in their work are likely to develop high LMX quality. High performance is an important exchange variable the follower can offer the leader in return for obtaining valuable resources (such as praise, recognition, task support). Consistent with this are findings showing that followers' proactivity (i.e., desire to initiate work activities; Li, Lang, & Crant, 2010), job competence (DelVecchio, 1998), and citizenship behavior (Bauer & Green, 1996) are reliably associated with higher LMX quality.

**Leader Characteristics.** There has been relatively less research examining leader antecedents of LMX than of follower antecedents. Part of the reason why has been the focus of research on understanding the LMX relationship from primarily the follower perspective. However, some of the antecedents examined for followers have also been explored in relation to the leader. For example, in terms of *personality* the findings are similar to those for the follower, showing leaders high on agreeableness, extraversion, and conscientiousness develop higher LMX with followers. Schyns (2015) suggests leader agreeableness is the most important personality dimension for determining LMX quality and that leaders with this characteristic are also likely to maintain a large number of positive relationships in their work team. This is to be expected, as people high in agreeableness tend to be trusting, helpful, and good-natured, which are qualities that should enhance effective relationship development (Schyns, Paul, Mohr, & Blank, 2005).

Leaders' behaviors have also been examined as antecedents of high LMX, such as delegation (Bauer & Green, 1996), ethical behavior (Mahsud, Yukl, & Prussia, 2010), transformational leadership (Wang, Law, Hackett, & Chen, 2005), and not violating psychological contracts (Restubog, Bordia, & Bordia, 2011).

**Interactional Variables.** LMX is a dyadic process, and therefore in order to understand it one needs to consider follower and leader antecedents not only separately but the interaction between them. In doing this most studies have focused on the congruence between the leader and follower on a range of antecedent variables. The general assumption is that leader–follower congruence is good for relationship development, as it reduces uncertainty and potential conflict, and this enhances LMX quality. The theoretical basis for this conjecture comes from relationship science and the "similarity-attraction" hypothesis (Byrne, 1971), which states that people prefer others who are similar to themselves on important dimensions, as this provides consensual validation of their attitudes and beliefs (see Thomas, Martin, Epitropaki, Guillaume, & Lee, 2013).

In terms of *personality congruence*, there are inconsistent findings with studies reporting congruence on different dimensions of the Big Five leading to high LMX quality (e.g., Zhang, Wang, & Shi, 2012). Better support for the similarity-attraction explanation of congruence comes from the finding that leader–follower similarity on attitudes (Phillips & Bedeian, 1994), values (Ashkanasy & O'Connor, 1997), positive affectivity (Bauer & Green, 1996), and power similarity (McClane, 1991) all predict high LMX quality. Furthermore, similarity of leader–follower liking is positively related to LMX quality (e.g., Wayne & Ferris, 1990).

It may not be *actual* congruence that is important, but rather *perceived* congruence in determining LMX quality. Such a distinction has been made in the social cognition literature with the view that feeling similar to others is often more important than actually being similar to them in determining outcomes. This is because people vary in their perceptions of the situations, employ a range of perceptual biases, and therefore perceived similarity is more proximal to (and therefore a better predictor of) LMX than actual similarity. Several studies support this view and show a positive relationship between perceived similarity (e.g., Phillips & Bedeian, 1994) and LMX quality. Furthermore, Liden et al. (1993), in a longitudinal study, found that perceived similarity between the follower and leader predicted future reports of LMX quality.

**Contextual Variables.** The final category of antecedent factors refers to contextual or organizational variables that predict LMX quality. As one might expect, team size and leader workload are negatively correlated with LMX quality (e.g., Green, Blank, & Liden, 1983; Schyns et al., 2005). Finally, research has examined the role of organizational (e.g., Tordera, González-Romá, & Peiró, 2008) and team (e.g., Tse, Dasborough, & Ashkanasy, 2008) climate on LMX.

**Outcomes of LMX.** As noted by Martin et al. (2010) in reviewing the literature, "If one was to be critical one might observe that there is a bewildering array of factors that have been identified as antecedents and outcomes of LMX. Indeed, one might be hard pressed to identify any variables within the I/O Psychology literature that have not, in some way, been linked to LMX" (p. 70). This quote reflects the fact that the literature examining outcomes of LMX not only is large but covers a wide range of variables. In order to summarize some of the main findings, we organize this research into the main type of outcomes examined: work attitudes and performance.

**Work Attitudes.** Meta-analytic reviews show reliable relationships between LMX quality and a wide range of work-related attitudes and reactions (e.g., Dulebohn et al., 2012). Martin et al. (2010) summarized some of the main outcomes at different levels of analysis: high LMX quality leading to *individual-level* outcomes (e.g., higher employee job satisfaction, job-related well-being, empowerment, organizational commitment and to lower job stress and turnover intentions), *dyadic-level* outcomes (e.g., better workplace friendships, leader support, leader delegation, consultation), and *organizational-level* outcomes (e.g., higher perceived justice). Clearly, having a high LMX quality is associated with many positive workplace reactions. What is noticeable in this research is not only the large effect sizes for many relationships (e.g., $\rho = .49$ with job satisfaction, $\rho = .47$ with organizational commitment; Dulebohn et al., 2012) but that the effects are consistent across many different characteristics of followers and leaders, jobs types, organizational sectors, and cultures.

Indeed, the positive effects of a high LMX quality on work attitudes have been so well documented that it led Epitropaki and Martin (2015, p. 139) to reflect, "Is there anything left unsaid or unexamined?" Their analysis focused principally on job satisfaction and organizational commitment, as they represent the most commonly examined LMX outcomes but could be applied more generally. They concluded that while this research has been comprehensive, there is more to learn by focusing on developing better theoretical models and methodological techniques.

**Performance.** One way a follower can "pay back" or reciprocate the benefits they receive from the leader is by developing a high LMX relationship (such as more attention, support, and opportunities) and to work hard to meet work goals. There has been less research examining the relation between LMX and performance than with work attitudes, presumably due to the difficulty of obtaining performance measures. However, more recently there has been a noticeable increase in studies examining performance, which has allowed for more robust findings to emerge.

There are specific issues that need to be considered when examining the relation between LMX and performance in order to interpret the findings. First, studies vary with respect to how they measure performance, with the most popular method being supervisor-rated, which might be open to a number of reporting biases (Duarte, Goodson, & Klich, 1993). Measures of work performance that are more objective in nature clearly have an advantage but tend to be less frequently utilized and, due to their nature, specific for certain types of work (e.g., salespeople). Second, there are different types of work performance, and studies tend to focus on different aspects. Rotundo and Sackett's (2002) useful three-component model of performance helps evaluate the different studies: *task* (or "in-role"), *citizenship* (or "extra-role"), and *counterproductive* performance (behaviors that harm the well-being of the organization). Third, one might assume that the relationship between LMX and performance is affected by whether LMX is judged by the follower or the leader. It might be the case that the leader equates LMX quality more closely with work performance than does the follower; that is, leaders are more likely to use good performance as a basis for judging high LMX.

In a comprehensive review, Martin et al. (2016) reported a meta-analysis of the relation between LMX and three outcomes of performance. They found a positive relationship between LMX and task (146 samples, $\rho = .30$) and citizenship (97 samples, $\rho = .34$) performance, and a negative relationship between LMX and counterproductive performance (19 samples, $\rho = -.24$). Therefore, having high LMX quality with the leader was associated with the follower performing better not just on direct in-role work duties but also on more extra-role activities that have benefits for the organization and beyond the immediate leader–follower context.

While there are strong main effects between LMX and performance, studies have further shown that the relationship is greater when the follower is high in conscientiousness (Kamdar & Van Dyne, 2007), low in extraversion (Bauer et al.,

2006), high in growth need strength (Graen, Novak, & Sommerkamp, 1982), high in goal commitment (Klein & Kim, 1998), and high in task autonomy (Ozer, 2008).

**Summary.** This section reviewed a range of factors that are antecedents and outcomes of LMX quality. While we reported results in separate categories to organize the review, in fact, most studies examine multiple antecedents within the same research design. This is important, as these antecedent factors do not occur in isolation but as clusters of factors that are associated with each leader–follower dyad. Given this, it might be that the impact of each antecedent variable on LMX quality is different when it occurs in conjunction with other antecedents than when examined alone. In addition, the majority of studies employ a cross-sectional research design and therefore are unable to establish if the antecedents *determine* LMX quality. Increasing use of longitudinal designs in the LMX literature is offering a better opportunity to examine the direction of effects for many examined variables (Thomas et al., 2013).

We also reviewed some of the main outcomes of LMX quality, such as work attitudes and performance. In terms of work attitudes and reactions, there is considerable evidence showing the positive benefits of a high LMX quality and a wide range of outcomes. There is also strong evidence showing that high LMX has benefits on a range of performance measures and that these benefits extend beyond the immediate leader–follower context to outcomes at a more organizational level.

It is important to acknowledge that research focusing on the causal effects of LMX on outcomes might be prone to problems associated with endogeneity. One cannot assume that LMX varies randomly in organizational settings. The LMX relationships may be shaped by a series of factors related to the leader, the follower, or the organizational environment. As a result, we cannot ignore the possibility that it is these factors (rather than LMX) that affect the LMX outcomes (Antonakis, Bendahan, Jacquart, & Lalive, 2014). This issue has been known in the leadership literature (House & Aditya, 1997). For example, Gerstner and Day (1997) noted in their meta-analysis: "We avoid discussing [the relationships found] in terms of causal inferences regarding the direction of these relationships. For purposes of the present analyses, we treat them all as correlates" (p. 829). Still, the majority of research examining LMX as an independent variable has overlooked the serious threat that endogeneity poses for estimate consistency and inference. It is thus important that future research on LMX outcomes employs rigorous research designs and statistical procedures that systematically address issues concerning endogeneity (Antonakis et al., 2014).

**LMX Agreement.** Whereas we might expect leader and follower perceptions of the LMX relationship to match, research indicates that this is not the case (*e.g.*, Schyns & Day, 2010). For example, Gerstner and Day (1997) identified 24 samples in their meta-analysis that measured LMX from both follower and leader perspectives and reported an average sample-weighted correlation of .29. Sin, Nahrgang, and Morgeson (2009) identified 64 samples and reported a true score correlation of .37 between leader and follower ratings. Such a perceptual asymmetry is intriguing: Why don't leaders and followers see eye to eye?

A possible explanation lies in the duration of the relationship (e.g., Graen et al., 2006), as leader–follower agreement on the relationship quality may take time to develop. Cogliser, Schriesheim, Scandura, and Gardner (2009) highlighted the possibility of individual differences (e.g., negative affectivity), socio-cognitive processes (e.g., leader and follower schemas), as well as contextual factors (e.g., span of leadership) as important predictors of LMX agreement. Another explanation may relate to the leaders' reluctance to admit that they differentiate among followers, as the observed higher overall LMX mean and lower variation of leaders' ratings may indicate (Tekleab & Taylor, 2003).

The different levels of rater difficulty (due to the fact that leaders rate multiple followers; Zhou & Schriesheim, 2009), as well as the differences in hierarchical levels that change the salience of aspects of the relationship (e.g., M. M. Harris & Schaubroeck, 1988), have also been highlighted. Recently, Zhou and Schriesheim (2010) proposed that leaders and followers focus on different LMX dimensions—thus the asymmetry in perceptions. They specifically found that leaders were more likely to use task-related exchange factors to evaluate LMX, whereas employees were more oriented toward the social aspects of the relationship. Measurement issues (such as measurement inequivalence of the follower and leader LMX scales and misalignments in scale referents) have been further indicated (Zhou & Schriesheim, 2009).

Recent studies have looked at the content and direction of LMX agreement. For example, Cogliser et al. (2009) proposed a typology of four combinations of leader and follower LMX ratings based on the degree of LMX agreement (balance) and the quality of the relationship (i.e., balanced/low LMX, balanced/high LMX, unbalanced/follower overestimation of LMX, and unbalanced/follower underestimation of LMX). They found that congruent and positive relationships had more favorable effects for the followers, whereas congruent but negative relationships had detrimental effects.

The well-documented asymmetry of LMX perceptions between leaders and followers is an important phenomenon in the context of relational leadership. It highlights the subjective nature of the relational reality and the need for a closer look at the factors that shape these differentiated perceptions.

### LMX Development: Insights From Relationship Science

Despite the empirical evidence demonstrating the significant influence of the leader–member relationship in assimilating employees into an organization and its impact on important outcomes, we still don't know enough about how the relationship develops over time (e.g., Day, 2014). Graen and Scandura (1987) highlighted three early stages (i.e., "role-taking," "role-making," and "routinization") as critical to the development of the relationship. Later, Graen and Uhl-Bien (1995), in their leadership-making model, also focused on the early stages of LMX development and described three phases: a "stranger phase," where leader–member exchanges are mainly formal; an "acquaintance phase," where increased social exchanges (beyond the employment contract) occur between leader and members; and a "mature partnership" phase, where exchanges between individuals are highly developed, and they are not only behavioral but also emotional. Mature partnerships are assumed to reflect high-quality LMX, and the model also assumes a variation in real time of how each dyad progresses through these stages. Although it is a more general model that encompasses all varieties of dyadic work relationships, Ferris et al. (2009) similarly propose that good-quality relationships can deteriorate and disintegrate in the face of consistently unmet expectations.

Interestingly, the few longitudinal studies that have been conducted have shown LMX to be a quick, intensive process that occurs very early in the relationship, and that once established LMX quality remains essentially stable thereafter (e.g., Liden, Wayne, & Stillwell, 1993; Nahrgang, Morgeson, & Ilies, 2009). Implicit in this view is that little extra effort, above and beyond the norms of exchange behaviors established early in the relationship, is necessary for LMX quality to be maintained. Increasingly, however, this assumption has been called into question, and numerous calls have been made for theory and research to go beyond the formative stages to reveal the dynamics played out across the life cycle of the LMX relationship (e.g., Erdogan & Bauer, 2014; Martin et al., 2010).

To this end, below we introduce theory and research from the multidisciplinary literature on relationship science (sometimes referred to as close or personal relationships; see Berscheid, 1999; Berscheid & Reis, 1998), which provides a more detailed exposition of relationship maintenance processes in close nonwork relationships. Although some distinctions can be made between personal and workplace relationships, there are more similarities than differences between close nonwork and leader–follower relationships. For example, both kinds of relationships are characterized by reciprocal liking, mutual influence, high trust, synchronized plans and goals, responsiveness, and the provision of various kinds of resources and support (for a more detailed discussion, see Thomas et al., 2013). Thus, it could be argued that theory and research on relationship science provides a valuable starting point for understanding how leader–follower relationships are maintained at a desired level.

Interdependence theory is the most prominent framework in relationship science, and like LMX theory it is built on the principles of social exchange and reciprocity (Blau, 1964). Building on interdependence theory, Rusbult's (1980) investment model posits that dependence increases to the extent that the relationship satisfies the individual's most important needs and the quality of alternatives for meeting such needs is low. Dependence leads to relationship commitment (i.e., the intent to persist, long-term orientation, and psychological attachment), which is enacted by both parties engaging in a variety of relationship maintenance strategies to ensure the perpetuation of the relationship at the desired level (Rusbult, 1980).

In a similar vein, LMX relationships are characterized by high levels of interdependence. The follower depends upon the leader for provision of resources (e.g., money, information, status, affiliation, service), but also the leader depends upon the follower for similar resources (Wilson et al., 2010). The level of investment, however, is likely to depend on the quality of the relationship. High-quality LMX relationships in which both leaders' and followers' needs are met are characterized by high levels of dependence, investment, and commitment, and thus higher motivation to engage in maintenance acts. In contrast, low-quality LMX relationships in which resource provision is low are typified by less dependence, investment, and commitment, and hence, less inclination to exert significant effort or endure great costs toward the goal of maintaining the relationship.

Broadly speaking, the investment model distinguishes between two kinds of relationship maintenance mechanisms: cognitive (benign attributions, positive illusions, and derogation of alternatives) and behavioral (accommodation, willingness to sacrifice, and forgiveness; Rusbult, Olsen, Davis, & Hannon, 2001). Cognitive maintenance strategies are preemptive by nature. For example, the generation of benign external attributions for relationship-threatening behavior can help to protect the status of high-quality LMX relationships. Behavioral maintenance strategies are more reactive and effortful. For instance, partners in high-quality relationships are more inclined to accommodate and constructively deal with minor relationship-based problems so as to prevent the deterioration of relationship quality (Fletcher, Thomas, & Durant, 1999). There is growing recognition, however, that more serious relationship problems occur in the workplace (e.g., Fehr & Gelfand, 2012), such as violations of trust and relationship norms (Dirks, Lewicki, & Zaheer, 2009)—transgressions that cannot be easily condoned or entirely explained away. In these circumstances, forgiveness is likely to be an effective maintenance or repair strategy, at least for high-quality LMX relationships (Thomas et al., 2013). Because committed individuals have invested heavily in their relationships and are dependent upon each other for the provision of important resources, they are likely to be motivated to forgive a partner's transgressions.

The motivation to engage in relationship maintenance behaviors is likely to be influenced by the attachment style of leaders and followers alike. A basic tenet of attachment theory—one of the most prominent theories in relationship science—is that individuals generate styles or cognitive working models that represent the degree of success of attachment-seeking efforts across the life-span of close relationships. Individuals can possess secure, insecure-anxious, or insecure-avoidant attachment styles. Securely attached individuals are more likely to seek interdependence with others, invest more heavily in close relationships, and adopt relationship-maintaining goals (Etcheverry, Le, Wu, & Wei, 2013). Conversely, people with an insecure-avoidant attachment style feel uncomfortable depending upon others and put little effort into developing and maintaining close relationships. By contrast, insecure-anxious individuals are anxiously preoccupied with establishing and maintaining close relationships to the extent that they are hypervigilant to challenges and threats to their relationships and thus can engage in less adaptive relationship maintenance behaviors (e.g., excessive support-seeking) that can alienate others (Tran & Simpson, 2009).

LMX researchers have begun to extend attachment theory to the context of leader–follower relationships (e.g., Hinojosa, McCauley, Randolph-Seng, & Gardner, 2014). In terms of LMX development, both attachment security at the individual level and leader–follower attachment congruence (i.e., both secure) at the dyadic level has been associated with higher-quality LMX relationships (e.g., Richards & Hackett, 2012). However, the link between attachment styles and LMX maintenance behavior is yet to be empirically examined.

**Summary.** LMX theory and research has largely overlooked the need for relationship maintenance behavior in order to sustain LMX relationships at their desired levels, despite frequent calls for researchers to go beyond the early stages of LMX development and examine how mature LMX relationships are maintained (e.g., Martin et al., 2010). As such, in this section we have integrated insights from the multidisciplinary literature on relationship science to address this lacuna. Guided by interdependence theory and the investment model (Rusbult, 1980), we outlined a range of cognitive (e.g., congenial attributions) and behavioral (e.g., accommodation, forgiveness) relationship maintenance strategies that are likely to be enacted in the context of LMX relationships, and how the motivation to engage in such strategies is likely to be influenced by attachment styles. To this end, we believe that this represents fertile ground for future research on relational leadership.

## Beyond the Dyad: Group and Collective Relational Perspectives

Almost 100 years ago Mary Parker Follett (1924) suggested that leadership emerges from dynamic interactions among organizational actors. However, it is only recently that systematic empirical work has emerged on collective leadership forms (e.g., Denis, Langley, & Sergi, 2012). Although all these forms are basically relational leadership manifestations, the review of this literature is beyond the scope of our chapter. In this chapter we will present two important strands of relational leadership that transcend the dyadic level and reside on the group and collective level: (a) LMX differentiation and (b) leadership and social networks research.

## LMX Differentiation: "Not All Relationships Are Created Equal"

Differentiation has been an inherent assumption of LMX theory since its inception, but the explicit examination of LMX differentiation is a relatively recent phenomenon. It is also one of the most important current areas of inquiry for LMX research (see Anand, Vidyarthi, & Park, 2015). LMX differentiation has been examined in three distinct ways: perceived LMX (e.g., Hooper & Martin, 2008), relative LMX (RLMX; e.g., Hu & Liden, 2013), and group-level LMX differentiation (e.g., Erdogan & Bauer, 2010).

Perceived LMX differentiation (e.g., Hooper & Martin, 2008) is a perceptual measure that captures perceived variability of LMX relationships within a group, whereas relative LMX and LMX differentiation directly incorporate the team context. RLMX captures the individual-within-group level (i.e., a meso-level of analysis; Anand et al., 2015). It is based on the notion that LMX relationships in a work group exist not only in absolute terms but also in relative terms (Hogg et al., 2005). Members compare their LMX with that of other team members, and the outcome of this social comparison may affect work outcomes over and above or in interaction with individual LMX (e.g., Festinger, 1954; Vidyarthi, Liden, Anand, Erdogan, & Ghosh, 2010). Finally, group-level LMX differentiation captures the degree of within-group variation that exists when a leader forms different-quality relationships with different members (e.g., Erdogan & Bauer, 2010).

Prior LMX differentiation research has argued that a high degree of variability creates conditions that promote competition and antagonism among team members as individuals maneuver for a larger proportion of available attention and resources (i.e., conditions of uncertainty and volatility). Conversely, low levels of variability might enhance cooperation and social harmony within the group (Hooper & Martin, 2008). Of interest, the overall evidence regarding the role of all three facets of LMX differentiation for individual outcomes remains inconclusive (e.g., T. B. Harris, Li, & Kirkman, 2014). Some researchers have found evidence for the positive role of differentiation (e.g., Henderson, Wayne, Shore, Bommer, & Tetrick, 2008; Ma & Qu, 2010), whereas others have found support for the negative impact of LMX differentiation on work attitudes but its positive effect on work behaviors (e.g., Erdogan & Bauer, 2010; Nishii & Mayer, 2009).

Recently, Gooty and Yammarino (2016) argued that LMX differentiation moderates the relationship between employees' LMX and job performance ratings. They found that the relationship between LMX and performance was weaker when LMX differentiation was high. Interestingly, Kauppila (2016) found the impact of LMX differentiation on work outcomes was stronger for employees with low rather than high LMX. His explanation was that when LMX differentiation is high, followers with low LMX see that it is possible to form high-quality relationships with the leader because some group members have succeeded in doing so. Epitropaki et al. (2016), in a two-study examination of all three levels of LMX differentiation (perceived LMX differentiation, relative LMX, and group-level LMX differentiation), found support for the interactive effect of political skill and both perceived and group-level LMX differentiation on LMX quality (Study 1) and relative LMX (Study 2). They further reported significant moderated indirect effects of political skill on task performance, OCB, and job satisfaction via relative LMX (Study 2). They concluded that politically skilled employees can navigate uneven relational terrains and see LMX differentiation as an opportunity rather than a threat. In conditions of high differentiation, they are able to develop improved relationships with the leader (both absolute and relative), which then translate to higher performance and satisfaction at work.

The above studies highlight the importance of context and boundary conditions. Differentiation is neither good nor bad. Its effects depend on situational variables (e.g., justice climate, perceived organizational support) as well as personal resources (e.g., political skill) that employees recruit to deal with the differentiated relational leadership environment in their work group.

## Social Network Relational Leadership

Although the vast majority of LMX research has focused on the dyad as the relevant level of analysis and it is only recently that we have seen an interest in group-level constructs such as LMX differentiation (discussed in the previous section), the need to adopt a social network lens in LMX research has been acknowledged by early LMX scholars. Graen and Scandura (1987, pp. 202–203), for example, discussed "dyadic subassemblies" extending beyond the leader–member relationship as networks that comprise an "organizational understructure" of relationships that contribute to individual and organizational effectiveness. Sparrowe and Liden (1997) also proposed that a member's "assimilation" into the organization depends on the sponsorship of his or her leader, with sponsorship defined as the leader's incorporation of members into his or her own network of close, trusted relations.

In their recent review, Carter et al. (2015) integrated leadership and social network research. They defined leadership as a relational phenomenon "situated in specific social contexts, involving patterned emergent processes, and encompassing both formal and informal influences" (p. 616). They further argued that social network approaches can offer theories and methodologies that can significantly advance relational leadership research. Existing studies were classified as (a) leadership in networks, (b) leadership as networks, and (c) leadership in and as networks.

*Leadership in networks* studies use a relational approach to model the social network context of leadership, but leadership itself is viewed via a nonrelational, individualistic, and personological perspective. Emphasis is placed on leadership emergence and effectiveness within a social network context, based on attributes of individuals (e.g., charisma, transformational leadership, social capital; e.g., Lau & Liden, 2008). *Leadership as networks* studies consider networks of leadership relationships and are based on the notion that leadership resides in the ties among individuals. Whereas many of the studies in the first category focus on formal leaders, most studies in the second category examine patterns of leadership relationships among all members of a collective (team or organization). Emphasis is placed on forms of leadership that are shared, collective, distributed, or plural (e.g., Carson, Tesluk, & Marrone, 2007). Finally, *leadership in and as networks* research emphasizes the interplay between social and leadership networks as well as the outcomes of their coevolving relationships. Research in this domain is still limited but underscores the importance of social structures in shaping leadership as a relational phenomenon (e.g., Sparrowe & Liden, 2005). Interestingly, the majority of existing research in the third and most promising domain examines LMX as a focal leadership variable.

Sparrowe and Emery (2015) have recently provided a narrative review of the development of the themes of structure and tie strength in LMX literature and further integrated LMX differentiation research with cognitive social networks. Cognitive social networks are mental representations of individual social networks characterized by actors and ties. Sparrowe and Emery suggested that when a member mentally represents the leader–member relationships within the group, a cognitive social network is activated (which may be different from the actual social network). These cognitive networks of leader–member relations are found to be salient (Sparrowe & Emery, 2015) and can open new and exciting paths in social networks and leadership research.

## Summary

LMX differentiation research has flourished in recent years and has broadened the LMX scope beyond the dyad. It has recognized that dyadic relationships are embedded in work groups that are characterized by interdependence and complexity. Each dyadic relationship does not exist in isolation but is relative to other LMX relationships in the work group, and as a result social comparison processes are of paramount importance for employee outcomes. Furthermore, social network approaches are a promising line of research that can address some of the foundational ideas of leadership such as its relational, patterned nature that involves both formal and informal influence.

## Social Constructionist Relational Leadership Perspectives

Whereas positivist and post-positivist approaches understand the self as a distinct entity that is clearly bounded when it engages in interactions with other entities, social constructionist perspectives see the self as "inconnection," created through interaction (Uhl-Bien, 2006). Social constructionists believe that social realities are intersubjectively constructed in everyday interactions and in relation to cultural and historical contexts (e.g., Morgan & Smirchich, 1980). Emphasis is placed on relationality, or the *space between* (Bradbury & Lichtestein, 2000). It is rooted in Mead's (1934) symbolic interactionism that rests on the assumption that people act on the basis of meaning, that meaning arises out of social interaction, and that meaning can be modified through social interaction.

In this paradigm, leadership emerges in a process of co-construction and does not exist prior to the relationship (Fairhurst, 2007). According to Endres and Weibler's (2016) three-component model of relational social constructionist leadership, leadership is based on three dynamic components: (a) a process of intersubjectively creating social realities through ongoing interpretation and interaction, (b) high-quality relating and communicating, and (c) emerging flows of influence. Relational social constructionist leadership challenges the individuality of the leader and shifts the perspective from leader to leadership (e.g., Crevani, Lindgren, & Packendorff, 2010). It further challenges the significance of leadership (e.g., Alvesson & Sveningsson, 2003) by adopting a critical management theory lens.

In this stream of relational leadership work, we highlight studies like the one conducted by Cunliffe and Eriksen (2011), who utilized Bakhtin's (1986) concept of *living conversation* and conceptualized leadership as embedded in the everyday relationally responsive dialogical practices of leaders. Relational leadership is not a theory or model but a way of *being in the world* that embraces a relationally responsive way of thinking and acting. They suggested that "relational leadership means recognizing the intersubjective nature of life, the inherently polyphonic and heteroglossic nature of relationships and the need to engage in *relational dialogue*" (p. 1437). Of interest is also Gittell and Douglass's (2012) conceptual paper in which they define relational leadership as a sensemaking process that is based on reciprocal interrelating between workers and managers that helps them determine what is to be done and how to do it. This process of reciprocal interrelating involves communicating through relationships of shared goals, shared knowledge, and mutual respect.

An interesting theoretical and methodological lens that relational social constructionist leadership could adopt in the future is that of *process studies* (e.g., Langley & Tsoukas, 2016). Process scholars address questions about how and why things emerge, develop, grow, or terminate over time. They prioritize activity over product, change over persistence, novelty over continuity, and emphasize concepts such as *becoming*, change, flux, and disruption. Viewing relational leadership as a process may significantly advance our understanding of its dynamic nature.

Uhl-Bien's (2006) theory attempts to bridge the two epistemological camps of relational leadership. She defined relational leadership as "a social influence process through which emergent coordination (i.e., evolving social order) and change (e.g., new values, attitudes, approaches, behaviors, and ideologies) are constructed and produced" (p. 655). She further proposed relational leadership theory as an approach that can encompass both individuated and connected perspectives by explaining both the emergence of leadership relationships (drawing on traditional individuated views that focus on the nature of the relationship, such as leader–member exchange) and the relational dynamics of organizing (including various constructionist views of leadership). Uhl-Bien and Ospina (2012) adopted this multitheoretical lens in their book *Advancing Relational Leadership Research* that invited an open dialogue among perspectives, a *paradigm interplay*. Their book is an excellent resource for the interested reader who wishes to delve into a broad and lively conversation among paradigmatic approaches on relational leadership.

## Summary

The "relationality" movement in leadership (Uhl-Bien & Ospina, 2012) has gathered exciting momentum and has attempted to move leadership research away from personological, static perspectives. Relational social constructionist leadership approaches, in particular, offer new insights on relational leadership and leadership in general. Leadership resides not in individual leaders or followers but "in the between space" of the relationship; it does not exist prior to the relationship, and it emerges through dialogue and intense communication. The majority of work in this area is conceptual, and the few studies conducted have employed qualitative methodologies such as ethnography (e.g., Cunliffe & Eriksen, 2011), discourse analysis (e.g., Fairhurst & Uhl-Bien, 2012), and case studies (e.g., Alvesson & Sveningsson, 2003).

## Relational Leadership: The Road Ahead

In this chapter we reviewed the diverse literature on relational leadership that spans across two levels of analysis (dyadic and collective) and two main epistemological camps (positivist/post-positivist/entity and social construction). Figure 5.1 attempts to bridge the two epistemological camps by depicting the differential quality of relationships between leaders and followers that develop in work groups (LMX quality and LMX differentiation processes) as well as the "between space" in which leadership resides in accordance with the social constructionist approaches.

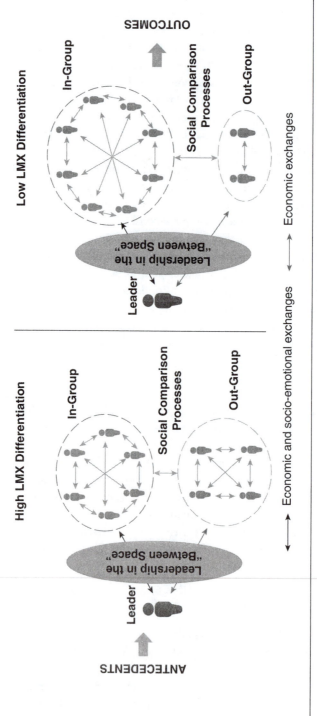

**Figure 5.1**  Dominant Relational Leadership Processes

It is important to acknowledge that despite our emphasis on the dyadic and collective level in this chapter, relational leadership research is fundamentally multilevel in nature. For example, individual follower perceptions of the LMX quality that have been commonly used as a measure of LMX, especially in the early studies, clearly reside on the individual level of analysis (e.g., Schriesheim, Castro, Zhou, & Yammarino, 2001). We explicitly choose to focus on the dyadic and collective levels in this chapter in order to emphasize the interdependent nature of relational leadership and the need for a multi-actor-focused research and analysis.

Given the fundamentally relational nature of leadership, relational leadership perspectives will continue being at the forefront of leadership research for the years to come. In addition to the suggestions we made in previous sections regarding relationship development based on insights from the close relationships literature, there are several paths that future research on relational leadership can explore.

## Relational Cognition: Relational and Network Schemas

Socio-cognitive approaches to leadership (e.g., Epitropaki et al., 2013; Shondrick & Lord, 2010), and relational schemas in particular, can open up exciting research possibilities. People do not approach relationships as *tabula rasa*. Their perceptions, expectancies, and understanding are guided by their relational schemas that have been developed through socialization processes and prior experiences of interpersonal relationships. Relational schemas are thus cognitive structures that represent regularities in patterns of interpersonal relatedness and include three elements: an interpersonal script, a self-schema, and a schema about the other person (Baldwin, 1992).

There has been one published study that has specifically looked at *relational schemas of leadership* (Huang, Wright, Chiu, & Wang, 2008). They found that leaders and members formed different relational schemas, focusing on work-related issues and interpersonal concerns, respectively. Epitropaki et al. (2013) also integrated individual leadership schemas such as implicit leadership (ILTs) and followership theories (IFTs) with relational leadership schemas. They proposed that in a dyadic leader–follower relationship, leaders utilize a relational schema encompassing a self-schema (ILTs), an other-schema (IFTs), and a leader–follower interpersonal script. Similarly, followers employ their relational schema consisting of a self-schema (IFTs), an other-schema (ILTs), and an interpersonal script. Such schemas may affect the quality of leader–follower interactions and related outcomes.

Furthermore, the development of leader–follower relationships over time as well as the relationship maintenance strategies that we reviewed in a previous section are likely to be affected by the nature of relationship cognition. Of particular relevance, research by Knee and colleagues (e.g., Knee, Patrick, & Lonsbary, 2003) has revealed that individuals possess *implicit theories of relationships* entailing schemas about what makes a good relationship (e.g., destiny and growth beliefs of relationships). Destiny theorists believe that relationship partners are either compatible (i.e., meant to be) or they are not, whereas growth theorists believe that all relationships have to be worked at and cultivated. Extending this logic to LMX relationships, it is plausible that leaders and followers possess implicit theories of leader–follower relationships that affect the process of LMX development and maintenance. Namely, individuals with destiny theories of the leader–follower relationship will most likely believe that LMX quality is largely predetermined by leader–follower similarity and compatibility, and thus will put little effort into maintaining or enhancing the relationship beyond normal exchange behaviors. Growth theorists, on the other hand, will be motivated to cultivate the relationship and redouble their efforts to maintain and repair the relationship in the face of relationship problems and challenges.

A third line of research that is of potential interest is that of *network schemas of leadership*. For example, Balkundi and Kilduff (2005) focused on network schemas and discussed the idea that a leader's cognitive representations of social networks determine both the choices leaders make as well as leadership effectiveness. They build on the idea that networks are both cognitive structures that reside in the mind of organizational actors as well as actual structures of relationships among them and specifically stated "network approach locates leadership not in the attributes of individuals but in the relationships connecting individuals" (p. 942). Sparrowe and Emery (2015) also highlighted the salience of cognitive networks of leader–member relations and their importance in the context of LMX research. Epitropaki et al. (2013) further suggested that in a network of shared leadership and followership roles, each organizational actor can utilize both ILTs and IFTs as part of their self-schema as well as of their other-schema for each of the actors with which they interact. Furthermore, a network leadership–followership script will emerge and subsequently determine the pattern of leader–follower interactions among network actors.

## Relational Emotion and Affect

It is impossible to talk about relationships and not address affective processes and emotions. A crucial area of the study of emotion in organizations is the leader–follower interaction (e.g., Ashkanasy & Humphrey, 2011). There are several studies that support the *emotional contagion hypothesis* (Hatfield, Cacioppo, & Rapson, 1994) in leader–follower relationships. For example, Sy, Cote, and Saavedra (2005) found that when leaders were in a positive mood, individual group members also experienced positive mood and were more likely to cooperate with one another. Glaso and Einarsen (2006) found leader–follower relationships to be strongly colored by positive and negative moods, emotions, and emotion-laden judgments, with four affective factors relevant to the supervisor–subordinate relationship, three of which were negative (frustration, violation, uncertainty, recognition). These factors correlated strongly with subordinates' perceptions of the quality of their LMX relation as well as with their job satisfaction.

Newcombe and Ashkanasy (2002) found nonverbal emotional cues to have a significant impact upon members' perception of LMX. Results showed that the leader's positively expressed emotion led to higher member ratings of LMX. Also, members' perceptions of leaders were associated with the level of congruency between the leader's verbal message and his or her nonverbally expressed emotion. An experience sampling study (Miner, Glomb, & Hulin, 2005) revealed that employees rated 80% of their interactions with their supervisors as positive and only 20% as negative; however, the effects of negative interactions on employee mood were, in general, five times stronger than the effects of positive interactions. These findings suggest that even though most supervisory interactions are positive, the overall net effect of interactions with supervisors may be slightly negative because of the stronger effect of negative interactions on employee moods. Dasborough, Ashkanasy, Tee, and Tse (2009) further argued that emotional contagion can affect the leaders as well, leading to an *emotional spiral*. A number of studies have also documented the positive effects of leader positive emotional displays on outcomes (e.g., Sy et al., 2005). Also, Totterdell et al. (2005) used a social network perspective and found evidence for affect convergence within work interaction groups.

Emotion is clearly an area of promise for future research on relational leadership. As Gooty, Connelly, Griffith, and Gupta (2010) argued, we need more theoretical and empirical work that explicitly addresses "the dyadic level (e.g., leader and follower emotions affecting each other's outcomes, agreement regarding what is felt versus displayed at the dyad level) [and] group level (e.g., the influence of group moods on leader moods, construct development of group emotional tone and the role of the leader)" (p. 998).

## Relational Identity

A fast-growing body of leadership literature has focused on leader and follower identity development dynamics, levels, co-construction, and effects (e.g., Epitropaki, Kark, Mainemelis, & Lord, 2017; Miscenko, Guenter, & Day, 2017). Brewer and Gardner's (1996) conceptualization of three fundamental self-representations—the individual self, the relational self, and the collective self—is of relevance here. Sluss and Ashforth (2007) built on Brewer and Gardner (1996) and argued that relational identity at work integrates person- and role-based identities and thereby the individual, interpersonal, and collective levels of self. They further suggested that in organizational settings individuals have multiple relational identities (e.g., with coworkers, leaders, subordinates, clients). Such multiplicity has implications for relational identity salience (which one is stronger, and why?) as well as for interactions and synergies among identities (do leadership and followership relational identities clash or harmoniously coexist in a person?).

In the context of leader and follower identity dynamics, identity negotiation and self-verification processes (e.g., Swann, Johnson, & Bosson, 2009) have also been used as main theoretical frameworks. DeRue and Ashford (2010), for example, described how leader and follower identities are claimed and granted as part of a dynamic relational and social process through which individuals acquire, internalize, and validate leader identities. Relational identity and leadership identity construction are hence exciting areas of future research on relational leadership (for a recent review, see Epitropaki et al., 2017).

# Conclusion

Relational leadership approaches capture the fundamental nature of leadership as a relational, dynamic, multilevel phenomenon. Research spans across epistemological camps and is characterized by plurality, vibrancy, and prolificacy. It is also one of the few leadership strands in which researchers have systematically attempted to establish an open dialogue among perspectives in order to attain multidisciplinary insights (e.g., Uhl-Bien & Ospina, 2012). The positivist paradigm has been clearly dominated by LMX research that, despite the conceptual and methodological criticisms it has received (e.g., Antonakis et al., 2014), remains one of the strongest lines of leadership research. Socio-constructionist views have emphasized the importance of dialogue and discourse as well as the leader–follower relationship as an identity space.

So what's next for relational leadership research? A clear theme that emerged from our discussion on future research is that of *relationship development over time*. Despite the acknowledgment of the dynamic nature of leadership phenomena, time remains "an unexplored dimension in leadership studies" (Shamir, 2011, p. 307). Relational leadership takes time to evolve and flourish. As we described earlier in this chapter, relationships develop over time, may get disintegrated over time through violations and betrayals, and may be maintained over time via various cognitive and behavioral relationship maintenance strategies. Thus, the temporal aspects of relational leadership need to be explicitly addressed by future research. Relationship development needs to be captured by rigorously designed longitudinal studies that have carefully considered the appropriate time scales (Day, 2014). Adopting a *process* rather than entity view of relational leadership phenomena can open new and exciting paths for relational leadership researchers across all epistemological perspectives.

Also, examining relational leadership as a phenomenon that extends beyond the dyad and resides within a multi-actor network of relationships will help us get a better grasp of its complexity and its multifaceted enactment in real organizational settings. Big data methodologies can be particularly helpful in this endeavor (e.g., Tonidandel, King, & Cortina, 2017).

In sum, our chapter reviewed dominant paradigms and research streams in relational leadership and offered a platform for possible future research. It becomes evident from our review that relational leadership is not only the past and present but pretty much the future of leadership research. As the nature of organizing is rapidly changing and the presence of technology has become widespread in our work relationships, new questions emerge as well as new methodological possibilities that can potentially revolutionize relational leadership research.

## Discussion Questions

1. What do you think the relational leadership approaches contribute to the study of leadership?
2. Which are the two main epistemological camps in the study of relational leadership? Which are, in your view, their main differences and points of convergence?

3.  Which are, in your opinion, the main methodological challenges of existing relational leadership research? Outline some key steps you would follow in the design of a study on leader–follower relationships on the dyadic or collective level.

4.  Which of the paths of future research identified in this chapter would you consider high priority? Can you think of additional avenues for future research on relational leadership?

## Recommended Readings

*   Bauer, T., & Erdogan, B. (Eds.). (2015). *The Oxford handbook of leader–member exchange.* Oxford, UK: Oxford University Press.
*   Uhl-Bien, M., & Ospina, S. (Eds.). (2012). *Advancing relational leadership research: A dialogue among perspectives.* Charlotte, NC: Information Age.

## Recommended Case Studies

*   **Case:** Cliffe, S. (2001, September). What a star, what a jerk! *Harvard Business Review, 37–48.*
*   **Case:** Gabarro, J. J., & Kaftan, C. (2011). Jamie Turner at MLI, Inc. Harvard Business School Brief Cases.

## Recommended Video

*   Heffernan, M. (2015). Margaret Heffernan: Why it is time to forget the pecking order at work. https://www.ted.com/talks/margaret_heffernan_why_it_s_time_to_forget_the_pecking_order_at_work

## References

Alvesson, M., & Sveningsson, S. (2003). The great disappearing act: Difficulties in doing "leadership." *The Leadership Quarterly, 14,* 359–381.

Anand, S., Vidyarthi, P. R., & Park, H. (2015). LMX differentiation: Understanding relational leadership at individual and group levels. In T. Bauer & B. Erdogan (Eds.), *The Oxford handbook of leader–member exchange* (pp. 263–291). Oxford, UK: Oxford University Press.

Antonakis, J., Bendahan, S., Jacquart, P., & Lalive, R. (2014). Causality and endogeneity: Problems and solutions. In D. V. Day (Ed.), *The Oxford handbook of leadership and organizations* (pp. 93–117). New York, NY: Oxford University Press.

Ashkanasy, N. M., & Humphrey, R. H. (2011). Current emotion research in organizational behavior. *Emotion Review, 3,* 214–224.

Ashkanasy, N. M., & O'Connor, C. (1997). Value congruence in leader–member exchange. *Journal of Social Psychology, 137,* 647–662.

Bakhtin, M. M. (1986). *Speech genres and other late essays* (V. McGee, Trans.) Austin: University of Texas Press.

Baldwin, M. W. (1992). Relational schemas and the processing of social information. *Psychological Bulletin, 112*(3), 461–484.

Balkundi, P., & Kilduff, M. (2005). The ties that lead: A social network approach to leadership. *The Leadership Quarterly, 16,* 941–961.

Bauer, T. N., & Erdogan, B. (2015). Leader–member exchange (LMX) theory: An introduction and overview. In T. N. Bauer & B. Erdogan (Eds.), *The Oxford handbook of leader–member exchange.* Oxford, UK: Oxford University Press.

Bauer, T. N., & Green, S. G. (1996). Development of leader–member exchange: A longitudinal test. *Academy of Management Journal, 39*, 1538–1567.

Bernerth, J. B., Armenakis, A. A., Field, H. S., Giles, W. F., & Walker, H. J. (2007). Is personality associated with perceptions of LMX? An empirical study. *Leadership & Organization Development Journal, 28*, 613–631.

Berscheid, E. (1999). The greening of relationship science. *American Psychologist, 54*, 260–266.

Berscheid, E., & Reis, H. T. (1998). Attraction and close relationships. In D. T. Gilbert, S. T. Fiske, & G. Lindzey (Eds.), *The handbook of social psychology* (Vol. 2, 4th ed., pp. 193–281). New York, NY: McGraw-Hill.

Blau, P. (1964). *Exchange and power in social life*. New York, NY: Wiley.

Bolino, M. C., & Turnley, W. H. (2009). Relative deprivation among employees in lower-quality leader–member exchange relationships. *The Leadership Quarterly, 20*, 276–286.

Bradbury, H., & Lichtenstein, B. M. (2000). Relationality in organizational research: Exploring the space between. *Organization Science, 11*, 551–564.

Brewer, M. B., & Gardner, W. (1996). Who is this "we"? Levels of collective identity and self representations. *Journal of Personality and Social Psychology, 71*, 83–93.

Brower, H. H., Schoorman, F. D., & Tan, H. H. (2000). A model of relational leadership: The integration of trust and leader–member exchange. *Leadership Quarterly, 11*, 227–250.

Byrne, D. (1971). *The attraction paradigm*. New York, NY: Academic Press.

Carroll, B. & Levy, L. 2010. Leadership development as identity construction. *Management Communication Quarterly, 24*(2): 211–231.

Carson, J. B., Tesluk, P. E., & Marrone, J. A. (2007). Shared leadership in teams: An investigation of antecedent conditions and performance. *Academy of Management Journal, 50*(5), 1217–1234.

Carter, D. R., DeChurch, L. A., Braun, M. T., & Contractor, N. S. (2015). Social network approaches to leadership: An integrative conceptual review. *Journal of Applied Psychology, 100*, 597–622.

Chang, C.-H. & Johnson, R. E. 2010. Not all leader-member exchanges are created equal: Importance of leader relational identity. *The Leadership Quarterly, 21*(5): 796–808.

Clifton, J. (2012). A discursive approach to leadership: Doing assessments and managing organizational meanings. *Journal of Business Communication, 49*, 148–168.

Clifton, J. (2014). Small stories, positioning, and the discursive construction of leader identity in business meetings. *Leadership, 10*, 99–117.

Cogliser, C. C., Schriesheim, C. A., Scandura, T. A., & Gardner, W. L. (2009). Balance in leader and follower perceptions of leader–member exchange: Relationships with performance and work attitudes. *Leadership Quarterly, 20*(3), 452–465.

Costa, P. T., Jr., & McRae, R. R. (1992). *Revised NEO Personality Inventory (NEO-PI-R) and NEO Five-Factor Inventory (NEO-FFI) professional manual*. Odessa, FL: Psychological Assessment Resources.

Crevani, L., Lindgren, M., & Packendorff, J. (2010) Leadership, not leaders: On the study of leadership as practices and interactions. *Scandinavian Journal of Management 26*(1), 77– 86.

Crosby, F. (1976). A model of egoistical relative deprivation. *Psychological Review, 83*(2), 85–113.

Cunliffe A., & Eriksen, M. (2011). Relational leadership. *Human Relations, 64*, 14–25.

Dasborough, M. T., Ashkanasy, N. M., Tee, E. Y. J., & Tse, H. H. M. (2009). What goes around comes around: How meso-level negative emotional contagion can ultimately determine organizational attitudes towards leaders. *The Leadership Quarterly, 20*, 571–585.

Day, D. V. (2014). Time and leadership. In A. J. Shipp & Y. Fried (Eds.), *Time and work* (Vol. 2, pp. 30–52). New York, NY: Psychology Press.

DelVecchio, S. K. (1998). The quality of salesperson–manager relationship: The effect of latitude, loyalty and competence. *The Journal of Personal Selling and Sales Management, 18*(1), 31–47.

Denis, J.-L., Langley, A., & Sergi, V. (2012). Leadership in the plural. *Academy of Management Annals, 6*, 211–283.

DeRue, D. S., & Ashford, S. J. (2010). Who will lead and who will follow? A social process of leadership identity construction in organizations. *Academy of Management Review, 35*(4), 627–647.

Dienesch, R. M., & Liden, R. C. (1986). Leader–member exchange model of leadership: A critique and further development. *Academy of Management Review, 11*, 618–634.

Dihn, J., Lord, R. G., Gardner, W., Meuser J. D., Liden, R. C., & Hu, J. (2014). Leadership theory and research in the new millennium: Current theoretical trends and changing perspectives. *The Leadership Quarterly, 25,* 36–62.

Dirks, K. T., Lewicki, R. J., & Zaheer, A. (2009). Repairing relationships within and between organizations: Building a conceptual foundation. *Academy of Management Review, 34,* 68–84.

Duarte, N. T., Goodson, J. R., & Klich, N. R. (1994). Effects of dyadic quality and duration on performance appraisal. *Academy of Management Journal, 37,* 499–521.

Dulebohn, J. H., Bommer, W. H., Liden, R. C., Brouer, R. L., & Ferris, G. R. (2012). A meta-analysis of antecedents and consequences of leader–member exchange: Integrating the past with an eye toward the future. *Journal of Management, 38*(6), 1715–1759.

Endres, S., & Weibler, J. (2016), Towards a three-component model of relational social constructionist leadership: A systematic review and critical interpretive synthesis. *International Journal of Management Reviews.* Advance online publication. doi:10.1111/ijmr.12095

Epitropaki, O., Kapoutsis, I., Ellen, B. P., III, Ferris, G. R., Drivas, K., & Ntotsi, A. (2016). Navigating uneven terrain: The roles of political skill and LMX differentiation in prediction of work relationship quality and work outcomes. *Journal of Organizational Behavior, 37,* 1078–1103.

Epitropaki, O., Kark, R., Mainemelis, C., & Lord, R. G. (2017). Leadership and followership identity processes: A multilevel review. *The Leadership Quarterly, 28,* 104–129.

Epitropaki, O., & Martin, R. (2013). Transformational-transactional leadership and upward influence: The role of relative leader–member exchanges (RLMX) and perceived organizational support (POS). *The Leadership Quarterly, 24*(2), 299–315.

Epitropaki, O., & Martin, R. (2015). Leader–member exchanges and work attitudes: Is there anything left unsaid or unexamined? In T. Bauer & B. Erdogan (Eds.), *The Oxford handbook of leader–member exchange.* Oxford, UK: Oxford University Press.

Epitropaki, O., Sy, T., Martin, R., Tram-Quon, S., & Topakas, A. (2013). Implicit leadership and followership theories "in the wild": Taking stock of information-processing approaches to leadership and followership in organizational settings. *The Leadership Quarterly, 24,* 858–881.

Erdogan, B., & Bauer, T. N. (2010). Differentiated leader–member exchanges: The buffering role of justice climate. *Journal of Applied Psychology, 95,* 1104–1120.

Erdogan, B., & Bauer, T. N. (2014). Leader–member exchange (LMX) theory: The relational approach to leadership. In D. Day (Ed.), *The Oxford handbook of leadership and organizations* (pp. 407–433). Oxford, UK: Oxford University Press.

Etcheverry, P. E., Le, B., Wu, T. F., & Wei, M. (2013). Attachment and the investment model: Predictors of relationship commitment, maintenance, and persistence. *Personal Relationships, 20,* 546–567.

Fairhurst, G. T. (2007). *Discursive leadership: In conversation with leadership psychology.* Thousand Oaks, CA: Sage.

Fairhurst, G., & Uhl-Bien, M. (2012). Organizational discourse analysis (ODA): Examining leadership as a relational process. *The Leadership Quarterly, 23*(6), 1043–1062.

Fehr, R., & Gelfand, M. J. (2012). The forgiving organization: A multilevel model of forgiveness at work. *Academy of Management Review, 37,* 664–688.

Ferris, G. R., Liden, R. C., Munyon, T. P., Summers, J. K., Basik, K. J., & Buckley, M. R. (2009). Relationships at work: Toward a multidimensional conceptualization of dyadic work relationships. *Journal of Management, 35,* 1379–1403.

Festinger, L. (1954). A theory of social comparison processes. *Human Relations, 7,* 117–140.

Feyerherm, A. E. (1994). Leadership in collaboration: A longitudinal study of two interorganizational rule-making groups. *The Leadership Quarterly, 5,* 253–270.

Fletcher, G. J. O., Thomas, G., & Durant, R. (1999). Cognitive and behavioral accommodation in close relationships. *Journal of Social and Personal Relationships, 16,* 705–730.

Foa, E. B., & Foa, U. G. (1974). *Societal structures of the mind.* Springfield, IL.: Charles C. Thomas.

Follett, M. P. (1924). *Creative experience* (reprint 1951). New York, NY: Peter Smith.

Gerstner, C. R., & Day, D. V. (1997). Meta-analytic review of leader–member exchange theory: Correlates and construct issues. *Journal of Applied Psychology, 82*, 827–844.

Gittell, G. H., & Douglass, A. (2012). Relational bureaucracy: Structuring reciprocal relationships into roles. *Academy of Management Review, 37*(4), 709–733.

Glaso, L., & Einarsen, S. (2006). Experienced affects in leader–subordinate relationships. *Scandinavian Journal of Management, 22*, 49–73.

Gooty, J., Connelly, S., Griffith, J., & Gupta, A. (2010). Leadership, affect and emotions: A state of the science review. *The Leadership Quarterly, 21*, 979–1004.

Gooty, J., & Yammarino, F. (2016). The leader–member exchange relationship: A multisource, cross-level investigation. *Journal of Management, 42*(4), 915–935.

Graen, G. B., Novak, M. A., & Sommerkamp, P. (1982). The effects of leader–member exchange and job design on productivity and satisfaction: Testing a dual attachment model. *Organizational Behavior and Human Performance, 30*, 109–131.

Graen. G. B., & Uhl-Bien, M. (1995). Relationship-based approach to leadership: Development of leader–member exchange (LMX) theory of leadership over 25 years: Applying a multi-level multi-domain perspective. *The Leadership Quarterly, 6*, 219–247.

Green, S. G., Blank, W., & Liden, R. C. (1983). Market and organizational influences on bank employees' work attitudes and behaviors. *Journal of Applied Psychology, 68*(2), 298–306.

Harris, M. M., & Schaubroeck, J. (1988). A meta-analysis of self-supervisor, self-peer, and peer–supervisor ratings. *Personnel Psychology, 41*, 43–62.

Harris, T. B., Li, N., & Kirkman, B. L. (2014). Leader–member exchange (LMX) in context: How LMX differentiation and LMX relational separation attenuate LMX's influence on OCB and turnover intention. *The Leadership Quarterly, 25*, 314–328.

Hatfield, E., Cacioppo, J. T., & Rapson, R. L. (1994). *Emotional contagion.* Cambridge, UK: Cambridge University Press.

Henderson, D. J., Wayne, S. J., Shore, L. M., Bommer, W. H., & Tetrick, L. E. (2008). Leader–member exchange, differentiation and psychological contract fulfilment: A multilevel examination. *Journal of Applied Psychology, 93*, 1208–1219.

Hinojosa, A. S., McCauley, K. D., Randolph-Seng, B., & Gardner, W. L. (2014). Leader and follower attachment styles: Implications for authentic leader–follower relationships. *The Leadership Quarterly, 25*, 595–610.

Hogg, M. A., Martin, R., Epitropaki, O., Mankad, A., Svensson, A., & Weeden, K. (2005). Effective leadership in salient groups: Revisiting leader–member exchange theory from the perspective of the social identity theory of leadership. *Personality and Social Psychology Bulletin, 31*(7), 991–1004.

Hollander, E. P. (1964). *Leaders, groups, and influence.* New York, NY: Oxford University Press.

Hooper, D., & Martin, R. (2008). Beyond personal leader–member exchange (LMX) quality: The effects of perceived variability on employee reactions. *The Leadership Quarterly, 19*, 20–30.

Hu, J., & Liden, R. C. (2013). Relative leader–member exchange within team contexts: How and when social comparison impacts individual effectiveness. *Personnel Psychology, 66*, 127–172.

Huang, X., Wright, R. P., Chiu, W. C. K., & Wang, C. (2008). Relational schemas as sources of evaluation and misevaluation in leader–member exchanges: Some initial evidence. *The Leadership Quarterly, 19*, 266–282.

Kamdar, D. & Van Dyne, L. 2007. The joint effects of personality and workplace social exchange relationships in predicting task performance and citizenship performance. *Journal of Applied Psychology, 92*(5): 1286–1298.

Kauppila, O. (2016). When and how does LMX differentiation influence followers' work outcomes? The interactive roles of one's own LMX status and organizational context. *Personnel Psychology, 67*, 359–393.

Klein, K. J., & Kim, J. S. (1998). A field study of the influence of situational constraints, leader–member exchange, and goal commitment on performance. *Academy of Management Journal, 41*, 88–89.

Knee, C. R., Patrick, H., & Lonsbary, C. (2003). Implicit theories of relationships: Orientations toward evaluation and cultivation. *Personality and Social Psychology Review, 7*, 41–55.

Koivunen, N. (2007). The processual nature of leadership discourses. *Scandinavian Journal of Management, 23*, 285–305.

Langley, A., & Tsoukas, H. (2016). *Process studies handbook*. Thousand Oaks, CA: Sage.

Lau, D. C., & Liden, R. C. (2008). Antecedents of coworker trust: Leader blessings. *Journal of Applied Psychology, 93*, 1130–1138.

Li, N., Liang, J., & Crant, J. M. (2010). The role of proactive personality in job satisfaction and organizational citizenship behavior: A relational perspective. *Journal of Applied Psychology, 95*, 395–404.

Liden, R. C., Wayne, S. J., & Stilwell, D. (1993). A longitudinal study on the early development of leader–member exchanges. *Journal of Applied Psychology, 78*, 662–674.

Ma, L., & Qu, Q. (2010). Differentiation in leader–member exchange: A hierarchical linear modeling approach. *The Leadership Quarterly, 21*(5), 733–744.

Mahsud, R., Yukl, G., & Prussia, G. (2010). Leader empathy, ethical leadership, and relations-oriented behaviors as antecedents of leader–member exchange quality. *Journal of Managerial Psychology, 25*(6), 561–577.

Maio, G. R., Thomas, G., Fincham, F. D., & Carnelley, K. B. (2008). Unraveling the role of forgiveness in family relationships. *Journal of Personality and Social Psychology, 94*, 307–319.

Martin, R., Epitropaki, O., Thomas, G., & Topakas, A. (2010). A critical review of leader–member relationship (LMX) research: Future prospects and directions. *International Review of Industrial and Organizational Psychology, 25*, 35–89.

Martin, R., Thomas, G., Guillaume, Y., Lee, A., & Epitropaki, O. (2016). Leader–member exchange (LMX) and performance: A meta-analytic review. *Personnel Psychology, 69*, 67–121.

McClane, W. E. (1991). The interaction of leader and member characteristics in the leader–member exchange (LMX) model of leadership. *Small Group Research, 22*, 283–300.

Mead, G. H. (1934). *Mind, self, and society*. Chicago, IL: University of Chicago Press.

Miner, A. G., Glomb, T. M., & Hulin, C. (2005). Experience sampling mood and its correlates at work. *Journal of Occupational and Organizational Psychology, 78*, 171–193.

Miscenko, D., Guenter, H., & Day, D. V. 2017. Am I a leader? Examining leader identity development over time. *The Leadership Quarterly*.

Morgan, G., & Smircich, L. (1980). The case for qualitative research. *The Academy of Management Review, 5*(4), 491–500.

Nahrgang, J. D. & Seo, J. J. 2015. How and why high leader -member exchange (LMX) relationships develop: Examining the antecedents of LMX. *The Oxford Handbook of Leader-Member Exchange*: 87–118.

Nahrgang, J. D., Morgeson, F. P., & Ilies, R. (2009). The development of leader–member exchanges: Exploring how personality and performance influence leader and member relationships over time. *Organizational Behavior and Human Decision Processes, 108*, 256–266.

Newcombe, M. J., & Ashkanasy, N. M. (2002). The role of affect and affective congruence in perceptions of leaders: An experimental study. *The Leadership Quarterly, 13*, 601–614.

Nishii, L. H., & Mayer, D. M. (2009). Do inclusive leaders help to reduce turnover in diverse groups? The moderating role of leader–member exchange in the diversity to turnover relationship. *Journal of Applied Psychology, 94*, 1412–1426.

Ozer, M. (2008). Personal and task-related moderators of leader–member exchange among software developers. *Journal of Applied Psychology, 93*, 1174–1182.

Phillips, A. S., & Bedeian, A. G. (1994). Leader–follower exchange quality: The role of personal and interpersonal attributes. *Academy of Management Journal, 37*, 990–1001.

Restubog, S., Bordia, P., & Bordia, S. (2011). Investigating the role of psychological contract breach on career success: Convergent evidence from two longitudinal studies. *Journal of Vocational Behaviour, 79*(2), 428–437.

Richards, D., & Hackett, R. D. (2012). Attachment and emotion regulation: Compensatory interactions and leader–member exchange. *The Leadership Quarterly, 23*, 686–701.

Rotundo, M., & Sackett, P. R. (2002). The relative importance of task, citizenship, and counterproductive performance to global aspects of job performance: A policy capturing approach. *Journal of Applied Psychology, 87*, 66–80.

Rusbult, C. E. (1980). Commitment and satisfaction in romantic associations: A test of the investment model. *Journal of Experimental Social Psychology, 16*, 172–186.

Rusbult, C. E., Olsen, N., Davis, J. L., & Hannon, P. (2001). Commitment and relationship maintenance mechanisms. In J. H. Harvey & A. Wenzel (Eds.), *Close romantic relationships: Maintenance and enhancement* (pp. 87–113). Mahwah, NJ: Lawrence Erlbaum.

Schriesheim, C. A., Castro, S. L., Zhou, X. T., & Yammarino, F. J. (2001). The folly of theorizing "A" but testing "B": A selective level-of-analysis review of the field and detailed leader–member exchange illustration. *The Leadership Quarterly, 12*(4), 515–551.

Schyns, B. (2015). Leader and follower personality and LMX. In T. Bauer & B. Erdogan (Eds.), *The Oxford handbook of leader–member exchange* (pp. 119–135). Oxford, UK: Oxford University Press.

Schyns B., & Day, D. (2010). Critique and review of leader–member exchange theory: Issues of agreement, consensus, and excellence. *European Journal of Work and Organizational Psychology, 19*, 1–29.

Schyns, B., Paul, T., Mohr, G., & Blank, H. (2005). Comparing antecedents and consequences of leader–member exchange in a German working context to findings in the US. *European Journal of Work and Organizational Psychology, 14*, 1–22.

Seers, A. (1989). Team-member exchange quality: A new construct for role-making research. *Organizational Behavior and Human Decision Processes, 43*, 118–135.

Shamir, B. (2011). Leadership takes time: Some implications of (not) taking time seriously in leadership research. *The Leadership Quarterly, 22*, 307–315.

Shondrick, S. J., & Lord, R. G. (2010). Implicit leadership and followership theories: Dynamic structures for leadership perceptions, memory and leader–follower processes. *International Review of Industrial and Organizational Psychology, 25*, 1–33.

Sin, H.-P., Nahrgang, J. D., & Morgeson, F. P. (2009). Understanding why they don't see eye-to-eye: An examination of leader–member exchange (LMX) agreement. *Journal of Applied Psychology, 94*(4), 1048–1057.

Sluss, D. M., & Ashforth, B. E. (2007). Relational identity and identification: Defining ourselves through work relationships. *Academy of Management Review, 32*, 9–32.

Sparrowe, R. T., & Emery, C. (2015). Tracing structure, tie strength, and cognitive networks in LMX theory and research. In T. N. Bauer & B. Erdogan (Eds.), *The Oxford handbook of leader–member exchange* (pp. 293–309). Oxford, UK: Oxford University Press.

Sparrowe, R. T., & Liden, R. C. (2005). Two routes to influence: Integrating leader–member exchange and social network perspectives. *Administrative Science Quarterly, 50*(4), 505–535.

Swann, W. B., Johnson, R. E., & Bosson, J. K. (2009). Identity negotiation at work. *Research in Organizational Behavior, 29*, 81–109.

Sy, T., Côté, S., & Saavedra, R. (2005). The contagious leader: Impact of leader's mood on the mood of group members, group affective tone, and group processes. *Journal of Applied Psychology, 90*, 295–305.

Tekleab, A. G., & Taylor, M. S. (2003). Aren't there two parties in an employment relationship? Antecedents and consequences of organization–employee agreement on contract obligations and violations. *Journal of Organizational Behavior, 24*, 585–608.

Thomas, G., Martin, R., Epitropaki, O., Guillaume, Y., & Lee, A. (2013). Social cognition in leader–follower relationships: Applying insights from relationship science to understanding relationship-based approaches to leadership. *Journal of Organizational Behavior, 34*, S63–S81.

Tonidandel, S., King, E. B., & Cortina, J. M. (2017). Big data methods. *Organizational Research Methods*. Advance online publication. doi:10.1177/1094428116677299

Tordera, N., González-Romá, V., & Peiró, J. M. (2008). The moderator effect of psychological climate on the relationship between leader–member exchange (LMX) quality and role overload. *European Journal of Work and Organizational Psychology, 17*, 55–72.

Totterdell, P., Wall, T., Diamond, H., Holman, D., & Epitropaki, O. (2004). Affect networks: A structural analysis of the relationship between work ties and job-related affect. *Journal of Applied Psychology, 89*, 854–867.

Tran, S., & Simpson, J. A. (2009). Pro–relationship maintenance behaviors: The joint roles of attachment and commitment. *Journal of Personality and Social Psychology, 97*, 685–698.

Tse, H. H. M., Dasborough, M. T., & Ashkanasy, N. M. (2008). A multi-level analysis of team climate and interpersonal exchange relationships at work. *The Leadership Quarterly, 19*, 195–211.

Uhl-Bien, M. (2006). Relational leadership theory: Exploring the social processes of leadership and organizing. *The Leadership Quarterly, 17*, 654–676.

Uhl-Bien, M., & Ospina, S. (Eds.). (2012). *Advancing relational leadership research: A dialogue among perspectives.* Charlotte, NC: Information Age.

Vidyarthi, P. R., Liden, R. C., Anand, S., Erdogan, B., & Ghosh, S. (2010). Where do I stand? Examining the effects of leader–member exchange social comparison on employee work behaviors. *Journal of Applied Psychology, 95*, 849–861.

Wang, H., Law, K. S., Hackett, R. D., Wang, D., & Chen, Z. X. (2005). Leader–member exchange as a mediator of the relationship between transformational leadership and followers' performance and organizational citizenship behavior. *Academy of Management Journal, 48*, 420–432.

Wayne, S. J., & Ferris, G. R. (1990). Influence tactics, affect, and exchange quality in supervisor–subordinate interactions: A laboratory experiment and field study. *Journal of Applied Psychology, 75*, 487–499.

Wilson, K., Sin, H., & Conlon, D. (2010). What about the leader in leader–member exchange? The impact of resource exchanges and substitutability on the leader. *Academy of Management Review, 35*, 358–372.

Zhang, Z., Wang, M., & Shi, J. (2012). Leader–follower congruence in proactive personality and work outcomes: The mediating role of leader–member exchange. *Academy of Management Journal, 55*(1), 111–130.

Zhou, X., & Schriesheim, C. (2009). Supervisor–subordinate agreement on leader–member exchange (LMX) quality: Review and testable propositions. *The Leadership Quarterly, 20*, 920–932.

Zhou, X., & Schriesheim, C. (2010). Quantitative and qualitative examination of propositions concerning supervisor–subordinate convergence in descriptions of leader–member exchange (LMX) quality. *The Leadership Quarterly, 21*, 826–843.

# CHAPTER 6

# Contingencies, Context, Situation, and Leadership

*Roya Ayman*

*Matthew Lauritsen*

---

## Opening Case: A Day in the Life of a Leader

Chris McAllister has just started a new job as a general manager. He has all the normative qualities of a good leader: good judgment, clear communication, and a history of success in his previous job, among others. His last job was at a manufacturing plant, where he was mostly responsible for managing his employees' workloads and making sure shipments were ready on time. The role required managing the revenue and costs of his business unit, and interaction with employees on the factory floor was uncommon.

Chris's new job is at a large design and innovation consulting firm. Creativity is the essence of the mission of this organization. There is no dress code at this company, and employees can set up camp anywhere they please within a large, open, and collaborative workspace. Most of the work is done in small, temporary teams with a flattened hierarchy. Those who take the lead in these teams are chosen based on team skills and personal enthusiasm for the current project, rather than their knowledge, skills, or seniority. Now, instead of managing inventory, he has to manage knowledge workers in a completely different environment.

When Chris arrived at his desk one morning only a few weeks after starting his job, he learned that one of the company's major clients was dissatisfied with a team's design project and requested that it be revised before the end of the week. He decided to put together a team that he thought was capable and offered them a monetary bonus if they completed the request on time. Much to his disappointment, the team was reluctant to start working, made little initial progress, lacked motivation, and began to feel bitter toward Chris every time he made a decision for the group. The team failed to meet the deadline, and Chris began to wonder where he had gone wrong. He was confident that his decisions were good for the business, but for some reason they were not resonating with the team.

## Discussion Questions

1. How can someone be successful in one environment but not in another?

2. What makes Chris's new job different from his old job? How does the situation make a difference?

3. How would events change if Chris had asked for the group's opinions before making a decision?

4. Would it make a difference if Chris were a woman? Why or why not?

# Chapter Overview

In leadership studies, we have observed two general lines of research proceeding in parallel. On one hand, many studies focused on the relationship between leader traits or behaviors and organizational outcomes. Others found themselves invoking contingencies, context, and situations to explain their findings (e.g., Judge, Bono, Ilies, & Gerhardt, 2002; Judge & Piccolo, 2004). This demonstrates that despite efforts to find simple explanations for leadership, there is a more complex picture to consider. Scholars continue to focus on context and contingencies (e.g., Liden & Antonakis, 2009; Porter & McLaughlin, 2006), demonstrating the importance of these factors in the study of leadership. As Fiedler (1992) commented, life exists within a pretzel-shaped universe and therefore needs pretzel-shaped theories to explain it. This is especially the case in the field of leadership research.

Historically, the 20th-century psychological exploration of leadership research started with the "great man" theory, which focused on leadership as a quality within an individual (e.g., Ayman, 1993; Chemers, 1997; Zaccaro, Kemp, & Bader, 2004). This philosophical school dominated the majority of the subsequent theoretical developments and empirical investigations as well as the practice of selection of leaders in organizations. Conversely, based on Marx and Engels's *Zeitgeist* or "spirit of the time" philosophical paradigm, leadership can be seen not within the person who becomes the leader, but rather in the situation and the time surrounding the person who becomes the leader. Thus, this approach focused more on the situational impact on leadership and leadership effectiveness (Ayman, 1993; Chemers, 1997) and was the backdrop of the contingency approaches to leadership in the 20th century. However, the dominant focus on the person of the leader within the leadership process is prevalent even after the introduction of contingency approaches. This is evident in the influential works of Big Five personality and leadership (Hogan, Curphy, & Hogan, 1994), full range of leadership theory (Antonakis, Avolio, & Sivasubramaniam, 2003), and leader–member exchange (Graen & Uhl-Bien, 1995). Despite this research, the empirical evidence attests that interest in contingencies and context persists (Porter & McLaughlin, 2006).

In this chapter, we first review the theories and models known within the contingency approaches of leadership. Subsequently, we analyze the definitions of contingencies, context, and situation present in leadership research, acknowledging the various variables and methodological approaches. In so doing, we present a conceptualization of these variables at the interpersonal and intrapersonal levels to assist model building regarding contingencies, context, and situation. In addition, methodological issues that facilitate the role of these concepts in understanding leadership will be discussed.

## Contingency Models and Theories of Leadership

Historically, the models and theories of leadership developed in the late 1960s through the 1970s demonstrated that leadership effectiveness is a result of the interaction between the characteristics of the leader and the situation (Fiedler, 1978). Some models focused on the leader's internal state and traits, such as the contingency model of leadership effectiveness and the cognitive resource theory (Fiedler, 1978; Fiedler & Garcia, 1987). Others focused on the leader's perceived behaviors, such as the normative decision-making model (Vroom & Jago, 1978; Vroom & Yetton, 1973), path-goal theory (House, 1971; House & Mitchell, 1974), and situational leadership theory (Hersey & Blanchard, 1969). More recently, leadership categorization has been presented as another contingency theory. Its placement in our scheme of the trait and behavioral contingency approaches to leadership is not as transparent; however, it seems that the focus is on both leader traits (e.g., Offermann, Kennedy, & Wirtz, 1994) and leader behaviors (Lord, Foti, & DeVader, 1984). As we explain later, leadership categorization demonstrates how expectations about leaders vary due to their role or the situation. In the following subsections, we briefly describe each of these models and present a matrix to compare the models and theories based on their approach to assessing the leader, the situation, and leadership outcomes (see Table 6.1).

## Leader Trait Contingency Models

Two contingency models exist that show the situational factors that intervene between the leader's characteristics and various outcomes: contingency model of leadership effectiveness and cognitive resource theory. In both these models, the characteristics of the leader relate to individual- and group-level outcomes, but the extent of this relationship depends upon the situation. In this section, we will review each model and discuss the contextual factors in detail.

**Table 6.1** Matrix Comparing Contingency Models' Treatment of the Leader, the Situation, and Outcomes

| | Contingency Model of Leadership Effectiveness | Cognitive Resource Theory | Normative Model of Leadership Decision Making | Path-Goal Theory | Situational Leadership Theory |
|---|---|---|---|---|---|
| **The Leader** | | | | | |
| Source | Leader | Leader | Mostly the leader; some from the subordinates | Subordinates | Subordinates |
| Characteristics | Trait (LPC scale): task and interpersonal orientation | Intelligence and experience | Decision strategies (five styles): autocratic I and II; consultative I and II; and group II | Supervisory behavior: participative, supportive, achievement-oriented, and directive | Supervisory behavior (LEAD): selling, telling, participating, and delegating |
| **The Situation** | | | | | |
| Source | The leader and experimenter | The leader | The leader and experimenter | The subordinate | The leader or experimenter |
| The Variables | Leader–member relationship<br>Task structure<br>Position power | Stress with boss<br>Stress with coworkers<br>Stress with task | Availability of information<br>Team support and cohesion<br>Time available<br>(These are simplified representations of 11 conditions.) | Subordinates' needs, values, and abilities<br>Subordinates' task structure and difficulty | Subordinates' willingness and ability (follower maturity index) |
| **Outcomes** | | | | | |
| Group | Performance satisfaction (with leader and subordinates) | Actual performance | Performance satisfaction | General satisfaction | General satisfaction |
| Individuals | Leader's stress | | | Team member's stress | |

**Contingency Model of Leadership Effectiveness.** Fiedler (1964) was the first to formulate a trait contingency model of leadership effectiveness, which became known as the contingency model of leadership effectiveness. In this model, Fiedler (1978) predicted leader or group success from the interaction of the leader's orientation (i.e., task or relationship) with the leader's situational control. A leader's orientation is an internal state and is not directly related to observed behaviors (Ayman, 2002). This orientation is fairly stable and is similar to the way in which personality is conceptualized. To measure a leader's orientation toward the work setting, the model uses the Least Preferred Coworker (LPC) scale (e.g., Ayman & Romano, 1998). Most initial studies in this paradigm were conducted in experimental settings (see Fiedler, 1978), where participants were chosen to act as leaders based on whether their LPC score was in the top one-third (relationship-oriented) or the bottom one-third (task-oriented).

Many procedures were used to substantiate the task orientation of those with low LPC scores and the relationship orientation of those with high LPC scores. To clarify these labels further, two studies (Chemers & Ayman, 1985; Rice, Marwick, Chemers, & Bentley, 1982) examined the impact of LPC scores on the relationship between an individual's job satisfaction and performance as evaluated by their boss. They found that when compared with relationship-oriented leaders, task-oriented leaders showed a significantly higher correlation between their satisfaction with work and their performance evaluation. Based on these findings, the LPC scale was further substantiated as a measure of the individual's focus and self-worth based on accomplishment of the task.

In this model, the leader's ability to control and influence the accomplishment of the group's task is his or her situational control. Situational control is based on three aspects: team climate, leader's task structure, and leader's position power. Team climate, better known as the leader–member relationship, assesses the cohesion of team members and their support of the leader. The leader's task structure includes two aspects of the leader's task: the task-structure dimensions and the leader's background (i.e., the leader's experience and training). Task structure is the amount of clarity and direction to achieve the task goal. The final task-structure score is determined by adjusting the task's structure score with the level of the leader's experience and training. For example, the task of a leader with more experience or training will be more structured than the task structure of a novice in the same position. Position power reflects the leader's legitimacy, as well as the authority for punishing and rewarding the team members (Ayman, 2002; Fiedler, 1978).

The order of importance of these three situational aspects is based on their contribution to the leader's sense of control and prediction in a situation. During decades of research, Fiedler (1978) concluded that the leader–member relationship is twice as important in contributing to the leader's control as task structure. Furthermore, task structure is twice as important as position power (Ayman, Chemers, & Fiedler, 1995, 1998). Subsequently, Ayman (2002) argued that a sense of control in a situation gives a person power. The order of importance of situational control aspects are closely representative of the relative importance associated with French and Raven's (1959) sources of power (Podsakoff & Schriesheim,

1985). For example, leader–member relation is analogous to referent power, and leader's task structure can be related to expert power.

The contingency model of leadership effectiveness, based on the leader-match concept, predicts that leaders who are relationship-oriented will be more effective in moderate situational control than will task-focused leaders, whereas leaders who are task-focused will be more effective in both high- and low-control situations. When leaders are in the situation where the model predicts their greatest effectiveness, they are considered in-match leaders. When they are in situations where the model predicts they will be less effective, they are referred to as being out-of-match leaders (Ayman, 2002).

Because this model views the leader's traits as stable, attempts to create in-match leaders require changing the situation, known as situation engineering (Fiedler & Chemers, 1984). Based on this model, leadership training programs were designed to assist the leader in learning how to change the situation to best fit his or her leader orientation. Burke and Day's (1986) meta-analysis of various managerial training models found leader match training (Fiedler, Chemers, & Mahar, 1976) to be most effective and generalizable to other situations. Furthermore, three separate meta-analyses (Peters, Hartke, & Pohlman, 1985; Schriesheim, Tepper, & Tetrault, 1994; Strube & Garcia, 1981) found support for the general predictions of the model and called for further development and extension (Ayman, 2002). A detailed review of this model and a discussion of its strengths and weaknesses are presented elsewhere (Ayman, 2002; Ayman, Chemers, & Fiedler, 1998).

Finally, the leader effectiveness criterion in this model has been primarily defined as group performance (Fiedler, 1978). In response to some criticisms that the model predicts only performance, Rice (1981) suggested that the model could also predict team satisfaction, which was subsequently supported empirically (Ayman & Chemers, 1991). In addition, Chemers, Hays, Rhodewalt, and Wysocki (1985) found that if the leaders were out of match, they experienced higher levels of stress and reported clinical symptoms of illness.

The model has been validated mostly at the group level of analysis (Ayman et al., 1995, 1998). However, these authors noted that the design of the model allows for it to function at other levels, such as the individual and the dyadic levels of analysis. For example, in Chemers et al. (1985), the analysis was at the level of the individual leader examining the model's prediction for the leader's stress. Results of two other studies, one laboratory (Chemers, Goza, & Plumer, 1978) and one field (Tobey-Garcia, Ayman, & Chemers, 2000), tentatively supported a dyadic level of analysis. These studies showed that in moderate situational control conditions, relationship-oriented leaders with task-oriented subordinates yield the highest satisfaction and performance. But in these same situations, task-oriented leaders with task-oriented subordinates who have important but conflicting information seemed to do the worst. This could be partially due to the lack of match experienced in this situation by task-oriented leaders, who therefore may be stressed and not open to new ideas. In this situation, if the subordinate negates the task-oriented leader's structure and/or ideas, the leader by nature may feel further threatened and thus will likely reject the information that is vital and lose the opportunity to succeed.

**Cognitive Resource Theory (CRT).** Cognitive resource theory is the second contingency model based on leader traits and characteristics (Fiedler & Garcia, 1987), where the leader's effectiveness can be predicted based on the interaction of two internal characteristics—intelligence and experience—with the situation. In CRT, the core proposition states that situational factors will dictate whether leader intelligence or experience predicts leadership effectiveness. Fiedler (2002) incorporated Sternberg's (1995) explanations of (a) intelligence referring to "fluid" intelligence versus (b) experience being akin to "crystallized" intelligence. The first refers to cognitive ability to deal with novelty, and the second refers to automatization of responses reflective of experiences and mastery. The situation in this theory is defined by the leader's level of stress. A leader can experience job stress in various ways, such as role conflict and overload, as well as from various sources, such as coworkers, the task, or the leader's own superior (Fiedler, 1993).

Fiedler (1993, 1995) summarized the findings of several studies in both the laboratory (e.g., Murphy, Blyth, & Fiedler, 1992) and the field (Potter & Fiedler, 1981) where, under high-stress conditions, the leaders' performance was positively related to their experience and negatively related to their intelligence. In low-stress situations, a leader's intelligence was positively related to performance and experience had less of an effect. Fiedler (2002) further concluded: "People can be experienced and bright or experienced and stupid. But the performance of a particular job requires the leader to give priority either to experience or to analytical or creative analysis in solving the particular problem" (p. 102).

A combination of the contingency model of leadership effectiveness with CRT could demonstrate that out-of-match leaders are stressed. These leaders then may need to rely more on their experience than their intelligence in order to perform well. Zaccaro (1995) considered CRT a promising starting point and encouraged theorists to consider the roles of multiple traits, such as ego resilience and social intelligence. In their quantitative review of the available literature, Judge, Colbert, and Ilies (2004) found some support for this model.

## Leader Behavioral Contingency Approaches

### Normative Model of Leadership Decision Making

Overall, the normative model focuses on the interaction between a leader's decision-making strategy choices and the decision situation. Vroom and Jago (1998) identified five leadership strategies for decision making (see Table 6.1). The strategies range from decision making by the leader, to the partial inclusion of the subordinates, to full involvement of the subordinates. The decision heuristics describe the situation based on four criteria: improve the quality of the decision, improve subordinate involvement, reduce the time spent, and develop the subordinates (Vroom & Jago, 1998). These criteria are also the basis for measuring the effectiveness of the decision. The leader is presented with a decision-making tree with yes/no responses reflecting the heuristics. The full representation of this decision process flowchart is available for review in other sources (e.g., Vroom & Jago, 1998).

If decision quality is critical, the leader has to assess his or her knowledge level, the degree of the problem structure, and the degree of the subordinate's agreeableness and knowledge pertaining to the decision at hand. For example, group involvement is the advised strategy when subordinates are more knowledgeable on an issue than the leader. When time is of concern, the involvement of the group becomes less practical. In time-pressured situations, most leaders use more autocratic decision-making strategies. Lastly, if development of subordinate interest, acceptance, and commitment is critical for the decision to be implemented favorably, then greater subordinate involvement is advised. In such situations, the leader may have to pay the cost of increased time and perhaps even sacrifice decision quality to ensure team support and cohesion. The goal of achieving a balance between quality, time, and maintenance of team support will affect whether the leader prioritizes the goal of reaching a high-quality decision over that of high acceptance by the team members, or vice versa.

The participative leadership model, or normative model of leadership decision making, has received support. Based on the evidence, the model demonstrates that the level of participative decision making should be gauged based on the situation and the effectiveness criteria used. Additionally, there seem to be other contingencies (e.g., gender, cultural values) that appear to monitor the effectiveness of the leader's choice of decision-making style.

**Path-Goal Theory.** According to path-goal theory, the leader helps to create a path for subordinates to reach their goals and the goals of the organization by engaging in different types of leadership (House, 1996). House (1971) identified directive, achievement-oriented, supportive, and participative leadership behaviors as the theory's independent variables (see Table 6.1). It should be noted that the first two are more task-focused (e.g., assigning tasks, scheduling, emphasizing deadlines) and the latter two are more considerate (e.g., making people feel at ease, being open to suggestions, encouraging team members). The effectiveness of these behaviors is moderated by the characteristics of the environment as well as of the follower.

Various authors have highlighted notable limitations of the path-goal theory. One issue seems to be related to the instruments used to measure leader behavior (Fisher & Edwards, 1988; Schriesheim & Von Glinow, 1977). Another issue is that most studies have examined either task or subordinate characteristics. Furthermore, Stinson and Johnson (1975) as well as Wofford and Liska (1993) recommended testing a multiple moderator model. Finally, Wofford and Liska also expressed concern that the majority of the studies testing the theory suffered from same-source bias (i.e., common methods variance). To conclude, Evans (1996) stated, "In light of the absence of studies testing the critical motivational hypothesis of the theory, it is hard to argue that the theory has undergone reasonable testing. It has not" (p. 307).

On a positive note, path-goal theory can be seen as an important development in leadership theory that encouraged the evolution of new leadership conceptualizations. It was the basis of the development of theories of charismatic leadership and substitutes for leadership (House, 1996) and potentially an impetus for the development of a vertical dyad linkage model (Dansereau, Graen, & Haga, 1975).

Although the empirical support for the model is mixed, it helped drive new thinking about leadership.

**Situational Leadership Theory.** Hersey and Blanchard (1969) proposed that the effectiveness of four leadership behaviors—selling, telling, participating, and delegating—depends on whether they complement the subordinates' task-related characteristics (e.g., ability, education, experience) and psychological maturity (e.g., willingness, self-esteem, motivation). Although the theory does have a measure to assess the leader's style—the Leadership Effectiveness and Adaptability Description (LEAD)—many of the empirical studies on this model seem to use the Leader Behavior Description Questionnaire (LBDQ) in measuring the leader's behaviors (e.g., Case, 1987; Vecchio, 1987; Vecchio & Boatwright, 2002).

Based on the major tenets of the theory, the leader should "delegate" (i.e., exhibit low consideration and low-structuring behaviors) in situations where subordinates are able and willing, having both the ability and the motivation to perform effectively. When subordinates are willing and unable, the appropriate leader behavior is to "sell" (i.e., engage in high consideration and high-structuring behaviors). In situations where the subordinates are unwilling but able, the leader should engage in "participative decision making" (i.e., show high consideration but low-structuring behaviors). When the subordinates are unwilling and unable, the leader needs to "tell" them what to do (i.e., demonstrate low consideration but high-structuring behaviors). Although situational leadership theory has intuitive appeal, it has undergone only limited empirical examination. Unfortunately, most reviews have been very critical of the model and have not found much empirical support for it (e.g., Fernandez & Vecchio, 1997; Vecchio, 1997; Vecchio & Boatwright, 2002; York, 1996).

## Contingencies, Context, and Situation Defined

In the previous section we presented traditional contingency leadership models and theories, which propose that leadership occurs in context. In most of those models, the operationalization of contingency is similar to that of Johns (2006). Johns stated that context, which can include constraints and opportunities for behavior, surrounds a phenomenon and is external to the individual. Similarly, leadership scholars who have written about leadership contingencies have conceptualized contingencies as context (Antonakis et al., 2003; Avolio, 2007; Chemers, 2000; Diedorff, Rubin, & Morgeson, 2009; Liden & Antonakis, 2009). Therefore, in leadership, the situation is the context or contingency that can influence the relation between the leader's behavior or characteristics and the outcome.

Some of these characteristics can be antecedents to leadership, or they can moderate the relationship between leadership behavior and outcome. As an antecedent, some researchers consider gender, for example, as a predictor of leader behavior that examines how men and women leaders differ (Eagly, Johannesen-Schmidt, & van Engen, 2003; see Chapter 10 in this volume). Others consider the gender of the leader a contingency or context of a leadership style and outcome (Antonakis et al., 2003). Also, the leader's role and gender, as well as culture, have impacted observers' descriptions of a manager or a leader based on research in Implicit Leadership Theory (see Chapters 4 and 9).

In addition, the leader's characteristics such as his or her personality, gender, intelligence, and experience can interact, and these interactions can create a situation or contingency that influences the relationship between leader behavior and outcomes. Again, for example, the gender of the leader is not an external situation or context, so the definition of contingency in this case seems to include a more intrapersonal aspect. In this section, we argue that contingencies in leadership can have an interpersonal or an intrapersonal aspect (see Figure 6.1).

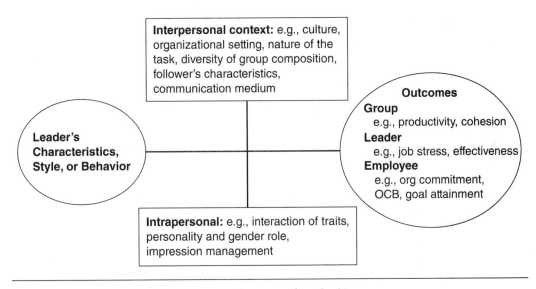

**Figure 6.1**     Interpersonal and Intrapersonal Aspects of Leadership

## Interpersonal Aspect

The interpersonal aspect of contingencies can be considered objectively or subjectively. Objective contingencies may consist of country, level in the organization (e.g., Antonakis et al., 2003; Lowe, Kroeck, & Sivasubramaniam, 1996), type of industry or field of work, tenure in the leadership relationship, and work group composition. The objective contingencies are usually proxies for power, values, and interpersonal interaction.

The subjective assessment of context is usually evaluated through the perspectives of the subordinates. Some examples of subjective assessment of context may include the leader's distance from the followers (e.g., Antonakis & Atwater, 2002), subordinates' values (Dvir & Shamir, 2003), and uncertainty (Waldman, Ramirez, House, & Puranam, 2001). Before we present the various factors that have gained recognition as contextual factors in leadership within the present framework, we will briefly review the substitutes-for-leadership theory. This theory expanded the classic work of the contingency models by developing a more inclusive list of contextual factors of leadership. This theory also provided a framework for the contextual factors that hinder or enhance a leader's impact.

**Substitutes-for-Leadership Theory.** Since the 1970s, contextual factors have played a role in leadership research; however, the conceptualization of these factors has not been well developed. It has been argued (that "we need a taxonomy of the situation, or at least dimensions on which the situations vary. Fiedler is one of the few psychologists to offer a language for describing both context and individual difference" (Sternberg & Vroom, 2002, p. 317). Fiedler (1978) presented a taxonomy (Ayman, 2002; Sternberg & Vroom, 2002) focusing on the leader's situation. Through the level of clarity in the situation, a leader gains control and power. In path-goal theory and subsequently substitutes-for-leadership theory, the focus is on the subordinates' situation.

The early contingency theories focused primarily on leadership in the work group or in a small-group paradigm. Substitutes-for-leadership theory considered leadership in the context of a dynamic organizational and cultural milieu. Based on Podsakoff, Mackenzie, and Bommer (1996), in Jermier and Kerr's (1997) discussion, a leader's behavior typically accounts for less variance in predicting relevant leadership outcomes than do situational factors (i.e., substitutes for leadership). Kerr and Jermier (1978) proposed a taxonomy of 14 situational contingencies that can be divided into three classes: (1) characteristics of subordinates, (2) the nature of the subordinates' tasks, and (3) organizational characteristics.

The key point to remember in this work is that the contingencies were originally conceived as substitutes for, or neutralizers of, a leader's behavior. To further clarify these concepts, Schriesheim (1997) described *substitutes* as factors that were directly related to the employee's outcomes and that replaced the need for leader behavior. *Neutralizers* were those factors that inhibit the leader's behavioral influence on the outcome. The distinction between the two factors is based on the relationship of the situational factor with the leader's behavior. In the substitutes-for-leadership paradigm, the situational factors and the outcome variables are positively related regardless of the leader's behavior. However, neutralizers are correlated with neither the leader's behavior nor the outcome, but they will nullify the effect of the leader's behavior on the outcome.

As Podsakoff and Mackenzie (1997) have argued, research on the substitutes-for-leadership theory supports the notion that leader behavior does not have a universal effect on outcomes. The results of empirical tests of the substitutes-for-leadership theory are mixed, but Podsakoff et al. (1996), through a meta-analysis of 22 studies, found some support for this theory, whereas Dionne, Yammarino, Atwater, and James (2002) found that the approach did not have much empirical support. Dionne et al. argued that the positive findings for the effects of substitutes for leadership on outcomes may be due to common-source ratings bias. Although the support for this model has been questioned, it has arguably contributed to a clearer conceptualization of the contingency variables from subordinates' perspectives as well as contributed to the study of moderators and mediators in leadership research.

## Context in Leadership

We use two group dynamic models to assist in conceptualizing the contextual factors in the study of leadership. The first is the systems approach to groups—namely, the input-process-output (I-P-O) model (Hackman & Morris, 1975), and the second is the model of team effectiveness, which includes the role of context (West, Borrill, & Unsworth, 1998). These models hold a dynamic perspective, which allows for reciprocal effects between inputs and processes and between processes and outputs. For the purposes of our discussion, the leadership process is the focus of interest.

The inputs to the group include cultural context and organizational context (i.e., reward structure, feedback systems, location of team members, communication medium, and time constraints, group composition, and task features).

Outputs or outcomes of the group can be either behavioral (e.g., turnover, performance, organizational citizenship) or attitudinal (e.g., satisfaction, stress) and can occur at the individual leader, subordinate, leader–subordinate dyad, or group levels. Both the input variables and outcomes have an important impact on the leader's characteristics and choice of action to achieve success.

Each of the four input factors may act as moderators, and thereby establish the contingencies between leadership processes and organizational outcomes. For the study of leadership and context we used these models of team effectiveness to stimulate consideration of a wide variety of interpersonal aspects of context variables. To further demonstrate the impact of input factors on leadership, the following section will highlight empirical examples of the role of cultural context, organizational context/climate, group composition, the nature of the task, follower characteristics on leaders' traits, and leaders' behaviors in relation to various outcomes.

**Culture.** Ayman (2004) argued that culture and leadership have a symbiotic relationship, in which one cannot exist without the other. Ayman and Korabik (2010) acknowledge the wide diversity of definitions provided for culture. However, for the operationalization of culture in leadership research, they identify two categories: visible (objective) indices of culture, as reflected by such differences between groups as country boundaries, and invisible (subjective) indices of culture, as reflected by the values and norms that a social group has agreed on over time.

Avolio (2007), Ayman (2004), and Chemers (2000) have offered ideas on how to integrate culture into theories and models of leadership. Two potential roles can be examined for culture in leadership: It can be considered (a) as an antecedent to leadership behavior, where leaders from different cultures may be perceived as acting differently (see Chapter 13), and (b) as a moderating effect of culture on the relationship between leadership (trait or behavior) and outcomes, such as performance or employee engagement.

Culture as a moderator in leadership or a context in leadership has been studied less frequently. However, a few studies have examined the contextual nature of culture in leadership. This can be conducted where the relationship of a particular leadership style in relation to outcomes or a leadership model is tested across countries or cultural values. It can also be studied when the leader and the followers have mixed cultural backgrounds. In this case, examining the variation of the relationship between particular leadership style characteristics and outcomes for various dyad compositions can be explored. The latter condition will be further discussed in the dyad/group composition section.

In the former types of these studies, culture was most often considered as subjective or invisible (cultural values). The three cultural values considered in most studies of leadership are individualism/collectivism, uncertainty avoidance, and power distance (Hofstede, 2001). In order to examine culture as a context (moderator) for leadership and outcome, we can look at a given leadership behavior and its relation to outcomes in various cultures to see if the relation holds. Another option is to examine the impact of culture when the leaders from one culture interact with followers from another. A study in India showed that culture and organizational-specific measures were the best predictor of employees' performance; their predictions were superior to the transformational leadership measure (Palrecha, Spangler, & Yammarino, 2012).

Examining collectivistic values' impact on transformational leadership and outcomes, Walumbwa and Lawler (2003) as well as Jung and Avolio (1999) found that transformational leadership is more effective among those with higher collectivist orientation. Examining collectivism and uncertainty avoidance in the Middle East showed that, while collectivism enhanced the relationship between transformational leadership and job involvement of employees, the presence of uncertainty avoidance reduced the magnitude of the relationship (Sheikh, Newman, & Al Azzeh, 2013).

In another study, teams with higher power distance and collectivistic values showed a stronger relationship between transformational leadership and group potency (Schaubroeck, Lam, & Cha, 2007). Kirkman, Chen, Farh, Chen, and Lowe (2009) also showed that the relationship between transformational leadership and organizational citizenship behavior was positive and stronger for those employees with lower power distance orientation.

Overall, many studies show that collectivism and uncertainty avoidance as cultural values strengthen the relation between transformational leadership and outcomes (Walumbwa & Lawler, 2003; Walumbwa, Lawler, & Avolio, 2007). Conversely, high power distance lowers the relation between transformational leadership and outcomes (Newman & Butler, 2014). In contrast, collectivist cultural values did not affect the relationship between transformational leadership and employee motivation (Wang & Gagné, 2013). Although cultural values have shown to moderate the relationship between leadership behavior and outcome, some studies did not find the expected cultural context effect (Cavazotte, Hartman, & Bahiense, 2014). Understanding and developing a conceptualization or theory as when cultural values are moderators and when they are not would help advance our understanding of the role of culture.

Examining culture from an objective standpoint and using the imposed-etic approach, we looked at cross-cultural studies on transformational and transactional leadership. Comparing Taiwanese and New Zealander leaders' style and employee satisfaction, Singer and Singer (1990) found that New Zealanders described their leaders as more transformational than transactional; whereas Taiwanese described their leaders as equal, but were more satisfied with transactional leaders than the New Zealanders. However, several studies in China showed that the relation between transformational leadership and employee performance was validated (Miao, Newman, & Lamb, 2012; Sun Xu, Shang, 2014: Tse & Chiu, 2012). Similar validations were presented for transformational leadership and outcomes such as employee organizational citizenship behavior (Cho & Dansereau, 2010). A meta-analysis on leader–member exchange and culture across 23 countries validated the LMX model and providing evidence for the universality of this leadership model (Rockstuhl, Dulebohn, Ang, & Shore, 2012).

In summary, using a common measure across cultures seems to show overall support for transformational and leader–member exchange models and their relation to outcomes. However, there is also evidence of the diversity of definitions, manifestations, and mediation variables that make these behaviors unique in various cultural settings.

**Organization.** Organizational context surrounds the work team and its leader. Organizational climate is reflective of organizational context, which includes normative social interactions and policies and procedures. Organizational climate can be defined objectively, such as a tall and flat hierarchy of the organization, its size, and the sector or industry. It can also be defined subjectively through shared beliefs and norms of interactions (Dennison, 1996). Porter and McLaughlin's (2006) review of leadership articles between 1990 and 2005 showed that the empirical studies on organizational context and leadership are limited, while many affirm its importance in the study of leadership effectiveness. In this section we will further highlight some empirical findings and update this information.

The impact of organizational norms on leadership has been established across a number of studies. For example, Shartle (1951) illustrated the importance of workplace norms on how leaders behave in demonstrating that the best predictor of a leader's behavior in organizations is the behavior of his or her boss, not the leader's personality. Across meta-analyses on transformational and transactional leadership (Judge & Piccolo, 2004; Lowe et al., 1996) there has been shown to be no effect associated with a leader's position in the hierarchy on his or her respective leadership styles or effectiveness. However, Chun, Yammarino, Dionne, Sosik, and Moon (2009) demonstrated that the closer the distance between the leader and the follower and the higher the frequency of interaction, the higher the level of commitment of the follower toward his or her supervisor.

On the other hand, Lowe et al. (1996) did find that transformational leader behavior is more effective in public sector organizations than in the private sector. Judge and Piccolo (2004) further explained that comparing across the four settings of business, college, military, and public sector, in business organizations, contingent reward was most effective compared to transformational leadership. This shows that although level in the organization did not affect the leader's behaviors, type of organization did.

Within the West et al. (1998) team effectiveness model, organizational contextual variables included, among others, physical conditions and affective reactions both to work groups and to the organization as a whole. However, in leadership research, only a few of these variables have been considered as moderators. To elaborate on the effect of space and physical conditions, earlier research on communication patterns (Leavitt, 1951) and seating arrangements (Howells & Becker, 1962) showed that these situational factors influenced leader identification and emergence. The main rationale behind such findings may be that greater eye contact gives more control and that, therefore, they are more likely to be identified as the leaders (Chemers, 1997; Shaw, 1981).

Contemporary leaders may not always engage in face-to-face interaction if work is conducted via computer-mediated environments. Along with the expansion of the virtual workplace, e-leadership gained greater attention (Antonakis & Atwater, 2002). Early research on e-leadership showed how technological structures or processes can moderate leadership effects on group process and outcomes (Avolio & Kahai, 2003).

More recently, therefore, researchers are viewing the medium of communication as an organizational contextual factor relevant to e-leadership. For example, Puranova and Bono (2009) demonstrated that although leaders behaving transformationally were valuable in both face-to-face and computer-mediated conditions, the impact was stronger in virtual teams. In contrast, Hambley, O'Neill, and Kline (2007) revealed no differences across transformational and transactional leadership styles, but face-to-face teams were more constructive in their feedback and video-conference teams were more cohesive than chat teams. Furthermore, Hoyt and Blascovich (2003) demonstrated that face-to-face conditions increased team members' satisfaction with a leader who was perceived as behaving in either transformational or transactional ways. Similarly, Golden and Veiga (2008) showed that employees who reported high-quality LMX also reported higher commitment and satisfaction even if they were working virtually. However, those with low LMX had significantly lower satisfaction and commitment the more extensively they worked virtually. Furthermore, Gajendran and Joshi (2012) demonstrated that for teams who are geographically distributed, high LMX will be positively related to employee involvement in decision making and innovation when there is high frequency of communication. Therefore, distance and virtual work settings demand high-quality relationships and frequent transformational leadership behaviors.

**Group Composition.** The input variable of group composition (West et al., 1998) covers research that examines both the size of the work group and the effects of the heterogeneity of group membership on group and individual outcomes. In today's diverse workforce, studies examining the role of group composition on leadership are of great value. Group composition can be examined at a group level or a dyadic level. In this section we are focused on the size of the group and the gender composition.

A small number of studies showed the effect of group size and composition on the relationship between leadership and outcomes. For example, to demonstrate the effect of organization or work group size on leadership and outcomes, Ling, Simsek, Lubatkin, and Veiga (2008) found that the impact of transformational leadership on the objective performance of the organization was higher in smaller organizations than in larger ones. On the other hand, in a study in Korea, researchers found that transformational leadership and various outcomes, such as team cohesion and interteam collaboration, were higher for those in larger teams (Cha, Kim, Lee, & Bachrach, 2015). Additionally, in a meta-analysis across eight studies, Mullen, Hu, and Salas (1989) reported the larger teams required more structuring behavior from the leader, which led to higher employee job satisfaction. Also studying research and development workers, Gumusluoglu, Karakitapoğlu-Aygün, and Hirst (2013) demonstrated that the span of control of the leader moderated the relationship between transformational leadership and supervisory commitment but not organizational commitment. Overall, this context variable has not been highly studied and has had varying effects, depending on the leadership behavior.

Gender composition of the group could affect group atmosphere and moderate the impact of a leader's behavior and the outcome. To date, the number of studies examining the role of group diversity and leadership is limited. Seong and Hong (2013) showed that it is group norms, not transformational leadership, that assisted a gender-diverse team to be more committed. It is important to acknowledge that the results also showed that cooperative group norms and perceptions of the leader's transformational leadership were positively correlated.

At a dyadic level, a few studies have examined gender composition as a moderator or context for leadership behaviors and outcomes. In their early meta-analysis, Eagly, Makhijani, and Klonsky (1992) highlighted that the gender of the follower as well as the workplace gender orientation has an impact on the devaluating of women's leadership behavior. In their discussion they particularly identified sports industry and manufacturing as highly male-dominated stereotyping work settings. The role of the subordinates' gender as a contextual factor on the relationship between the gender of the leader, the leadership behavior, and effectiveness was less clear in their discussion.

Subsequent studies may shed light on this finding. Ayman, Korabik, and Morris (2009) demonstrated that dyad gender composition moderated the relationship between leaders' transformational leadership and their leadership performance. Male subordinates devalued female transformational leaders as compared with male transformational leaders. Similarly, Fleener, Ayman, and Elington (2011) found that when employees' goals were difficult, male subordinates of women charismatic leaders were less successful than were other subordinates. Examining the moderating effect of dyad gender composition for LMX and satisfaction with supervision, Ayman, Rinchiuso, and Korabik (2004) found that men with female subordinates who had moderate leader–member exchange (LMX) relationships had the least-satisfied subordinates compared to all other dyads. Additionally, when the relationship is good and the dyads are dissimilar, the satisfaction is highest. These findings show that the gender dyad of leaders and followers can moderate the effect of the leadership behavior on outcomes. This evidence further substantiates the need for using gender composition of dyads and teams as a context rather than only examining the main effect of the leader's gender on perceived leader behavior and outcome.

**Nature of the Task.** The nature of the group task holds implications for the process and outcome of the work completed. The nature of a task may be assessed in many ways (for more information on task typologies, refer to Hackman, 1968; McGrath, 1984). For example, tasks may vary in type, difficulty, complexity, degree of dependence on communication for task completion (Hollingshead & McGrath, 1995), or even gender orientation (Wentworth & Anderson, 1984).

The uncertainty and complexity of the task and its effect on leadership outcome relation was examined in various contingency models from the leaders' and the subordinates' perspectives (e.g., contingency model of leadership effectiveness, path-goal theory). In addition, the complexity and certainty of the organization's task environment as perceived by top management moderated the impact of the CEO's charismatic leadership on financial outcomes (Waldman, Ramirez, House, & Puranam, 2001). Thus, we can see that regardless of how we define leadership, the nature of the goal or task at hand can affect the success of that leader/follower. Keller (2006) found that managers perceived as transformational were more effective in research projects, but those rated higher on structuring behavior were more effective in development projects.

**Followers' Characteristics.** The characteristics of the follower have been repeatedly treated as a contextual factor in leadership research in path-goal theory and implicit leadership theory. More recently, the follower's core self-evaluation and engagement have been shown to moderate the relationship between transformational leadership and outcomes. Roger and Ayman (2001) showed that sales managers who were perceived as transformational had higher employee performance when the employee reported low job involvement. That is, employees who were highly job involved did not rely on their manager's transformational leadership to perform. Then again, Zhu, Avolio, and Walumbwa (2009) found that transformational leadership has a stronger positive relation with employee work engagement when the follower had positive characteristics. Furthermore, Kim, Liden, Kim, and Lee (2015) found that transformational leadership further enhanced the relation between core self-evaluation and employee outcomes. The role of follower characteristic on transformational leadership and outcome needs further examination to see if follower characteristic can be a substitute for transformational leadership or if it behaves like an enhancer.

**Organization and Group Outcomes.** Organization and group outcomes seem to be a moderator of leader and outcome. As previously mentioned, the West et al. (1998) model of team effectiveness recognizes that outcomes can be either attitudinal (e.g., satisfaction) or behavioral (e.g., turnover) and can occur at leader, individual subordinate, or group levels.

Judge and Piccolo's (2004) meta-analysis of transformational leadership and contingent reward demonstrated that criteria for outcomes can be a moderator between leader behavior and outcomes. More specifically, transformational leadership was not as strongly related to leader job performance and contingent reward was not as strongly related to group or organizational performance. Additionally, Judge, Bono, Ilies, and Gerhardt (2002) showed that examining emergence of a leader instead of the leader's effectiveness related to different traits.

Additionally, Table 6.1 shows that most classical contingency models tend to use more subjective measures of outcomes, such as satisfaction, commitment, and stress (e.g., path-goal theory, normative model). The contingency model of leadership effectiveness, however, tends to use more objective measures, such as meeting goals.

Overall, the team effectiveness model provides a theoretical group perspective to the potential substitutes or enhancers for leadership, in addition to stimulating researchers to consider other contingencies, such as cultural context. Additionally, researchers need to focus on the contextual factors that are most relevant today, such as the medium of communication, the effects of leadership behavior across hierarchical levels (e.g., Kane & Tremble, 2000), and the effects of distal (indirect) and proximal (direct) leadership (e.g., Avolio, Zhu, Koh, & Puja, 2004).

## Intrapersonal Aspect

At the intrapersonal level, relevant contingencies include different leader characteristics that may affect one another and thereby influence the person's ability to lead. For example, do personality traits, such as self-monitoring, impact leadership effectiveness the same way for men as they do for women? (See Chapter 2 for more information.)

In this section we briefly highlight the possibility of the interaction of personality traits and other leader characteristics on leadership effectiveness. Different aspects of a person may interact with each other and diminish a leader's strength or exacerbate a weakness. For example, women generally score lower than men on scales of self-monitoring, a trait shown to be associated with leadership (Day, Schleicher, Unckless, & Hiller, 2002). From this logic one could surmise that women are lacking a key personality trait that could help them be more effective leaders. However, one study (Becker, Ayman, & Korabik, 2002) demonstrated that women with high self-monitoring scores in male-dominated work settings have less agreement with their subordinates about their behavior than the men. This was almost reversed for men in a more gender-neutral setting. This may mean that the impact of self-monitoring on leadership is more complex than reflected in the meta-analysis, and further investigation will be helpful.

Ayman and Chemers (1991) examined the role of self-monitoring and the concept of leader-match. They demonstrated that leaders who were low self-monitors and in-match performed better than the high self-monitors who were also in-match. However, high self-monitor leaders who were out-of-match recognized their situation and managed their responses. For example, a high self-monitor and task-oriented leader with moderate situational control performed better than his or her low self-monitor counterpart. That is, the task-oriented leader who is a high self-monitor, when out of match will be more attentive to situational cues and manage his or her responses so as to be more appropriate. More research exploring the role of self-monitoring in moderating the effect of personality and leader behavior would be informative.

Additionally, the interplay of sociodemographic gender and gender role needs more exploration. The little research available shows that it is the gender role orientation of the leader that matters, not their gender (Korabik & Ayman 2007), when predicting the relationship between transformational leadership and outcomes such as satisfaction and stress. This line of research can also help us reduce our stereotype of women and men and focus on the underlying values individuals hold (Ayman & Korabik, 2010; Korabik & Ayman, 2007).

## Summary and Conclusion

To address the contingency and contextual approaches to leadership, this chapter has two main sections. The first part consists of a review of classical contingency models. The second part offers a conceptualization of the type of variables used to test context in leadership research. In our review of classic contingency theories of leadership, we classified the theories into two types: (a) those based on the relationship between the leader's traits and outcomes (i.e., contingency model of leadership effectiveness and cognitive resource theory) and (b) those based on the relationship between the leader's behavior and outcomes (i.e., the normative decision-making model, situational leadership theory, and path-goal theory).

In most of the earlier research, the context was generally conceptualized in terms of aspects of the situation. In this chapter, we recommended considering two different types of context/contingencies: interpersonal (i.e., an interaction at the dyad or group level) and intrapersonal (i.e., an interaction of various aspects of the leader's traits, socio-demographics, and values). For the interpersonal aspects of context/contingencies, we recommended considering the West et al. (1998) model of team effectiveness, advocating consideration of group inputs and group outcomes as potential contextual factors. For intrapersonal contingencies, we proposed such concepts as leaders' self-monitoring, gender, and culture.

The key issue to remember when thinking of contingency approaches to leadership is that the approach is strongly based in a person–situation fit framework. The models in this approach have demonstrated that effective leaders respond to the situation in multiple ways: by changing their behaviors, by being perceived as behaving differently, or by choosing and managing their situation. This position is similar to Sternberg's (1988) definition of intelligent functioning, which refers to the individual's "purposive adaptation to, selection of and shaping of real-world environment relevant to one's life and abilities" (p. 65).

Finding an optimal match is what Chemers (1997) referred to as *mettle*. As noted by Chemers, "Mettle captures the sense of a confident and optimistic leader whose perceptions, thoughts and mood provide a reservoir of enthusiasm and energy for meeting the challenges presented by the leadership task" (p. 166). This state is somewhat similar to Csikszentmihalyi's (1990) concept of "flow," referring to when an individual's skill and knowledge are neither more nor less than the situation needs. In this state, leaders manifest the height of their potential, expressing optimism and feeling efficacious (Chemers, 2002). Fiedler (1978) referred to this state as a leader being in-match. When the situation is congenial to the leader's characteristics, the leader functions optimally and with ease.

At first glance, some may perceive a contradiction in the concept of leaders being stable and consistent as well as being flexible to meet situational needs. In essence, however, there is no difference between the two. In either case, the leader's persona does not change. For example, a high self-monitoring leader does not become a low self-monitor; nor does a high LPC leader become a low LPC leader. Instead, leaders engage in behaviors and strategies that bring them closer to being in-match with the situation and experiencing flow or mettle.

So, for example, a low LPC leader in a moderate control situation (out-of-match) may realize that she or he needs to include other team members in the decision-making process, as recommended by Vroom's decision-making tree. The leader may then use a nominal group technique to have a structured method of managing the situation. Another alternative is to use a consultative style, some of the control over the outcome, which is demanded by the leader's personality trait. Thus, a simple matter of accepting drop-ins versus meeting by appointment only may seem to be a small issue, but it may have implications in the situational match of a leader. Therefore, when we talk about flexibility, it is in reference to behaviors that manage the situation, not to changing one's traits or personality.

In many of the previous works, the ability to adjust and be flexible is recognized as an important competency for a leader (e.g., Lord et al., 1986). Flexibility can be considered an intrapersonal contingency and is also present in social/emotional intelligence (Van Rooy & Viswesvaran, 2004) and cultural intelligence (Triandis, 2006). Leaders facing a diverse workforce frequently find themselves in situations and contexts that need to be managed by adjusting their behaviors.

Other conceptualizations of context presented in this chapter included context as an antecedent instead of a moderator. In the West et al. (1998) model, contextual variables are a part of the inputs to group processes. However, we provided several examples in this chapter showing how these input variables can act as moderator variables. Thus, in leadership research the input variables have a place in being considered as a moderator as well.

Additionally, we discussed the nature of the measurement of context as objective (visible) or subjective (invisible). In their purest definition, context or contingencies, from a research design perspective, are mostly moderators rather than predictors. But a given variable can be considered as both a context as well as a predictor. The majority of studies that include context have measured it through the perception of the leader or the subordinates. When objective context has been used, invariably they act as a proxy for subjective interpretations. For example, *country* can be further expanded on by the values people have rather than simply the geographical location, and *gender* can be explained by the roles people adopt rather than mere biological differences.

## Future Research

With such strong and consistent evidence that situation, context, and contingencies matter in understanding and studying leadership, is there a place for direct impact of a leader's traits and behavior on organizational and personal outcomes related to leaders and followers? In the future, scholars may consider this issue when exploring new paradigms of leadership behaviors, such as authenticity or servant leadership. In studying traits of the leader, researchers may want to consider the situational factors when examining the relationship between traits and outcomes to enhance the meaning of these findings.

Additionally, future research may explore the impact of data source and the nature of context. That is, when assessing context it could be beneficial to examine both objective and subjective operationalization or to triangulate the information by collected data from multiple perspectives.

## Implication for Practice

Reflecting back to our opening anecdote, Chris McAllister's experience could be explained by much of the evidence provided by research throughout this chapter. For example, working with R&D employees requires different leadership behaviors than with manufacturing employees (Keller, 2006). Also, being a man or a woman leading different-gender employees can have an impact on the transferability of those leadership behaviors (Fleener et al., 2001).

Practitioners use leadership knowledge either for training and development or for evaluation processes in selection and performance reviews. To consider the situation, job analysis prior to identification of competencies and abilities may clarify the nature of the job, the scope of the position, and the context of the work. Thus, this procedure may allow for a more accurate prioritization of competencies, skills, and abilities (Dierdorff, Rubin, & Morgeson, 2009). Practitioners assessing leaders' performance may need to be mindful of other contingencies, such as gender or ethnicity. Results of some studies demonstrated that competencies considered for the manager's performance vary based on the gender of the leader (Frame, Roberto, Schwab, & Harris, 2010; Ostroff, Atwater, & Feinberg, 2004).

Overall, the contingency approach to leadership has alluded to the fact that leaders consciously, or unconsciously, try to reach their optimal level of performance by being aware of their situation and responding accordingly. Therefore, leadership training programs such as Leader Match (Fiedler & Chemers, 1984) and situational leadership (Hersey & Blanchard, 1982) facilitate leaders to become more sensitive, responsive, and flexible. Additionally, the practice of 360-degree feedback, as a means to develop leaders, gives leaders a chance to see themselves through the eyes of others (i.e., in an interpersonal context). Training outcomes can be attained either by the behavior adjustment of the leader, as described by the subordinates, or through the leader's description of how he or she managed the situation.

To conclude, contingencies, context, and the situation are important factors to consider when we select, train, and develop leaders. In our leadership theories, we need to integrate and conceptualize these factors more effectively. A combination of skills and competencies—such as sensitivity, responsiveness, and flexibility—may help a leader reach mettle (Chemers, 2002). These competencies can be manifested in various ways through particular traits, skills, or behaviors depending on the person, the method of assessment, and the leadership situation. Therefore, contingencies in leadership cannot be ignored, as they are inevitably connected to fully understanding leadership processes.

## Discussion Questions

1. Knowing the role of contingencies and context, what should be considered when selecting leaders? Use both trait and behavioral approaches in your discussion.
2. How should leadership studies be designed so as to be attentive to contingencies? What are the options and strategies?

3. Consider a leader of your choice. Describe how her or his personality and behaviors in various situations could lead to success or failure.

## Recommended Readings

- Hannah, S. T., Uhl-Bien, M., Avolio, B. J., & Cavarretta, F. L. (2009). A framework for examining leadership in extreme contexts. *The Leadership Quarterly, 20,* 897–919.
- James, E. H., & Wooten, L. P. (2005). Leadership as (un)usual: How to display competence in times of crisis. *Organizational Dynamics, 34,* 141–152.
- Kaplan, R. E., & Kaiser, R. B. (2003). Developing versatile leadership. *MIT Sloan Management Review, 44*(4), 19–26.
- Sally, D. (2002). Co-leadership: Lessons from republican Rome. *California Management Review, 42*(4), 84–99.
- Snowden, D., & Boone, M. (2007). A leader's framework for decision making. *Harvard Business Review, 85*(11), 68–76.

## Recommended Case Studies

- **Case:** Mitchell, J., & Konrad, A. (2011). Christina Gold leading change at Western Union. Richard Ivey School of Business Case 9B06M007.
- **Case:** Schwartz, M. S., & Copp, H. (2011). Difficult hiring decision at Central Bank. Richard Ivey School of Business Case 9B06C004.

## Recommended Videos

- McChrystal, S. (2011). Stanley McChrystal: Listen, learn . . . then lead. https://www.ted.com/talks/stanley_mcchrystal?language=en
- Obeing, E. (2012). Smart failure for a fast-changing world. https://www.ted.com/talks/eddie_obeng_smart_failure_for_a_fast_changing_world?language=en

## References

Antonakis, J., & Atwater, L. (2002). Leader distance: A review and a proposed theory. *The Leadership Quarterly, 13,* 673–704.

Antonakis, J., Avolio, B. J., & Sivasubramaniam, N. (2003). Context and leadership: An examination of the nine factor full range leadership theory using the Multifactor Leadership Questionnaire. *The Leadership Quarterly, 14,* 261–295.

Avolio, B. J. (2007). Promoting more integrative strategies for leadership theory building. *American Psychologist, 62,* 25–33.

Avolio, B. J., & Kahai, S. (2003). Effects of leadership style, anonymity, and rewards on creativity-relevant processes and outcomes in an electronic meeting system context. *The Leadership Quarterly, 14*(4–5), 499–524.

Avolio, B. J., Zhu, W., Koh, W., & Puja, B. (2004). Transformational leadership and organizational commitment: Mediating role of psychological empowerment and moderating role of structural distance. *Journal of Organizational Behavior, 25,* 951–968.

Ayman, R. (1993). Leadership perception: The role of gender and culture. In M. M. Chemers & R. Ayman (Eds.), *Leadership theory and research: Perspectives and directions* (pp. 137–166). New York, NY: Academic Press.

Ayman, R. (2002). Contingency model of leadership effectiveness. In L. L. Neider & C. A. Schriesheim (Eds.), *Leadership* (pp. 197–228). Greenwich, CT: Information Age.

Ayman, R. (2004). Culture and leadership. In C. Spielberger (Ed.), *Encyclopedia of applied psychology* (Vol. 2, pp. 507–519). San Diego, CA: Elsevier.

Ayman, R., & Chemers, M. M. (1991). The effects of leadership match on subordinate satisfaction in Mexican organizations: Some moderating influences of self-monitoring. *Applied Psychology: An International Review, 44,* 299–314.

Ayman, R., Chemers, M. M., & Fiedler, F. (1995). The contingency model of leadership effectiveness and its levels of analysis. *The Leadership Quarterly, 6,* 147–167.

Ayman, R., Chemers, M. M., & Fiedler, F. (1998). The contingency model of leadership effectiveness and its levels of analysis. In F. Yammarino & F. Dansereau (Eds.), *Leadership: The multi-level approaches* (pp. 73–96). New York, NY: JAI Press.

Ayman, R., & Korabik, K. (2010). Leadership: Why gender and culture matter. *American Psychologist, 65,* 157–170.

Ayman, R., Korabik, K., & Morris, S. (2009). Is transformational leadership always perceived as effective? Male subordinates' devaluation of female transformational leaders. *Journal of Applied Social Psychology, 39,* 852–879.

Ayman, R., Rinchiuso, M., & Korabik, K. (2004, August). *Organizational commitment and job satisfaction in relation to LMX and dyad gender composition.* Paper presented at the International Congress of Psychology, Beijing, China.

Ayman, R., & Romano, R. (1998). Measures and assessments for the contingency model of leadership. In F. Yammarino & F. Dansereau (Eds.), *Leadership: The multi-level approaches* (pp. 97–114). New York, NY: JAI Press.

Becker, J., Ayman, R., & Korabik, K. (2002). Discrepancies in self/subordinates' perceptions of leadership behavior: Leader's gender, organizational context, and leader's self-monitoring. *Group & Organizational Management, 27,* 226–244.

Burke, M. J., & Day, R. R. (1986). A cumulative study of the effectiveness of managerial training. *Journal of Applied Psychology, 71,* 242–245.

Case, B. (1987). Leadership behavior in sport: A field test of the situation leadership theory. *International Journal of Sport Psychology, 18,* 256–268.

Cavazotte, F., Hartman, N. S., & Bahiense, E. 2014. Charismatic Leadership, Citizenship Behaviors, and Power Distance Orientation. *Cross-Cultural Research, 48*(1): 3–31.

Cha, J., Kim, Y., Lee, J., & Bachrach, D. G. (2015). Transformational leadership and inter-team collaboration: Exploring the mediating role of teamwork quality and moderating role of team size. *Group and Organizational Management, 40*(6), 715–743.

Chemers, M. M. (1997). *An integrative theory of leadership.* Mahwah, NJ: Lawrence Erlbaum.

Chemers, M. M. (2000). Leadership research and theory: A functional integration. *Group Dynamics: Theory, Research, and Practice, 4,* 27–43.

Chemers, M. M. (2002). Efficacy and effectiveness: Integrating models of leadership and intelligence. In R. E. Riggio, S. E. Murphy, & F. J. Pirossolo (Eds.), *Multiple intelligences and leadership* (pp. 139–160). Mahwah, NJ: Lawrence Erlbaum.

Chemers, M. M., & Ayman, R. (1985). Leadership orientation as a moderator of the relationship between performance and satisfaction of Mexican managers. *Personality and Social Psychology Bulletin, 11,* 359–367.

Chemers, M. M., Goza, B., & Plumer, S. I. (1978, August). *Leadership style and communication process.* Paper presented at the annual meeting of the American Psychological Association, Toronto, ON, Canada.

Chemers, M. M., Hays, R., Rhodewalt, F., & Wysocki, J. (1985). A person-environment analysis of job stress: A contingency model explanation. *Journal of Personality and Social Psychology, 49,* 628–635.

Cho, J. & Dansereau, F. 2010. Are transformational leaders fair? A multi-level study of transformational leadership, justice perceptions, and organizational citizenship behaviors. *The Leadership Quarterly, 21*(3): 409–421.

Chun, J. U., Yammarino, F. J., Dionne, S. D., Sosik, J. J., & Moon, H. K. (2009). Leadership across hierarchical levels: Multiple levels of management and multiple levels of analysis. *The Leadership Quarterly, 20*(5), 686–707.

Csikszentmihalyi, M. (1990). *Flow: The psychology of optimal experience.* New York, NY: Harper Perennial.

Dansereau, F., Graen, G. B., & Haga, W. (1975). A vertical dyad linkage approach to leadership in formal organizations: A longitudinal investigation of the managerial role-making process. *Organizational Behavior and Human Performance, 13,* 46–78.

Dansereau, F., & Yammarino, F. J. (Eds.). (1998a). *Leadership: The multiple-level approaches—Classical and new wave.* Stamford, CT: JAI Press.

Dansereau, F., & Yammarino, F. J. (Eds.). (1998b). *Leadership: The multiple-level approaches—Contemporary and alternative.* Stamford, CT: JAI Press.

Day, D. V., & Lord, R. G. (1988). Executive leadership and organizational performance: Suggestions for a new theory and methodology. *Journal of Management, 14,* 453–464.

Day, D. V., Shleicher, D. J., Unckless, A. L., & Hiller, N. J. (2002). Self-monitoring personality at work: A meta-analytic investigation of construct validity. *Journal of Applied Psychology, 87*(2), 390–401.

Dennison, D. R. (1996). What is the difference between organizational culture and organizational climate? A native's point of view on a decade of paradigm wars. *Academy of Management Review, 21,* 619–654.

Dierdorff, E. C., Rubin, R. S., & Morgeson, F. P. (2009). The milieu of managerial work: An integrative framework linking work context to role requirements. *Journal of Applied Psychology, 94,* 972–988.

Dionne, S. D., Yammarino, F. J., Atwater, L. E., & James, L. R. (2002). Neutralizing substitutes for leadership theory: Leadership effects and commonsource bias. *Journal of Applied Psychology, 87,* 454–464.

Eagly, A. H., & Carli, L. L. (2007). *Through the labyrinth: The truth about how women become leaders.* Boston, MA: Harvard Business School Press.

Eagly, A. H., Johannesen-Schmidt, M. C., & van Engen, M. L. (2003). Transformational, transactional, and laissez-faire leadership styles: A meta-analysis comparing women and men. *Psychological Bulletin, 129,* 569–591.

Eagly, A. H., & Karau, S. J. (1991). Gender and the emergence of leader: A meta-analysis. *Journal of Personality and Social Psychology, 60,* 685–710.

Eagly, A. H., Karau, S. J., & Makhijani, M. G. (1995). Gender and leader effectiveness: A meta-analysis. *Psychological Bulletin, 117,* 125–145.

Eagly, A. H., Makhijani, M. G., & Klonsky, B. G. (1992). Gender and the evaluation of leaders: A meta-analysis. *Psychological Bulletin, 111*(1), 3–22.

Evans, M. G. (1996). R. J. House's "a path-goal theory of leader effectiveness." *The Leadership Quarterly, 7,* 305–309.

Fernandez, C. F., & Vecchio, R. P. (1997). Situational leadership theory revisited: A test of an across jobs perspective. *The Leadership Quarterly, 8,* 67–84.

Fiedler, F. E. (1964). A contingency model of leadership effectiveness. In L. Berkowitz (Ed.), *Advances in experimental social psychology* (Vol. 1, pp. 149–190). New York, NY: Academic Press.

Fiedler, F. E. (1978). The contingency model and the dynamics of the leadership process. In L. Berkowitz (Ed.), *Advances in experimental social psychology* (Vol. 11, pp. 59–112). New York, NY: Academic Press.

Fiedler, F. E. (1992). Life in a pretzel-shaped universe. In A. Bedeian (Ed.), *Management laureates: A collection of autobiographical essays* (Vol. 1, pp. 301–334). Greenwich, CT: JAI Press.

Fiedler, F. E. (1993). The leadership situation and the black box in contingency theories. In M. Chemers & R. Ayman (Eds.), *Leadership theory and research: Perspectives and directions* (pp. 2–28). New York, NY: Academic Press.

Fiedler, F. E. (1995). Cognitive resource and leadership performance. *Applied Psychology: An International Review, 44,* 5–28.

Fiedler, F. E. (2002). The curious role of cognitive resources in leadership. In R. Riggio, S. Murphy, & F. Pirozzolo (Eds.), *Multiple intelligences and leadership* (pp. 91–104). Mahwah, NJ: Lawrence Erlbaum.

Fiedler, F. E., & Chemers, M. M. (1984). *Improving leadership effectiveness: The leader match concept* (2nd ed.). New York, NY: John Wiley.

Fiedler, F. E., Chemers, M. M., & Mahar, L. 1976. Improving leadership effectiveness: The leader match concept: John Wiley & Sons.

Fiedler F. E., & Garcia, J. E. (1987). *New approaches to effective leadership: Cognitive resources and organizational performance.* New York, NY: John Wiley.

Fisher, B. M., & Edwards, J. E. (1988). Consideration and initiating structure and their relationships with leader effectiveness: A meta-analysis. *Academy of Management Best Paper,* 201–205.

Fleener, B., Ayman, R., & Elington, K. (2011, April). *A multi-level, multi-sources study of Charismatic leadership, gender, and performance.* Presented at Society of Industrial and Organizational Psychology, Chicago, IL.

Frame, M. C., Roberto, K. J., Schwab, A. E., & Harris, C. T. (2010). What is important on the job? Differences across gender, perspective, and job level. *Journal of Applied Social Psychology, 40,* 36–56.

French, J. R., & Raven, B. (1959). The basis of social power. In D. Cartwright (Ed.), *Studies in social power* (pp. 150–167). Ann Arbor: Institute for Social Research, University of Michigan.

Gajendran, R. S., & Joshi, A. (2012). Innovation in globally distributed teams: The role of LMX, communication frequency, and member influence on team decisions. *Journal of Applied Psychology, 97*(6), 1252–1261.

Golden, T. D., & Veiga, J. F. (2008). The impact of superior–subordinate relationships on the commitment, job satisfaction, and performance of virtual workers. *The Leadership Quarterly, 19*(1), 77–88.

Graen, G. B., & Uhl-Bien, M. (1995). Relationship based approach to leadership: Development of leader-member exchange (LMX) theory of leadership over 25 years: Applying a multi-level multi-domain perspective. *The Leadership Quarterly, 6,* 219–247.

Gumusluoglu, L., Karakitapoğlu-Aygün, Z., & Hirst, G. (2013). Transformational leadership and R&D workers' multiple commitments: Do justice and span of control matter? *Journal of Business Research, 66*(11), 2269–2278.

Hackman, J. R. (1968). Effects of task characteristics on group products. *Journal of Experimental Social Psychology, 4,* 162–187.

Hackman, J. R., & Morris, C. G. (1975). Group task, group interaction process, and group performance effectiveness: A review and proposed integration. In L. Berkowitz (Ed.), *Advances in experimental social psychology* (Vol. 8). New York, NY: Academic Press.

Hambley, L. A., O'Neill, T. A., & Kline, T. J. B. (2007). Virtual team leadership: The effects of leadership style and communication medium on team interaction styles and outcomes. *Organizational Behavior and Human Decision Processes, 103*(1), 1–20.

Hanges, P. J., Lord, R. G., & Dickson, M. W. (2000). An information-processing perspective on leadership and culture: A case for connectionist architecture. *Applied Psychology: An International Review, 49,* 133–161.

Hersey, P., & Blanchard, K. (1969). Life cycle theory of leadership. *Training and Development Journal, 23,* 26–34.

Hersey, P., & Blanchard, K. (1982). *Management of organizational behavior* (4th ed.). Englewood Cliffs, NJ: Prentice Hall.

Hofstede, G. (2001). *Culture's consequences: Comparing values, behaviors, institutions, and organizations across nations* (2nd ed.). Thousand Oaks, CA: Sage.

Hogan, R., Curphy, G. J., & Hogan, J. (1994). What we know about leadership: Effectiveness and personality. *American Psychologist, 49,* 493–504.

Hollingshead, A. B., & McGrath, J. E. (1995). Computer-assisted groups: A critical review of the empirical research. In R. A. Guzzo, E. Salas, & Associates (Eds.), *Team effectiveness and decision-making in organizations* (pp. 46–78). San Francisco, CA: Jossey-Bass.

House, R. J. (1971). A path-goal theory of leadership effectiveness. *Administrative Quarterly, 16,* 312–338.

House, R. J. (1996). Path-goal theory of leadership: Lessons, legacy, and a reformulated theory. *The Leadership Quarterly, 7,* 323–352.

House, R. J., & Mitchell, T. R. (1974). Path-goal theory of leadership. *Journal of Contemporary Business, 9,* 81–97.

Howells, L. T., & Becker, S. W. (1962). Seating arrangement and leadership emergence. *Journal of Abnormal and Social Psychology, 64,* 148–150.

Hoyt, C. L., & Blascovich, J. (2003). Transformational and transactional leadership in virtual and physical environments. *Small Group Research, 34,* 678–715.

Jermier, J. M., & Kerr, S. (1997). "Substitutes for leadership: Their meaning and measurement"—Contextual recollections and current observations. *The Leadership Quarterly, 8,* 95–102.

Johns, G. (2006). The essential impact of context on organizational behavior. *Academy of Management Review, 31,* 386–408.

Judge, T. A., Bono, J. E., Ilies, R., & Gerhardt, M. W. (2002). Personality and leadership: A qualitative and quantitative review. *Journal of Applied Psychology, 87*, 765–780.

Judge, T. A., Colbert, A. E., & Ilies, R. (2004). Intelligence and leadership: A quantitative review and test of theoretical propositions. *Journal of Applied Psychology, 89*, 542–552.

Judge, T. A., & Piccolo, R. F. (2004). Transformational and transactional leadership: A meta-analytic test of their relative validity. *Journal of Applied Psychology, 89*, 755–768.

Jung, D. I., & Avolio, B. J. (1999). Leadership style and followers' cultural orientation on performance in group and individual task conditions. *Academy of Management Journal, 42*, 208–218.

Kane, T. D., & Tremble, T. R. (2000). Transformational leadership effects at different levels of the Army. *Military Psychology, 12*, 137–160.

Keller, R. T. (2006). Transformational leadership, initiating structure, and substitutes for leadership: A longitudinal study of research and development project team performance. *Journal of Applied Psychology, 91*(1), 202–210.

Kerr, S., & Jermier, J. M. (1978). Substitutes for leadership: Their meaning and measurement. *Organizational Behavior and Human Performance, 22*, 375–403.

Kim, T., Liden, R. C., Kim, S., & Lee, D. (2015). The interplay between follower core self-evaluation and transformational leadership: Effects on employee outcomes. *Journal of Business and Psychology, 30*(2), 345–355.

Kirkman, B. L., Chen, G., Farh, J. L., Chen, Z. X., & Lowe, K. B. (2009). Individual power distance orientation and follower reaction to transformational leaders: A cross-level, cross-cultural examination. *Academy of Management Journal, 52*(4), 744–764.

Klein, K. J., & Kozlowski, S. W. J. (Eds.). (2000). *Multilevel theory, research, and methods in organizations: Foundations, extensions, and new directions.* San Francisco, CA: Jossey-Bass.

Korabik, K., & Ayman, R. (2007). Gender and leadership in the corporate world: A multiperspective model. In J. C. Lau, B. Lott, J. Rice, & J. Sanchez-Hudes (Eds.), *Transforming leadership: Diverse visions and women's voices* (pp. 106–124). Malden, MA: Blackwell.

Leavitt, H. J. (1951). Some effects of certain communication patterns on group performance. *Journal of Abnormal and Social Psychology, 46*, 38–50.

Liden, R. C., & Antonakis, J. (2009). Considering context in psychological leadership research. *Human Relations, 62*, 1587–1605.

Ling, Y., Simsek, Z., Lubatkin, M. H., & Veiga, J. F. (2008). Impact of transformational CEOs on the performance of small to medium firms: Does organizational context matter? *Journal of Applied Psychology, 93*, 923–934.

Lord, R. G., DeVader, C. L., & Alliger, G. M. (1986). A meta-analysis of the relation between personality traits and leadership: An application of validity generalization procedures. *Journal of Applied Psychology, 71*, 402–410.

Lord, R. G., & Emrich, C. G. (2001). Thinking outside the box by looking inside the box: Extending the cognitive revolution in leadership research. *The Leadership Quarterly, 11*, 551–579.

Lord, R. G., & Maher, K. J. (1991). *Leadership and information processing: Linking perceptions and performance.* Boston, MA: Routledge.

Lowe, K. B., Kroeck, G., & Sivasubramaniam, N. (1996). Effectiveness correlates of transformational and transactional leadership: A meta-analytic review of the MLQ literature. *The Leadership Quarterly, 7*, 385–425.

McGrath, J. E. (1984). A typology of tasks. *Groups, interaction and performance* (pp. 53–66). Englewood Cliffs, NJ: Prentice Hall.

Miao, Q., Newman, A., & Lamb, P. 2012. Transformational leadership and the work outcomes of Chinese migrant workers: The mediating effects of identification with leader. *Leadership, 8*(4): 377–395.

Mitchell, T. R., & James, L. R. (2001). Building better theory: Time and the specification of when things happen. *Academy of Management Review, 26*, 530–547.

Mullen, B., Symons, C., Hu, L., & Salas, E. (1989). Group size, leadership behavior, and subordinate satisfaction. *Journal of General Psychology, 116*(2), 155–170.

Mumford, M. D., Dansereau, F., & Yammarino, F. Y. (2000). Followers, motivations, and levels of analysis: The case of individualized leadership. *The Leadership Quarterly, 11*, 313–340.

Murphy, S. E., Blyth, D., & Fiedler, F. E. (1992). Cognitive resource theory and the utilization of the leader's and group members' technical competence. *The Leadership Quarterly, 3,* 237–255.

Offermann, L. R., Kennedy, J. K., Jr., & Wirtz, P. W. (1994). Implicit leadership theories: Content, structure, and generalizability. *The Leadership Quarterly, 5,* 43–58.

Ostroff, C., Atwater, L. E., & Feinberg, B. J. (2004). Understanding self-other agreement: A look at rater and ratee characteristics, context, and outcomes. *Personnel Psychology, 57,* 333–375.

Palrecha, R., Spangler, W. D., & Yammarino, F. J. (2012). A comparative study of three leadership approaches in India. *The Leadership Quarterly, 23*(1), 146–162.

Peters, L. H., Hartke, D. D., & Pohlmann, J. F. (1985). Fiedler's contingency theory of leadership: An application of the metaanalysis procedures of Schmitt and Hunter. *Psychological Bulletin, 97,* 274–285.

Podsakoff, P. M., & Mackenzie, S. B. (1997). Kerr and Jermier's substitutes for leadership model: Background, empirical assessment, and suggestions for future research. *The Leadership Quarterly, 8,* 117–125.

Podsakoff, P. M., MacKenzie, S. B., & Bommer, W. H. (1996). Meta-analysis of the relationships between Kerr and Jermier's substitutes for leadership and employee job attitudes, role perceptions, and performance. *Journal of Applied Psychology, 81,* 380–399.

Podsakoff, P. M., & Schriesheim, C. A. (1985). Field studies of French and Raven's bases of power: Critique, reanalysis, and suggestions for future research. *Psychological Bulletin, 97,* 387–411.

Polyashuk, Y., Ayman, R., & Roberts, J. L. (2008, April). *Relationship quality: The effect of dyad composition diversity and time.* Poster session presented at the meeting of the Society of Industrial and Organizational Psychology, San Francisco, CA.

Porter, L. W., & McLaughlin, G. B. (2006). Leadership and the organizational context: Like the weather? *The Leadership Quarterly, 17,* 559–576.

Potter, E. H., III, & Fiedler, F. E. (1981). The utilization of staff members' intelligence and experience under high and low stress. *Academy of Management Journal, 24,* 361–376.

Preacher, K. J., Rucker, D. D., & Hayes, A. F. (2007). Addressing moderated mediation hypotheses: Theory, methods, and prescriptions. *Multivariate Behavioral Research, 42,* 185–227.

Puranova, R. K., & Bono, J. E. (2009). Transformational leadership in context: Face to face and virtual teams. *The Leadership Quarterly, 20,* 343, 357.

Rice, W. R. (1981). Leader LPC and follower satisfaction: A review. *Organizational Behavior and Human Performance, 28,* 1–25.

Rice, W. R., Marwick, N. J., Chemers, M. M., & Bentley, J. C. (1982). Task performance and satisfaction: Least preferred coworker (LPC) as a moderator. *Personality and Social Psychology Bulletin, 8,* 534–541.

Rockstuhl, T., Dulebohn, J. H., Ang, S., & Shore, L. M. (2012). Leader-Member Exchange (LMX) and culture: A meta-analysis of correlates of LMX across 23 countries. *Journal of Applied Psychology, 97,* 1097–1130.

Rogers, T. & Ayman, R. (2001, July). The role of transformational leadership in salesperson's motivation and performance. Paper presented at the 7th European Congress of Psychology, London, U.K.

Schaubroeck, J., Lam, S. S., & Cha, S. E. 2007. Embracing transformational leadership: team values and the impact of leader behavior on team performance. *Journal of Applied Psychology, 92*(4): 1020.

Schneider, R. J., & Hough, L. M. (1995). Personality and industrial/organizational psychology. In C. L. Cooper & I. T. Robertson (Eds.), *International review of industrial and organizational psychology* (Vol. 10). New York, NY: John Wiley.

Schriesheim, C. A. (1997). Substitutes-for-leadership theory: Development and basic concepts. *The Leadership Quarterly, 8,* 103–108.

Schriesheim, C. A., Tepper, B. J., & Tetrault, L. A. (1994). Least preferred coworker score, situational control and leadership effectiveness: A meta-analysis of contingency model performance predictions. *Journal of Applied Psychology, 79,* 561–573.

Schriesheim, C. A., & Von Glinow, M. A. (1977). The path-goal theory of leadership: A theoretical and empirical analysis. *Academy of Management Journal, 20,* 398–405.

Seong, J. Y., & Hong, D. (2013). Gender diversity: How can we facilitate its positive effects on teams? *Social Behavior and Personality, 41*(3), 497–508.

Shartle, C. L. (1951). Studies of naval leadership, part I. In H. Guetzkow (Ed.), *Groups, leadership and men: Research in human relations* (pp. 119–133). Pittsburgh, PA: Carnegie Press.

Shaw, M. E. (1981). *Group dynamics: The psychology of small group behavior* (3rd ed.). New York, NY: McGraw-Hill.

Sheikh, A. Z., Newman, A., & Al Azzeh, S. A.-F. 2013. Transformational leadership and job involvement in the Middle East: the moderating role of individually held cultural values. *The International Journal of Human Resource Management, 24*(6): 1077–1095.

Singer, M. S., & Singer, A. E. (1990). Situational constraints on transformational versus transactional leadership behavior, subordinates' leadership preference, and satisfaction. *The Journal of Social Psychology, 130*(3), 385–396.

Staw, B. M., & Ross, J. (1980). Commitment in an experimenting society: A study of the attribution of leadership from administrative scenarios. *Journal of Applied Psychology, 65*(3), 249–260.

Sternberg, R. J. (1988). *The triarchic mind: A new theory of human intelligence.* New York, NY: Penguin Books.

Sternberg, R. J. (1995). A triarchic view of "cognitive resource and leadership performance." *Applied Psychology: An International Review, 44,* 29–32.

Sternberg, R. J., & Vroom, V. (2002). The person versus situation in leadership. *The Leadership Quarterly, 13,* 301–323.

Stinson, J. E., & Johnson, T. W. (1975). The path-goal theory of leadership: A partial test and suggested refinement. *Academy of Management Journal, 18,* 242–252.

Stogdill, R. M. (1974). *Handbook of leadership.* New York, NY: Free Press.

Strube, M. J., & Garcia, J. E. (1981). A meta-analytical investigation of Fiedler's contingency model of leadership effectiveness. *Psychological Bulletin, 90,* 307–321.

Sun, W., Xu, A., & Shang, Y. 2014. Transformational leadership, team climate, and team performance within the NPD team: Evidence from China. *Asia Pacific Journal of Management, 31*(1): 127–147.

Tobey-Garcia, A., Ayman, R., & Chemers, M. (2000, July). *Leader–subordinate trait dyad composition and subordinate satisfaction with supervision: Moderated by task structure.* Paper presented at the XXVII International Congress of Psychology, Stockholm, Sweden.

Triandis, H. C. (2006). Cultural intelligence in organizations. *Group & Organizational Management, 31,* 20–26.

Van Rooy, D. L., & Viswesvaran, C. (2004). Emotional intelligence: A meta-analytic investigation of predictive validity and nomological net. *Journal of Vocational Behavior, 65,* 71–95.

Vecchio, R. P. (1987). Situational leadership theory: An examination of a prescriptive theory. *Journal of Applied Psychology, 72,* 444–451.

Vecchio, R. P. (1997). Situational leadership theory: An examination of a prescriptive theory. In R. P. Vecchio (Ed.), *Leadership: Understanding the dynamics of power and influence in organizations* (pp. 334–350). Notre Dame, IN: University of Notre Dame Press.

Vecchio, R. P., & Boatwright, K. J. (2002). Preferences for idealized styles of supervision. *The Leadership Quarterly, 13,* 327–342.

Vroom V. H., & Jago, A. G. (1978). On the validity of the Vroom-Yetton model. *Journal of Applied Psychology, 63,* 151–162.

Vroom, V. H., & Jago, A. G. (1988). *The new leadership: Managing participation in organizations.* Englewood Cliffs, NJ: Prentice Hall.

Vroom, V. H., & Jago, A. G. (1998). Situation effects and levels of analysis in the study of leader participation. In F. Yammarino & F. Dansereau (Eds.), *Leadership: The multi-level approaches* (pp. 145–159). Stamford, CT: JAI Press.

Vroom, V. H., & Yetton, P. W. (1973). *Leadership and decision-making.* Pittsburgh, PA: University of Pittsburgh Press.

Waldman, D. A., Ramirez, G. G., House, R. J., & Puranam, P. (2001). Does leadership matter? CEO leadership attributes and profitability under conditions of perceived environmental uncertainty. *Academy of Management Journal, 44*(1), 134–143.

Waldman, D. A., & Yammarino, F. J. (1999). CEO charismatic leadership: Levels-of-management and levels-of-analysis effects. *Academy of Management Review, 24,* 266–285.

Walumbwa, F. O., & Lawler, J. J. (2003). Building effective organizations: Transformational leadership, collectivist orientation, work-related attitudes, and withdrawal behaviors in three emerging economies. *International Journal of Human Resource Management, 14,* 1083–1101.

Walumbwa, F. O., Lawler, J. J., & Avolio, B. J. (2007). Leadership, individual differences, and work-related attitudes: A cross-cultural investigation. *Applied Psychology: An International Review, 56*(2), 212–230.

Wang, Z., & Gagné, M. (2013). A Chinese–Canadian cross-cultural investigation of transformational leadership, autonomous motivation, and collectivistic value. *Journal of Leadership & Organizational Studies, 20,* 134–142.

Wentworth, D. K., & Anderson, L. R. (1984). Emergent leadership as a function of sex and task type. *Sex Roles, 11,* 513–524.

West, M. A., Borrill, C. S., & Unsworth, K. L. (1998). Team effectiveness in organizations. In C. L. Cooper & I. T. Robertson (Eds.), *International review of industrial and organizational psychology* (pp. 1–48). Chichester, UK: Wiley.

Wofford, J. C., & Liska, L. Z. (1993). Pathgoal theories of leadership: A meta-analysis. *Journal of Management, 19,* 857–876.

Yammarino, F. J., & Dansereau, F. (Eds.). (2009). *Multi-level issues in organizational behavior and leadership* (Vol. 8). Bingley, UK: Emerald.

York, R. O. (1996). Adherence to situational leadership theory among social workers. *Clinical Supervisor, 14,* 5–26.

Yukl, G., & Van Fleet, D. D. (1992). Theory and research on leadership in organizations. In M. D. Dunnette & L. M. Hough (Eds.), *Handbook of industrial and organizational psychology* (2nd ed., Vol. 3, pp. 147–198). Palo Alto, CA: Consulting Psychologist Press.

Zaccaro, S. J. (1995). Leader resource and the nature of organizational problems. *Applied Psychology: An International Review, 44,* 32–36.

Zaccaro, S. J. (2007). Trait-based perspectives of leadership. *American Psychologist, 62,* 6–16.

Zaccaro, S. J., Kemp, C., & Bader, P. (2004). Leader traits and attributes. In J. Antonakis, A. T. Cianciolo, & R. J. Sternberg (Eds.), *The nature of leadership* (pp. 102–124). Thousand Oaks, CA: Sage.

Zhu, W., Avolio, B. J., & Walumbwa, F. O. (2009). Moderating role of follower characteristics with transformational leadership and follower work engagement. *Group & Organization Management, 34*(5), 590–619.

# CHAPTER 7

# Shared Leadership

*Christina L. Wassenaar*

*Craig L. Pearce*

---

## Opening Case: A Day in the Life of a Leader

Miena walked into work today with mixed emotions. She felt excited, nervous, passionate, and hopeful, but most of all she wanted to do the best possible job in her new position as head chef at this trendy restaurant. She knew that she had been given this job because she was a gifted chef, and she was very proud of her accomplishments and the recognition that she regularly received for her talents. This new job was the culmination of 10 years of study and hard work.

Because this was a new kitchen, with only a few people with whom she had previously worked, Miena was also wondering what kind of environment she would be walking into when she entered the kitchen. Sure, during her interviews people were nice and seemed open to working together to create wonderful menus and exciting food. But now, when it was really time to get to work, there would be other talented cooks who had also hoped to have the job she had; how should she get the best performance out of them?

Miena continued to ponder this question as she put on her apron. She thought back to a mentor of her own, Thomas. She thought about his focus on unyielding quality and the desire to serve innovative food, every day, all the time. She remembered that he expected his people to be creative; beyond that goal he also said, "I hired you because you are the best. I won't tell you what you need to be doing every moment. You know what you have to do, so if you have an idea or skill that will help us succeed, step forward and show us what you can do."

Miena knew that this way of leading was unusual in a kitchen. Normally, the chef is like an absolute monarch—a king or queen. All of the cooks who work under the head chef are merely tools to create the chef's art. Kitchens are usually hierarchically structured: Under the head chef is the sous-chef, and then there are the various section chefs and their assistants. The head chef gives the vision and coordinates everything, and those below execute, usually without question. This tradition of organizing a kitchen, the classical French way, is sacrosanct.

Miena knew that it was likely that every person she would work with today had been trained in this kind of hierarchically structured kitchen. But she also knew that she had become the chef she was today because of Thomas and his style of leading, where he encouraged others to lead, take initiative, and grow. Miena realized, as she walked through the swinging doors into the main kitchen, she wanted to do the same with her new role. She wanted to teach, learn, and excel, and in doing so, allow others the opportunity that she had experienced in her own training.

### Discussion Questions

1.  What would you suggest Miena do first when she speaks to her new team?

2.  Miena is not just thinking about empowering people; she is planning to try to share the lead. What are some of the steps she should take to make this strategic goal successful?

3.  How do you think Miena's new team will react to her planned style of leading them?

## Chapter Overview

> It is amazing how much people get done if they do not worry about who gets the credit.
>
> —Swahili proverb

When we consider the nature of leadership, it conjures deep and profound considerations (Antonakis, Cianciolo, & Sternberg, 2004). In this regard, shared leadership theory moves us from a perspective on leadership as a hierarchical role to that of leadership as a dynamic social process (Pearce & Conger, 2003; Pearce & Wassenaar, 2015; Pearce, Wassenaar, & Manz, 2014). The notion of nature in human social behavior implies that the activities that are engaged in are inherent or characterological, that our instinct takes over our decisions, or that certain attributes or behaviors are innate. It implies that the actions that we take in our daily lives are part of a predetermined character that is formed through our environment, upbringing, and cultural history. As members of a community, as parents, children, employees, and finally as leaders, our nature—the foundation of who we are—is integral to how we interact with those around us.

But is that enough? Can we rely on our personal and traditional understanding of societal rules in a world that is clearly moving in new directions, driven primarily by technology but also by demography, the rise and fall of various embedded norms, and by new geopolitical paradigms? At some level, we are part of a brave new world—but how many times have our ancestors wrestled with change? Even more relevant to the topic at hand, *who* led this change?

Accordingly, the purpose of this chapter is to offer a foundational view of the theory of shared leadership. In the past few decades, this particular form of leadership—which has been present in our society for ages—has gained relevance both in its practical application through the workplace and in scientific research. Shared leadership is defined as "a dynamic, interactive influence process among individuals in groups for which the objective is to lead one another to the achievement of group or organizational goals or both" (Pearce & Conger, 2003, p. 1). In other words, shared leadership occurs when group members actively and intentionally shift the role of leader to one another as needed by the environment or circumstances in which the group operates. Although this is markedly different from the more traditional models of leadership where the influence and decision making travels downstream from the vertical leader to the followers (Day, Gronn, & Salas, 2004, 2006; Day & O'Connor, 2003; Pearce & Sims, 2000, 2002; Riggio, Chaleff, & Lipman-Blumen, 2008), it is *not* our intention to promote the idea that studying shared leadership supersedes or replaces the study of hierarchical leadership or the more traditionally understood forms of leadership (Pearce, Conger, & Locke, 2008). Rather, with shared leadership, the role of leadership does not reside in one person's hands but in the group's arms as they move together toward common objectives.

Clearly, this type of leadership is a departure from the traditional understanding of the hierarchical leader. Our typical notion is that of a single person around whom the rest of the group circles and who is the arbiter of decisions and purpose. Throughout history, we have read about these celebrated souls (Bass & Bass, 2008; Carlyle, 1841/1894; Figueira, Brennan, & Sternberg, 2009)—and yes, we do celebrate them, for better or for worse. We aspire to achieve their status, or at least their acceptance. Because of this, the primary focus in the study of leadership has been on the attitudes, behaviors, and activities of these leaders with the hope of understanding, demystifying, and perhaps even emulating them (Bass & Bass, 2008).

Pearce and Conger (2003) suggest that lately some in the scholarly community have divested themselves from this norm and taken to the notion that leadership is actually a *process* that can be taught, shared, distributed, and collectively enacted. These scholars have also begun to popularize the view that leadership can be a shared influence process and that the role of leadership does *not* have to originate solely from a hierarchical leader. Rather, leadership can derive from any member of a group or social system who can offer the skills and talent that are needed by the project or system at the time (Hunt, 2004; Ropo, Eriksson, & Hunt, 1997). Of course, at this point there exists far less empirical study in this area than in the older, more established leadership theories, but in the past two decades, momentum in the study of shared leadership has grown and taken great strides.

Therefore, in this chapter we will cover four main areas regarding shared leadership. First, we identify the historical theoretical precursors to the development of shared leadership theory. Then, we provide an overview of studies of shared leadership that have begun to document its antecedents and outcomes. Our third section focuses on how to implement shared leadership in practice, offering concrete advice to would-be leaders. Finally, we close with a view toward the future of leadership in organizations.

Sometimes, in order to go forward, we first need to go back. In the case of leadership study, Bass and Avolio (1993) point out that "new" theories related to the field of leadership are often repioneered versions of older theories (Yukl, 2012). In order not to fall into the selective memory trap, we will spend just a little time reviewing some of the historical underpinnings of shared leadership and how our current understanding of the shared leadership experience has been influenced by offerings from the fields of organizational behavior, psychology, teamwork, sociology, and leadership.

# Historical Bases of Shared Leadership

It generally appears that prior to the Industrial Revolution, very little thought was given to the scientific study of leading others, or leadership. It was during this period, especially toward the 1830s on, that the impact from the changes that were occurring at an increasingly rapid pace began to be studied in any scientific manner (Nardinelli, 2008). Of course, there were many people, from manufacturers to philosophers, who were writing about the phenomena that were affecting the global stage, but the main focus of their work centered on the transfer and movement of knowledge about technological advances (Stewart, 1998, 2003). However, Stewart (2003) noted that as late as the end of the 18th century, many of those who were considered scientists also began to address the scientific measurement of the social and managerial occurrences of the day. It was at the beginning of the 19th century when economists such as Jean Baptiste Say (1803/1964) wrote that entrepreneurs "must possess the art of superintendence and administration" (p. 330). The main interests of economists prior to his writing this were land and labor, and to some extent, capital. Eventually, the idea that leadership did have a role in business began to be more understood; however, this idea of leading others still focused mainly on the command-and-control activities that would be generated from the hierarchical leader. It was only later in that century that slight hints of shared leadership can be detected in management writing as another form of leading others (Pearce & Conger, 2003).

One of the earliest management thinkers in the area of systemic organizational and leadership approaches was Daniel C. McCallum. He developed one of the first groupings of principles related to management that could span various industries and were mainly focused on leadership. One of these principles was unity of command, where orders came from the top and work was carried out by those down subsequent levels of the hierarchy (Wren, 1994). The overwhelming majority of the Industrial Revolution writing on leadership was focused on a top-down, command-and-control perspective (e.g., Montgomery, 1836, 1840; Wren, 1994). This perspective became firmly ensconced by the turn of the 20th century and was captured in what came to be known as "scientific management" (Gantt, 1916; Gilbreth, 1912; Gilbreth & Gilbreth, 1917; Taylor, 1903, 1911).

If we simply rested on the writing of the aforementioned authors and social philosophers, we could easily draw the conclusion that the absolute control of employee behavior by the employers is the only way our forbearers knew. However, if we step outside of these scholars, we notice small leadership nudges in another direction. One of the people who noticed and then wrote about her dissonant observations was a management consultant and community activist named Mary Parker Follett. She wrote about a concept called the *law of the situation* (Follett, 1924). She thought that instead of following the articulated leader in any and all situations, it sometimes made more sense to follow the person in the group who had the most knowledge about the situation in which the group was operating. Clearly, her ideas were a sharp departure from the normally accepted, hierarchical leadership model of the day, yet they also appear to be quite closely associated with the idea of shared leadership theory.

Although Follett was a popular management consultant and speaker during the 1920s, the majority of the business community of the time discounted many of her ideas and writings. Some of this was a result of the economic reality of the time; things were so uncertain, especially during the 1930s and 1940s, that the idea of losing control to anyone was anathema to the organizational leadership of the time (Drucker, 1954). However, Peter Drucker (1995) calls her "the brightest star in the management firmament" for that era (p. 2).

Another pivotal pillar of the development of shared leadership in our historical review was the writing done by Hollander (1961) and quickly followed by others, which dealt with the idea that a leader can emerge or be selected by members of a leaderless group (e.g., Bartol & Martin, 1986; Hollander, 1978; Stein & Heller, 1979). It is clear that this type of theory building is integral to our deeper understanding of the psychological underpinnings for the emergence of a leader who has not been "chosen" by the upper management. The difference between shared leadership and emergent leadership is that whereas emergent leadership deals mainly with the choosing of an ultimate leader, the concept of shared leadership deals more with the idea that multiple leaders can and will emerge over time, based on the needs and situation in which the group finds itself (Pearce, 1997; Pearce & Sims, 2002).

An additional component that allows us a foundational look at the development of shared leadership theory is the literature on substitutes for leadership (e.g., Kerr & Jermier, 1978). Those writings suggest that there are possible substitutes for a hierarchical leader that can manifest themselves under certain circumstances. For example, in work that is highly routinized, the need for a leader or supervisor to oversee all facets of each individual's work is unnecessary. Taking this idea a step further, shared leadership can also serve as a substitute for a more formally designated leader.

The concept of self-leadership (Manz, 1986) can also be seen as emergent from the theory of leadership substitutes. Manz and Sims (1980) identified self-management, or self-leadership, as a possible substitute for a more traditionally appointed, vertical leader. They believed that (1) the more individuals knew about and understood the organization's needs, (2) the more highly skilled they were, and (3) the more motivated they were to engage in activities that were productive, the more likely their ability to lead themselves would mitigate the need for proximal control, direction, and supervision. Taking this idea just a little further, we can draw the conclusion that this could also work well at the group level and lead to the development of shared leadership in a group as each individual displayed his or her abilities, skills, organizational understanding, and motivation to achieve (Pearce & Conger, 2003).

Finally, the theory of empowerment should be briefly explored as a foundational component to shared leadership. This is a topic that has interested many in the field of leadership (e.g., Blau & Alba, 1982; Conger & Kanungo, 1988; Conger & Pearce, 2009; Cox, Pearce, & Sims, 2003; Manz, 1986; Manz & Sims, 1989, 1990; Mohrman, Cohen, & Mohrman, 1995; Pearce & Sims, 2000, 2002) and deals mainly with the issue of power (e.g., Conger & Kanungo, 1988). Often, the primary focus in management research is on those at the top of the organization and their activities. Empowerment, however, focuses on the devolvement of hierarchical power, usually to followers, rather than describing the dynamic social processes involved in shared leadership.

Most of the literature and research in empowerment is focused on the individual (e.g., Conger & Kanungo, 1988), although there are some who are researching this phenomenon at the group level (e.g., Mohrman et al., 1995). It must be clearly noted that although empowering leadership or empowerment is definitely the act of sharing leadership, it is also not the equivalent of the shared leadership that can be created by a group. In order for shared leadership to fully exist in a group, members must be actively engaged and participative in the leadership process (Conger & Pearce, 2009). Because of this, it is evident that empowerment is a critical and necessary component for the development of shared leadership in a group.

In this section, we have very briefly discussed some of the most important historical underpinnings of the development of shared leadership theory—from the Industrial Revolution, which began in Great Britain but which quickly spread to the rest of the globe, to the pioneers in the area of "scientific management," to several interesting and valuable streams of research that allow us more clarity when beginning our own exploration of shared leadership theory. See which is adapted from Pearce and Conger (2003), for a comprehensive list of the theoretical and research foundations of shared leadership theory.

In the following section, we will delve further into the literature on shared leadership, exploring both the antecedents and outcomes of this important leadership concept.

**Table 7.1**  Historical Bases of Shared Leadership

| Theory/Research | Key Issues | Representative Authors |
| --- | --- | --- |
| Law of the situation | • Let the situation, not the person, determine the "orders." | • Follett (1924) |
| Human relations and social systems perspectives | • One should pay attention to the social and psychological needs of employees. | • Turner (1933); Mayo (1933); Barnard (1938) |

| Theory/Research | Key Issues | Representative Authors |
|---|---|---|
| Role differentiation in groups | • Members of groups typically assume different types of roles. | • Benne and Sheats (1948) |
| Co-leadership | • Concerns the division of the leadership role between two people—primarily research examines mentor and protégé relationships. | • Solomon, Loeffler, and Frank (1953); Heenan and Bennis (1998) |
| Social exchange theory | • People exchange punishments and rewards in their social interactions. | • Festinger (1954); Homans (1958) |
| Management by objectives and participative goal setting | • Subordinates and superiors jointly set performance expectations. | • Drucker (1954); Erez and Arad (1986); Locke and Latham (1990) |
| Emergent leadership | • Leaders can "emerge" from a leaderless group. | • Hollander (1961) |
| Mutual leadership | • Leadership can come from peers. | • Bowers and Seashore (1966) |
| Expectation states theory and team member exchange | • Team members develop models of status differential between various team members. | • Berger, Cohen, and Zelditch (1972); Seers (1989) |
| Participative decision making | • Under certain circumstances, it is advisable to elicit more involvement by subordinates in the decision-making process. | • Vroom and Yetton (1973) |
| Vertical dyad linkage/leader–member exchange | • Examines the process between leaders and followers and the creation of in-groups and out-groups. | • Graen (1976) |
| Substitutes for leadership | • Situation characteristics (e.g., highly routinized work) diminish the need for leadership. | • Kerr and Jermier (1978) |
| Self-leadership | • Employees, given certain conditions, are capable of leading themselves. | • Manz and Sims (1980) |
| Self-managing work teams | • Team members can take on roles that were formerly reserved for managers. | • Manz and Sims (1987, 1993) |
| Followership | • Examines the characteristics of good followers. | • Kelley (1988) |
| Empowerment | • Examines power sharing with subordinates. | • Conger and Kanungo (1988) |
| Shared cognition | • Examines the extent to which team members share similar mental models about key internal and external environmental issues. | • Cannon-Bowers and Salas (1993); Klimoski and Mohammed (1994); Ensley and Pearce (2001) |
| Connective leadership | • Examines how well leaders are able to make connections to others both inside and outside the team. | • Lipman-Blumen (1996) |

SOURCE: Craig L. Pearce and Jay A. Conger (2003) Shared Leadership: Reframing the Hows and Whys of Leadership. Thousand Oaks, CA: SAGE.

# Overview of Evidence on the Antecedents and Outcomes of Shared Leadership

Recently, shared leadership has been receiving increased attention in both the practitioner (e.g., Pearce, Manz, & Sims, 2014) and academic literature (e.g., D'Innocenzo, Mathieu, & Kukenberger, 2014; Nicolaides et al., 2014; Wang, Waldman, & Zhang, 2014; Wassenaar & Pearce, 2015). Although the vast majority of the writing on shared leadership has been conceptual in nature, a modicum of empirical advance is worth noting. This empirical work has identified both antecedents and outcomes of shared leadership in a wide variety of contexts. For example, Pearce et al. (2014) recently documented 21 qualitative analyses of shared leadership across contexts ranging from hospitals, to research and development, to airlines, to the blue-collar world of manufacturing, to the white-collar world of virtual teams of knowledge workers, and even to the c-suite ranks of top management teams, as well as across multiple national contexts, including Asia, Europe, and North America. Below, we briefly provide an overview of the empirical evidence on shared leadership to date. Our purpose here is not to provide an exhaustive review of all the literature on shared leadership, but rather to provide a representative review.

## Antecedents Associated With Shared Leadership

One of the most fascinating angles when studying any phenomenon in organizational behavior is to investigate its antecedents, or more simply put, what potential activities or behaviors result in an outcome. Lately, researchers have been focusing their efforts on developing a richer and deeper understanding of the precursors to the evolution of shared leadership in groups and organizations. In this vein, they have discovered three main groups of antecedents to shared leadership, which we will briefly explain in the following paragraphs.

**Hierarchical/Vertical Leaders.** Not surprisingly, hierarchical or vertical leaders have been found to have a considerable influence on the development and occurrence of shared leadership. For example, top leader support has been found to be related to shared leadership development (Hess, 2015), while trust in the hierarchical leader is directly correlated to the shared leadership formation in groups (George et al., 2002; Olson-Sanders, 2006), as it serves as a facilitating force for smooth social interactions (Dirks & Ferrin, 2002), which in turn directly affect the group's ability to share leadership effectively.

Masal (2015) found transformational leadership to be related to the development of shared leadership in a study of police. Shamir and Lapidot (2003) were able, in their study of the Israeli Defense Forces, clearly to conclude that leader and follower goal alignment contribute to the development of shared leadership. They also confirmed that group members' trust in, and satisfaction with, their leaders is directly related to the degree to which shared leadership exists in those groups.

Similarly, Elloy (2008) discovered that when the vertical leader allows group members latitude in decision making, the incidence of shared leadership increased, while Chiu (2014) found leader humility to be predictive of shared leadership, and Fausing, Joensson, Lewandowski, and Bligh (2015) found empowering leader behavior to result in shared leadership.

The gender of the vertical leader has been found to be important when considering the development of shared leadership. In their study that was conducted in several major Finnish health care organizations, Konu and Viitanen (2008) uncovered that teams who have a female vertical leader are more likely to share leadership among group members. Their research also suggests that the reason for this higher incidence of shared leadership in these female-led groups is that these leaders are more likely to be inclined to nurture those around them than are their male counterparts (Paris, Howell, Dorfman, & Hanges, 2009).

Finally, the behavior of the vertical leader has been found to be integrally important to the development of shared leadership in a group (Hooker & Csikszentmihalyi, 2003; Pearce et al., 2014). In the qualitative work done by Hooker and Csikszentmihalyi (2003), six vertical leader behaviors were found to support the development of shared leadership: (1) valuing excellence, (2) providing clear goals, (3) giving timely feedback, (4) matching challenges and skills, (5) diminishing distractions, and (6) creating freedom. Pearce et al. (2014) found empowering leadership, visionary leadership, and leader focus on purpose/values to be related to the development of shared leadership. Taken together, these studies identify the important role that vertical leadership has in the display and development of shared leadership.

**Support Structures.** Another important group of antecedents that have been studied in the past few years are those that enhance our understanding of the support structures that are in place or can be developed to aid in a group's development of shared leadership. For example, technology has been, is, and will continue to be a foundational underpinning to the development of shared leadership in groups (Wassenaar et al., 2010). Cordery, Soo, Kirkman, Rosen, and Mathieu (2009) realized that critical components in the development and sustainability of shared leadership in virtual teams are the support structures—both social and technological—that enable group members to communicate more easily, fluidly transporting information across time and geography. These support mechanisms can be constituted of the technical infrastructure that is in place, which supports communication between members of a group or others, and training (employee training, orientations, or other organized learning environments) that augments the skills of the group.

Pearce et al. (2014) documented that selection systems, compensation systems, education, and training and development systems were all linked to the development of shared leadership. DeRue, Nahrgang, and Ashford (2015) found network patterns and warmth perceptions affected shared leadership. Furthermore, Hess (2015) identified institution-wide focus on team outcomes and equity in team member recruitment to facilitate shared leadership. Elloy (2008) discovered that when an organization provided team training, and when it encouraged and facilitated communication among employees within a paper mill, the development of shared leadership was greatly facilitated. Another line of research that has been gaining momentum in both the academic and practitioner literatures is specifically related to executive coaching (Bono, Purvanova, Towler, & Peterson, 2009; Elmhirst, 2008; Leonard & Goff, 2003). The incidence of coaching in organizations has been extolled as essential in leader and team development, yet very little empirical research has, as of yet, been done—particularly as it relates to groups. However, Carson et al. (2007), as well as Cordery et al. (2009), did uncover that coaching was positively related to the demonstration of shared leadership.

**Culture and Empowerment.** Context of leadership has been gaining increasing attention in the literature (e.g., Antonakis, Avolio, & Sivasubramaniam, 2003). Clearly, there must be more ways that cause or lead to an environment in which leadership is shared than just the activities of the vertical leader or how much support a group or its members receive. One of these is culture (Pearce, 2008). For example, Konu and Viitanen (2008) learned that a group's values are an important predictor of shared leadership. Similarly, Pearce et al. (2014) found culture and empowerment to be related to shared leadership. Moreover, in the same study, in which they explored coaching and its contribution to sharing leadership, Carson et al. (2007) and Serban and Roberts (2016) found that internal environment—a concept similar to cultural values—was also a contributor to shared leadership, thus further providing confirmation for our belief that organizational culture or context is a contributing factor in the development of shared leadership.

Wood (2005) also discovered that if a team and its members perceive that they are empowered, they are more likely to behave in a way that shares leadership. He was exploring the question of whether members of top management teams in church organizations could even occur in what is normally considered a highly developed hierarchical organization. It was a revealing outcome, especially when taking into account our previous explorations of the incidence of shared leadership throughout history and how, against our initial expectations or knowledge, it also did occur in many religious denominations, particularly through the Middle Ages (Coss, 1996).

**Other Antecedents.** There are four other interesting and valuable antecedents that have been explored in the research literature as precursors to shared leadership. The first is relationship longevity. Ropo and Sauer (2003) conducted a longitudinal qualitative study of orchestras, uncovering the fact that the length of relationships between various members, such as orchestra leaders, sponsors, members, or other possible group members, is an important foreshadowing to sharing leadership between the various orchestral constituents. Chiu (2014) found that proactivity of team members facilitated the development of shared leadership, while Paunova and Lee (2016) found team learning orientation facilitated shared leadership. Similarly, Pearce et al. (2014) found such items as proactivity, trust, and openness to be facilitators of shared leadership. Hooker and Csikszentmihalyi (2003), in their study of university research teams, discovered that flow (Csikszentmihalyi, 1990) and the development of a state of flow were a foundational link in the development of shared leadership in the creative group. Fausing et al. (2015) found team member interdependence to be related to the development of shared leadership. Muethel, Gehrlein, and Hoegl (2012) found sociodemographic characteristics of groups to affect shared leadership. Serban and Roberts (2016) found task cohesion to be associated with shared leadership. Our final antecedent is proximity. It was studied by Balthazard, Waldman, Howell, and Atwater (2004) and Hess (2015), all of whom found that face-to-face teams are more likely to develop shared leadership than virtual teams, which builds on the work of Antonakis and Atwater (2002).

**Summary.** As we can clearly observe from the varied possible antecedents that we have reviewed, there are many precursors or potential causes that enable shared leadership to occur in groups. As researchers, we are merely at the beginning of the exploration of these antecedents, and there is enormous opportunity for further research in this area. Developing a more complete understanding of these causes will only further enable organizations and groups to capitalize on the benefits or outcomes of sharing leadership, which we will explore in some detail in the next section.

## Outcomes Associated With Shared Leadership

Broadly speaking, there are three levels of analysis regarding outcomes in organizational behavior and leadership research—individual-, group-, and organization-level outcomes—and outcome variables span from intermediate-type outcomes, such as attitudes, behaviors, and cognitions, to effectiveness or performance outcomes (Luthans, 2010). Below, we provide an overview of the outcomes empirically associated with shared leadership.

**Individual-Level Outcomes.** At least seven individual-level outcomes have been associated with shared leadership. Individual satisfaction is one of the most widely researched individual-level variables in organizational behavior (e.g., Cranny, Smith, & Stone, 1992), and two studies have specifically examined the effects of shared leadership on satisfaction. First, Avolio, Jung, Murray, and Sivasubramaniam (1996), in a study of undergraduate project teams, found team member satisfaction to be positively related to shared leadership. Next, Shamir and Lapidot (2003), in a study of Israeli military officer training, found that shared leadership was positively related to satisfaction with, as well as trust in, hierarchical leaders. Thus, shared leadership has been linked to satisfaction with both team members and team leaders.

Building on the work of Bandura (1986), George et al. (2002), in a nursing study, found shared leadership to be directly related to follower self-efficacy. Also in the hospital environment, Klein, Zeigert, Knight, and Xiao (2006) found shared leadership to be positively associated with the skill development of junior medical staff, which was also found in Pearce et al. (2014). Moreover, Peter, Braun, and Frey (2015) and Gu, Chen, Huang, and Lui (2016) found shared leadership to be positively related to individual creativity, while Grille and Kauffeld (2015) found shared leadership to be associated with feelings of autonomy. Finally, Hooker and

Csikszentmihalyi (2003), in a study of R&D laboratories, found mimetic effects of shared leadership. That is, as followers learned shared leadership from the lead scientist in their original PhD training laboratory, they mimicked those lead scientist behaviors to develop shared leadership in their own laboratories. This is similar to what Bass, Waldman, Avolio, and Bebb (1987) called the "falling dominoes effect," noted for transformational leadership mimetic effects. Accordingly, shared leadership has been empirically associated with multiple individual-level outcomes.

**Group/Team-Level Outcomes.** Wang et al. (2014) published a meta-analysis on the outcomes of shared leadership at the group/team-level of analysis. Their analyses were based on 42 independent studies comprising 3,439 individuals. Twenty-three of the studies were published, while 19 were unpublished. Eleven of the studies used student teams, while 31 of the studies were of groups/teams in work settings. The vast majority of the studies were from North America.

Wang et al. (2014) found that shared leadership is a moderately strong predictor of group outcomes, with a mean corrected correlation of .34, which is fairly robust in social science research. They also found that context does matter: Shared leadership is a better predictor of outcomes in complex environments.

Interestingly, Wang et al. (2014) postulated, and found, that shared leadership results are more robust with what they called "new-genre" shared leadership behavior than with "traditional" behavior. They defined new-genre behavior as encompassing transformation and empowering types of behaviors, while they defined traditional behaviors as encompassing directive and transactional types of behaviors. Wang et al. examined the methods used to assess shared leadership and found that measurement protocols do affect results. The most important finding, however, from their study is that shared leadership predicts more variance in outcome variables than hierarchical leadership.

The other two meta-analyses mentioned earlier (D'Innocenzo, 2014; Nicolaides et al., 2014) found results consistent with the Wang et al. (2014) study. The most important finding from the D'Innocenzo (2014) study was that network-based measures of shared leadership provide a greater account of variance in outcome variables, while the most important finding from the Nicolaides et al. (2014) study is that team confidence partially mediates the relationship between shared leadership and team performance.

More recent studies are consistent with all three meta-analyses. For example, Mathieu, Kukenberger, D'Innocenzo, and Reilly (2015) found shared leadership to be positively related to team cohesion, while Grille and Kauffeld (2015) found shared leadership to be positively related to team performance. Furthermore, Sousa and Van Dierendonck (2015) found shared leadership to be related to the development of behavioral integration in teams, while Gu et al. (2016) found shared leadership to be positively related to team creativity.

**Organization-Level Outcomes.** Although the effects of shared leadership on individuals and groups are important, perhaps most important, one should consider the effects of shared leadership at the organizational level of analysis. In this regard, several studies help to shed some light. First, O'Toole, Galbraith, and Lawler (2003), in a qualitative study of shared leadership at the top of organizations of 25 firms, concluded that 17 firms experienced positive effects, whereas eight experienced negative effects. Potentially more significant, using multiple regression analysis, Ensley, Hmieleski, and Pearce (2006) conducted a two-sample study of shared leadership in entrepreneurial firms. Their first sample of 66 firms was drawn from the Inc. 500 list, which is of the fastest growing, privately held firms in the United States. Their second sample was a random national sample of U.S.–based firms, drawn from Dun & Bradstreet's market identifiers database. In both samples, they found that while controlling for CEO leader behavior, shared leadership predicted the financial performance of the firms.

More recently, Hmieleski, Cole, and Baron (2012) also found a positive effect of shared leadership on entrepreneurial firm performance. Furthermore, Pearce et al. (2014) reported qualitative studies of organizations across a range of industries and countries and clearly found strong evidence of shared leadership and organizational performance. As such, the initial evidence on shared leadership indicates that it can have a potential powerful effect on organizational performance outcomes. Finally, Zhou (2016) found shared leadership to be related to entrepreneurial team performance in China.

**Summary.** In sum, shared leadership appears to be an important predictor of several outcome variables that span attitudinal, behavioral, cognitive, and effectiveness outcomes at the individual, group, and organizational levels of analysis. In the following section, we offer concrete advice for the implementing, maintaining, and developing of shared leadership.

# The Practice of Shared Leadership

Although much of this chapter is devoted to exploring the development of shared leadership theory, we now shift to practical advice for implementing shared leadership in organizations. Specifically, what are the overarching pieces of advice that we can offer regarding shared leadership? The lessons, as we reflect on the evidence, span four major categories: (1) individual-level advice; (2) group/team-level advice; (3) organization-level advice; and (4) human resources practices advice (see Figure 7.1). Using these four overarching categories, below we provide a comprehensive guide to action for the development of shared leadership in organizations.

**Individual-Level Advice.** The first piece of advice for individuals desiring to develop shared leadership is to look back at the Swahili proverb that opened this chapter. For shared leadership, it is critical that individuals keep their egos in check. This is not easy, especially for people high in need for achievement. Nonetheless, by setting individual egos aside it is possible to move from "I" to "we" as a reference point. In the complex world of organizations, the overwhelming majority of work

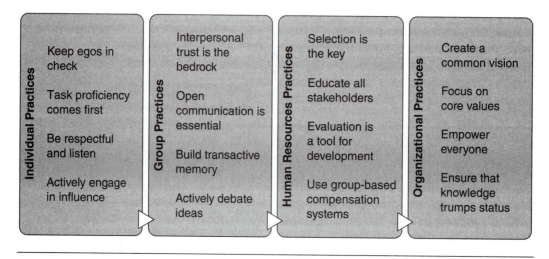

**Figure 7.1**    Four Practices and 16 Actions to Enable Shared Leadership

SOURCE: Pearce.

requires collaborative efforts. As such, it is imperative to move beyond the egos of individuals.

In addition to the focus on collective identification, individuals desiring shared leadership need to have well-developed listening skills and demonstrate respect for others' ideas, opinions, and perspectives. Finally, the individuals involved must be leaders in their own right; they must engage in appropriate influence toward others. It does not matter how brilliant a particular individual is if he or she does not actively contribute leadership to the group. Shared leadership requires the leadership of all, depending on the knowledge, skills, and abilities of the individuals involved and the task requirements of the situation at hand. Otherwise, shared leadership will fail. As such, these are the key pieces of advice for individuals when it comes to implementing shared leadership.

**Group/Team-Level Advice.** The most fundamental piece of advice for developing shared leadership in groups and teams is to focus on interpersonal trust. Trust is critical for shared leadership: Without trust, shared leadership is a pipe dream. To wit, trust is so foundational to social endeavors that research in neuro-economics has found that trust is related to the economic success of nations. Groups (and teams) are the fundamental units of larger societal entities. As such, it is in groups and teams that trust must be developed. Open communication enables the sharing of knowledge within groups, discourages second-guessing of other group members, and helps to develop trust, all of which facilitate the development of shared leadership.

While open communication is important, if shared leadership is to be truly effective, members of groups must develop what scholars call transactive memory—being aware of which group members have which knowledge, skills, and abilities that are relevant to the tasks of the group. This transactive memory facilitates smooth leadership transitions and prevents the hording of power by one person or a select subgroup of individuals.

What if the group does not have a well-developed transactive memory, such as might be the case early in the life of the group or team? Here, our advice centers on encouraging the active debate of ideas. Create group and team norms that stress the importance of constructively challenging one another's ideas. Research in this area very clearly documents how active debate of ideas is strongly related to unit performance. As such, these are our primary pieces of advice for the development of shared leadership to apply at the group/team level.

**Organization-Level Advice.** As we start to move to larger collectives of people, such as organizations, different issues rise to the fore when it comes to implementing productive shared leadership. Most fundamental here is that there is a clear vision regarding the purpose of the organization, if shared leadership is to thrive. If there is no clear and common vision it is most likely that groups and subgroups within the organization will work toward cross-purposes (at best). One of the interesting things to consider here is that common vision and shared leadership can work in tandem. What we mean is that shared leadership be specifically utilized to help to shape the common vision, if hierarchical leaders are very purposeful. A recent article by Berson, Waldman, and Pearce (2016) goes into far more detail on this specific point.

While shared vision is key to shared leadership in organizations, shared values are also of upmost importance. There is no one set of values that is the key in this regard, other than a sincere focus on fairness and ethics. The reality is that shared cultural values are the only long-term source of competitive advantage that is not easily copied, and they provide a strong basis upon which shared leadership can be developed, thereby augmenting competitive advantage.

Obviously, we advocate empowering everyone, at least somewhat. It is an unusual person who is not capable of assuming some leadership responsibility and positively contributing to organizational success. In this vein, knowledge should always trump status. It is very important to encourage those with the most relevant knowledge on a given task to provide the leadership for that situation, rather than deferring to those with the highest status in the room. This is often uncomfortable, but it can clearly be rather rewarding. These are the key components of advice we offer for the encouragement of shared leadership at the organizational level.

**Human Resources Practice Advice.** Selection is undoubtedly the absolute most important thing that can ever be done in any organization, large or small—ask any husband or wife. The issue here is looking for person/job, person/organization, and person/situation fit. Different circumstances, naturally, call for different individual characteristics. With that said, most people do an abysmal job of selecting people for specific jobs. There are a couple of exemplars, highlighted in Pearce et al. (2014), that we strongly advocate emulating in this regard—Southwest Airlines and W. L. Gore. It is outside of our scope to go into detail here, regarding all of their selection procedures, but suffice it to say that they are way more selective than the most prestigious Ivy League college you might admire.

While selection is paramount, shared leadership also requires ongoing support in the form of education, training, and development (ETD). As opposed to typical ETD, which is focused on appointed leaders or so-called high potentials, shared leadership ETD efforts need to be far more inclusive. Similarly, evaluation, which is generally used to justify remuneration, needs to be used for development. Finally, when it comes to compensation we need to totally rethink how it is distributed in most organizations. While nearly all organizations hail teamwork as critical, very few actually reward based on team outcomes. As such, we strongly advise the appropriate use of group-based compensation, such as gainsharing, to encourage shared leadership throughout an organization. Taken together, these various approaches facilitate the development of shared leadership. Of course, every scenario will be different and will call for a tailored approach.

## The Future of Organizational Leadership

As we forge further into the knowledge era, our models of leadership will continue to evolve to embrace the paradigmatic shift away from leadership as merely a hierarchical role to leadership as an unfolding social process, in a shared leadership-type perspective (Wassenaar et al., 2010). This evolutionary process, as with many others, brings to light several questions beginning with the most simple: Can leadership be shared effectively? Yes. Pearce, Manz, and Sims (2014) have uncovered numerous organizations where shared leadership is affecting real outcomes. Examples include how the medical team at a trauma center treats patients more quickly and safely; how sharing leadership in Alcoholics Anonymous helps people who are struggling to heal their addictions more effectively; and how Southwest Airlines attributes its success not to how it structures its costs, but rather to how its corporate culture of feedback from all points of the hierarchy can enable leadership to originate from any level.

Is developing shared leadership challenging? Yes. Having said that, we firmly believe that most people are capable of being both followers *and* leaders, and that shared leadership is an organizational imperative in the age of knowledge work (Pearce, 2010). Although there are circumstances where shared leadership approaches might not work, the research evidence demonstrates that shared leadership can positively affect individual- group- and organizational-level outcomes, including organizational performance.

Does this mean that shared leadership is a panacea? No. There will nearly always be a need for hierarchical leadership in our modern organizations (Leavitt, 2005). As documented by several studies (e.g., Ensley et al., 2006; Hooker & Csikszentmihalyi, 2003; Pearce & Sims, 2002; Shamir & Lapidot, 2003), shared and hierarchical leadership work in tandem to affect individual, group, and organizational outcomes.

Are there circumstances where we do not advocate shared leadership? Yes. For example, shared leadership is applicable only to tasks where there is interdependency among the individuals involved. To force fit any particular potential organizational process simply does not seem wise. We might further speculate that certain other preconditions are necessary for shared leadership to flourish. For instance, it seems important that the individuals involved should have well-developed knowledge, skills, and abilities—not only for the technical aspects of their tasks, but also for how to engage effectively as both followers and leaders—if shared leadership is to be effective. These are but a few caveats regarding shared leadership: Shared leadership, and related approaches, require far more research, not only on their outcomes but also on their antecedents and moderators. As research continues to delve deeper into leadership processes, it will yield more insights for the organizations of the future.

## Discussion Questions

1. Where have you experienced shared leadership? What were some of the positive aspects? Why? Were there things about shared leadership that you felt could work better?
2. Are there some situations in which shared leadership might work better than others?
3. What advice would you give a designated leader regarding shared leadership?

## Recommended Readings

- Manz, C. C., & Pearce, C. L. (in press). *Twisted leadership.* Palmyra, VA: Maven House Press.
- Pearce, C. L. (2008, July 7). Follow the leaders. *Wall Street Journal,* p. R8.
- Pearce, C. L., & Wassenaar, C. L. (2014). Leadership, like fine wine, is something that is meant to be shared, globally. *Organizational Dynamics, 43*(1), 9–16.
- Pearce, C. L., Wassenaar, C. L., & Manz, C. C. (2014). Is shared leadership the key to responsible leadership? *Academy of Management Perspectives, 28,* 275–288.

## Recommended Case Studies

This book contains 21 real-life case studies from multiple industries, countries, and both for-profit and not-for-profit organizations:

- Pearce, C. L., Manz, C. C., & Sims, H. P., Jr. (2014). *Share, don't take the lead.* Charlotte, NC: Information Age.

## Recommended Video

- Talgam, I. (2009). Lead like the great conductors. https://www.ted.com/talks/itay_talgam_lead_like_the_great_conductors/

## References

Antonakis, J., & Atwater, L. (2002). Leader distance: A review and a proposed theory. *The Leadership Quarterly, 13,* 673–704.

Antonakis, J., Avolio, B. J., & Sivasubramaniam, N. (2003). Context and leadership: An examination of the nine-factor full-range leadership theory using the Multifactor Leadership Questionnaire. *The Leadership Quarterly, 14,* 261–295.

Antonakis, J., Bendahan, S., Jacquart, P., & Lalive, R. (2010). On making causal claims: A review and recommendations. *The Leadership Quarterly, 21*(6), 1086–1120.

Antonakis, J., Cianciolo, A. T., & Sternberg, R. J. (2004). *The nature of leadership.* Thousand Oaks, CA: Sage.

Avolio, B. J., Jung, D., Murray, W., & Sivasubramaniam, N. (1996). Building highly developed teams: Focusing on shared leadership process, efficacy, trust, and performance. In M. M. Beyerlein, D. A. Johnson, & S. T. Beyerlein (Eds.), *Advances in interdisciplinary studies of work teams* (pp. 173–209). Greenwich, CT: JAI.

Balthazard, P., Waldman, D., Howell, J., & Atwater, L. (2004, January). Shared leadership and group interaction styles in problem-solving virtual teams. In *Proceedings of the 37th annual Hawaii international conference on system sciences,* 43 (HICSS, Vol. 1, p. 10043b).

Bandura, A. (1986). *Social foundations of thought and action: A social cognitive theory.* Englewood Cliffs, NJ: Prentice Hall.

Barnard, C. I. 1938. The functions of the executive. Cambridge, Mass.,: Harvard University Press.

Bartol, K. M., & Martin, D. C. (1986). Women and men in task groups. In R. D. Ashmore & F. K. Del Boca (Eds.), *The social psychology of female–male relations* (pp. 259–310). New York, NY: Academic Press.

Bass, B. M., & Avolio, B. J. (1993). Transformational leadership: A response to critiques. In J. G. Hunt, B. R. Baliga, H. P. Dachler, & C. A. Schriesheim (Eds.), *Emerging leadership vistas* (pp. 29–40). Lexington, MA: D. C. Heath.

Bass, B. M., & Bass, R. (2008). *The Bass handbook of leadership: Theory, research, and managerial applications.* New York, NY: Simon & Schuster.

Bass, B. M., Waldman, D. A., Avolio, B. J., & Bebb, M. (1987). Transformational leadership and the falling dominoes effect. *Group & Organization Studies, 12,* 73–87.

Benne, K. D. & Sheats, P. 1948. Functional roles of group members. *Journal of Social Issues, 4*(2): 41–49.

Berger, J., Cohen, B. P., & Zelditch Jr, M. 1972. Status characteristics and social interaction. American Sociological Review: 241–255.

Blau, J. R., & Alba, R. D. (1982). Empowering nets of participation. *Administrative Science Quarterly, 27,* 363–379.

Bono, J., Purvanova, R., Towler, A., & Peterson, D. (2009). A survey of executive coaching practices. *Personnel Psychology, 62,* 361–404.

Bowers, D. G. & Seashore, S. E. 1966. Predicting organizational effectiveness with a four-factor theory of leadership. *Administrative Science Quarterly,* 11: 238–263.

Carlyle, T. (1894). *On heroes and hero worship and the heroic in history.* London, UK: Chapman and Hall. (Original work published 1841)

Carson, J., Tesluk, P., & Marrone, J. (2007). Shared leadership in teams: An investigation of antecedent conditions and performance. *Academy of Management Journal, 50,* 1217–1234.

Chiu, C. Y. (2014). *Investigating the emergence of shared leadership in teams: The roles of team proactivity, internal social context, and leader humility.* Buffalo: State University of New York at Buffalo.

Conger, J. A., & Kanungo, R. N. (1988). The empowerment process: Integrating theory and practice. *Academy of Management Review, 13,* 639–652.

Conger, J. A., & Pearce, C. L. (2009) Using empowerment to motivate people to engage in effective self- and shared leadership. In E. A. Locke (Ed.), *Principles of organizational behavior* (pp. 201–216). New York, NY: John Wiley.

Converse, S., Cannon-Bowers, J., & Salas, E. 1993. Shared mental models in expert team decision making. Individual and group decision making: Current(1993): 221.

Cordery, J., Soo, C., Kirkman, B., Rosen, B., & Mathieu, J. (2009). Leading parallel global virtual teams: Lessons from Alcoa. *Organizational Dynamics, 38,* 204–216.

Coss, P. R. (1996). *The knight in medieval England.* Conshohocken, PA: Combined Books.

Cox, J. F., Pearce, C. L., & Sims, H. P., Jr. (2003). Toward a broader agenda for leadership development: Extending the traditional transactional–transformational duality by developing directive, empowering and shared leadership skills. In S. E. Murphy & R. E. Riggio (Eds.), *The future of leadership development* (pp. 161–180). Mahwah, NJ: Lawrence Erlbaum.

Cranny, C. J., Smith, P. C., & Stone, E. F. (1992). *Job satisfaction: How people feel about their jobs and how it affects their performance.* Lexington, MA: Lexington Books.

Csikszentmihalyi, M. (1990). *Flow: The psychology of optimal experience.* New York, NY: Harper & Row.

Day, D. V., Gronn, P., & Salas, E. (2004). Leadership capacity in teams. *The Leadership Quarterly, 15,* 857–880.

Day, D. V., Gronn, P., & Salas, E. (2006). Leadership in team-based organizations: On the threshold of a new era. *The Leadership Quarterly, 17,* 211–216.

Day, D. V., & O'Connor, P. M. G. (2003). Leadership development: Understanding the process. In S. E. Murphy & R. E. Riggio (Eds.), *The future of leadership development* (pp. 11–28). Mahwah, NJ: Lawrence Erlbaum.

DeRue, D. S., Nahrgang, J. D., & Ashford, S. J. (2015). Interpersonal perceptions and the emergence of leadership structures in groups: A network perspective. *Organization Science, 26*(4), 1192–1209.

D'Innocenzo, L., Mathieu, J. E., & Kukenberger, M. R. (2014). A meta-analysis of different forms of shared leadership–team performance relations. *Journal of Management, 42*(7), 1964–1991.

Dirks, K. T., & Ferrin, D. L. (2002). Trust in leadership: Meta-analytic findings and implications for research and practice. *Journal of Applied Psychology, 87,* 611–628.

Drucker, P. F. (1954). *The practice of management.* New York, NY: Harper & Row.

Drucker, P. F. (1995). *Management in time of great change.* New York, NY: Penguin Putnam.

Elloy, D. F. (2008). The relationship between self-leadership behaviors and organization variables in a self-managed work team environment. *Management Research News, 31,* 801–810.

Elmhirst, K. (2008). Executive coaching. *Leadership Excellence, 25*(1), 11.

Ensley, M. D., Hmieleski, K. M., & Pearce, C. L. (2006). The importance of vertical and shared leadership within new venture top management teams: Implications for the performance of startups. *The Leadership Quarterly, 17,* 217–231.

Erez, M. & Arad, R. 1986. Participative goal-setting: Social, motivational, and cognitive factors. *Journal of Applied Psychology, 71*(4): 591.

Evans, C. R., & Dion, K. L. (1991). Group cohesion and performance: A meta-analysis. *Small Group Research, 22,* 175–186.

Fausing, M. S., Joensson, T. S., Lewandowski, J., & Bligh, M. (2015). Antecedents of shared leadership: Empowering leadership and interdependence. *Leadership & Organization Development Journal, 36*(3), 271–291.

Figueira, T. J., Brennan, T. C., & Sternberg, R. H. (2009). *Wisdom from the ancients: Leadership lessons from Alexander the Great to Julius Caesar.* New York, NY: Fall River Press.

Follett, M. P. (1924). *Creative experience.* New York, NY: Longmans Green.

Gantt, H. L. (1916). *Industrial leadership.* New Haven, CT: Yale University Press.

George, V., Burke, L. J., Rodgers, B., Duthie, N., Hoffmann, M. L., Koceja, V., . . . Gehring, L. L. (2002). Developing staff nurse shared leadership behavior in professional nursing practice. *Nursing Administration Quarterly, 26*(3), 44–59.

Gerstner, C. R., & Day, D. V. (1997). Meta-analytic review of leader–member exchange theory: Correlates and construct issues. *Journal of Applied Psychology, 82,* 827–844.

Gilbreth, F. B. (1912). *Primer of scientific management.* New York, NY: Van Nostrand Reinhold.

Gilbreth, F. B., & Gilbreth, L. M. (1917). *Applied motion study.* New York, NY: Sturgis & Walton.

Grille, A., & Kauffeld, S. (2015). Development and preliminary validation of the Shared Professional Leadership Inventory for Teams (SPLIT). *Psychology, 6*(1), 75.

Gu, J., Chen, Z., Huang, Q., Liu, H., & Huang, S. (2016). A multilevel analysis of the relationship between shared leadership and creativity in inter-organizational teams. *The Journal of Creative Behavior.* Advance online publication. doi:10.1002/jocb.135

Heenan, D. A. & Bennis, W. 1999. Co-leaders: The power of great partnerships: John Wiley & Sons.

Hess, J. P. (2015). Enabling and sustaining shared leadership in autonomous teams. *European Scientific Journal, 1,* 82–95.

Hmieleski, K. M., Cole, M. S., & Baron, R. A. (2012). Shared authentic leadership and new venture performance. *Journal of Management, 38*(5), 1476–1499.

Hofstede, G. H. (1980). *Culture consequences: International differences in work-related values*. London, UK: Sage.

Hollander, E. P. (1961). Some effects of perceived status on responses to innovative behavior. *Journal of Abnormal and Social Psychology, 63*, 247–250.

Hollander, E. P. (1978). *Leadership dynamics: A practical guide to effective relationships*. New York, NY: Free Press.

Hooker, C., & Csikszentmihalyi, M. (2003). Flow, creativity, and shared leadership: Rethinking the motivation and structuring of knowledge work. In C. L. Pearce & J. A. Conger (Eds.), *Shared leadership: Reframing the hows and whys of leadership* (pp. 217–234). Thousand Oaks, CA: Sage.

House, R. J., Hanges, P. J., Ruiz-Quintanilla, S. A., Dorfman, P. W., Javidan, M., Dickson, M., et al. (1999). Cultural influences on leadership in organizations: Project GLOBE. In W. H. Mobley, M. J. Gessner, & V. Arnold (Eds.), *Advances in global leadership* (Vol. 1, pp. 171–234). Stamford, CT: JAI.

Hunt, J. G. (2004). What is leadership? In J. Antonakis, A. T. Cianciolo, & R. J. Sternberg (Eds.), *The nature of leadership* (pp. 19–47). Thousand Oaks, CA: Sage.

Kelley, R. E. 1988. In praise of followers: Harvard Business Review Case Services.

Kerr, S., & Jermier, J. (1978). Substitutes for leadership: Their meaning and measurement. *Organizational Behavior and Human Performance, 22*, 374–403.

Klein, K. J., Ziegert, J. C., Knight, A. P., & Xiao, Y. (2006). Dynamic delegation: Shared, hierarchical, and deindividualized leadership in extreme action teams. *Administrative Science Quarterly, 51*, 590–621.

Klimoski, R. & Mohammed, S. 1994. Team mental model: Construct or metaphor? *Journal of Management, 20*(2): 403-437.

Konu, A., & Viitanen, E. (2008). Shared leadership in Finnish social and health care. *Leadership in Health Services, 21*, 28–40.

Leavitt, H. J. (2005). *Top down: Why hierarchies are here to stay and how to manage them more effectively*. Boston, MA: Harvard Business School Press.

Leonard, H. S., & Goff, M. (2003). Leadership development as an intervention for organizational transformation. *Consulting Psychology Journal, 55*, 58–67.

Liden, R. C., & Antonakis, J. (2009). Considering context in psychological leadership research. *Human Relations, 62*, 1587–1605.

Locke, E. A. (2003). Leadership: Starting at the top. In C. L. Pearce & J. A. Conger (Eds.), *Shared leadership: Reframing the hows and whys of leadership* (pp. 271–284). Thousand Oaks, CA: Sage.

Luthans, F. (2010). *Organizational behavior*. New York, NY: McGraw-Hill.

Manz, C. C. (1986). Self-leadership: Toward an expanded theory of self-influence processes in organizations. *Academy of Management Review, 11*, 585–600.

Manz, C. C., Shipper, F., & Stewart, G. L. (2009). Everyone a team leader: Shared influence at W. L. Gore & Associates. *Organizational Dynamics, 38*, 239–244.

Manz, C. C., & Sims, H. P., Jr. (1980). Self-management as a substitute for leadership: A social learning theory perspective. *Academy of Management Review, 5*, 361–367.

Manz, C. C., & Sims, H. P., Jr. (1989). *Super leadership: Leading others to lead themselves*. New York, NY: Prentice Hall.

Masal, D. (2015). Shared and transformational leadership in the police. *Policing: An International Journal of Police Strategies & Management, 38*(1), 40–55.

Mathieu, J. E., Kukenberger, M. R., D'Innocenzo, L., & Reilly, G. (2015). Modeling reciprocal team cohesion–performance relationships, as impacted by shared leadership and members' competence. *Journal of Applied Psychology, 100*(3), 713.

Mohrman, S. A., Cohen, S. G., & Mohrman, A. M. (1995). *Designing team-based organizations: New forms for knowledge work*. San Francisco, CA: Jossey-Bass.

Montgomery, J. (1836). *The theory and practice of cotton spinning; or the carding and spinning master's assistant*. Glasgow, Scotland: John Niven, Trongate.

Montgomery, J. (1840). *The cotton manufacture of the United States of America contrasted and compared with that of Great Britain*. London, UK: John N. Van.

Muethel, M., Gehrlein, S., & Hoegl, M. (2012). Socio-demographic factors and shared leadership behaviors in dispersed teams: Implications for human resource management. *Human Resource Management, 51*(4), 525–548.

Mundlak, Y. (1978). Pooling of time-series and cross-section data. *Econometrica, 46*(1), 69–85.

Nardinelli, C. (2008). *Industrial revolution and the standard of living.* Retrieved from http://www.econlib.org/library/Enc/IndustrialRevolutionandtheStandardofLiving.html

Nicolaides, V. C., LaPort, K. A., Chen, T. R., Tomassetti, E. J., Weis, E. J., Zaccaro, S., & Cortina, J. M. (2014). The shared leadership of teams: A meta-analysis of proximal, distal, and moderating relationships. *The Leadership Quarterly, 25,* 923–942.

Olson-Sanders, T. (2006). Collectivity and influence: The nature of shared leadership and its relationship with team learning orientation, vertical leadership and team effectiveness (Doctoral dissertation). Retrieved from ABI/INFORM Global (Publication No. AAT 3237041).

O'Toole, J., Galbraith, J., & Lawler, E. E., III. (2003). The promise and pitfalls of shared leadership: When two (or more) heads are better than one. In C. L. Pearce & J. A. Conger (Eds.), *Shared leadership: Reframing the hows and whys of leadership* (pp. 250–268). Thousand Oaks, CA: Sage.

Paris, L., Howell, J., Dorfman, P., & Hanges, P. (2009). Preferred leadership prototypes of male and female leaders in 27 countries. *Journal of International Business Studies, 40,* 1396–1405.

Paunova, M., & Lee, Y. T. (2016). Collective global leadership in self-managed multicultural teams: The role of team goal orientation. *Advances in Global Leadership* (Vol. 9, pp. 187–210). Bingley, UK: Emerald Group.

Pearce, C. L. (1997). *The determinants of change management team (CMT) effectiveness: A longitudinal investigation.* (Unpublished doctoral dissertation), University of Maryland, College Park.

Pearce, C. L. (2008, July 7). Follow the leaders. *Wall Street Journal,* p. R8.

Pearce, C. L. (2010). Leading knowledge workers: Beyond the era of command and control. In C. L. Pearce, J. A. Maciariello, & H. Yamawaki (Eds.), *The Drucker difference* (pp. 35–46). New York, NY: McGraw-Hill.

Pearce, C. L., & Conger, J. A. (Eds.). (2003). *Shared leadership: Reframing the hows and whys of leadership.* Thousand Oaks, CA: Sage.

Pearce, C. L., Conger, J. A., & Locke, E. (2008). Shared leadership theory. *The Leadership Quarterly, 19,* 622–628.

Pearce, C. L., Manz, C. C., & Sims, H. P., Jr. (2009). Where do we go from here? Is shared leadership the key to team success? *Organizational Dynamics, 38,* 234–238.

Pearce, C. L., Manz, C. C., & Sims, H. P., Jr. (2014). *Share, don't take the lead.* Charlotte, NC: Information Age.

Pearce, C. L., & Osmond, C. P. (1999). From workplace attitudes and values to a global pattern of nations: An application of latent class modeling. *Journal of Management, 25,* 759–778.

Pearce, C. L., & Sims, H. P., Jr. (2000). Shared leadership: Toward a multi-level theory of leadership. In M. M. Beyerlein, D. A. Johnson, & S. T. Beyerlein (Eds.), *Advances in interdisciplinary studies of work teams* (pp. 115–139). Greenwich, CT: JAI.

Pearce, C. L., & Sims, H. P., Jr. (2002). Vertical versus shared leadership as predictors of the effectiveness of change management teams: An examination of aversive, directive, transactional, transformational, and empowering leader behaviors. *Group Dynamics, Theory, Research, and Practice, 6,* 172–197.

Pearce, C. L., & Wassenaar, C. L. (2014). Leadership, like fine wine, is something meant to be shared, globally. *Organizational Dynamics, 43*(1), 9–16.

Pearce, C. L., Wassenaar, C. L., & Manz, C. C. (2014). Is shared leadership the key to responsible leadership? *Academy of Management Perspectives, 28,* 275–288.

Pearce, C. L., Yoo, Y., & Alavi, M. (2004). Leadership, social work, and virtual teams: The relative influence of vertical versus shared leadership in the nonprofit sector. In R. E. Riggio & S. Smith Orr (Eds.), *Improving leadership in nonprofit organizations* (pp. 160–203). San Francisco, CA: Jossey-Bass.

Peter, T., Braun, S., & Frey, D. (2015, January). How shared leadership affects individual creativity and support for innovation. *Academy of Management Proceedings.* doi:10.5465/AMBPP.2015.16212abstract

Riggio, R. E., Chaleff, I., & Lipman-Blumen, J. (Eds.). (2008). *The art of followership: How great followers create great leaders and organizations.* San Francisco, CA: Jossey-Bass.

Rodríguez, C. (2005). Emergence of a third culture: Shared leadership in international strategic alliances. *International Marketing Review, 22,* 67–95.

Ropo, A., Eriksson, P., & Hunt, J. G. (1997). Reflections on conducting processual research on management and organizations. *Scandinavian Journal of Management, 13,* 331–335.

Ropo, A., & Sauer, E. (2003). Partnerships of orchestras: Towards shared leadership. *International Journal of Arts Management, 5*(2), 44–55.

Say, J. B. (1964). *A treatise on political economy.* New York, NY: Augustus M. Kelley. (Original work published 1803)

Seibert, S. E., Sparrowe, R. T., & Liden, R. C. (2003). A group exchange structure approach to leadership in groups. In C. L. Pearce & J. A. Conger (Eds.), *Shared leadership: Reframing the hows and whys of leadership* (pp. 173–192). Thousand Oaks, CA: Sage.

Serban, A., & Roberts, A. J. (2016). Exploring antecedents and outcomes of shared leadership in a creative context: A mixed-methods approach. *The Leadership Quarterly, 27*(2), 181–199.

Shamir, B., & Lapidot, Y. (2003). Shared leadership in the management of group boundaries: A study of expulsions from officers' training courses. In C. L. Pearce & J. A. Conger (Eds.), *Shared leadership: Reframing the hows and whys of leadership* (pp. 235–249). Thousand Oaks, CA: Sage.

Solomon, A., Loeffler, F. J., & Frank, G. H. 1953. An analysis of co-therapist interaction in group psychotherapy. *International Journal of Group Psychotherapy, 3*(2): 171–180.

Sousa, M., & Van Dierendonck, D. (2015). Introducing a short measure of shared servant leadership impacting team performance through team behavioral integration. *Frontiers in Psychology, 6.*

Stein, R. T., & Heller, T. (1979). An empirical analysis of the correlations between leadership status and participation rates reported in the literature. *Journal of Personality and Social Psychology, 37,* 1993–2002.

Stewart, L. (1998). A meaning for machines: Modernity, utility, and the eighteenth century British public. *Journal of Modern History, 70,* 259–294.

Stewart, L. (2003). Science and the eighteenth-century public: Scientific revolutions and the changing format of scientific investigation. In M. Fitzpatrick, P. Jones, C. Knelworf, & I. McAlmon (Eds.), *The Enlightenment world* (pp. 234–246). London, UK: Routledge.

Taylor, F. W. (1903). *Shop management.* New York, NY: Harper & Row.

Taylor, F. W. (1911). *Principles of scientific management.* New York, NY: Harper & Brothers.

Turner, C. 1933. Test room studies in employee effectiveness. *American Journal of Public Health and the Nations Health, 23*(6): 577–584.

Wang, D., Waldman, D. A., & Zhang, Z. (2014). A meta-analysis of shared leadership and team effectiveness. *Journal of Applied Psychology, 99*(2), 181.

Wassenaar, C. L., & Pearce, C. L. (2012). Shared leadership 2.0: A 2010 glimpse into the state of the field. In M. Uhl-Bien & S. Ospina (Eds.), *Relational leadership theory.* Charlotte, NC: Information Age.

Wassenaar, C. L., & Pearce, C. L. (2015). Shared leadership in action. *Academy of Management Perspectives.* Advance online publication. doi:10.5465/amp.2015.0175

Wassenaar, C. L., Pearce, C. L., Hoch, J., & Wegge, J. (2010). Shared leadership meets virtual teams: A match made in cyberspace. In P. Yoong (Ed.), *Leadership in the digital enterprise: Issues and challenges* (pp. 15–27). Hersey, PA: IGI Global.

Wood, M. S. (2005). Determinants of shared leadership in management teams. *International Journal of Leadership Studies, 1*(1) 64–85.

Wren, D. A. (1994). *The evolution of management thought* (4th ed.). New York, NY: John Wiley.

Yukl, G. A. (2012). *Leadership in organizations* (8th ed.). Englewood Cliffs, NJ: Prentice Hall.

Zhou, W. (2016). When does shared leadership matter in entrepreneurial teams: The role of personality composition. *International Entrepreneurship and Management Journal, 12*(1), 153–169.

# CHAPTER 8

# Evolutionary, Biological, and Neuroscience Perspectives

*Mark van Vugt*

---

## Opening Case: A Day in the Life of a Leader

Everyone in the group expected the conflict to escalate at some point, but when it finally did it wreaked havoc in the community and upset many. Jack, the leader of the group, had been challenged a number of times by Tom, his underling. They were usually fighting over resources, and up until now each conflict had always been settled in favor of the powerful, overbearing leader, Jack. But this time it was different. Tom was not going to accept Jack's authority this time. He mounted a leadership challenge. Tom stood face to face with Jack and unlike previous times, Tom did not look away when Jack was intimidating him with his piercing eyes, which was in clear violation of the group's rules concerning hierarchy. Tom made himself look bigger by erecting his body and spreading his arms and legs wide, like a boxer before entering the ring. Jack was quick to interpret this as a challenge to his leadership, and he made himself even bigger. They started delivering blows to each other with their hands and feet. This was not going to be settled peacefully. The group stood by and watched. Were they going to wait until the fight was over and side with the winner? No. Peter, who was friends with Tom, made a move to help his friend, and now it was two against one. Just when Jack's allies were preparing to come to his aid, out of the group Mary emerged and approached the combatants. Being the oldest female in the group, she was held in high esteem by everyone. If someone could intervene successfully in this conflict it would be her. She stepped in between the two males and delivered a few blows to the bodies of Jack and Tom, and then the fight was over. The two angry males went their separate ways, and reconciled shortly afterward by hugging each other and patting each other on the back. Jack had survived this particular leadership challenge, but he knew that Tom would be trying again to seize the leadership position as soon as Jack looked weak and indecisive.

Now, you may think the above example concerns humans, but it does not. Instead, it represents a typical leadership challenge in chimpanzees. The chimpanzee (together with the bonobo) is the closest genetic relative of us humans, and we share a common ancestry from around 5 to 7 million years ago. Chimpanzees live in small groups with dominance hierarchies and an alpha male as their "leader." The leader faces frequent leadership challenges from subordinate males in the group who sometimes team up against each other to overthrow the alpha. According to primatologist Frans de Waal (1982), who has studied chimpanzees in Arnhem Zoo in the Netherlands, when such challenges arise sometimes older females step in as peacekeepers.

## Discussion Questions

1. What are the main similarities and differences between leadership in humans and nonhuman primates?

2. What do you think are the benefits of being a leader in a group of chimpanzees?

3. What are the nonverbal indicators of leadership and followership in humans?

4. Give examples of dominant leaders in business or politics who behave like alphas.

# Chapter Overview

When a honey bee returns to its hive after foraging for nectar, it performs a dance for the other bees. The bee skips around making a figure-eight movement, waggling its abdomen as it does so. In 2005, scientists found out that the dancer is indicating through its moves the location and quality of a foraging site (Riley, Greggers, Smith, Reynolds, & Menzel, 2005). The direction the bee is facing points to the direction of the food source relative to the sun; the duration of the waggle dance represents how far the source lies and its quality. Scientists proved it by setting up artificial food sources and monitoring the behavior of the bees that scrutinized a waggle dance. When the hive was moved 250 meters, the follower bees flew to a site that was 250 meters away from the artificial source, proving that the follower bees were following navigational instructions encoded in the waggle dance. It proved a theory first put forward by Nobel Prize–winning biologist Karl von Frisch in the 1960s. The dancer bee is in fact acting as a leader by scouting out food resources for the hive. The best dancers recruit the most followers, and this interaction produces a very efficient group performance.

The waggle dance of the honey bee is one of many leadership and followership displays that take place in the animal kingdom, from the migration patterns of birds and fish, and foraging activities among dolphins and hyenas, to food sharing among nonhuman primates (Smith et al., 2015).

Humans are animals too. Although our leadership patterns are, in many ways, more sophisticated than those of our animal relatives, maybe there are lessons to be learned from taking a closer look at the evolutionary history of leadership and drawing cross-species comparisons. In this chapter, I will explain why leadership has emerged in various social species, not just humans, and what forms it takes. Questions about the evolutionary origins and functions of leadership are seldom asked by social and behavioral scientists studying leadership. They tend primarily to be interested in the mechanics of leadership—how does it work?—rather than questions about the deeper-evolved functions of leadership. Addressing questions about both the proximate and ultimate causes of leadership could help to integrate leadership theories and generate novel hypotheses.

There is an increasing awareness among leadership scholars of the importance of building comprehensive theories by integrating knowledge from the natural, biological, and social sciences that all have interesting things to say about leadership (Antonakis, 2011; Bennis, 2007; Colarelli & Arvey, 2015). Anthropologists, biologists, cognitive neuroscientists, economists, political scientists, primatologists, psychologists, and zoologists have been studying various aspects of leadership emergence, yet so far there has been very little cross-fertilization among these areas in developing models and theories of leadership that are consistent with one another (cf. King, Johnson, & van Vugt, 2009; Smith et al., 2015). In addition, social scientists studying leadership have provided many good middle-level theories—such as personality, cognitive, situational, and contingency theories of leadership (e.g., Bass, 1985; Fiedler, 1995; Graen & Uhl-Bien, 1995; House, 1996; Shamir, House, & Arthur, 1993)—yet they are not always well connected to higher-order theories (cf. Bennis, 2007; van Vugt, Hogan, & Kaiser, 2008). Finally, most leadership theorists base their ideas on data from modern, complex organizations such as businesses, the military, and government, yet these are novel structures on an evolutionary time scale. Humans spent more than 95% of their evolutionary history in small-scale societies with informal, shared, and egalitarian leadership arrangements (van Vugt & Ronay, 2014; von Rueden & van Vugt, 2015). Understanding leadership in small-scale societies helps test theories of why leadership exists at all and what contributes to leader emergence and effectiveness in any society.

Evolutionary theory (as I will explain shortly) may provide an overarching framework that can connect these separate lines of inquiry into leadership. Darwin's (1871) theory of evolution through natural selection makes clear that the human mind is ultimately a product of biological evolution—in the same way that our bodies are evolutionary products—consisting of many different traits and mechanisms that evolved because they enabled humans to cope better with the demands of the social and physical environments in which they evolved.

In this chapter, I will put forward a new theoretical perspective on leadership—evolutionary leadership theory, or in short, EvoL theory—which is guided by the principles of Darwin's evolutionary theory, and explains how our leadership and followership psychology may have been shaped through selection pressures operating on humans in ancestral environments (van Vugt & Ronay, 2014). I will define leadership broadly here in terms of a process of influence over the establishment of goals, logistics of coordination, monitoring of effort, and reward or punishment strategies (Bass, 2008; Yukl, 2014). In this chapter, I will first provide a very brief introduction into evolutionary theory, and focus in particular on the growing field of evolutionary psychology. This field applies Darwinian thinking to human psychology and behavior. Second, I will argue why evolutionary psychology may be particularly relevant for understanding leadership and followership, and address various evolved functions of leadership. Third, I will put forward a short natural history of leadership, addressing how leadership may have evolved in steps from a rather crude device for synchronizing the activities of simple organisms to complex social structures able to coordinate the activities of millions of humans dispersed across space and time. Fourth, I will present recent data on leadership collected by behavioral scientists—using a variety of methods from mathematical models to ethnographies and from animal behavior observations to neuroscience experiments—showing the richness and diversity of an evolutionary perspective on leadership. Finally, I will address some implications of adopting an evolutionary perspective for developing further theory and research on leadership with a particular focus on the mismatch hypothesis.

## The Evolutionary Psychology of Leadership

EvoL theory starts with the recognition that the physiological, neurological, and psychological processes involved in producing human behaviors are first and foremost products of biological evolution. It follows, therefore, that conceptual insights of evolutionary theory, when applied with rigor and care, can produce novel discoveries about human behaviors in the same way as they can about the behaviors of other animals (Buss, 2015; van Vugt & Ronay, 2014; van Vugt & Schaller, 2008). Cultural processes matter too, of course, in understanding human behavior, but culture is also a product of biology, as humans have evolved psychological mechanisms for imitation and social learning (Henrich & Gil-White, 2001; Richerson & Boyd, 2006; Tooby & Cosmides, 2005).

Charles Darwin is the (grand)father of modern evolutionary theory. In his 19th-century voyage on the *Beagle* to the Galápagos Islands, Darwin noted that different species were beautifully adapted to their environments. After much study, he concluded that different species were not created by a divine hand, but they arose as a consequence of their environment. Members of a species displaying certain features—say, a giraffe boasting a long neck—flourished in their environment, the African savannah, better than less well-equipped members—short-necked giraffes. A long-necked giraffe would have access to more food resources (leaves high in the tree tops), and this advantage would give long-necked members a survival advantage. Over time, this could result in differential reproduction: long necks get more offspring than short necks and, given enough time, long necks would become a universal feature of giraffes. This feature, neck size, is then referred to as an adaptation. This, Darwin reasoned, explained why creatures seemed so perfectly suited to their natural environments.

Darwin postulated that natural selection operates via three very simple rules:

- There is variation in traits between individuals within the same species.
- Some of this variation is heritable (which is why offspring resemble parents).
- Some of these trait variations give individuals an edge in the competition for resources.

These three rules form the backbone of evolutionary theory.

Darwin's insights have been proven right so many times that evolutionary theory is no longer treated as a hypothetical possibility, but rather as a law of nature (Coyne, 2010). To understand evolutionary theory, one does not necessarily need to know anything about heritability, genes, or alleles. Yet it is good to realize, first, that adaptations (such as the giraffe's neck) are underpinned by genes that operate as units of selection. Any gene first emerges as a random mutation, and usually only spreads through a population if it gives the organism an edge in the competition for resources. Going back to our example, at some point in history, a baby giraffe was born with a spontaneous gene mutation giving it a longer neck than the other giraffes. Because this gene produced a giraffe that was better adapted to its environment, this particular gene survived, and over many generations, it has spread through the population so that every giraffe nowadays carries the "long neck" gene—in evolutionary terms, this trait has gone to "fixation." It is important to realize that when evolutionary biologists talk about a "gene for trait X," this is overly simplistic because most traits are underpinned by multiple genes operating in complex combinations; for example, human height is influenced by almost 700 genes, according to genome-wide association studies (Wood et al., 2014). Finally, when evolutionary biologists talk about "traits," they refer to any feature of an organism that is expressed when an organism's genes interact with their environment, including physical features (such as height and eye color), neurophysiological mechanisms (such as brain areas, neurotransmitters, and hormones), psychological mechanisms (such as cognitions, emotions), and behaviors (such as risk taking, sociability, followership). Natural selection can operate on any aspect of an organism's design, if it is under the control of genes. For further details on evolutionary biology and evidence for evolution, I refer readers to popular science books written by distinguished evolutionary theorists such as Jerry Coyne (2010), Ernst Mayr (2001), or Richard Dawkins (2009).

Evolutionary leadership theory is inspired by *evolutionary psychology*, a branch of psychology that applies the principles and theories of evolutionary biology to human psychology and behavior (Buss, 2015; Pinker, 2002; Tooby & Cosmides, 2005). Evolutionary psychology integrates theory and research from different branches of psychology and connects them to knowledge from the biological sciences to generate a unifying theoretical framework based on the premise of evolutionary theory. The core tenet underlying evolutionary perspectives in psychology is that the human mind is a product of evolution through natural selection: Evolution has shaped the human brain (and its products such as hormones, emotions, cognitions, and behaviors) in the same way as it has shaped the human body and the bodies and minds of other animals. In effect, this means that humans are viewed as part of the living world, being subject to the same laws of biology and evolution as other species.

Evolutionary psychology proposes that human minds contain a number of specialized psychological mechanisms—or adaptations—that enable humans to solve many different problems affecting their reproductive success (Buss, 2015). Humans likely possess specialized adaptive mechanisms for heat regulation, predator avoidance, foraging, mate selection, parental investment, face recognition, language, social interaction, and leadership. These psychological mechanisms are functional and domain-specific in the sense that they are extremely good at solving specific problems, but not others (Barrett & Kurzban, 2006). For instance, language is a highly efficient device for sharing social information, but it is not good for keeping a body warm.

It is instructive to think of these evolved mechanisms as cognitive heuristics, or "if–then" computational rules, that have been selected over evolutionary time to respond to certain environmental inputs, and produce outputs in terms of adaptive behavioral, psychological, and physiological responses. An example of an adaptive computational rule would be something like "Only follow an individual who appears trustworthy." It is easy to see that this rule works better, on average, than the rule "Just follow anyone indiscriminately" and would, over the course of evolution, have been selected for. Evolutionary psychologists further assume that evolved psychological mechanisms (a) operate automatically (without requiring much conscious effort; cf. Kahneman, 2011); (b) do not require extensive learning or training; (c) are relatively culture-free; (d) follow stable developmental pathways; and (e) are highly sensitive to relevant environmental inputs (Tooby & Cosmides, 2005).

Finally, it is good to realize that because biological evolution is a painstakingly slow process, psychological mechanisms are adapted to past environments. This means that they may not necessarily produce adaptive responses in modern environments, especially if environmental and social conditions rapidly change. For instance, the heuristic "Follow a physically strong leader" may have been a functional mechanism in ancestral human environments in which physical strength of leaders mattered in, for instance, conflict resolution (Spisak et al., 2011; von Rueden & van Vugt, 2015). Yet this computational rule may backfire in modern environments in which the physical qualities of leaders arguably matter less (although it is still possible that tall and physically strong leaders attract more followers because they are seen as more influential). We refer to these discrepancies between ancestral and modern environments as evolutionary *mismatches* (van Vugt, Johnson, Kaiser, & O'Gorman, 2008), and we will address the implications later on.

Evolutionary scientists often apply four questions to find evidence for adaptive mechanisms (Tinbergen, 1963). Wondering why humans have vision, one answer would be that it helps them find food and detect dangers. This why-question concerns the ultimate, evolutionary function of vision. An additional question is through what particular series of steps vision evolved, the phylogenetic question. Other questions concern the mechanics of the eye—how does vision work?—and how vision develops across an animal's lifetime, the ontogenetic question. Although the answers to these four questions are very different, they complement each other in providing a full description of an adaptation: vision.

In the same way, we could ask about the *function, phylogeny, ontogeny,* and *mechanics* of leadership to get a complete account (Smith et al., 2015; van Vugt & Ahuja, 2010). The first question concerns the role of leadership in promoting the survival and reproductive success of individuals. The second *phylogenetic* question is through what series of steps leadership evolved, and when it first appeared in the human lineage (Brosnan, Newton-Fisher, & van Vugt, 2009). The third question concerns the mechanics of leadership—how does it work?—and this is what generally most interests psychologists and other behavioral scientists studying leadership: People with which personalities make good leaders, and which particular leadership styles attract most followers? The final question concerns the *ontogenetic* processes and asks how leadership and followership develop across the lifespan of an organism. For instance, it has been proposed that mimicry and gazing are early developmental stages of followership—infants follow the gaze of adults from the age of 9 months onward (van Vugt, 2014).

## The Evolutionary Functions of Leadership

Why do humans have leadership, and why do leader–follower relations form automatically and spontaneously? The probable answer lies deep in human evolutionary history (van Vugt & Ahuja, 2010). Humans are highly social animals (Baumeister & Leary, 1995; Richerson & Boyd, 2006; Smith et al., 2015). For a large part of human history—the genus Homo is approximately 2.5 million years old—humans lived in small, seminomadic family groups of hunter-gatherers who were highly interdependent, cooperative, and egalitarian. The likely place of our origins was the savanna in Africa (Foley, 1997). For early humans, coordinating activities were important for their survival. One of the more fundamental coordination challenges involves the movement of the group from one place, say a waterhole, to another. House's (1971) path-goal theory acknowledges this primary function of leadership: Effective leaders clarify the path to help their followers get from where they are to where they want to be, and they make the journey along the path easier by removing roadblocks. Ancestral humans needed to move quite literally from one place to another, and—in light of the dangers of predators and opportunities for collective action—it was adaptive to move as a group (King, Johnson, & van Vugt, 2009). But when does a group move, and where? Leadership offers a solution. Leadership for the purpose of group movement has been documented across animal societies, from social insects to fish, and from birds to mammals (Couzin et al., 2005; King et al., 2009; Smith et al., 2015). This suggests that leadership and followership may not require complex computational rules. Simple rules such as "Move if hungry" or "Stay close to one's neighbor" can produce something akin to leadership and followership. Furthermore, if we assume state or trait differences in the likelihood of a first move—such as one individual being hungrier or bolder than the other—it will automatically generate "leaders" and "followers," as our game theory models show (Couzin et al., 2005; van Vugt, 2006).

Once these rudimentary mechanisms for leadership and followership are in place, they can be co-opted to solve more complex coordination problems. Evolutionary leadership theory suggests various additional functions of leadership pertaining to, for instance, resource acquisition, alliance formation, conflict management, intergroup relations, and teaching in humans. These functions come out of the comparative and anthropological literatures on small-scale human societies (Hooper et al., 2010; Smith et al., 2015; von Rueden & van Vugt, 2015)—these latter

Photos A–D courtesy: ©iStockphoto.com/kietisak; ©iStockphoto.com/ Inventori; ©iStockphoto.com/skynesher; ©iStockphoto.com/FatCamera

**Figure 8.1**    Some Examples of Leadership and Followership Across the Animal World

(A) Tandem running in ants: The ant on the left is following the other to a known food source, and is led via tactile communication. Image courtesy of Tom Richardson and Nigel Franks. (B) Honey bee "waggle" dance signalling the location and quality of potential nest sites to colony members. Image courtesy of Jürgen Tautz and Marco Kleinhenz. (C) Side-flop display by an informed lead dolphin, used to coordinate shifts in activity patterns in group-mates. Image courtesy of Susan and David Lusseau. (D) Graduation ceremony at Harvard University, led by music, hierarchical costumes, a myriad of signals, and ritualized ceremony. Image courtesy of Dominic Johnson. Printed with permission from Elsevier.

offer a plausible model of group life among early humans. Concerning resource opportunities, the honey bee example shows that scout bees act as leaders in pointing the hive to new foraging and migration sites. In hunter-gatherer societies, there are individual leaders for hunting. For instance, among Native American tribes in eastern California there are leaders for rabbit hunts, and whale hunts among the Inuit require coordination of a boat crew overseen by a captain (von Rueden & van Vugt, 2015). Conflict management is another recurrent feature of small-scale societies that requires leadership. The social lives of hunter-gatherers involve constant conflict, both within and between groups, and anthropological studies show the emergence of war and peace leaders. For instance, among various Native American tribes such as the Cheyenne and Crow, younger, more aggressive war leaders exercise authority over raids, but more senior peace leaders take over during peace time (von Rueden & van Vugt, 2015).

Our closest relative—the chimpanzee—also practices warfare and peacekeeping, suggesting phylogenetic consistency. For instance, in *Chimpanzee Politics* primatologist Frans De Waal (1996) describes an instance of peace "leadership" among the chimpanzee colony of Arnhem Zoo in the Netherlands:

> A quarrel between Mama and Spin got out of hand and ended in fighting and biting. Numerous apes rushed up to the two warring females and joined in the fray. A huge knot of fighting, screaming apes rolled around in the sand, until Luit [the alpha male] leapt in and literally beat them apart. He did not choose sides in the conflict, like others; instead anyone who continued to act received a blow from him. (p. 129)

Another leader function concerns the distribution of resources, such as food beyond the family. In small-scale societies Big Men leaders emerge who generously provide resources and in so doing attract followers (cf. potlatches; van Vugt, Hogan, et al., 2008). Leaders also emerge if group coordination becomes more complex. Plains Indian bands generally do not have leaders, but during the summer buffalo hunt they elect tribal chiefs to oversee food production and to punish thieves and free-riders (von Rueden & van Vugt, 2015).

Finally, there is a role for leaders in small-scale societies to teach group members relevant skills and knowledge, for instance, about the workings of the natural world. In various hunter-gatherer societies such as the Hmong in East Asia there are *shaman* leaders who coordinate religious rituals and form the bridge between the group and the spiritual world of ancestors (Harner, 1980).

In sum, evolutionary leadership theory (van Vugt & Ahuja, 2010; van Vugt & Ronay, 2014) assumes that leadership emerged as a simple coordination mechanism among group-living species. In addition, leadership facilitated the solution of more complex social problems that our hunter-gatherer ancestors faced, such as such as policing groups, punishing free-riders, planning raids and battles, peacekeeping, teaching, and managing group resources. The anthropological literature on small-scale societies, which provide good models of ancestral human group life, provide support for each of these distinctive functions of leadership (Hooper et al., 2010; von Rueden & van Vugt, 2015).

The logic underlying EvoL theory is as follows. Effective leadership in these various domains would have contributed to group effectiveness and individual survival and reproduction. As a thought experiment, imagine two groups of humans living in the same region and competing for the same resources. One band is characterized by internal discord, defective group decision making, and coordination failures. The second is characterized by harmony, effective group decision making, and smooth coordination if the situation requires leadership. Over time the members of the second group flourish and do better reproductively such that their genes—and the associated physiological and psychological mechanisms for which these genes code—will be passed on to the next generations until they spread through the entire human population. This evolutionary process of leadership and followership mechanisms likely took place through biological evolution in the first place. Yet in humans information is passed on through both genes and culture (which is a product of biological evolution as well). Cultural selection operates via the same Darwinian mechanisms of variation, selection, and retention but can operate at a much faster rate (Richerson & Boyd, 2006). It is probable that cultural practices of leadership, such as having formal hierarchies with institutionalized leaders (chiefs, generals, CEOs), were successful cultural innovations. Once these structures emerged after the Agricultural Revolution, they spread quickly and successfully through human societies. If we want to understand the differences between humans and nonhumans in manifestations of leadership, we have to consider the interplay between biological and cultural evolution, which is what gene-culture coevolutionary models do (Henrich et al., 2015; Smith et al., 2015; cf. niche-construction theory; Spisak, O'Brien, Nicholson, & van Vugt, 2015).

## A Brief Natural History of Leadership

Moving away from the evolutionary functions of leadership, what can we say about its phylogeny? How did leadership evolve across evolutionary time, and what can we say about the evolution of leadership in humans and nonhumans? A review of the human and nonhuman leadership literature suggests at least four major evolutionary transitions in the emergence of leadership (King et al., 2009; van Vugt, Hogan et al., 2008; see Table 8.1): (1) Leadership first emerged in prehuman species dating back many tens of millions of years ago as a mechanism to solve simple group coordination problems, where an individual initiated a movement and others followed; leadership was co-opted in our species, and perhaps other primates such as chimpanzees (with whom we shared a common ancestor some 5 to 7 million years ago), to foster collective action in situations involving significant conflicts of interest among individuals, such as conflict management and internal peacekeeping, in which physically dominant or socially important individuals emerged as leaders. (2) Dominance, a heritage of our primate nature, was attenuated in early human egalitarian societies, dating back some 2.5 million years ago, and this paved the way for prestige-based leadership and more democratic, participatory forms of group decision making, especially after the emergence of language about 100,000 years ago.

(3) The increase in the scale and social complexity of human societies that took place after the Agricultural Revolution some 13,000 years ago produced powerful, formally appointed leaders to manage complex coordination challenges—the chiefs, priests, and kings. At best, they acted as Big Men leaders by providing important public goods, and at worst, they abused their powers to exploit followers as though they were slaves (see Table 8.1). (4) Since only around 250 years ago, nation-states emerged with democratically elected presidents and, after the Industrial Revolution, major companies with elected CEOs and educated workers, and large urban areas with highly educated citizens. Leadership is still hierarchical, but it is also participatory in most parts of the globe, and followers can choose to leave these organizations and move elsewhere.

**Table 8.1**    A Natural History of Leadership

| Stage | Time Period | Society | Group Size | Leadership Structure | Leader | Leader–Follower Relations |
|---|---|---|---|---|---|---|
| 1 | > 2.5 million years ago | Prehuman | Variable | Situational | Any individual, often the dominant group member (alpha) | Situational or hierarchical (nonhuman primates) |
| 2 | 2.5 million–13,000 years ago | Band, clan, tribe | Dozens to hundreds | Informal, prestige- or expertise-based | Big man, head man | Egalitarian and situational |
| 3 | 13,000–250 years ago | Chiefdoms, kingdoms, warlord societies | Thousands | Centralized, institutionalized (sometimes hereditary) | Chiefs, kings, warlords | Hierarchical, prestige- or dominance-based |
| 4 | 250 years ago–present | Nations, states, large businesses | Thousands to millions | Centralized, democratic | Heads of state, CEOs | Hierarchical, but participatory |

SOURCE: M. Van Vugt, R. Hogan, and R. Kaiser. (2008). Leadership, Followership, and Evolution: Some Lessons from the Past. *American Psychologist, 63*, 182–196.

# Testing Evolutionary Hypotheses About Leadership

How do evolutionary-minded psychologists acquire knowledge about leadership? Evolutionary psychology represents an enormously diverse set of theories, methods, and analytical perspectives that can be usefully applied to study leadership and followership (Price & van Vugt, 2014; van Vugt & Tybur, 2015). This diversity results from the fact that evolutionary psychology, and evolutionary behavioral sciences more generally, attracts contributions from scientists with an unusually diverse range of scholarly backgrounds—not just scholars with different kinds of training within psychology, but scholars from biology, primatology, zoology, anthropology, economics, political science, and many other academic disciplines. The diversity is also a functional response to the high standards of evidence required for theory development and hypotheses testing in evolutionary psychology. A truly convincing support for an evolutionary-informed theory or hypothesis about leadership needs to show not only that it is activated in evolutionarily relevant situations but also that it functions in ways that would have promoted people's reproductive success. The first part is relatively easy. The second part is reasonably hard.

First, evolutionary psychologists frequently begin with a general theory—often from the core principles of evolutionary biology—that heuristically guides attention toward potential psychological adaptations. Common theories used by evolutionary psychologists include parental investment theory, sexual selection theory, life-history theory, and costly signaling theory (Gangestad & Simpson, 2007). If a hypothesized adaptation flows directly from a theory under the general paradigm of evolution, then evolutionary psychologists can express more confidence in the existence of an adaptation. For instance, a higher parental investment among females leads to the hypothesis that women have evolved to be interested in sexual partners who are good, reliable providers of resources. Furthermore, costly signaling theory suggests that (1) women should have evolved to pay attention to honest signals from potential mates about their resource-holding ability or potential and (2) men should be keen to send these honest, costly signals to desirable partners. This in turn gives rise to the hypothesis that men signal their mate value through achieving high-status positions—because status is linked to resources (van Vugt & Tybur, 2015). This yields testable predictions in the domain of leadership such that (1) men should be more motivated to obtain top-management positions, especially when the monetary and prestige benefits associated with these positions are substantial; (2) women should find male leaders more attractive as romantic partners, whereas the opposite is not necessarily true: women leaders do not attract more sexual interest from men; and (3) men should enact costly leadership behaviors in the presence of attractive women (the opposite should not be true for women leaders acting in the presence of men). Many of these predictions have received empirical support (e.g., Iredale & van Vugt, 2008; Jensen-Campbell, Graziano, & West, 1995), and some still require testing.

Second, evolutionary theorists can apply game theory to study the emergence of leadership. Game theory models interactions among individuals as the outcomes of social strategies that are in competition against each other (van Vugt, 2006). These models show, for instance, that leader–follower relations emerge faster when the interests of individuals in a coordination game are aligned rather than in conflict, and when one individual is informed and others in the group are not (Couzin et al., 2005).

Third, computer simulations and agent-based models can be used to test the validity of hypotheses underlying the emergence of leadership. For instance, computer simulations can help identify conditions under which groups move from an egalitarian structure with informal leaders as decision makers to a hierarchical structure with formal leadership (Hooper et al., 2010).

Fourth, experimental methods of behavioral economics and social psychology are useful in testing evolutionary hypotheses about leadership. The experimental (economics) games method studies interactions between players in games such as the prisoner's dilemma game, public goods game, or weak-link coordination game, in which players make interdependent decisions. This can produce insights into many questions, for instance, regarding which personality types are more likely to take the lead in a coordination game with sequential play, in which one player moves first and the rest follow (Gillet, Cartwright, & van Vugt, 2011).

Fifth, evidence for any hypothesized leadership and followership mechanism could emerge from recent advances in social neuroscience. The nascent field of organizational cognitive neuroscience applies neuroscience techniques to organizational behaviors such as leadership (Lee, Senior, & Butler, 2012; Waldman, Wang, & Fenters, 2016). Brain imaging studies (fMRI) have the potential to provide data attesting to specific physiological structures associated with specific kinds of organizational behaviors (Adolphs, 1999). Functional MRI research can be used to detect where there is brain activity when leaders successfully coordinate group activities, make fair allocation offers, or punish individuals harming group goals (Fehr & Camerer, 2007). A very recent technique called TMS, or transcranial magnetic simulation, has emerged that disrupts activity in brain areas thought to be responsible for social and economic decisions. This technique has found, for example, that disruption of the left frontal pre-cortex hinders people's ability to build a favorable social reputation (Knoch, Schneider, Schunk, Hohmann, & Fehr, 2009), a prerequisite for effective leadership.

Hormonal studies can help identify the hormonal correlates of leadership emergence or effectiveness. Individual differences in baseline hormone levels, such as cortisol, serotonin, and testosterone, predict how well individuals perform in high-status positions (van Vugt & Tybur, 2015). For instance, Josephs et al. (2006) reported a mismatch effect in an experimental study by showing that high-testosterone individuals do better on a complex cognitive task in a high-status position, whereas low-testosterone individuals perform better on this task in a low-status position. In addition, recent research among company employees suggests that when individuals try to climb the organizational hierarchy, basal testosterone is associated with a more directive, authoritarian leadership style, but when they have already secured a position of leadership, testosterone is unrelated to an authoritarian leadership style (Van der Meij, Schaveling, & van Vugt, 2016).

Sixth, behavior genetics studies help to provide an indication of whether leadership emergence has a substantial genetic component. A high heritability index suggests that there may be important individual differences in these traits. Employing twin design methods on longitudinal population data, De Neve et al. (2013) estimated the heritability of leadership role occupancy at 24%. Further research on genetic markers suggested that leadership role is associated with a single gene allele that regulates dopamine released in the brain. In addition to direct genetic effects, there are some promising results of studies showing that stable personality differences that are known to have a reasonably high heritable component (between 40% and 60%; Ilies, Arvey, & Bouchard, 2006) systematically predict leadership emergence (such as extraversion and intelligence).

Seventh, methods of experimental cognitive psychology are also often used by evolutionary psychologists to find evidence for evolved psychological mechanisms. Regarding leadership, cognitive experiments can be used to find out if people automatically recognize particular individuals as leaders. One study examined if people make spontaneous, automatic associations with leadership when they rate people's faces. For instance, people prefer a more masculine-looking leader in war time but a feminine-looking leader in peace time (Spisak et al., 2011; van Vugt & Grabo, 2015). Such prototypes are present among people across various cultures and across different age groups. There is indeed cross-cultural agreement on what the face of a leader looks like (Berggren, Jordahl, & Poutvarra, 2010). This indicates that these prototypes are automatic, evolved decision rules that may not require extensive learning (unlike what implicit leadership theories assume; cf. Epitropaki & Martin, 2004; Lord, De Vader, & Alliger, 1986). Indeed, a study found that children as young as 5 years old can pick the winners of political election outcomes that they know nothing about just by judging the competence of the candidates' faces (Antonakis & Dalgas, 2009). Other research reveals that both adults and children make similar snapshot judgments of various leadership attributes (dominance, trustworthiness) based on very minimal exposure (100ms) to faces (Cogsdill, Todorov, Spelke, & Banaji, 2014; Todorov, Olivola, Dotsch, & Mende-Siedlecki, 2015).

Eighth, psychological surveys can provide support for evolutionary hypotheses about leadership by examining self-reported data about people's experiences with leadership and followership in the real world. For instance, survey evidence from around the world reveals that there are some traits that are universally perceived to be associated with good leadership, such as vision, integrity, and trustworthiness (Den Hartog, House, Hanges, Ruiz-Quintanilla, & Dorfman, 1999). In addition, there are traits that are more important considerations in some cultures but not in others, such as a leader's generosity and dominance (Den Hartog et al., 1999). This suggests that some decision rules are relatively biologically fixed, such as "Follow a leader I can trust." Yet other rules are more flexible and possibly the product of local cultural norms such as "Follow an authoritarian leader."

Ninth, anthropological and ethnographic databases can provide additional evidence for evolutionary hypotheses about leadership, testing the extent to which leadership phenomena are universal across human cultures, from small-scale to large-scale societies (von Rueden & van Vugt, 2015). This kind of evidence is necessary to differentiate between phenomena that have deeper, evolutionary roots, and those that are more superficial, culture-specific manifestations. For instance, research on small-scale societies, which are good models of ancestral group living, has found that prestigious leaders (e.g., those who excel in hunting or political diplomacy) sire more offspring than average (von Rueden et al., 2011).

Tenth, and finally, cross-species evidence is instrumental in testing speculations about the evolutionary history of any alleged leadership mechanism or trait. In both human and elephant groups, for instance, older individuals take on leadership positions when traditional knowledge is required, such as the way to a long-forgotten waterhole (King et al., 2009; van Vugt & Ahuja, 2010). In addition, experiments on nonhuman primates reveal that unfair offers from "leaders" are being rejected by "followers" (Brosnan & De Waal, 2005). This finding implies that the underlying evolved psychological mechanism or decision rule—act fairly—either is the product of convergent evolution (where two species, not closely related, come up with the same solution to a problem) or was maintained when humans and nonhuman primates (in this case, capuchin monkeys) split from their last common ancestor millions of years ago (Brosnan et al., 2009). Primate studies, and animal research more generally, enhance our understanding of the evolution of important adaptive mechanisms such as fairness, empathy, and leadership (Preston & De Waal, 2013; Smith et al., 2015).

When considered in conjunction, the findings from these diverse lines of inquiry can produce new insights into leadership, its mechanisms, its development, and evolutionary functions. The utility of an evolutionary approach becomes apparent to just about anyone who seriously employs such an approach. For illustrative purposes, the following is a list of 9 recent empirical findings that have been discovered by evolutionarily inspired research programs on leadership with a diverse methodology, ranging from mathematical models to neuroscience studies. Although not one of these findings tells a definitive story, together they point to the existence of specialized evolved systems for leader–follower relations. A growing body of empirical evidence, in other words, shows the value of adopting an evolutionary-biological approach to leadership.

1. Agent-based models show that in groups with a heterogeneity in preferences between members yet a limited time to reach consensus, leadership emerges spontaneously (Gavrilets, Auerbach, & van Vugt, 2016). The leader position is then taken by the most stubborn group member—the individual least willing to shift their position. This result explains why under time pressure democratic groups revert to a more hierarchical decision-making structure.

2. A recent twin study reveals that about 40% of the variation in leadership emergence behaviors is explained by genetic factors (Chaturvedi, Zyphur, Arvey, Aviolo, & Larsson, 2012). This suggests that there is a heritable component to leadership. Yet it is rather unlikely that there is a single gene responsible for the difference between born leaders and born followers (cf. De Neve et al., 2014).

3. A brain imaging study shows that when followers receive an unfair offer from their leader in an ultimatum game, it elicits brain activity in areas related to emotion (anterior insula), suggesting that emotions play a role in deciding whether or not to follow a leader (Sanfey, 2007). This suggests that fast, intuitive, affective judgments play a role in how we evaluate our leaders.

4. Anthropological data obtained among the Tsimane in Bolivia show that physically formidable men often hold high-status positions in this hunter-gatherer society, they have more wives, and they sire more offspring (von Rueden et al., 2011). Physically strong men are likely to receive high status among the Tsimane because they are (seen as) better warriors and diplomats.

5.  An experimental study revealed that individuals with high baseline levels of testosterone were more likely to abuse their power position in an economic game. High-testosterone individuals with a greater number of followers (a proxy for power) were more likely to keep money for themselves than to distribute it evenly among themselves and their followers (Bendahan, Zehnder, Pralong, & Antonakis, 2015).

6.  A hyperscanning (fNIRS) experiment shows that dyads with a leader and a follower synchronize their neural activities more than leaderless dyads (Jiang et al., 2015). This study suggests that leader emergence is characterized by high levels of interpersonal neural synchronization between leaders and followers, and that the quality of communications matters more than the frequency in getting these pairs to synchronize neutrally.

7.  Data from management executive programs show that higher-ranked managers in work organizations have lower levels of cortisol (the "stress" hormone) than lower-ranked employees (Sherman et al., 2012). This suggests that high-status positions in society (such as leadership) come with lower stress levels and ultimately predict better health.

8.  A laboratory experiment shows that groups with punitive leaders reach higher levels of cooperation than groups without leaders (O'Gorman, Henrich, & van Vugt, 2009). The implication of this study is that leadership may have evolved partly to tackle the fundamental free-rider problem in (ancestral) human societies.

9.  A cognitive experiment using the well-known gaze cue paradigm shows that after being primed with danger cues participants followed the eye gaze of dominant-looking faces more than nondominant-looking faces (Ohlsen, Van Zoest, & van Vugt, 2013). This suggests that in danger, people may be using an automatic "follow-the-strong-leader" heuristic, which may be an evolutionary heritage.

# Implications of Evolutionary Leadership Theory

In this final section, I will note some implications of adopting an evolutionary perspective for leadership research and practice comparing leadership in modern organizations with leadership in small-scale societies in which humans evolved. Some of these implications can also be derived from other, proximate theories of leadership such as path-goal theory, leader–member exchange theory, social identity theory, transformational or leader categorization theories (Avolio et al., 2009; Epitropaki et al., this volume; van Knippenberg, this volume). Yet each of these theories must ultimately turn to evolution to explain its own assumptions (e.g., why are we attracted to charismatic leaders? why do we associate particular physical traits with leadership? where does the cultural variation in leader structures emerge from?). Furthermore, EvoL theory also sheds light on core leadership questions that have not yet been sufficiently addressed in the literature, such as why some people are followers rather than leaders, why there is a consistent preference for tall and healthy-looking leaders, and why women CEOs tend to attract hostility. Finally, an evolutionary framework also seems to generate a broader variety of implications for research and practice than other theoretical perspectives (van Vugt & Ronay, 2014; von Rueden & van Vugt, 2015), for instance, the way we should design leadership in organizations in light of the constraints of human-evolved psychology (e.g., is it prudent that organizations replace face-to-face leadership with remote leadership?).

## Why Follow?

An evolutionary approach highlights the importance of studying followership. Understanding the psychology of followership is in principle more interesting than leadership because there are more followers than leaders, and it is puzzling from an evolutionary perspective why individuals voluntarily give up their personal autonomy to follow another individual. Yet it is hardly studied (see Brown, this volume, for a follower-centric approach to leadership). EvoL theory suggests that followership evolved in response to coordination problems such as group movement, group defense, conflict resolution, and teaching that were significant and recurrent in our evolutionary history. This implies that followership should emerge more quickly in these evolutionarily relevant situations and that there are differences in followership styles depending on the problem at hand.

Although this hypothesis has not been tested explicitly, it is consistent with prior findings. People are more likely to follow a leader under conditions of external threat such as a crisis or natural disaster (Baumeister, Chesner, Senders, & Tice, 1989; Hamblin, 1958). Intergroup conflict also encourages the emergence of followership. In the famous Robber Cave experiment, individuals who did not know each other were brought together, and they promptly chose team leaders to represent them (Sherif, 1966). Finally, conformity research suggests that when people are uncertain about the best course of action, they are more likely to take the advice of another individual, the leader. The classic Milgram and Asch experiments in social psychology demonstrate that people quickly adhere to a rule—"Follow what most people do"—even if it is the morally or intellectually wrong decision. This implies that human minds are effectively tuned to followership—a heritage of our ancestral past—which is consistent with EvoL theory.

A different implication of EvoL theory is that individuals may not want to have a structural leader when they face a relatively simple coordination problem among a small group of people with little or no conflict of interest. This is consistent with the research on leadership substitutes (Kerr & Jermier, 1978). Installing leaders could even undermine team performance in these situations. For instance, highly cohesive groups do less well in performing a routine task with a formally appointed leader (Haslam et al., 1998).

The leadership literature could benefit from adopting a follower-centric approach (Brown, this volume; Uhl-Bien et al., 2014; Wayne & Ferris, 1990). Follower styles may be at least as variable and differentiated as leadership styles across contexts and personalities (Uhl-Bien et al., 2014; van Vugt et al., 2008). People follow with different levels of commitment, from being reluctant to being overzealous followers (Kellerman, 2008). In addition, some people follow because they want to learn something new ("apprentices"), identify strongly with leaders ("fans"), or are being forced to by someone higher up the hierarchy (subordinates of managers). An evolutionary lens places followership at the forefront of the study of leadership and is a good starting point for developing new followership theory and research (van Vugt & Ronay, 2014).

## How Important Is Context?

Another strength of EvoL theory is that it provides a solid foundation for contingency approaches to leadership by showing that different adaptive problems that early humans faced select for different kinds of leadership. Extrapolating from modern hunter-gatherer societies, leadership was flexible and, depending on conditions, different leaders emerged—for instance, the best hunter leads the hunting party, the wisest elder resolves internal conflicts, the fiercest warrior leads battles (von Rueden & van Vugt, 2015). An implication is that, despite stable individual (and heritable) differences in the likelihood of emerging as leaders across situations, who emerges as leader is contingent upon situations. Twin research suggests, indeed, that only about 25% of variance in leadership emergence is due to heritable differences in personality (Ilies, Gerhardt, & Le, 2004).

EvoL theory assumes that different leadership styles reflect evolved mechanisms that respond differently in different situations with (slightly) different payoff structures. So, for instance, we prefer a more aggressive, masculine leader with a dominant personality during war time, but in peace we prefer a more trustworthy, feminine leader (Little et al., 2007; Spisak et al., 2011). Thus, cognitive prototypes of leadership change depending upon what adaptive domain is salient (van Vugt & Grabo, 2015). EvoL theory also accounts for the fact that some leadership attributes are universally valued in leaders (such as fairness), whereas the importance of other attributes is culturally more flexible (Den Hartog & Dickson, this volume; Hofstede, 1980; Richerson & Boyd, 2006). For instance, participative, democratic styles prevail in the United States and Europe, where leaders have been forced to share power with citizens because of economic or geographical pressures (Acemoglu & Robinson, 2012). In contrast, more authoritarian leadership styles are found in places in which, for instance, intergroup conflicts or pathogen risks are prevalent (such as sub-Saharan Africa and Asia). There, stronger conformity pressures and punitive measures are necessary to maintain the peace or prevent the spread of infection risks (cf. individualistic versus collectivistic cultures; Fincher, Thornhill, Murray, & Schaller, 2008).

## Why Are Leader–Follower Relations Ambivalent?

A third strength of EvoL theory is that it explains the fundamental ambivalence in leader–follower relations (van Vugt et al., 2008). An evolutionary approach suggests that there are two different hierarchies in the animal world (van Vugt & Tybur, 2015). The first is the classic dominance hierarchy that results from competition for scarce resources, where the strongest and most determined individuals prevail, controlling group resources and activities. The second form of hierarchy emerges by consensus when hierarchical decision-making structures benefit group performance (Ronay et al., 2012). These two models offer very different accounts of leadership. The dominance model characterizes the various nonhuman primates such as gorillas and chimpanzees in which alpha males direct and control group activities and followers are intimidated by threat of force. This picture is, however, quite different for humans. Due to our particular evolutionary history as a cooperative, egalitarian species, human hierarchies are much flatter than in nonhuman primates, and leadership is primarily based on prestige rather than coercion (Henrich & Gil-White, 2001; van Vugt et al., 2004). We refer to this as the service-for-prestige theory of leadership (Price & van Vugt, 2014): Individuals who provide public services such as coordinating a hunt or a raid are conferred with status and prestige by the group. In small-scale societies, such individual "leaders" are indeed admired and respected, and their status is converted into reproductive success—they have more wives and children (von Rueden et al., 2011).

Dominance, however, is part of our primate heritage, and humans have likely evolved psychological mechanisms for forming dominance-submission relationships too (van Vugt & Ronay, 2014). Hence, there is always a risk in organizations that leaders will use their powers to exploit followers if the conditions are right (Padilla, Hogan, & Kaiser, 2007). This makes the leader–follower relationship inherently ambivalent. On one hand, there will be a temptation to extract resources from others in the organization. Thus, humans have likely evolved a leadership psychology with a set of decision rules that elicits dominance behaviors in appropriate situations (such as when they hold power). On the other hand, humans have evolved a followership psychology that includes a set of mechanisms, or decision rules, to avoid being dominated and exploited by leaders.

The anthropological and psychological literatures reveal several psychological mechanisms that individuals possess to increase their power base. "Big Men" leaders in small-scale societies are known to redistribute resources fairly and generously, and this enhances their powers—these are universally desirable leadership attributes (Brown, 1991; Dorfman et al., 2004; Henrich et al., 2015). Leaders can also induce external group threats to consolidate their power base (Cohen et al., 2004). Leaders sometimes "buy" support through engaging in nepotistic and corruptive practices (Altemeyer, 1981; Gandossy & Sonnenfeld, 2004), which furthers their reproductive interests (von Rueden & van Vugt, 2015). With the advent of language, another powerful tool emerged for leaders to dominate—the invention of ideologies. Throughout history, leaders have used or even created religions to maintain power—for example, the Sun Language religion of Kemal Ataturk—and turned their rule into a hereditary position to benefit themselves and their kin, a clear indication of nepotism (van Vugt & Ahuja, 2010).

At the same time, various mechanisms likely evolved to ensure that humans benefitted from following leaders without being exploited. In the anthropological literature such anti-exploitation devices are referred to as "levelling mechanisms (Boehm, 1999) or STOPs—strategies to overcome the powerful (van Vugt & Ahuja, 2010). The first is to accept and endorse authority only in areas where leaders have proven expertise (von Rueden & van Vugt, 2015). A second mechanism is the use of gossip and ridicule to keep leaders in place. In small-scale societies, if a chief misbehaves, he is publicly criticized, and if he tries to give commands, he is often rebuffed (Boehm, 1999).

Shunning exploitative leaders also acts as a powerful tool to level power differences. Ostracism presumably had severe consequences for excluded individuals in our evolutionary past, as it still has today (Williams, 2007). The ultimate sanction against exploitative leaders in small-scale societies is homicide. In hunter-gatherer societies, a dominating individual runs the risk of being killed, usually by a member of his own family, to avoid conflict between clans (Boehm, 1999). In the United States, disgruntled citizens have attempted to assassinate 15 of the 45 presidents, making it one of the most dangerous jobs in the world (Oliver & Marion, 2010).

## Are There Mismatches Between Ancestral and Modern Environments?

Finally, EvoL theory provides an answer to why modern leadership arrangements may fail by suggesting that there is a mismatch between our evolved leadership psychology and the challenges of modern environments. Human leadership psychology evolved in small groups in which leadership was personal, informal, and consensual. The mismatch hypothesis assumes that this evolved psychology still affects the way we select and respond to leaders today, sometimes creating mismatch challenges (van Vugt, Johnson, et al., 2008; von Rueden & van Vugt, 2015).

## Who Is the Leader?

EvoL theory explains why leadership correlates with physical traits such as height, voice pitch, and facial masculinity that, on the face of it, have little to do with good leadership—something not easily explained by existing leadership theories. Successful leaders in modern societies tend to be taller (Blaker et al., 2013; Judge & Cable, 2004; Stulp et al., 2013), although this may not necessarily be the case in team sports, where a player's age is more important for leadership than their height (Elgar, 2016). Leaders are generally also more masculine in terms of their facial and bodily characteristics (Little et al., 2007; Spisak et al., 2012). Male CEOs with deeper voices manage larger companies and enjoy longer tenures (von Rueden & van Vugt, 2015). These are indicators of physical strength (Sell et al., 2009), which in small-scale ancestral societies were particularly important because leadership was often physical, requiring dominance (e.g., for conflict resolution) or stamina (e.g., for group movement). Yet in modern societies leadership is often not a physical matter—although some leadership contests can be grueling physically, such as the U.S. presidential race—and followers rarely meet their leaders face to face. Yet such physical features continue to influence our leadership perceptions today. As Todorov et al. (2015) recently remarked about the validity of face cues: "When making social attributions of faces, people are making too much out of too little information" (p. 27).

Mismatch may also explain why narcissistic, Machiavellian, and even psycho-pathic individuals emerge at the pinnacle of modern organizations (Babiak & Hare, 2006; Judge & Bono, 2000)—these are referred to as dark triad leaders. Such individuals come across initially as charming, competent, and inspiring, yet there is no evidence that such leaders promote the interests of followers, and they could even harm them (Brunell et al., 2008). In small-scale societies people knew their leaders intimately, and it would be relatively easy to infer people's competence from their actual deeds. Displays of narcissism or psychopathy would result in punishment by the group (Boehm, 1999). However, in modern organizational structures in which people move jobs easily and mechanisms are often lacking to monitor people's actual performance, it is relatively difficult to distinguish competence from inflated self-beliefs. Thus, there are arguably more niches for dark triad leaders to emerge in modern organizations (von Rueden & van Vugt, 2015).

The current selection process of leaders creates another potential mismatch. In ancestral human societies, leaders emerged from the bottom up through their knowledge, personality, or moral virtues. In modern industrial and bureaucratic organizations, leaders are appointed top-down, by managers more senior in the organizational hierarchy. Pleasing superiors is an important predictor of career success in modern organizations, which did not exist to the same extent in the small-scale societies in which humans evolved. It is noteworthy that executives are more likely to succeed if subordinates are included in the selection process (Sessa, Kaiser, Taylor, & Campbell, 1998), which is a way to avoid mismatch.

The mismatch hypothesis also provides a clue about another current social issue: the prejudice against female leadership (Carli & Eagly, this volume). Male leadership was the norm in small-scale human societies, as leadership is often a matter of physical strength (Sell et al., 2009). Yet it remains to be seen how beneficial the bias toward male leadership is in modern complex organizations that increasingly emphasize interpersonal skills and coaching skills (Eagly & Carli, 2003). Despite many similarities, men and women are somewhat different in their biological makeup as a result of pursuing different mating strategies (Geary, 1998). Unlike what social role theorists claim, sex differences exist not just in physical traits, but also in psychological traits (Pinker, 2002). Women, on average, have better verbal memory, empathy, and communication skills—presumably as a result of evolutionary selection pressures on females to maintain close social networks for protection and child-rearing (van Vugt, 2006). Males, on average, are better at building larger, looser networks and functioning in hierarchical relationships (Benenson, 2013). Presumably this is because ancestral men played a more direct role in warfare, selecting for larger coalitions and more directive leaders (van Vugt et al., 2007; van Vugt & Spisak, 2008). Such evolved differences offer a plausible explanation for why men lead in a more authoritarian way and women in a more participative way (Eagly & Johnson, 1990).

## How Effective Is the Leader?

There are also likely to be mismatches in leader effectiveness. First, leadership in small-scale societies tends to operate informally and in face-to-face interactions with followers. The success of transformational, charismatic leaders may result in part from an evolved follower psychology that expects an intimate, personal relationship with leaders (van Vugt & Ronay, 2014). As physical distance between leaders and followers increases, organizations must work around this problem to render leadership effective. Over the past few decades, the globalization of the workforce and advances in information technologies have given rise to new work arrangements such as telecommuting, remote and digital work, and flexible work time agreements, often causing managers to lead subordinates at a distance (Antonakis & Atwater, 2002; Kelley & Kelloway, 2012). For instance, 10% of the U.S. and Canadian workforce works remotely at least 8 hours per week, and 96% of today's employees rely on the Internet, e-mail, or cell phones to stay in touch with work communications (U.S. Bureau of Labor Statistics, 2002). Such trends have resulted in a relatively new form of leadership characterized by electronically mediated communication between geographically and physically isolated leaders and followers—remote leadership. But how effective is remote leadership? Studies reveal that workers tend to prefer face-to-face interactions with their managers and that face-to-face communications are more persuasive (Le Ngoc et al., 2016). By creating virtual environments with richer social cues, organizations may work around the problem of an evolved psychology that responds to face-to-face leadership.

Second, leadership in small-scale societies tends to be shared and distributed. The individual most qualified for the task at hand—be it hunting, diplomacy, or warfare—can exercise influence, but only within this narrow domain of expertise (von Rueden & van Vugt, 2015). Furthermore, important group decisions are often made based on consensus, and information is pooled from a range of individuals (the "wisdom of the crowd" effect). Yet modern organizations make one individual—the CEO or manager—responsible for managing different functions well beyond their domain of expertise. This may partly be based on the belief that skill in one domain predicts skill in another (Yukl, 2014). Apparently, humans have evolved social learning mechanisms that tend to favor the broad imitation of successful individuals such as leaders (Henrich et al., 2015; Price & van Vugt, 2014). Yet it is questionable whether such biases are functional in evaluating leaders in modern, complex organizations. Followers have overly optimistic expectations about leaders ("the romance of leadership"), yet few leaders have the right skills to perform a wide array of duties. This is the problem of leader versatility—the ability to perform multiple, even competing roles (Kaiser, Lindberg, & Craig, 2007). Failure to share leadership and involve stakeholders may account for the relatively high failure rate of topflight leaders (van Vugt et al., 2008; Pearce & Wassenaar, this volume).

A third potential mismatch is the status difference between leaders and followers in modern times. Leadership is often rewarded with high salaries and considerable prestige and privileges. Research suggests that payment of CEOs is far higher than what people believe to be fair. In modern business environments, the average salary for CEOs is almost 200 times the average pay for workers (Norton & Ariely, 2011). Psychological studies show that power, which is associated with a high salary difference, increases the potential for abuse (Kipnis, 1972) and decreases the ability to empathize with subordinates (Galinsky, Magee, Inesi, & Gruenfeld, 2006). The highly asymmetric payoffs for modern business leaders may be at odds with our evolved psychology and encourage a kind of management that employees naturally resist. In the small-scale societies that humans evolved in, there were minimal wealth and status differences between individuals. This raises the question: Why would anyone want to be a leader? One possibility is that leaders themselves, or their direct kin, profit from coordination—for instance, defending their territory. Another is that successful leaders, like hunters or diplomats, are reciprocated by receiving prestige benefits (the service-for-prestige theory; Price & van Vugt, 2014; cf. von Rueden et al., 2011). A final possibility is that leadership acts as an honest signal (see earlier section) that reflects valuable personal qualities, such as courage or resource potential, to attract allies or sexual mates. To the extent that such signals are more costly, they are harder to fake and so, according to this logic, people should be keen to pay attention to individuals enacting good leadership behaviors.

In sum, the mismatch hypothesis can explain various biases in leadership emergence and effectiveness that are likely to form obstacles for leadership in modern organizations. Nevertheless, future research will need to discount alternative explanations for mismatch. For example, someone's physical strength or narcissism may be a reliable signal, even in modern times, of their intelligence or their ability to recruit allies to form larger social networks from which organizations can profit (von Rueden & van Vugt, 2015). Also, in modern societies, differences in status and wealth may be acceptable as long as they do not translate into differences in reproductive opportunities between high- and low-status individuals. Thus, despite vast social inequalities in modern societies, this may not in fact produce mismatch.

# Conclusions

Inspired by evolutionary psychology, evolutionary leadership theory is a new approach to the study of leadership that connects the diverse lines of research and provides an overarching framework that is consistent, ultimately, with the principles from evolutionary biology. I have argued why it is important to study the evolutionary functions of leadership. I have shown what evolutionary psychology can contribute to research on leadership, generating many novel hypotheses and testing them with a diversity of different methodologies, from behavioral genetics to neuroscience, and from experimentation to game theory. I have also outlined various implications of adopting an evolutionary perspective for leadership theory, research, and practice. I hope this new field of inquiry will generate interest from leadership researchers and practitioners who are interested, as I am, in understanding the true nature of leadership.

## Discussion Questions

1. Do nonhuman animals have leadership? If so, how is it similar to human leadership? How is it different?
2. How can neuroscience research contribute to understanding leadership and followership?

3. Does power corrupt? Discuss evidence for or against this claim using insights from evolutionary psychology.
4. Why would there have been a preference for taller leaders in ancestral environments? How would you investigate this claim?

## Recommended Readings

- van Vugt, M., & Ahuja, A. (2010). *Naturally selected: Why some people lead, why others follow, and why it matters.* London, UK: Profile.
- van Vugt, M., & Grabo, A. E. (2015). The many faces of leadership: An evolutionary-psychology approach. *Current Directions in Psychological Science, 24,* 6484–6489.
- van Vugt, M., Jiang, J., Chen, C., Shi, G., Ding, G., Liu, L., & Lu, C. (2015). Leader emergence through interpersonal neural synchronization. *Proceedings of the National Academy of Sciences, 112,* 4274–4279.
- von Rueden, C., & van Vugt, M. (2015). Leadership in small-scale societies: Some implications for theory, research, and practice. *The Leadership Quarterly, 26*(6), 978–990.

## Recommended Case Studies

- **Film Case:** *Geronimo: An American legend* (1993).
- **Case:** Brown, T. (2012). From blueprint to genetic code: The merits of an evolutionary approach to design. Harvard Business School Case ROT165-PDF-ENG.

## Recommended Video

- De Waal, F. (2012). Primatologist Frans De Waal about morality in primates. https://youtu.be/GcJxRqTs5nk

## References

Acemoglu, D., & Robinson, J. (2012). *Why nations fail: The origins of power, prosperity, and poverty.* New York, NY: Crown.

Adolphs, R. (1999). Social cognition and the human brain. *Trends in Cognitive Sciences, 3,* 469–479.

Altemeyer, B. (1981). *Right-wing authoritarianism.* Winnipeg, Canada: University of Manitoba Press.

Anderson, C., & Kilduff, G. J. (2009). Why do dominant personalities attain influence in face-to-face groups? The competence-signaling effects of trait dominance. *Journal of Personality and Social Psychology, 96,* 491–503.

Antonakis, J. (2011). Predictors of leadership: The usual suspects and the suspect traits. In A. Bryman, D. Collinson, K. Grint, B. Jackson, & M. Uhl-Bien (Eds.), *The Sage handbook of leadership* (pp. 269–285). Thousand Oaks, CA: Sage.

Antonakis, J., Ashkanasy, N. M., & Dasborough, M. (2009). Does leadership need emotional intelligence? *The Leadership Quarterly, 20,* 247–261.

Antonakis, J., & Atwater, L. (2002). Leader distance: A review and a proposed theory. *The Leadership Quarterly, 13,* 673–704.

Antonakis, J., & Dalgas, O. (2009). Predicting elections: Child's play. *Science, 323,* 1183.

Avolio, B., Walumbwa, F. O., & Weber, T. J. (2009). Leadership: Current theories, research, and future directions. *Annual Review of Psychology, 60,* 421–449.

Babiak, P., & Hare, R. D. (2006). *Snakes in suits: When psychopaths go to work*. New York, NY: Harper.

Barrett, H. C., & Kurzban, R. (2006). Modularity in cognition: Framing the debate. *Psychological Review, 113*, 628–647.

Bass, B. M. (1985). *Leadership and performance beyond expectations*. New York, NY: Free Press.

Bass, B. M. (2008). *Bass and Stogdill's handbook of leadership: Theory, research, and managerial applications*. New York, NY: Free Press.

Baumeister, R. F., Chesner, S. P., Senders, P. S., & Tice, D. M. (1989). Who's in charge here? Group leaders do lend help in emergencies. *Personality and Social Psychology Bulletin, 14*, 17–22.

Baumeister, R. F., & Leary, M. (1995). The need to belong: Desire for interpersonal attachments as a fundamental human motivation. *Psychological Bulletin, 117*, 497–529.

Bendahan, S., Zehnder, C., Pralong, F. P., & Antonakis, J. (2015). Leader corruption depends on power and testosterone. *The Leadership Quarterly, 26*, 101–122.

Benenson, J. F. (2013). The development of human female competition: Allies and adversaries. *Philosophical Transactions of the Royal Society B, 368*.

Bennis, W. (2007). The challenges of leadership in the modern world. *American Psychologist, 62*, 2–5.

Berggren, N., Jordahl, H., & Poutvaara, P. (2010). The looks of a winner: Beauty and electoral success. *Journal of Public Economics, 94*, 8–15.

Blaker, N. M., Rompa, I., Dessing, I. H., Vriend, A. F., Herschberg, C., & van Vugt, M. (2013). The height leadership advantage in men and women: Testing evolutionary psychology predictions about the perceptions of tall leaders. *Group Processes and Intergroup Relations, 16*, 17–27.

Boehm, C. (1999). *Hierarchy in the forest*. Cambridge, MA: Harvard University Press.

Brosnan, S. F., & de Waal, F. B. M. (2003). Monkeys reject unequal pay. *Nature, 425*(6955), 297–299.

Brosnan, S. F., Newton-Fisher, N. E., & van Vugt, M. (2009). A melding of minds: When primatology meets personality and social psychology. *Personality and Social Psychology Review, 13*, 129–147.

Brown, D. (1991). *Human universals*. Boston, MA: McGraw-Hill.

Brunell, A. B., Gentry, W. A., Campbell, W. K., Hoffman, B. J., Kuhnert, K. W., & DeMarree, K. G. (2008). Leader emergence: The case of the narcissistic leader. *Personality and Social Psychology Bulletin, 34*, 1663–1676.

Buss, D. M. (20105). *Handbook of evolutionary psychology*. Hoboken, NJ: John Wiley.

Chaturvedi, S., Zyphur, M. J., Arvey, R. D., Avolio, B., & Larsson, G. (2012). The heritability of emergent leadership: Age and gender as moderating factors. *The Leadership Quarterly, 23*, 219–232.

Cogsdill, E. J., Todorov, A. T., Spelke, E. S., & Banaji, M. R. (2014). Inferring character from faces: A developmental study. *Psychological Science, 25*(5), 1132–1139.

Colarelli, S., & Arvey, R. (2015). *Handbook of the biology of organizational behavior*. Chicago, IL: University of Chicago Press.

Couzin, I. D., Krause, J., Franks, N. R., & Levin, S. A. (2005). Effective leadership and decision-making in animal groups on the move. *Nature, 433*, 513–516.

Darwin, C. (1871). *The descent of man*. London, UK: Appleton.

Dawkins, R. (2009). *The greatest show on earth: The evidence for evolution*. New York, NY: Free Press.

De Waal., F. B. M. (1996). *Good natured: The origins of right and wrong in humans and other animals*. Cambridge, MA: Harvard University Press.

Den Hartog, D. N., House, R. J., Hanges, P. J., Ruiz-Quintanilla, S. A., & Dorfman, P. W. (1999). Culture-specific and cross-culturally generalizable implicit leadership theories: A longitudinal investigation. *The Leadership Quarterly, 10*, 219–256.

Dorfman, P. W., Hanges, P. J., & Brodbeck, F. C. (2004). Leadership and cultural variation: The identification of culturally endorsed leadership profiles. In R. J. House, P. J. Hanges, M. Javidan, P. W. Dorfman, & V. Gupta (Eds.), *Culture, leadership, and organizations: The GLOBE study of 62 societies* (pp. 669–719). Thousand Oaks, CA: Sage.

Eagly, A. H., & Carli, L. L. (2003). The female leadership advantage: An evaluation of the evidence. *The Leadership Quarterly, 14*, 807–834.

Eagly, A. H., & Johnson, B. T. (1990). Gender and leadership style: A meta-analysis. *Psychological Bulletin, 108*, 233–256.

Elgar, M. A. (2016). Leader selection and leadership outcomes: Height and age in a sporting model. *The Leadership Quarterly, 27*, 588–601.

Epitropaki, O., & Martin, R. (2004). Implicit leadership theories in applied settings: Factor structure, generalizability, and stability over time. *Journal of Applied Psychology, 89*, 293–310.

Fehr, E., & Camerer, C. (2007). Social neuroeconomics: The neural circuitry of social preferences. *Trends in Cognitive Sciences, 11*, 419–427.

Fiedler, F. E. (1967). *A theory of leadership effectiveness*. New York, NY: McGraw-Hill.

Fiedler, F. E. (1995). Cognitive resources and leadership performance. *Applied Psychology, 44*(1), 5–28.

Fincher, C., Thornhill, R., Murray, D., & Schaller, M. (2008). Pathogen prevalence predicts human cross-cultural variability in individualism/collectivism. *Proceedings of the Royal Society B, 275*, 1279–1285.

Foley, R. A. (1997). The adaptive legacy of human evolution: A search for the environment of evolutionary adaptedness. *Evolutionary Anthropology, 4*, 194–203.

Galinsky, A. D., Magee, J. C., Inesi, M. E., & Gruenfeld, D. H. (2006). Power and perspectives not taken. *Psychological Science, 17*, 1068–1077.

Gandossey, R., & Sonnenfeld, J. A. (2004). *Leadership and governance from the inside out*. London, UK: Wiley.

Gangestad, S., & Simpson, J. A. (2007). *The evolution of the mind*. New York, NY: Guilford.

Gavrilets, S., Auerbach, J., & van Vugt, M. (2016). *Convergence to consensus in heterogeneous groups and the emergence of informal leadership*. Unpublished manuscript.

Geary, D. (1998). *Male/female: The evolution of human sex differences*. Washington, DC: APA Press.

Gillet, J., Cartwright, E., & van Vugt, M. (2011). Selfish or servant leadership? Leadership personalities in coordination games. *Personality and Individual Differences, 51*(3), 231–236.

Graen, G. B., & Uhl-Bien, M. (1995). Development of leader–member exchange (LMX) theory of leadership over 25 years: Applying a multi-level domain perspective. *The Leadership Quarterly, 6*, 219–247.

Greenleaf, R. (2002). *Servant leadership* (25th anniv. ed.). Mahwah, NJ: Paulist Press.

Hackman, J. R., & Wageman, R. (2007). Asking the right questions about leadership. *American Psychologist, 62*, 43–47.

Hamblin, R. L. (1958). Leadership and crises. *Sociometry, 21*, 322–335.

Haslam, A., McGarty, C., Brown, P., Eggins, R., Morrison, B., & Reynolds, K. (1998). Inspecting the emperor's clothes: Evidence that random selection of leaders can enhance group performance. *Group Dynamics, 2*, 168–184.

Henrich, J., & Gil-White, F. (2001). The evolution of prestige: Freely conferred deference as a mechanism for enhancing the benefits of cultural transmission. *Evolution and Human Behavior, 22*, 165–196.

Hofstede, G. (1980). *Culture's consequences: International differences in work-related values*. Beverly Hills, CA: Sage.

Hogan, R., & Kaiser, R. (2005). What we know about leadership. *Review of General Psychology, 9*, 169–180.

Hooper, P. L., Kaplan, H. S., & Boone, J. L. (2010). A theory of leadership in human cooperative groups. *Journal of Theoretical Biology, 265*, 633–646.

House, R. J. (1971). A path-goal theory of leader effectiveness. *Administrative Science Quarterly, 16*, 321–339.

House, R. J. (1996). Path-goal theory of leadership: Lessons, legacy, and a reformulated theory. *The Leadership Quarterly, 7*(3), 323–352.

Ilies, R., Arvey, R., & Bouchard, T. (2006). Darwinism, behavioral genetics, and organizational behavior: A review and agenda for future research. *Journal of Organizational Behavior, 27*, 121–141.

Ilies, R., Gerhardt, M., & Le, H. (2004). Individual differences in leadership emergence: Integrating meta-analytic findings and behavior genetics estimates. *International Journal of Selection and Assessment, 12*, 207–219.

Iredale, W., Vugt, M. V., & Dunbar, R. 2008. Showing Off in Humans: Male Generosity as a Mating Signal. *Evolutionary Psychology, 6*(3): 386–392.

Jensen-Campbell, L. A., Graziano, W. G., & West, S. G. (1995). Dominance, prosocial orientation, and female preferences: Do nice guys really finish last? *Journal of Personality and Social Psychology, 68*, 427–440.

Jiang, J., Chen, C., Shi, G., Ding, G., Liu, L., & Lu, C. (2015). Leader emergence through interpersonal neural synchronization. *Proceedings of the National Academy of Sciences, 112,* 4274–4279.

Josephs, R. A., Sellers, J. G., Newman, M. L., & Metha, P. (2006). The mismatch effect: When testosterone and status are at odds. *Journal of Personality and Social Psychology, 90,* 999–1013.

Judge, T. A., Bono, J., Ilies, R., & Gerhardt, M. (2002). Personality and leadership: A qualitative and quantitative review. *Journal of Applied Psychology, 87,* 765–780.

Judge, T. A., & Cable, D. M. (2004). The effect of physical height on workplace success and income: A preliminary test of a theoretical model. *Journal of Applied Psychology, 89,* 428–441.

Judge, T. A., Colbert, A. E., & Ilies, R. (2004). Intelligence and leadership: A quantitative review and test of theoretical propositions. *Journal of Applied Psychology, 89,* 542–552.

Kahneman, D. (2011). *Thinking, fast and slow* (1st ed.). New York, NY: Farrar, Straus and Giroux.

Kaiser, R., Lindberg, J., & Craig, S. (2007). Assessing the flexibility of managers: A comparison of methods. *International Journal of Selection and Assessment, 16,* 40–55.

Kellerman, B. (2008). *Followership.* Boston, MA: Harvard Business School Press.

Kelley, E., & Kelloway, E. K. (2012). Context matters: Testing a model of remote leadership. *Journal of Leadership & Organizational Studies, 19,* 4437–4449.

Kerr, S., & Jermier, J. (1978). Substitutes for leadership: Their meaning and measurement. *Organizational Behavior and Human Performance, 22,* 374–403.

King, A. J., Johnson, D. D. P., & van Vugt, M. (2009). The origins and evolution of leadership. *Current Biology, 19,* R911–R916.

Kipnis, D. (1972). Does power corrupt? *Journal of Personality and Social Psychology, 24,* 33–41.

Knoch, D., Schneider, F., Schunk, D., Hohmann, M., & Fehr, E. (2009). Disrupting the prefrontal cortex diminishes the human ability to build a good reputation. *Proceedings of the National Academy of Sciences of the United States of America, 106,* 20895–20899.

Krause, J., Ruxton, G. D., & Krause, S. (2010). Swarm intelligence in animals and humans. *Trends in Ecology & Evolution, 25,* 28–34.

Lee, N., Senior, C., & Butler, M. (2012). Leadership research and cognitive neuroscience: The state of this union. *The Leadership Quarterly, 23,* 213–218.

Le Ngoc, M., Lehmann-Willenbrock, N., Oostrom, J., Sipman, M., & Van Vugt, M. (2017). Obstacles for remote leadership in the workplace: An evolutionary hypothesis.

Little, A., Buriss, R. P., Jones, B., & Roberts, S. C. (2007). Facial appearance affects voting decisions. *Evolution and Human Behavior, 28,* 18–27.

Lord, R. G., De Vader, C. L., & Alliger, G. M. (1986). A meta-analysis of the relation between personality traits and leadership perceptions: An application of validity generalization procedures. *Journal of Applied Psychology, 71,* 402–410.

Mayr, E. (2001). *What evolution is.* New York, NY: Basic Books.

Mezulis, A., Abramson, L., Hyde, J. S., & Hankin, B. L. (2004). Is there a universal positivity bias in attributions? A meta-analytic review of individual, developmental, and cultural differences in the self-serving attributional bias. *Psychological Bulletin, 130,* 711–746.

Norton, M. I., & Ariely, D. (2011). Building a better America—One wealth quintile at a time. *Perspectives on Psychological Science, 6,* 9–12.

O'Gorman, R. O., Henrich, J., & van Vugt, M. (2009). Constraining free-riding in public goods games: Designated solitary punishers can sustain human cooperation. *Proceedings of Royal Society B, 276,* 323–329.

Ohlsen, G., Van Zoest, W., & van Vugt, M. (2013). Gender and facial dominance in gaze cuing: Emotional context matters in the eyes that we follow. *PLoS ONE, 8.*

Oliver, W. M., & Marion, N. E. (2010). *Killing the president: Assassinations, attempts, and rumored attempts on U.S. commanders-in-chief.* Santa Barbara, CA: Praeger.

Padilla, A., Hogan, R., & Kaiser, R. B. (2007). The toxic triangle: Destructive leaders, vulnerable followers, and conducive environments. *The Leadership Quarterly, 18,* 176–194.

Pinker, S. (2002). *The blank slate.* London, UK: Penguin Classics.

Preston, S. D., & de Waal, F. B. M. (2002). Empathy: Its ultimate and proximate bases. *Behavioral and Brain Sciences, 25*(1), 1–20.

Price, M. E., & van Vugt, M. (2014). The evolution of leader–follower reciprocity: The theory of service-for-prestige. *Frontiers in Human Neuroscience, 8,* 363.

Richerson, P. J., & Boyd, R. (2006). *Not by genes alone: How culture transformed human evolution.* Chicago, IL: University of Chicago Press.

Riley, J. R., Greggers, U., Smith, A., Reynolds, D., & Menzel, R. (2005). The flight paths of honey bees recruited by the waggle dance. *Nature, 435,* 205–207.

Ronay, R., Greenaway, K., Anicich, E. M., & Galinsky, A. D. (2012). The path to glory is paved with hierarchy: When hierarchical differentiation increases group effectiveness. *Psychological Science, 23,* 669–677.

Sanfey, A. (2007). Social decision making: Insights from game theory and neuroscience. *Science, 318,* 598–602.

Sell, A., Tooby, J., Cosmides, L., Sznycer, D., von Rueden, C., & Gurven, M. (2009). Human adaptations for the visual assessment of strength and fighting ability from the body and face. *Proceedings of the Royal Society-B, 276,* 575–584.

Sessa, V. I., Kaiser, R., Taylor, J. K., & Campbell, R. J. (1998). *Executive selection.* Greensboro, NC: Center for Creative Leadership.

Shamir, B., House, R. J., & Arthur, M. B. (1993). The motivational effects of charismatic leadership: A self-concept based theory. *Organization Science, 4*(4), 577–594.

Sherif, M. (1966). *In common predicament.* Boston, MA: Houghton Mifflin.

Sherman, G. D., Lerner, J. S., Josephs, R. A., Renshon, J., & Gross, J. J. (2016). The interaction of testosterone and cortisol is associated with attained status in male executives. *Journal of Personality and Social Psychology, 110*(6), 921.

Simonton, D. K. (1994). *Who makes history and why?* New York, NY: Guilford.

Smith, J. E., Gavrilets, S., Borgerhoff Mulder, M., Hooper, P. L., El Moulden, C., Nettle, D., . . . Smith, E. A. (2015). Leadership in mammalian societies: Emergence, distribution, power, and pay-off. *Trends in Ecology and Evolution, 31,* 54–66.

Spisak, B. R., Homan, A. C., Grabo, A., & van Vugt, M. (2011). Facing the situation: Testing a biosocial contingency model of leadership in intergroup relations using masculine and feminine faces. *The Leadership Quarterly, 23,* 273–280.

Spisak, B. R., O'Brien, M. J., Nicholson, N., & van Vugt, M. (2015). Niche construction and the evolution of leadership. *Academy of Management Review, 40,* 291–306.

Stulp, G., Buunk, A. P., Verhulst, S., & Pollet, T. V. (2013). Tall claims? Sense and nonsense about the importance of height of US presidents. *The Leadership Quarterly, 24*(1), 159–171.

Tinbergen, N. (1963). On the aims and methods in ethology. *Zeitschrift for Tierpsychology, 20,* 410–433.

Todorov, A., Olivola, C. Y., Dotsch, R., & Mende-Siedlecki, P. (2015). Social attributions from faces: Determinants, consequences, accuracy, and functional significance. *Annual Review of Psychology, 66,* 519–545.

Tooby, J., & Cosmides, L. (2005). The theoretical foundations of evolutionary psychology. In D. M. Buss (Ed.), *The handbook of evolutionary psychology* (2nd ed., Vol. 1, pp. 3–87). Hoboken, NJ: John Wiley.

Uhl-Bien, M., Riggio, R. E., Lowe, K. B., & Carsten, M. K. (2014). Followership theory: A review and research agenda. *The Leadership Quarterly, 25,* 83–104.

Van der Meij, L., Schaveling, J., & van Vugt, M. (2016). Basal testosterone, leadership and dominance: A field study and meta-analysis. *Psychoneuroendocrinology, 72,* 72–79.

van Vugt, M. (2006). The evolutionary origins of leadership and followership. *Personality and Social Psychology Review, 10,* 354–372.

van Vugt, M. (2009). Despotism, democracy, and the evolutionary dynamics of leadership and followership. *American Psychologist, 64,* 54–56.

van Vugt, M. (2014). On gazes, faces, votes and followers: Evolutionary and neuroscience approaches to leadership. In J. Decety & Y. Christen (Eds.), *New frontiers in social neuroscience* (pp. 93–110). Heidelberg Germany: Springer.

van Vugt, M., & Ahuja, A. (2010). *Naturally selected: Why some people lead, why others follow, and why it matters.* London, UK: Profile.

van Vugt, M., & De Cremer, D. (1999). Leadership in social dilemmas: The effects of group identification on collective actions to provide public goods. *Journal of Personality and Social Psychology, 76,* 587–599.

van Vugt, M., & Grabo, A. E. (2015). The many faces of leadership: An evolutionary-psychology approach. *Current Directions in Psychological Science, 24,* 6484–6489.

van Vugt, M., Hogan, R., & Kaiser, R. (2008). Leadership, followership, and evolution: Some lessons from the past. *American Psychologist, 63,* 182–196.

van Vugt, M., Jepson, S. F., Hart, C. M., & De Cremer, D. (2004). Autocratic leadership in social dilemmas: A threat to group stability. *Journal of Experimental Social Psychology, 40,* 1–13.

van Vugt, M., Johnson, D., Kaiser, R., & O'Gorman, R. (2008). Evolution and the social psychology of leadership: The mismatch hypothesis. In C. R. Hoyt, G. R. Goethals, & D. R. Forsyth (Eds.), *Leadership at the crossroads: Vol. 1. Leadership and psychology* (pp. 267–282). London, UK: Praeger.

van Vugt, M., & Ronay, R. (2014). The evolutionary psychology of leadership: Theory, review, and roadmap. *Organizational Psychology Review, 4,* 74–95.

van Vugt, M., & Schaller, M. (2008). Evolutionary perspectives on group dynamics: An introduction. *Group Dynamics, 12,* 1–6.

van Vugt, M., & Spisak, B. R. (2008). Sex differences in leadership emergence during competitions within and between groups. *Psychological Science, 19,* 854–858.

van Vugt, M., & Tybur, J. M. (2015). *The evolutionary foundations of status hierarchy. The handbook of evolutionary psychology* (Vol. 2). New York, NY: John Wiley.

von Rueden, C., Gurven, M., & Kaplan, H. (2010). Why do men seek status? Fitness payoffs to dominance and prestige. *Proceedings of the Royal Society B: Biological Sciences,* rspb20102145.

von Rueden, C., & van Vugt, M. 2015. Leadership in small-scale societies: Some implications for theory, research, and practice. *The Leadership Quarterly, 26*(6), 978–990.

Waldman, D. A., Wang, D., & Fenters, V. (2016). The added value of neuroscience methods in organizational research. *Organizational Research Methods.* Advance online publication. doi:10.1177/1094428116642013.

Wayne, S. J., & Ferris, G. R. (1990). Influence tactics, affect and exchange quality in supervisor–subordinate interactions: A laboratory experiment and field study. *Journal of Applied Psychology, 75,* 487–499.

Williams, K. D. (2007). Ostracism. *Annual Review of Psychology, 58,* 425–452.

Wilson, D. S. (2007). *Evolution for everyone.* New York, NY: Delta.

Wilson, E. O. (1975). *Sociobiology: The new synthesis.* Cambridge, MA: Harvard University Press.

Wood, A. R., Esko, T., Yang, J., Vedantam, S., Pers, T. H., Gustafsson, S., . . . Frayling, T. M. (2014). Defining the role of common variation in genomic and biological architecture of adult human height. *Nature Genetics, 46,* 1173–1186.

Yukl, G. A. (2014). *Leadership in organizations.* Englewood Cliffs, NJ: Prentice Hall.

# PART III

# Current Topics in Leadership

# CHAPTER 9

# Social Cognition, Social Perception, and Leadership

*Konstantin O. Tskhay*

*Nicholas O. Rule*

---

## Opening Case: A Day in the Life of a Leader

Amy is an executive recruiter meeting a number of highly qualified candidates for the top-shelf positions at the most innovative companies and not-for-profit organizations in New York City, Toronto, and London. She speaks to people with impressive résumés, documenting continuous leadership excellence, achievement, and great technical skills. Her job is difficult at times because she has to identify leaders who not only possess exceptional leadership skills (having been in a number of directorial and managerial positions) but also are ready to lead organizations. Furthermore, the few candidates she forwards to the company's board must satisfy a number of the organization's internal demands, such as a fit with the corporate culture.

Today, Amy met two candidates, Stephen and Matthew, whom she is considering for an executive position at a social innovation organization. The candidates are equally qualified for the position: Both have similar accomplishments, previously led multiple teams, and had diverse technical training. Additionally, they each have a pleasant disposition and are well spoken. The meetings went smoothly. Now, Amy faces a decision about which candidate to forward to the company's representatives.

Amy ponders which candidate seems to better fit this particular company. Stephen presented himself with dominance, ambition, drive, and analytic thinking—advantages for communicating goals and directives internally. However, she felt that he might be too extraverted and seemed inauthentic at times—she thinks that this "trying too hard" feeling could be attributed to Stephen's enthusiasm about the position but could hurt the company's relationship with external stakeholders if that were his stable disposition. Matthew, on the other hand, appeared authentic, charismatic, and intelligent—all great attributes for communicating with the press, partner organizations, and shareholders. Yet he seemed to lack the dominance and determination that may be needed day to day. Additionally, Amy thinks that people may not take Matthew seriously due to his babyish facial appearance, which might lead him to be misconstrued as immature and inexperienced. Aside from her general impressions, Amy considers other factors, such as the candidates' ages, travel flexibility, and potential for economic impact in an executive position. The clock just hit midnight; the final decision needs to be delivered in the morning.

### Discussion Questions

1. Which candidate should Amy forward to meet the company representatives? Why?

2. Is Amy correct in evaluating the candidates on seemingly arbitrary traits? What would be a better strategy?

3. Do you think looks should be considered in this situation? Is there a kernel of truth in appearance?

# Chapter Overview

Although laypeople may not have the same experience as Amy in finding and vetting new employees for corporations, they process information about others from briefly observing them (Macrae & Quadflieg, 2010), including their leadership ability and success (Antonakis & Dalgas, 2009; Benjamin & Shapiro, 2009; Rule & Ambady, 2008, 2009, 2010; Sanchez-Cortes, Aran, Mast, & Gatica-Perez, 2010; Todorov, Mandisodza, Goren, & Hall, 2005; Tskhay, Xu, & Rule, 2014; see also Poutvaara, Jordahl, & Berggren, 2009). At any given moment, people evaluate each other on a number of characteristics, starting with basic assessments of sex, race, and age, and continuing to more complex questions about personality traits and social status (Bruce & Young, 1986). This information-processing ability is at the core of social cognition and perception (Bodenhausen & Todd, 2010). In the current chapter, we examine this prowess of the human mind, focusing specifically on how people process leadership.

At any given moment, the human brain processes an enormous amount of information, ranging from the perception of basic elements in the environment (e.g., ambient sounds) to inferring complex social information (e.g., others' emotional states). Thus, we must perceive information effectively and efficiently, store this information for long periods of time, and use it to predict events that include other people's motivations, desires, and behaviors. The study of this information-processing module is referred to as social cognition (Fiske & Taylor, 2013; Gallese, Keysers, & Rizzolatti, 2004).

To describe leadership from this socio-cognitive perspective, we have divided this chapter into two broad sections. First, we review the socio-cognitive framework, discussing how various aspects of human perception and cognition lead to the construction of mental models and representations that help people navigate their social environments. In the second part of the chapter, we focus specifically on leadership, highlighting studies that have utilized the methods and models of social cognition to identify who emerges as a leader and whether leadership emergence yields leadership success. Finally, we conclude by outlining potential mediating models, trying to explain how the perception and cognition of leadership translates to real-world outcomes.

# The Social Cognitive Model of Information Processing

Models of social cognition posit that the human mind has developed a special module for processing and integrating social information that helps people understand the world (Macrae & Quadflieg, 2010). This putative module stores information about other people and their relationships to facilitate successful interactions. As such, social cognition is thought to have arisen as an evolutionary adaptation that allows individuals to successfully mate, cooperate, compete, and choose leaders (Caporael, 1997; Herrmann, Call, Hernández-Lloreda, Hare, & Tomasello, 2007; Stevens & Fiske, 2013). In this section, we discuss some of the fundamental concepts and processes of social cognition: mental representations, social perception, and person construal.

## Mental Representations

Mental representations are the basic units of socio-cognitive processing (Bodenhausen & Todd, 2010). Broadly, they constitute the ideas and thoughts people have about each other. However, this definition does not place limits on the complexity of such thoughts and ideas. As such, mental representations may include physical features (e.g., facial hair), traits (e.g., masculinity), and representations of individuals' identity or group membership (e.g., man). Socio-cognitive theory posits that the mind organizes mental representations of people hierarchically, starting from basic featural aspects that aggregate toward trait perceptions and then climax as complex mental representations (Freeman & Ambady, 2011). For example, when people think about facial hair, they infer masculinity (Neave & Shields, 2008), which in turn results in construing the person as male.

Naturally, facial hair is not the only feature that leads a person to think that someone is a man (e.g., E. Brown & Perrett, 1993). For example, people may represent men as having broad shoulders, thick eyebrows, and pronounced jaws (Antoszewska & Wolański, 1991; E. Brown & Perrett, 1993; Crosby & Nyquist, 1977; Johnson & Tassinary, 2005; Kozlowski & Cutting, 1977). The same physical and dynamic features may also activate related representations of dominance, assertiveness, and aggression, which then connect back to "man-ness," or masculinity (Freeman & Ambady, 2011). As such, networks of features, traits, and other attributes converge to form the mental representation from which the person construal arises. Psychologists refer to this network as a schema—the cognitive tool used to organize complex information into manageable categories based on relationships between different attributes (Bodenhausen & Todd, 2010; see also Rosch, 1975).

Although the idea of a schema as a composition of attributes is intuitive, the human mind must store multiple categories that define both highly and scarcely visible aspects of identity (e.g., age, sexual orientation; Brewer, 1988; Tskhay & Rule, 2013). Thus, the mind organizes all of these representations into connected networks where multiple schemata affect each other differentially (Read, Vanman, & Miller, 1997; E. R. Smith, 1996). For example, the activation of the "male" representation should inhibit an opposing "female" construal due to the contrast of features that define each (Freeman & Ambady, 2011). Indeed, facial hair would rarely activate the representation of a woman because the two concepts are usually incompatible (Macrae & Martin, 2007; Tskhay & Rule, 2015). At the same time, activating a male representation would trigger both leadership and dominance schemata (Carli & Eagly, 2012). As such, the human mind organizes schemata and their related traits into hierarchically interrelated networks.

Indeed, people use a number of mental representations to decide about others' group memberships, personality traits, and (ultimately) their identities (e.g., Bruce & Young, 1986). Much of the information that composes one's mental representations comes from the individual's previous encounters with others (E. R. Smith, 1996). For instance, although children can distinguish basic and obvious social dimensions early in life (e.g., sex; Wild et al., 2000), more complex attributes (e.g., leadership ability) are learned as they mature (Heider, 1944; Matthews, Lord, & Walker, 1990, as cited in D. J. Brown, 2012; see also Antonakis & Dalgas, 2007). Mental representations are thus acquired over time through experience with the environment.

## Social Perception

Just as the perception of shapes, lines, and sounds comprise basic cognitive processing, social perception is the initiation point for social cognition (Brewer, 1988). Social perception research therefore aims to understand how people use information in their social environment to process social stimuli and create mental models. Critically, the study of social perception has allowed researchers to understand not only what inferences people make about each other, but also how they form these perceptions in the first place (e.g., Quinn & Macrae, 2005).

Social perception can be described as a three-stage process (Gilbert, Pelham, & Krull, 1988). First, people categorize each other into groups. Next, they translate this initial categorization into a more refined inference about what an individual may be like. Finally, they evaluate the circumstances and situational variables surrounding the person perceived, making adjustments to their inference (Gilbert, Krull, & Malone, 1990; Gilbert et al., 1988). The process of perceiving others thus involves extracting information from the environment, aggregating this information and related cognitions to make an inference, and reevaluating the information in consideration of the surrounding context. Generally speaking, researchers agree that the first two stages account for most of social perception, meaning that people largely rely on their first impressions when making inferences. However, the last stage suggests that people can augment these perceptions when additional information is available (see Gilbert et al., 1990; Rule, Tskhay, Freeman, & Ambady, 2014).

On a more technical level, perception begins by encoding the basic features of a stimulus. In the case of social stimuli, these features originate in static and dynamic cues consciously or nonconsciously expressed by a person (Ambady, Hallahan, & Rosenthal, 1995; Ambady & Rosenthal, 1992; Freyd, 1987; Gosling, Ko, Mannarelli, & Morris, 2002). These include one's facial structure (Zebrowitz, 1997), body movement (Johnson & Tassinary, 2005), vocal characteristics (Pittam & Gallois, 1986), and even one's odor (Baron, 1983), among other cues. For example, people's impressions of cooperation and trust depend on the width of the person's face (Stirrat & Perrett, 2010), and movements of the hips and shoulders provide valid and reliable information about a person's sex and sexual orientation (Johnson, Gill, Reichman, & Tassinary, 2007; Johnson & Tassinary, 2005). People additionally use vocal qualities to accurately perceive others' ethnic backgrounds (Kalin & Rayko, 1978). Indeed, the human mind habitually extracts patterns from the social environment to differentiate adaptive signals from distracting noise, though mistakes can still be made (Jussim, 1991; McArthur & Baron, 1983). Here, we briefly review the most prominent theories of how people extract and learn relevant cues from the environment (see Table 9.1).

**Table 9.1**  Summary of Theoretical Models Relating to the Social Perception and Cognition of Leadership

| Theory | Key Concepts | Conclusion |
| --- | --- | --- |
| **The Ecological Model of Social Perception** (McArthur & Baron, 1983) | 1. Perception serves a survival-enhancing purpose<br>2. Information is revealed through dynamic events<br>3. Information permits affordances (adaptations)<br>4. Perceivers attune to affordances | People learn relevant information about others in their environment |
| **Brusnwik's Lens Model** (Brunswik, 1956) | 1. Cue utility = cues that people use<br>2. Cue validity = cues targets actually display<br>3. Inference is probabilistic | People achieve accuracy when cue utility matches cue validity (i.e., when they use valid cues) |
| **The Realistic Accuracy Model** (Funder, 1995) | 1. Cue must be relevant to perceivers<br>2. Cue must be available to perceivers<br>3. Perceiver must detect the cue<br>4. Perceiver must use the cue | People achieve accuracy when valid cues are available and detected |

*(Continued)*

**Table 9.1**   (Continued)

| Theory | Key Concepts | Conclusion |
|---|---|---|
| **The Dynamic Interactive Model of Person Construal** (Freeman & Ambady, 2011) | 1. People possess mental models about others<br>2. Patterns of activation (inhibition) lead to person construal<br>3. People aggregate lower-level features and higher-order cognitions to arrive at stable representations | People dynamically aggregate information to form complete and stable person construals |
| **Leadership Categorization Theory I** (Lord et al., 1984) | 1. People possess implicit leadership theories<br>2. Implicit leadership theories form a leadership schema<br>3. Leadership schemata give rise to leadership prototypes<br>4. If a stimulus matches the leadership prototype, leadership perception occurs<br>5. The person is selected as a leader | People's implicit theories form leadership prototypes, which result in leadership perception and facilitate leaders' emergence |
| **Leadership Categorization Theory II** (Lord et al., 2001) | 1. People possess implicit leadership theories<br>2. Implicit leadership theories are organized as a network<br>3. The network gives rise to leadership prototypes<br>4. If a stimulus matches the prototype, leadership perception occurs<br>5. The person is selected as a leader | People's implicit theories interconnect to form leadership prototypes, which trigger perceptions of leadership and facilitate the emergence of leaders |

**The Ecological Model of Social Perception.** The Ecological Model of Social Perception argues that perceptions of others have adapted over the course of human evolution because they serve survival-enhancing purposes (Gibson, 1986/2014; McArthur & Baron, 1983; see also van Vugt's chapter in this volume for a discussion of evolutionary perspectives on leadership). Some of these environmental adaptations may be ingrained from birth (such as the avoidance of disgusting smells; Rozin, Haidt, & McCauley, 1999), whereas others are learned through continuous exposure to the physical and social environment (e.g., leadership; D. J. Brown, 2012). Importantly, this premise suggests that humans use and attend to cues in the environment, encoding only the most relevant to survival (McArthur & Baron, 1983).

Naturally, numerous cues in the environment are important for survival. Some of these are static (such as rocks that one may need to avoid), whereas others are more dynamic (like the emotions expressed on other people's faces). Although both present important information, the mind typically attends to those deemed immediately important, regardless of whether they change or remain constant over time. Indeed, it would be difficult to focus on all environmental cues and design an "action plan" for each. Thus, the important cues must capture one's attention, relate to one's imminent goals, and create opportunities for action in order to reach the main stage of awareness.

The Ecological Model of Social Perception thus posits that the mind will principally attend to social cues that afford survival-enhancing information. These cues will then be encoded and stored as mental representations that one may later generalize across situations (Zebrowitz, Kikuchi, & Fellous, 2007). Accordingly, the mind not only extracts information based on one's current motivations, but also learns associations that help organize the social world more broadly.

**Brunswik's Lens Model.** Supplementing the inferential portion of the Ecological Model of Social Perception, Brunswik's Lens Model attempts to explain how people accurately infer social information by addressing the valid cues that targets send and how perceivers may or may not use them (Brunswik, 1956). For example, individuals send multiple cues into the world signaling whether they are introverted or extraverted. Perceivers may then attend to the cues that they believe communicate extraversion (e.g., assertiveness, expressiveness, positive affect) and use them to infer the trait (Nestler & Back, 2013; R. E. Riggio & Friedman, 1986). However, suppose that extraverted individuals only display greater expressiveness and positive affect, but not submissiveness or assertiveness—rendering only the former two cues valid indicators of that particular target's underlying disposition. Perceivers' accuracy therefore depends on whether they use *valid* cues when making inferences. At the same time, the cues that each perceiver uses depend on that person's previous interaction with extraverted individuals. In other words, the model proposes that perceivers probabilistically compute which traits are relevant for making an inference as they interact with multiple targets, storing and updating this information in their mental representations of a particular characteristic at each encounter.

Though prominent and often used (e.g., Gosling et al., 2002), Brunswik's Lens Model suffers from simplicity. Individuals may not display the same indicating cues across different situations, contexts can constrain or amplify perceivers' ability to detect them, and the model does not account for people's motivations or biases (West & Kenny, 2011). Although it works well in experimental design and analysis, the model may lack the resolution needed for parsing everyday life.

**The Realistic Accuracy Model.** Funder (1995) proposed the Realistic Accuracy Model as a sequential stage process that integrates the adaptive function of the Ecological Model with the accuracy measurement of the Lens Model across four stages: relevance, availability, detection, and utilization. Stage 1 notes that the cues people use to judge others must be relevant to the underlying trait. Stage 2 then addresses the necessity that the cue be visible and expressed by the target so that it is available for perception. These first two stages thus focus on cues and target characteristics, whereas the latter two stages focus on the perceiver and his or her biases. Accordingly, Stage 3 refers to the perceiver's need to ably detect the relevant and available target cue from among the cacophony of interfering noise in one's environment. Finally, Stage 4 requires that the perceiver then use the detected information to render a judgment. With all four stages satisfied, one achieves accurate perception.

Naturally, some perceivers may be "good judges"—that is, they are better than others at detecting social information. The relevance of the environment and characteristics of the perceiver thus remain implicit in the model and have subsequently inspired explorations of characteristics that promote perceivers' ability for accurate judgment (Colvin & Bundick, 2001). Likewise, the focus on targets' availing relevant cues suggests additional contingent factors that may moderate the ultimate accuracy and/or reliability of the perception.

## The Dynamic Interactive Theory of Person Construal

People's construals of others are the product of multiple lower-level representations that adhere into a prototype, or holistic representation of an identity. Critically, they constitute the point at which the mind decides about a person's identity, group membership, and trait characteristics. People then use this information to decide whether to affiliate, cooperate, mate, compete, or otherwise interact with others (Herrmann et al., 2007).

According to the Dynamic Interactive Theory of Person Construal (Freeman & Ambady, 2011), schemata become activated or inhibited once the mind has aggregated its intake of information about a person. Yet the process does not end there: The mind continues to perform this task iteratively to integrate new confirmatory or contradictory information. Thus, not only do representations of others get continuously updated on the fly, people may actually reinitiate their inferences about others every time they encounter the person (Rule et al., 2014). Social cognition, though somewhat stable, is therefore also dynamic.

Given these complexities, social cognition researchers still have much exploration to do. Yet they have made sizable gains in understanding how people process information about each other. Researchers know that the mind stores multiple representations of other people (Bodenhausen & Todd, 2010); that people adeptly learn social cues from the environment; and that social perception leads to person construal, which results in decision making. Critically, the investigation of social cognition is not limited to psychology and has been applied to understanding leadership as well (Lord, Foti, & De Vader, 1984).

# Social Cognition and Leadership

Following the principles of social cognition, leaders possess and project characteristics that activate representations about leadership in others' minds. In this section, we describe how people think about leaders (i.e., implicit leadership theories; Offerman, Kennedy, & Wirtz, 1994) and how those thoughts aggregate to form holistic mental representations of leadership (D. J. Brown, 2012; E. R. Smith, 1996). Specifically, we discuss leadership categorization theory, explaining how people use traits to identify and select leaders (Lord et al., 1984). We then briefly review how followers' perceptions contribute to leaders' emergence (see also Brown's chapter in this volume). Finally, we outline how perceptions of leaders translate into outcomes (e.g., leadership success; Rule & Ambady, 2008).

## Implicit Leadership Theories and Leadership Categorization Theory

Individuals' implicit leadership theories (ILTs; i.e., their beliefs about the behaviors and traits that distinguish leaders from nonleaders) have received decades of attention from researchers of leadership and organizational behavior (e.g., Eden & Leviatan, 1975; House, Javidan, Hanges, & Dorfman, 2002; Lord et al., 1984; see also Brown's chapter in this volume for a more detailed treatment). For instance, one may implicitly believe that a leader should be more attractive, dominant, masculine, and powerful than a nonleader. Thus, people's beliefs about leaders typically refer to representations of their traits (Lord, Brown, Harvey, & Hall, 2001; J. A. Smith & Foti, 1998). Low-level featural information therefore needs to be organized into meaningful trait schemata before construing one as a leader, which then aggregate into a leadership prototype (Lord & Dinh, 2014; Lord et al., 1984).

Leadership Categorization Theory (Lord et al., 1984) describes how ILTs produce holistic representations of leadership. Specifically, it proposes that ILTs are arranged into leadership schemata—networks of traits that aggregate into leader and nonleader prototypes (Lord et al., 2001). Thus, following connectionist models of cognition, various inputs to the cognitive system generate patterns of activation and inhibition, which result in the construction of representational output nodes (see E. R. Smith, 1996; J. A. Smith & Foti, 1998). In other words, internal connections between representations flexibly incorporate information from lower-level perceptual features with higher-order cognitions to arrive at a leader representation (e.g., environmental demands and other contingencies; Lord et al., 2001; see also Lord & Dinh, 2014). Activating the representation and aligning it with the perception of an individual yields an impression of leadership effectiveness.

As displayed in Figure 9.1, information about the target from the environment enters the perceiver's mind (i.e., the social cognition module) via low-level perceptual characteristics. These characteristics are then integrated with the leadership schema, a network of traits that coactivate, to construe the target as either a leader or nonleader—the system's output. This decision precipitates leader emergence (as in Lord et al.'s [2001] connectionist model). Subsequently, this categorization translates into leader effectiveness, as it is practically impossible to produce leadership outcomes and influence others if the followers do not consider one to be a leader.

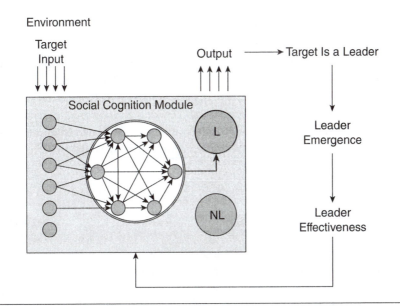

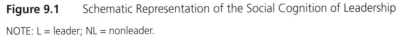

**Figure 9.1**    Schematic Representation of the Social Cognition of Leadership

NOTE: L = leader; NL = nonleader.

Finally, leader effectiveness feeds back into the system to reinforce the image of the person as a leader in the eyes of followers (more on this below).

# Social Cognition and Leadership Research

We have thus far discussed the core aspects of social cognition and spoken about how cognitive models of information processing explain people's perception and identification of leaders. In the next section, we review some of the empirical evidence demonstrating the socio-cognitive system's role in leadership perception and how those perceptions relate to measures of leadership effectiveness.

## From Physical Features to Leadership Perception

Although much of the research examining leadership perception, leader proto-types, and leadership effectiveness has focused on traits (Lord & Dinh, 2014), several studies have identified physical features that promote perceptions of leadership and presage leaders' outcomes. Evolutionary theories suggest that physical characteristics signaling formidability and dominance translate into perceptions of leadership, but with some nuance (Murray & Schmitz, 2011; H. R. Riggio & Riggio, 2010; van Vugt, Hogan, & Kaiser, 2008; van Vugt & Ronay, 2014). For instance, people prefer taller and more masculine leaders in times of war but not in times of peace, suggesting that physical traits that convey aggression may be valued in leaders more when the context requires aggressive behavior (Re, DeBruine, Jones, & Perrett, 2013). Similarly, CEOs with higher facial width-to-height ratios (a physiognomic product of high pubertal testosterone levels that otherwise correlates with aggressive behavior; Carré, McCormick, & Mondloch, 2009) predict better financial outcomes in corporate structures where power is fairly centralized (Wong, Ormiston, & Haselhuhn, 2011). Finally, having a wide mouth (indicative of greater biting abilities in primates, an important correlate of interpersonal competition and combat) predicts leadership selection, correlates with CEOs' company profits, and explains election results in the U.S. Senate (Re & Rule, 2016). Although such face measurements explain about 9%–14% of the variance in leadership outcomes, they likely encourage other parallel and higher-order perceptions (i.e., trait inferences) that cooperatively support perceptions of leadership.

## Leadership Traits

Since the introduction of ILTs, researchers have attempted to identify the traits that people attribute to leaders. In their seminal study, Lord et al. (1984) asked people to provide 10 attributes for 11 leadership categories (e.g., in business, education, and the military). After examining these attributes, they found that people consistently associated intelligence with leadership in 10 of the 11 domains. Although other trait descriptors were less consistent, many still received a high score on leader prototypicality. For example, traits related to competition (e.g., agency and power), traits related to cooperation (e.g., communion and warmth), and organizational skills received high scores, whereas dishonesty and unemotionality did not. Offermann et al. (1994) extended this work using more advanced methodologies and more diverse samples. Organizing ILTs according to prototypicality, they identified six prototypic traits (sensitivity, dedication, attractiveness, intelligence, strength, and charisma) and two antiprototypic traits (tyranny and masculinity) that produced 41 different lower-level ILTs. Epitropaki and Martin (2004) subsequently reduced the number of traits from eight to six (sensitivity, intelligence, dedication, dynamism, tyranny, and masculinity) and the number of ILTs from 41 to 21. This new set of ILT traits showed stability across changes in time, context, and different groups of respondents.

Although much of this research relied on self-reports, separate work shows that people evaluate leadership the moment they encounter someone (Ballew & Todorov, 2007). Research has documented that people evaluate others' leadership ability from mere glimpses of their faces (e.g., Antonakis & Dalgas, 2009; Rule & Ambady, 2008; Todorov et al., 2005). Such studies have also shown that multiple individuals share similar impressions about the traits that constitute effective leadership. Most of these studies have shown that traits like competence, dominance, and power predict leadership selection and success in Western cultures, regardless of the leader's race or sex (e.g., Livingston & Pearce, 2009; Rule & Ambady, 2009). Importantly, and consistent with the Ecological Model of Social Perception, leaders exhibit these traits through their behaviors, suggesting that perceivers' ILTs reflect the leaders' actual characteristics (e.g., Judge, Colbert, & Ilies, 2004; Tskhay et al., 2014). The composition of traits that people use to detect leadership may therefore emerge from their individual experiences interacting with leaders (see also D. J. Brown, 2012).

## Mental Representations, Schemas, and Prototypes of Leadership

Naturally, leadership emergence only begins with ILTs, beyond which they aggregate to form prototypes. Lord et al. (1984) reasoned that the traits most central to leadership should activate leadership prototypes faster than less prototypical traits. To test this, they generated 25 items that described prototypical, neutral, and antiprototypical behavioral traits and asked participants to rate them for how well they described leaders. They found a moderate negative correlation between prototypicality ratings and reaction times: Participants reacted faster to more (vs. less) prototypical traits, suggesting that more prototypical items activated leadership representations faster (e.g., Collins & Loftus, 1975).

Additional research has demonstrated that activating leadership schemata can cloud participants' memory for prototypical leadership traits. Research in social cognition has shown that when people forget the details of others' attributes, they refer to their internally stored prototypes to fill the gaps in their memory (Sherman & Hamilton, 1994; Valentine, 1991). Accordingly, people attribute more prototypical leadership behaviors to others who have been labeled as effective leaders (Phillips, 1984; Phillips & Lord, 1982), suggesting that ILTs may contribute to leadership prototypes.

Indeed, particular traits or conceptions of leadership can weigh heavily into individuals' choices of leaders. One line of research has demonstrated that naive observers can predict who wins political elections (Armstrong, Green, Jones, & Wright, 2010; Todorov et al., 2005). This finding has been replicated multiple times across governments in Asia, Australia, Europe, North America, and South America (Antonakis & Dalgas, 2009; Lawson et al., 2010; Little et al., 2007; Martin, 1978; Rule et al., 2010). Particular traits seem to predict these choices. Numerous studies have shown that perceivers' inferences of the competence of political candidates predict their electoral success in Western nations (e.g., Ballew & Todorov, 2007), though different traits may predict electoral outcomes in East Asia. Rule et al. (2010) and Na, Kim, Oh, Choi, and O'Toole (2015) both found that competence judgments did not predict the outcomes of Japanese and Korean elections, respectively. Rather, traits related to warmth (e.g., trustworthiness, likeability) played a greater role in East Asian voters' judgments and East Asian candidates' success. Interestingly, American and Japanese participants in Rule et al.'s research continued to apply their own expectations about the traits associated with leadership when judging the electoral success of candidates from the other nation. These results suggest that people may project their own ILTs (here, culturally clustered) onto others.

Such ILTs may develop early in cognition. Antonakis and Dalgas (2009) presented young children (about 10 years old, on average) with 57 pairs of faces of politicians and asked them to indicate who would be the better captain of a boat, finding that the children's choices corresponded to the winning candidate in the pair in about 71% of cases—on par with the performance of adults. The children's accuracy suggests that consensual ideas about success and leadership are ingrained in people since childhood. Indeed, 3–6-year-old children's ideas about core social attributes (e.g., competence, dominance, and trustworthiness) largely align with those of adults but become more defined with age (Cogsdill, Todorov, Spelke, & Banaji, 2014; Matthews et al., 1990). People may therefore absorb information from their immediate surroundings to foster constructs of leadership as their minds develop.

Yet other data suggest that some aspects of leadership perception may rely on innate responses. In further evidence of how consensual leadership prototypes interface with basic cognition, Rule et al. (2011) demonstrated that activation in the amygdala of the human brain correlates with perceptions of leaders. Participants in Rule et al.'s study exhibited greater left amygdala activation when viewing photos of the faces of CEOs, despite no knowledge or mention that the individuals were leaders. Afterward, they rated each face for leadership ability. The higher their ratings of leadership for any given target, the greater was the amygdala's response. Moreover, these judgments of leadership corresponded to one measure of the CEOs' actual success as leaders (the profitability of their companies), which also correlated with the amygdala's response (i.e., more successful CEOs provoked a stronger response from the amygdala). Given the amygdala's central role in physiological arousal (e.g., Anderson et al., 2003), this suggests that more successful and prototypically leader-like individuals may be more arousing.

## From Leadership Cognition to Leadership Effectiveness

Numerous studies have examined how leadership perception translates to leadership performance. For example, leaders perceived as intelligent perform better (see Judge et al., 2004) and CEOs who look powerful (i.e., competent, dominant, and facially mature) lead more profitable companies (e.g., Rule & Ambady, 2008). Similar perceptions of power from the faces of law firm managing partners also predict the financial performance of their firms (Rule & Ambady, 2011a). More surprising, however, is that judgments of the law firm managing partners predicted their firms' performance equally well regardless of whether they were based on current photos or photos taken when they were college students—on average 35 years earlier (Rule & Ambady, 2011b). This suggests that the look of power in leaders' faces may be present relatively early in their careers, allowing for interesting speculation about how their facial appearance may reflect their dispositional traits or provide them with opportunities to develop as leaders.

Indeed, although previous research suggests that first impressions are sticky (Rule et al., 2014), they may be revised as new contextual information enters the cognitive system (Gilbert et al., 1990). In other words, contextual factors affect the relationship between perceptions of leadership and leadership success. For instance, cross-cultural studies suggest that the traits apparent from leaders' faces may relate to their success differently, depending on the collective values of a given nation. Examining political candidates, Rule and colleagues found that American and Canadian voters elected leaders who appeared powerful, whereas Japanese voters elected leaders who appeared warm (Rule & Ambady, 2010; Rule et al., 2010). Similarly, Harms, Han, and Chen (2012) found that Western perceivers expected perceptions of intelligence and dominance to predict the success of Chinese CEOs (but they did not), and et al. (2011) also found that Americans' perceptions of power from the faces of Japanese CEOs correlated with their perceptions of leadership from their faces but not with their actual leadership success.

Additional research suggests that subcultural differences within a nation can affect leaders' success as well. Specifically, perceptions of warmth-related traits predict the success of Black CEOs because they disarm the prevalent stereotype of Black men as overly dominant, powerful, or aggressive (Livingston & Pearce, 2009). Likewise, although perceptions of power-related traits predict the success of female CEOs (Rule & Ambady, 2009), female business leaders appear more communal than male business leaders of similar rank (Pillemer, Graham, & Burke, 2014).

Furthermore, research also demonstrates that people can overcome their first impressions. For example, although people generally view women as less competent than men, they do not show this bias when told that a target female team member has contributed to her group's work product to the same degree as the male team members (see Heilman & Haynes, 2005). People similarly revise their impressions when provided with additional information about the female candidate's qualifications and previous work performance, or when presented in a context that is less male dominated (Eagly, Makhijani, & Klonsky, 1992; Heilman, Martell, & Simon, 1988; Tosi & Einbender, 1985). Together, these results suggest that individuals' ILTs may affect not only who is chosen for leadership, but how effective the person is in recruiting and leading followers.

Studies of leaders' nonverbal behaviors also show that people's perceptions and cognitions about leadership may affect outcomes. Expressive nonverbal behavior has consistently been regarded as a marker of charismatic leadership and greater social status (e.g., Conger & Kanungo, 1994; Den Hartog & Verburg, 1998; Friedman, Prince, Riggio, & DiMatteo, 1980; Newcombe & Ashkanasy, 2002; Tskhay, Zhu, & Rule, 2017). Research confirms that political candidates who demonstrate more expressive affect and eye gaze are evaluated more positively (McGovern & Tinsley, 1978). To test the relationship between ILTs, leadership prototypes, and performance outcomes, Tskhay et al. (2014) examined the nonverbal behaviors of orchestra conductors. Specifically, they showed participants silent videos of conductors in action, asking them to judge their expressiveness and likely success as leaders. As expected, the participants perceived conductors with more expressive body language to be more successful, and they were: More expressive conductors had garnered more recognitions, earned more awards, and performed at more venues, suggesting that perceptions of leadership track not only monetary outcomes, but reputational outcomes as well.

Furthermore, some research has shown that people can learn the charismatic behaviors needed to improve perceptions of their leadership ability. Antonakis, Fenley, and Liechti (2011) taught charismatic leadership tactics (e.g., greater expressiveness; see also Friedman et al., 1980) to company managers and business students by providing them with information on the traits and behaviors that constitute effective and charismatic leadership, showing them videos of successful leaders, and asking them to practice the techniques with each other. They then observed a reliable and significant improvement in the participants' Multifactor Leadership Questionnaire scores (Bass & Avolio, 1995) following the training, suggesting that enacting the behaviors of leadership can lead to better leadership skills.

Although a growing body of research suggests that leader perceptions may reflect leaders' ability to some degree, it is important to consider the limitations of this research. For instance, Rule et al. (2013) found that people are not accurate in making inferences of corporate executives', military officers', or undergraduate students' trustworthiness. This can be particularly troubling in organizational contexts, where candidates for positions are often evaluated via face-to-face interviews based on evaluators' gut feelings (see Posthuma, Morgeson, & Campion, 2002; see also Rule, Bjornsdottir, Tskhay & Ambady, 2016). To overcome the biases that potentially lead to suboptimal organizational productivity, hiring managers may want to impart a consistent structure to their interviewing practices (see Campion, Pursell, & Brown, 1988) and rely more on objective indicators of cognitive ability and performance, such as general intelligence (see Heilman & Haynes, 2005; Schmidt & Hunter, 1998).

In sum, a small but growing body of research examines how cognitions and perceptions about leaders translate to various performance metrics. Some of this research has examined traits and cues that are relatively static (e.g., inferences of personality from facial appearance), whereas other studies have investigated dynamic behaviors and cues (e.g., nonverbal expressiveness). Furthermore, these apply to outcomes based on other people's subjective evaluations (e.g., professional awards) and to objective outcomes (e.g., measures of an overall organization's profits). Race, culture, and sex may moderate these relationships. Importantly, perceptions of leadership may not always produce desirable outcomes, as these perceptions may be quite inaccurate under certain conditions. Next, we highlight several possible explanations for these relationships between perceptions of leadership and leadership success.

## From Social Cognition to Leadership Effectiveness: A Mechanistic View

Although many studies have reported correlations between trait characteristics, leadership perceptions, and leadership effectiveness (e.g., Rule & Ambady, 2008; Todorov et al., 2005; Tskhay et al., 2014), few have examined the mechanisms connecting cognitions to leadership outcomes (Antonakis, 2012; van Knippenberg & Sitkin, 2013). Although the link between ILTs and leadership prototypes seems theoretically plausible, the question about how various characteristics of the face and nonverbal expression might affect leadership effectiveness remains to be answered. Here, we provide several plausible accounts aiming to connect perceptions and cognitions about leaders to outcomes, hoping that future researchers might explore various pathways to leadership effectiveness.

Beginning with the link between CEOs' appearance and their companies' performance, one can see that the direction of the effects is unspecified: CEOs with more leader-like faces could improve companies' performance, or perhaps better-performing companies hire CEOs who look like better leaders to serve as their public face (e.g., Ranft, Zinko, Ferris, & Buckley, 2006). One study has suggested that men who look (but do not actually act) more competent are more likely to be hired as CEOs (Graham, Harvey, & Puri, 2010), favoring the latter hypothesis. However, several other studies have shown that perceptions based on CEOs' faces predict their companies' success within the CEO's specific tenure at the company, degrading the possibility that the CEO achieved success because he was merely chosen to ride an already fast horse (e.g., Re & Rule, 2016; Wong et al., 2011).

Moreover, the leaders of law firms differ critically from CEOs in how they are selected, yet show converging results regarding facial appearance and leadership success (Rule & Ambady, 2011a). Unlike companies whose executives and leaders may engage in a fair bit of horizontal movement, law firms operate on a "tenure-like" vertical promotion system (Galanter & Palay, 1994). Candidates for the top leadership position must therefore obtain an undergraduate degree, gain admission to law school, get hired at a firm, and make partner at the firm before being eligible to serve as managing partner. This steep winnowing process should rule out anyone who might gain a position based solely on his or her looks. However, the processes underlying the relationship between facial appearance and leadership success may not be so straightforward. Recall that Rule and Ambady (2011b) found that judgments based on photos taken of the managing partners of the United States' top 100 law firms before they had even entered law school predicted their organizations' financial success. This could suggest either that their faces honestly advertised their leadership ability or that looking like a leader provided them with more opportunities to develop the leadership skills needed for success. Finally, it could simply be that facial appearance matters only as a tie-breaker among leadership candidates in cases where the direct qualifications for leadership have already reached ceiling levels (see Rule & Tskhay, 2014). Theory and research in social cognition may help to identify the multiple paths through which this might occur.

One of the ways in which appearances can shape behavior is through self-fulfilling prophecies (e.g., McArthur & Baron, 1983). That is, individuals may attribute a trait to another person, motivating that individual to then develop that trait. For example, Rosenthal and Jacobson (1968) provided schoolchildren with mock intelligence tests, subsequently informing their teachers that specific students (actually a random selection) would make substantial intellectual gains by the end of the school year. Upon returning to examine the children, they found that the teachers' expectations about their intelligence stimulated their pupils' academic gains, presumably because they devoted more attention to the students they believed had greater potential. Such an effect could apply to leadership as well: If people think of someone as a leader, that individual will likely be selected for leadership (Lord et al., 1984) and may then gain the experience, training, and mentorship needed to succeed as a leader, fulfilling those expectations. The perception of leadership may also become enhanced by occupying a leadership position. For example, aside from gaining the experience of leadership, occupying one leadership role may lead to appointment to another. This may cyclically build one's record of leadership in a way that perpetuates or provides credibility to the notion that someone is an effective leader.

Similarly, the experience of leadership could cause one to look more leader-like over time. Interacting with other leaders may provide models for an individual for how effective leaders ought to behave, just as interacting with followers may allow a leader to develop a sense of how leaders perform (D. J. Brown, 2012). This could even lead to one's facial appearance changing to look more leader-like, a phenomenon known as the Dorian Gray effect (Zebrowitz, Collins, & Dutta, 1998). Indeed, feelings of power and success can make a person stand up tall and display other behaviors that communicate leadership (Carney, Cuddy, & Yap, 2010; Cuddy, Wilmuth, Yap, & Carney, 2015).

Although speculation about the mechanisms linking leadership ability, behavior, and appearance is intriguing, it is also important to understand how perceptions of leaders (valid or not) may affect followers. Among the many positive feelings that leaders may inspire among their followers, they can also sometimes invoke threat, aggression, and dominance (Keating, 2002, 2011)—all traits that automatically capture the cognitive and attentional resources of the human mind (Öhman, 1986). Furthermore, leadership itself is partly defined as the ability to influence others to generate collective action toward an organizational goal (Bass, 1985; Conger & Kanungo, 1994; Shamir, Arthur, & House, 1993). In fact, Drath et al. (2008) have proposed that a leader's goal is to provide followers with a common direction, align their motion toward a common goal, and generate commitment to the vision or goal that the leader has put forward (see Avolio & Bass, 1988; Bass, 1985; Conger &

Kanungo, 1994; House, 1977). To succeed at this, leaders may need to be attention-grabbing "zeitgebers" who entrain followers to their own rhythms and then channel them toward their intended goal (Bluedorn & Jaussi, 2008; see also Rule et al., 2011).

Theories of charismatic leadership support this view. Researchers examining charismatic leadership often speak about the leader's ability to maintain followers' attention, inspiring them toward a greater purpose (e.g., Bass, 1985; House, 1977; Shamir et al., 1993; Weber, 1978/1922). Through this mechanism, leaders might elicit emotional contagion, spreading their feelings to their followers (Cherulnik, Donley, Wiewel, & Miller, 2001). Furthermore, Keating (2002, 2011) argued that charismatic individuals might influence others more if they stimulate both approach and avoidance reactions in others, which orient and improve attention.

# Conclusion

In this chapter, we attempted to paint a picture of leadership from the perspective of social cognition, highlighting the mechanisms that may play a central role in leadership perception, leadership emergence, and leadership effectiveness. In doing so, we discussed the socio-cognitive literature on representations and prototype formation and how those concepts directly apply to leadership through ILTs and Leadership Categorization Theory (see Lord et al., 1984; Lord et al., 2001). Finally, we attempted to demonstrate that people's cognitions about leaders might translate into real-world outcomes on the organizational level, discussing some potential mechanisms and contingencies worthy of consideration by future researchers. In doing so, we hope that our delineation of the levels at which people perceive and think about leadership will help readers to better understand how theories of social cognition and information processing may describe and structure theories of leadership and generate new avenues for expanding how leaders and followers come to find their roles.

## Discussion Questions

1. How do ILTs appear in the mind? Are the traits clustering around ILTs innate or learned?
2. Is being seen by others as a leader always positive? Why or why not?
3. We discussed several ways that ILTs and leadership prototypes affect the performance of groups and organizations. What other ways might social cognition impact real-world outcomes?
4. How much does appearance contribute to leadership, and leadership contribute to appearance and other nonverbal behaviors?

## Recommended Readings

- Freeman, J. B., & Ambady, N. (2011). A dynamic interactive theory of person construal. *Psychological Review, 118,* 247–279.
- Halvorson, H. G. (2015, January). A second chance to make the right impression. *Harvard Business Review.* https://hbr.org/2015/01/a-second-chance-to-make-the-right-impression

- Re, D. E., & Rule, N. O. (2015). CEO facial appearance, firm performance, and financial success. In M. Fetscherin (Ed.), *CEO branding: Meaning, measuring, managing* (pp. 219–238). New York, NY: Routledge.

## Recommended Case Studies

- **Case:** Gino, F., & Staats, B. R. (2015). Mary Caroline Tillman at Egon Zehnder: Spotting talent in the 21st century. *Harvard Business Review* Case 416017-PDF-ENG.
- **Case:** Seijts, G., Gandz, J., & Crossan, M. M. (2014). Invictus: Introducing leadership competencies, character, and commitment. *Harvard Business Review* Case W14042-PDF-ENG.

## Recommended Videos

- Brooks, D. (2011). David Brooks: The social animal. https://www.ted.com/talks/david_brooks_the_social_animal
- Todorov, Alexander (2007). Elections How Voters Really Think and Feel. https://youtu.be/eLrDiBhHYNY.

## References

Ambady, N., Hallahan, M., & Rosenthal, R. (1995). On judging and being judged accurately in zero-acquaintance situations. *Journal of Personality and Social Psychology, 69*, 518–529.

Ambady, N., & Rosenthal, R. (1992). Thin slices of expressive behavior as predictors of interpersonal consequences: A meta-analysis. *Psychological Bulletin, 111*, 256–274.

Anderson, A. K., Christoff, K., Stapin, I., Panitz, D., Ghahremani, D. G., Glover, G., . . . Sobel, N. (2003). Dissociated neural representations of intensity and valence in human olfaction. *Nature Neuroscience, 6*, 196–202.

Antonakis, J. (2012). Transformational and charismatic leadership. In J. Antonakis & D. Day (Eds.), *The nature of leadership* (2nd ed., pp. 256–288). Thousand Oaks, CA: Sage.

Antonakis, J., & Dalgas, O. (2009). Predicting elections: Child's play! *Science, 323*, 1183.

Antonakis, J., Fenley, M., & Liechti, S. (2011). Can charisma be taught? Tests of two interventions. *Academy of Management Learning & Education, 10*, 374–396.

Antoszewska, A., & Wolański, N. (1991). Sexual dimorphism in newborns and adults. *Studies in Human Ecology, 10*, 23–38.

Armstrong, J. S., Green, K. C., Jones, R. J., & Wright, M. J. (2010). Predicting elections from politicians' faces. *International Journal of Public Opinion Research, 22*, 511–522.

Avolio, B. J., & Bass, B. M. (1988). Transformational leadership, charisma and beyond. In J. G. Hunt, B. R. Baliga, H. P. Dachler, & C. A. Schriesheim (Eds.), *Emerging leadership vistas* (pp. 29–50). Lexington, MA: Lexington Books.

Ballew, C. C., & Todorov, A. (2007). Predicting political elections from rapid and unreflective face judgments. *Proceedings of the National Academy of Sciences of the United States of America, 104*, 17948–17953.

Baron, R. A. (1983). "Sweet smell of success"? The impact of pleasant artificial scents on evaluations of job applicants. *Journal of Applied Psychology, 68*, 709–713.

Bass, B. M. (1985). *Leadership and performance beyond expectations.* New York, NY: Free Press.

Bass, B. M., & Avolio, B. J. (1995). *MLQ multifactor leadership questionnaire for research: Permission set.* Redwood City, CA: Mindgarden.

Benjamin, D. J., & Shapiro, J. M. (2009). Thin-slice forecasts of gubernatorial elections. *Review of Economics and Statistics, 91*, 523–536.

Bluedorn, A. C., & Jaussi, K. S. (2008). Leaders, followers, and time. *The Leadership Quarterly, 19*, 654–668.

Bodenhausen, G. V., & Todd, A. R. (2010). Social cognition. *WIREs Cognitive Science, 1*, 160–171.

Brewer, M. B. (1988). A dual process model of impression formation. In R. S. Wyer Jr. & T. K. Srull (Eds.), *Advances in social cognition* (Vol. 1, pp. 1–36). Hillsdale, NJ: Lawrence Erlbaum.

Brown, D. J. (2012). In the mind of followers: Follower-centric approaches to leadership. In J. Antonakis & D. Day (Eds.), *The nature of leadership* (2nd ed., pp. 331–362). Thousand Oaks, CA: Sage.

Brown, E., & Perrett, D. I. (1993). What gives a face its gender? *Perception, 22*, 829–840.

Bruce, V., & Young, A. (1986). Understanding face recognition. *British Journal of Psychology, 77*, 305–327.

Brunswik, E. (1956). *Perception and the representative design of psychological experiments* (2nd ed.). Berkeley: University of California Press.

Campion, M. A., Pursell, E. D., & Brown, B. K. (1988). Structured interviewing: Raising the psychometric properties of the employment interview. *Personnel Psychology, 41*, 25–42.

Caporael, L. R. (1997). The evolution of truly social cognition: The core configurations model. *Personality and Social Psychology Review, 1*, 276–298.

Carli, L. L., & Eagly, A. H. (2012). Leadership and gender. In J. Antonakis & D. Day (Eds.), *The nature of leadership* (2nd ed., pp. 417–476). Thousand Oaks, CA: Sage.

Carney, D. R., Cuddy, A. J., & Yap, A. J. (2010). Power posing brief nonverbal displays affect neuroendocrine levels and risk tolerance. *Psychological Science, 21*, 1363–1368.

Carré, J. M., McCormick, C. M., & Mondloch, C. J. (2009). Facial structure is a reliable cue of aggressive behavior. *Psychological Science, 20*, 1194–1198.

Cherulnik, P. D., Donley, K. A., Wiewel, T. S. R., & Miller, S. R. (2001). Charisma is contagious: The effect of leaders' charisma on observers' affect. *Journal of Applied Social Psychology, 31*, 2149–2159.

Cogsdill, E. J., Todorov, A. T., Spelke, E. S., & Banaji, M. R. (2014). Inferring character from faces a developmental study. *Psychological Science, 25*, 1132–1139.

Collins, A. M., & Loftus, E. F. (1975). A spreading-activation theory of semantic processing. *Psychological Review, 82*, 407–428.

Colvin, C. R., & Bundick, M. J. (2001). In search of the good judge of personality: Some methodological and theoretical concerns. In J. A. Hall & F. J. Bernieri (Eds.), *Interpersonal sensitivity: Theory and measurement* (pp. 47–65). Mahwah, NJ: Lawrence Erlbaum.

Conger, J. A., & Kanungo, R. N. (1994). Charismatic leadership in organizations: Perceived behavioral attributes and their measurement. *Journal of Organizational Behavior, 15*, 439–443.

Crosby, F., & Nyquist, L. (1977). The female register: An empirical study of Lakoff's hypothesis. *Language in Society, 6*, 313–322.

Cuddy, A. J., Wilmuth, C. A., Yap, A. J., & Carney, D. R. (2015). Preparatory power posing affects nonverbal presence and job interview performance. *Journal of Applied Psychology, 100*, 1286–1295.

Den Hartog, D. N., & Verburg, R. M. (1998). Charisma and rhetoric: Communicative techniques of international business leaders. *The Leadership Quarterly, 8*, 355–391.

Drath, W. H., McCauley, C. D., Palus, C. J., Van Velsor, E., O'Connor, P. M., & McGuire, J. B. (2008). Direction, alignment, commitment: Toward a more integrative ontology of leadership. *The Leadership Quarterly, 19*, 635–653.

Eagly, A. H., Makhijani, M. G., & Klonsky, B. G. (1992). Gender and the evaluation of leaders: A meta-analysis. *Psychological Bulletin, 111*, 3–22.

Eden, D., & Leviatan, U. (1975). Implicit leadership theory as a determinant of the factor structure underlying supervisory behavior scales. *Journal of Applied Psychology, 60*, 736–741.

Epitropaki, O., & Martin, R. (2004). Implicit leadership theories in applied settings: Factor structure, generalizability, and stability over time. *Journal of Applied Psychology, 89*, 293–310.

Fiske, S. T., & Taylor, S. E. (2013). *Social cognition: From brains to culture* (2nd ed.). Thousand Oaks, CA: Sage.

Freeman, J. B., & Ambady, N. (2011). A dynamic interactive theory of person construal. *Psychological Review, 118*, 247–279.

Freyd, J. J. (1987). Dynamic mental representations. *Psychological Review, 94,* 427–438.

Friedman, H. S., Prince, L. M., Riggio, R. E., & DiMatteo, M. R. (1980). Understanding and assessing nonverbal expressiveness: The Affective Communication Test. *Journal of Personality and Social Psychology, 39,* 333–351.

Funder, D. C. (1995). On the accuracy of personality judgment: A realistic approach. *Psychological Review, 102,* 652–670.

Galanter, M., & Palay, T. (1994). *Tournament of lawyers: The transformation of the big law firm.* Chicago, IL: University of Chicago Press.

Gallese, V., Keysers, C., & Rizzolatti, G. (2004). A unifying view of the basis of social cognition. *Trends in Cognitive Sciences, 8,* 396–403.

Gibson, J. J. (2014). *The ecological approach to visual perception: Classic edition.* New York, NY: Psychology Press. (Original work published 1986)

Gilbert, D. T., Krull, D. S., & Malone, P. S. (1990). Unbelieving the unbelievable: Some problems in the rejection of false information. *Journal of Personality and Social Psychology, 59,* 601–613.

Gilbert, D. T., Pelham, B. W., & Krull, D. S. (1988). On cognitive busyness: When person perceivers meet persons perceived. *Journal of Personality and Social Psychology, 54,* 733–740.

Gosling, S. D., Ko, S. J., Mannarelli, T., & Morris, M. E. (2002). A room with a cue: Personality judgments based on offices and bedrooms. *Journal of Personality and Social Psychology, 82,* 379–398.

Graham, J. R., Harvey, C. R., & Puri, M. (2010). *A corporate beauty contest* (No. w15906). Cambridge, MA: National Bureau of Economic Research.

Harms, P. D., Han, G., & Chen, H. (2012). Recognizing leadership at a distance: A study of leader effectiveness across cultures. *Journal of Leadership & Organizational Studies, 19,* 164–172.

Heider, F. (1944). Social perception and phenomenal causality. *Psychological Review, 51,* 358–374.

Heilman, M. E., & Haynes, M. C. (2005). No credit where credit is due: Attributional rationalization of women's success in male–female teams. *Journal of Applied Psychology, 90,* 905–916.

Heilman, M. E., Martell, R. F., & Simon, M. C. (1988). The vagaries of sex bias: Conditions regulating the undervaluation, equivaluation, and overvaluation of female job applicants. *Organizational Behavior and Human Decision Processes, 41,* 98–110.

Herrmann, E., Call, J., Hernández-Lloreda, M. V., Hare, B., & Tomasello, M. (2007). Humans have evolved specialized skills of social cognition: The cultural intelligence hypothesis. *Science, 317,* 1360–1366.

House, R. J. (1977). A 1976 theory of charismatic leadership. In J. G. Hunt & L. L. Larson (Eds.), *Leadership: The cutting edge.* Carbondale: Southern Illinois University Press.

House, R., Javidan, M., Hanges, P., & Dorfman, P. (2002). Understanding cultures and implicit leadership theories across the globe: An introduction to Project GLOBE. *Journal of World Business, 37,* 3–10.

Johnson, K. L., Gill, S., Reichman, V., & Tassinary, L. G. (2007). Swagger, sway, and sexuality: Judging sexual orientation from body motion and morphology. *Journal of Personality and Social Psychology, 93,* 321–334.

Johnson, K. L., & Tassinary, L. G. (2005). Perceiving sex directly and indirectly: Meaning in motion and morphology. *Psychological Science, 16,* 890–897.

Judge, T. A., Colbert, A. E., & Ilies, R. (2004). Intelligence and leadership: A quantitative review and test of theoretical propositions. *Journal of Applied Psychology, 89,* 542–552.

Jussim, L. (1991). Social perception and social reality: A reflection-construction model. *Psychological Review, 98,* 54–73.

Kalin, R., & Rayko, D. S. (1978). Discrimination in evaluative judgments against foreign-accented job candidates. *Psychological Reports, 43,* 1203–1209.

Keating, C. F. (2002). Charismatic faces: Social status cues put face appeal in context. In G. Rhodes & L. A. Zebrowitz (Eds.), *Facial attractiveness* (pp. 153–192). Westport, CT: Ablex.

Keating, C. F. (2011). Channelling charisma through face and body status cues. In D. Chadee & A. Kostic (Eds.), *Social psychological dynamics* (pp. 93–111). Kingston, Jamaica: University of West Indies Press.

Kozlowski, L. T., & Cutting, J. E. (1977). Recognizing the sex of the walker from a dynamic point-light display. *Perception and Psychophysics, 21,* 575–580.

Lawson, C., Lenz, G. S., Baker, A., & Myers, M. (2010). Looking like a winner: Candidate appearance and electoral success in new democracies. *World Politics, 62*, 561–593.

Little, A. C., Burriss, R. P., Jones, B. C., & Roberts, S. C. (2007). Facial appearance affects voting decisions. *Evolution and Human Behavior, 28*, 18–27.

Livingston, R. W., & Pearce, N. A. (2009). The teddy-bear effect: Does having a baby face benefit black chief executive officers? *Psychological Science, 20*, 1229–1236.

Lord, R. G., Brown, D. J., Harvey, J. L., & Hall, R. J. (2001). Contextual constraints on prototype generation and their multilevel consequences for leadership perceptions. *The Leadership Quarterly, 12*, 311–338.

Lord, R. G., & Dinh, J. E. (2014). What have we learned that is critical in understanding leadership perceptions and leader-performance relations? *Industrial and Organizational Psychology, 7*, 158–177.

Lord, R. G., Foti, R. J., & De Vader, C. L. (1984). A test of leadership categorization theory: Internal structure, information processing, and leadership perceptions. *Organizational Behavior and Human Performance, 34*, 343–378.

Macrae, C. N., & Martin, D. (2007). A boy primed Sue: Feature-based processing and person construal. *European Journal of Social Psychology, 37*, 793–805.

Macrae, C. N., & Quadflieg, S. (2010). Perceiving people. In S. Fiske, D. T. Gilbert, & G. Lindzey (Eds.), *The handbook of social psychology* (5th ed., pp. 428–463). New York, NY: McGraw-Hill.

Martin, D. S. (1978). Person perception and real life electoral behavior. *Australian Journal of Psychology, 30*, 255–262.

Matthews, A. M., Lord, R. G., & Walker, J. B. (1990). *The development of leadership perceptions in children.* Unpublished manuscript, University of Akron.

McArthur, L. Z., & Baron, R. M. (1983). Toward an ecological theory of social perception. *Psychological Review, 90*, 215–238.

McGovern, T. V., & Tinsley, H. E. (1978). Interviewer evaluations of interviewee nonverbal behavior. *Journal of Vocational Behavior, 13*, 163–171.

Murray, G. R., & Schmitz, J. D. (2011). Caveman politics: Evolutionary leadership preferences and physical stature. *Social Science Quarterly, 92*, 1215–1235.

Na, J., Kim, S., Oh, H., Choi, I., & O'Toole, A. (2015). Competence judgments based on facial appearance are better predictors of American elections than of Korean elections. *Psychological Science, 26*, 1107–1113.

Neave, N., & Shields, K. (2008). The effects of facial hair manipulation on female perceptions of attractiveness, masculinity, and dominance in male faces. *Personality and Individual Differences, 45*, 373–377.

Nestler, S., & Back, M. D. (2013). Applications and extensions of the lens model to understand interpersonal judgments at zero acquaintance. *Current Directions in Psychological Science, 22*, 374–379.

Newcombe, M. J., & Ashkanasy, N. M. (2002). The role of affect and affective congruence in perceptions of leaders: An experimental study. *The Leadership Quarterly, 13*, 601–614.

Offermann, L. R., Kennedy, J. K., & Wirtz, P. W. (1994). Implicit leadership theories: Content, structure, and generalizability. *The Leadership Quarterly, 5*, 43–58.

Öhman, A. (1986). Face the beast and fear the face: Animal and social fears as prototypes for evolutionary analyses of emotion. *Psychophysiology, 23*, 123–145.

Phillips, J. S. (1984). The accuracy of leadership ratings: A cognitive categorization perspective. *Organizational Behavior and Human Performance, 33*, 125–138.

Phillips, J. S., & Lord, R. G. (1982). Schematic information processing and perceptions of leadership in problem-solving groups. *Journal of Applied Psychology, 67*, 486–492.

Pillemer, J., Graham, E. R., & Burke, D. M. (2014). The face says it all: CEOs, gender, and predicting corporate performance. *The Leadership Quarterly, 25*, 855–864.

Pittam, J., & Gallois, C. (1986). Predicting impressions of speakers from voice quality: Acoustic and perceptual measures. *Journal of Language and Social Psychology, 5*, 233–247.

Posthuma, R. A., Morgeson, F. P., & Campion, M. A. (2002). Beyond employment interview validity: A comprehensive narrative review of recent research and trends over time. *Personnel Psychology, 55*, 1–81.

Poutvaara, P., Jordahl, H., & Berggren, N. (2009). Faces of politicians: Babyfacedness predicts inferred competence but not electoral success. *Journal of Experimental Social Psychology, 45*, 1132–1135.

Quinn, K. A., & Macrae, C. N. (2005). Categorizing others: The dynamics of person construal. *Journal of Personality and Social Psychology, 88,* 467–479.

Ranft, A. L., Zinko, R., Ferris, G. R., & Buckley, M. R. (2006). Marketing the image of management: The costs and benefits of CEO reputation. *Organizational Dynamics, 35,* 279–290.

Re, D. E., DeBruine, L. M., Jones, B. C., & Perrett, D. I. (2013). Facial cues to perceived height influence leadership choices in simulated war and peace contexts. *Evolutionary Psychology, 11,* 89–103.

Re, D. E., & Rule, N. O. (2016). The big man has a big mouth: Mouth width correlates with perceived leadership ability and actual leadership performance. *Journal of Experimental Social Psychology, 63,* 86–93.

Read, S. J., Vanman, E. J., & Miller, L. C. (1997). Connectionism, parallel constraint satisfaction processes, and Gestalt principles: (Re)introducing cognitive dynamics to social psychology. *Personality and Social Psychology Review, 1,* 26–53.

Riggio, H. R., & Riggio, R. E. (2010). Appearance-based trait inferences and voting: Evolutionary roots and implications for leadership. *Journal of Nonverbal Behavior, 34,* 119–125.

Riggio, R. E., & Friedman, H. S. (1986). Impression formation: The role of expressive behavior. *Journal of Personality and Social Psychology, 50,* 421–427.

Rosch, E. (1975). Cognitive representations of semantic categories. *Journal of Experimental Psychology: General, 104,* 192–233.

Rosenthal, R., & Jacobson, L. (1968). *Pygmalion in the classroom: Teacher expectation and pupils' intellectual development.* New York, NY: Holt, Rinehart & Winston.

Rozin, P., Haidt, J., & McCauley, C. R. (1999). Disgust: The body and soul emotion. In T. Dalgleish & M. Power (Eds.), *Handbook of cognition and emotion* (pp. 429–445). Chichester, UK: John Wiley.

Rule, N. O., & Ambady, N. (2008). The face of success: Inferences from chief executive officers' appearance predict company profits. *Psychological Science, 19,* 109–111.

Rule, N. O., & Ambady, N. (2009). She's got the look: Inferences from female chief executive officers' faces predict their success. *Sex Roles, 61,* 644–652.

Rule, N. O., & Ambady, N. (2010). First impressions of the face: Predicting success and behavior. *Social and Personality Psychology Compass, 4,* 506–516.

Rule, N. O., & Ambady, N. (2011a). Face and fortune: Inferences of personality from managing partners' faces predict their firms' financial success. *The Leadership Quarterly, 22,* 690–696.

Rule, N. O., & Ambady, N. (2011b). Judgments of power from college yearbook photos and later career success. *Social Psychological and Personality Science, 2,* 154–158.

Rule, N. O., Ambady, N., Adams, R. B., Jr., Ozono, H., Nakashima, S., Yoshikawa, S., & Watabe, M. (2010). Polling the face: Prediction and consensus across cultures. *Journal of Personality and Social Psychology, 98,* 1–15.

Rule, N. O., Bjornsdottir, R. T., Tskhay, K. O., & Ambady, N. (2016). Subtle perceptions of male sexual orientation influence occupational opportunities. *Journal of Applied Psychology, 101,* 1687–1704.

Rule, N. O., Ishii, K., & Ambady, N. (2011). Cross-cultural impressions of leaders' faces: Consensus and predictive validity. *International Journal of Intercultural Relations, 35,* 833–841.

Rule, N. O., Krendl, A. C., Ivcevic, Z., & Ambady, N. (2013). Accuracy and consensus in judgments of trustworthiness from faces: Behavioral and neural correlates. *Journal of Personality and Social Psychology, 104,* 409–426.

Rule, N. O., Moran, J. M., Freeman, J. B., Whitfield-Gabrieli, S., Gabrieli, J. D. E., & Ambady, N. (2011). Face value: Amygdala response reflects the validity of first impressions. *NeuroImage, 54,* 734–741.

Rule, N. O., & Tskhay, K. O. (2014). The influence of economic context on the relationship between chief executive officer facial appearance and company profits. *The Leadership Quarterly, 25,* 846–854.

Rule, N. O., Tskhay, K. O., Freeman, J. B., & Ambady, N. (2014). On the interactive influence of facial appearance and explicit knowledge in social categorization. *European Journal of Social Psychology, 44,* 529–535.

Sanchez-Cortes, D., Aran, O., Mast, M. S., & Gatica-Perez, D. (2010). Identifying emergent leadership in small groups using nonverbal communicative cues (pp. 8–12). International Conference on Multimodal Interfaces and the Workshop on Machine Learning for Multimodal Interaction, Beijing, China.

Schmidt, F. L., & Hunter, J. E. (1998). The validity and utility of selection methods in personnel psychology: Practical and theoretical implications of 85 years of research findings. *Psychological Bulletin, 124,* 262–274.

Shamir, B., House, R. J., & Arthur, M. B. (1993). The motivational effects of charismatic leadership: A self-concept based theory. *Organization Science, 4*, 577–594.

Sherman, J. W., & Hamilton, D. L. (1994). On the formation of interitem associative links in person memory. *Journal of Experimental Social Psychology, 30*, 203–217.

Smith, E. R. (1996). What do connectionism and social psychology offer each other? *Journal of Personality and Social Psychology, 70*, 893–912.

Smith, J. A., & Foti, R. J. (1998). A pattern approach to the study of leader emergence. *The Leadership Quarterly, 9*, 147–160.

Stevens, L. E., & Fiske, S. T. (1995). Motivation and cognition in social life: A social survival perspective. *Social Cognition, 13*, 189–214.

Stirrat, M., & Perrett, D. I. (2010). Valid facial cues to cooperation and trust: Male facial width and trustworthiness. *Psychological Science, 21*, 349–354.

Todorov, A., Mandisodza, A. N., Goren, A., & Hall, C. C. (2005). Inferences of competence from faces predict election outcomes. *Science, 308*, 1623–1626.

Tosi, H. L., & Einbender, S. W. (1985). The effects of the type and amount of information in sex discrimination research: A meta-analysis. *Academy of Management Journal, 28*, 712–723.

Tskhay, K. O., & Rule, N. O. (2013). Accuracy in categorizing perceptually ambiguous groups a review and meta-analysis. *Personality and Social Psychology Review, 17*, 72–86.

Tskhay, K. O., & Rule, N. O. (2015). Sexual orientation across culture and time. In S. Safdar & N. Kosakowska-Berezecka (Eds.), *Psychology of gender through the lens of culture* (pp. 55–73). New York: Springer International.

Tskhay, K. O., Xu, H., & Rule, N. O. (2014). Perceptions of leadership success from nonverbal cues communicated by orchestra conductors. *The Leadership Quarterly, 25*, 901–911.

Tskhay, K. O., Zhu, R., & Rule, N. O. (2017). Perceptions of charisma from thin slices of behavior predict leadership prototypicality judgments. *The Leadership Quarterly.* Advance online publication. doi:10.1016/j.leaqua.2017.03.003

Valentine, T. (1991). A unified account of the effects of distinctiveness, inversion, and race in face recognition. *The Quarterly Journal of Experimental Psychology, 43*, 161–204.

van Knippenberg, D., & Sitkin, S. B. (2013). A critical assessment of charismatic–transformational leadership research: Back to the drawing board? *The Academy of Management Annals, 7*, 1–60.

van Vugt, M., Hogan, R., & Kaiser, R. B. (2008). Leadership, followership, and evolution: Some lessons from the past. *American Psychologist, 63*, 182–196.

van Vugt, M., & Ronay, R. (2014). The evolutionary psychology of leadership: Theory, review, and roadmap. *Organizational Psychology Review, 4*, 74–95.

Weber, M. (1978). *Economy and society: An outline of interpretive sociology.* Berkley: University of California Press. (Original work published 1922)

West, T. V., & Kenny, D. A. (2011). The truth and bias model of judgment. *Psychological Review, 118*, 357–378.

Wild, H. A., Barrett, S. E., Spence, M. J., O'Toole, A. J., Cheng, Y. D., & Brooke, J. (2000). Recognition and sex categorization of adults' and children's faces: Examining performance in the absence of sex-stereotyped cues. *Journal of Experimental Child Psychology, 77*, 269–291.

Wong, E. M., Ormiston, M. E., & Haselhuhn, M. P. (2011). A face only an investor could love: CEOs' facial structure predicts their firms' financial performance. *Psychological Science, 22*, 1478–1483.

Zebrowitz, L. A. (1997). *Reading faces: Window to the soul?* Boulder, CO: Westview.

Zebrowitz, L. A., Collins, M. A., & Dutta, R. (1998). The relationship between appearance and personality across the life span. *Personality and Social Psychology Bulletin, 24*, 736–749.

Zebrowitz, L. A., Kikuchi, M., & Fellous, J. M. (2007). Are effects of emotion expression on trait impressions mediated by babyfaceness? Evidence from connectionist modeling. *Personality and Social Psychology Bulletin, 33*, 648–662.

# CHAPTER 10

# Leadership and Gender

*Linda L. Carli*

*Alice H. Eagly*

---

## Opening Case: A Day in the Life of a Leader

Angela Merkel, the chancellor of Germany, rises in the morning between 6:00 and 6:30 a.m. in her unpretentious, rent-controlled apartment located in the center of Berlin. She makes breakfast and eats with her husband sometime between 8:00 and 9:00 a.m. After being transported in an armored vehicle to the chancellor's office, she meets with her close advisers and discusses world news and other issues for which her staff has prepared background information. This being Wednesday, the day of weekly cabinet meetings, she meets with them at 9:30 a.m. and discusses, among other issues, the continuing refugee crisis. As chair of this meeting, she invites discussion but skilfully mediates to settle matters that become contentious. Among these cabinet ministers and advisers, women are well represented, with Beate Baumann serving as her office manager, speechwriter, and gatekeeper.

A working lunch follows, where she discusses the Syrian crisis with her defense minister, Ursula Von der Leyen, and other advisers. She then meets with Julia Klöckner, chair of the Christian Democratic Union Party in the state of Rhineland-Palatinate, who arrived together with several of her associates. A keen strategist, Merkel advises them how to overcome the political challenges they are facing from opposition parties.

Because the Bundestag (i.e., parliament) is meeting this afternoon, she immediately goes there to deliver a planned speech on the refugee crisis. As usual, she is wearing her signature black pants and bright-colored blazer. Just before speaking at this televised event, she has a quick visit with her hair stylist. In this speech, she reviews the recent history of the refugee crisis and current situation. In particular, she adroitly defends the agreement that she brokered with Turkey to retain refugees and to pass on only Syrian nationals to Germany and the rest of Europe. She delivers this speech in her usual calm style, which is free from bombast and high-flying rhetoric. She presents facts and concrete solutions in a straightforward, low-key manner. The speech is generally well received, consistent with the German public having accorded her a high approval rating and bestowing on her the nickname of "Mutti," or "Mommy." However, she is worried because the welcoming policy that she has fostered in the refugee crisis has already threatened the high level of trust that she has enjoyed.

After leaving the Bundestag, Merkel returns to her office, where she works at a simple writing table instead of the large, imposing desk inherited from her predecessor, Gerhard Schroeder. The wall above her writing desk displays a portrait of Konrad Adenauer, the first chancellor of postwar West Germany. On a shelf behind her desk sits a small, framed portrait of Catherine the Great, the German-born Russian empress who set transformative change in motion in 18th-century Russia. Yet, in the presence of these inspiring role models, Merkel faces the mundane task of looking over and signing documents that her staff bring to her. She also listens to a report from several of her advisers about civil unrest involving right-wing protesters of the surge in immigration. This meeting extends to a working dinner at the chancellery.

Merkel returns to her apartment sometime after 10 p.m. She is in bed by midnight, allowing 6 to 7 hours of sleep before beginning her routine the next day.[1]

## Discussion Questions

1. How would you characterize Angel Merkel's leadership style? Do you think her gender has affected the way she leads?

2. What characteristics of Merkel do you believe make her a particularly strong leader? What weaknesses do you think she has?

3. How are expectations, and, consequently, the evaluations of female leaders, affected by the cultural context? Compare and contrast what one would probably find in the U.S. versus Norway."

# Chapter Overview

In many societies, women have made considerable progress in attaining leader roles, as symbolized by the ascension of Angela Merkel to the very powerful position of chancellor of Germany. However, gender equality remains a distant goal, with men currently possessing considerably more power and authority than women in organizations and governments. Patriarchy, although weakened, still prevails. In this chapter, we review the social science for why gender inequality remains, while still slowly diminishing.

We focus on leadership exercised in formal positions, not the informal leadership that often goes unrecognized and unrewarded. In accounting for the relative deficit of

---

1. See Kreller (2014); Orth (2014); Packer (2014); Rinke & Brown (2010).

**Table 10.1**    Summary of Findings Testing Theoretical Explanations for the Gender Gap in Leadership

| Explanation | Finding |
| --- | --- |
| Human capital | Women favored in education and general school extracurricular activities; men in business schools and school sports |
| Family responsibilities | Men favored; due to family, women more often quit and work part-time |
| Leadership styles | Women favored in use of transformational style and rewards, and in avoiding punishment, waiting to act, and laissez-faire leadership, unclear effect of democratic leadership |
| Effectiveness | Mixed findings on financial outcomes for organizations; for ratings of leader effectiveness, women and men favored in different contexts |
| Evolutionary approach | Evidence favors flexibility in gender roles; female and male leaders favored in different contexts |
| Trait differences | No clear advantage in the Big Five traits or intelligence; unclear relevance of aggressiveness and competition |
| Discrimination | Men favored; women discriminated against in hiring, promotion, and pay |
| Stereotyping | Men favored overall because women are subject to the double bind, although context affects the male advantage |
| Organizational obstacles | Men favored due to demand for long hours and women's lack of access to networks, mentors, and desirable assignments |

women in leader roles, we consider five factors. First, does women's lesser human capital contribute to the deficit? Second, is women's leadership style disadvantageous? The third explanation considers whether men's nature gives them an advantage. The fourth explanation focuses on prejudice and discrimination, and the fifth considers organizational barriers. We begin by reviewing women's current status as leaders.

# Representation of Women and Men in Leadership Roles

In most developed societies, women have gained considerable access to management. In the United States, women currently hold 39% of all managerial positions, up from 11% in 1940 (U.S. Census Bureau, 2016). Although the proportion of women declines with higher organizational rank (Helfat, Harris, & Wolfson, 2006), across all organizations, 28% of chief executive officers are women (U.S. Bureau of Labor Statistics, 2016, Table 11). In nonprofit organizations, women fare better, constituting 43% of chief executive officers and 43% of board members, but are less common in the larger, wealthier nonprofits (Stiffman, 2015). In the Fortune or S&P 500, women constitute 25% of senior executives and managers, 19% of board members, but only 4% of chief executive officers (Catalyst, 2016).

Globally, the percentage of female managers has risen in the last decade and ranges from 59% in Jamaica to 3% in Pakistan (International Labor Organization, 2015a). A study of large listed corporations in 39 nations reported 11% median female corporate board representation, with the highest representation in Iceland (48%), Norway (37%), and France (30%), all nations with quotas requiring a minimum female membership (Deloitte, 2015).

Despite gradual increases, women remain underrepresented in political leadership (United Nations, 2015). Currently, U.S. women hold 19% of congressional seats and 25% in state legislatures (Center for American Women and Politics, 2015). Globally, women hold 23% of parliamentary seats: 19% in Asia, 23% in Africa, 27% in the Americas, and 24% in Europe excluding the Nordic nations, which are highest at 41% (International Parliamentary Union, 2016).

A few women have emerged in very high places. Currently, women lead governments as presidents or prime ministers in 19 nations, including Germany, where Angela Merkel continues as chancellor (Christensen, 2016; Kent, 2015), and a woman serves as managing director of the International Monetary Fund. Thus, instead of the impenetrable barrier implied by the *glass ceiling* metaphor, women face challenges that are difficult but not impossible to overcome. To symbolize women's often challenging paths to leadership, we offer the metaphor of the *labyrinth* (Eagly & Carli, 2007). Some women do make it to the center of the labyrinth and attain leadership, but compared with the men's relatively straight paths, women's less direct routes require more careful navigation. We now consider what forms the labyrinth takes. Why do women remain underrepresented as leaders?

# Human Capital Investments and Family Responsibilities

## Human Capital of Women and Men

One explanation for the leadership gender gap is that women lack human capital due to deficiencies in the skills, knowledge, and psychological attributes that enable leadership. However, in industrialized countries, women typically now exceed men in education (United Nations, 2015). In the United States in 2014, women received 57% of bachelor's degrees, 60% of master's degrees, and 52% of PhDs (National Center for Education Statistics, 2015, Table 318.30). In the United States (Voyer & Voyer, 2014) and many industrialized countries (United Nations, 2015), women and girls earn higher grades than men and boys.

More women are earning the MBA degree—a usual credential for high-level managerial careers. Worldwide, in 2015, women took 44% of graduate management admissions tests and were 40% of the applicant pool for full-time MBA programs (Bruggeman & Chan, 2016). Moreover, more women—now 47% of applicants—are seeking finance degrees (Bruggeman & Chan, 2016). Still, gender gaps remain. One study found that men's higher grades and greater representation in finance were associated with women's lower earnings (Bertrand, Goldin, & Katz, 2010). Yet sharp critiques have faulted the masculine cultures of elite business schools for disadvantaging women (e.g., Wittenberg-Cox & Symons, 2015).

Young people's experiences outside of classrooms could build human capital in the form of self-confidence and competitiveness (Fitzsimmons & Callan, 2016). U.S. studies reveal that boys participate more in sports and girls in other activities such as clubs and student government (e.g., Ingels, Dalton, & LoGerfo, 2008; Kort-Butler & Hagewen, 2011). These extracurricular activities are associated with well-being, pro-social behavior, and other outcomes (see review by Farb & Matjasko, 2012), including self-rated leadership ability (Hancock, Dyk, & Jones, 2012), and the association is clearer for nonsport than sport activities. In college, men continue to participate more in sports (Quadlin, 2016) and women more in student government except in the leadership roles of president and treasurer (American Student Government Association, 2016). Although such research suggests that extracurricular activity advantages women at least as much as men, there is some limited evidence that participation in competitive sports fosters a taste for competition (Comeig, Grau-Grau, Jaramillo-Gutiérrez, & Ramírez, 2015). Although some economists have argued that women's labor market outcomes are adversely affected by their lesser competitiveness (e.g., Reuben, Sapienza, & Zingales, 2015), the available evidence is sparse.

Occupational interests and preferences are aspects of human capital that shape career decisions. Compared with men, women prefer (Diekman & Steinberg, 2013) and are employed in occupations that fulfill communal goals—that is, helping and interacting with people (e.g., Lippa, Preston, & Penner, 2014). Furthermore, in research on the specific attributes that people indicate that they seek in jobs, a meta-analysis revealed some gender differences: Women preferred working with people, opportunity to help others, easy commute, resource adequacy, and opportunity to make friends, whereas men preferred solitude and leisure (Konrad, Ritchie, Lieb, & Corrigall, 2000). Women's communal orientation could enhance their interest in management, even while shaping the type of managerial careers that they undertake. For example, a survey of 300,000 U.S. business students found that women outnumbered men by two to one or more in seeking jobs in nonprofits, government and public service, and health care, as well as in retail, fashion, and apparel; marketing and advertising; and consumer goods (Goudreau, 2010).

Women are less attracted than men to political leadership. This finding emerged robustly in three U.S. national surveys of persons employed in the professions from which most political candidates emerge (e.g., lawyers, political activists, business leaders; see Lawless, 2015). Two causes have received considerable support: Women are less likely to be recruited to run for office, and women have lower self-efficacy in relation to running. A national survey of U.S. high school and college students found that this political ambition gender gap increased from high school to college, as men became progressively more involved than women in political activities through courses, political organizations, media consumption, and conversations (Fox & Lawless, 2014).

Women's overall career ambition is similar to that of men. In fact, self-reported desire for a high-paying job is now greater among young women than young men in the United States (Patten & Parker, 2012). Male and female employees appear to be equally committed to their employing organizations (e.g., Meyer, Stanley, Herscovitch, & Topolnytsky, 2002). Also, a study of 1,000 employees of U.S. public and private organizations found that more women than men aspired to top management when they entered these organizations. However, over time, women's aspirations had faded relative to those of the men (Coffman & Neuenfeld, 2014).

All in all, we have a nuanced story to tell about human capital. Women excel in amount of education even though they may face some disadvantage in business schools. Girls, like boys, gain additional capital outside of schoolwork, although boys may gain more experience in competitive contexts. Women's stronger communal orientation attracts them more to some types of leader roles. Finally, women's considerable ambition for leadership may fade as they navigate the labyrinth—an issue we address in the remainder of this chapter.

## Women's and Men's Family Responsibilities

According to human capital theory, family responsibilities undermine women's careers. There is little doubt that, on average, women spend more time than men on childcare and housework in all nations (U.S. Bureau of Labor Statistics, 2015a, Tables A-6, A-7; World Bank, 2013). Because much domestic work is obligatory and routine, opting out of it because of job responsibilities is generally not feasible. Therefore, women typically sacrifice personal time and, as a result, experience less leisure time than men do (e.g., Sayer, 2016).

Although job turnover is slightly higher in men than in women (see meta-analysis by Griffeth, Hom, & Gaertner, 2000), a large-scale study of professionals and managers in Fortune 500 companies found a 36% higher quit rate among women than men (Hom, Roberson, & Ellis, 2008). This difference attenuated in positions occupied by more women because of a higher male quit rate in such jobs. Women quit more than men only in the early years of job tenure and more often for family reasons (e.g., Bertrand, Goldin, & Katz, 2010; see Theodossiou & Zangelidis, 2009, for European data). In general, employees suffer long-term income loss from job breaks for family responsibilities, which are more costly than breaks taken for reasons such as obtaining additional training (Theunissen, Verbruggen, Forrier, & Sels, 2011).

Part-time employment, which also slows women's advancement, has been increasing, especially among women (International Labor Organization, 2015b). In 2010, some 26% of women in Europe and 13% in the United States worked fewer than 30 hours a week, compared with 4% to 5% of men (Blau & Kahn, 2013). Having a spouse or children is associated with part-time work for women but with increased hours for men (Greenhaus & Powell, 2012). Even women in high-status occupations often reduce their work hours to accommodate family responsibilities (Herr & Wolfram, 2012).

In sum, part-time schedules and breaks from employment lower women's human capital relative to that of men and thereby contribute substantially to gender gaps in pay, advancement, and authority (Abendroth, Maas, & van der Lippe, 2013; Blau & Kahn, 2013; Mandel & Semyonov, 2014). Such findings can raise questions about the adequacy of female leaders' performance. Do women perform as well as men when they do occupy leadership roles?

# The Leadership Styles of Women and Men

## Research on Leadership Styles of Women and Men

If women lack adequacy as leaders, perhaps their leadership style is at fault—that is, their typical modes of interacting with their superiors, peers, and subordinates. Because styles influence leaders' effectiveness (Yukl, 2013), any sex differences in style could affect women's advancement.

Meta-analyses of gender differences in leadership style based on people's ratings of individual leaders' typical behaviors found that women overall adopted a somewhat less autocratic and more democratic leadership style, by involving subordinates in decision making (Eagly & Johnson, 1990; van Engen & Willemsen, 2004). Indeed, leading "from behind," as the term is known in the United States, involves working with others to reach collective decisions, a signature effort of German chancellor Angela Merkel. In contrast, women and men did not differ in their task-oriented versus interpersonally oriented leadership—the extent to which they emphasized maintaining rules and procedures versus attending to followers' needs, although women were more interpersonally oriented in nonmanagerial samples, especially among university students.

Eagly and Johnson (1990) suggested that women's preference for democratic and participative leadership styles could stem from gender norms discouraging women from leading in a top-down, autocratic manner (see subsection Restrictions on Women's Agency). Yet norms about appropriate managerial behavior likely differ across organizations, given that women tended to manifest more democratic and more interpersonally oriented styles than men in leader roles that were less male-dominated. Thus, there may be more leeway for culturally feminine relational and participative styles with greater numbers of women in leader roles.

In the 1980s and 1990s, many researchers shifted their research to transformational leadership: a style that is future oriented rather than present oriented and that strengthens organizations by inspiring followers' commitment and ability to contribute creatively to organizations. Transformational leadership involves establishing oneself as a role model by gaining followers' trust and confidence (Bass, 1998). Transformational leaders state future goals, develop plans to achieve those goals, and innovate, even when their organization is generally successful. By mentoring and empowering followers, such leaders encourage them to develop their full potential and thus to contribute more effectively to their organization.

Researchers contrasted transformational leaders with *transactional* leaders, who appeal to subordinates' self-interest by establishing exchange relationships with them. This type of leadership involves clarifying subordinates' responsibilities, rewarding them for meeting objectives, and correcting them for failing to meet objectives. In addition to these two styles, researchers distinguished a *laissez-faire* style that is marked by a general failure to take responsibility for managing (see Antonakis, Chapter 3, this volume).

Because transformational leadership combines masculine qualities with feminine communal ones, especially in its individualized consideration dimension, the style is likely to be more attractive to female leaders than more masculine styles (Eagly & Carli, 2007). Testing this idea, a meta-analysis compared men's and women's transformational, transactional, and laissez-faire styles of leadership (Eagly, Johannesen-Schmidt, & van Engen, 2003). The findings revealed small sex differences (reported as means in the *d* metric of standardized differences, with differences in the male direction given a positive sign, see Women were generally more transformational and more transactional on the transactional subscale of providing rewards for satisfactory performance. Women's transformational leadership differed most from men's in *individualized consideration*, focusing on developing and mentoring followers and attending to their individual needs. In contrast, compared with women, men showed more transactional leadership by emphasizing followers' mistakes and failures and waiting until problems become severe before intervening. Men were also more laissez-faire than women. These differences were replicated in large-scale studies by Antonakis, Avolio, and Sivasubramaniam (2003) and Desvaux and Devillard (2008).

In summary, women's leadership style tends to be more democratic and participative, compared with men's more autocratic and directive style. Female managers also tend to adopt a transformational style somewhat more than men do. Transactionally, female managers use more rewards than men do. In contrast, men, more than women, attend to subordinates' failures to meet standards and display the more problematic styles that involve delay in solving problems or being absent or uninvolved at critical times. Similar findings emerged in a study of people's beliefs, or stereotypes, about female and male leadership styles, suggesting that people are generally aware of these relatively subtle behavioral differences (Vinkenburg, van Engen, Eagly, & Johannesen-Schmidt, 2011).

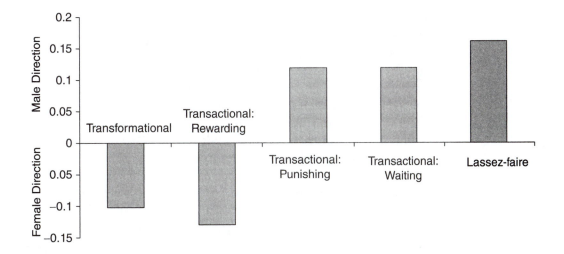

**Figure 10.1**   Effect Sizes Reflecting Gender Differences in Transformational, Transactional, and Laissez-Faire Leadership

SOURCE: Adapted from "Transformational, transactional, and laissez-faire leadership styles: A meta-analysis comparing women and men," by A. H. Eagly, M. C. Johannesen-Schmidt, & M. van Engen, 2003. Psychological Bulletin, 129, p. 571.

## Leadership Style and Leaders' Effectiveness

Do these findings on leadership style advantage either male or female leaders? With respect to democratic and participative styles, the answer is not clear. Assertiveness, an aspect of autocratic style that consists of actively pursuing and defending one's own interests, is most effective at moderate levels; high levels can damage social relationships, whereas low levels limit goal achievement (Ames & Flynn, 2007). Additional research could determine whether women's typically more democratic style usually places them in this advantageous middle ground.

The implications of transformational and transactional leadership are clearer. As confirmed meta-analytically (Judge & Piccolo 2004; see also Wang, Oh, Courtright, & Colbert, 2011), the behaviors somewhat characteristic of women, the transformational style and the component of transactional style that involves providing rewards, were correlated with effectiveness. In contrast, of the behaviors somewhat more characteristic of men, transactional leadership involving punishment was only weakly associated with effectiveness, and delaying problem-solving and the laissez-faire style were associated with impaired effectiveness.

Some caution about this female advantage generalization is appropriate. One reason for caution is that these style differences are quite small. A second reason for caution is the possibility of a selection bias whereby, to attain leader roles, women have to meet higher promotion standards than men (see Blau & DeVaro, 2007). Given such ambiguities, we review other ways of examining the relative effectiveness of female and male leaders.

In business contexts, one way to study effectiveness involves examining the relations between the proportion of female leaders and companies' financial performance. Some early studies found that gender diversity was associated with better financial outcomes (e.g., Desvaux, Devillard-Hoellinger, & Baumgarten, 2007). These and other early studies initiated the so-called *business case* whereby female leadership is said to bring about higher corporate profits. However, basing conclusions on simple group comparisons or correlational analyses is not sufficient to indicate that women cause greater profits. Such associations may suffer from endogeneity—that is, statistical anomalies such as reverse causation, omitted variables, selection biases, and flawed measures (Antonakis, Bendahan, Jacquart, & Lalive, 2010).

In fact, newer research with appropriate statistical controls for endogeneity has not routinely supported the business case (see Adams, 2016). For example, in a large sample of U.S. firms, Adams and Ferriera (2009) found an overall negative average effect of the gender diversity of corporate boards when controlling for individual firm characteristics. However, this effect was moderated by how well governed firms were. Specifically, the presence of female directors reduced attendance problems of boards and increased monitoring of CEOs, holding them accountable for poor performance. This monitoring benefited firms with weak governance, but was counterproductive for firms that were well governed. This study illustrates one way in which differences in female and male behavior may have unexpected consequences.

A meta-analysis of 140 studies examining the effects of increasing board gender diversity on firm financial outcomes revealed a tiny, but significant, positive zero-order correlation ($r = .03$) (Byron & Post, 2016). All in all, the business case for women on boards lacks support, although some individual studies have produced positive outcomes (see Eagly, 2016). Research has also found considerably more evidence associating women's board participation with enhanced social outcomes, such as corporate responsibility, than with financial outcomes (Byron & Post, 2016).

A final method of assessing leaders' performance is based on ratings of the effectiveness of individual leaders. In a meta-analysis of 96 studies comparing the effectiveness of men and women holding comparable leadership roles, there was no overall sex difference (Eagly, Karau, & Makhijani, 1995). A later meta-analysis of leaders' effectiveness encompassing 95 studies also found no overall sex difference (Paustian-Underdahl, Walker, & Woehr, 2014). However, perceived effectiveness depended on whether leadership was rated by the leaders themselves or by others. With others' ratings, women appeared to be more effective than men, whereas with self-ratings, men appeared to be more effective than women. The type of organization affected results in both meta-analyses. In contexts that were male dominated (e.g., military, government), men received higher effectiveness ratings, whereas in contexts that were more female-dominated (e.g., education, middle management), women were perceived as more effective than men. Such contextual findings suggest an influence of gender stereotypes. In male-dominated settings, people may equate good leadership with stereotypically masculine behaviors, creating doubt about women's competence. Similarly, in female-dominated settings, leadership may be infused to some extent with more feminine qualities (Koenig, Eagly, Mitchell, & Ristikari, 2011).

In conclusion, research on leaders' style and effectiveness suggests that style differences between women and men are unlikely to hinder women's performance as leaders but instead could even enhance their performance. Also, findings on leaders' effectiveness suggest neither male nor female advantage, although contextual effects abound. Overall, there is little ground for concluding either that women have ineffective leadership styles or are generally less effective than their male counterparts.

# The Nature Arguments: Men as Naturally Dominant

## Evolutionary Psychology Theory

Evolutionary psychologists ascribe current psychological sex differences to the differing reproductive pressures on males and females in the early history of the human species (e.g., Buss, 2016). According to one evolutionary approach (Trivers, 1972), because women invested more than men in their offspring (e.g., through gestation and nursing), women consequently became choosier about potential mates. This choosiness presumably took the form of ancestral women preferring mates who could provide resources to support them and their children. As a result, ancestral men competed with other men to obtain resources and sexual access to women, and the winners in these competitions were more likely to have their genes carried on to the next generation. By this logic, men who fared better in these competitions were dominant, aggressive, risk taking, competitive, and status seeking—attributes that facilitated leadership. Such men's greater control of resources and higher status facilitated their reproductive success, and these qualities became ingrained in men as evolved traits.

Other evolutionary scientists have emphasized the extreme environmental variability and changing adaptive challenges present during human evolution (e.g., Richerson & Boyd, 2005), arguing that this evolutionary history would have enhanced cognition, producing humans capable of responding flexibly to environmental changes (e.g., Lieberman, 2012; Potts, 2012). Also because, over eons, humans lived in groups of increasing size, their evolutionary niche advantaged those who had social skills enabling communication and persuasion. Given this sociality, along with advanced cognition, humans gained the capacity to form different types of social structures, depending on external conditions (Gintis, van Schaik, & Boehm, 2015).

These assumptions about human flexibility suggest that male dominance would not be a human universal. Indeed, anthropological scholarship reveals that most very simple foraging societies were organized into nonhierarchical and nonpatriarchal band structures (e.g., Boehm, 1999; Gintis et al., 2015). In such societies, men and women were likely relatively mutually dependent for their subsistence, depending on each society's environment and ecology. Both sexes would have reaped advantages from pair bonds with effective resource providers. Despite sex-based task specialization, relations between the sexes were probably relatively egalitarian.

Patriarchy emerged along with a variety of economic and social developments, including warfare and intensive agriculture (Wood & Eagly, 2012). With the advent of settled societies that accumulated wealth, roles in the nondomestic economies increasingly required specialized training, intensive energy expenditure, and travel away from the home. Because of men's freedom from the gestation and nursing of infants, they were better positioned to occupy these roles and, ultimately, roles that entailed primary responsibility for providing resources for family units. Women's labor became more confined to the private, domestic sphere because birth rates remained high while nondomestic work moved out of homes and farms and eventually into factories and offices. Therefore, women generally lost power relative to men. Inequality increased, and men came to dominate leadership roles (Miller, 2015).

Given the presumption that the predominance of male leaders reflects the broader social structure, some evolutionary psychologists have theorized contingencies in the expression of male dominance. Espousing what is known as an *evoked culture* approach, they argue that genetically programmed sex differences in qualities such as aggressiveness and dominance can be differentially evoked by contextual factors (Buss, 2016; van Vugt & Ronay, 2014). From the evoked culture perspective, whether people favor leaders with masculine or feminine qualities would depend on the prevailing conditions. Research illustrating the contextual quality of such preferences has shown that priming participants with threats of death elicited a preference for more agentic and masculine leadership (Hoyt, Simon, & Innella, 2011), whereas priming with threats of crime or unemployment elicited a preference for social change and female leadership (Brown, Diekman, & Schneider, 2011). Moreover, female leaders tend to be preferred for organizations in crisis, in part because they signal the potential for change (Ryan et al., 2016; see section Organizational Obstacles to Women's Leadership). Such findings suggest that the prevalence of male leaders reflects sociocultural conditions at least as much as evolved tendencies.

## Sex Differences in Leadership Traits

Personality traits have also been implicated as important determinants of leadership ability. Most contemporary psychologists take the view that sex differences in traits and behaviors follow from both nature and nurture (Eagly & Wood, 2013). Consistent with this interactionist view, tendencies toward leadership appear to be partially heritable (Ilies, Arvey, & Bouchard, 2006), yet responsive to socialization whereby children and young people can gain leadership skills in many settings.

Of special interest are the gender differences in traits that may be relevant to leadership, which may include aggressiveness and assertiveness. Indeed, meta-analyses have found greater aggressiveness in men than women, particularly for physical rather than verbal aggression (Archer, 2004; Bettencourt & Miller, 1996). A meta-analysis on workplace aggression (Hershcovis et al., 2007) also showed greater male participation. Men also scored higher than women on self-report personality measures of overall assertiveness (Costa, Terracciano, & McCrae, 2001). Consistent with these trends, men show greater motivation to manage in a traditional, hierarchic command-and-control manner (see meta-analysis by Eagly, Karau, Miner, & Johnson, 1994).

Sex differences in competitiveness have also been of interest, given the logic that people often compete for leader positions. As noted in the section Human Capital of Women and Men, behavioral economists have studied competitiveness in laboratory and field settings (see review by Niederle & Vesterlund, 2011). The general finding is that men compete more than women, reflecting both men's overconfidence and their more favorable attitudes toward competition. In research on competitiveness in bargaining and mixed-motive games, a meta-analysis revealed a small sex difference, with men behaving more competitively than women (Walters, Stuhlmacher, & Meyer, 1998; see also Balliet, Wu, & De Dreu, 2014). However, a meta-analysis of social dilemma research found small effects whereby male–male interactions were more cooperative than female–female interactions and mixed-sex interactions produced more competition and less cooperation in men than women (Balliet, Li, Macfarlan, & van Vugt, 2011).

Other research further demonstrates the contextual quality of male and female competitiveness. For example, one experiment showed greater female than male competitiveness in a task related to the stereotypically feminine domain of fashion but greater male competitiveness or no difference in other domains (Wieland & Sarin, 2012). Also, a Chinese experiment showed greater competitiveness of men than women for a monetary incentive but equal competitiveness for an incentive that benefitted children (Caesar, Wordofa, & Zhang, in press).

Although findings on aggressiveness and competitiveness more often lean in the male than the female direction overall, there is little reason to believe that these qualities typically make leaders more effective. Physical aggression is hardly a means of advancement in modern professional organizations. Of course, verbal aggression, negative assertion, and competitiveness may facilitate leader emergence in some contexts. Yet characteristics akin to these dominating qualities, such as arrogance, self-centered ambition, or having an intimidating or abrasive style, are also known to derail leaders (Judge, Piccolo, & Kosalka, 2009).

Much research on the effects of personality on leadership has been focused on the five-factor model of personality, known as the Big Five (e.g., McCrae & Costa, 1987). A meta-analysis of studies assessing these traits' relations to leadership has shown that extraversion, openness to experience and, conscientiousness have small to moderate associations with leader emergence, and along with agreeableness, also relate to performing effectively as a leader. In contrast, neuroticism relates negatively to leader emergence and effectiveness (Judge, Bono, Ilies, & Gerhardt, 2002). Regression analyses demonstrated that leader emergence was most strongly predicted by extraversion and conscientiousness and leader effectiveness by extraversion and openness to experience; neuroticism and agreeableness were of little importance. Another meta-analysis found general intelligence also associated with leader emergence and also effectiveness (Judge, Colbert, & Ilies, 2004).

And how do men and women fare in these traits? Comparing their traits suggests that neither sex has a clear overall advantage in leadership. A large cross-cultural study found that women showed higher levels of neuroticism, extraversion, agreeableness, and conscientiousness, with differences ranging from moderate in the case of neuroticism to small for the other traits (Schmitt, Realo, Voracek, & Allik, 2008). Women and men do not differ in overall intelligence (Halpern, 2012). Thus, women have a disadvantage in neuroticism and an advantage in agreeableness, neither of which has much relevance to leadership. Women show more conscientiousness and extraversion, which do predict leadership.

For effective leadership, managerial experts typically advocate an androgynous mix of qualities that include negotiation, cooperation, diplomacy, team building, and inspiring and nurturing others. Under contemporary conditions, it is thus unlikely that effective leadership derives mainly from traditionally masculine command-and-control behaviors or that men's ascendance to elite leadership roles reflects their natural dominance. Therefore, we turn to the possibility of prejudice and discrimination.

# Prejudice and Discrimination Against Female Leaders

## Gender Discrimination

Economic studies show that human capital accounts for only a portion of the gender gaps in pay and advancement, suggesting that discrimination probably contributes to the unexplained gaps (Johnston & Lee, 2012; Mandel & Semyonov,

2014). Lending credibility to claims of discrimination, a study of U.S. federal employees found that women had to have higher performance ratings than men to be promoted (Pema & Mehay, 2010). Moreover, studies showing a constant level of discrimination across organizational levels suggest that women face a steady attrition that yields fewer women at higher levels (e.g., Elliot & Smith, 2004).

Evidence of discrimination also comes from experiments that compare the evaluation of male and female job applicants with identical qualifications. Experiments involving actual hiring situations, in which employers evaluate applicants or job applications, show that men are favored for jobs providing higher status and wages and for male-dominated positions, whereas women are favored only for female-dominated jobs (see review by Riach & Rich, 2002). Other experiments involve simulated hiring decisions in which students, managers, or other participants evaluate female or male applicants who have identical résumés. A meta-analysis of 136 such studies revealed that male raters prefer men over women for male-dominated, female-dominated, and integrated jobs, with the biggest male advantage accorded for male-dominated jobs (Koch, D'Mello, & Sacket, 2015). Female raters did not favor either sex except for giving men an advantage for female-dominated jobs.

Organizational studies also reveal discrimination: A meta-analysis of such studies found that women performed as well as men but obtained fewer promotions and less income, especially in prestigious and male-dominated positions (Joshi, Son, & Roh, 2015). Similar results were obtained in another organizational meta-analysis showing that women received higher performance evaluations but were rated as less promotable (Roth, Purvis, & Bobko, 2012). And other experiments show that, even with comparable professional work experience, mothers but not fathers were targets of workplace discrimination (e.g., Correll, Benard, & Paik, 2007; Heilman & Okimoto, 2008). Finally, research shows that it is unlikely that female employees merely avoid authority positions because of family obligations (Corrigall & Konrad, 2006; Galinsky, Aumann, & Bond, 2008). Rather, discrimination may undermine women's ambition (see subsection Human Capital of Women and Men) and may underlie the gender gap in authority by providing women smaller gains in workplace authority than men for similar human capital investments and conferring fewer advantages in job autonomy, challenging work, and income (Mintz & Krymkowski, 2010; Schieman, Schafer, & McIvor, 2013).

## Stereotypes About Women, Men, and Leaders and the Double Bind

Discrimination against female leaders occurs mainly because people believe that women lack the capacity to be effective leaders. According to role incongruity theory, prejudice toward female leaders derives from gender roles—consensual beliefs about the attributes of women and men; these beliefs are either *descriptive* expectations about what women and men are like or *injunctive* expectations about what women and men ought to be like (Eagly & Karau, 2002). Prejudice against women as leaders flows from the incongruity that people often perceive between the characteristics typical of women and the requirements of leader roles.

According to research in many nations, people expect men to be agentic—assertive, dominant, competent, and authoritative—and women to be communal—warm, supportive, kind, and helpful (e.g., J. E. Williams & Best, 1990). People also ascribe predominantly agentic qualities to leaders, making beliefs about leaders similar to beliefs about men, as Schein (1973) demonstrated in her "think manager, think male" studies. In Schein's studies, participants rated a man, a woman, or a successful leader on gender-stereotypical traits; correlational analyses then tested whether the leader traits were more similar to the traits of men or women. A meta-analytic review of studies in the think manager, think male paradigms (and two related paradigms) revealed that although the association of leadership and masculine characteristics has weakened over time, leaders continue to be perceived as more like men than women (Koenig et al., 2011), and especially in highly male-dominated and higher-status leader roles. Prejudice is thus more likely when there is more incongruity between a leader role and the female gender role.

Stereotypes can be self-fulfilling. Thinking about negative portrayals of one's group can cause group members to become concerned about fulfilling the stereotype, and this concern can derail their performance in the stereotypic domain. For example, in one *stereotype threat* experiment, students viewed television commercials featuring female-stereotypic (vs. neutral) content (Davies, Spencer, & Steele, 2005). Women, but not men, exposed to the female-stereotypic portrayals expressed less preference for a leadership role versus a nonleadership role. Although stereotype threat usually undermines performance, other reactions are possible, such as distancing oneself from the threatened domain or even challenging the stereotype by behaving counterstereotypically (see review by Hoyt & Murphy, 2016).

Stereotypes bring women other unique challenges as leaders. On one hand, women are perceived as lacking the agency to be effective leaders; on the other hand, because of injunctive norms about female communion, female leaders are perceived as lacking sufficient warmth if they behave too agentically (Eagly & Carli, 2007). The challenge for women leaders is to balance the leader role's demand for agency and the female role's demand for communion, creating a *double bind*. As a result of the double bind, female leaders also face a *double standard*, such that for comparable levels of performance, female leaders overall receive somewhat lower evaluations than male leaders, especially in male-dominated settings (see meta-analysis by Eagly, Makhijani, & Klonsky, 1992). In studies of military cadets (Boldry, Wood, & Kashy, 2001) and managers (Heilman, Block, & Martell, 1995), men received higher evaluations than women who performed equally well. Except in feminine settings, women must display greater evidence of skill than men to be considered equally competent (e.g., Biernat & Kobrynowicz, 1997; Carli, 1990). As a result, women have more difficulty influencing others (Carli, in press).

These challenges that gender stereotypes produce for women leaders are often compounded by cultural stereotypes about race and ethnicity. These other stereotypes also contain some attributes disadvantageous for leadership—for example, African Americans are stereotyped as less competent, Hispanics as less ambitious, and Asian Americans as less assertive (e.g., Gavami & Peplau, 2012). Minority women thus face different challenges than White women (see Rosette, Koval, Ma, & Livingston, 2016). White women are sometimes evaluated less favorably than Black women for comparable performance (Biernat & Sesko, 2013), although under conditions of poor performance, Black women may receive especially low ratings of competence (Rosette & Livingston, 2012).

## Restrictions on Women's Agency

Paradoxically, becoming prototypical of desirable leadership does not ordinarily protect women from prejudice. Unlike traditional women, who are considered warm and nice but not especially instrumentally competent, women who excel and display leadership are considered instrumentally competent but not particularly warm (Glick, Diebold, Bailey-Werner, & Zhu, 1997). This perceived gender-role violation can, in turn, lower evaluations of women in leadership roles.

Compared with men, women's ability to lead is more dependent on their adherence to a constricted range of behaviors (Carli, 1999). In particular, behaviors that convey dominance, negative assertion, self-promotion, or lack of warmth conflict with the communal demands of the female gender role and therefore interfere with female influence. For example, a meta-analytic review revealed that women are more influential using communal rather than agentic influence tactics, but men were equally influential regardless of type of tactic used (Smith et al., 2013). Another meta-analysis demonstrated that people dislike explicit displays of dominance in women more than in men but react more favorably to subtle displays (see meta-analysis by M. J. Williams & Tiedens, 2016). Moreover, competent behavior yields greater benefits for men than women (Biernat, Tocci, & Williams, 2012; Brescoll, 2011). In general, women in powerful positions are seen as less legitimate than their male counterparts, triggering consequences such as reduced cooperation (see review by Vial, Napier, & Brescoll, 2016).

Although both men and women have been found to be more critical of female than male leaders, this tendency is stronger among men than women. Data from 31 countries show that men endorse sexist attitudes more than women do (Napier, Thorisdottir, & Jost, 2010). Men, more than women, associate leadership with masculine traits (Koenig et al., 2011), give less favorable evaluations to female than male leaders (Eagly et al., 1992; Eagly et al., 1995), and are less inclined to hire women (Koch et al., 2015).

One way that women can increase their likableness and thereby increase their influence with men is to "feminize" their behavior by increasing their interpersonal warmth. Warm women are better liked, which results in their increased influence (Carli, in press). Female leaders may therefore display an amalgam of agentic and communal qualities to gain influence and lead effectively. In one experiment, female leaders had to show both communion and agency to be seen as effective, whereas male leaders needed to show only agency (Johnson, Murphy, Zewdie, & Reichard, 2008). Pressures on women leaders to conform to gender roles likely contribute to women's motivation to avoid autocratic forms of leadership and their reliance on more democratic and transformational leadership styles.

In summary, gender roles cause people to expect and prefer women to be communal, creating a double bind for female leaders, who must demonstrate exceptional competence to be seen as equal in ability to men and must also avoid threatening others with dominance and lack of warmth. Thus, Chancellor Angela Merkel finesses the double bind with her calm, even-tempered style that is free of the bombast and macho posturing of her predecessor, Gerhard Schroeder. That Schroeder could maintain his leadership with such a style illustrates men's freedom from backlash for dominance. Nor are men penalized for exhibiting moderate communality, creating an advantage for them because they can display a wider range of behaviors, tailoring their leadership style to the demands of the situation. Moreover, men's greater resistance to female leadership also slows women's advancement to higher levels of leadership. Research thus provides strong evidence that stereotypes are a major factor accounting for women's rarity in elite leadership roles.

## Organizational Obstacles to Women's Leadership

Because men have traditionally held positions of authority, organizations are structured to suit the life experiences of men. Consequently, organizations often establish norms that appear on the surface to be gender-neutral, but that inherently advantage men (e.g., Martin, 2003). In particular, many organizations have increased demands on their managerial and professional workforce, requiring long hours and personal sacrifices. Such demands implicitly presume an ideal employee that fits a traditional male image, with few outside responsibilities and complete devotion to the organization (J. C. Williams, Berdahl, & Vandello, 2016).

These changes have increased the prevalence of *extreme jobs* among professionals and managers that require very long hours of demanding work (Hewlett, 2007) and pressures to work longer and faster, to foreswear breaks, to travel a lot, and to be available 24/7 (McCann, Morris, & Hassard, 2008). These demands are especially pronounced in high-status executive and professional positions, where long hours lead to faster advancement and higher pay (Cha & Weeden, 2014). As a result, people employed in management and related fields usually work longer than average hours (U.S. Bureau of Labor Statistics, 2015a, Table 5). Rewarding employees for long hours presents a particular challenge to women, who have the bulk of domestic responsibilities (Gascoigne, Parry, & Buchanan, 2015). With their fewer domestic duties and more leisure time, men find it easier to commit to such extreme jobs.

These problems are most serious among women in high-intensity careers. Men have less pressure, given that they often have wives who are not employed. Even at high levels, female executives and professionals often have considerable family responsibilities that create stresses in meeting ideal employee standards. An example is Anne-Marie Slaughter's much-discussed article in *The Atlantic,* "Why Women Can't Have It All," which recounted her travails in balancing the demands of a high-level U.S. State Department position with her responsibilities toward her husband and two young sons (Slaughter, 2012).

Fathers also report stresses in reconciling their jobs with their family life because they generally profess a desire to devote equal effort to their families and their jobs (Harrington, Van Deusen, & Humberd, 2011). Nevertheless, a common division of labor is what J. C. Williams et al. (2016) label the *neo-traditional family,* defined by the father having a big, demanding job and the mother having a less time-consuming job allowing her to undertake more domestic work and thus support his career. Ambivalence about mothers' high-intensity careers is reflected in a Pew survey, revealing that 70% of respondents endorsed full-time employment for fathers of young children, compared with only 12% for mothers (Parker, 2015).

Women's greater family responsibilities can also undermine their ability to form work-related networks, which depend on socializing at bars and restaurants after work and through activities such as golfing or attending sports events. Regardless of whether women are welcome in such venues, mothers no doubt find that such activities interfere with time with their children. Consequently, women have less access to powerful career networks than men do (Burt, 1998; Dreher & Cox, 1996). Yet having networks and mentors is associated with increased salary and promotions (see meta-analysis by Ng, Eby, Sorensen, & Feldman, 2005). Thus, women's relative lack of social capital impedes their leadership opportunities.

Women face other challenges in traditional male corporate cultures. Female executives have reported difficulty fitting in with the culture of their organizations and obtaining developmental work assignments and international travel opportunities (e.g., Hoobler, Lemmon, & Wayne, 2014; Lyness & Thompson, 2000). Part of the reason why women advance less rapidly than men is they receive fewer challenging developmental assignments (King et al., 2012). Mirroring this phenomenon, in an experiment in which pairs of men and women negotiated about working on challenging or easy assignments, women were equally interested in the challenging work but ultimately received less of it than the men did (De Pater et al., 2009).

In general, managers view female employees as having less career motivation than male employees and treat them accordingly (Hoobler et al., 2014). Therefore, it is not surprising that corporate women more than men exit corporations or shift into staff management roles instead of the line management roles that typically lead to senior management (Barsh & Yee, 2012). However, women are more often given highly risky, high-level assignments where they are likely to fail, a phenomenon known as the *glass cliff* (see review by Ryan et al., 2016). Consequently, women are denied achievable challenging assignments but receive more ill-fated assignments that are unlikely to advance their careers.

Given in-group favoritism, it might be that women fare better in organizations in which women have more decision-making power. Providing evidence that senior women benefit the advancement of female subordinates, one national sample of 20,000 U.S. firms found that the percentage of women in senior management predicted subsequent increases in the percentage of women in middle management (Kurtulus & Tomaskovic-Devey, 2012). Yet other studies have produced inconsistent findings (see review by Kunze & Miller, 2014). Moreover, not all senior women are equally supportive of female subordinates: Some are *queen bees,* who distance themselves from junior women (Derks, Van Laar, & Ellemers, 2016). Although this behavior exacerbates gender inequality, it appears to be a response to existing gender discrimination and the social identity threats experienced by token female leaders.

In conclusion, organizational structure and culture implicitly favor men. Because men typically lack women's domestic duties, men can more easily satisfy the corporate demands for long work hours and continuous availability. Corporate cultures and male networks are also often unwelcoming to women, undermining their ability to create valuable social capital on the job. And women have difficulty obtaining desirable assignments with advancement potential. These obstacles discriminate against women and contribute to their relative absence from leadership positions.

## The Rise and Future of Female Leaders

Despite barriers, women are rising into leadership roles in many nations, and not merely into lower and midlevel roles, but slowly into visible roles at the tops of organizations and governments. Powerful women such as Angela Merkel, Janet Yellen, and Christine Lagarde now receive routine coverage in the popular media. We now discuss the changes that have enabled at least some women to rise into leadership roles that women have very rarely occupied in the past.

One important factor in women's rise is their increasing educational advantage relative to men that we noted earlier. Also, the domestic division of labor has changed, with housework and childcare shared more equally by women and men (Bianchi, 2011). This shift reflects changing attitudes about family and employment roles. Endorsement of traditional gender roles in the United States is at an all-time low, especially among younger Americans (Galinsky et al., 2008).

Women and men have converged considerably in employment and income: Whereas in 1973, 79% of men and 45% of women were in the labor force, by 2015, those percentages were 69% and 57%, respectively (U.S. Bureau of Labor Statistics, 2016, Table 2). Furthermore, in 38% of married couples, the highest percentage ever, women are the primary or sole wage earners (U.S. Bureau of Labor Statistics, 2015b, Table 26).

As women shift more of their time from domestic labor to paid labor, they assume the personal characteristics required to succeed in these new roles (Eagly & Wood, 2012). Research tracking sex differences over time reveals that as women have entered formerly male-dominated roles, they have become more agentic, and increasingly assertive, dominant, risk-taking, and interested in science, math, and engineering (see review by Wood & Eagly, 2012).

The qualities that now are seen as characteristic of good leadership have become more androgynous over time, incorporating more feminine, communal qualities (see Koenig et al., 2011). These new themes reflect organizational environments marked by accelerated technological growth, increasing workforce diversity, and a weakening of geopolitical boundaries. Leadership experts now recommend that leaders employ more communal qualities: democratic relationships, participatory decision making, delegation of responsibility, developing subordinates, and relying on team-based skills (e.g., Kanter, 1997; Lipman-Blumen, 2000).

If women have become more masculine and leader roles more feminine, could characteristics ascribed to women eventually match leadership roles as well as those ascribed to men? We think so, but as we have shown, gender prejudice and discrimination have diminished but not disappeared. People still associate leadership more strongly with male than female traits. Women's agency is still met with resistance, particularly in male-dominated and traditionally masculine settings. The domestic division of labor remains unequal, and women continue to earn less and advance more slowly. Moreover, effective leadership in some situations may favor an authoritative, directive approach, which may elicit backlash and be risky for women.

Still, organizations are experimenting with a wide range of reforms, such as family-oriented work-life practices, to achieve greater gender diversity in their managerial ranks. These practices, especially family-friendly leave arrangements and direct provision of services (e.g., childcare or eldercare) can have positive effects, but generally only after a substantial time lag and only in some organizational contexts (see Kalysh, Kulik, & Perera, 2016). Moreover, the potential benefits of family-friendly reforms are often countered by *flexibility stigma*—negative reactions against those who take advantage of such practices (e.g., J. C. Williams et al., 2016), and this can result in underuse of these benefits. In response, some organizations have attempted to destigmatize options such as flextime and flexplace. Others have focused on making work practices more efficient to shorten long work weeks (J. C. Williams et al., 2016) or on reducing employee's gender stereotypes through education and diversity training (e.g., Carnes et al., 2015). Still other interventions, often based on government mandates, modify selection and promotion procedures to increase the representation of women and minorities. Examples include mandating affirmative action, goal-setting targets, reporting requirements, and the institution of quotas. These policies usually do increase female leadership, but can have unintended effects (see Sojo, Wood, Wood, & Wheeler, 2016). Companies sometimes take actions to avoid being included in the mandate. Also, such interventions can stigmatize the women targeted to benefit from them, antagonize those who do not benefit from them, and foster stresses in work groups (e.g., Heilman & Haynes, 2006). Finally, research is required to determine which interventions are most effective and under what conditions (e.g., Dobbin, Schrage, & Kalev, 2015).

The rise of women into elite leadership roles has gained momentum in recent years. In progressive circles, female leaders have come to symbolize modernity and future-oriented leadership. For example, when Justin Trudeaux, prime minister of Canada, was asked why he chose equal numbers of women and men for his cabinet, he replied, "Because it's 2015" (Editorial Board, 2015). Although the effects of increased female leadership are not fully understood, the addition of women greatly increases the pool of leadership talent. Therefore, both the rationality of bureaucratic organizations in capitalist societies and the fundamental fairness that is highly valued in democratic societies should facilitate women's increasing entry into the ranks of leaders in the future.

## Discussion Questions

1. What can employers do to reduce conflicts between family obligations and workplace responsibilities?
2. What popular images are there in the media of male and female leaders? Are there more images of male than female leaders? Have these images changed over time?
3. How can the double bind be addressed beyond encouraging women to lead with a mix of masculine and feminine qualities? Can people be educated about gender stereotypes and the challenges that women leaders face?
4. Imagine that you had to make the case for more women in positions of authority to organizational leaders and male coworkers. What arguments would you make?

## Recommended Readings

- Bohnet, I. (2016). *What works: Gender equality by design*. Cambridge, MA: Harvard University Press.
- Eagly, A. H., & Carli, L. L. (2007). Women and the labyrinth of leadership. *Harvard Business Review, 85*, 62–71.
- Glass, C., & Cook, A. (2016). Leading at the top: Understanding women's challenges above the glass ceiling. *The Leadership Quarterly, 27*, 51–63.
- Sanchez-Hucles, J. V., & Davis, D. D. (2010). Women and women of color in leadership: Complexity, identity, and intersectionality. *American Psychologist, 65*, 171–181.
- Williams, J., & Dempsey, R. (2014). *What works for women at work: Four patterns working women need to know*. New York, NY: New York University Press.

## Recommended Case Studies

- **Case:** Gentile, M. (1994). *Anne Livingston and Power Max Systems*. Boston, MA: Harvard Business School Publishing.
- **Case:** Kantor, J. (2013, September 7). Harvard Business School case study: Gender equity. *New York Times*. Retrieved from http://www.nytimes.com/

## Recommended Video

- Tomasdottir, A. (2010). Halla Tomasdottir: A feminine response to Iceland's financial crash. http://www.ted.com/talks/halla_tomasdottir?language=en

## References

Abendroth, A., Maas, I., & van der Lippe, T. (2013). Human capital and the gender gap in authority in European countries. *European Sociological Review, 29*, 261–273.

Adams, R. B. (2016). Women on boards: The superheroes of tomorrow? *The Leadership Quarterly, 27*(3), 371–386.

Adams, R. B., & Ferreira, D. (2009). Women in the boardroom and their impact on governance and performance. *Journal of Financial Economics, 94*, 291–309.

American Student Government Association. (2016). *SG database: Percentage of women serving in collegiate student governments nationwide.* Retrieved from http://www.asgaonline.com/

Ames, D. R., & Flynn, F. J. (2007). What breaks a leader? The curvilinear relation between assertiveness and leadership. *Journal of Personality and Social Psychology, 92,* 307–324.

Antonakis, J., Avolio, B. J., & Sivasubramaniam, N. (2003). Context and leadership: An examination of the nine-factor full-range leadership theory using the Multifactor Leadership Questionnaire. *The Leadership Quarterly, 14,* 261–295.

Antonakis, J., Bendahan, S., Jacquart, P., & Lalive, R. (2010). On making causal claims: A review and recommendations. *The Leadership Quarterly, 21,* 1086–1120.

Archer, J. (2004). Sex differences in aggression in real-world settings: A meta-analytic review. *Review of General Psychology, 8,* 291–322.

Balliet, D., Li, N. P., Macfarlan, S. J., & van Vugt, M. (2011). Sex differences in cooperation: A meta-analytic review of social dilemmas. *Psychological Bulletin, 137,* 881–909.

Balliet, D., Wu, J., & De Dreu, C. K. W. (2014). Ingroup favoritism in cooperation: A meta-analysis. *Psychological Bulletin, 140,* 1556–1581.

Barsh, J., & Yee, L. (2012). *Unlocking the full potential of women at work.* Retrieved from http://www.mckinsey.com/business-functions/organization/our-insights/unlocking-the-full-potential-of-women-at-work

Bass, B. M. (1998). *Transformational leadership: Industry, military, and educational impact.* Mahwah, NJ: Lawrence Erlbaum.

Bertrand, M., Goldin, C., & Katz, L. F. (2010). Dynamics of the gender gap for young professionals in the financial and corporate sectors. *American Economic Journal: Applied Economics, 2,* 228–255.

Bettencourt, B. A., & Miller, N. (1996). Gender differences in aggression as a function of provocation: A meta-analysis. *Psychological Bulletin, 119,* 422–447.

Bianchi, S. M. (2011). Family change and time allocation in American families. *The Annals of the American Academy of Political and Social Science, 638,* 21–44.

Biernat, M., & Kobrynowicz, D. (1997). Gender- and race-based standards of competence: Lower minimum standards but higher ability standards for devalued groups. *Journal of Personality and Social Psychology, 72,* 544–557.

Biernat, M., & Sesko, A. K. (2013). Evaluating the contributions of members of mixed-sex teams: Race and gender matter. *Journal of Experimental Social Psychology, 49,* 471–476.

Biernat, M., Tocci, M. J., & Williams, J. C. (2012). The language of performance evaluations: Gender-based shifts in content and consistency of judgment. *Social Psychology and Personality Science, 3,* 186–192.

Blau, F. D., & DeVaro, J. (2007). New evidence on gender differences in promotion rates: An empirical analysis of a sample of new hires. *Industrial Relations: A Journal of Economy and Society, 46,* 511–550.

Blau, F. D., & Kahn, L. M. (2013). Female labor supply: Why is the United States falling behind? *American Economic Review, 103,* 251–256.

Boehm, C. (1999). *Hierarchy in the forest.* Cambridge, MA: Harvard University Press.

Boldry, J., Wood, W., & Kashy, D. A. (2001). Gender stereotypes and the evaluation of men and women in military training. *Journal of Social Issues, 57,* 689–705.

Brescoll, V. L. (2011). Who takes the floor and why: Gender, power, and volubility in organizations. *Administrative Science Quarterly, 56,* 622–641.

Brown, E. R., Diekman, A. B., & Schneider, M. C. (2011). A change will do us good: Threats diminish typical preferences for male leaders. *Personality and Social Psychology Bulletin, 73,* 930–941.

Bruggeman, P., & Chan, H. (2016, March). *Minding the gap: Tapping the potential of women to transform business.* Reston, VA: GMAC Research Reports. Retrieved from http://www.gmac.com/

Burt, R. S. (1998). The gender of social capital. *Rationality and Society, 10,* 5–46.

Buss, D. M. (2016). *Evolutionary psychology: The new science of the mind* (5th ed.). New York, NY: Routledge.

Byron, K., & Post, C. (2016). Women on boards of directors and corporate social performance: A meta-analysis. *Corporate Governance: An International Review, 24,* 448–442.

Caesar, A., Wordofa, F., & Zhang, Y. J. (in press). Competing for the benefit of offspring eliminates the gender gap in competitiveness. *Proceedings of the National Academy of Sciences.*

Carli, L. L. (1990). Gender, language, and influence. *Journal of Personality and Social Psychology, 59,* 941–951.

Carli, L. L. (1999). Gender, interpersonal power, and social influence. *Journal of Social Issues, 55,* 81–99.

Carli, L. L. (in press). Social influence and gender. In K. Williams & S. Harkins (Eds.), *Oxford handbook of social influence.* Oxford, UK: Oxford University Press.

Carnes, M., Devine, P. G., Manwell, L. B., Byars-Winston, A., Fine, E., Ford, C. E., . . . Sheridan, J. (2015). The effect of an intervention to break the gender bias habit for faculty at one institution: A cluster randomized, controlled trial. *Academic Medicine, 90,* 221–230.

Catalyst. (2016, February 3). Knowledge center: Women in S&P 500 companies. Retrieved from http://www .catalyst.org/knowledge/women-sp-500-companies

Center for American Women and Politics. (2016). *Levels of office.* Retrieved from http://www.cawp.rutgers.edu/ history-women-us-congress

Cha, Y., & Weeden, K. A. (2014). Overwork and the slow convergence in the gender gap in wages. *American Sociological Review, 79,* 457–484.

Christensen, M. I. (2016). *Worldwide guide to women in leadership.* Retrieved from http://www.guide2 womenleaders.com/Female_Leaders.htm

Coffman, J., & Neuenfeld, B. (2014). Everyday moments of truth: Frontline managers are key to women's career aspirations. Retrieved from http://www.bain.com/

Comeig, I., Grau-Grau, A., Jaramillo-Gutiérrez, A., & Ramírez, F. (2015). Gender, self-confidence, sports, and preferences for competition. *Journal of Business Research, 69,* 1418–1422.

Correll, S. J., Benard, S., & Paik, I. (2007). Getting a job: Is there a motherhood penalty? *American Journal of Sociology, 112,* 1297–1338.

Corrigall, E. A., & Konrad, A. M. (2006). The relationship of job attribute preferences to employment, hours of paid work, and family responsibilities: An analysis comparing women and men. *Sex Roles, 54,* 95–111.

Costa Jr, P. T., Terracciano, A., & McCrae, R. R. 2001. Gender differences in personality traits across cultures: Robust and surprising findings. *Journal of Personality and Social Psychology, 81*(2): 322–331.

Davies, P. G., Spencer, S. J., & Steele, C. M. (2005). Clearing the air: Identity safety moderates the effects of stereotype threat on women's leadership aspirations. *Journal of Personality and Social Psychology, 88,* 276–287.

De Pater, I. E., Van Vianen, A. E. M., Humphrey, R. H., Sleeth, R. G., Hartman, N. S., & Fischer, A. H. (2009). Individual task choice and the division of challenging tasks between men and women. *Group & Organization Management, 34,* 563–589.

Deloitte. (2015). *Women in the boardroom: A global perspective* (4th ed.). Retrieved from http://www2.deloitte.com/ content/dam/Deloitte/global/Documents/Risk/gx-ccg-women-in-the-boardroom-a-global-perspective4.pdf

Derks, B., Van Laar, C., & Ellemers, N. (2016). The queen bee phenomenon: Why women leaders distance themselves from junior women. *The Leadership Quarterly, 27*(3), 456–469.

Desvaux, G., & Devillard, S. (2008). *Women matter 2.* Retrieved from http://www.mckinsey.com/

Desvaux, G., Devillard-Hoellinger, S., & Baumgarten, P. (2007). *Women matter: Gender diversity, a corporate performance driver.* Paris, France: McKinsey.

Diekman, A. B., & Steinberg, M. (2013). Navigating social roles in pursuit of important goals: A communal goal congruity account of STEM pursuits. *Social and Personality Psychology Compass, 7,* 487–501.

Dobbin, F., Schrage, D., & Kalev, A. (2015). Rage against the iron cage: The varied effects of bureaucratic personnel reforms on diversity. *American Sociological Review, 80,* 1014–1044.

Dreher, G. F., & Cox, T. H., Jr. (1996). Race, gender, and opportunity: A study of compensation attainment and the establishment of mentoring relationships. *Journal of Applied Psychology, 81,* 297–308.

Eagly, A. H. (2016). When passionate advocates meet research on diversity, does the honest broker stand a chance? *Journal of Social Issues, 72,* 199–222.

Eagly, A. H., & Carli, L. L. (2007). *Through the labyrinth: The truth about how women become leaders.* Cambridge, MA: Harvard Business School Press.

Eagly, A. H., Johannesen-Schmidt, M. C., & van Engen, M. L. (2003). Transformational, transactional, and laissez-faire leadership styles: A meta-analysis comparing women and men. *Psychological Bulletin, 129,* 569–591.

Eagly, A. H., & Johnson, B. T. (1990). Gender and leadership style: A meta-analysis. *Psychological Bulletin, 108,* 233–256.

Eagly, A. H., & Karau, S. J. (2002). Role congruity theory of prejudice toward female leaders. *Psychological Review, 109,* 573–598.

Eagly, A. H., Karau, S. J., & Makhijani, M. G. (1995). Gender and the effectiveness of leaders: A meta-analysis. *Psychological Bulletin, 117,* 125–145.

Eagly, A. H., Karau, S. J., Miner, J. B., & Johnson, B. T. (1994). Gender and motivation to manage in hierarchic organizations: A meta-analysis. *The Leadership Quarterly, 5,* 135–159.

Eagly, A. H., Makhijani, M. G., & Klonsky, B. G. (1992). Gender and the evaluation of leaders: A meta-analysis. *Psychological Bulletin, 111,* 3–22.

Eagly, A. H., & Wood, W. (2012). Social role theory. In P. van Lange, A. Kruglanski, & E. T. Higgins (Eds.), *Handbook of theories in social psychology* (Vol. 2, pp. 458–476) Thousand Oaks, CA: Sage.

Eagly, A. H., & Wood, W. (2013). The nature–nurture debates: 25 years of challenges in understanding the psychology of gender. *Perspectives on Psychological Science, 8,* 340–357.

Editorial Board. (2015, Nov. 12). Antidote to cynicism. *New York Times.* Retrieved from http://www.nytimes.com/2015/11/12/opinion/an-antidote-to-cynicism-in-canada.html?_r=0

Elliott, J. R., & Smith, R. A. (2004). Race, gender, and workplace power. *American Sociological Review, 69,* 365–386.

Farb, A. F., & Matjasko, J. L. (2012). Recent advances in research on school-based extracurricular activities and adolescent development. *Developmental Review, 32,* 1–48.

Fitzsimmons, T. W., & Callan, V. J. (2016). Applying a capital perspective to explain continued gender inequality in the C-suite. *The Leadership Quarterly, 27*(3), 354–370.

Fox, R. L., & Lawless, J. L. (2014). Uncovering the origins of the gender gap in political ambition. *American Political Science Review, 108,* 499–519.

Galinsky, E., Aumann, K., & Bond, J. T. (2008). *Times are changing: Gender and generation at work and at home.* New York, NY: Families and Work Institute. Retrieved from http://familiesandwork.org/site/research/reports/Times_Are_Changing.pdf

Gascoigne, C., Parry, E., & Buchanan, D. (2015). Extreme work, gendered work? How extreme jobs and the discourse of "personal choice" perpetuate gender inequality. *Organization, 22,* 457–475.

Ghavami, N., & Peplau, L. A. (2012). An intersectional analysis of gender and ethnic stereotypes: Testing three hypotheses. *Psychology of Women Quarterly, 37,* 113–127.

Gintis, H., van Schaik, C., & Boehm, C. (2015). Zoon politikon. *Current Anthropology, 56*(3), 327–353.

Glick, P., Diebold, J., Bailey-Werner, B., & Zhu, L. (1997). The two faces of Adam: Ambivalent sexism and polarized attitudes toward women. *Personality and Social Psychology Bulletin, 23,* 1323–1334.

Goudreau, J. (2010, June 21). Top 20 industries favored by M.B.A. women. *Forbes.* Retrieved from http://www.forbes.com/

Greenhaus, J. H., & Powell, G. N. (2012). The family-relatedness of work decisions: A framework and agenda for theory and research. *Journal of Vocational Behavior, 80,* 246–255.

Griffeth, R. W., Hom, P. W., & Gaertner, S. (2000). A meta-analysis of antecedents and correlates of employee turnover: Update, moderator tests, and research implications for the next millennium. *Journal of Management, 26,* 463–488.

Halpern, D. F. (2012). *Sex differences in cognitive abilities* (4th ed.). New York, NY: Psychology Press.

Hancock, D., Dyk, P. H., & Jones, K. (2012). Adolescent involvement in extracurricular activities: Influences on leadership skills. *Journal of Leadership Education, 11,* 84–101.

Harrington, B., Van Deusen, F., & Humberd, B. (2011). *The new dad: Caring, committed, conflicted.* Boston, MA: Boston College Center for Work and Family.

Heilman, M. E., Block, C. J., & Martell, R. F. (1995). Sex stereotypes: Do they influence perceptions of managers? *Journal of Social Behavior and Personality, 10*(6), 237–252.

Heilman, M. E., & Haynes, M. C. (2006). Affirmative action: Unintended adverse effects. In M. F. Karsten (Ed.), *Gender, race, and ethnicity in the workplace* (Vol. 2, pp. 1–24). Westport, CT: Praeger.

Heilman, M. E., & Okimoto, T. G. (2008). Motherhood: A potential source of bias in employment decisions. *Journal of Applied Psychology, 93,* 189–198.

Helfat, C. E., Harris, D., & Wolfson, J. P. (2006). The pipeline to the top: Women and men in the top executive ranks of U.S. corporations. *Academy of Management Perspectives, 20,* 42–64.

Herr, J. L., & Wolfram, C. D. (2012). Work environment and opt-out rates at motherhood across high-education career paths. *Industrial & Labor Relations Review, 65,* 928–950.

Hershcovis, M. S., Turner, N., Barling, J., Arnold, K. A., Dupré, K. E., Inness, M., . . . Sivanthan, N. (2007). Predicting workplace aggression: A meta-analysis. *Journal of Applied Psychology, 92,* 228–238.

Hewlett, S. A. (2007). *Off-ramps and on-ramps: Keeping talented women on the road to success.* Boston, MA: Harvard Business School Press.

Hom, P. W., Roberson, L., & Ellis, A. D. (2008). Challenging conventional wisdom about who quits: Revelations from corporate America. *Journal of Applied Psychology, 93,* 1–34.

Hoobler, J. M., Lemmon, G., & Wayne, S. J. (2014). Women's managerial aspirations: An organizational development perspective. *Journal of Management, 40,* 703–730.

Hoyt, C. L., & Murphy, S. E. (2016). Managing to clear the air: Stereotype threat, women, and leadership. *The Leadership Quarterly, 27*(3), 387–399.

Hoyt, C. L., Simon, S., & Innella, A. N. (2011). Taking a turn toward the masculine: The impact of mortality salience on implicit leadership theories. *Basic & Applied Social Psychology, 33*(4), 374–381.

Ilies, R., Arvey, R. D., & Bouchard, T. J., Jr. (2006). Darwinism, behavioral genetics, and organizational behavior: A review and agenda for future research. *Journal of Organizational Behavior, 27,* 121–141.

Ingels, S. J., Dalton, B. W., & LoGerfo, L. (2008). *Trends among high school seniors, 1972–2004* (National Center for Education Statistics 2008–320). Washington, DC: National Center for Education Statistics. Retrieved from http://files.eric.ed.gov/fulltext/ED501757.pdf

International Labor Organization. (2015a). *Women in business and management: Gaining momentum: Global report.* Geneva, Switzerland: International Labor Organization. Retrieved from http://www.ilo.org

International Labor Organization. (2015b). *World employment and social outlook: The changing nature of jobs.* Geneva, Switzerland: International Labor Organization. Retrieved from http://www.ilo.org

International Parliamentary Union. (2015). *Women in National Parliaments.* Retrieved from http://www.ipu.org/wmn-e/world.htm

Johnson, S. K., Murphy, S. E., Zewdie, S., & Reichard, R. J. (2008). The strong, sensitive type: Effects of gender stereotypes and leadership prototypes on the evaluation of male and female leaders. *Organizational Behavior and Human Decision Processes, 106,* 39–60.

Johnston, D. W., & Lee, W. (2012). Climbing the job ladder: New evidence of gender inequity. *Industrial Relations, 51,* 129–151.

Joshi, A., Son, J., & Roh, H. (2015). When can women close the gap? A meta-analytic test of sex differences in performance and rewards. *Academy of Management Journal, 58,* 1516–1545.

Judge, T. A., Bono, J. E., Ilies, R., & Gerhardt, M. W. (2002). Personality and leadership: A qualitative and quantitative review. *Journal of Applied Psychology, 87,* 765–780.

Judge, T. A., Colbert, A. E., & Ilies, R. (2004). Intelligence and leadership: A quantitative review and test of theoretical propositions. *Journal of Applied Psychology, 89,* 542–552.

Judge, T. A., & Piccolo, R. F. (2004). Transformational and transactional leadership: A meta-analytic test of their relative validity. *Journal of Applied Psychology, 89,* 755–768.

Judge, T. A., Piccolo, R. F., & Kosalka, T. (2009). The bright and dark sides of leader traits: A review and theoretical extension of the leader trait paradigm. *The Leadership Quarterly, 20,* 855–875.

Kalysh, K., Kulik, C., & Perera, S. (2016). Help or hindrance? Work-life practices and women in management. *The Leadership Quarterly, 27*(3), 504–518.

Kanter, R. M. (1997). *On the frontiers of management.* Boston, MA: Harvard Business School Press.

Kent, L. (2015, July 30). *Number of women leaders around the world has grown, but they're still a small group.* Washington, DC: Pew Research Center. Retrieved from http://www.pewresearch.org/

King, E. B., Botsford, W., Hebl, M. R., Kazama, S., Dawson, J. F., & Perkins, A. (2012). Benevolent sexism at work: Gender differences in the distribution of challenging developmental experiences. *Journal of Management, 38,* 1835–1866.

Koch, A. J., D'Mello, S. D., & Sackett, P. R. (2015). A meta-analysis of gender stereotypes and bias in experimental simulations of employment decision making. *Journal of Applied Psychology, 100,* 128–161.

Koenig, A. M., Eagly, A. H., Mitchell, A. A., & Ristikari, T. (2011). Are leader stereotypes masculine? A meta-analysis of three research paradigms. *Psychological Bulletin, 137,* 616–642.

Konrad, A. M., Ritchie, J. E., Jr., Lieb, P., & Corrigall, E. (2000). Sex differences and similarities in job attribute preferences: A meta-analysis. *Psychological Bulletin, 126,* 593–641.

Kort-Butler, L. A., & Hagewen, K. J. (2011). School-based extracurricular activity involvement and adolescent self-esteem: A growth curve analysis. *Journal of Youth & Adolescence, 40,* 568–581.

Kreller, A. (2014, July 17). Angela Merkel: So sieht ein tag im leben der kanzlerin aus. *Web.de—Magazine.* Retrieved from http://web.de/magazine/

Kunze, A., & Miller, A. R. (2014). *Women helping women? Evidence from private sector data on workplace hierarchies* (No. w20761). Cambridge, MA: National Bureau of Economic Research.

Kurtulus, F. A., & Tomaskovic-Devey, D. (2012). Do female top managers help women to advance? A panel study using EEO-1 records. *Annals of the American Academy of Political and Social Science, 639,* 173–197.

Lawless, J. L. (2015). Female candidates and legislators. *Annual Review of Political Science, 18,* 349–366.

Lieberman, P. (2012). *The unpredictable species. What makes humans unique?* Princeton, NJ: Princeton University Press.

Lipman-Blumen, J. (2000). *Connective leadership: Managing in a changing world.* New York, NY: Oxford University Press.

Lippa, R. A., Preston, K., & Penner, J. (2014). Women's representation in 60 occupations from 1972 to 2010: More women in high-status jobs, few women in things-oriented jobs. *PLoS ONE, 9*(5).

Lyness, K. S., & Thompson, D. E. (2000). Climbing the corporate ladder: Do female and male executives follow the same route? *Journal of Applied Psychology, 85,* 86–101.

Mandel, H., & Semyonov, M. (2014). Gender pay gap and employment sector: Sources of earnings disparities in the United States, 1970–2010. *Demography, 51,* 1597–1618.

Martin, P. Y. (2003). "Said and done" versus "saying and doing": Gender practices, practicing gender at work. *Gender & Society, 17,* 342–366.

McCann, L., Morris, J., & Hassard, J. (2008). Normalized intensity: The new labour process of middle management. *Journal of Management Studies, 45,* 343–371.

McCrae, R. R., & Costa, P. T., Jr. (1987). Validation of the five-factor model of personality across instruments and observers. *Journal of Personality and Social Psychology, 52,* 81–90.

Meyer, J. P., Stanley, D. J., Herscovitch, L., & Topolnytsky, L. (2002). Affective, continuance, and normative commitment to the organization: A meta-analysis of antecedents, correlates, and consequences. *Journal of Vocational Behavior, 61,* 20–52.

Miller, L. F. (2015). Fine-tuning the ontology of patriarchy: A new approach to explaining and responding to a persisting social injustice. *Philosophy & Social Criticism, 41,* 885–906.

Mintz, B., & Krymkowski, D. H. (2010). The ethnic, race, and gender gaps in workplace authority: Changes over time in the United States. *The Sociological Quarterly, 51,* 20–45.

Napier, J. L., Thorisdottir, H., & Jost, J. T. (2010). The joy of sexism? A multinational investigation of hostile and benevolent justifications for gender inequality and their relations to subjective well-being. *Sex Roles, 62,* 405–419.

National Center for Education Statistics. (2015). *Digest of education statistics, 2015.* Retrieved from https://nces.ed.gov/programs/digest/2015menu_tables.asp

Ng, T. W. H., Eby, L. T., Sorensen, K. L., & Feldman, D. C. (2005). Predictors of objective and subjective career success: A meta-analysis. *Personnel Psychology, 58,* 367–408.

Niederle, M., & Vesterlund, L. (2011). Gender and competition. *Annual Review of Economics, 3,* 601–630.

Orth, M. (2014, November 24). Angela's asserts. *Vanity Fair.* Retrieved from http://www.vanityfair.com/

Packer, G. (2014, December 1). The quiet German. *The New Yorker.* Retrieved from http://www.newyorker.com/magazine/2014/12/01/quiet-german

Parker, K. (2015). *Women more than men adjust their careers for family life.* Washington, DC: Pew Research Center. Retrieved from http://www.pewresearch.org/fact-tank/

Patten, E., & Parker, K. (2012). A gender reversal on career aspirations. Washington, DC: Pew Research Center. Retrieved from http://www.pewsocialtrends.org/

Paustian-Underdahl, S. C., Walker, L. S., & Woehr, D. J. (2014). Gender and perceptions of leadership effectiveness: A meta-analysis of contextual moderators. *Journal of Applied Psychology, 99,* 1129–1145.

Pema, E., & Mehay, S. (2010). The role of job assignment and human capital endowments in explaining gender differences in job performance and promotion. *Labour Economics, 17,* 998–1009.

Post, C., & Byron, K. (2015). Women on boards and firm financial performance: A meta-analysis. *Academy of Management Journal, 58,* 1546–1571.

Potts, R. 2012. Evolution and Environmental Change in Early Human Prehistory. *Annual Review of Anthropology,* 41(1): 151–167.

Quadlin, N. Y. (2016). Gender and time use in college: Converging or diverging pathways? *Gender & Society, 30,* 361–385.

Reuben, E., Sapienza, P., & Zingales, L. (2015). *Taste for competition and the gender gap among young business professionals* (National Bureau of Economic Research Working Paper 21695). Cambridge, MA: National Bureau of Economic Research.

Riach, P. A., & Rich, J. (2002). Field experiments of discrimination in the market place. *The Economic Journal, 112,* F480–F518.

Richerson, P. J., & Boyd, R. (2005). *Not by genes alone: How culture transformed human evolution.* Chicago, IL: University of Chicago Press.

Rinke, A., & Brown, S. (2010, November 12). Special report: The two lives of Angela Merkel. *Reuters, U.S. Edition.* Retrieved from http://www.reuters.com/article/us-merkel-idUSTRE6AB24W20101112

Rosette, A. S., Koval, C. Z., Ma, A., & Livingston, R. (2016). Race matters for women leaders: Intersectional effects on agentic deficiencies and penalties. *The Leadership Quarterly, 27*(3), 429–445.

Rosette, A. S., & Livingston, R. W. (2012). Failure is not an option for Black women: Effects of organizational performance on leaders with single versus dual-subordinate identities. *Journal of Experimental Social Psychology, 48,* 1162–1167.

Roth, P. L., Purvis, K. L., & Bobko, P. (2012). A meta-analysis of gender group differences for measures of job performance in field studies. *Journal of Management, 38,* 719–739.

Ryan, M. K., Haslam, S. A., Morgenroth, T., Rink, F., Stoker, J., & Peters, K. (2016). Getting on top of the glass cliff: Reviewing a decade of evidence, explanations, and impact. *The Leadership Quarterly, 27*(3), 446–455.

Sayer, L. C. (2016). Trends in women's and men's time use, 1965–2012: Back to the future? In S. M. McHale, V. King, J. Van Hook, & A. Booth (Eds.), *Gender and couple relationships* (pp. 43–77). New York, NY: Springer International.

Schein, V. E. (1973). The relationship between sex role stereotypes and requisite management characteristics. *Journal of Applied Psychology, 57,* 95–100.

Schieman, S., Schafer, M. H., & McIvor, M. (2013). The rewards of authority in the workplace: Do gender and age matter? *Sociological Perspectives, 56,* 75–96.

Schmitt, D. P., Realo, A., Voracek, M., & Allik, J. (2008). Why can't a man be more like a woman? Sex differences in Big Five personality traits across 55 cultures. *Journal of Personality and Social Psychology, 94,* 168–182.

Slaughter, A. M. (2012, July–August). Why women still can't have it all. *The Atlantic,* 84–102.

Smith, A. N., Watkins, M. B., Burke, M. J., Christian, M. S., Smith, C. E., Hall, A., & Simms, A. (2013). Gendered influence: A gender role perspective on the use and effectiveness of influence tactics. *Journal of Management, 39,* 1156–1183.

Sojo, V. E., Wood, R. E., Wood, S. A., & Wheeler, M. A. (2016). Reporting requirements, targets, and quotas for women in leadership. *The Leadership Quarterly, 27*(3), 519–536.

Stiffman, E. (2015, September). *Women nonprofit leaders still make less than men, survey finds.* Retrieved from https://philanthropy.com/article/Women-Nonprofit-Leaders-Still/233129

Theodossiou, I., & Zangelidis, A. (2009). Should I stay or should I go? The effect of gender, education and unemployment on labour market transitions. *Labour Economics, 16,* 566–577.

Theunissen, G., Verbruggen, M., Forrier, A., & Sels, L. (2011) Career sidestep, wage setback? The impact of different types of employment interruptions on wages. *Gender, Work & Organization, 18,* e110–e131.

Trivers, R. L. (1972). Parental investment and sexual selection. In B. Campbell (Ed.), *Sexual selection and the descent of man: 1871–1971* (pp. 136–179). Chicago, IL: Aldine.

United Nations. (2015). *The world's women 2015: Trends and statistics.* Retrieved from http://unstats.un.org/unsd/gender/worldswomen.html

U.S. Bureau of Labor Statistics. (2015a). *American time use: Databases, tables and calculators by subject.* Retrieved from http://www.bls.gov/news.release/archives/atus_06242015.pdf

U.S. Bureau of Labor Statistics. (2015b). *Women in the labor force: A databook (2015 edition).* Retrieved from http://www.bls.gov/

U.S. Bureau of Labor Statistics. (2016). *Labor force statistics from the current population survey.* Retrieved from http://www.bls.gov/cps/tables.htm

U.S. Census Bureau. (2016). *Women in the workforce.* Retrieved from https://www.census.gov/newsroom/pdf/women_workforce_slides.pdf

van Engen, M. L., & Willemsen, T. M. (2004). Sex and leadership styles: A meta-analysis of research published in the 1990s. *Psychological Reports, 94,* 3–18.

van Vugt, M., & Ronay, R. (2014). The evolutionary psychology of leadership: Theory, review, and roadmap. *Organizational Psychology Review, 4,* 74–95.

Vial, A. C., Napier, J. L., & Brescoll, V. (2016). A bed of thorns: Female leaders and the self-reinforcing cycle of illegitimacy. *The Leadership Quarterly, 27*(3), 400–414.

Vinkenburg, C. J., van Engen, M. L., Eagly, A. H., & Johannesen-Schmidt, M. C. (2011). An exploration of stereotypical beliefs about leadership styles: Is transformational leadership a route to women's promotion? *The Leadership Quarterly, 22*(1), 10–21.

Voyer, D., & Voyer, S. D. (2014). Gender differences in scholastic achievement: A meta-analysis. *Psychological Bulletin, 140,* 1174–1204.

Walters, A. E., Stuhlmacher, A. F., & Meyer, L. L. (1998). Gender and negotiator competitiveness: A meta-analysis. *Organizational Behavior and Human Decision Processes, 76,* 1–29.

Wang, G., Oh, I., Courtright, S. H., & Colbert, A. E. (2011). Transformational leadership and performance across criteria and levels: A meta-analytic review of 25 years of research. *Group & Organization Management, 36,* 223–270.

Wieland, A., & Sarin, R. (2012). Domain specificity of sex differences in competition. *Journal of Economic Behavior & Organization, 83,* 151–157.

Williams, J. C., Berdahl, J. L., & Vandello, J. A. (2016). Beyond work-life "integration." *Annual Review of Psychology, 67,* 515 –539.

Williams, J. E., & Best, D. L. (1990). *Measuring sex stereotypes: A multination study.* Newbury Park, CA: Sage.

Williams, M. J., & Tiedens, L. Z. (2016). The subtle suspension of backlash: A meta-analysis of penalties for women's implicit and explicit dominance behavior. *Psychological Bulletin, 142,* 165–197.

Wittenberg-Cox, A., & Symons, L. (2015, April 27). How women are faring at business schools worldwide. *Harvard Business Review.* Retrieved from https://hbr.org/

Wood, W., & Eagly, A. H. (2012). Biosocial construction of sex differences and similarities in behavior. In J. M. Olson & M. P. Zanna (Eds.), *Advances in experimental social psychology* (Vol. 46, pp. 55–123). London, UK: Elsevier.

World Bank. (2013). *Gender at work: A companion to the world development report on jobs.* Retrieved from http://www.worldbank.org/

Yukl, G. (2013). *Leadership in organizations* (8th ed.). New York, NY: Pearson.

# CHAPTER 11

# Power and Leadership

*Rachel E. Sturm*

*Lucas Monzani*

---

### Opening Case: A Day in the Life of a Leader[1]

Sorensen and two other colleagues who were the boss's "closest and most trusted subordinates" were looking forward to their boss's return from his first European vacation and the surprise that awaited him. In his absence, the three subordinates designed and built a new model of a car following the world-renowned success of a prior car model. After unveiling the new car to their boss, the boss slowly walked around it a few times, carefully surveying it. Suddenly, the boss latched onto one of the doors, yanked it off the hinges, and then proceeded to violently demolish the rest of the car with his bare hands and feet from one end to the other (Jardim, 1970).

This car was a modest upgrade to the vaulted Model T, and this boss was none other than Henry Ford, who had already become one of the richest men in the world because of his desire to make a vehicle for the common man. Ford's reaction to the new model was both shocking and hurtful to his subordinates; he even moved one of his most gifted engineers to another department to keep this person as far away from engineering as possible (Jardim, 1970). However, signs of Ford's rigidity against changing the Model T (a car that was virtually unchanged from 1908 until its demise

---

1. Rachel E. Sturm would like to acknowledge graduate assistant Eric Strohecker, MBA 2016, for his help in writing this case.

in 1927 after more than 15 million copies had been made) had been building for some time.

Henry Ford was beginning not to tolerate any questions or suggestions for design improvement of his ideas. In addition, Sorensen and other executives were being played against one another by Ford (Nye, 1979). There were no titles for workers at the company, as each person proved their worth through pleasing Ford with whatever whim struck him (Jardim, 1970). Multiple employees were often put on the same problem without initially knowing that they were actually competing against each other to see whose results would win Ford's favor (Jardim, 1970). His distrust of anyone who was, or became, an expert was well known—his belief was that they had lost their ability to think outside the box but instead only relied upon what they had learned and already experienced (Grandin, 2009). Whereas these actions led many employees to be fearful and voluntarily leave the organization, a number stayed committed to working under Ford for a variety of reasons, including that they may have actually enjoyed having to be "on their toes" all the time, liked being associated with Ford's reputation, and may have lacked other attractive work alternatives; Ford's $5 a day for 8 hours' work made him a legend worldwide, as it doubled the standard wage at the time.

## Discussion Questions

1. Why do you think people were interested in working under Henry Ford's leadership?

2. How did becoming one of the world's richest men affect Henry Ford's leadership?

3. What were some mistakes that Henry Ford made as his career progressed?

# Chapter Overview

When people think about the concept of power, they often think about political leaders. In fact, *Forbes*'s annual ranking of the most powerful leaders in the world usually ranks a number of top governmental officials and heads of state from different countries as their most powerful. In 2015, for example, Vladimir Putin (of Russia), Angela Merkel (of Germany), Barack Obama (of the United States), and Xi Jinping (of China) were all listed within the top five most powerful leaders of the world. What is it about these leaders that makes them so powerful? According to *Forbes*, the actions of these leaders can "move the planet" because of four dimensions: (1) They have power over lots of people; (2) they control financial resources that are relatively large compared to their peers; (3) they are powerful in multiple spheres; and (4) they actively use their power. These dimensions still raise the question, though, of what exactly is power? And they also pose the provocative question that many of us have also pondered: Do these powerful leaders use their power for good? In other words, are these leaders moving the planet toward positive, prosocial outcomes for the collective well-being? To answer these questions and to further understand what power does to the leaders who possess it, as was demonstrated in the opening case with Henry Ford, we begin by looking at how power has been operationalized over time.

# What Is Power?

## Philosophical Background

Power is a topic that has interested many famous philosophers, including Plato (428 BCE–348 BCE) and Aristotle (384 BCE–322 BCE). In *The Republic*, Plato draws from an ancient myth, the "Ring of Gyges," to account for the nature of morality and virtue, and how it relates to leaders holding power (Plato, 1901). In short, Gyges was a shepherd at the service of King Candaules of Lydia. After surviving an earthquake, Gyges ventured into a cave looking for a lost sheep. Within the cave, Gyges found a golden ring, which made its wearer invisible. After taming the ring's power, Gyges offered to update King Candaules about the status of the flocks in order to gain access to the king's castle. Once inside, Gyges used the ring to seduce the queen, and together they killed the king so Gyges could take his place on the throne. In *The Republic*, Plato elaborated on what would occur if such a mythical ring existed. Could allegedly good leaders resist the temptation of acting without consequences? Would they remain moral, or are leaders only as good as society forces them to be? For Plato, individuals who lacked *strength of character* should be excluded from office (i.e., leadership positions) because they would be most inclined to use power for self-serving reasons. In fact, Plato criticized "the naïve view that leaders are as a matter of course motivated by the honorable advancement of a community's aims" (Williamson, 2008, p. 397). Hence, Plato believed that rulers should be carefully selected and developed to govern, and that only the virtuous—those with a highly developed sense of justice—should be allowed to exercise power (Williamson, 2008).

Aristotle echoes Plato's sentiments of carefully choosing leaders to govern in society. Yet whereas Plato trusted the governing class that surrounded the leader (e.g., aristocracy) to limit the leader's power, Aristotle instead believed that all individuals should be first, and above all, "leaders of themselves." Thus, for Aristotle, leadership—and by extension, being able to exercise power—was only meant for those who could master their passions through a leadership of self, because such self-mastery would prevent rulers from succumbing to the corruptive nature of power (i.e., becoming tyrants; Aristotle, 1999). Plato and Aristotle agreed that only those who are among the wisest men have the strongest claim to rule because wisdom enables leaders to build regimes that emphasize the common good. For Aristotle, wisdom plays a central role in ensuring virtuous leadership, because it enables leaders to balance their character strengths to deal with everyday contingencies in a harmonic, adaptive, and prosocial way (Aristotle, 1999). We will discuss this notion of virtue in more detail toward the end of the chapter.

## Defining Power

Building upon the foundation set forth by Plato and Aristotle, as well as other philosophers, writers, and scientists, scholars in the 20th and 21st centuries have considered a number of important characteristics of power in their research. In reviewing a great deal of this scholarly work, Sturm and Antonakis (2015) identified three defining characteristics of power that have emerged in definitions and measurements of power from the past 75 years of research: that power involves having the (1) discretion and (2) means to (3) enforce one's will. Discretion refers to the choices and latitude of action available to powerholders to enforce their will. As we saw in the opening paragraph, *Forbes* indicates the importance of powerholders actively using their power to be deemed most powerful; hence, these individuals are demonstrating the importance of having discretion and the choice to be powerful.

In terms of having the means to enforce one's will, these means can be innate (e.g., physical appearance, charisma), acquired through training and expertise, or structural—that is, tied to one's position (e.g., rewards, punishment; French & Raven, 1959). As the *Forbes* ranking suggests, controlling financial resources tends to be an important means used by the powerful and helps explain why political leaders (those who have executive control over a country's wealth) tend to top its annual list. Rounding out the top five in its 2015 most powerful list, though, is Pope Francis, whose means of power extends past monetary resources to things such as legitimacy and likeability.

Last, what one *wills* has to do with regulating, controlling, or being able exogenously to impact aspects of one's environment or others. According to Bendahan, Zehnder, Pralong, and Antonakis (2015), leaders enforcing their will over others refers to those who are dependent on the leader, and thus the more followers that leaders have, the more power they possess. This defining characteristic of power is also evident in *Forbes*'s annual ranking, which includes the dimension of having power over lots of people (and in multiple spheres of influence).

Taking stock of these three defining characteristics of power, we apply Sturm and Antonakis's (2015) definition of power as having the discretion and the means to asymmetrically enforce one's will over entities, to help explain the nature of leadership. The term *entity* can include others (such as employees in an organization), as well as policies, practices, systems, organizational structure (Hambrick & Mason, 1984), and so forth. For instance, Karl Marx, a famous German philosopher, viewed power in terms of social classes and social systems. He argued that power rests in the domination and subordination of social classes based on economic activities and the division of labor. As such, "power centers" (i.e., leaders) of the organization attempt to influence the social coercion and conflict that occur within these systems (Etzioni, 1964). In addition to systems, even time can be considered an entity that can be manipulated by powerful leaders, such as Hugo Chávez moving Venezuela into its own time zone in 2007 so that the country did not have to share a time zone with the United States (*The Economist*, 2015). Thus, power can be applied to various levels of analysis, going from a dyadic analysis where leaders enforce their will on one follower to being able to enforce their will on entire countries.

As we have been learning throughout this book, leadership is a process that involves personal characteristics of the leader, the interaction between the leader and follower(s), and situational pressures. We will find that the dynamics of power mirror the leadership process because they are also rooted in context (Emerson, 1962) and include the dynamics and structure of personality (e.g., McClelland, 1975).

Hence, power is a function of the leader, followers, and the situation (Hughes, Ginnett, & Curphy, 1999). As Russell (1938) suggests, power is a basic force in social relationships; thus, the focus of power in this chapter will be on interpersonal power and how leaders can carry out their will over others (e.g., followers).

## Scientific Background on the Definition of Power

The opening chapter of this book asserts that "the ability to lead others . . . requires that one has power." Having just defined power, we now take a step back and review some of the past research on the operationalization of power in order to build a foundation for why power is important to exercising leadership. In Chapter 3 of this book, we learned that Weber (1947) popularized the term *charisma*. In terms of power, we find that Weber also made a significant impact; that is, his classic definition of power as the probability that a person can carry out his or her own will despite resistance (Weber, 1947) has paved the way for most conceptualizations of power. Weber's definition emphasizes discretion, as do more current descriptions of power, which include a general striving for agency (van Dijke & Poppe, 2006), agency without influence by others (Lammers, Stoker, & Stapel, 2009), and being able to control one's resources (Galinsky, Gruenfeld, & Magee, 2003). As such, not only do leaders take purpose-driven action that brings about change (Bryman, 1992), but by engaging in this agency, they become more powerful and can better enforce their will on others.

Some leaders naturally aspire toward leadership positions as a way to fulfill an inherent desire for power. McClelland (1975) identified this desire as the *need for power* and believed that individuals vary in the amount of psychological satisfaction they derive from controlling others. Thus, leaders who have a high need for power will seek out positions that afford them access to different means of power so they can enforce their will on others. In addition, albeit not without limitation, measures of trait dominance have been used as a proxy for power in past empirical research (Anderson & Berdahl, 2002; Weick & Guinote, 2006). Although important, a desire for power or dominance is not enough to understand leader emergence, as it is quite common for some individuals to "land" in a leadership position even though their desire to be powerful is not strong (e.g., a forced promotion). Moreover, culture may also facilitate the "rise to power." For instance, the term *power distance* refers to the extent to which less powerful individuals accept that power is distributed unequally (Hofstede, 1991). Followers who are high on power distance will tend to obey aspirational leaders without questioning their leadership competence especially if, for example, these leaders already possess some amount of power, or if a powerful entity validates their claim (e.g., an executive board, union representatives, or even a political party). Thus, personal characteristics of leaders can inform their attraction to power and how they respond to powerful others, but a more holistic approach is needed in order to fully understand a leader's power.

Whereas some leaders may be predisposed to wanting power, the dynamics and structure of their personality alone do not ensure that they will become powerful. As is the case with leadership, power also involves an interaction of some sort.

According to Emerson (1962, p. 32), for example, the power of Actor A over Actor B is the amount of resistance on the part of B that can be potentially overcome by A; Actor A becomes more powerful when Actor B becomes more dependent upon Actor A for scarce and valuable resources. When conceptualizing power as a property of a social relation, we see power as being much more than an ability of a person, especially the ability or capacity to influence (Lewin, 1951/1997), as it is often described in textbooks (cf. Hughes et al., 1999; Whetten & Cameron, 2016; Yukl, 2002). That being said, though, power tends to go hand in hand with social influence and persuasion. Influence, which represents the process of affecting the thoughts, behavior, and feelings of another person, is vital to the discussion of leader power because the nature of leadership is an influencing process (Antonakis, Bastardoz, Jacquart, & Shamir, 2016). We see influence, in terms of being influential, as a possible source or outcome of power. For instance, a leader can use various influence tactics (e.g., pressure, ingratiation, rational persuasion) to gain power by evoking basic human tendencies to respond favorably to a request: reciprocation, consistency, social validation/proof, liking, authority, and scarcity (Cialdini, 2001; Cialdini & Goldstein, 2004). According to Magee and Galinsky (2008), though, power does not necessitate some sort of action (e.g., a change in behavior) by either party in the relationship.

When thinking about leadership in the dispositional sense (i.e., that it is informal, not tied to one's position in the organization), we can see how power can also be informal (Etzioni, 1964)—that it can arise from referent or symbolic sources (French & Raven, 1959), and not just from control over valued resources, such as rewards or punishment (which you would find is often tied to one's position). For example, a highly charismatic individual in a work group can exert power in that group even if she or he is not in the formal position of manager. Therefore, not only is power different from authority, but the typical requirement in many current definitions of power that power should be defined as control over resources (e.g., Galinsky et al., 2003; Jordan, Sivanathan, & Galinsky, 2011; Rucker, Dubois, & Galinsky, 2011) is necessarily restrictive. By broadening the conceptualization of power past "control over valued resources," we can see how other qualitatively different variables, such as culture, can enable powerholders to exert their will on others. For instance, "if men are allowed to vote in a certain society and women are not, then these men have more power than the women—that is, these men can exert their will through their votes because of their gender and other cultural injunctions" (Sturm & Antonakis, 2015, p. 142). As such, the operationalization of power in terms of discretion, means, and enforcing one's will over others shifts the notion of power from being merely tied to a position to being a social process that is informed by context.

Building on this notion of context a bit further, including in this book a chapter that explores what power means to leadership and how a leader can gain power might be deemed quite "North American" in its cultural orientation (Whetten & Camerson, 2016). This is so because national cultures that emphasize collectivism (over individualism) and ascription (over achievement) may take a more negative view on power, and thus discussing how any individual can enforce their will on others may seem contrary to the social order (Whetten & Camerson, 2016). While recognizing this perspective, we also believe that power plays a vital role in economic, political, and social interactions (Fehr, Herz, & Wilkening, 2013), and is therefore important to practicing leaders. As such, understanding what power is and how leaders can achieve it helps us to understand how social interactions work. In addition, this chapter is unique from other chapters on power in leadership textbooks in that we describe what power actually does, both good and bad, to the powerholder. In particular, we explain the importance of who the leader is when it comes to the outcomes of his or her power expression.

## Where Does Power Come From?

Power can come from many sources. As shown in Figure 11.1, these sources (i.e., antecedents) can be structural, cognitive, from traits, and physical in nature as well (Sturm & Antonakis, 2015). These different sources of power are evident in the "means" aspect of the definition of power, which suggests that power can be gained and enforced through a variety of mechanisms (such as sitting in a higher-status chair).

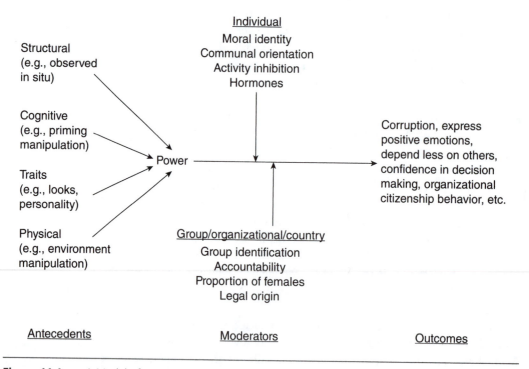

**Figure 11.1**  A Model of Interpersonal Power

SOURCE: From Sturm, R.E., & Antonakis, J. 2015. Interpersonal Power: A Review, Critique, and Research Agenda. *Journal of Management*, 41(1): p 147.

## Structural Sources

To start, structural means of power tend to be rooted in position, as well as titles, task assignments, and authority. According to French and Raven (1959), positional sources of power include reward, coercive, and legitimate power. Reward power relates directly to control over valued resources—a leader can control a subordinate's salary and promotion—while coercive power links to a leader being able to cause an unpleasant experience for a follower (through threats of punishment, abuse); for instance, a leader on the board of directors team can vote to fire the current CEO of a company. In addition, leaders can have power based on their position in a formal hierarchy (i.e., legitimate authority), wherein both a leader and follower(s) agree that the leader has influential rights based on position. For example, the head coach of a National Football League team has power over his players as a result of his position as coach. Other structural sources of power include bureaucratic structures, political coalitions and alliances within organizations, resource dependencies, and social networks (Anderson & Brion, 2014); aligned with these sources, individuals tend to think that powerholders have stronger political skills (Stern & Westphal, 2010).

Whetton and Cameron (2016, p. 237) identified four characteristics tied to position that can help leaders gain power in an organization: (1) *Centrality* refers to access to information in a communication network; (2) *flexibility* refers to the amount of discretion bestowed upon a position; (3) *visibility* refers to the degree to which task performance is seen by influential people in the organization; and (4) *relevance* refers to alignment of assigned tasks and organizational priorities. In general, research has demonstrated the importance of network centrality and having access to, and control of, information in terms of acquiring power (Anderson & Brion, 2014). For example, network centrality has been found to be positively related to perceptions of power, the likelihood of promotion (Brass, 1984), and the leader's attribution of charisma (Balkundi, Kilduff, & Harrison, 2011). In addition, Burt (2000) found that individuals who bridged structural holes in organizations by connecting two otherwise disconnected individuals benefitted in negotiation settings by playing individuals off one another.

In addition to the leader's position in the organization, situational pressures play a role in how leaders exert their power. In a study on bank managers, Mulder, de Jong, Koppelar, and Verhage (1986) found that leaders tend to exercise their power more during times of crisis. Specifically, their study revealed that leaders were more likely to use coercive and legitimate means of power in a crisis situation than in relatively calm periods of time. Moreover, Rucker, Galinsky, and Dubois (2012) identified that when structural sources of power are viewed in terms of social roles (e.g., employee, spouse, friend, community volunteer), these sources can create shifts in the experience of power if there is a temporary change in structure. An actor, for instance, may feel powerful while acting but relatively powerless coming home to a spouse who disapproves of the excessive amount of time spent away from the family. Thus, a leader's power can change depending on the situation/context and the social role that they are in.

## Cognitive Sources

Cognitive means of power shift the focus from social roles and positions to the individual level. Specifically, this approach assumes that power is experienced by most individuals at one time or another (Galinsky et al., 2003) and is therefore embedded within individuals (Rucker et al., 2012). As a result, when it comes to measuring power from this perspective, researchers believe they can manipulate power by priming, or cognitively exposing, individuals to power. A popular example of this prime is having participants think about a time they had power and then write about it (Galinsky et al., 2003; Galinsky, Rucker, & Magee, 2016). However, it is likely that this power prime is biased (i.e., is confounded and not ecologically valid) because asking participants in the treatment group to write about power hints at what is expected of them, which means these participants are being exposed to the purpose of the experiment (while participants in the control group are not because they were told to write about what they did yesterday); as such, participants in the treatment group may form, and act on, expectations for how they should behave (because they are aware that power is being manipulated) versus how they would actually behave if they had been given real power. Accordingly, Sturm and Antonakis (2015) suggest that researchers use caution when solely using this recall prime (and related tasks; e.g., Malhotra & Gino, 2011) in empirical research because it cannot establish that only power was manipulated.

Moving from an experimental setting into the field, research has found that power can be "mentally transferred" from one individual to another simply by interpersonal interaction. For example, Goldstein and Hays (2011) found that individuals who had a brief but cooperative interaction with powerful others mentally adopted the others' power as if it were their own; these individuals, especially the men, proceeded to act as if they themselves were powerful even outside the boundaries of the interaction. This research finding, coupled with the priming study previously mentioned, provides important implications for studying the consequences of cognitively feeling powerful. Yet we agree with research that suggests that the consequences of feeling powerful are distinct from the consequences of being powerful (i.e., having real power; e.g., Flynn, Gruenfeld, Molm, & Polzer, 2011). As Sturm and Antonakis (2015) state, power involves enforcing your will over others, and although leaders may feel powerful, they may not actually be able to enforce their will. Along similar lines (and building upon the previous discussion on structural sources of power), an informal leader in an organization may be better able to exert their will on others compared to a leader in a formal position of authority.[2]

## Traits as a Source of Power

In terms of traits as a means of power, we are interested in the personal attributes and characteristics of a leader that afford them power. As Anderson and Brion (2014) point out, power is often given to those who are perceived as having superior

---

2. The next time you are in the presence of both a formal and informal leader in a group, watch to see how well they each can get others to do what they wish.

individual characteristics (e.g., expertise). According to French and Raven (1959), two important personal sources of power are expert and referent power. Expertise refers to work-related knowledge and skills (Whetton & Cameron, 2016), and Blau and Scott (1962) demonstrated that individuals who are perceived to be the most competent are given more power. It is possible, though, for leaders to gain power by being perceived as having expertise even if this is not necessarily true. However, Yukl (2002) asserts that having actual expertise becomes important when others depend on the leader for advice.

Referent or symbolic power, on the other hand, is about interpersonal attraction and occurs when followers have a desire to please the leader because they have strong feelings of affection, admiration, and loyalty toward the leader (Yukl, 2002). As we learned in Chapter 3, charisma is rooted in values and feelings and can create exceptional followership. Specifically, leaders can use charisma to signal to followers that they should be accorded status (Antonakis et al., 2016), and can therefore help leaders build their referent means of power. In addition to charisma, we see other referent means of power associated with many of the individuals in *Forbes*'s annual list of the most powerful leaders in the world. For example, Pope Francis appears to have an authentic way of carrying himself that makes people trust him. According to a study by Monzani, Ripoll, and Peiró (2014), authentic leadership increased followers' loyalty, and therefore the leaders' referent power as well. In addition, Pope Francis is quite likeable, and Whetten and Cameron (2016) suggest that a leader may be able to gain power by finding ways to enhance their likeability.[3]

As was previously stated when defining power, power differences can also arise from basic human motives and individual-difference variables, including the *need for power* and having high trait dominance. Furthermore, sex, age, and race can also impact how much power a leader has (Anderson & Brion, 2014). Social role theory indicates that power is ascribed more often to certain demographic groups (Eagly, 1987) and research supports this assertion by demonstrating that women do not emerge as leaders in small groups as often as men do (Eagly & Karau, 1991); even in *Forbes*'s 2015 annual list of the most powerful leaders in the world, we see only two female leaders represented in the top 10 leaders on the list. Moreover, and perhaps most interestingly, physical characteristics of an individual, such as height and facial features, have also been found to be associated with perceptions of power. For instance, in a sample of Canadian workers, Gawley, Perks, and Curtis (2009) found that physical height positively correlated with holding a position of authority. A similar finding was found in the sports industry, wherein soccer referees tended to be taller than their assistants and taller referees seemed to have more authority in controlling the game (Stulp, Buunk, Verhulst, & Pollet, 2012).

---

3. It is important to note here that likeability is not synonymous with agreeableness. Research suggests that agreeableness is not related to leader effectiveness and is actually negatively associated with leader emergence (Judge, Bono, Ilies, & Gerhardt, 2002). Interestingly, Barrick and Mount (1993) found that managers in high-autonomy jobs (i.e., had access to power because they had discretion and decision-making authority) who were low in agreeableness performed better than those who were high in agreeableness in these jobs.

## Physical Environment

In addition to physical characteristics of the leader (e.g., gender, height) being an important source of power, the physical environment surrounding the leader is also an important source of power that can be (and often is) manipulated. In a series of experiments that had individuals assume expansive body postures either consciously or inadvertently, Yap, Wazlawek, Lucas, Cuddy, and Carney (2013) found that environments that expanded the body fostered a sense of power in people; in a clever field study, these researchers revealed that automobiles with more expansive driver's seats were more likely to be illegally parked in New York City. Another example of such primes includes getting participants to sit in the chair of a high-status individual, as opposed to a lower-status chair, and then to observe their decisions (Chen, Lee-Chai, & Bargh, 2001). From a methodological standpoint, these primes are effective in generating a sense of power in people because they are unobtrusive and induce nonconscious information processing (as opposed to the cognitive primes listed in the cognitive sources section, which can possibly alert participants to the true purpose of the experiment). However, these types of power-posing primes have also come under increasing scrutiny. Ranehill et al. (2015), for instance, found that power posing only increased self-reported feelings of power but had no effect on hormone levels of testosterone and risk preference, which we will discuss in the next section.

From a follower perspective, the physical environment can also be manipulated to influence how others view the leader in power. For example, research has found that powerful individuals are often portrayed from below (so that people have to look up to them), whereas those with less power are often portrayed from above (Giessner, Ryan, Schubert, & Van Quaquebeke, 2011). Furthermore, using vertical angles in pictures to signal height was also used in *Time* magazine's list of the 100 most influential people (Giessner et al., 2011).

In summarizing this section on the different sources of power, it is important to note that these sources of power are not mutually exclusive of one another. Hence, at any one point in time, leaders may have access to multiple sources of power. For example, there are theories that highlight the importance of traits but also overlap with some of the other sources of power (e.g., structural). According to Yukl (2002), individuals are often given power in exchange for favors (because one has something, such as expertise, that the other needs) and also when their subunit (e.g., functional department, which is structural) acquires power. Additionally, research has found that when the same guest lecturer was introduced to several college classes, he was perceived as being taller with each increase in academic status (Wilson, 1968). In particular, when he was introduced as a lecturer to one class but as a professor to another, the students in the latter class thought he was taller when guessing his height. Hence, how one introduces someone to a group (e.g., structural source of power because it is tied to position and title) can impact the perceptions of their physicality (e.g., traits as a source of power in terms of height). Moreover, in terms of looking at the physical environment as a source of power, we learned that manipulating the space around someone, such as having them sit in a high-status chair, can prime them to cognitively experience power.

# What Does Power Do to Leaders?

When individuals possess power, they experience changes (Jordan et al., 2011; Keltner, Gruenfeld, & Anderson, 2003). These changes can be cognitive (related to thoughts) and affect how leaders process information, such as how much they stereotype. These changes can also be affective (pertaining to emotions and feelings) and influence one's emotional display. Behavioral changes can occur too, thus affecting how one acts, such as engaging in risky conduct. There are even neurological (and physiological) changes that can occur. In the following paragraphs, we will detail the cognitive, affective, behavioral, and neurochemical changes that can occur to powerholders in order to illustrate important outcomes of power; please refer to Table 11.1 as a summary of these findings. We will then explain what power does to leaders overall, taking these specific changes into account, thus setting up the discussion of whether powerful leaders tend to use their power for good or not.

**Table 11.1**　Summary of Changes to Powerholders

| Type of Change | Outcome |
| --- | --- |
| Cognitive | • Enables goal setting and prioritization among goals<br>• Decreases distraction from details<br>• Increases abstract and analytical thinking<br>• Increases stereotyping<br>• Increases hypocrisy<br>• Both decreases and increases perspective taking<br>• Increases creativity<br>• Leads to confidence (and overconfidence) |
| Affective | • Increases positive affect (e.g., desire, enthusiasm, optimism, pride)<br>• Increases displays of pleasure but reduces displays of sadness<br>• Decreases compassion and lessens being attuned to others' suffering<br>• Leads to prioritizing themselves over others |
| Behavioral | • Increases behavioral action<br>• Leads to approaching rewarding outcomes<br>• Increases money spent on themselves<br>• Increases resistance to others' social influence<br>• Increases touching and flirting behaviors<br>• Decreases social conformity and increases the violation of social norms<br>• Increases risk-seeking behavior |
| Neurochemical | • Increases testosterone and thus increases aggressive impulses<br>• Decreases cortisol and thus buffers against stress<br>• Increases dopamine levels, therefore activating reward centers in the brain<br>• Increases serotonin and thus feelings of self-worth<br>• In some contexts, increases oxytocin, and thus a preference for the in-group |

## Changes in Cognition

In terms of cognitive performance, power has been shown to enhance the setting and pursuit of goals (Anderson & Brion, 2014). Research has found that power not only enables individuals to set, initiate, and prioritize among goals (Guinote 2007), but that it can also make powerholders see themselves as less constrained in their goal attainment (Whitson et al., 2013). Related to this finding, Yap and colleagues (2013) found that powerholders may even underestimate the physical size of others in pursuing their goals. In addition, the focus on obtaining goal-relevant outcomes improved motor task performance for powerholders on golf putting and throwing darts (Burgmer & Englich, 2013). These benefits to goal setting may exist because powerholders tend to be less distracted by details and are therefore better at extracting the gist from incoming information in the environment (Smith & Trope, 2006). In other words, high-power leaders are better able to see the forest through the trees compared to low-power leaders. These leaders are also more prone to abstract and analytical thinking (Miyamoto & Ji, 2011; Smith & Trope, 2006).

Whereas power can help leaders focus their attention and efforts on goal attainment, which has numerous benefits, there can also be some drawbacks to this. For example, power tends to make powerholders less individuating (Erber & Fiske, 1984), which could help explain why they tend to stereotype more (Fiske & Dépret, 1996) and are hypocritical at times (Lammers, Stapel, & Galinsky, 2010). Research has also found that power can decrease perspective taking (Galinsky, Magee, Inesi, & Gruenfeld, 2006), but these results are inconclusive because other research has found power actually to increase perspective taking (Mast, Jonas, & Hall, 2009). Moreover, power increases creativity (Galinsky, Magee, Gruenfeld, Whitson, & Liljenquist, 2008) and confidence-inducing states in powerholders (Fast, Sivanathan, Mayer, & Galinsky, 2012), while decreasing the anticipated threat associated with loss (Inesi, 2010). Fast et al. (2012), for example, found that high-power individuals were more likely to overestimate the accuracy of their knowledge compared to low-power individuals. Taken together, these findings have important implications for leadership; specifically, they demonstrate the importance of the content of the goals that leaders set because powerful leaders will work hard to attain their goals. Moreover, if leaders have inaccurate or false information related to their goals, and power makes them overly confident, they may not see problems with their thinking that others do see.

## Changes in Affect

With regard to how powerful leaders experience and express emotion, power in general increases positive affect in powerholders, whereas reduced power increases negative affect (Keltner et al., 2003). Research has found this expression of positive affect to include desire, enthusiasm, happiness, optimism, and pride (Anderson & Galinsky, 2006; Berdahl & Martorana, 2006; Fast, Gruenfeld, Sivanathan, & Galinsky, 2009; Keltner et al., 2003). For example, Berdahl and Martorana (2006) found that those who were given power because they were assigned to lead discussion groups about a controversial social issue (e.g., abortion) experienced more positive emotions (i.e., happiness and interest) compared to the other group members (i.e., those with less power) who reported experiencing more negative emotions (i.e., discomfort and fear). Furthermore, powerholders tend to display smiles of pleasure more (Keltner, Young, Heerey, Oemig, & Monarch, 1998), and sadness is often more difficult to detect in them (Kemper, 1991).

There are a number of possible reasons why powerholders are likely to experience and express positive affect. One important reason is that they may be less attuned to others' suffering. For example, van Kleef et al. (2008) found powerholders to be less compassionate and less distressed when others were distressed. Relatedly, Blader and Chen (2012) found power to be negatively related to justice toward others. In addition, across three studies, Stellar, Manzo, Kraus, and Keltner (2011) found that compared to higher-class individuals (i.e., those who identified more as middle class to upper class), lower-class individuals reported higher levels of compassion. Though social class and power are not the same thing (a salient example would be Gandhi), status can afford leaders access to the different means of power (such as legitimacy). In a similar yet somewhat different vein, another reason why powerholders have more positive affect could be that they prioritize themselves over others because this is emotionally rewarding for them (van Kleef, Oveis, Homan, van der Löwe, & Keltner, 2015); in particular, van Kleef et al. (2015) found that powerholders were more inspired by themselves than by others. Thus, taken together, the findings presented here suggest that while powerful leaders can be more positive, they may be less inclined to understand (and respond to) others' emotions.

## Changes in Behavior

In general, power increases an action orientation (Galinsky et al., 2003; Keltner et al., 2003), which means that high-power leaders are more likely to take action than low-power leaders. Though we already see this characteristic represented in the definition of power (i.e., that leaders must choose to exercise their power), the practical implications of this characteristic are quite broad. For example, powerful leaders not only take action, but are more likely to approach rewarding outcomes (Gruenfeld, Inesi, Magee, & Galinsky, 2008; Keltner et al., 2003). Research has found that power increases the amount of money that consumers spend on themselves (Rucker et al., 2011), which seems to suggest that power can make people more behaviorally selfish. As evidenced with Bendahan et al.'s (2015) study on corruption, powerholders were more prone to using their power to violate social norms and serve themselves to the detriment of the common good; such behavior can occur because power makes leaders less dependent on others (Emerson, 1962) and also makes them feel more distant from others (Magee & Smith, 2013). Also, powerful leaders may experience other psychological processes that may buffer them from experiencing guilt when knowing they are violating social norms (Bendahan et al., 2015).

One reason why power may blind leaders to social norms and thus make them behave in socially inappropriate ways is that it makes them more resistant to others' social influence (Berdahl & Martorana, 2006), which allows them to express themselves more freely. For example, powerholders are more likely to engage in touching and flirting behaviors (Guinote, Judd, & Brauer, 2002; Keltner et al.,

2003). As mentioned before, powerholders are also more creative and, specifically, less influenced by salient examples when generating creative ideas (Galinsky et al., 2008). As a result, it seems that high-power leaders engage in less social conformity and may violate social norms more frequently (Galinsky et al., 2008). In addition, power increases risk-seeking behavior (Anderson & Galinsky, 2006), which often extends from their overconfidence. In summary, as we have been seeing so far, power seems to be enhancing the self in multiple ways, such as taking action to reach rewarding outcomes.

## Changes in Neurochemistry

Power can change leaders' cognition, affect, and behavior, all of which presumably represent a leader's "software." However, could power also affect leaders' "hardware" by altering their brain chemistry? Before we answer this question, we must first briefly describe the anatomy of the human brain—we will then look at how the brain reacts to stimuli that arise from power-related situations.

The brain is a network of neurophysiological structures that conform systems, which in healthy adults act as a holistic, highly coordinated entity (Bullmore & Sporns, 2012). Each system has specific functions that affect how humans experience and process stimuli from the outside world. For example, the deeper, more primitive structures that conform the limbic system can quickly assess the threat that an external stimulus poses to one's social status, and intuitively estimate the "chances" of surviving a confrontation (i.e., "fight or flight" responses; Gray, 1994). The limbic system is also what elicits most of our primal emotions, including fear, anger, anxiety, and joy. Conversely, the upper, more complex structures of the brain that conform the neocortex are responsible for processing the incoming raw information into cognitions, and therefore regulate the intensity of such primal emotions and behavioral responses (Kandel, Schwartz, Jessell, Siegelbaum, & Hudspeth, 2013).

All across this complex network of systems, information is transmitted using neurotransmitters (e.g., dopamine, serotonin) and hormones (e.g., testosterone, cortisol, and oxytocin). Dopamine and serotonin are neurotransmitters traditionally associated with feelings of reward, achievement, and well-being, respectively (Mogenson, Jones, & Yim, 1980). Testosterone is an androgen hormone (i.e., develops and maintains masculine features), which has been linked to competitive, status-enhancing behaviors (Mazur & Booth, 1998), while cortisol is a hormone linked to stress, and fight-or-flight behaviors. Oxytocin, on the other hand, has been widely associated with trust, prosocial, communal, and group-oriented behaviors (Campbell, 2010).

Neurotransmitters travel across synaptic connections within the brain with a quick but short-lived effect, whereas hormones reach the brain through the blood stream and have a more lasting effect. As both neurotransmitters and hormones travel through neural pathways (the brain's analog to "roads" that connect one system with another), they leave a chemical trail as they pass by. The resultant chemical trails create a temporary chemical imbalance in the brain that communicates important information to your body (such as telling your heart to beat). However, in healthy adults, once the external stimulus that triggered the neurochemical response disappears, the neurotransmitters and hormones mutually regulate, thus restoring balance to the brain (Plaff, Arnold, Fahrbach, Etgen, & Rubin, 2002). Recent research has begun to look into whether the frequent exposure to power-related situations could create a constant neurochemical imbalance in the brain, which could gradually reshape powerholders' neurophysiological structures and neural pathways in a way analogous to how drugs affect addicts (Zilioli & Watson, 2014). In addition, a number of recent studies have focused on exploring the effects that power-related stimuli have on hormones and neurotransmitters. For example, powerholders were found to have lower heart rates following stressful tasks (Schmid & Schmid Mast, 2013), which suggests that power can act as a buffer against stress.

Because humans and other mammals share common evolutionary ancestors, studying power-oriented behaviors in modern rodents can be quite informative about the neurochemical processes that occur in humans in power-related situations. For example, we know that in rodents, testosterone and cortisol interact in situations where an individual's social status is at stake—that is, when there is a clear and present struggle for power (Fuxjager & Marler, 2010). Furthermore, linkages between testosterone and dopamine provide some insights as to why some individuals see the possession of power as a very rewarding experience that can become especially addictive (Schwartzer, Ricci, & Melloni, 2013). Finally, unpacking both the interaction between testosterone on cortisol and the antagonistic effect of serotonin and oxytocin on testosterone helps to explain why powerholders differ in self- versus group-oriented behaviors (Edwards & Kravitz, 1997). To illustrate such effects, we will consider social status, which is one form of symbolic power described by French and Raven (1959), in the example below.

Social status usually derives from winning in a social competition. In animals, social competitions mostly involve establishing dominance over the herd or the pack, but for humans, examples of social competitions include sports matches, a job interview, or even taking part in a high school debate team. Because of evolution, humans' basic neurochemical response to the awareness of being part of a social competition is an increase in testosterone and a reduction in cortisol levels. Such imbalance increases aggressive impulses and focus, and reduces self-directed negative emotions (Mazur & Booth, 1998; Mehta & Josephs, 2010), explaining some of the powerholders' aforementioned behaviors. After winning a social competition, the brain releases more testosterone, which in turn reduces levels of cortisol. Alongside testosterone and cortisol, dopamine also plays a crucial role in social competitions. During competition, dopamine boosts cognitive performance, but its effect is even more relevant after a social competition, because it triggers reward centers, eliciting feelings of satisfaction. Thus, this *winner effect* not only is ego-affirming and rewarding, but creates a strong drive for winners to take part in future competitions. The opposite neurochemical response occurs for losers, for whom after losing the confrontation, cortisol levels increase while testosterone decreases. This increase in cortisol is an evolutionary adaptive stress response that prepares these individuals for future fights; however, if these individuals lose in subsequent fights, they will eventually burn out, and the winner's new social status will be consolidated (Sapolsky, 1995).

Some evidence suggests that winning every possible confrontation, and thus holding power for long periods of time, tends to affect behavioral patterns in both rodents and humans. For example, in line with the winner effect, unchallenged power leads to less empathy and concern for those lower on the social ladder (Robertson, 2012). This effect occurs because testosterone drives powerholders to defend their newly acquired social status by means of testosterone-infused aggression and/or other social dominance mechanisms. For animals, being dominant is not only is less stressful, but also provides tangential rewards (e.g., better access to food, territory, or partner coupling).

The brain uses oxytocin and serotonin to prevent individuals from constantly engaging in testosterone-induced aggressive behavior. For example, the orbito-frontal cortex, a neocortical region that regulates aggressive behavior, is rich in serotonin receptors (Mehta & Beer, 2010). Hence, when serotonin levels increase, this regulatory structure activates and aggressive impulses decrease. Similarly, oxytocin, through its ability to reduce aggressive behaviors toward in-group members, plays a crucial role in the establishment and maintenance of social relationships. For example, several studies link oxytocin to emotional attachment and maternal behaviors, cooperation, empathy, generosity, trust, and altruism (Barraza, McCullough, Ahmadi, & Zak, 2011; Baumgartner, Heinrichs, Vonlanthen, Fischbacher, & Fehr, 2008; Hurlemann et al., 2010; Zak, Stanton, & Ahmadi, 2007). Oxytocin receptors are also found in some cortical areas where testosterone receptors have been observed, possibly explaining the chemistry behind the more social aspect of interrelational power, which involves the relationship between the leader, the group they lead (i.e., the in-group), and those outside of it (i.e., the out-group). In fact, in highly affiliative species (such as the prairie vole), there is an abundant amount of oxytocin receptors in the brain's reward centers, which suggests that for these species taking care of others is a highly positive, reinforcing experience (Insel, 2010). Similarly, humans may seek those contexts whose stimuli create a sustained neurochemical imbalance in which there is an excess of oxytocin. Not surprisingly, the stimulation of endogenous oxytocin systems is a key neurochemical substrate underlying the prosocial and empathogenic effects of party drugs such as MDMA (ecstasy; McGregor & Bowen, 2012).

A cautionary note for those interested in exploring the neurochemical implications of power: The human brain is among the most complex networks of systems known to date, and therefore reducing the richness of human experience to a number of neurochemicals is a very simplistic and reductionist conception of the human being (Rose, 2003). Moreover, such reductionism, combined with the lack of an overarching integrative theoretical framework to guide research, could be severely misleading. For example, even though there seems to be a consensus on the positive effects of oxytocin on trust and affiliative behaviors, without the regulatory effect of an antagonist hormone such as testosterone, excessive oxytocin could lead to xenophobia and aggression toward the out-group (De Dreu, Greer, Van Kleef, Shalvi, & Handgraaf, 2011). To make matters worse, concerns were recently raised about a possible publication bias in oxytocin studies (Lane, Luminet, Nave, & Mikolajczak, 2016). A publication bias occurs when researchers choose to report only expected results, and neglect reporting undesired or null findings. Such underreporting is reinforced further by the reluctance of major journals to review, let alone accept for publication, such null reports. For example, Lane et al. (2016) admit that from a total of eight studies exploring the relation to oxytocin and trust, they only reported four, wherein only one of those four studies included null findings (Lane et al., 2015).

When it comes to leadership and power, neurochemistry, affect, cognition, and behavior are highly intertwined. As a result, for those interested in studying the linkages between leadership and power, we recommend adopting an integrative approach that contemplates all these dimensions into their theory-building and posterior empirical research (Avolio, 2007).

## Self-Enhancement Effect of Power

As we have been learning in this section so far, it seems that the changes that are occurring to powerful leaders are generally making them more self-focused. As evidenced in the preceding paragraphs, those who experience power are more likely to feel liberated to take action to achieve rewarding outcomes and to satisfy their own needs; these individuals are also more likely to violate social norms and are less likely to take on others' suffering. Hence, it seems that power acts as a catalyst to reveal a leader's true self (Hirsh, Galinsky, & Zhong, 2011). With this in mind, it is understandable why Plato and Aristotle warned us to be careful of who we select into positions of leadership because these individuals will have access to power, which enhances self-expression. In particular, this focus on placing greater importance on one's own self-interests has led many to believe that power corrupts. As Lord Acton once asserted, "Power tends to corrupt, and absolute power corrupts absolutely" (Acton & Himmelfarb, 1948, pp. 335–336). Taken another way, though, this self-enhancement effect of power could possibly lead to prosocial outcomes if those wielding the power are inherently prosocial. For example, power has been found to enhance moral awareness (which subsequently decreased self-interest) for those with a strong moral identity (DeCelles, DeRue, Margolis, & Ceranic, 2012); it has also enabled communally oriented individuals to act more altruistically (Chen et al., 2001). In the next section, we delve into more detail on the importance of who the leader is when it comes to the consequences of how they use their power.

## Who Should Be Elected Into Positions of Power?

We have established that power magnifies a leader's characteristics. Such magnification can be functional to leadership up to a certain point, but after a specific threshold is reached, power becomes corruptive. Power-induced corruption implies that leaders are using power to increase their personal gain in a way that contravenes social norms and is detrimental to the common good (Bendahan et al., 2015). In order to resist the corruptive nature of power, leaders not only must be exceptionally good at leading the organization and others, but also need to truly master "leadership of self" (Crossan, Vera, & Nanjad, 2008); as Lao Tzu, the founder of

Taoism, once proclaimed, "Mastering others is strength. Mastering yourself is true power." With the aim of understanding what type of leader will be able to wield power in such a way, we will first demonstrate how power-induced corruption can occur. In particular, we will discuss structural corruption, which is more chronic and less susceptible to change, and situational corruption, which dissipates once power-related stimuli disappear. Second, we will learn how *virtuous* leaders can navigate both of these types of corruption that are often found in conducive organizations, susceptible followers, and even ego-distorted selves, so as to overcome the corruptive effects of power (Padilla, Hogan, & Kaiser, 2007).

## The Corruptive Impact of Power

Some organizations are destructive and antisocial from their very inception (e.g., gangs). Others have been created for prosocial purposes but may have lost their way, becoming structurally corrupt. For example, the negative influence of pseudo-transformational leaders can reshape an organization's culture into a conducive environment for their toxic leadership (Barling, Christie, & Turner, 2008). In the corporate world, some of the characteristics of structurally corrupt organizations would be (1) a monopolistic, profit-driven strategy with zero social responsibility; (2) a highly competitive climate; and (3) a highly authoritarian culture. On the other hand, situationally corrupt organizations would be those that have a culture of prosocial values, but because of threats or instability resort to unethical policies and practices at times. Examples of such threats are the need to maintain the leading position in the market with the addition of new competition, shareholder pressure to sustain share-value at any cost, or even the interference of public governmental bodies in daily operations. The prognosis is much better for virtuous leaders in situationally corrupt organizations than in structurally corrupt ones, because in the latter, the pressure of such a toxic environment is most likely to erode the character of leaders over time, forcing them either to take radical action to drive change (increasing the chances of them becoming a self-proclaimed tyrant) or eventually to leave the organization.

Power-induced corruption is also likely to affect how leaders lead others. Team leaders and project managers at lower levels of the organization are susceptible to power-induced corruption that derives from their social status within a group. For example, recent studies evaluating the social dynamics of leadership (Haslam, Reicher, & Platow, 2011; Hogg & Terry, 2000; Steffens et al., 2014) showed that power is not only claimed by leaders but also granted by the group they seek to lead (DeRue & Ashford, 2010). Thus, granted power may be highly corruptive as well. One of the main findings of this line of inquiry is that social groups are more likely to give their leaders increased leeway if they perceive them to be highly representative of the shared characteristics of the group (i.e., prototypicality). Leaders' prototypicality is so influential that followers will endorse prototypical leaders even if these leaders fail to achieve their promised goals, display a reduced sense of accountability, have a lower frequency of team-oriented behaviors (Giessner & van Knippenberg, 2008; Giessner, van Knippenberg, van Ginkel, & Sleebos, 2013), or even commit breaches of procedural fairness (Ullrich, Christ, & van Dick, 2009).

Virtuous leaders, though, will use this prototypical leeway to sustain their rule in tough times, or "bend the bureaucracy" so that it truly serves the interests of the common good (as Plato expected). Instead, structurally destructive leaders (e.g., corporate psychopaths; Boddy, 2014) are more likely to abuse this informal power to satisfy their own selfish needs.

Finally, in certain situations even otherwise virtuous individuals are susceptible to succumbing to power-induced corruption. For example, during the Renaissance, Niccolò Machiavelli wrote *The Prince* as a critique of the corrupt Florentine aristocracy. Machiavelli concluded that only a prince who is "strong as a lion" but also "astute as a fox" could rule without being nullified by such a corrupt ruling class. However, current research finds fault with Machiavelli's thinking because whereas seeking and holding power (in its many forms) is functional, and to some extent essential for sustaining leadership, trying to hold absolute power indefinitely, and at any cost, is probably the most basic form of leadership hubris (Claxton, Owen, & Sadler-Smith, 2015). In a biographical study of 100 U.S. presidents and British prime ministers, 18 leaders were found to have succumbed to the hubris syndrome, which is a collection of symptoms evoked by holding power that cannot be explained by prior stable personality disorders (e.g., narcissism, bipolar disorder) but that remits when power fades (Owen & Davidson, 2009).

The hubris syndrome is highly aligned with the aforementioned effects of power-induced neurochemical imbalances. For example, even though the testosterone-driven winner effect is highly affirming for the leader, it has a dark side because remaining unchallenged after several confrontations can lead to an escalation of power-seeking behaviors. As it occurs with substance abuse, such escalation seeks to satisfy the aforementioned need for power at any cost, and is very likely to impair the leader's judgment about possible threats facing the organization they lead (Robertson, 2012). Furthermore, when a power-related situation fosters a persistent excess of oxytocin, this can also be highly detrimental to effective leadership. Whereas high levels of oxytocin foster trust and in-group cooperation, leaders can become overly attached to the groups they lead, and in turn direct their aggression toward other groups that may pose a threat to their group, thus influencing followers to engage in social exclusion, xenophobia, intergroup prejudice, and eventually aggression (Bartels, 2012). In fact, recent studies show that high doses of oxytocin in humans relate to ethnocentrism, the tendency to view one's group as superior to other groups (De Dreu et al., 2011). Such evidence suggests that even a strong attachment and concern for one's peers may have a corruptive effect on leaders, and again highlights the importance for leaders to find balance between pursuing self-serving interests and a selfless service to others and the organization.

## The Importance of Virtuousness for Powerful Leaders

As evidenced in the preceding paragraphs, power-induced corruption is not just the leader's issue—it can take root and affect many within the organization as well as impact society as a whole. Although Aristotle's teachings were written centuries ago, he provides us with an important way of dealing with the corruptive effects of power. Under the notion of *virtue,* Aristotle collected those behaviors we would label today as functional, adaptive, and prosocial (Crossan, Mazutis, Seijts, & Gandzs, 2013). For Aristotle, power is not inherently bad in itself, but is corruptive only if it breaks the harmonic balance of one's behavior, turning virtues into vices and thus weakening one's character, which tends to happen more often than not.

According to Aristotle, positive and virtuous character is the consequence of frequently displaying virtuous behaviors. Building upon this notion, current research views character as a set of virtues that are universally considered to be important to well-being and excellence (Peterson & Seligman, 2004; Seijts, Gandz, Crossan, & Reno, 2015). Modern psychology views character as consisting of distal (stable, inherited traits such as conscientiousness) and proximal (malleable, context-dependent, and acquired traits such as self-efficacy) personality traits that are aligned with prosocial values and are expressed in behaviorally virtuous ways. For example, Crossan and colleagues (2013) proposed 11 character strengths (i.e., judgment, courage, humanity, justice, temperance, transcendence, accountability, drive, collaboration, humility, and integrity) that are essential for virtuous leadership and positive organizational performance (Seijts et al., 2015; Sosik, Gentry, & Chun, 2012). Thus, the display of character in a leadership role would represent what we understand today as good leadership (Seijts & Gandz, 2013) and demonstrates why a growing number of scholars propose that virtuousness should be the gold standard by which the quality of decisions of those in power should be assessed. In particular, these scholars posit that a leader's virtuousness cannot be assessed outside the context in which such a decision is made, as what may be seen as virtuous in one context may be less so in another (Cameron, 2011; Wright & Goodstein, 2007).

The emphasis on character helps us to understand how a balance of virtue can enable leaders to overcome the corruptive effects of power. The vice aspect of power results from a distorted excess in the intensity of self-referential cognition, affect, and the frequency of self-oriented behaviors, to the detriment of other-oriented cognition, affect, and behavior. As mentioned earlier, powerholders experience more optimism and display a higher frequency of risk-taking behaviors compared to the less powerful (Anderson & Galinsky, 2006). In excess, such behaviors express the vice of recklessness (i.e., unbalanced or too much courage). Similarly, power influences the powerholder's emotional displays (Kemper, 1991) and the likelihood of acting rashly (Galinsky et al., 2003), revealing a lack of prudence, which represents one facet of the virtue of temperance. Finally, power affects how powerholders see others, making them more susceptible to adopting, assuming, or even generating negative social stereotypes (Fiske & Dépret, 1996). Such harshness and closed-mindedness are vices that result from a lack of both humanity and judgment.

In order to develop virtuous leadership, Aristotle held practical wisdom as the most important virtue, because in short, it allows one to identify and understand the particularities of each situation (Aristotle, 1999). Nowadays, we use the term *judgment* to signal depth of character, which means knowing which character dimension should be used when. A solid sense of judgment is essential for leaders to cope with the challenges and temptations of exercising power. Specifically, good judgment enables leaders to avoid the vices of power (which leads to corruption), ensuring that power only magnifies their virtuousness. In addition, we believe that depth of character enables leaders to short-circuit the effects that power has on the brain's neurochemistry. Unfortunately, we do not yet have enough evidence to show linkages between character strengths and neurochemical processes or structures, but future research in this area is definitely worthwhile. For example, testosterone might activate neocortical areas linked to the character strengths of courage and drive, whereas oxytocin may activate on structures related to collaboration and humanity. Similarly, as dopamine activates neocortical reward centers in the brain, linkages to justice and accountability might exist, whereas serotonin might activate structures that reduce testosterone-infused aggression and therefore may have some connection to temperance and integrity. Whereas there is no silver-bullet for preventing the corruption of power, we encourage leaders to fully commit to developing virtuous character to help stave off power's corruptive nature.

# Conclusion

As we saw with *Forbes*'s 2015 annual list of the most powerful leaders in the world, leaders must choose to activate on their power, can gain and maintain it through a variety of ways, and can wield their power to create worldwide change. Though desirable to leaders, power proves to be a heavy burden for those who are not wise enough to bear it. As we learned earlier in this chapter with Plato's tale of the "Ring of Gyges," there are costs associated with holding power because it can corrupt its bearer. We see the corruptive nature of a ring that makes its wearer invisible in full effect in J. R. R. Tolkien's *The Hobbit* and *The Lord of the Rings*. For Tolkien, the ring of power is an actively malevolent force that necessarily decays the morality of the wearer. In these stories, we see the travails of Bilbo and Frodo as they are exposed to this mythical ring. We support this popular knowledge by summarizing modern-day scientific findings that describe the cognitive, affective, behavioral, and neurochemical changes that can occur to powerholders. Moreover, our chapter demonstrates the importance of who (i.e., what kind of leader) is afforded with power. Echoing the sentiments of Plato and Aristotle, we believe that virtuous leaders are the ones best suited to wield power because they will use it in prosocial ways. Thus, in light of the ever-expanding list of power abuses by leaders, we see that we might not be in a crisis of power and corruption today, but one of a lack of leader character.

## Discussion Questions

1. Is power inherently evil?
2. If you were in charge of succession planning in an organization, how would you select potential leaders, knowing that these individuals will have greater access to power? Also, how would you train them to be more prosocial once they have power?

## Recommended Readings

- Heimans, J., & Timms, H. (2014). Understanding "new power." *Harvard Business Review, 92*(12), 48–56.
- How power-hungry bosses keep their power. (2015). *Harvard Business Review, 93*(5), 24–25.
- Seijts, G. H., Gandz, J., Crossan, M., & Reno, M. (2015). Character matters: Character dimensions' impact on leader performance and outcomes. *Organizational Dynamics, 44*(1), 65–74.

## Recommended Case Studies

- **Case:** Clawson, J. G., & Yemen, G. (2007). *Tough guy.* Darden School of Business.
- **Case:** Snook, S. A., Perlow, L. A., & Delacey, B. J. (2005). *Coach knight: The will to win.* Harvard Business School.
- **Case:** Lundberg, K., & Heymann, P. (2003). *Robust web of corruption: Peru's intelligence chief Vladimiro Montesinos.* Harvard Kennedy School.

## Recommended Videos

- Liu, E. (2014). Why ordinary people need to understand power. https://www.youtube.com/watch?v=Cd0JH1AreDw
- Schwartz, B. (2009). Our loss of wisdom. http://www.ted.com/talks/barry_schwartz_on_our_loss_of_wisdom

## References

Acton, J. E. E. D. A., & Himmelfarb, G. (1948). *Essays on freedom and power.* Boston, MA: Beacon Press.

Anderson, C., & Berdahl, J. L. (2002). The experience of power: Examining the effects of power on approach and inhibition tendencies. *Journal of Personality and Social Psychology, 83,* 1362–1377.

Anderson, C., & Brion, S. (2014). Perspectives on power in organizations. *Annual Review of Organizational Psychology and Organizational Behavior, 1,* 67–97.

Anderson, C., & Galinsky, A. D. (2006). Power, optimism, and risk-taking. *European Journal of Social Psychology, 36*(4), 511–536.

Antonakis, J., Bastardoz, N., Jacquart, P., & Shamir, B. (2016). Charisma: An ill-defined and ill-measured gift. *Annual Review of Organizational Psychology and Organizational Behavior, 3*(1), 293–319.

Aristotle. (1999). *Nicomachean ethics* (T. Irwin, Trans.). Indianapolis, IN: Hacket.

Avolio, B. J. (2007). Promoting more integrative strategies for leadership theory-building. *American Psychologist, 62*(1), 25–33.

Balkundi, P., Kilduff, M., & Harrison, D. A. (2011). Centrality and charisma: Comparing how leader networks and attributions affect team performance. *Journal of Applied Psychology, 96*(6), 1209–1222.

Barling, J., Christie, A., & Turner, N. (2008). Pseudo-transformational leadership: Towards the development and test of a model. *Journal of Business Ethics, 81*(4), 851–861.

Barraza, J. A., McCullough, M. E., Ahmadi, S., & Zak, P. J. (2011). Oxytocin infusion increases charitable donations regardless of monetary resources. *Hormones and Behavior, 60*(2), 148–151.

Barrick, M. R., & Mount, M. K. (1993). Autonomy as a moderator of the relationships between the Big 5 personality dimensions and job-performance. *Journal of Applied Psychology, 78,* 111–118.

Bartels, A. (2012). Oxytocin and the social brain: Beware the complexity. *Neuropsychopharmacology, 37*(8), 1795–1796.

Baumgartner, T., Heinrichs, M., Vonlanthen, A., Fischbacher, U., & Fehr, E. (2008). Oxytocin shapes the neural circuitry of trust and trust adaptation in humans. *Neuron, 58*(4), 639–650.

Bendahan, S., Zehnder, C., Pralong, F. P., & Antonakis, J. (2015). Leader corruption depends on power and testosterone. *The Leadership Quarterly, 26*(2), 101–122.

Berdahl, J., & Martorana, P. (2006). Effects of power on emotion and expression during a controversial group discussion. *European Journal of Social Psychology, 36,* 497–509.

Blader, S. L., & Chen, Y.-R. (2012). Differentiating the effects of status and power: A justice perspective. *Journal of Personality and Social Psychology, 102,* 994–1014.

Blau, P. M., & Scott, W. R. (1962). *Formal organizations: A comparative approach.* San Francisco, CA: Chandler.

Boddy, C. R. (2014). Corporate psychopaths, conflict, employee affective well-being and counterproductive work behavior. *Journal of Business Ethics, 121,* 107–121.

Brass, D. J. (1984). Being in the right place: A structural analysis of individual influence in an organization. *Administrative Science Quarterly, 29,* 518–539.

Bryman, A. (1992). *Charisma and leadership in organizations.* London, UK: Sage.

Bullmore, E., & Sporns, O. (2012, May). The economy of brain network organization. *Nature Reviews Neuroscience, 13,* 336–349.

Burgmer, P., & Englich, B. (2013). Bullseye! How power improves motor performance. *Social Psychological and Personality Science, 4,* 224–232.

Burt, R. S. (2000). The network structure of social capital. *Research in Organizational Behavior, 22,* 345–423.

Cameron, K. S. (2011). Responsible leadership as virtuous leadership. *Journal of Business Ethics, 98,* 25–35.

Campbell, A. (2010). Oxytocin and human social behavior. *Personality and Social Psychology Review, 14*(3), 281–295.

Chen, S., Lee-Chai, A. Y., & Bargh, J. A. (2001). Relationship orientation as moderator of the effects of social power. *Journal of Personality and Social Psychology, 80,* 183–187.

Cialdini, R. B. (2001). Harnessing the science of persuasion. *Harvard Business Review, 79,* 72–79.

Cialdini, R. B., & Goldstein, N. J. (2004). Social influence: Compliance and conformity. *Annual Review of Psychology, 55,* 591–621.

Claxton, G., Owen, D., & Sadler-Smith, E. (2015). Hubris in leadership: A peril of unbridled intuition? *Leadership, 11*(1), 57–78.

Crossan, M., Mazutis, D., Seijts, G., & Gandz, J. (2013). Developing character in business programs. *Academy of Management Learning and Education, 12*(2), 285–305.

Crossan, M., Vera, D., & Nanjad, L. (2008). Transcendent leadership: Strategic leadership in dynamic environments. *The Leadership Quarterly, 19*(5), 569–581.

De Dreu, C. K. W., Greer, L. L., Van Kleef, G. A., Shalvi, S., & Handgraaf, M. J. J. (2011). Oxytocin promotes human ethnocentrism. *Proceedings of the National Academy of Sciences, 108*(4), 1262–1266.

DeCelles, K. A., DeRue, D. S., Margolis, J. D., & Ceranic, T. L. (2012). Does power corrupt or enable? When and why power facilitates self-interested behavior. *Journal of Applied Psychology, 97,* 681–689.

DeRue, D. S., & Ashford, S. J. (2010). Who will lead and who will follow? A social process of leadership identity construction in organizations. *Academy of Management Review, 35*(4), 627–647.

Eagly, A. H. (1987). *Sex differences in social behavior: A social-role interpretation.* Hillsdale, NJ: Lawrence Erlbaum.

Eagly, A. H., & Karau, S. J. (1991). Gender and the emergence of leaders: A meta-analysis. *Journal of Personality and Social Psychology, 60,* 685–710.

*The Economist.* (2015). Rulers of time: Clocks and calendars provide a timeless way for regimes to illustrate their power. Retrieved from http://www.economist.com/news/leaders/21660980-clocks-and-calendars-provide-timeless-way-regimes-illustrate-their-power-rulers-time

Edwards, D. H., & Kravitz, E. A. (1997). Serotonin, social status and aggression. *Current Opinion in Neurobiology, 7*(6), 812–819.

Emerson, R. M. (1962). Power-dependence relations. *American Sociological Review, 27,* 31–40.

Erber, R., & Fiske, S. T. (1984). Outcome dependency and attention to inconsistent information. *Journal of Personality and Social Psychology, 47*, 709–726.

Etzioni, A. (1964). *Modern organizations.* Englewood Cliffs, NJ: Prentice-Hall.

Fast, N. J., Gruenfeld, D. H., Sivanathan, N., & Galinsky, A. D. (2009). Illusory control: A generative force behind power's far-reaching effects. *Psychological Science, 20*, 502–508.

Fast, N. J., Sivanathan, N., Mayer, N. D., & Galinsky, A. D. (2012). Power and overconfident decision-making. *Organizational Behavior and Human Decision Processes, 117*, 249–260.

Fehr, E., Herz, H., & Wilkening, T. (2013). The lure of authority: Motivation and incentive effects of power. *American Economic Review, 103*, 1325–1359.

Fiske, S. T., & Dépret, E. (1996). Control, interdependence and power: Understanding social cognition in its social context. *European Review of Social Psychology, 7*(1), 31–61.

Flynn, F. J., Gruenfeld, D., Molm, L. D., & Polzer, J. T. (2011). Social psychological perspectives on power in organizations. *Administrative Science Quarterly, 56*, 495–500.

*Forbes.* (2015). The world's most powerful people 2015. Retrieved from http://www.forbes.com/sites/davidewalt/2015/11/04/the-worlds-most-powerful-people-2015/#762b53f01868

French, J., & Raven, B. (1959). *The bases of social power.* In D. Cartwright (Ed.), *Studies in social power* (pp. 150–167). Ann Arbor: University of Michigan.

Fuxjager, M. J., & Marler, C. A. (2010). How and why the winner effect forms: Influences of contest environment and species differences. *Behavioral Ecology, 21*(1), 37–45.

Galinsky, A. D., Gruenfeld, D. H., & Magee, J. C. (2003). From power to action. *Journal of Personality and Social Psychology, 85*(3), 453–466.

Galinsky, A. D., Magee, J. C., Gruenfeld, D. H., Whitson, J. A., & Liljenquist, K. A. (2008). Power reduces the press of the situation: Implications for creativity, conformity, and dissonance. *Journal of Personality and Social Psychology, 95*, 1450–1466.

Galinsky, A. D., Magee, J. C., Inesi, M. E., & Gruenfeld, D. H. (2006). Power and perspectives not taken. *Psychological Science, 17*, 1068–1074.

Galinsky, A. D., Rucker, D. D., & Magee, J. C. (2015). Power: Past findings, present considerations, and future directions. In M. Mikulincer & P. R. Shaver (Eds.), *APA handbook of personality and social psychology* (pp. 421–460). Washington, DC: American Psychological Association.

Gawley, T., Perks, T., & Curtis, J. (2009). Height, gender, and authority status at work: Analyses for a national sample of Canadian workers. *Sex Roles, 60*(3–4), 208–222.

Giessner, S. R., Ryan, M. K., Schubert, T. W., & Van Quaquebeke, N. (2011). The power of pictures: Vertical picture angles in power pictures. *Media Psychology, 14*(4), 442–464.

Giessner, S. R., & van Knippenberg, D. (2008). "License to fail": Goal definition, leader group prototypicality, and perceptions of leadership effectiveness after leader failure. *Organizational Behavior and Human Decision Processes, 105*(1), 14–35.

Giessner, S. R., van Knippenberg, D., van Ginkel, W., & Sleebos, E. (2013). Team-oriented leadership: The interactive effects of leader group prototypicality, accountability, and team identification. *Journal of Applied Psychology, 98*(4), 658–667.

Goldstein, N. J., & Hays, N. A. (2011). Illusory power transference: The vicarious experience of power. *Administrative Science Quarterly, 56*, 593–621.

Grandin, G. (2009). *Fordlandia: The rise and fall of Henry Ford's forgotten jungle city.* New York, NY: Picador.

Gray, J. A. (1994). Three fundamental emotion systems. In P. Ekman & R. J. Davidson (Eds.), *The nature of emotion: Fundamental questions.* New York, NY: Oxford University Press.

Guinote, A. (2007). Behavior variability and the situated focus theory of power. *European Review of Social Psychology, 18*, 256–295.

Guinote, A., Judd, C. M., & Brauer, M. (2002). Effects of power on perceived and objective group variability: Evidence that more powerful groups are more variable. *Journal of Personality and Social Psychology, 82*, 708–721.

Hambrick, D. C., & Mason, P. A. (1984). Upper echelons—The organization as a reflection of its top managers. *Academy of Management Review, 9,* 193–206.

Haslam, S. A., Reicher, S. D., & Platow, M. J. (2011). *The new psychology of leadership.* New York, NY: Psychology Press.

Hirsh, J. B., Galinsky, A. D, & Zhong, C.-B. (2011). Drunk, powerful, and in the dark. *Perspectives on Psychological Science, 6,* 415–427.

Hofstede, G. (1991). *Cultures and organizations: Software of the mind.* New York, NY: McGraw-Hill.

Hogg, M. A., & Terry, D. J. (2000). Social identity and self-categorization in organizational contexts. *Academy of Management Review, 25,* 121–140.

Hughes, R. L, Ginnett, R. C., & Curphy, G. J. (1999). *Leadership: Enhancing the lessons of experience.* New York, NY: Irwin McGraw-Hill.

Hurlemann, R., Patin, A., Onur, O. A., Cohen, M. X., Baumgartner, T., Metzler, S., . . . Kendrick, K. M. (2010). Oxytocin enhances amygdala-dependent, socially reinforced learning and emotional empathy in humans. *Journal of Neuroscience, 30,* 4999–5007.

Inesi, M. E. (2010). Power and loss aversion. *Organizational Behavior and Human Decision Processes, 112,* 58–69.

Insel, T. R. (2010). The challenge of translation in social neuroscience: a review of oxytocin, vasopressin, and affiliative behavior. *Neuron, 65*(6), 768–779.

Jardim, A. (1970). *The first Henry Ford: A study in personality and business leadership.* Cambridge, MA: MIT Press.

Jordan, J., Sivanathan, N., & Galinsky, A. D. (2011). Something to lose and nothing to gain: The role of stress in the interactive effect of power and stability on risk taking. *Administrative Science Quarterly, 56,* 530–558.

Judge, T. A., Bono, J. E., Ilies, R., & Gerhardt, M. W. (2002). Personality and leadership: A qualitative and quantitative review. *Journal of Applied Psychology, 87,* 765–780.

Kandel, E. R., Schwartz, J. H., Jessell, T. M., Siegelbaum, S. A., & Hudspeth, A. J. (2013). *Principles of neural science* (5th ed.). New York, NY: McGraw-Hill.

Keltner, D., Gruenfeld, D. H., & Anderson, C. (2003). Power, approach, and inhibition. *Psychological Review, 110,* 265–284.

Keltner, D., Young, R. C., Heerey, E. A., Oemig, C., & Monarch, N. D. (1998). Teasing in hierarchical and intimate relations. *Journal of Personality and Social Psychology, 75,* 1231–1247.

Kemper, T. D. (1991). Predicting emotions from social relations. *Social Psychology Quarterly, 54*(4), 330–342.

Lammers, J., Stapel, D. A., & Galinsky, A. D. (2010). Power increases hypocrisy: Moralizing in reasoning, immorality in behavior. *Psychological Science, 21,* 737–744.

Lammers, J., Stoker, J. I., & Stapel, D. A. (2009). Differentiating social and personal power opposite effects on stereotyping, but parallel effects on behavioral approach tendencies. *Psychological Science, 20,* 1543–1549.

Lane, A., Luminet, O., Nave, G., & Mikolajczak, M. (2016). Is there a publication bias in behavioural intranasal oxytocin research on humans? Opening the file drawer of one laboratory. *Journal of Neuroendocrinology, 28*(4). http://doi.wiley.com/10.1111/jne.12384

Lane, A., Mikolajczak, M., Treinen, E., Samson, D., Corneille, O., de Timary, P., & Luminet, O. (2015). Failed replication of oxytocin effects on trust: The envelope task case. *PLoS ONE, 10*(9).

Lewin, K. (1997). Behavior and development as a function of the total situation. In D. Cartwright (Ed.), *Field theory in social psychology* (pp. 337–381). Washington, DC: American Psychological Association. (Original work published 1951)

Luthans, F., & Avolio, B. J. (2009). The "point" of positive organizational behavior. *Journal of Organizational Behavior, 30,* 291–307.

Magee, J. C., & Galinsky, A. D. (2008). Social hierarchy: The self-reinforcing nature of power and status. *Academy of Management Annals, 2,* 351–398.

Magee, J. C., & Smith, P. K. (2013). The social distance theory of power. *Personality and Social Psychology Review, 17,* 158–186.

Malhotra, D., & Gino, F. (2011). The pursuit of power corrupts: How investing in outside options motivates opportunism in relationships. *Administrative Science Quarterly, 56,* 559–592.

Mast, M. S., Jonas, K., & Hall, J. A. (2009). Give a person power and he or she will show interpersonal sensitivity. *Journal of Personality and Social Psychology, 97,* 835–850.

Mazur, A., & Booth, A. (1998). Testosterone and dominance in men. *Behavioral and Brain Sciences, 21,* 353–397.

McClelland, D. C. (1975). *Power: The inner experience.* New York, NY: Halsted Press.

McGregor, I. S., & Bowen, M. T. (2012). Breaking the loop: Oxytocin as a potential treatment for drug addiction. *Hormones and Behavior, 61,* 331–339.

Mehta, P. H., & Beer, J. (2010). Neural mechanisms of the testosterone–aggression relation: The role of orbito-frontal cortex. *Journal of Cognitive Neuroscience, 22,* 2357–2368.

Mehta, P. H., & Josephs, R. A. (2010). Testosterone and cortisol jointly regulate dominance: Evidence for a dual-hormone hypothesis. *Hormones and Behavior, 58,* 898–906.

Miyamoto, Y., & Ji, L.-J. (2011). Power fosters context-independent, analytic cognition. *Personality and Social Psychology Bulletin, 37,* 1449–1458.

Mogenson, G. J., Jones, D. L., & Yim, C. Y. (1980). From motivation to action: Functional interface between the limbic system and the motor system. *Progress in Neurobiology, 14*(2–3), 69–97.

Monzani, L., Ripoll, P., & Peiro, J. M. (2014). Followers' agreeableness and extraversion and their loyalty towards authentic leadership. *Psicothema, 26*(1), 69–75.

Mulder, M., de Jong, R. D., Koppelar, L., & Verhage, J. (1986). Power, situation, and leaders' effectiveness. *Journal of Applied Psychology, 71,* 566–570.

Nye, D. E. (1979). *Henry Ford, ignorant idealist.* Port Washington, NY: Kennikat Press.

Owen, D., & Davidson, J. (2009). Hubris syndrome: An acquired personality disorder? A study of US presidents and UK prime ministers over the last 100 years. *Brain: A Journal of Neurology, 132*(5), 1396–1406.

Padilla, A., Hogan, R., & Kaiser, R. B. (2007). The toxic triangle: Destructive leaders, susceptible followers, and conducive environments. *The Leadership Quarterly, 18,* 176–194.

Peterson, C., & Seligman, M. E. (2004). *Character strengths and virtues: A classification and handbook.* Washington, DC: American Psychological Association.

Plaff, D. W., Arnold, A. P., Fahrbach, S. E., Etgen, A. M., & Rubin, R. T. (2002). *Hormones, brain and behavior.* San Diego, CA: Academic Press.

Plato. (1901). *The Republic of Plato; an ideal commonwealth* (Rev. ed.; B. Jowett, Trans.). New York, NY: The Colonial Press.

Platow, M. J., van Knippenberg, D., Haslam, S. A., van Knippenberg, B., & Spears, R. (2006). A special gift we bestow on you for being representative of us: Considering leader charisma from a self-categorization perspective. *The British Journal of Social Psychology, 45*(2), 303–320.

Ranehill, E., Dreber, A., Johannesson, M., Leiberg, S., Sul, S., & Weber, R. A. (2015). Assessing the robustness of power posing: No effect on hormones and risk tolerance in a large sample of men and women. *Psychological Science, 26,* 653–656.

Robertson, I. H. (2012). *The winner effect: How power affects your brain.* London, UK: Bloomsbury.

Rose, N. (2003). Neurochemical selves. *Society, 41*(1), 46–59.

Rucker, D. D., Dubois, D., & Galinsky, A. D. (2011). Generous paupers and stingy princes: Power drives consumer spending on self versus others. *Journal of Consumer Research, 37,* 1015–1029.

Rucker, D. D., Galinsky, A. D., & Dubois, D. (2012). Power and consumer behavior: How power shapes who and what consumers value. *Journal of Consumer Psychology, 22,* 352–368.

Russell, B. (1938). *Power: A new social analysis.* London, UK: Allen and Unwin.

Sapolsky, R. M. (1995). Social subordinance as a marker of hypercortisolism. *Annals of the New York Academy of Sciences, 771,* 626–639.

Schmid, P. C., & Schmid Mast, M. (2013). Power increases performance in a social evaluation situation as a result of decreased stress responses. *European Journal of Social Psychology, 43,* 201–211.

Schwartzer, J. J., Ricci, L. A., & Melloni, R. H. (2013). Prior fighting experience increases aggression in Syrian hamsters: Implications for a role of dopamine in the winner effect. *Aggressive Behavior, 39*(4), 290–300.

Seijts, G. H., & Gandz, J. (2013). Good leaders learn. *Developing Leaders, 12,* 50–56.

Seijts, G. H., Gandz, J., Crossan, M., & Reno, M. (2015). Character matters: Character dimensions' impact on leader performance and outcomes. *Organizational Dynamics, 44*(1), 65–74.

Smith, P. K., & Trope, Y. (2006). You focus on the forest when you're in charge of the trees: Power priming and abstract information processing. *Journal of Personality and Social Psychology, 90,* 578–596.

Sosik, J. J., Gentry, W. A., & Chun, J. U. (2012). The value of virtue in the upper echelons: A multisource examination of executive character strengths and performance. *The Leadership Quarterly, 23,* 367–382.

Steffens, N. K., Haslam, S. A., Reicher, S. D., Platow, M. J., Fransen, K., Yang, J., . . . Boen, F. (2014). Leadership as social identity management: Introducing the Identity Leadership Inventory (ILI) to assess and validate a four-dimensional model. *The Leadership Quarterly, 25*(5), 1001–1024.

Stellar, J. E., Manzo, V. M., Kraus, M. W., & Keltner, D. (2012). Compassion and class: Socioeconomic factors predict compassionate responding. *Emotion, 12,* 449–459.

Stern, I., & Westphal, J. D. (2010). Stealthy footsteps to the boardroom: Executives' backgrounds, sophisticated interpersonal influence behavior, and board appointments. *Adimnstrative Science Quarterly, 55,* 278–319.

Stulp, G., Buunk, A. P., Verhulst, S., & Pollet, T. V. (2012). High and mighty: Height increases authority in professional refereeing. *Evolutionary Psychology, 10*(3), 588–601.

Sturm, R. E., & Antonakis, J. (2015). Interpersonal power: A review, critique, and research agenda. *Journal of Management, 41*(1), 136–163.

Ullrich, J., Christ, O., & van Dick, R. (2009). Substitutes for procedural fairness: Prototypical leaders are endorsed whether they are fair or not. *Journal of Applied Psychology, 94*(1), 235–44.

van Dijke, M., & Poppe, M. (2006). Striving for personal power as a basis for social power dynamics. *European Journal of Social Psychology, 36,* 537–556.

van Kleef, G. A., Oveis, C., Homan, A., van der Löwe, I., & Keltner, D. (2015). Power gets you high: The powerful are more inspired by themselves than by others. *Social Psychological and Personality Science, 6,* 472–480.

van Kleef, G. A., Oveis, C., van der Löwe, I., LuoKogan, A., Goetz, J., & Keltner, D. (2008). Power, distress, and compassion: Turning a blind eye to the suffering of others. *Psychological Science, 19,* 1315–1322.

Weber, M. (1947). *The theory of social and economic organization* (A. M. Henderson & T. Parsons, Trans.). New York, NY: Oxford University Press.

Weick, M., & Guinote, A. (2008). When subjective experiences matter: Power increases reliance on ease-of-retrieval. *Journal of Personality and Social Psychology, 94,* 956–970.

Whetten, D. A., & Cameron, K. S. (2016). *Management skills.* Englewood Cliffs, NJ: Prentice Hall.

Whitson, J. A., Liljenquist, K. A., Galinsky, A. D., Magee, J. C., Gruenfeld, D. H., & Cadena, B. (2013). The blind leading: Power reduces awareness of constraints. *Journal of Experimental Social Psychology, 49,* 579–582.

Williamson, T. (2008). The good society and the good soul: Plato's *Republic* on leadership. *The Leadership Quarterly, 19,* 397–408.

Wilson, P. R. (1968). The perceptual distortion of height as a function of ascribed academic status. *Journal of Social Psychology, 74,* 97–102.

Wright, T. A., & Goodstein, J. (2007). Character is not "dead" in management research: A review of individual character and organizational-level virtue. *Journal of Management, 33,* 928–958.

Yap, A. J., Wazlawek, A. S., Lucas, B. J., Cuddy, A. J. C., & Carney, D. R. (2013). The ergonomics of dishonesty: The effect of incidental expansive posture on stealing, cheating, and traffic violations. *Psychological Science, 24,* 2281–2289.

Yukl, G. (2002). *Leadership in organizations.* Englewood Cliffs, NJ: Prentice Hall.

Zak, P. J., Stanton, A. A., & Ahmadi, S. (2007). Oxytocin increases generosity in humans. *PLoS ONE, 2*(11), e1128.

Zilioli, S., & Watson, N. V. (2014). Testosterone across successive competitions: Evidence for a "winner effect" in humans? *Psychoneuroendocrinology, 47,* 1–9.

# CHAPTER 12

# Leadership and Identity

*Daan van Knippenberg*

---

## Opening Case: A Day in the Life of a Leader

Alice Dupont was considering the challenges ahead of her. The biggest she was facing was to convince her employees of a major change in her company's focus: a shift away from the services on which the company was built—indeed, that seemed to define the company's identity—to new products that seemed a disconnect with the company's past. She could sense all the ways in which her employees would resent and resist the change, perceiving the decision to drop what used to be their signature products as a betrayal of what the company stood for. She also realized that this was no trivial issue. She dearly needed her people to have a sense of ownership of the change and to work to make the change a success. She realized the change was doomed to fail if her people would be dragging their feet or worse. She was sympathetic to her people's concerns, at least in the sense that she could appreciate that they felt a strong connection with the company and saw the work they did and the services they delivered as capturing the essence of the company—a shared identity that they valued and would seek to protect and preserve. At the same time, she realized the change was necessary, inevitable, for the company to be viable in years to come. Importantly, she also saw that dropping their old focus and shifting to a new portfolio of services was not the disconnection many people would perceive. In fact, the shift fit perfectly with her company's mission of delivering high-quality, state-of-the-art, business-to-business services—and as the company's founder, she should know! She also realized this was her core strength in the matter. Not only could she clearly see that the shift was *not* a disconnect, not a betrayal of what the company represented, but a logical development of the company in changing times; as the company's founder and owner, she was also uniquely positioned to convey this message with full legitimacy. If anyone could stake a claim about what the company stood for—indeed, about the company's very identity—it was her. This, then, was the only and obvious way forward: presenting a powerful message of how the change was a natural development of why she started the company in the first place.

## Discussion Questions

1. How do identity concerns play a role in Alice Dupont's employees' resistance to the change?

2. How can Alice Dupont's leadership address these identity concerns?

# Chapter Overview

Leadership is a core and integral aspect of human groups, organizations, and societies. Indeed, it is hard to think of social groupings without some sort of leadership structure, even if only informal. Leadership also has the potential to be a major influence on the functioning and performance of groups, organizations, and societies. Not surprisingly, then, leadership has been high on the agenda of behavioral research in management, psychology, and the social sciences for more than a century. What is surprising, however, is that leadership research has historically paid little attention to the notion that leadership typically takes place in the context of a shared group membership, where leaders are also a member of the group (team, organization, nation) they lead—or with a leader external to the group at least sharing membership in the overarching group in which the group is embedded (e.g., an organizational leader dealing with a team that is part of the same organization even when the leader is not part of the team; Hogg, van Knippenberg, & Rast, 2012b; D. van Knippenberg, 2011). What this means is that the effects of leadership are influenced by processes related to the psychology of group membership. This is the focal issue highlighted in this chapter.

Central to the psychology of group membership is *identity*—the perception of self and others in terms of a shared group membership. Identity plays an important role in the leadership process (or the self-concept; self and identity are constructs that can be used interchangeably). Follower identity both influences responses to leadership and is influenced by leadership (Lord, Brown, & Freiberg, 1999; Shamir, House, & Arthur, 1993; D. van Knippenberg & Hogg, 2003; D. van Knippenberg, van Knippenberg, De Cremer, & Hogg, 2004). Although this analysis puts a premium on understanding the role of group identity—the shared social identity of leaders and followers—it can easily be extended to cover two other core aspects of identity and self-conception that are not necessarily specifically tied to a shared group membership (but can be): self-evaluations, and conceptions of identity change and continuity over time. These issues, too, are addressed in this chapter. The same identity principles can also be extended to include the influence of leader identity on leadership—not only in terms of the shared group membership but also in terms of the role identity as a leader (i.e., in group identity terms, the membership in an abstracted leader category). This issue, too, is addressed, albeit more briefly, given the more limited empirical evidence.

Although leadership research has been slow to connect with the role of self and identity, this has changed dramatically during the past 25 years. The aim of the current chapter is to capture this development and to provide a state-of-the-science overview of research in leadership, self, and identity. To do so, I first address what is arguably the core of research in leadership, self, and identity: the notion of social (group) identity and the social identity perspective on leadership. This core aspect captures both the ways in which follower social identity informs responses to leadership and leadership's influence on follower social identity. The discussion then moves on to the roles of self-evaluation, identity change and continuity, and leader identity.

## Social Identity and Leadership

If we think about ourselves, one of the things that come to mind in capturing who we are is our belongingness to social groups. Whether it is our nationality, ethnicity, organizational membership, profession, or yet other group memberships, we tend to take our membership in social groups (i.e., teams, organizations, nations, demographic categories) as describing, to a greater or lesser extent, important aspects of ourselves. This self-defining quality of social group memberships is captured by theories of social identity, self-categorization, and self-construal (Hogg, 2003; Tajfel & Turner, 1986; Turner, Hogg, Oakes, Reicher, & Wetherell, 1987), more recently increasingly grouped under the heading *social identity approach* (Haslam, 2004). The social identity approach describes how individuals see themselves not only in individual terms (i.e., characteristics that identify the self as a unique individual, the individual self or identity, "I") but also in terms of group or organizational memberships (i.e., characteristics that identify the self as a group member, the collective self or social identity, "we").

The social identity approach was developed as a perspective on intergroup relations to explain why people tend to be biased in favor of their membership groups ("in-group"; Tajfel & Turner, 1986). However, the essence of the approach—social self-definition—captures what is perhaps the core aspect of the psychology of group membership and has far broader implications for our understanding of social attitudes and behavior than just intergroup relations, as more recent developments in social identity research show (for reviews, see, e.g., Haslam, 2004; Hogg, 2003). Self-definition as a group member (social identity) exerts an important influence on perceptions, attitudes, and behavior. Because it implies seeing the self through the lens of group membership, social identity entails taking the group's best interest to heart—indeed, experiencing the group interest as the self-interest (i.e., the interest of an inclusive "we"; D. van Knippenberg, 2000)—and experiencing the group identity as both self-describing and self-guiding (Turner et al., 1987). These two processes are of particular importance to the social identity analysis of leadership. In a nutshell, follower social identity leads followers to favor leaders who are perceived to be *group prototypical* (i.e., embodying the group identity and thus the social reality shared by the group) and to be serving the group's best interest. Moreover, effective leadership may derive from leaders' ability to build followers' identification with the collective and to change followers' understanding of this collective identity.

## Group Prototypicality and Group-Serving Orientation

The social identity approach describes how social groups are mentally represented as group prototypes—fuzzy sets of characteristics that capture what defines the group, what group members have in common, and what distinguishes the group from other groups (Hogg, 2001; Turner et al., 1987). Such group prototypes are subjective representations and capture not so much the group average as an idealized image of the group—what is judged to be truly group-defining. Group prototypes capture the socially shared reality of the group. They describe what the group values, believes, and considers important, and what are seen as appropriate and desirable behaviors and courses of action. In effect, group prototypes capture what is group-normative. Thus, the group prototype is a source of influence on those who identify with the group (i.e., self-define in terms of the group membership; Ashforth & Mael, 1989; Tajfel & Turner, 1986), as identification leads one to ascribe group-defining characteristics to the self and motivates the individual to conform to group norms (Abrams & Hogg, 1990; Turner et al., 1987).

Core to the social identity analysis of leadership is the fact that group members, and therefore also group leaders, may differ in the extent to which they represent or embody the group prototype (i.e., are group prototypical). To the extent that a leader of a collective (i.e., group, team, organization, nation) is perceived to be group prototypical (i.e., to embody the collective identity), the leader derives influence from the (implicit) perception that he or she represents what is group-normative (Hogg, 2001). Moreover, group prototypicality also induces trust in the leader's intentions. Because they embody the group identity, group prototypical leaders are trusted to pursue the group's best interests (B. van Knippenberg & van Knippenberg, 2005; D. van Knippenberg & Hogg, 2003). Because identification results in the internalization of group interests, serving the group is a quality that individuals who identify highly with their group prioritize in their leaders (Haslam & Platow, 2001; Platow & van Knippenberg, 2001). Accordingly, the trust in leaders' group-serving orientation elicited by leader group prototypicality contributes to leadership effectiveness (Giessner & van Knippenberg, 2008; Giessner, van Knippenberg, & Sleebos, 2009).

Evidence for the role of leader group prototypicality is found in lab experiments (e.g., Hains, Hogg, & Duck, 1997) as well as field research (e.g., B. van Knippenberg & van Knippenberg, 2005). It is also found in evidence for the effectiveness of individuals in formal leadership positions (e.g., Pierro, Cicero, Bonaiuto, van Knippenberg, & Kruglanski, 2005; Platow & van Knippenberg, 2001) and for emergent leaders (Fielding & Hogg, 1997; D. van Knippenberg, van Knippenberg, & van Dijk, 2000). Indicators of effectiveness include follower perceptions and attitudes such as perceived leadership effectiveness and job satisfaction (e.g., Giessner & van Knippenberg, 2008; Hogg, Hains, & Mason, 1998; Pierro et al., 2005) as well as more objective indicators of leadership effectiveness such as task performance (B. van Knippenberg & van Knippenberg, 2005) and creativity (Hirst, van Dick, & van Knippenberg, 2009). Moreover, support derives from studies from a range of countries on different continents (Australia, the Americas, Asia, and Europe; D. van Knippenberg, 2011) testifying to the robustness of this analysis across cultures.

More anecdotally, too, the notion of leader group prototypicality seems instrumental in explaining the effectiveness of business and political leaders. Reicher and Hopkins (2001, 2003), for instance, discuss how national leaders like Thatcher (United Kingdom), Sukarno (Indonesia), and Gandhi (India) derived influence from their followers' perception that they were the embodiment of the nation (see also below for the active role that leaders may play in fostering such perceptions). Business leaders, too, may in part base their influence and appeal on their perceived group prototypicality—for example, because as the business founder, he or she has become the embodiment of the company (e.g., Steve Jobs at Apple) or because his or her personal history is closely linked to the company (e.g., former Philips CEO Gerard Kleisterlee).

One question that this emphasis on leader group prototypicality may give rise to is, what about group diversity? Can group prototypicality still play a role in leadership when group members differ widely in terms of their demographic characteristics (age, gender, ethnicity) and/or job-related characteristics (functional and educational background)? This is no trivial matter, as organizations and societies are growing increasingly diverse and diversity clearly is not without consequence for group process and performance (D. van Knippenberg & Schippers, 2007). In this respect, it is important to realize that group prototypicality does not revolve around being as similar as possible to the group on as many attributes as possible. Rather, it concerns the extent to which the leader represents the ideal type of the group in terms of *group-defining* characteristics. For instance, the fact that a research and development team has male as well as female members may be irrelevant to team members' sense of identity derived from the team membership. In contrast, the sense that the team is deeply committed to breakthrough innovations and undertakes whatever risky or unconventional way is required to get there may be an important part of team identity. The issue, then, would not be whether the leader represents the team's composition in terms of gender but, rather, whether the leader embodies the do-or-die commitment of the team to realizing innovative products. Diversity should not be mistaken for an absence of shared identity (cf. D. van Knippenberg, Haslam, & Platow, 2007), and group prototypicality may play a similar role in leadership effectiveness for more diverse and more homogeneous groups. Demographic attributes may play a role in leader group prototypicality, but a high degree of group member diversity does not preclude the possibility of a leader's embodying the group identity. In fact, demographics may be more likely to play a role in leader group prototypicality the more they are shared. Even when demographics are not core to how the team sees itself, a leader deviating from the team in demographic attributes shared by the team (e.g., the male leader of an all-female team or the female leader of an all-male team) may be faced with at least the initial impression that the leader is different from the team and unlikely to embody what the group stands for. In such situations, the leader's active role in managing perceptions of the team's identity and the leader's representativeness of that team identity become all the more important.

The proposition that group members favor leaders whom they perceive to serve the group and act in the group's best interest (i.e., to which part of leader group prototypicality's link with effectiveness is attributed) also implies that acts that are (or can be interpreted as) indicative of the leader's group-serving motivation feed into leadership effectiveness (Haslam & Platow, 2001; D. van Knippenberg & Hogg, 2003). Consistent with this analysis, leadership effectiveness has been linked to such behaviors as leader self-sacrifice on behalf of the group (Yorges, Weiss, & Strickland, 1999), leader allocation decisions that favor the group over other groups (Platow, Hoar, Reid, Harley, & Morrison, 1997), and leader expressions of commitment to the group (De Cremer & van Vugt, 2002).

The social identity analysis advanced both leader group prototypicality and leader group-oriented behavior as key elements of effective leadership. Leader group prototypicality engenders trust in leaders' group-serving orientation (B. van Knippenberg & van Knippenberg, 2005) and, in part, derives its effectiveness from this trust (Giessner & van Knippenberg, 2008). Thus, in part, leader group prototypicality and leader group-oriented behavior derive their effectiveness from the same mechanism—the perception of leader group-serving orientation. Accordingly, leader group prototypicality and leader group-oriented behavior may be expected to have an interactive influence on leadership effectiveness, such that one in a sense compensates for the other. Given one element, the other's relationship with leadership effectiveness becomes weaker (D. van Knippenberg & Hogg, 2003). This, indeed, is what is found across a number of different operationalizations of leader group-serving orientations, such as allocation decisions (Platow & van Knippenberg, 2001), self-sacrifice (B. van Knippenberg & van Knippenberg, 2005), and appeals to the collective interest (vs. the self-interest; Platow, van Knippenberg, Haslam, van Knippenberg, & Spears, 2006): Group prototypical leaders are effective regardless of whether or not they engage in group-oriented behavior, but nonprototypical leaders are more effective when they engage in group-oriented acts than when they do not.

All other things being equal, the effects of leader group prototypicality, leader group-serving behavior, and their interaction should hold. Core to the social identity analysis, however, is that these leadership influences are rooted in follower identification with the collective. Accordingly, these influences are expected to be stronger, with higher follower identification and social identity salience

(Hogg, 2001).[1] Thus, if follower social identity lies at the root of group prototypical leaders' effectiveness, the relationship between prototypicality and effectiveness should be moderated by identification, which has been shown to be the case (Fielding & Hogg, 1997; Hains et al., 1997; Hogg et al., 1998). In a similar vein, research has shown that followers respond more positively to leader group-oriented behavior the more they identify with the collective (De Cremer, van Knippenberg, van Dijke, & Bos, 2006; De Cremer & van Vugt, 2002; Platow et al., 1997). Further validating this analysis, the interactive influence of leader group prototypicality and leader group-oriented behavior was also shown to be contingent on follower identification (Platow & van Knippenberg, 2001).

The social identity model of leadership advances prototypicality and group-orientedness as two core aspects of effective leadership. These aspects directly follow from an analysis of the psychology of group membership in terms of social identity and self-categorization theories. More recently, this analysis has been extended with insights that have a shorter tradition in the social identity approach but are, nevertheless, well grounded in this approach: the role of uncertainty and change in leadership, and leader fairness. Moreover, throughout its development, cross-links and integrations with other approaches to leadership have been established that may provide the building blocks for more integrative and broad-ranging theories of leadership (Hogg, van Knippenberg, & Rast, 2012a, 2012b). These issues are addressed in the following sections.

## Extension and Integration

**Prototypicality, Uncertainty, and Change.** An important leadership function—some would argue the core of leadership—lies in bringing about change and managing uncertainty. It is not self-evident that what makes leaders effective as change agents or in managing and reducing uncertainty is the same as what makes leaders effective in more stable times (cf. Conger & Kanungo, 1987). The relationship between leadership, change, and uncertainty is an important issue to consider.

Uncertainty plays an important role in the social identity approach to leadership. Hogg (2007) advanced a desire for uncertainty reduction as a key motive underlying affiliation with social groups. Uncertainty is an aversive psychological state that

---

1. Whereas identification captures the extent to which an individual conceives of the self in terms of the group membership, social identity salience refers to the extent that the identification is cognitively activated—is influential in the here and now rather than dormant (i.e., the fact that someone identifies with a group does not mean that this identification is always equally central to the person's thoughts and actions). For instance, the competition between one's group and another group may render one's group identification more salient than it would have been without the competition. Identification can be seen as the more chronic or enduring influence, whereas identity salience can be seen as the more contextual activation of that influence (Haslam, 2004). To a large extent, however, identification and salience may be expected to be functionally equivalent and, indeed, to a certain extent, positively related. I will focus on the more enduring influence of identification, which is also more widely studied in the leadership literature, and take this also to apply to social identity salience.

individuals will desire to resolve or at least reduce. Social identity may be important in this respect because it captures a shared social reality that may help reduce uncertainty. Social identity helps define what is important, valued, and even what is "real," and it may provide guidance as to appropriate responses to uncertain situations. Accordingly, a desire to reduce uncertainty may lead individuals to rely on their group memberships and to think and act more on the basis of their social identity (Hogg, 2007). Uncertainty also invites a desire for leadership. When people are uncertain, they look to leadership to reduce this uncertainty (D. van Knippenberg et al., 2000). In combination, these propositions suggest that individuals desiring to reduce subjective uncertainty will be particularly sensitive to leader group prototypicality—leadership that is perceived to embody a shared social reality.

In support of this proposition, D. van Knippenberg et al. (2000) show that prototypical group members are more likely to emerge as leaders when task uncertainty is high. Research by Pierro and colleagues suggests that individual-level influences on the desire for uncertainty reduction moderate the relationship between leader group prototypicality and leadership effectiveness. Pierro et al. (2005) focused on individual differences in the need for closure (the desire to avoid uncertainty, ambiguity, and unresolved issues) and found that leader group prototypicality was more strongly related to leadership effectiveness for followers with a greater need for closure. Extending this analysis to more situational rather than dispositional indicators of a desire to reduce uncertainty, Cicero, Pierro, and van Knippenberg (2007, 2010) obtained similar moderated relationships for follower job stress and role ambiguity (i.e., both are associated with a greater need for closure). Providing further support for the social identity basis of these relationships, Pierro et al. (2007) showed that the interactive effect of prototypicality and need for closure was moderated by follower identification.

These findings may also have important implications for leadership of change, because change is typically associated with uncertainty. As a case in point, Pierro et al. (2007) conducted their study in the context of organizational change and found that leader prototypicality predicted follower openness to change as a function of follower need for closure and identification. Change also puts another issue on the agenda in the form of potential changes to collective identity. In the course of their lives, people change and develop, as does their identity. The same holds for social identities. Over time, group, organizational, and national identities may change. This alone is unproblematic; however, people value a sense of continuity in individual and social identity (Sani, 2008). This may render people resistant to collectives changes, because these can be perceived as a threat to the continuity of a valued identity (Rousseau, 1998; D. van Knippenberg, van Knippenberg, Monden, & de Lima, 2002). Because collective changes rely heavily on the active cooperation of the members of the collective, such resistance to change is a major challenge for leadership of change (Conner, 1995).

From an identity perspective, then, an important role for leadership of change is to act not only as agents of change, but also as agents of continuity of identity to remove resistance to change (D. van Knippenberg & Hogg, 2003; cf. Shamir, 1999). Leadership of change is more effective if it conveys the message that despite all changes, the core aspects of the collective identity are maintained. The message of change should also convey that "we will still be us" (Rousseau, 1998). As a case in point, Reicher and Hopkins (2003) argue that successful leadership of change may actually convey the message that as a consequence of change, the collective will become *more* true to its "real" or authentic identity. As an illustrative corporate example in this respect, D. van Knippenberg and Hogg (2003) point to Apple founder Steve Jobs's return to the company after years of absence. Originally, Jobs had helped create an organizational identity as an unconventional and creative company, but after Jobs's departure, these aspects of identity gradually faded. On returning to Apple, Jobs's strategy to change matters at Apple appears to have included advocating a return to Apple's roots of being unconventional and creative—in a sense, returning the company to its "true identity" from which it had strayed. Framed like this, Jobs's message of change was not just a message of continuity of identity; it was a call to *increase* continuity of identity *through* the change.

D. van Knippenberg, van Knippenberg, and Bobbio (2008) discuss evidence that leader group prototypicality may be particularly effective in instilling such a sense of continuity of identity in times of change. Prototypical leaders' representativeness of the shared identity builds trust that the leader will act as an agent of continuity. Group prototypical leaders are trusted to ensure that treasured aspects of the collective identity will survive the change. In support of this prediction, D. van Knippenberg et al. discussed evidence from two experimental studies focusing on organizational change in the form of a merger, showing that a group prototypical leader was more effective in building the willingness to contribute to the change than a nonprototypical leader because the group prototypical leader was seen more as an agent of continuity of the organizational identity. In addition, the second study provided further evidence for the role of continuity of identity by manipulating the size of the discontinuity threat (i.e., the extent to which the change could potentially change the organization's identity) and showing that the effect of leader group prototypicality was stronger with greater threat to the continuity of the organizational identity.

Leadership of change is an understudied issue (Yukl, 2002), and these studies, too, in a sense, only scratch the surface of the issues at stake in leadership of change. Even so, they testify to the promise and broader applicability of the social identity approach to leadership. As such, they invite further exploration of the issue from an identity angle.

**Social Identity and Leader Fairness.** There is a long-running academic interest in the psychology of justice (Lind & Tyler, 1988; Thibaut & Walker, 1975). This research has identified the perceived fairness of the outcomes one receives (distributive justice), the procedures used to arrive at these outcomes (procedural justice), and the fairness of interpersonal treatment (interactional justice) as important determinants of people's responses to treatment by and relationships with authorities (Colquitt, Conlon, Wesson, Porter, & Ng, 2001). Only relatively recently, however, has research started to engage with the implications of the fact that in organizational contexts, these authorities are often leaders. The analysis of organizational justice, thus, is very much also an analysis of leader fairness (D. van Knippenberg,

De Cremer, & van Knippenberg, 2007). Indeed, many of the outcomes studied in this area of research, such as follower satisfaction, motivation, cooperation, and performance, can be understood in terms of leadership effectiveness.

Analyses of the psychology of justice have also recognized that there is an important social identity function to fairness, in particular to procedural and interactional fairness (Lind & Tyler, 1988; Tyler & Blader, 2000). The way an authority (e.g., one's leader) chooses to treat one (i.e., procedural and interactional fairness) conveys one's standing with the authority (Koper, van Knippenberg, Bouhuijs, Vermunt, & Wilke, 1993). Recent social identity analyses of fairness have proposed that identification with the group or organization leads one to be more sensitive to procedural fairness because of a greater concern with such social evaluations from one's identity group. In support of this proposition, these studies have shown that the impact of leader procedural fairness is stronger for followers with higher levels of identification (Lind, Kray, & Thompson, 2001; Tyler & De Cremer, 2005).

More firmly integrating research on leader fairness into the social identity analysis of leadership, research also suggests that the trust in group prototypical leaders extends to trust in the leader's fairness (Janson, Levy, Sitkin, & Lind, 2008; van Dijke & De Cremer, 2008). What this also implies is that analogously to the prototypicality group-oriented behavior interactions proposed in the social identity analysis of leadership, leader group prototypicality and leader fairness interact in predicting leadership effectiveness. This is exactly what Janson et al. (2008) proposed and found for leader interactional fairness. Ullrich et al. (2009) obtained similar findings for procedural fairness and, moreover, showed that this interaction was moderated by follower identification, as one would expect if the effect is rooted in social identity.

Janson et al. (2008) also extended this logic to leader group-oriented behavior (self-sacrificial leadership) and showed that self-sacrifice and interactional fairness interacted in such a way that the positive influence of one was attenuated under high levels of the other. De Cremer and van Knippenberg (2002) reported similar findings for the interactive effects of leader self-sacrifice and leader procedural fairness, albeit that their analysis emphasized leadership's role in building follower collective identification (more on this below). In sum, then, a social identity approach to leader fairness seems to offer a viable perspective to advance our understanding of this important aspect of leadership and to more firmly integrate it into other perspectives on leadership (for a review of the literature on leader fairness, see D. van Knippenberg et al., 2007).

Summarizing the key points of the social identity theory of leadership outlined in this and the previous sections, Figure 12.1 captures how leader group prototypicality may have a positive effect on leadership effectiveness, mediated by trust in the leader's group-serving motivation. This relationship is moderated by leader group-serving behavior and leader fairness, which both represent alternative ways in which leaders can instill trust in their group-servingness, and moderated by member group identification and member desire for uncertainty reduction, which both render members more sensitive to the extent to which the leader is group prototypical and represent the shared social reality.

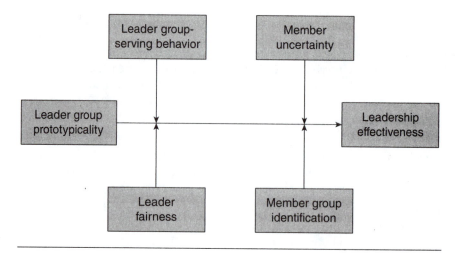

**Figure 12.1**    A Summary of Core Notions of the Social Identity Analysis of Leadership

**Group Versus Leader Prototypicality.** The concept of leader group prototypicality, which is central to the social identity analysis of leadership, can be traced back to categorization theory in cognitive psychology. There is another perspective in leadership that also revolves around the notion of prototypicality, and that also traces its roots back to the same work in cognitive psychology: leadership categorization theory (Lord & Maher, 1991; Chapter 4). The important difference, however, is that leadership categorization theory does not refer to group prototypicality, but to the prototypicality of an abstracted category of leaders (e.g., the leader role)—mental representations capturing the ideal type of a leader. Although leadership categorization theory is the only other leadership theory that explicitly uses the concept of prototypicality, there are a number of similar approaches revolving around individuals' mental representations of leadership that, therefore, may be grouped under the heading of *leadership categorization theories* (D. van Knippenberg & Hogg, 2003). This includes work on implicit leadership theories (Eden & Leviatan, 1975), the romance of leadership (Meindl, Ehrlich, & Dukerich, 1985), role congruity theory of gender and leadership (Eagly & Karau, 2002; Chapter 10), and cross-cultural differences in leadership perceptions.

What all these approaches share is that they are *follower-centric* (Meindl, 1995; Shamir, Pillai, Bligh, & Uhl-Bien, 2007). They put the notion center stage that leadership is in the eye of the beholder. That is, all these approaches, in one way or another, advance the notion that one's understanding of leadership (i.e., one's leadership prototype) is an implicit standard against which (potential) leaders are judged. Individuals with characteristics more prototypical of leaders (i.e., as per the perceiver's implicit understanding of leadership) are more likely to be judged as effective leaders. Eagly and Karau's (2002) role congruity theory, for instance, applies this principle to explain gender biases in leadership perceptions: For many individuals, their implicit leader prototypes emphasize male over female characteristics, which biases their perceptions to see more leadership qualities in male than in female (potential) leaders—even when, objectively, such differential perceptions are unjustified.

The social identity analysis of leadership advances a highly similar process, but the implicit standard differs. Leaders are proposed to be implicitly judged in terms of their group prototypicality rather than their leader prototypicality. Although these propositions seem to be at odds, they are in fact easily reconciled (Lord & Hall, 2003; D. van Knippenberg & Hogg, 2003). A line of research by Hogg and colleagues (Fielding & Hogg, 1997; Hains et al., 1997; Hogg et al., 1998; see also Platow & van Knippenberg, 2001) identifies follower identification as the key moderator of the relative importance of group prototypicality versus leader prototypicality in responses to leadership. With higher follower identification, group prototypicality becomes a more important basis for leadership effectiveness compared to leader prototypicality. More recently, Hogg et al. (2006) showed that this analysis also applies specifically to gender and leadership. When follower identification was high, it was leader group prototypicality that drove perceptions of leadership effectiveness, not leader gender.

Giessner and colleagues extended this integration to the study of responses to leader performance (Giessner et al., 2009; Giessner & van Knippenberg, 2008). Leadership categorization theories have established a tendency to overattribute performance to leadership. That is, people have a tendency to see success as an indicator of good leadership and failure as an indicator of bad leadership, and to discount nonleadership influences on these outcomes (Lord, Binning, Rush, & Thomas, 1978; Meindl et al., 1985). Part of what this means is that leaders will be held responsible for negative outcomes and will, in effect, be judged as poor leaders after failure to achieve collective goals. Giessner and colleagues argued that leader group prototypicality attenuates this tendency. Specifically, they proposed that the greater trust in group prototypical leaders extends to perceptions of the leader's performance, so that group prototypical leaders would suffer less negative leadership evaluations after failure. Their studies supported this proposition. They showed that the attenuating effect of group prototypicality was stronger with higher follower identification and was contingent on the extent to which the performance goal allowed leeway in interpreting leader failure (i.e., when the failure was more ambiguous, group prototypicality was more able to protect the leader against negative evaluations).

Leadership categorization processes are important both because they introduce biases (and therefore issue a warning against relying on subjective assessments of leadership qualities in research as well as practice; Eagly & Karau, 2002; Lord & Maher, 1991) and because they may set the stage for behavioral indicators of leadership effectiveness (i.e., followers are likely to be more open to the influence of leaders they perceive as possessing "the right stuff"). A further integration of group identity and leadership categorization theories may have important value for the development of follower-centric approaches to leadership (cf. D. van Knippenberg, van Knippenberg, & Giessner, 2007) and thus for our understanding of an important aspect of the leadership process.

**Group-Based Versus Interpersonal Leadership.** The social identity analysis of leadership emphasizes the group-based nature of leadership processes more than most other approaches to leadership, with the exception of shared leadership and team leadership. In an interesting counterpoint, there is a long-standing research tradition in leadership that champions the interpersonal, dyadic nature of leadership: leader–member exchange (LMX) theory (Dansereau, Graen, & Haga, 1975; Gerstner & Day, 1997; Graen & Uhl-Bien, 1995). LMX theory builds on the more general social exchange theory of human relations (Homans, 1958) to understand how leader–follower relationship quality develops over time and influences leadership effectiveness. In a nutshell, its basic tenet is that leader–follower relationships are based on the exchange of material (e.g., a bonus) and immaterial (e.g., respect) goods, and that the quality of the leader–follower relationship is captured by the quality of this social exchange. Exchange quality is understood here both in terms of the quality of the goods exchanged (i.e., better relationships involve more exchanges and are of higher value) and in terms of the balance in the exchange. The value of goods received should match the value of goods given (i.e., there should be fairness in the exchange). The quality of the exchange relationship may differ from follower to follower, and therefore a leader may have better relationships with some followers than with others. In LMX theory, it therefore is the interpersonal relationship between leader and follower that is key to leadership effectiveness, not the relationship between leader and followers in terms of their shared group membership.

At first blush, the LMX perspectives may seem in opposition to the social identity analysis. Nonetheless, the integration of these perspectives is relatively straightforward and lies in the moderating role of follower identity. Hogg et al. (2005) demonstrated that social identification moderates the extent to which followers approach the relationship with their leader in interpersonal terms or, rather, in terms of the shared group membership. Consistent with this proposition, their findings indicated that a leadership style of approaching followers in terms of their work group membership as opposed to an interpersonal basis (e.g., exchange quality with the leader) was more effective in that the more followers identified with the group. D. van Knippenberg, van Dick, and Tavares (2007) obtained comparable findings for organizational identification as moderator of the relationship between leader support (a core variable in social exchange analysis of organizational behavior; Rhoades & Eisenberger, 2002) and turnover intentions as an indicator of leadership effectiveness. Leader support (i.e., reflecting the leader's input in the social exchange relationship) was more effective with lower follower identification (i.e., when the relationship presumably was conceived of more in interpersonal terms). It may be noted that studies like these are only a first step toward more fully exploring the potential for integration of these perspectives. But follower identity manifests itself as an important determinant of the relative impact of different leadership processes.

A more recent development is focused on *intergroup leadership*—leadership in situations in which members of multiple groups have to collaborate to realize shared objectives (Hogg, van Knippenberg, & Rast, 2012a). In such situations, leaders may be less able to call upon a shared group membership to mobilize collaborative efforts. The typical notion of invoking a shared superordinate group ("we are all Americans") may often backfire as people either resist the superordinate identity that is seen to deny the group identity that is more self-defining, or project the group identity upon the superordinate identity and judge other groups that deviate from this identity construction negatively ("they are not *real* Americans"; Hogg et al., 2012a). Addressing this issue, Hogg et al. (2012a) argue that such situations call for the construction of an intergroup relational identity and leadership embodying that identity (i.e., being prototypical of the intergroup relational identity). Intergroup relational identity is understood to capture group identity defined in terms of the relationship of the group with other groups. For instance, being a teacher is defined by the teacher–student relationship, and being a nurse can be understood to derive meaning in substantive part by the nurse–doctor relationship. Empirical research addressing these issues should emerge in years to come, but the conceptual work points to the possibility of developing integrative identity theory across the interpersonal, intragroup, and intergroup levels of analysis.

## Leadership as Shaping Identity

Follower identity is not only something that motivates responses to leadership; it is also something that may be affected by leadership. The important thing to realize is that identity is not set in stone. Not only may identity change gradually over time (Sani, 2008), but situational factors may have relatively quick influences on identity. Part of our identity, sometimes referred to as the working self-concept (Lord & Brown, 2004; Markus & Nurius, 1986), is quite fluid and may vary as a function of situational cues. Self-categorization theory's treatment of social identity salience (Turner et al., 1987; note 1) is a case in point, where situational cues (e.g., a threat to the group) may make group identity salient, whereas group identity may withdraw to the background once the situational cues that triggered its activation are no longer present. Aside from this relatively "on-and-off" influence captured by notions of the working self-concept and identity salience, self-conception may also undergo less short-lived changes under the influence of contextual factors. As one's team becomes more successful, for instance, one may increasingly grow to identify with it. Given the important role of identity in motivation and behavior, an important aspect of leadership effectiveness may therefore revolve around leaders' ability to temporarily or more permanently change follower self-conception (Shamir et al., 1993; D. van Knippenberg et al., 2004). Research has highlighted this especially in leadership's influence on collective identification.

One of the core challenges facing leadership is to unite a diverse group of individuals in the pursuit of shared team, organizational, or societal goals, objectives, and missions. Different people have different interests, and it is often not self-evident to individuals that they would prioritize the collective interest over their individual pursuits. Achieving such a transformation of motives (such as from self-interests to collective interests) is key to mobilizing followers' cooperative efforts in realizing collective objectives (Burns, 1978). Along these lines, collective identification may drive the prioritization of collective interest (Ashforth & Mael, 1989). As recognized by social identity analyses of leadership and analyses of charismatic/transformational leadership alike, leadership thus can mobilize and motivate followers for collective endeavors by building follower identification (D. van Knippenberg & Hogg, 2003a).

In line with this analysis, a number of studies show that the effectiveness of aspects of leadership can be explained by their influence on follower identification. For instance, De Cremer and van Knippenberg (2002) established a mediating role for collective identification in a study of the interactive effects of leader self-sacrifice and leader procedural fairness, showing that self-sacrifice and procedural fairness attenuated each other's positive effect on follower cooperation because both resulted in higher follower identification. De Cremer and van Knippenberg (2004) studied the interactive influence of leader self-sacrifice and self-confidence and showed that these aspects of leadership enhanced each other's influence on leadership effectiveness and that these effects were mediated by collective identification.

In combination with the evidence for the moderating role of follower identification in the leadership processes, this suggests a dynamic model in which leadership that builds identification (e.g., group-serving leadership) can set the stage for its future effectiveness. This is not to say that identification is the only process through which leadership is effective, but it does testify to the important role that follower collective identification may play in the leadership process, such as in motivating cooperation and other collective efforts.

These analyses also point to an issue that is far less explored in leadership research: the *content* of the collective identity. As D. van Knippenberg (2000) argued, identification motivates the pursuit of the collective interest, but it is the perception of what is the collective interest that determines if and how identification translates into action (e.g., identification leads to performance only if performance is seen as important to the group). Reicher and Hopkins's (2003) analysis implies that such perceptions can be closely linked to perceptions of the collective identity itself and that leaders can, in this respect, be effective by acting as *entrepreneurs of identity*, actively shaping followers' understanding of what the collective identity is and, by implication, how it is best served (cf. Voss, Cable, & Voss, 2006). This is a process we know far less about, but based on our knowledge about the importance of leadership's influence on follower identification, it seems it should be higher on the research agenda than it currently is.

In relation to this issue, an important element of Reicher and Hopkins's (2003) analysis is that leadership may not only shape followers' understanding of the collective identity, but also affect follower perceptions of leader group prototypicality. Their analysis suggests, for instance, that political leaders like Thatcher, Sukarno, and Gandhi not only derived influence from their group prototypicality, but actively construed a public self-image that conveyed their prototypicality. It is not so much that they just "happened to be" group prototypical, but that they actively contributed to the perception that they were. By and large, however, this work is qualitative and anecdotal, and important contributions are still to be made in complementing this work with quantitative, hypothesis-testing research. Although firmer conclusions should await the outcomes of such research, an important implication is that being an *entrepreneur of identity* not only can make one highly effective as a leader, but may also be a competency that can, to a certain extent, be developed.

Being an entrepreneur of identity may be an aspect of leadership that is of particular importance in the context of group diversity, where it may sometimes be challenging to see what unites and defines the group or what grounds there would be to see the leader as group prototypical. Under such conditions, in particular, it may be an important leadership skill to be able to define group identity in such a way that it is able both to instill a sense of collective identity among group members and to engender the perception that the leader embodies this identity. As perhaps a somewhat extreme example of what this might look like, consider this brief excerpt from an influential speech given by U.S. president John F. Kennedy to an audience in West Berlin at the height of the Cold War, just after the East Germans had added a second barrier behind the original Berlin Wall:

> Two thousand years ago, the proudest boast was *civis Romanus sum*. Today, in the world of freedom, the proudest boast is *Ich bin ein Berliner*. All free men, wherever they may live, are citizens of Berlin, and, therefore, as a free man, I take pride in the words *Ich bin ein Berliner*.

President Kennedy was not born in Berlin and, indeed, was not even German. Out of context, the claim to be a citizen of Berlin—*Ich bin ein Berliner*—would seem to be merely a quaint touch, but what this quote shows is that what President Kennedy was really doing was defining a group—*all free men, wherever they may live*—in which he and his audience share a membership. Especially against the backdrop of the notion, then more salient than ever, that America is the leader of the free world, by proudly claiming to be *ein Berliner*, President Kennedy may have conveyed an image that fed straight into his audience's perception of him as a leader in the context of this shared group membership—as *their* leader.

There is more to identity than collective identification, and other aspects of identity and self-conception may play important roles in leadership. Leadership research has highlighted self-evaluations and, to a more modest extent, future identities. In setting the stage for the following discussion, I note that self-evaluations and future identities are not aspects of identity separate from identifications. Rather, self-evaluations and future identities may be conceived at different levels of self-construal (D. van Knippenberg et al., 2004). At the level of individual identity, self-evaluations and future identities concern the individual as a unique person separate from others; at the level of collective identity, self-evaluations and future identities concern the membership group—identity in the sense of "we." Table 12.1 captures this schematically, quoting the most frequently studied instantiations of self-evaluations and future identities at the individual and collective levels of self-construal.

**Table 12.1**     Aspect of Self/Identity by Level of Self-Construal

|  | *Level of Self-Construal* | |
| --- | --- | --- |
| **Aspect of self** | Individual identity | Collective identity |
| Self-evaluation | Self-esteem, self-efficacy | Collective self-esteem, collective efficacy |
| Self in time | Self-continuity, possible selves | Collective self-continuity, collective possible selves |

## Self-Evaluations and Leadership

People are evaluators. They cannot help passing judgment on virtually anything they encounter, including other people and, indeed, themselves. Self-evaluations play an important role in motivation, and therefore also in leadership. Self-evaluations are typically discussed either as self-esteem, which often tends to emphasize the evaluation of the social self (how well one is regarded by others), or as the more capability-oriented concept of self-efficacy in one's assessments of personal capabilities to accomplish certain goals (Bandura, 1997). However, there is reason to believe that self-esteem and self-efficacy both are instantiations of the higher-order concept of self-evaluations (Judge, Locke, & Durham, 1997). Of particular interest to leadership researchers, and especially in a social identity analysis of leadership, self-evaluations not only capture one's assessment of the individual self (i.e., self-esteem or self-efficacy) but may also capture one's (shared) assessment of the group, the collective self (collective self-esteem; Crocker & Luhtanen, 1990; collective efficacy; Bandura, 1997). Self-evaluations are important to motivation, because higher self-evaluations inspire higher achievement goals.

The implication for leadership is that leadership may derive part of its effectiveness from building follower, individual, and collective self-esteem and self-efficacy, because higher levels of (collective) self-evaluation may inspire more ambitious achievement goals (Shamir et al., 1993). This is shown, for instance, in research on leader procedural fairness (De Cremer et al., 2005), empowering leadership (Mathieu, Ahearne, & Taylor, 2007), and leader self-efficacy (Hoyt, Murphy, Halverson, & Watson, 2003).

An important thing to note, however, is that the evidence that leadership may build follower self-evaluations is more robust than the evidence that higher follower performance follows from leadership's influence on self-evaluations (D. van Knippenberg et al., 2004). A complication is highlighted by the work of Vancouver and colleagues on self-efficacy (e.g., Vancouver, More, & Yoder, 2008). These authors showed that whereas self-efficacy may inspire more ambitious performance goals (which are good for performance), it may simultaneously inspire lower investment of effort (which is bad for performance). That is, high confidence in one's capabilities may actually motivate one to invest less effort, on the assumption that one will be able to achieve one's goals anyway. In relationship to leadership and performance, follower self-evaluations may be somewhat of a double-edged sword.

It would be particularly worthwhile for research to determine the conditions under which leadership's influence on follower self-evaluations can be expected to have desired behavioral effects.

Self-evaluations may also moderate responses to leadership. Research on organizational justice shows that low self-esteem may render individuals more sensitive to authorities' procedural fairness (Vermunt, van Knippenberg, van Knippenberg, & Blaauw, 2001), suggesting the same might hold for leader procedural fairness and follower self-esteem. De Cremer (2003) showed exactly this. Other research more tentatively suggests that follower self-evaluations moderate responses to leadership (e.g., Murphy & Ensher, 1999), but this evidence is far from definitive (D. van Knippenberg et al., 2004). The current state of the science thus suggests that it may be worthwhile to consider follower self-evaluations both as a mediator and as a moderator of leadership effectiveness, but at the same time, it suggests that more definite conclusions should await more conclusive evidence.

# Follower Identity Over Time

I have previously addressed in this chapter the notion of identity change and continuity of identity. This points to a broader issue, which is that there is a temporal dimension to identity. People have a sense of the relationship between their past, present, and future identity, and they value a sense of continuity of identity (Sani, 2008; Shamir et al., 1993). In addition to a sense of continuity of identity, there is another major component to the temporal aspect of identity: Individuals may also have more or less well-defined notions about who they could be in the future (i.e., *possible selves*; Markus & Nurius, 1986). Such selves can take the form of ideal selves (images of who one ideally would be) as well as ought selves (images of who one should be). An ideal self for a young lawyer at a law firm at the start of her career may, for instance, be that of a successful senior partner. The importance of such possible selves lies in the fact that they may motivate and guide goal pursuit. Individuals tend to be more persistent and better at self-regulating their efforts in goal pursuit for goals that are tied to possible selves (Banaji & Prentice, 1994). The better articulated and developed a possible self, the more it may become a "self-guide" and regulate the individual's actions—that is, the more it may become a source of motivation.

Based on these notions regarding the motivating and self-regulating potential of possible selves, Lord et al. (1999) and D. van Knippenberg et al. (2004) have proposed that leadership may be more effective if it can invite follower formation of possible selves that are aligned with collective goals and missions. Building on these conceptual analyses, Stam, van Knippenberg, and Wisse (2010) showed that leader visionary speeches that more explicitly invite followers to form an ideal self that is based on a core vision are more effective in motivating vision-congruent performance (mediated by possible selves), especially for followers with a promotion focus (Higgins, 1987) who are more sensitive to such ideal images. Possible selves, and, more generally, the temporal aspects of the self, are largely uncharted territory in leadership research, providing a clear challenge for future research efforts (see also Stam, Lord, van Knippenberg, & Wisse, 2014).

Possible selves and, more generally, the development of a particular identity over time not only are relevant to understanding the psychology of followers in the leadership process, but also may be of particular relevance to our understanding of the psychology of leaders. As will be discussed in the next section, self-conception as a leader may be an important driver of leader behavior, and among other things, this raises the question of how identity as a leader develops over time.

## Leader Identity

At the core of the identity approach to leadership is the notion that identity shapes perceptions, attitudes, and behavior, and that identity, therefore, may be a powerful motivating force. Clearly, a focus on follower identity is instrumental in understanding leadership effectiveness, but an identity perspective may also be applied to understand what motivates leadership itself—leader identity can also be the focus of inquiry. Although the bottom line for leadership research is leadership effectiveness (i.e., in terms of effects on followers), there is also a long tradition in studying the determinants of leadership. The traditional perspective on these determinants has been a personality perspective (e.g., Judge & Bono, 2000; D. van Knippenberg, 2012), but an identity perspective may be at least as suited to tackle this issue.

In recognition of this, research has recently started to consider the role of leader self and identity in shaping leadership. Some of this work is closely aligned with the social identity analysis of leadership (e.g., D. van Knippenberg et al., 2000) and has emphasized leader identity as a determinant of leader self-serving versus group-serving behavior. Giessner, van Knippenberg, Sleebos, and van Ginkel (2013) showed that self-perceived group prototypicality was positively related to leader group-serving behavior, whereas leaders with low perceived prototypicality were only group-serving to the extent that they felt accountable and identified with the group. Focusing on leader identification with the collective, van Dick, Hirst, Grojean, and Wieseke (2007) demonstrate how leader organizational identification may lay the basis for follower organizational identification.

Identity in terms of the group membership shared with followers is not the only important aspect of leader identity to consider. For leaders, an important part of their identity may also be role related and revolve around the extent to which they conceive of themselves as a leader (cf. the contrast between the social identity analysis and leadership categorization theories)—leader self-definition as a leader or leader role identification (cf. Stets & Burke, 2000). It is not self-evident that people in formal leader roles would see themselves as leaders and would have a strong sense of self that emphasizes that leader role. Leaders differ in the extent to which being a leader is an important part of their identity (Rus, van Knippenberg, & Wisse, 2010). This is no minor point, because just as group identification invites taking group prototypes as a referent, leader role identification may invite taking one's ideal type of a leader as a referent and may influence leader actions.

In a qualitative case study, Kramer (2003) argued that self-conception in terms of the leader role may have a powerful motivating influence on leaders' behavior. Focusing his analysis on U.S. president Lyndon Johnson's decisions concerning America's involvement in Vietnam, Kramer suggests that President Johnson made a number of decisions that were informed more by his conception of what it meant to be a great American president and his self-image as fitting that category than by sound judgment of what would be advisable courses of action (even when President Johnson could be deemed very capable of arriving at these sound judgments). In a quantitative counterpoint to this, Rus et al. (2010) studied self-definition as a leader as a determinant of leader-self versus group-serving behavior. They argued and found that stronger self-definition as a leader invites leaders to rely more on normative information about what good leaders should do or what most leaders would do in making decisions that have consequences along the self-serving versus group-serving continuum.

Studies like these not only suggest that the effects of leader role identification are deserving of more research attention, they also beg the question of what leads to the development of a leader identity (Day & Harrison, 2007; Day, Harrison, & Halpin, 2009). Such development, in fact, need not be restricted to people in a formal leader role—individuals in nonleadership positions, too, may conceive of themselves to a greater or lesser extent in terms of their leadership qualities (van Quaquebeke, van Knippenberg, & Brodbeck, 2011). In that sense, the development of a leader identity can start well before one holds a formal leadership position and may express itself in leadership behavior even when one does not hold a formal leadership position. Lord and Hall (2005) accord the development of possible selves as a leader an important role in leadership development (cf. Ibarra, 1999). That is, it may not be so much seeing oneself as a leader in the present as it is having a future image of the self as a leader that motivates and guides leadership development. A possible self as a leader may invite one to develop the necessary leadership skills and to experiment with leadership behaviors. DeRue and Ashford (2010) argue that in collaborative contexts, this may invite mutually reinforcing processes, in which others' responses to one's leadership attempts may affirm one's emergent leader identity, which in turn may invite other acts of leadership that bolster others' acknowledgment of one's leadership (cf. Ridgeway, 2003).

Part of the challenge of this line of research is that there is good theory and emergent evidence to suggest that the development of leader identity is important, but that such identity development would typically be expected to take place over the course of many years (Day et al., 2009). Accordingly, empirical work to substantiate and stimulate theoretical developments would have to be longitudinal in nature and cover larger time spans than are typically seen in leadership research. Such complications should not discourage researchers from undertaking such endeavors. There is clear promise in furthering the analysis of leadership identity empirically.

Whereas the study of self-definition as a leader revolves around individuals' understanding of what it means to be a leader, a related but different focus is on individuals' assessment of their own capabilities as a leader in the form of leadership self-efficacy (e.g., Anderson, Krajewski, Griffin, & Jackson, 2008; Paglis &

Green, 2002; Singer, 1991). Following the basic self-efficacy logic outlined previously (Bandura, 1997), leaders with higher leadership self-efficacy are expected to engage more proactively with the leadership role and thus to be more effective. There is some evidence suggesting that this may be the case (Chemers, Watson, & May, 2000; Hoyt et al., 2003; Ng, Ang, & Chan, 2008; Paglis & Green, 2002). The same caveat identified earlier also applies here. Specifically, although leadership self-efficacy may fuel leadership ambitions, it does not necessarily mean that leaders with higher leadership self-efficacy will invariably exert greater efforts in pursuit of their goals (Vancouver et al., 2008).

The issue is not just with identity and self-evaluation as a leader, however. Johnson, Venus, Lanaj, Mao, and Chang (2012) show that leader personal and collective identities predict different aspects of leadership—abusive supervision and transformational leadership, respectively. The latter construct suffers from validity issues, but the Johnson et al. study does illustrate the promise of developing theory to link leader identifications to leader behaviors.

Leadership research has a long history of studying leader personality as determinant of leader behavior and leadership effectiveness, and attention to the role of leader identity in this respect is still at an embryonic stage. Even so, given the somewhat modest success of the personality perspective on leadership (Judge, Bono, Ilies, & Gerhardt, 2002; D. van Knippenberg, 2012), it seems worthwhile to explore the possibility that a leader identity perspective may complement the personality perspective and substantially add to our understanding of the determinants of leadership. More research efforts in this area seem clearly warranted.

## The Road Ahead

In leadership, identity matters. Research in the social identity analysis, in particular, has yielded a substantial body of highly consistent results to support that conclusion. This evidence also seems strong enough to warrant further investigation of the less explored issues suggested by this analysis, such as the determinants of leaders' ability and motivation to be an entrepreneur of identity and to actively make the identity dynamics identified in the social identity analysis work for them. In other areas, such as the role of the temporal aspects of the self in leadership effectiveness or of leader identity, analyses are still quite nascent. Given the strong evidence for the viability of other aspects of the identity analysis, it would seem reasonable to suspect promise in these areas too, however, and to invest substantial research efforts in these emerging areas.

The identity perspective on leadership is also a perspective that engages with other perspectives in leadership (e.g., leadership categorization theories, LMX theory), rather than developing in isolation. In that sense, further development of the identity perspective may be instrumental in providing integration in the leadership field and in building more broad-ranging accounts of leadership (D. van Knippenberg & Hogg, 2003). From this perspective, the available evidence in the identity analysis of leadership issues a call for further research in the area.

## Discussion Questions

1. In recent political elections, can you identify evidence that candidates try to use social identity dynamics to mobilize support? What do such tactics look like, and what effects do they appear to have? Do you see evidence that the winning candidate is getting more mileage out of these dynamics than the competition?

2. Reflecting on your work experience, what motivates you? To what extent is this related to how you see yourself, your sense of who you are? If you think of very good and very bad experiences you have had with leadership, to what extent do these speak to your sense of identity? What do the answers to these questions tell you about the identity role of leadership in your own personal work experience?

3. Can you describe your own identity as a leader? Do you have one at this point in your life? If you imagine yourself as a leader, what would you ideally be like? What would it take to achieve this? What do the answers to these questions tell you about the development of (your) role identity as a leader?

## Recommended Reading

- Wright, R. (2010, June 1). Is Steve Jobs big brother? *New York Times Online Opinionator.* https://nyti.ms/2uB37lN

## Recommended Case Study

- **Case:** Mark, K., & Konrad, A. (2005). Anita Jairam at Metropole Services. Richard Ivey School of Business.

## Recommended Video

- Canadian Institute for Advanced Research. (2014). Prof. Alex Haslam on why leaders need to care about group identity. https://www.youtube.com/watch?v=nwcf_E9pUUA

## References

Abrams, D., & Hogg, M. A. (1990). Social identification, self-categorization and social influence. *European Review of Social Psychology, 1,* 195–228.

Anderson, D. W., Krajewski, H. T., Griffin, R. D., & Jackson, D. N. (2008). A leadership self-efficacy taxonomy and its relation to effective leadership. *The Leadership Quarterly, 19,* 595–608.

Ashforth, B. E., & Mael, F. (1989). Social identity theory and the organization. *Academy of Management Review, 14,* 20–39.

Banaji, M. R., & Prentice, D. A. (1994). The self in social contexts. *Annual Review of Psychology, 45,* 297–332.

Bandura, A. (1997). *Self-efficacy: The exercise of self-control.* New York, NY: Freeman.

Burns, J. M. (1978). *Leadership.* New York, NY: Harper & Row.

Chemers, M. M., Watson, C. B., & May, S. (2000). Dispositional affect and leadership effectiveness: A comparison of self-esteem, optimism, and efficacy. *Personality and Social Psychology Bulletin, 26,* 267–277.

Cicero, L., Pierro, A., & van Knippenberg, D. (2007). Leader group prototypicality and job satisfaction: The moderating role of job stress and team identification. *Group Dynamics, 11,* 165–175.

Cicero, L., Pierro, A., & van Knippenberg, D. (2010). Leadership and uncertainty: How role ambiguity affects the relationship between leader group prototypicality and leadership effectiveness. *British Journal of Management, 21,* 411–421.

Colquitt, J. A., Conlon, D. E., Wesson, M. J., Porter, C. O. L. H., & Ng, K. Y. (2001). Justice at the millennium: A meta-analytic review of 25 years of organizational justice research. *Journal of Applied Psychology, 86,* 425–445.

Conger, J. A., & Kanungo, R. N. (1987). Toward a behavioral theory of charismatic leadership in organizational settings. *Academy of Management Review, 12,* 637–647.

Conner, D. R. (1995). *Managing at the speed of change: How resilient managers succeed and prosper where others fail.* New York, NY: Villard Books.

Crocker, J., & Luhtanen, R. (1990). Collective self-esteem and ingroup bias. *Journal of Personality and Social Psychology, 58,* 60–67.

Dansereau, F., Graen, G., & Haga, W. J. (1975). A vertical dyad linkage approach to leadership within formal organizations: A longitudinal investigation of the role making process. *Organizational Behavior and Human Performance, 13,* 46–78.

Day, D. V., & Harrison, M. M. (2007). A multilevel, identity-based approach to leadership development. *Human Resource Management Review, 17,* 360–373.

Day, D. V., Harrison, M. M., & Halpin, S. M. (2009). *An integrative approach to leader development.* New York, NY: Routledge.

De Cremer, D. (2003). Why inconsistent leadership is regarded as procedurally unfair: The importance of social self-esteem concerns. *European Journal of Social Psychology, 33,* 535–550.

De Cremer, D., van Knippenberg, B., van Knippenberg, D., Mullenders, D., & Stinglhamber, F. (2005). Rewarding leadership and fair procedures as determinants of self-esteem. *Journal of Applied Psychology, 90,* 3–12.

De Cremer, D., & van Knippenberg, D. (2002). How do leaders promote cooperation? The effects of charisma and procedural fairness. *Journal of Applied Psychology, 87,* 858–866.

De Cremer, D., & van Knippenberg, D. (2004). Leader self-sacrifice and leadership effectiveness: The moderating role of leader self-confidence. *Organizational Behavior and Human Decision Processes, 95,* 140–155.

De Cremer, D., & van Knippenberg, D. (2005). Cooperation as a function of leader self-sacrifice, trust, and identification. *Leadership and Organization Development Journal, 26,* 355–369.

De Cremer, D., van Knippenberg, D., van Dijke, M., & Bos, A. E. R. (2006). Self-sacrificial leadership and follower self-esteem: When collective identification matters. *Group Dynamics, 10,* 233–245.

De Cremer, D., & van Vugt, M. (1999). Social identification effects in social dilemmas: A transformation of motives. *European Journal of Social Psychology, 29,* 871–893.

De Cremer, D., & van Vugt, M. (2002). Intergroup and intragroup aspects of leadership in social dilemmas: A relational model of cooperation. *Journal of Experimental Social Psychology, 38,* 126–136.

DeRue, D. S., & Ashford, S. J., (2010). Who will lead and who will follow? A social process of leadership identity construction in organizations. *Academy of Management Review, 35,* 627–647.

DeRue, D. S., Ashford, S. J., & Cotton, N. C. (2009). Assuming the mantle: Unpacking the process by which individuals internalize a leader identity. In L. M. Roberts & J. E. Dutton (Eds.), *Exploring positive identities in organizations* (pp. 217–236). New York, NY: Routledge.

Eagly, A. H., & Karau, S. J. (2002). Role congruity theory of prejudice toward female leaders. *Psychological Review, 109,* 573–598.

Eden, D., & Leviatan, V. (1975). Implicit leadership theory as a determinant of the factor structure underlying supervisory behavior. *Journal of Applied Psychology, 60,* 736–741.

Fielding, K. S., & Hogg, M. A. (1997). Social identity, self-categorization, and leadership: A field study of small interactive groups. *Group Dynamics: Theory, Research, and Practice, 1,* 39–51.

Gerstner, C. R., & Day, D. V. (1997). Meta-analytic review of leader–member exchange theory: Correlates and construct issues. *Journal of Applied Psychology, 82,* 827–844.

Giessner, S. R., & van Knippenberg, D. (2008). "License to fail": Goal definition, leader group prototypicality, and perceptions of leadership effectiveness after leader failure. *Organizational Behavior and Human Decision Processes, 105,* 14–35.

Giessner, S. R., van Knippenberg, D., & Sleebos, E. (2009). License to fail? How leader group prototypicality moderates the effects of leader performance on perceptions of leadership effectiveness. *The Leadership Quarterly, 20,* 434–451.

Giessner, S. R., van Knippenberg, D., Sleebos, E. P., & van Ginkel, W. P. (2013). Team-oriented leadership: The interactive effects of leader group prototypicality, accountability, and team identification. *Journal of Applied Psychology, 98,* 658–667.

Graen, G. B., & Uhl-Bien, M. (1995). Relationship-based approach to leadership: Development of leader–member exchange (LMX) theory of leadership over 25 years: Applying a multi-level multi-domain approach. *The Leadership Quarterly, 6,* 219–247.

Hains, S. C., Hogg, M. A., & Duck, J. M. (1997). Self-categorization and leadership: Effects of group prototypicality and leader stereotypicality. *Personality and Social Psychology Bulletin, 23,* 1087–1100.

Haslam, S. A. (2004). *Psychology in organisations: The social identity approach* (2nd ed.). London, UK: Sage.

Haslam, S. A., & Platow, M. J. (2001). Your wish is our command: The role of shared social identity in translating a leader's vision into followers' action. In M. A. Hogg & D. J. Terry (Eds.), *Social identity processes in organizational contexts* (pp. 213–228). Philadelphia, PA: Psychology Press.

Higgins, E. T. (1987). Self-discrepancy: A theory relating self and affect. *Psychological Review, 94,* 319–340.

Hirst, G., van Dick, R., & van Knippenberg, D. (2009). A social identity perspective on leadership and employee creativity. *Journal of Organizational Behavior, 30,* 963–982.

Hogg, M. A. (2001). A social identity theory of leadership. *Personality and Social Psychology Review, 5,* 184–200.

Hogg, M. A. (2003). Social identity. In M. R. Leary & J. P. Tangney (Eds.), *Handbook of self and identity* (pp. 462–479). New York, NY: Guilford.

Hogg, M. A. (2007). Uncertainty-identity theory. In M. P. Zanna (Ed.), *Advances in experimental social psychology* (Vol. 39, pp. 69–126). San Diego, CA: Academic Press.

Hogg, M. A., Fielding, K. S., Johnson, D., Masser, B., Russell, E., & Svensson, A. (2006). Demographic category membership and leadership in small groups: A social identity analysis. *The Leadership Quarterly, 17,* 335–350.

Hogg, M. A., Hains, S. C., & Mason, I. (1998). Identification and leadership in small groups: Salience, frame of reference, and leader stereotypicality effects on leader evaluations. *Journal of Personality and Social Psychology, 75,* 1248–1263.

Hogg, M. A., Martin, R., Epitropaki, O., Mankad, A., Svensson, A., & Weeden, K. (2005). Effective leadership in salient groups: Revisiting leader–member exchange theory from the perspective of the social identity theory of leadership. *Personality and Social Psychology Bulletin, 31,* 991–1004.

Hogg, M. A., van Knippenberg, D., & Rast, D. E., III (2012a). Intergroup leadership in organizations: Leading across group and organizational boundaries. *Academy of Management Review, 37,* 232–255.

Hogg, M. A., van Knippenberg, D., & Rast, D. E., III. (2012b). The social identity theory of leadership: Theoretical origins, research findings, and conceptual developments. *European Review of Social Psychology, 23,* 258–304.

Homans, G. C. (1958). Social behavior as exchange. *American Journal of Sociology, 63,* 597–606.

Hoyt, C. L., Murphy, S. E., Halverson, S. K., & Watson, C. B. (2003). Group leadership: Efficacy and effectiveness. *Group Dynamics: Theory, Research, and Practice, 7,* 259–274.

Ibarra, H. (1999). Provisional selves: Experimenting with image and identity in professional adaptation. *Administrative Science Quarterly, 44,* 764–791.

Janson, A., Levy, L., Sitkin, S., & Lind, A. E. (2008). Fairness and other leadership heuristics: A four-nation study. *European Journal of Work and Organizational Psychology, 17,* 251–272.

Johnson, R. E., Venus, M., Lanaj, K., Mao, C., & Chang, C. H. (2012). Leader identity as an antecedent of the frequency and consistency of transformational, consideration, and abusive leadership behaviors. *Journal of Applied Psychology, 97,* 1262–1272.

Judge, T. A., & Bono, J. E. (2000). Five-factor model of personality and transformational leadership. *Journal of Applied Psychology, 85,* 751–765.

Judge, T. A., Bono, J. E., Ilies, R., & Gerhardt, M. (2002). Personality and leadership: A qualitative and quantitative review. *Journal of Applied Psychology, 87,* 765–780.

Judge, T. A., Locke, E. A., & Durham, C. C. (1997). The dispositional causes of job satisfaction: A core self-evaluations approach. *Research in Organizational Behavior, 19,* 151–188.

Koper, G., van Knippenberg, D., Bouhuijs, F., Vermunt, R., & Wilke, H. (1993). Procedural fairness and self-esteem. *European Journal of Social Psychology, 23,* 313–325.

Kramer, R. M. (2003). The imperatives of identity: The role of identity in leader judgment and decision making. In D. van Knippenberg & M. A. Hogg (Eds.), *Leadership and power: Identity processes in groups and organizations* (pp. 184–196). London, UK: Sage.

Lind, E. A., Kray, L., & Thompson, L. (2001). Primacy effects in justice judgments: Testing predictions from fairness heuristic theory. *Organizational Behavior and Human Decision Processes, 85,* 189–210.

Lind, E. A., & Tyler, T. R. (1988). *The social psychology of procedural justice.* New York, NY: Plenum.

Lord, R. G., Binning, J. F., Rush, M. C., & Thomas, J. C. (1978). The effect of performance cues and leader behavior on questionnaire ratings of leadership behavior. *Organizational Behavior and Human Performance, 21,* 27–39.

Lord, R. G., Brown, D. J., & Freiberg, S. J. (1999). Understanding the dynamics of leadership: The role of follower self-concepts in the leader/follower relationship. *Organizational Behavior and Human Decision Processes, 78,* 1–37.

Lord, R., & Hall, R. (2003). Identity, leadership categorization, and leadership schema. In D. van Knippenberg & M. A. Hogg (Eds.), *Leadership and power: Identity processes in groups and organizations* (pp. 48–64). London, UK: Sage.

Lord, R. G., & Hall, R. J. (2005). Identity, deep structure and the development of leadership skill. *The Leadership Quarterly, 16,* 591–615.

Lord, R. G., & Maher, K. J. (1991). *Leadership and information processing: Linking perceptions and performance.* Boston, MA: Unwin Hyman.

Markus, H., & Nurius, P. (1986). Possible selves. *American Psychologist, 41,* 954–969.

Mathieu, J., Ahearne, M., & Taylor, S. R. (2007). A longitudinal model of leader and salesperson influences on sales force technology use and performance. *Journal of Applied Psychology, 92,* 528–537.

Meindl, J. R. (1995). The romance of leadership as a follower-centric theory: A social constructionist approach. *The Leadership Quarterly, 6,* 329–341.

Meindl, J. R., Ehrlich, S. B., & Dukerich, J. M. (1985). The romance of leadership. *Administrative Science Quarterly, 30,* 78–102.

Murphy, S. E., & Ensher, E. A. (1999). The effects of leader and subordinate characteristics in the development of leader–member exchange quality. *Journal of Applied Social Psychology, 29,* 1371–1394.

Ng, K.-Y., Ang, S., & Chan, K.-Y. (2008). Personality and leader effectiveness: A moderated mediation model of leadership self-efficacy, job demands, and job autonomy. *Journal of Applied Psychology, 93,* 733–743.

Paglis, L. L., & Green, S. G. (2002). Leadership self-efficacy and managers' motivation for leading change. *Journal of Organizational Behavior, 23,* 215–235.

Pierro, A., Cicero, L., Bonaiuto, M., van Knippenberg, D., & Kruglanski, A. W. (2005). Leader group prototypicality and leadership effectiveness: The moderating role of need for cognitive closure. *The Leadership Quarterly, 16,* 503–516.

Pierro, A., Cicero, L., Bonaiuto, M., van Knippenberg, D., & Kruglanski, A. W. (2007). Leader group prototypicality and resistance to organizational change: The moderating role of need for closure and team identification. *Testing, Psychometrics, Methodology in Applied Psychology, 14,* 27–40.

Platow, M. J., Hoar, S., Reid, S., Harley, K., & Morrison, D. (1997). Endorsement of distributively fair and unfair leaders in interpersonal and intergroup situations. *European Journal of Social Psychology, 27,* 465–494.

Platow, M. J., & van Knippenberg, D. (2001). A social identity analysis of leadership endorsement: The effects of leader ingroup prototypicality and distributive inter-group fairness. *Personality and Social Psychology Bulletin, 27,* 1508–1519.

Platow, M. J., van Knippenberg, D., Haslam, S. A., van Knippenberg, B., & Spears, R. (2006). A special gift we bestow on you for being representative of us: Considering leader charisma from a self-categorization perspective. *British Journal of Social Psychology, 45,* 303–320.

Reicher, S., & Hopkins, N. (2003). On the science and art of leadership. In D. van Knippenberg & M. A. Hogg (Eds.), *Leadership and power: Identity processes in groups and organizations* (pp. 197–209). London, UK: Sage.

Rhoades, L., & Eisenberger, R. (2002). Perceived organizational support: A review of the literature. *Journal of Applied Psychology, 87,* 698–714.

Ridgeway, C. L. (2003). Status characteristics and leadership. In D. van Knippenberg & M. A. Hogg (Eds.), *Leadership and power: Identity processes in groups and organizations* (pp. 65–78). London, UK: Sage.

Rousseau, D. M. (1998). Why workers still identify with organizations. *Journal of Organizational Behavior, 19,* 217–233.

Rus, D., van Knippenberg, D., & Wisse, B. (2010). Leader self-definition and leader self-serving behavior. *The Leadership Quarterly, 21,* 509–529.

Sani, F. (2008). *Self-continuity: Individual and collective perspectives.* New York, NY: Psychology Press.

Shamir, B. (1999). Leadership in boundaryless organizations: Disposable or indispensable? *European Journal of Work and Organizational Psychology, 8,* 49–71.

Shamir, B., House, R., & Arthur, M. B. (1993). The motivational effects of charismatic leadership: A self-concept based theory. *Organization Science, 4,* 577–594.

Shamir, B., Pillai, R., Bligh, M. C., & Uhl-Bien M. (2007), *Follower-centered perspectives on leadership: A tribute to the memory of James R. Meindl.* Greenwich, CT: Information Age.

Singer, M. (1991). The relationship between employee sex, length of service and leadership aspirations: A study from valence, self-efficacy and attribution perspectives. *Applied Psychology: An International Review, 40,* 417–436.

Stam, D., Lord, R. G., van Knippenberg, D., & Wisse, B. (2014). An image of who we might become: Vision communication, possible selves, and vision pursuit. *Organization Science, 25,* 1172–1194.

Stam, D., van Knippenberg, D., & Wisse, B. (2010). Focusing on followers: The role of regulatory focus and possible selves in explaining the effectiveness of vision statements. *The Leadership Quarterly, 21,* 457–468.

Stets, J. E., & Burke, P. J. (2000). Identity theory and social identity theory. *Social Psychology Quarterly, 63,* 284–297.

Tajfel, H., & Turner, J. C. (1986). The social identity theory of intergroup behavior. In S. Worchel & W. Austin (Eds.), *Psychology of intergroup relations* (pp. 7–24). Chicago, IL: Nelson-Hall.

Thibaut, J., & Walker, L. (1975). *Procedural justice: A psychological analysis.* Hillsdale, NJ: Lawrence Erlbaum.

Turner, J. C., Hogg, M. A., Oakes, P. J., Reicher, S. D., & Wetherell, M. S. (1987). *Rediscovering the social group: A self-categorization theory.* Oxford, UK: Blackwell.

Tyler, T. R., & Blader, S. (2000). *Cooperation in groups: Procedural justice, social identity, and behavioral engagement.* Philadelphia, PA: Psychology Press.

Tyler, T. R., & De Cremer, D. (2005). Process-based leadership: Fair procedures and reactions to organizational change. *The Leadership Quarterly, 16,* 529–545.

Ullrich, J., Christ, O., & van Dick, R. (2009). Substitutes for procedural fairness: Prototypical leaders are endorsed whether they are fair or not. *Journal of Applied Psychology, 94,* 235–244.

van Dick, R., Hirst, G., Grojean, M. W., & Wieseke, J. (2007). Relationships between leader and follower organizational identification and implications for follower attitudes and behaviour. *Journal of Occupational and Organizational Psychology, 80,* 133–150.

van Dijke, M., & De Cremer, D. (2008). How leader prototypicality affects followers' status: The role of procedural fairness. *European Journal of Work and Organizational Psychology, 17,* 226–250.

van Knippenberg, B., & van Knippenberg, D. (2005). Leader self-sacrifice and leadership effectiveness: The moderating role of leader prototypicality. *Journal of Applied Psychology, 90,* 25–37.

van Knippenberg, D. (2000). Work motivation and performance: A social identity perspective. *Applied Psychology: An International Review, 49,* 357–371.

van Knippenberg, D. (2011). Embodying who we are: Leader group prototypicality and leadership effectiveness. *Leadership Quarterly, 22,* 1078–1091.

van Knippenberg, D., De Cremer, D., & van Knippenberg, B. (2007). Leadership and fairness: The state of the art. *European Journal of Work and Organizational Psychology, 16,* 113–140.

van Knippenberg, D., Haslam, S. A., & Platow, M. J. (2007). Unity through diversity: Value-in-diversity beliefs as moderator of the relationship between work group diversity and group identification. *Group Dynamics, 11,* 207–222.

van Knippenberg, D., & Hogg, M. A. (2003). A social identity model of leadership effectiveness in organizations. *Research in Organizational Behavior, 25,* 243–295.

van Knippenberg, D., & Schippers, M. C. (2007). Work group diversity. *Annual Review of Psychology, 58,* 515–541.

van Knippenberg, D., van Dick, R., & Tavares, S. (2007). Social identity and social exchange: Identification, support, and withdrawal from the job. *Journal of Applied Social Psychology, 37,* 457–477.

van Knippenberg, D., van Knippenberg, B., & Bobbio, A. (2008). Leaders as agents of continuity: Self continuity and resistance to collective change. In F. Sani (Ed.), *Self-continuity: Individual and collective perspectives* (pp. 175–186). New York, NY: Psychology Press.

van Knippenberg, D., van Knippenberg, B., De Cremer, D., & Hogg, M. A. (2004). Leadership, self, and identity: A review and research agenda. *The Leadership Quarterly, 15,* 825–856.

van Knippenberg, D., van Knippenberg, B., & Giessner, S. R. (2007). Extending the follower-centered perspective: Leadership as an outcome of shared social identity. In B. Shamir, R. Pillai, M. C. Bligh, & M. Uhl-Bien (Eds.), *Follower-centered perspectives on leadership: A tribute to the memory of James R. Meindl* (pp. 51–70). Greenwich, CT: Information Age.

van Knippenberg, D., van Knippenberg, B., Monden, L., & de Lima, F. (2002). Organizational identification after a merger: A social identity perspective. *British Journal of Social Psychology, 41,* 233–252.

van Knippenberg, D., van Knippenberg, B., & van Dijk, E. (2000). Who takes the lead in risky decision making? Effects of group members' individual riskiness and prototypicality. *Organizational Behavior and Human Decision Processes, 83,* 213–234.

van Quaquebeke, N., van Knippenberg, D., & Brodbeck, F. C. (2011). More than meets the eye: The role of subordinates' self-perceptions in leader categorization processes. *Leadership Quarterly, 22,* 367–382.

Vancouver, J. B., More, K. M., & Yoder, R. J. (2008). Self-efficacy and resource allocation: Support for a discontinuous model. *Journal of Applied Psychology, 93,* 35–47.

Vermunt, R., van Knippenberg, D., van Knippenberg, B., & Blaauw, E. (2001). Self-esteem and outcome fairness: Differential importance of procedural and outcome considerations. *Journal of Applied Psychology, 86,* 621–628.

Voss, Z. G., Cable, D. M., & Voss, G. B. (2006). Organizational identity and firm performance: What happens when leaders disagree about "who we are"? *Organization Science, 17,* 741–755.

Yukl, G. (2002). *Leadership in organizations* (5th ed.). New York, NY: Prentice Hall.

# CHAPTER 13

# Leadership, Culture, and Globalization

*Deanne N. Den Hartog*

*Marcus W. Dickson*

---

## Opening Case: A Day in the Life of a Leader

When the multinational, Berlin-based auto parts manufacturer acquired the company she worked for in her native Colombia, Nathalie wasn't worried. She had risen steadily through the ranks, and felt ready for her management position. She had presumed it would be an easy transition, because she knew the industry well. However, she now managed manufacturing operations in several different countries, overseeing a "team" of plant managers. *Team* felt like the wrong term, as their geographic separation implied that most team communication happened through e-mail, with only occasional videoconference meetings of the whole group. Additionally, because of time zone differences, Nathalie only actually *spoke* to some plant managers, but with others—who worked while she slept—Nathalie had less of a personal connection. Consequently, there wasn't much of a "team feeling" so much as there were independent relationships between Nathalie and her plant managers around the world.

Today's challenges included getting information and input from her team, and building consensus on how to move forward. Nathalie had sent out draft budget projections for the unit, and asked team members to provide feedback. Three new e-mails in her inbox highlighted Nathalie's frustrations. The first, from Lingfei at a plant outside Tokyo, recommended further team discussions about the budget projections Nathalie had shared. Nathalie sensed that Lingfei didn't agree with the projections, but the e-mail never quite said that. The second e-mail, from Hasan in Indonesia, seemed vague, saying nothing about what he thought of the budgeting process, or whether the projections were remotely accurate. The third, from Christopher in England, clearly expressed frustration that the budgeting process was taking longer than scheduled, and seemed not to follow the company's standard budgeting process, because of Susan's efforts to get input from the rest of the team. Christopher e-mailed that "time is money, you know." A fourth team member, Cyrille from France, had not replied by the requested deadline . . . again.

Nathalie sighed as she looked over these e-mails. Her boss in Berlin told her yesterday that she needed to take command of her team and provide clear and consistent direction. Though she was trying, that approach was just so foreign to her. She was used to building consensus in teams with strong relationships and personal loyalty. Those sorts of relationships seemed to form naturally "back home," but hadn't happened now, and Nathalie wasn't sure where to start. She sensed issues weren't just related to specific team members, but instead to the cultures they came from. Should she try to change her style to meet their preferences, or change them to meet hers?

### Discussion Questions

1.  How can Nathalie think about cultural differences that might be affecting her team without resorting to cultural stereotyping?

2.  Does the lack of face-to-face communication contribute to Nathalie's problem? If so, how?

3.  If we believe that cultural value differences are affecting the team's efforts, what should be Nathalie's next steps?

# Chapter Overview

Although business is done all over the globe, differences exist in what is seen as acceptable or effective behavior around the world. Cultural differences in what is considered effective leadership also clearly exist. There are many political leaders who are immensely popular in their home countries for reasons that people in other areas of the world do not understand. Similarly, managers who succeed in their home countries often struggle when they become expatriates. What leaders do is influenced by what is customary in their environment, and what people from different backgrounds expect from leaders reflects the values held in their groups. Cultural values are defined as a set of beliefs and norms—often anchored in the morals, laws, customs, and practices of a society—that define what is right and wrong and specify general preferences (e.g., Adler, 2002).

Globalization of business means that leaders increasingly need to deal with people from different cultures (e.g., Javidan, Dorfman, DeLuque, & House, 2006).

In addition, in many countries, the workforce is growing more culturally diverse. Thus, people from different cultures increasingly come into contact at work, and leaders need to convincingly present the organization's vision to a diverse multicultural workforce in an unpredictable and increasingly global environment. Leaders thus need to act in a culturally sensitive manner. Insight into leadership in different cultures can thus be of use to managers doing business in another culture or working in multicultural settings.

Leadership as a function in human groups is found all over the world, and stories emphasizing the importance of leadership are found throughout history (e.g., Bass & Bass, 2008). Leadership everywhere has to do with disproportionate influence, and the leadership role is associated with power and status. For example, Pickenpaugh (1997) assessed symbols of leadership in traditional cultures from the Pacific Islands, sub-Saharan Africa, and lowland South America and found that their leaders (kings, chiefs) often wear necklaces of large canine teeth from the most powerful and ferocious animals in their respective environments. Elsewhere, power and status may be conveyed through such things as job titles, business cards, office size, or other symbols recognizable as status and power related by those witnessing them (e.g., Gupta, de Luque, & House, 2004).

In this chapter, we focus on organizational leadership around the globe. However, when looking at leadership cross-culturally, it is important to remember that concepts such as leadership, participation, or cooperation do not mean the same thing in every cultural context. As cultures vary, so too do the institutions within those cultures, and leadership as a central component of institutional functioning does as well (Dickson, Den Hartog, & Castaño, 2009). For instance, in the "West," participation usually refers to having influence on a decision, whereas in Japan it refers to the consensus-oriented approach, bottom-up procedures, and lobby consultations of the *ringi* system (Steers, Nardon, & Sanchez-Runde, 2009).

Even the term *leadership* itself can be interpreted differently across cultures. *Leader* and *leadership* have a positive connotation in Anglo-Saxon countries, conjuring up heroic images of outstanding individuals. However, elsewhere the direct translation of *leader* may invoke images of dictatorship. Other translation issues abound. For example, in egalitarian societies literally translating *follower* or *subordinate* may be less appropriate: In the Netherlands, subordinates are typically referred to as *medewerkers* or coworkers, not subordinates (Dickson et al., 2009). Such examples show that even with careful attention to translation, there may be unrecognized, subtle nuances of meaning that vary across languages and cultures. This poses obvious measurement problems: How can we be sure we are even measuring the same construct? If we are not, to what should found differences be attributed? This forms a concern in all cross-cultural research, including leadership research.

The Global Leadership and Organizational Behavior Effectiveness (GLOBE) Project is a large-scale research project designed to assess both similarities and differences in the cultural semantic definition of leadership. GLOBE defined leadership as "the ability of an individual to influence, motivate, and enable others to contribute toward the effectiveness and success of the organizations of which they are members." This intentionally broad definition of leadership was acceptable to a group of leadership scholars representing a wide range of cultures, while allowing for its culture-specific nature (e.g., Den Hartog et al., 1999; House et al., 2004; House, Dorfman, Javidan, Hanges, & DeLuque, 2014). In other words, while leadership exists everywhere, what is seen as effective leader behavior may vary in different societies, resulting in different leader behaviors and practices.

An older study on how people can be prepared for future leadership roles can illustrate this. Stewart, Barsoux, Kieser, Ganter, and Walgenbach (1994) compared the education and careers of British and German middle managers. In Britain, talented graduates of any discipline were recruited for management careers. In Germany, management was perceived more functionally, and a direct relationship between the content of vocational training and the job was more common. In career development, the British emphasized mobility, variety, and generalized knowledge and skills. Companies prepared their future leaders through frequent changes of jobs and functions. In contrast, in Germany less emphasis on mobility existed. Managers spent more time in each job, and development of specialized expertise was valued. These different approaches in developing leaders reflect differences in ideas on what makes leaders effective in these cultures.

Below, we present examples of studies on leader behavior from around the globe. To date, leadership theorizing has been strongly influenced by North American values. However, these values are not necessarily shared in other cultures. Thus, we describe different dimensions of societal cultures and the ways in which they might lead to differences in approaching leadership and discuss leadership perceptions around the world, showing similarities and differences in the way people view effective leadership across cultures.

## Leadership Research in Different Countries

Most leadership research to date was conducted in North America and Western Europe (e.g., Dickson, Castaño, Magomaeva, & Den Hartog, 2012). During the last two decades, leadership was also investigated in regions of the world that traditionally did not study leadership much. For example, Bealer and Bhanugopan (2014) studied transformational and transactional leadership in the United Arab Emirates; Pellegrini and Scandura (2006) studied leader–member exchange (LMX) and delegation in Turkey; and Chen, Eberly, Chiang, Farh, and Cheng (2014) addressed paternalistic leadership in China. Many such leadership studies in non-Western regions of the world are carried out in a single country.

Comparative leadership research is also done, although studies often only compare small numbers of countries. For example, using GLOBE data, Abdalla and Al-Homoud (2001) compared Kuwaitis' and Qataris' views of outstanding leadership and found these groups stress similar characteristics (e.g., integrity; visionary, inspirational, administrative skills; and performance orientation). Many other examples of smaller comparative studies exist (e.g., Bu, Craig, & Peng, 2001; Wanasika, Howell, Littrell, & Dorfman, 2011). Some comparative studies assess differences between groups with a different cultural background within a certain country, as managers from different cultural backgrounds may (not) demonstrate different leader behaviors. For example, Xin and Tsui (1996) compared influence styles of Asian American and Caucasian American managers and found only minor differences. This highlights that people need not behave differently in leadership roles solely based on ethnicity or country of origin. Though cultural values influence behavior, so do individual differences.

An example of a more elaborate project involving more than 40 countries is the research on event management (e.g., Smith, Peterson, & Schwartz, 2002). In handling events, managers can use different sources of information and meaning (e.g., rules/regulations; national norms; widespread beliefs; information from superiors, peers, or subordinates; unwritten rules). Preferences differ across nations. For example, participation-oriented sources of guidance such as relying on subordinates were found mostly in Western Europe. Managers from other regions such as Africa tended to rely on more hierarchically oriented sources of information such as superiors and rules. Managers in yet other countries relied more strongly on widespread beliefs as a source of guidance (Smith et al., 2002).

Finally, some work focuses on "global leadership" (e.g., Mendenhall et al., 2012). Global leadership research has a somewhat different focus than comparative cross-cultural leadership research and more holistically tries to understand who global leaders are, what they do, and how the environment they operate in affects them. This work suggests that requirements for leaders to be effective in a global context include developing multicultural effectiveness, learning to manage paradoxes, and appreciating every individual's uniqueness in the context of cultural differences (Dickson et al., 2012). Several measures relating to global leadership or global leader mindsets have now been developed, although because these constructs are still being debated, defined, and developed, the focus of these measures differs. An example is the Global Mindset Inventory (Javidan & Teagarden, 2012), which assesses several elements of an individual's intellectual capital, psychological capital, and social capital related to experiences and relationships across cultures. Below, we focus on cross-cultural leadership and comparative studies.

## North American Bias

The applicability of theories and concepts developed in one part of the world should not be taken for granted elsewhere, and although leadership studies are now conducted in many countries, there is still a North American bias in leadership models and measures. That is, "individualistic rather than collectivistic; emphasizing assumptions of rationality rather than aesthetics, religion, or superstition; stated in terms of individual rather than group incentives; stressing follower responsibilities rather than rights; assuming hedonistic rather than altruistic motivation and assuming centrality of work and democratic value orientation" (House, 1995, p. 443). Many cultures do not share these assumptions. Careful consideration of cultural differences and how these affect the meaning, enactment, and effectiveness of leader behaviors is needed when applying leadership models around the globe.

An example of a widely used construct/measure of U.S. origin is Bass and colleagues' Multifactor Leadership Questionnaire (MLQ), tapping transactional and transformational leadership (e.g., Antonakis, Avolio, & Sivasubramaniam, 2003).

This questionnaire is used in countries around the globe, and findings show that a preference for transformational leadership exists in most cultures and that it generally correlates more positively with positive outcomes than transactional leadership (Bass, 1997). For example, a study among bank employees in the United States, China, and India showed that transformational leadership related positively to follower efficacy, commitment, and satisfaction in all three samples (Walumbwa, Lawler, Avolio, Wang, & Shi, 2005). Yet the items in the MLQ are phrased rather abstractly and such leadership does not necessarily look exactly the same in different cultures, as it can be enacted in different ways (e.g., Dickson et al., 2012). For example, charismatic leaders articulate an ideological message, set a personal example, and convey self-confidence—resulting in being trusted and respected by their followers. However, charisma can be shown highly assertively (e.g., Winston Churchill) or in a quiet, nonaggressive manner (e.g., Aung San Suu Kyi). Thus, although concepts such as transformational leadership may be universally valid, specific behaviors shown may vary. For instance, "Indonesian inspirational leaders need to persuade their followers about the leaders' own competence, a behavior that would appear unseemly in Japan" (Bass, 1997, p. 132). Transformational leadership may also take more or less participative forms (Bass & Bass, 2008), which is likely linked to societal norms and values regarding the distribution of power. In an egalitarian society such as the Netherlands, transformational leader behaviors correlate highly with participation (Den Hartog et al., 1999). Thus, in egalitarian societies, to be seen as transformational, leaders may allow more participation than in high power distance societies, where transformational leadership may more readily take a directive form.

One major study assessing leadership preferences and behaviors in many cultures is the GLOBE Project, directed toward the development of knowledge concerning how societal and organizational cultures affect leadership and organizational practices (House et al., 2004, 2014). In the first GLOBE study, teams of researchers from some 62 different countries from all over the world participated. Measures of culture and leadership preferences were developed. Over 17,000 middle managers from 800 organizations described leader attributes and behavior that they perceived to enhance or impede outstanding leadership. The latest GLOBE study in 24 societies focused on how societal culture influences expected leadership behaviors and whether success depends on the match of CEO leadership to these societal expectations (House et al., 2014). The results of these studies were reported in articles (e.g., Den Hartog et al., 1999; Dorfman et al., 2012) and books (Chhokar, Brodbeck, & House, 2007; House et al., 2004, 2014). At various points below, GLOBE results are described.

## Dimensions of Societal Culture Related to Leadership

Culture forms a set of relatively stable, basic, and shared practices and values that help human social groups or societies find solutions to fundamental problems. Schein (1992) focused on two such challenges, namely, how to survive, grow, and adapt to the environment and how to achieve sufficient internal integration to permit daily functioning and ensure the ability to adapt and survive. When people come together as a group, they develop shared beliefs and assumptions about the world and the people in it. These beliefs help the group survive. Value orientations, beliefs, and assumptions refer to the basic nature of people, human relationships, as well as relationships with nature, time, and activity (e.g., Hofstede, 2001; Kluckhohn & Strodtbeck, 1961; Nardon & Steers, 2009; Schwartz, 1999).

One way to study culture is through culture dimensions. Several typologies of societal culture dimensions have been developed. The most widely known is Hofstede's (1980, 2001) framework. His original study (among IBM employees in over 40 countries) identified four culture dimensions: power distance, uncertainty avoidance, masculinity–femininity, and collectivism–individualism. Later, long-/ short-term orientation and indulgence/restraint were added. See Table 13.1 for descriptions of these dimensions.

Hofstede's work has been criticized for presenting an overly simplistic, dimensional conceptualization of culture, the original sample coming from a single multinational corporation, culture being malleable over time, measures being not

**Table 13.1**   Hofstede's Culture Dimensions and Their Descriptions

| *Dimension* | *Meaning* |
|---|---|
| Power distance | • The extent to which a society accepts and embraces power in institutions and organizations being distributed unequally. |
| Uncertainty avoidance | • The extent to which a society feels threatened by uncertain and ambiguous situations and tries to avoid these situations by providing greater (career) stability, establishing formal rules, rejecting deviant ideas and behaviors, and believing in absolute truths and the attainment of expertise. |
| Masculinity–femininity | • The extent to which a society mostly has "masculine" values such as assertiveness and toughness, competitiveness, and material achievement or "feminine" ones such as concern for others, quality of relationships, quality of life, and care for the weak. |
| Collectivism–individualism | • How society views the desirability of interdependence versus independence. In collectivist societies, people are expected to place the interest of the collective before personal interest, whereas in individualist societies people are expected to take care of themselves and look after their own interest. |
| Long-/short-term orientation | • How society views time and the importance of past, present, and the future. Long-term orientation stresses the future, persistence, thrift, and perseverance. Short-term orientation focuses on the present or past, valuing traditions, fulfilling social obligation, immediate gratification, and saving face. |
| Indulgence/restraint | • The extent to which society endorses pursuit of "the good things in life." Indulgent cultures allow/support individuals following their impulse and focus energy on building and maintaining friendships. In restrained cultures fulfilling one's duty is more celebrated than pursuing one's impulses, and friendships are subordinate to meeting one's obligations. |

SOURCE: Based on Hofstede (1980, 2001, 2011).

sufficiently well developed, and ignoring within-country cultural heterogeneity (see e.g., Sivakumar & Nakata, 2001; McSweeney, 2002, for critiques; see Kirkman, Lowe, & Gibson, 2006, for an overview of research using Hofstede's dimensions). Below, we discuss Hofstede's four original dimensions alongside several others proposed by GLOBE or others. The GLOBE study has also received some criticism (see, e.g., Hofstede, 2006, and the rejoinder by Javidan, House et al., 2006; Peterson & Castro, 2006, and the rejoinder by Hanges & Dickson, 2006). For example, Hofstede (2006) criticizes GLOBE's measurement. GLOBE views culture as consisting of both (1) values, that is, what is considered desirable in society, as well as (2) practices, that is, actual ways in which members of a culture go about dealing with their collective challenges (e.g., Javidan, House, et al., 2006). Although, theoretically, cultural values are often proposed to drive cultural practices (e.g., Hofstede, 2001), that assumption had not been tested yet. GLOBE aimed to construct measures that would allow for that.

Cultural practices and values were measured using isomorphic items. For example, a cultural practice item of the power distance dimension (reverse coded) is:

In this society, power is . . .

| 1 | 2 | 3 | 4 | 5 | 6 | 7 |
|---|---|---|---|---|---|---|
| *concentrated at the top* | | | | | | *shared throughout the society* |

The related value question is:

In this society, power should be . . .

| 1 | 2 | 3 | 4 | 5 | 6 | 7 |
|---|---|---|---|---|---|---|
| *concentrated at the top* | | | | | | *shared throughout the society*[1] |

Unexpectedly, for six of the nine culture dimensions investigated by GLOBE, correlations between values and practices dimensions were negative. The most notable relationships between values and practices are seen in societies with practice scores in the extreme regions, either high or low. For example, societies with the lowest future orientation practices scores show the highest upward move in their aspirations. In contrast, societies with the highest assertiveness orientation practices show the largest downward move in their aspirations. Javidan, House, et al. (2006) thus concluded that the assumption of a simple linear relationship between values and practices does not hold.

Note that negative correlations between the practices and values scores do not mean that a score above the midpoint (i.e., 4) on the one is associated with a score below the midpoint (i.e., 4) on the other. For example, respondents from virtually all societies report a higher value score on performance orientation than their practices score. The average values score is 5.94 and the average practice score is 4.10,

---

1. Similar questions assessed culture at the organizational level of analysis.

yet they correlate negatively. The negative correlation occurs because for societies with higher practices scores the increment desired is smaller than for those with lower practices scores. This holds for performance orientation, future orientation, humane orientation, and in a reverse sense for power distance (societies prefer less power distance). The interpretation of the cultural practices scales is thus easier than that of the values scales.

## Masculinity

Having an aggressive attitude in the "Western" business world has a relatively positive connotation. Aggressive implies being tough, fast, and forceful, as opposed to weak and vulnerable (Den Hartog, 2004). According to Hofstede (2001), "aggressive" carries a positive connotation only in masculine countries. Hofstede described differences between "masculine" versus "feminine" societies in the desirability of assertive and tough behavior versus modest and tender behavior. Doney, Cannon, and Mullen (1998) contrasted masculinity and femininity in terms of valuing individual achievement versus norms for solidarity and service, a norm for confrontation versus cooperation, and norms stressing independent thought and action versus honoring moral obligations. Hofstede linked this dimension to gender differences. High cultural masculinity characterizes societies in which men are expected to be tough and women to be tender. Femininity characterizes societies where both men and women are expected to be modest and tender. Hofstede (2001) holds that masculine and feminine cultures create different leader hero types. The masculine manager is assertive, aggressive, and decisive. Conversely, the hero in feminine cultures seeks consensus, is less visible, and is intuitive rather than tough and decisive.

One critique of masculinity–femininity is that it includes too many different topics (e.g., gender role division, assertiveness in social relationships, being humane or focused on quality of life, being performance/achievement-oriented). In the GLOBE study, these are measured separately with dimensions labeled assertiveness, gender egalitarianism, performance orientation, and humane orientation. For instance, GLOBE assertiveness is defined as the degree to which individuals in societies are assertive, dominant, and aggressive in social relationships (Den Hartog, 2004). Assertiveness is linked to the preferred use of language in society. Assertiveness is a style of responding that implies making one's wants known to others, which is why in assertive cultures, being direct and unambiguous is acceptable. For example, a negative relationship between assertiveness and indirect language use exists in the United States and conversational indirectness correlates negatively with social desirability (Holtgraves, 1997). Thus, in assertive societies, people will tend to be direct, clear, and explicit. In less assertive cultures, a less direct manner of responding may be valued and indirect, more ambiguous, and subtle communication is typical. Being indirect can be linked to "face management." People are motivated to collectively manage each other's face or public identity, and they do this by phrasing remarks politely and indirectly (Den Hartog, 2004).

## Uncertainty Avoidance

Uncertainty avoidance describes a society's reliance on social norms and procedures to alleviate the unpredictability of the future and refers to the extent to which members in a society feel uncomfortable with and try to avoid ambiguous and uncertain situations (e.g., Hofstede, 2001). In high uncertainty avoidance societies, people tend to prefer (career) stability and formal rules, whereas people from low uncertainty avoidance cultures tend to prefer more flexibility in roles and jobs and are more mobile regarding jobs. High uncertainty avoidance countries also foster a belief in experts (Hofstede, 2001). The aforementioned study by Stewart et al. (1994) comparing managerial careers in Germany and the United Kingdom illustrates. Germany ranks high and the United Kingdom low on uncertainty avoidance, a difference reflected in the managers' typical career patterns where the British emphasized mobility, whereas the Germans valued developing expertise by staying longer in a job. Also, British managers emphasized resourcefulness and improvisation, whereas German managers expected reliability, punctuality, strict planning, and sticking to agreed plans. In Germany, business plans are highly detailed. Customers prefer such planning and expect transactions to be adhered to by the letter, on time, and as agreed. Meeting customer expectations is linked to careful and detailed planning. In contrast, in Ireland (low uncertainty avoidance), customers have less respect for plans, show unplanned behavior themselves, and expect high flexibility. Planning too much is seen as rendering business owners inflexible and making it harder to meet customer demands. Rauch, Frese, and Sonnentag (2000) compared German and Irish entrepreneurs running small companies and found that the influence of detailed planning on small-business success was positive in Germany and negative in Ireland.

Shane (1993) found that uncertainty-accepting societies are more innovative than are uncertainty-avoiding societies. Shane, Venkataraman, and MacMillan (1995) examined the relationship between culture dimensions and preferences for innovation championing strategies in 30 countries. When uncertainty avoidance was high, people preferred champions to work through organizational norms, rules, and procedures to promote innovation, whereas in uncertainty-accepting societies, champions' efforts to overcome organizational inertia to innovation by violating organizational rules and regulations were endorsed more.

## Relationships With Others: Collectivism

Another well-known culture dimension is individualism versus collectivism. Hofstede (2001) described cultures characterized by *individualism* as loosely knit social frameworks in which people are supposed to take care of themselves and look after their own interests and those of their close families only. In contrast, a tight social framework in which people distinguish between in-groups and out-groups is the key characteristic of cultures high on collectivism. In-groups are cohesive and strong. People expect their in-group to look after them throughout life and, in exchange, feel they owe the in-group absolute loyalty, including looking out for others in the in-group.

Schwartz (1999) has a slightly different approach, focusing on the extent to which people are autonomous versus embedded in the group. In cultures high on embeddedness, people are perceived as part of the collective, and they find meaning and direction in life through participating in the group and identifying with its goals. Organizations tend to take responsibility for members in all domains of life and, in return, expect members to identify with and work toward organizational goals. In contrast, individuals in autonomous cultures are perceived as autonomous entities who find meaning in life through their uniqueness.

Schwartz (1999) further distinguished between intellectual autonomy (i.e., individuals are encouraged to follow their own ideas and intellect) and affective autonomy (i.e., people are encouraged to independently find positive experiences for themselves). In cultures that emphasize intellectual autonomy, organizations and their leaders are more likely to treat their members as independent actors with their own interests, preferences, abilities, and allegiances. Employees are typically granted autonomy and encouraged to generate their own ideas and act on them (Sagiv & Schwartz, 2000). In a 47-nation study, Schwartz and Sagie (2000) found that socioeconomic development and democratization increased the importance of independent thought and action, openness to change, concern for the welfare of others, and self-indulgence, and decreased the importance of conformity, tradition, and security.

## Hierarchy, Status, and Power Distance

Within all societies, there are status and power differentials. These are obviously related to leadership. Power distance is related to a concentration of authority (Hofstede, 2001). In cultures with a large power distance, organizations typically have many layers and the chain of command is very important. In high power distance societies, leaders who contribute to society may be revered and emulated by others in the culture, whereas more egalitarian societies emphasize the role of the leader less (Dickson et al., 2012).

In high power distance countries, subordinates are typically more reluctant to challenge their supervisors than are employees in low power distance countries. Employees in high power distance cultures have been found to be more fearful in expressing disagreement with their managers (Adsit, London, Crom, & Jones, 2001). For example, people in high power distance countries are less likely to provide negative feedback to superiors informally. Furthermore, the idea that subordinates would be allowed to provide ratings of their leader (e.g., 360-degree feedback systems) is also more likely to be rejected in high power distance countries, as this may be perceived as threatening status positions (Kirkman & Den Hartog, 2004). How managers typically handle events also relates to power distance. Smith et al. (2002) show that managers in high power distance countries report more use of rules and procedures and less reliance on subordinates or their own experience in dealing with everyday events than are managers from more egalitarian countries.

Authoritarian leadership and autocratic decision making are likely to be accepted and expected in high power distance cultures. In egalitarian cultures, employees expect to have a say in decisions affecting their work. Hofstede (2001) reported that subordinates in high power distance countries saw their managers primarily as well-meaning autocrats, whereas subordinates in low power distance countries saw them primarily as resourceful democrats. Shane et al. (1995) found that the greater the power distance in a society, the more people preferred innovation champions to focus on gaining the support of those in authority before other actions are taken on an innovation (rather than on building a broad base of support for new ideas among organization members).

An issue confronting any society is how to guarantee the necessary responsible behavior of its members (Schwartz, 1999). Hierarchical cultures rely on hierarchical systems of ascribed roles and perceive the unequal distribution of power as legitimate. Individuals are socialized to comply with their roles as well as the rules and obligations attached to their position in society. Organizations emphasize top-down goal setting, the chain of authority, and well-defined roles in a hierarchical structure. Employees are expected to comply and put the interests of the organization before their own. In contrast, egalitarian cultures encourage people to view each other as moral equals. Organizations emphasize cooperative negotiation, and employees flexibly enact roles as they try to attain organizational goals. Leaders motivate others by enabling them to share in goal setting and by appealing to them to act on behalf of the joint welfare of all (Sagiv & Schwartz, 2000).

Relatedly, research addressed the willingness to accept supervisory direction. For example, Bu et al. (2001) compared the tendency to accept a supervisor's direction among Chinese, Taiwanese, and U.S. employees. Overall, the Chinese employees in their sample demonstrated the strongest tendency to accept direction and the U.S. employees the least. Peer consensus had more influence in the United States. Also, Chinese employees were more sensitive to the consistency between the supervisory direction and company policies and were less responsive to their own assessment of the merit of the directions they were given.

Another issue related to power and status arises from the question of whether status is based on achievement or ascription (Parsons & Shils, 1951). Whereas some societies accord status to people on the basis of their achievements, others ascribe it to people based on age, gender, social class, profession, or other criteria, such as family membership. Achieved status is based on what one has done or accomplished, and ascribed status is based on who one "is." Achievement-oriented societies tend to accord status based on members' accomplishments and performance. Ascribing cultures confer status on the individual and not on the task or the individual's accomplishments. In ascribing societies where seniority and age are major requirements, for example, it is usually unacceptable to have people report to bosses who are younger than they are. In the United States, the idea that anyone can become president is a strong reflection of achievement orientation, whereas in France, becoming president without attending the right *grande école* or having the right connections still seems impossible. In Japan, promotion to higher positions was historically based on seniority, gender, and age (e.g., Javidan, 2004), though this is beginning to change. Employees recognize these practices and shape their expectations accordingly.

In a study among leaders and their followers in the PRC and the United States, Kirkman et al. (2009) focused on individual-level differences in power distance orientation. They found that both individuals' power distance orientation and their group's shared perceptions of transformational leadership were positively related to procedural justice perceptions. Power distance orientation moderated the relationship between transformational leadership and procedural justice (stronger when power distance orientation was lower). Procedural justice, in turn, was linked with followers' organizational citizenship behavior. This study highlights that besides the role of societal culture in leadership, taking individual-level culture orientation effects into account in studying leadership is of interest.

## Examples of Other Dimensions

Another basic value on which cultures differ is their assumptions on the nature of human beings (Kluckhohn & Strodtbeck, 1961): Are people generally neutral, good, or evil? Within groups viewing humans as basically good, people will tend to trust others' intentions. In leadership terms, less emphasis on control and direct supervision of employees is needed if a basic belief exists that people have good intentions. In contrast, distrust prevails in cultures where people are believed to be evil, and more monitoring and closer supervision of employees is likely (e.g., Brannen et al., 2004). Whether a culture views humans as changeable or not is also of interest. In cultures where people are viewed as changeable, organizations and their leaders are more likely to invest in training their employees, including training to develop leadership skills. In cultures where people are considered to be less changeable, the emphasis is more on selecting the correct person for the job, including selection into leadership roles (e.g., Brannen et al., 2004).

Another interesting element of culture pertains to the perceived nature of the relationship with the outside world (Kluckhohn & Strodtbeck, 1961). Societies can view this relationship as one of subjugation, harmony, or dominance. The latter reflects the assumption that nature can be controlled and manipulated, a pragmatic orientation toward the nature of reality, and a belief in human perfectibility. This also relates to the above assumption of whether humans are able to change or not. In societies holding a dominance view, "it is taken for granted that the proper thing to do for people is to take charge and actively control their environment" (Schein, 1992, p. 127). At the other extreme, the assumption is that nature is powerful and humanity is subservient to nature. This implies a kind of fatalism, as one cannot influence nature and must therefore accept one's destiny and enjoy what one has (e.g., Javidan, 2004).

Similarly, Schwartz (1999) described mastery cultures that encourage people to master, change, and exploit the environment in order to attain goals. Here, organizations and their leaders need to be dynamic, competitive, and oriented toward achievement and success. In contrast, in harmony cultures, people try to understand and integrate with their natural environment rather than to change or exploit it. Leaders take a holistic view and try to understand the social and environmental implications of actions and seek nonexploitative ways to achieve goals (Sagiv & Schwartz, 2000).

Trompenaars and Hampden-Turner (1997) label this internal versus external cultures, akin to Rotter's (1954) work on internal and external locus of control. Culture-related differences exist in the degree to which people feel they have control over themselves and their lives (internal) or that they are controlled by external forces (external). For instance, choosing between the statements "What happens to them is their own doing" or "Sometimes I feel that I do not have enough control over the directions my life is taking," over 80% of U.S. managers chose the former (control over own destiny) versus 40% of Russian or Chinese managers. Internal cultures have a dominating and controlling attitude toward nature. Conflict and resistance imply one has strong convictions. The focus is on the self and one's own group, competition is valued, and playing "hard ball" is legitimate, which affects the preferred leadership style within a culture. In contrast, in external cultures, being at ease with the cycles of nature, willingness to compromise, seeking harmony, and responsiveness are seen as desirable characteristics for leaders. The focus is on the "other," and softness, persistence, politeness, and patience are needed to succeed (Den Hartog, 2004).

These and other culture dimensions provide one approach to differentiating between societal cultures and their preferred leadership styles. Certainly, other factors are also relevant, including the degree of economic development of the society. Thus, we now turn to culture and leadership in the developing world.

## Culture and Leadership Beyond the "Western" World

Models and research on leadership and culture were developed in and thus mostly focus on industrialized countries as opposed to "developing" countries (Aycan, 2004). However, these latter countries represent almost 80% of the world population and comprise a large, growing market and labor force, spread among extremely diverse countries (Punnett, 2004). Recognizing that these terms are value-laden, we use the term *industrialized* to refer to the Organisation for Economic Co-operation and Development (OECD) countries and Western Europe, and the term *developing* for other countries. On average, the industrialized countries have higher per capita income and rank higher on the United Nations Human Development Index (indicating the presence of good education, health care, and quality of life). Increasingly, businesses recognize the potential of the growing markets and young labor force in developing countries. Some such countries are physically large and have vast natural resources (e.g., Brazil); others have many well-trained people (e.g., India), good infrastructures (e.g., Zimbabwe), or good medical facilities (e.g., Cuba)—all characteristics that may provide a good environment for business opportunities (Punnett, 2004).

Developing countries are diverse, and a single, unified portrayal of their cultural characteristics is impossible. Yet Aycan (2004) notes that many share key elements in historical background (e.g., autocratic rule, colonialism), subsistence systems (e.g., reliance on agriculture), political environments (e.g., instability), economic conditions (e.g., scarcity), and/or demographic makeup (e.g., young workforce, unequal opportunity to access education). Economic/political environments and historical events shape cultures. Thus, some aspects of the cultures of these countries are likely similar. However, substantial differences also exist between and within developing countries. These may be regional or reflect differences between ethnic or religious groupings. Differences in values or behavior can also relate to the organizations people work for or to education, socioeconomic status, or age. For example, the values and behavior of a highly educated Indian manager, trained abroad and working for an American multinational corporation in an urban area, may resemble the values of other U.S. managers more than the values of an Indian manager with less education working for a small family business in a rural area. Such subcultural variations exist everywhere, but may be larger in developing countries (Aycan, 2004).

Cultures of developing countries tend to be somewhat more collectivistic, external, and higher on power distance. Feelings of helplessness and fatalism are relatively common culturally (Aycan et al., 2000). Often, relationships and networks are more important than rules and procedures, which can lead to favoritism among in-group members and discrimination against out-group members. Within-group loyalty and harmony are often important, as is interdependence, with personal achievement less valued; getting along is more important than getting ahead (Abdalla & Al-Homoud, 2001). This ensures smoothly running work processes, though not necessarily efficient ones. Communication is often indirect, nonassertive, nonconfrontational, and usually downward. Negative feedback is often avoided or given indirectly, as it is quickly seen as destructive (face management) and disruptive to harmony (Aycan, 2004).

Regarding leadership, one relatively common theme across these societies is a "paternalistic" leadership style that is high on status orientation, high on involvement in nonwork lives, and highly directive (e.g., Aycan, 2004; Chen et al., 2014). In these societies, organizations are generally expected to take care of their workers and workers' families. Leaders tend to establish close interpersonal relationships with subordinates. Subordinates expect personalized relationships, protection, close guidance, and supervision. The paternalistic relationship is strongly hierarchical. Leaders protect and provide for subordinates, whereas subordinates voluntarily submit, showing loyalty and deference. The leader is assumed to "know what is best" for subordinates, guiding them in different aspects of life (Aycan, 2004; Pellegrini & Scandura, 2008).

Paternalistic leadership is, for instance, strong in Mexico. An example described by Martinez and Dorfman (1998) involved an inspirational Mexican entrepreneur who involved himself in the private lives of his employees, as he felt this was required of him. For example, when a secretary remarked that her husband was going into the hospital for an operation, this leader called the doctor to discuss the matter and ensure the operation was legitimate. Other examples of paternalistic behaviors include attending congratulatory and condolence ceremonies of employees as well as their immediate family members (e.g., weddings, funerals); providing financial assistance (e.g., donations, loans) to employees for housing, health care, and children's education expenses; and mediating in interpersonal conflicts among employees (Aycan, 2004). A problem that can occur is the differential treatment of workers and related problems such as rivalry and jealousy (e.g., Sinha, 1995).

Aycan (2004) holds that paternalism is a leadership style that is not well understood in industrialized countries. Individualistic values endorsed in many industrialized nations imply a striving for autonomy and self-reliance, which is at odds with the guiding role of the paternalistic leader. The strong involvement in subordinates' personal lives would seem intrusive there, and the highly personal nature of the relationship unprofessional. However, in many developing countries, reciprocal consent for these paternalistic relationships between superior and subordinate exists. Such patterns may, of course, change over time.

In the previous section, we discussed culture and how it might impact leader behavior. Research shows that being perceived as a leader is a prerequisite for being able to go beyond a formal role in influencing others (Lord & Maher, 1991). To be successful, leaders need to show characteristics or behaviors recognized as "leadership." Thus, perceptual processes on the part of followers play a crucial role in the leadership process. As is clear from the above, attributes and behaviors that are seen as characteristic for effective leaders vary across cultures. In the following section, we explore this in more depth.

# Leadership Perceptions Across Cultures

People form ideas about what makes a leader effective. These ideas are influenced by culture. When thinking of a prototypical leader, a bold, autonomous, and decisive hero may typically come to mind in some cultures, whereas different images prevail elsewhere. For instance, an ideal leader may be a mature person whose experience and wisdom are admired and valued. Lord and Maher (1991) already suggested that societal culture and its values and ideologies should impact leadership prototypes and implicit leadership theories. In strong/uniform cultures, prototypes are widely shared, whereas countries with weak cultures or multiple subcultures will show a wider variance among individual prototypes (Hunt, Boal, & Sorenson, 1990). House et al. (2004) refer to these shared beliefs as culturally endorsed implicit leadership theories (CLTs). One question is whether we can distinguish leader behaviors and characteristics in these CLTs that are universally accepted and effective across cultures and ones that are differentially valued across cultures.

## Universally Endorsed and Culturally Contingent Leader Characteristics

As noted, the GLOBE Project is the largest cross-cultural leadership research project to date (Dorfman et al., 2012). Early results of the GLOBE project reported which leadership attributes were (1) found to be universally endorsed as contributing to outstanding leadership, (2) seen as undesirable, or (3) culturally contingent. For instance, in all participating countries, an outstanding leader is expected to be encouraging, positive, motivational, a confidence builder, dynamic, and to have foresight. Such a leader is excellence oriented, decisive, and intelligent. Outstanding leaders are good at team building, communicating, and coordinating. Integrity is valued, as such leaders are trustworthy, just, and honest. Attributes universally viewed as ineffective include being noncooperative, ruthless, nonexplicit, a loner, irritable, and dictatorial (Den Hartog et al., 1999; Dorfman, Hanges, & Brodbeck, 2004).

The importance of other leader attributes varies across cultures. These culturally contingent attributes had high means in some cultures, indicating this characteristic facilitated outstanding leadership there, and low means in other cultures, indicating this characteristic was seen to impede outstanding leadership there. For instance, country means for "risk taking" ranged from 2.14 to 5.96 on a 7-point scale, for "sensitive" from 1.96 to 6.35, for "class-conscious" from 2.53 to 6.09, and for "autonomous" from 1.63 to 5.17 (see Den Hartog et al., 1999, for the complete list).

Cultural differences play a role. For instance, differences in the appreciation of characteristics such as "subdued" and "enthusiastic" reflect differences in cultural norms regarding the appropriate expression of emotion. In some (Asian) cultures, displaying emotion is interpreted as a lack of self-control and thus a sign of weakness. Not showing one's emotions is the norm. In other cultures (e.g., Latin), effective communicators vividly express emotions. Other leader attributes that vary across cultures reflect power distance. For example, "status-conscious," "class-conscious," "elitist," and "domineering" are appreciated in high, but not in low, power distance cultures. Others reflect uncertainty avoidance, including risk taking, habitual, procedural, able to anticipate, formal, cautious, and orderly impeding outstanding leadership in some countries and enhancing it in others. Finally, being autonomous, unique, and independent seems to reflect cultural preferences for individualism and is found to contribute to outstanding leadership in some but not other cultures. Thus, while images of outstanding leaders around the world share some characteristics, vast differences in what is seen as desirable for leaders also exist (Den Hartog et al., 1999).

## Variations in the Enactment of Universal Leader Characteristics

The above shows a "universal" appreciation of certain leadership attributes and a more varied appreciation of others. However, as mentioned, even when attributes are universally valued, such attributes may not necessarily be enacted in the same way across cultures. The behavior reflecting an attribute may vary. Dickson, Hanges, and Lord (2001) address the various meanings of "universal" findings. Of most relevance here is the distinction between simple universals, in which the principle and enactment are the same across contexts, and variform universals, in which the principle is consistent across contexts but the enactment differs.

A specific example of a variform universal is that *visionary* is seen as a positive leader attribute in most cultures, but what one needs to do to be seen as visionary varies from one culture to another. For instance, as mentioned, effective styles of communicating visions differ. Whereas macho-oratory is linked to effective vision communication in some cultures, Fu, Wu, Yang, and Ye (2007) hold that a vision in China is normally expressed in a nonaggressive manner. Confucian values (e.g., kindness, benevolence) may make people wary of leaders giving pompous talks without engaging in specific action, and lead people to dislike leaders who are arrogant and distant.

Another example is that some authors hold that some risk taking is part of transformational leadership, a style endorsed in many countries. Yet the GLOBE results suggest that risk taking is not universally valued in leaders. Moreover, what is considered risk taking in one context may not be in another. The Mexican entrepreneur described by Martinez and Dorfman (1998), for instance, appointed someone from the Mexican lower class as a member of the administrative staff, despite objections of stockholders, based on her hard work, education, and expertise. Where in many countries, one would not find anything particularly strange about this decision, a person's social status is extremely important in Mexico. Thus, there this behavior was seen as risky, illustrating that the same behavior can take on a very different meaning in cultures that differ in their core shared values.

Another example relates to leader integrity, a universally desired leader characteristic in GLOBE. Still, culturally contingent understandings of integrity, and especially of disintegrity, were found to differ. For example, promoting a subordinate to a leadership position over others with more seniority was described as unethical in Taiwan, but not elsewhere. Thus, the "big picture" construct of integrity is universally desired and seen as necessary for effective leadership, yet the details of behaviors connoting leader integrity vary across cultures (Martin et al., 2013; Resick et al., 2011).

## Leadership Profiles, Culture Clusters, and Organizational Culture

GLOBE findings demonstrate that members of cultures share a common frame of reference regarding effective leadership. Some leader attributes are universally appreciated and others are endorsed in some but not other cultures. The GLOBE leadership attributes were also statistically grouped into six global leadership dimensions (Hanges & Dickson, 2004). These six dimensions were (1) charismatic/value-based leadership (e.g., visionary, inspirational, integrity, decisive); (2) team-oriented leadership (e.g., collaborating, integrating, diplomatic); (3) participative leadership (e.g., nonautocratic, allowing participation); (4) autonomous leadership (e.g., individualistic, independent, unique); (5) humane leadership (e.g., modesty, tolerance, sensitivity); and (6) self-protective leadership (e.g., self-centered, face-saver). Does the endorsement of these dimensions differ in different parts of the world?

Scholars suggest different ways to group countries into cultural clusters, using geographical proximity, mass migrations and ethnic social capital, religious and linguistic communality, social variables such as attitudes and values, and economic or sociopolitical development (Gupta, Hanges, & Dorfman, 2002). GLOBE focuses on 10 clusters. The meta-Western region includes Nordic Europe, Germanic Europe, Anglo, Latin America, and Latin Europe clusters; the meta-Eastern region consists of Southern Asia, Confucian Asia, Central/Eastern Europe, sub-Saharan Africa, and the Middle East (Arabic) clusters (see the GLOBE-focused March 2002 special issue of the *Journal of World Business*). Leadership profiles were developed for these clusters using the six leadership dimensions. These profiles highlight common elements of leadership as well as culturally unique ones (Dorfman et al., 2004).

Charismatic and team-oriented leadership were strongly endorsed in all 10 clusters. Humane leadership contributed somewhat to effective leadership everywhere, but not as strongly. Southern Asia, Anglo, and sub-Saharan Africa score somewhat higher and Latin and Nordic Europe somewhat lower on humane leadership. Autonomous leadership was mostly neutral regarding its contribution to effective leadership, but for some of the cultures it formed a factor that contributed slightly (e.g., Eastern and Germanic Europe), and for some others a factor that inhibited slightly (e.g., Latin Europe, Middle East). The self-protective CLT dimension formed an inhibitor of effective leadership everywhere. However, it was seen as more inhibiting in the Nordic, Germanic, and Anglo clusters and less so in the Middle Eastern, Confucian, and Southern Asian clusters. Participative leadership contributes to effective leadership for all culture clusters; however, considerable variation exists. The Germanic, Anglo, and Nordic clusters were particularly attuned to participative leadership, whereas the Middle Eastern, Eastern European, Confucian, and Southern Asian clusters were not (Dorfman et al., 2004).

The most recent GLOBE study involved CEOs and top management team members in 24 societies and focused both on how a society's culture influences the leadership behaviors expected in that culture and on whether leadership success depends on a CEO matching his or her leadership style to these expectations. Overall, the findings of the study reinforce the importance of CEOs to different organizational outcomes, the influence that culture has on what is expected of leaders in society, and the importance of CEOs matching their leader behaviors to the leadership expectations within the society (House et al., 2014). Almost 70 researchers in 24 societies collected survey data from over 1,000 CEOs and over 5,000 top management team members, and CEOs were also interviewed.

One aim was to see how societal culture influences the expected leadership behaviors in a society. The findings show cultural values affect culturally endorsed leadership expectations, and in turn, these affect CEO behavior. Leaders tend to understand what is expected in a culture and operate in a socially desirable fashion. For instance, cultures valuing performance orientation such as the United States and Germany expect leaders to be participative, and leaders in such cultures showed some of the highest levels of participative leadership.

Several CEO leadership behaviors generally across the participating societies had positive effects in terms of leading to effective top teams and organizational success. Most notably, charismatic or visionary leadership behavior most strongly affected both the outcome of top management team dedication and firm performance. The most influential charisma-related behaviors were being visionary, inspirational, integrity, and performance-oriented. CEO team-oriented leader behavior was the next most important style in terms of these outcomes, followed by humane-oriented leadership. Participative leadership was moderately related to top management team dedication but not to firm performance. Autonomous and self-protective leadership were generally ineffective.

In addition, as shown in Figure 13.1, better-performing CEOs match their behavior to societal expectations and exceed such expectations in terms of being even higher than expected on most leadership dimensions, especially including charismatic and team-oriented leadership. Underperforming CEOs, on the other hand, tend to fall short of expectations on most leadership dimensions, yet are more autonomous than is expected of leaders in their respective societies. Figure 13.1 presents data that were standardized at the country level. In other words, each country's leadership expectations are set to zero, and the figure shows (in standardized units) the average extent to which CEOs exceeded or fell below those cultural expectations. CEOs were classified as most or least successful for this figure based on their top management teams' level of commitment; the pattern of results is very similar for competitive firm performance, though with smaller effects. The match between the CEOs' leader behavior and the leadership expectations within a society is important and predicts top management team dedication and firm performance (see House et al., 2014, for a detailed account of this research).

Whereas results show that societal values clearly impact the shared perceptions of effective leader behaviors as well as outcomes, the GLOBE Project was also among the first studies to allow large-scale assessment of the relative impact of *societal* culture as well as *organizational* culture on these perceptions. For example, the first GLOBE study (House et al., 2004) showed that the performance orientation of culture was related to charismatic/value-based leadership and participative leadership CLTs at both the organizational and societal levels of culture. Thus, societies and organizations valuing a strong performance orientation seem to look to charismatic leaders with the ability to paint the picture of an ambitious and exciting future. They also value a leader who involves others in building this future in a participative manner (Javidan, 2004). In many cases, the impact of organizational culture on the leadership belief system, or CLT, was at least as strong as that of societal culture (Dorfman et al., 2004).

Values that characterize a society are likely to be reflected in the values held by members of organizations. Dickson, BeShears, and Gupta (2004) described mechanisms by which this influence is likely to occur. These include the simple fact that people who make up organizations come from some societal culture and are likely to hold the values that characterize that society; the pressures placed on organizations to

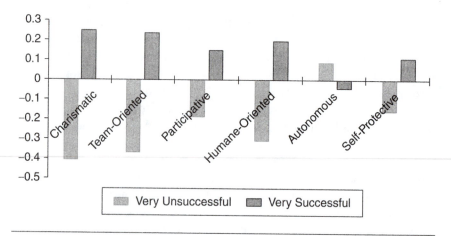

**Figure 13.1**   Very Successful and Very Unsuccessful CEOs' Leadership Behaviors Compared to Cultural Expectations, as related to Top Management Team Commitment

SOURCE: Based on House et al. (2014).

conform to the values of the society, through either subtle rewards or perceived advantages for conformity and punishments for nonconformity (i.e., coercive, normative, and mimetic isomorphic pressures); resource dependency pressures, in which conformity is required in order to acquire and retain necessary physical and human resources; and social network pressures, through which the patterns of interactions and dependence relationships compel organizations toward adopting and/or reflecting societal values.

Leaders of organizations embed and transmit culture in the thinking, feeling, and behavior of the group. Thus, Bass and Bass (2008) suggest leaders can function as founders of cultures or countercultures, as culture builders, and as agents of change in the dominant culture. Trice and Beyer (1991) add the leader's role in maintaining culture. Schein (1992) holds that "leadership is originally the source of the beliefs and values that get a group moving to deal with its internal and external problems. If what a leader proposes works and continues to work, what once was only the leader's assumption gradually comes to be a shared assumption" (pp. 26–27). The founder of the organization thus plays a crucial role in culture formation by choosing the basic mission, the group members, the context in which to operate, and the initial responses of the group to succeed and integrate within this environment. Dickson, Resick, and Hanges (2006) focus on the strength of organizational culture or climate and show, based on GLOBE data, that unambiguous climates tend to be stronger. Strong cultures can inhibit or promote the effects of leaders' efforts, depending on whether the influence attempts are in line with the dominant values in that culture. In that vein, Schein ironically suggested that often culture may manage management more than management manages culture.

# Conclusions

In this chapter on leadership and culture, we aimed to show that we should not take for granted that models and theories developed in one place will work similarly in another. We described culture and showed how culture can affect implicit leadership theories and behavior and showed that even when preferred leader characteristics and behaviors are similar, their enactment might differ across cultures. Clearly, more research on leadership in different cultures is needed. Large-scale comparative studies involving comparable samples from many different countries are of interest. Preferably, such studies can be repeated over time to gain more insight in the changing nature of leadership. However, at the other extreme, more indigenous, local, and rich studies, yielding more culture-specific models, are also of interest.

We did not describe in detail the many potential problems and methodological pitfalls that need to be addressed in cross-cultural research, which is beyond the scope of this chapter. With the support of the Society for Industrial-Organizational Psychology, Dickson et al. (2016) are pursuing a series of studies designed to address three controversies with the cross-cultural research literature, with specific focus on the proper steps to justify aggregation and then to aggregate culture-level data, the implications for culture-level means and variances of different forms of culture-related questions, and the measurement equivalence of societal level constructs. Measurement invariance is another such issue. Another potential obstacle is the problem of translation. How do we ensure that respondents interpret questions similarly or that constructs have the same meaning? What happens if respondents complete questionnaires in a nonnative language? Sampling provides another challenge in cross-cultural research. For example, using national borders as cultural boundaries may not be appropriate in countries with large or numerous subcultures.

Also, studies risk committing the "ecological fallacy"—that is, assuming isomorphic relationships between variables across differing levels of analysis, such as assuming characteristics or relationships existing at the cultural level automatically apply to other levels of analysis, such as the individual. However, what applies for individuals may or may not apply for groups, and vice versa (e.g., Dorfman et al., 2004). This problem can be minimized by paying careful attention to levels of analysis in theory building and in collecting and analyzing data. For instance, in questionnaire research aimed at the culture level, culture items can be phrased to refer explicitly to groups, organizations, or societies rather than to individuals. Whether individual responses can then be aggregated to group levels can be tested statistically.

These examples of methodological challenges show that studying leadership in different cultures is not easy. However, well-designed studies will help develop a better understanding of the differences and similarities in what is acceptable and effective organizational leadership around the world. Clearly, enhanced understanding in this area is crucial in the increasingly globalized world of work.

## Discussion Questions

1. Ralph Waldo Emerson, the American lecturer, philosopher, essayist, and poet, used to greet friends by asking, "What has become clear to you since last we met?" In that spirit, what has become clear in the literature on cross-cultural leadership in recent years? What research questions remain to be answered?

2. Some argue that culture is becoming less important, or less meaningful as a construct, due to globalization. Others argue that as globalization increases, so does adherence to core cultural values. Does the evidence suggest that leaders in multicultural settings still need to attend to issues of culture, or is that need fading?

3. Does the meaning of cross-cultural leadership differ for practicing leaders compared to scholarly researchers? If so, how could we promote greater alignment between practical and scholarly understandings of cross-cultural leadership? What does the current literature offer to the practicing leader?

4. What types of dilemmas and problems does this type of research face?

5.  What does this research suggest about the common practice of sending expatriate managers or executives to work in countries other than their own? What barriers are likely to emerge related to cultural differences? What sort of person might be effective in that role?

6.  How can organizations be proactive to try to prevent problems arising from people of different cultural backgrounds having different expectations of leaders and different understandings of what leadership is? Should organizations attempt to make cultural values—which are generally implicit—more explicit, so that they can be discussed and addressed to increase effectiveness and reduce misunderstandings? Or will such efforts yield the opposite effect, highlighting differences rather than ways to overcome or work together despite differences?

7.  Are there particular dimensions of culture where differences between managers, or between managers and subordinates, on that dimension would be more likely to lead to organizational problems, misunderstandings, or ineffectiveness? Why would differences on those dimensions be particularly problematic?

8.  If you were placed in the role of leader of a multicultural team that has never worked together, how would you begin your interactions together? Would you do anything specifically to address your cultural background and its impact on you as the leader? Are there things you would do to address the multicultural background of your team members? How would you move forward to ensure the best performance from the talented but different people who are now working for you?

## Recommended Readings

- Biermeier-Hanson, B., Liu, M., & Dickson, M. W. (2015). Alternate views of global leadership: Applying global leadership perspectives to leading global teams. In R. Griffith & J. Wildman (Eds.), *Leading global teams: Translating the multidisciplinary science to practice* (pp. 195–224). New York, NY: Springer.
- Javidan, M., Dorfman, P., de Luque, M. S., & House, R. J. (2006). In the eye of the beholder: Cross-cultural lessons in leadership from Project GLOBE. *Academy of Management Perspectives, 20*(1), 67–90.
- Javidan, M., Teagarden, M., & Bowen, D. (2010). Making it overseas. *Harvard Business Review, 88*(4), 109–113.

## Recommended Case Studies

1.  **Case:** Fischer, W. A., & Chung, R. (2006). Learning to lead in China: Antonio Scarsi takes command. IMD-3–1696.

2.  **Case:** Maznevski, M., & Leger, K. (2008). Petter Eiken at Skanska: Leading change. IMD-3–1823.

    **Mini-Case Series.** Although these are a bit older, they are very short and provide opportunities for undergraduates or others less familiar with case methodology to begin to use the approach and to apply them to the cross-cultural domain. The titles mentioned are three of the eight cases, though most of them are appropriate for this topic.

    **Case:** de Bettignies, H., & Butler, C. (1995). Blowing in the wind. INSEAD 495-028-1.

    **Case:** DeLong, T .J., & Neeley, T. (2009). Managing a global team: Greg James at Sun Microsystems, Inc. (A) and (B). Harvard Business Cases 9-409-003.

    **Case:** Meyer, E., & Gupta, S. (2009). Leading across cultures at Michelin (A; prize winner). INSEAD 409-008-1.

## Recommended Videos

- Pattanaik, D. (2009). Devdutt Pattanaik: East vs. West—the myths that mystify. https://www.youtube.com/watch?v=I7QwxbImhZI
- Sirolli, E. (2012). Ernesto Sirolli: Want to help someone? Shut up and listen! https://www.youtube.com/watch?v=chXsLtHqfdM

## References

Abdalla, I. A., & Al-Homoud, M. A. (2001). Exploring the implicit leadership theory in the Arabian Gulf States. *Applied Psychology: An International Review, 50*, 506–531.

Adler, N. J. (2002). *International dimensions of organizational behavior* (4th ed.). Cincinnati, OH: South-Western College.

Adsit, D. J., London, M., Crom, S., & Jones, D. (2001). Cross-cultural differences in upward ratings in a multinational company. *The International Journal of Human Resource Management, 8*, 385–401.

Antonakis, J., Avolio B. J., & Sivasubramaniam, N. (2003). Context and leadership: An examination of the nine-factor full-range leadership theory using the Multifactor Leadership Questionnaire. *The Leadership Quarterly, 14*, 261–295.

Aycan, Z. (2004). Managing inequalities: Leadership and teamwork in the developing country context. In H. W. Lane, M. L. Maznevski, M. E. Mendenhall, & J. McNett (Eds.), *The Blackwell handbook of global management: A guide to managing complexity* (pp. 406–423). Malden, MA: Blackwell.

Aycan, Z., Kanungo, R., Mendonca, M., Yu, K., Deller, J., Stahl, G., & Kurshid, A. (2000). Impact of culture on human resource management practices: A 10-country comparison. *Applied Psychology: An International Review, 49*, 192–221.

Bass, B. M. (1997). Does the transactional–transformational leadership paradigm transcend organizational and national boundaries? *American Psychologist, 52*, 130–139.

Bass, B. M., & Bass, R. (2008). *The Bass handbook of leadership: Theory, research, and managerial applications* (4th ed.). New York, NY: Free Press.

Bealer, D., & Bhanugopan, R. (2014). Transactional and transformational leadership behaviour of expatriate and national managers in the UAE: A cross-cultural comparative analysis. *The International Journal of Human Resource Management, 25*(2), 293–316.

Brannen, M. Y., Gomez, C., Peterson, M. F., Romani, L., Sagiv, L., & Wu, P. C. (2004). People in global organizations: Culture, personality, and social dynamics. In H. W. Lane, M. L. Maznevski, M. E. Mendenhall, & J. McNett (Eds.), *The Blackwell handbook of global management: A guide to managing complexity* (pp. 26–54). Malden, MA: Blackwell.

Bu, N., Craig, T. J., & Peng, T. K. (2001). Acceptance of supervisory direction in typical workplace situations: A comparison of US, Taiwanese and PRC employees. *International Journal of Cross-Cultural Management, 1*, 131–152.

Chen, X. P., Eberly, M. B., Chiang, T. J., Farh, J. L., & Cheng, B. S. (2014). Affective trust in Chinese leaders linking paternalistic leadership to employee performance. *Journal of Management, 40*(3), 796–819.

Chhokar, J. S., Brodbeck F. C., & House, R. J. (Eds.). (2007). *Culture and leadership across the world: The GLOBE book of in-depth studies of 25 societies.* New York, NY: Lawrence Erlbaum.

Den Hartog, D. N. (2004). Assertiveness. In R. J. House, P. J. Hanges, M. Javidan, P. W. Dorfman, V. Gupta, & GLOBE Associates (Eds.), *Culture, leadership, and organizations: The GLOBE study of 62 societies* (pp. 395–436). Thousand Oaks, CA: Sage.

Den Hartog, D. N., House, R. J., Hanges, P., Dorfman, P., Ruiz-Quintanilla, A., . . . Zhou, J. (1999). Culture specific and cross-culturally endorsed implicit leadership theories: Are attributes of charismatic/transformational leadership universally endorsed? *The Leadership Quarterly, 10*, 219–256.

Dickson, M. W., BeShears, R. S., & Gupta, V. (2004). The impact of societal culture and industry on organizational culture: Theoretical explanations. In R. J. House, P. J. Hanges, M. Javidan, P. W. Dorfman, V. Gupta, & GLOBE Associates (Eds.), *Culture, leadership, and organizations: The GLOBE study of 62 societies* (pp. 74–90). Thousand Oaks, CA: Sage.

Dickson, M. W., Castaño, N., Magomaeva, A., & Den Hartog, D. N. (2012). Conceptualizing leadership across cultures. *Journal of World Business, 47*(4), 483–492.

Dickson, M. W., Den Hartog, D. N., & Castaño, N. (2009). Understanding leadership across cultures. In R. S. Bhagat & R. M. Steers (Eds.), *Cambridge handbook of culture, organizations, and work* (pp. 219–244). Cambridge, UK: Cambridge University Press.

Dickson, M. W., Hanges, P. J., Den Hartog, D., Keating, M., Kwantes, C., & Shaw, J. (2016). Investigating current measurement and aggregation controversies in the cross-cultural organizational literature. Funded proposal to the Society for Industrial-Organizational Psychology's International Research and Collaboration Grant competition.

Dickson, M. W., Hanges, P. J., & Lord, R. M. (2001). Trends, developments, and gaps in cross-cultural research on leadership. In W. Mobley & M. McCall (Eds.), *Advances in global leadership* (Vol. 2, pp. 75–100). Stamford, CT: JAI.

Dickson, M. W., Resick, C. J., & Hanges, P. J. (2006). When organizational climate is unambiguous, it is also strong. *Journal of Applied Psychology, 91*, 351–364.

Doney, P. M., Cannon, J. P., & Mullen, M. R. (1998). Understanding the influence of national culture on the development of trust. *Academy of Management Review, 23*, 601–620.

Dorfman, P. W., Hanges, P. J., & Brodbeck, F. C. (2004). Leadership and cultural variation: The identification of culturally endorsed leadership profiles. In R. J. House, P. J. Hanges, M. Javidan, P. W. Dorfman, V. Gupta, & GLOBE Associates (Eds.), *Culture, leadership, and organizations: The GLOBE study of 62 societies* (pp. 669–720). Thousand Oaks, CA: Sage.

Dorfman, P., Javidan, M., Hanges, P., Dastmalchian, A., & House, R. (2012). GLOBE: A twenty year journey into the intriguing world of culture and leadership. *Journal of World Business, 47*, 504–518.

Fu, P. P., Wu, R., Yang, Y., & Ye, J. (2007). Chinese culture and leadership in China. In J. S. Chhokar, F. C. Brodbeck, & R. J. House (Eds.), *Culture and leadership across the world: The GLOBE book of in-depth studies of 25 societies* (pp. 877–907). New York, NY: Lawrence Erlbaum.

Gupta, V., de Luque, M. S., & House, R. J. (2004). Multisource construct validity of GLOBE scales. In R. J. House, P. J. Hanges, M. Javidan, P. W. Dorfman, V. Gupta, & GLOBE Associates (Eds.), *Culture, leadership, and organizations: The GLOBE study of 62 societies* (pp. 152–177). Thousand Oaks, CA: Sage.

Gupta, V., Hanges, P. J., & Dorfman, P. (2002). Cultural clusters: Methodology and findings. *Journal of World Business, 37*, 11–15.

Hanges, P. J., & Dickson, M. W. (2004). The development and validation of the GLOBE culture and leadership scales. In R. J. House, P. J. Hanges, M. Javidan, P. W. Dorfman, V. Gupta, & GLOBE Associates (Eds.), *Culture, leadership, and organizations: The GLOBE study of 62 societies* (pp. 122–151). Thousand Oaks, CA: Sage.

Hanges, P. J., & Dickson, M. W. (2006). Agitation over aggregation: Clarifying the development of and the nature of the GLOBE scales. *The Leadership Quarterly, 17*, 522–536.

Hofstede, G. (1980). *Culture's consequences: International differences in work-related values.* Beverly Hills, CA: Sage.

Hofstede, G. (2001). *Culture's consequences: Comparing values, behaviors, institutions, and organizations across nations* (2nd ed.). Thousand Oaks, CA: Sage.

Hofstede, G. (2006). What did GLOBE really measure? Researchers' minds versus respondents' minds. *Journal of International Business Studies, 37*, 882–896.

Hofstede, G. (2011). Dimensionalizing cultures: The Hofstede model in context. *Online Readings in Psychology and Culture, 2*(1), 1–26.

Holtgraves, T. (1997). Styles of language use: Individual and cultural variability in conversational indirectness. *Journal of Personality and Social Psychology, 73*, 624–637.

House, R. J. (1995). Leadership in the twenty-first century: A speculative enquiry. In A. Howard (Ed.), *The changing nature of work* (pp. 411–450). San Francisco, CA: Jossey Bass.

House, R. J., Dorfman, P. W., Javidan, M., Hanges, P. J., & DeLuque, M. S. (2014). *Strategic leadership: The GLOBE study of CEO leadership behavior and effectiveness across cultures.* Thousand Oaks, CA: Sage.

House, R. J., Hanges, P. J., Javidan, M., Dorfman, P.W., Gupta, V., & GLOBE Associates (Eds.). (2004). *Culture, leadership, and organizations: The GLOBE study of 62 societies.* Thousand Oaks, CA: Sage.

Hunt, J. G., Boal, K. B., & Sorenson, R. L. (1990). Top management leadership: Inside the black box. *The Leadership Quarterly, 1,* 41–65.

Javidan, M. (2004). Performance orientation. In R. J. House, P. J. Hanges, M. Javidan, P. W. Dorfman, V. Gupta, & GLOBE Associates (Eds.), *Culture, leadership, and organizations: The GLOBE study of 62 societies* (pp. 239–281). Thousand Oaks, CA: Sage.

Javidan, M., Dorfman, P. W., DeLuque, M. S., & House, R. J. (2006). In the eye of the beholder: Cross cultural lessons in leadership from Project GLOBE. *Academy of Management Perspectives, 20,* 67–90.

Javidan, M., House, R. J., Dorfman, P. W., Hanges, P. J., & de Luque, M. S. (2006). Conceptualizing and measuring cultures and their consequences: A comparative review of GLOBE's and Hofstede's approaches. *Journal of International Business Studies, 37,* 897–914.

Javidan, M., & Teagarden, M. B. (2011). Conceptualizing and measuring global mindset. *Advances in Global Leadership, 6*(1), 13–39.

Kirkman, B. L., Chen, G., Fahr, J. L., Chen, Z. X., & Lowe, K. B. (2009). Individual power distance orientation and follower reactions to transformational leaders: A cross-level, cross-cultural examination. *Academy of Management Journal, 52,* 744–764.

Kirkman, B. L., & Den Hartog, D. N. (2004). Performance management in global teams. In H. W. Lane, M. L. Maznevski, M. E. Mendenhall, & J. McNett (Eds.), *The Blackwell handbook of global management: A guide to managing complexity* (pp. 250–272). Malden, MA: Blackwell.

Kirkman, B. L., Lowe, K. B., & Gibson, C. B. (2006). A quarter century of *Culture's Consequences*: A review of empirical research incorporating Hofstede's cultural values framework. *Journal of International Business Studies, 37,* 285–320.

Kluckhohn, F., & Strodtbeck, F. L. (1961). *Variations in value orientations.* Westport, CT: Greenwood Press.

Lord, R. G., & Maher, K. J. (1991*). Leadership and information processing.* London, UK: Routledge.

Martin, G. S., Keating, M. A., Resick, C. J., Szabo, E., Kwan, H. K., & Peng, C. (2013). The meaning of leader integrity: A comparative study across Anglo, Asian, and Germanic cultures. *The Leadership Quarterly, 24,* 445–461.

Martinez, S. M., & Dorfman, P. W. (1998). The Mexican entrepreneur: An ethnographic study of the Mexican empressario. *International Studies of Management & Organization, 28,* 97–123.

McSweeney, B. (2002). Hofstede's model of national cultural differences and their consequences: A triumph of faith—a failure of analysis. *Human Relations, 55,* 89–118.

Mendenhall, M., Osland, J., Bird, A., Oddou, G., Maznevski, M., Stevens, M., & Stahl, G. (Eds.). (2012). *Global leadership: Research, practice, and development.* New York, NY: Routledge.

Nardon, L., & Steers, R. M. (2009). The culture theory jungle: Divergence and convergence in models of national culture. In R. S. Bhagat & R. M. Steers (Eds.), *Cambridge handbook of culture, organizations, and work* (pp. 3–22). Cambridge, UK: Cambridge University Press.

Parsons, T., & Shils, E. A. (1951). *Toward a general theory of action.* Cambridge, MA: Harvard University Press.

Pellegrini, E. K., & Scandura, T. A. (2006). Leader–member exchange (LMX), paternalism, and delegation in the Turkish business culture: An empirical investigation. *Journal of International Business Studies, 37,* 264–279.

Pellegrini, E. K., & Scandura, T. A. (2008). Paternalistic leadership: A review and agenda for future research. *Journal of Management, 34,* 566–593.

Peterson, M. F., & Castro, S. L. (2006). Measurement metrics at aggregate levels of analysis: Implications for organization culture research and the GLOBE project. *The Leadership Quarterly, 17,* 506–521.

Pickenpaugh, T. E. (1997). Symbols of rank, leadership and power in traditional cultures. *International Journal of Osteoarcheaology, 7,* 525–541.

Punnett, B. J. (2004). The developing world: Toward a managerial understanding. In H. W. Lane, M. L. Maznevski, M. E. Mendenhall, & J. McNett (Eds.), *The Blackwell handbook of global management: A guide to managing complexity* (pp. 387–405). Malden, MA: Blackwell.

Rauch, A., Frese, M., & Sonnentag, S. (2000). Cultural differences in planning/success relationships: A comparison of small enterprises in Ireland, West Germany, and East Germany. *Journal of Small Business Management, 38*, 28–41.

Resick, C. J., Martin, G. S., Keating, M. A., Dickson, M. W., Kwan, H. K., & Peng, C. (2011). What ethical leadership means to me: Asian, American, and European perspectives. *Journal of Business Ethics, 101*, 435–457.

Rotter, J. B. (1954). *Social learning and clinical psychology.* New York, NY: Prentice-Hall.

Sagiv, L., & Schwartz, S. H. (2000). Value priorities and subjective well-being: Direct relations and congruity effects. *European Journal of Social Psychology, 30,* 177–198.

Schein, E. H. (1992). *Organizational culture and leadership* (2nd ed.). San Francisco, CA: Jossey-Bass.

Schwartz, S. H. (1999). Cultural value differences: Some implications for work. *Applied Psychology: An International Review, 48,* 23–48.

Schwartz, S. H., & Sagie, G. (2000). Value consensus and importance: A cross-national study. *Journal of Cross-Cultural Psychology, 31,* 465–497.

Shane, S. (1993). Cultural influences on national rates of innovation. *Journal of Business Venturing, 8,* 59–73.

Shane, S., Venkataraman, S., & MacMillan, I. (1995). Cultural differences in innovation championing strategies. *Journal of Management, 21,* 931–952.

Sinha, J. B. P. (1995). *The cultural context of leadership and power.* New Delhi, India: Sage.

Sivakumar, K., & Nakata, C. (2001). The stampede toward Hofstede's framework: Avoiding the sample design pit in cross-cultural research. *Journal of International Business Studies, 32,* 555–574.

Smith, P. B., Peterson, M. F., & Schwartz, S. H. (2002). Cultural values, sources of guidance, and their relevance to managerial behavior: A 47-nation study. *Journal of Cross-Cultural Psychology, 33,* 188–208.

Steers, R. M., Nardon, L., & Sanchez-Runde, C. (2009). Culture and organization design: Strategy, structure, and decision-making. In R. S. Bhagat & R. M Steers (Eds.), *Cambridge handbook of culture, organizations, and work* (pp. 71–117). Cambridge, UK: Cambridge University Press.

Stewart, R., Barsoux, J. L., Kieser, A., Ganter, H. D., & Walgenbach, P. (1994). *Managing in Britain and Germany.* London, UK: St. Martin's Press/MacMillan Press.

Trice, H. M., & Beyer, J. M. (1991). Cultural leadership in organizations. *Organization Science, 2,* 149–169.

Trompenaars, F., & Hampden-Turner, C. (1997). *Riding the waves of culture: Understanding cultural diversity in business* (2nd ed.). London, UK: Nicholas-Brealey.

Walumbwa, F. O., Lawler, J. J., Avolio, B. J., Wang, P., & Shi, K. (2005). Transformational leadership and work-related attitudes: The moderating effects of collective and self-efficacy across cultures. *Journal of Leadership and Organizational Studies, 11,* 2–16.

Wanasika, I., Howell, J. P., Littrell, R., & Dorfman, P. (2011). Managerial leadership and culture in Sub-Saharan Africa. *Journal of World Business, 46*(2), 234–241.

Xin, K. R., & Tsui, A. S. (1996). Different strokes for different folks? Influence tactics by Asian-American and Caucasian-American managers. *The Leadership Quarterly, 7,* 109–132.

# CHAPTER 14

# Leadership Development

## The Nature of Leadership Development

*David V. Day*

*Aiden M. A. Thornton*

---

### Opening Case: A Day in the Life of a Leader

Zara is a process improvement consultant with the Performance Excellence Group, a global management consulting firm. She joined 4 years ago through the graduate program after completing an undergraduate degree in economics and organizational behavior. In this role, Zara typically works on projects with mid- to large-sized organizations to reduce cost through making business processes more efficient.

Zara has been promoted quickly from consultant to senior consultant to manager because of her strong technical skills in financial modeling, quantitative analysis, and structured problem solving. She has been identified as high-potential talent, which has resulted in her being placed on an accelerated career path.

While she has relied on technical skills for her success to date, Zara now needs to focus on developing leadership skills, because managers are required to lead small (three- to seven-person) project teams. She recently began attending a leader development program that covers key topics for first-time team leaders including communication, giving feedback, coaching fundamentals, and team dynamics.

The first module required her to complete a 360-degree assessment in which senior leaders, peers, and junior consultants rated their perceptions of Zara's leadership skills. Zara was debriefed on the results and found the experience to be somewhat confronting. She learned that while senior leaders appreciated her leadership potential, others perceived her to struggle on a number of fronts with her people skills.

Several of her peers and junior consultants believed she was too authoritative, noncollaborative, and often did not listen to others' perspectives. The coach conducting the debriefing made a number of development suggestions. As a result, she agreed to practice her listening skills in meetings by preparing at least three open-ended questions to ask, to take on a new consulting project that involved highly diverse stakeholder perspectives, and to write a short journal entry every week to reflect on changes she noticed in herself and her relationships. Over the following months, Zara noticed subtle changes in her ability to ask more frequently than to tell, to listen for the meaning behind others' responses, and to build greater levels of trust in her relationships that she never thought possible.

## Discussion Questions

1. What should Zara do to follow up on her developmental activities?

2. Why are these leadership skills important for Zara's development at this point in her career?

3. What are some alternative approaches the coach might have used to support Zara's development?

# Chapter Overview

Understanding the nature of leadership development is not straightforward, given the complexity of the topic. Leadership alone is a highly complex construct, which some commentators have claimed is "curiously unformed" as a scholarly discipline (Hackman & Wageman, 2007, p. 43). Development is an equally complex construct, especially given that it involves change and is a process of inherent gains and losses (Baltes, 1987). Although progress has been made in terms of the statistical modeling of change over time (e.g., McArdle, 2009; Ployhart & Vandenberg, 2010), aspects of development pertaining to time and the timing of when things occur continue to be theoretically underdeveloped and often imprecisely specified in theory and research (Mitchell & James, 2001).

Given the vast number of publications on the topic of leadership development, it is easy to assume that a great deal is known about it from a scientific perspective. Unfortunately, this does not appear to be the case. As noted by others in the field, volume does not necessarily correlate with quality when it comes to the leadership development literature (Avolio, Sosik, Jung, & Berson, 2003). More generally and historically, there is wide gap between leadership theory and practice (Zaccaro & Horn, 2003). Partly as a result of this gap, the field of leadership development has been mainly a collection of disparate "best practices" (e.g., 360-degree feedback, coaching, on-the-job experience, mentoring) rather than a coherent, ongoing, theoretically guided, and evidence-based process (Day, 2000). Fortunately, the times are changing.

Relatively recent advances in the field make the possibility of building an evidence-based science of leadership development more than a pipe dream. Unfortunately, the field is still dominated by practitioners and others of uncertain motives who often assert that they can prescribe *the* answer on how best to develop leaders and leadership in organizations, or promote the use of assessment instruments of suspect validity to diagnose leadership needs (e.g., Myers-Briggs Type Indicator; see Zaccaro & Horn, 2003). But the good news is that reputable researchers have begun to explore some of the underlying process issues theoretically and empirically. One example is a meta-analysis of 200 lab and field studies evaluating the impact of leadership interventions (Avolio et al., 2009). Results indicated overall positive effects for leadership training and development interventions (but with noted variability in respective effect sizes associated with the underlying theoretical approach).

Despite such advances, there is much we do not yet know about the nature of leadership and its development. One of the primary limitations of current empirical evidence is the limited scope of research methods applied to answer such questions. A number of empirical studies draw inferences about the efficacy of development approaches by comparing the growth of trained to untrained leaders, which is an unfair and meaningless comparison (Cooper & Richarson, 1986; Shadish, Cook, & Campbell, 2002). Rigorous application of the scientific method to social constructs such as leadership require stronger methods, including the use of experimental field designs with randomized allocation of leaders to groups, comparisons of multiple treatment conditions, longitudinal evaluation over multiple time intervals, and measurement of outcomes at multiple levels (e.g., change in individual and teams). Limited application of such methods constrains the extent to which we can be confident about inferring causality or understanding the efficacy of many development approaches examined in the following research. One purpose of this chapter is to review the emerging literature on the topic of leadership development and integrate it with several key questions and underlying assumptions about its nature. A relevant place to begin is with clearly describing what is meant by leadership development.

It is surprising and perhaps a bit unsettling how often an operational definition or a clear description of leadership development is assumed rather than clearly stated. The dominant thinking appears to assume that leadership development involves developing leadership, which would seem to make sense. Nonetheless, there are reasons to question such a simplistic approach. Although leadership has proven difficult to define precisely, many scholars assert that leadership involves a social interaction among two or more individuals in pursuit of a mutual goal (e.g., Bennis, 2007; although see the definition offered in Chapter 1 of this volume for another example). For this reason, it has been proposed that most of what passes for leadership development is more appropriately termed *leader development*

(Day, 2000). Whereas leaders can work to develop their leadership-related knowledge, skills, and competencies, because of its goal-oriented interpersonal and relational nature leadership cannot be developed directly unless intact dyads, work groups, or the organization as a whole are the focus of development.

Based on this distinction between leader and leadership development, the constructs can be described in these ways: *Leader development* is the expansion of an individual's capacity to be effective in leadership roles and processes, whereas *leadership development* is the expansion of an organization's capacity to enact basic leadership tasks needed to accomplish shared, collective work (McCauley, Van Velsor, & Ruderman, 2010). From these descriptions it can be inferred that what is typically labeled as leadership development is more appropriately termed *leader development* (hence our use of the term *leader/ship development* to indicate both leader and leadership development). Instead of focusing mainly on organization position, hierarchy, or status to denote leadership, the notion of roles and processes refers to behaviors or other actions enacted by anyone regardless of formal role that facilitate setting direction, creating alignment, and building commitment. These fundamental "leadership tasks" are functional, adaptable, and pragmatic, which is more fitting for the ever-increasing kinds of challenges that require collaborative forms of leadership (Drath et al., 2008).

This presents us with the first general question or underlying assumption about leader/ship development: What is the available evidence that people can become better leaders? Perhaps great leaders are born with their talent already genetically bestowed upon them and little can be done for others who lack these genetic advances. That is, how much of development as a leader is due to heritable factors such as genetics (i.e., nature), and how much is due to experiences in the environment (i.e., nurture)?

## Are Leaders Born or Made?

It has been estimated that U.S. organizations invest between US$20 billion and US$40 billion annually in leader/ship development programs and other supporting management education activities (Lamoureux, 2007). A 2014 survey of 2,500 business and HR leaders in 94 countries indicated that broadening, deepening, and accelerating leader/ship development was rated as *urgent* or *important* by 86% of respondents (O'Leonard & Krider, 2014). Given these vast investments and perceived importance, it certainly seems that organizations believe that leadership can be developed. Nonetheless, there is a difference between inferring that leadership is something that might be developed based on financial investments and demonstrating it with hard data.

A relevant question raised by researchers is whether there is a specific leadership gene (Antonakis, Day, & Schyns, 2012). When that question was posed, no one had isolated the leadership gene, but more recent research suggested there might be such a gene in predicting *leadership role occupancy* (i.e., whether someone holds a supervisory position or not)—which might be more accurately termed *supervisory role occupancy*. De Neve et al. (2013) designed research using twin design methods involving identical and fraternal twins as participants who share either 100% or 50% of their genetic material, respectively. The results from two such longitudinal panels indicated that leadership role occupancy is associated with a genetic feature called rs4950, a "single nucleotide polymorphism residing on a neuronal acetylchlorine receptor gene CHRNB3" (p. 45). In addition, results indicated that the hereditability ($h^2$) of leadership role occupancy is estimated at approximately 24% (i.e., about a quarter of the variance in role occupancy is due to genetic factors). This is consistent with other twin study research involving leadership role occupancy as the outcome, indicating approximately 30% heritability (Arvey et al., 2006; Arvey, Zhang, Avolio, & Krueger, 2007). Additional analyses in these studies suggested that work experiences explained approximately 11.5% of the variance in leadership role occupancy, with other environmental influences explaining the remainder.

Other research using twins designs (Zhang, Ilies, & Arvey, 2009) sought to examine potential environmental moderators of the noted relationship between genetic influences and leadership role occupancy. The general approach is grounded in theory and research on gene-environment interactions in which aspects of the social environment modify the influence of an individual's genetic makeup either strengthening or weakening $h^2$ effects on various outcomes (Plomin, DeFries, & Loehlin, 1977). Results suggested that the genetic influences on leadership role occupancy were weaker for individuals reared in enriched social environments (e.g., higher family socioeconomic status, higher perceived parental support, and lower perceived conflict with parents). Conversely, genetic effects were stronger for twins reporting generally poorer social environments.

These findings appear to offer relatively good news to scientists and practitioners interested in the topic of leader development. Although some nontrivial proportion of inherited capabilities is associated with ascendency into supervisory leadership roles (approximately 24%–30%), a far larger proportion of the variance was associated with nonshared environmental influences. Put somewhat differently, by virtue of "good genes" some individuals appear to have a genetic advantage when it comes to emerging or ascending into leadership-related roles; however, the results also suggest that anyone might become a better leader and increase their odds of occupying formal or informal leadership roles through deliberate practice and experience.

Along these lines, research using managers as participants has shown that the relationship between the amount of developmental challenge in work experiences and leadership skill development shows an overall pattern of diminishing returns. When a developmental challenge reaches high levels (i.e., the experience is very difficult) the amount learned from those challenges is reduced; however, access to feedback (support) was shown to offset diminishing returns associated with high levels of developmental challenge (DeRue & Wellman, 2009). The amount of available environmental support is an important resource for developing leaders.

Having answered affirmatively the question that leader development in the form of predicting leadership role occupancy is more than genetics, the next question examines evidence that leaders actually can develop over time.

## Do Leaders Develop (i.e., Change Over Time)?

Although the research base is not large, there is emerging evidence from longitudinal designs on the question of whether leaders develop (i.e., change) over time, and if so, what factors predict this development. This question gets at core issues involving the psychology of change. Relevant studies take a longitudinal perspective (involving a minimum of three waves of data tracking the same core constructs) focusing on the development of indicators of leadership emergence (i.e., is someone seen as a leader) and/or effectiveness as a leader (i.e., is someone good at being a leader)—which are different but related questions. Because of some challenges associated with generalizing from case studies, we excluded them and other forms of anecdotal evidence (e.g., biographies of leaders) in this review of the evidence of longitudinal leader development.

The earliest published studies of psychological factors related to leadership advancement (a form of emergence) was the AT&T Management Progress Study (Bray, Campbell, & Grant, 1974) that pioneered the use of the assessment center for selection as well as development. The study began in 1956 and was still active several decades later. The focus of the longitudinal research was to address these core questions (Bray, 1982): (1) What significant changes take place as lives develop in a large business enterprise? (2) What expected changes do not occur? (3) What lies behind these changes and stabilities?

The study director wrote that he thought "the most significant single finding . . . is that success as a manager is highly predictable" (Bray, 1982, p. 183). Note that Bray (1982) frames results in terms of predicting success as a manager rather than as a leader; however, contemporary researchers frame similar career advancement issues in terms of leadership role occupancy (e.g., Arvey et al., 2006, 2007; De Neve et al., 2013). One of the most important personality factors in the study was *leadership motivation*, which was significantly related to assessment factors such as *leadership skills* and *work motivation*. Other personality factors related to multiple assessment factors were *ambition* and *optimism*. It is interesting to note the parallel between these results and more recent efforts directed at developing and testing a *motivation to lead* construct (Chan & Drasgow, 2001), as well as the role of optimism as a positive psychological capacity that is thought to be developed as part of authentic leader development (Luthans & Avolio, 2003).

The Fullerton Longitudinal Study (FLS) is an ongoing long-term project designed to study child development through adolescence and into adulthood. The project began in 1979 with 130 participants receiving yearly assessments through age 17, then again at age 24 and age 29. Leadership assessments were gathered at this last assessment period to date. This study provides a unique opportunity to trace the developmental pathways from individual differences in early childhood to self-rated adult leadership potential as well as leadership role occupancy (self-reported frequency of engagement in work-related leadership duties). Results from one set of analyses indicated that children who were more approaching of new people, places, and experiences at ages 2–16 tended to become more extraverted adolescents (age 17) with greater social skills as adults (age 29) and more work-related leadership responsibilities and higher transformational leadership potential (Guerin et al., 2011).

A second study from this larger FLS project sought to investigate potential relationships between intelligence, childhood intrinsic motivation, adolescent intrinsic motivation, and motivation to lead in adulthood (Gottfried et al., 2011). There were no significant relationships between intelligence and any of the motivation outcomes. But childhood intrinsic motivation predicted adolescent intrinsic motivation, which predicted the affective-identity ("I like to lead") and noncalculative ("I will lead even if there are no benefits to me") components of motivation to lead. There was no relationship between adolescent motivation and social-normative ("I have a duty to lead") motivation to lead.

Taken together, the FLS research provides insights into the early influences on leader development. Childhood intrinsic motivation and approach temperaments appear to be related to adolescent motivation and personality (extraversion) that predict aspects of motivation to lead and self-appraised leadership potential in adulthood. One potential implication of these findings is that more introverted children and adolescents might benefit from youth leadership initiatives designed to help draw out and prepare them for future leadership roles. Consistent with the literature on personality and leadership (Judge, Bono, Ilies, & Gerhardt, 2002), more extraverted individuals might have an advantage in emerging as a leader although there may be less of an influence on their subsequent effectiveness. Going forward with the FLS project, researchers plan to collect independent leadership ratings as the participants move further into adulthood and have the opportunity to take on additional leadership responsibilities.

*Developmental trajectory studies* involve research designed to chart and understand (i.e., model) the evolution of outcomes over time (Nagin, 2005). Trajectories are relevant to the study of leader development in that the respective leadership skills, competence, and effectiveness may traverse much of the adult lifespan (Day, Harrison, & Halpin, 2009). Modeling leader development trajectories could provide insight into different forms or shapes of trajectories, given that individuals are unlikely to start at the same level of knowledge or skill, or develop in the same way or at the same time, and to identify individual factors that predict differences in these trajectories.

Using data from the National Longitudinal Survey of Youth, 1979 (U.S. Department of Labor), researchers examined aspects of leader emergence (i.e., leadership role occupancy and leader advancement) across 10 years with a sample ($N = 1,747$) of full-time working adults (Li, Arvey, & Song, 2011). The researchers examined the influence of general mental ability, self-esteem, and family socioeconomic status on these two forms of leader emergence, and also examined the moderating role of gender. Leadership data were collected on five separate occasions and modeled using two-part random effect modeling for semicontinuous longitudinal data (Muthén, 2004). Results suggested a linear growth model fit the data better than alternatives (e.g., no growth; quadratic model). Self-esteem had a significant and positive effect on leadership role occupancy for both men and women and on leadership advancement in terms of number of employees supervised over time for women. Family socioeconomic status was found to have a negative effect on the leadership advancement of women, and general mental ability was found to have no effect on leader emergence over time for either sex.

Perhaps the most intriguing result from this study is that women leaders raised in higher socioeconomic environments were more likely to stall in their careers compared to women raised in lower economic status families. Although these results are interesting, there is not a clear explanation for this finding. More affluent women were not more likely to quit work, because everyone in the sample was employed full-time across the 10-year period. Instead, the authors point to work in the fields of child development (e.g., Luthar, 2003) and counseling psychology (Lapour & Heppner, 2009) to suggest that there is price for privilege, which may affect women to a greater extent than men when it comes to career development.

Another study estimating and predicting developmental trajectories examined university students ($N = 1,315$) engaged in community service–action learning projects in conjunction with a course on leadership and team building (Day & Sin, 2011). The participants worked in project teams across 13 weeks to conceptualize, design, implement, and evaluate a project that would benefit the local community in some way. Each team consisted of approximately six members plus a peer learning adviser (i.e., coach). There were no formal leaders assigned or appointed in the teams. Among other things, the peer adviser provided ratings of each team member four times on his or her effectiveness as a leader in the team. The research was designed as a partial test of a comprehensive and integrative model of leader development (Day et al., 2009). Central to the model are the proposed underlying processes of leader identity construction and self-regulation, which are further supported at the deepest level by the adult development processes associated with selective adaptation and compensation (Baltes, 1997).

A surprising finding from this study was that the prevailing trajectory of leader effectiveness was mainly negative, with a slight positive upturn at the final rating period (quadratic model). This reinforces an important point that development is not necessarily a positive, linear function. In the present case, putting young adults into a team environment in which they need both to perform and learn under stressful conditions can challenge their effectiveness as leaders. Nonetheless, there were conditions that moderated this overall trajectory. Identifying more strongly as a leader and adopting a stronger learning goal orientation (Dweck, 1986) were shown to be related to more effective (less negative) trajectories. Growth mixture modeling procedures (Wang & Bodner, 2007) revealed a second class of trajectories for about 10% of the sample consisting of positive and linear development of rated leadership effectiveness. Additional evidence suggested that aspects of adult development processes differentiated reliably between the two subclasses of developmental trajectories.

The foregoing discussion provides robust evidence that individuals do not experience or benefit from leader development in the same ways. Furthermore, various theoretically driven individual differences in the form of leader identity construction, goal orientation, and adult development processes were associated with more effective trajectories of leader development. These individual difference factors, as well as those identified in other longitudinal studies (e.g., personality, psychosocial developmental level, motivation to lead, self-esteem), might eventually prove to be important in enhancing and otherwise facilitating the development of effective leaders. This is particularly relevant if future research identifies treatment-trait interactions (Gully & Chen, 2010) in which individual differences partially determine the extent to which leader development initiatives achieve their intended outcomes.

This section reviewed longitudinal investigations demonstrating that leaders can and do develop over time and that individual differences can predict development and its forms (i.e., trajectories). The next section examines what develops as a function of leadership development initiatives. Put differently, if leaders can emerge or become more effective through taking part in developmental initiatives, then what is developed that is associated with this enhanced emergence and effectiveness?

## What Develops in Leader Development?

Determining what develops as a function of leader development initiatives is integral to advancing research as well as practice. From a research perspective, the answer determines the outcome variable(s) of interest that are measured in evaluating the degree of change that has occurred. There is a wide range of potential criteria to consider. What have become extremely popular—and controversial—are leadership competency models. Although the term *competency* apparently "has no meaning apart from the particular definition with whom one is speaking" (Schippmann et al., 2000, p. 706), one way to consider competencies is as bundles of leadership-related knowledge, skills, and abilities. Critics argue that competency models are a best practice "that defies logic, experience, and data" (Hollenbeck, McCall, & Silzer, 2006, p. 399), but others have countered that competency models provide an overarching framework that helps focus individuals and organizations in developing leadership skills. Specifically, competency models help individuals by outlining a leadership framework that can be used to help select, develop, and understand leadership effectiveness, and also employed as a basis for leadership training and developmental initiatives within an organization. Such models also potentially help organizations by communicating which general forms of leader behaviors are important and purportedly offering a leadership framework that is relevant across positions and situations.

**Developing the Expert Leader.** Regardless of one's perspective on leadership competency models, they provide taxonomy of various leadership-related skills, subskills, and skills bundles (i.e., competencies). A generic model of leadership skill requirements across organizational levels is the so-called leadership skills *strataplex* (T. V. Mumford, Campion, & Morgeson, 2007). At its core, the model proposes that leadership skills requirements can be understood in terms of four general categories: (1) cognitive, (2) interpersonal, (3) business, and (4) strategic skills. Various subskills for each general category have also been proposed and tested (see Table 14.1).

**Table 14.1**    Two Views on Essential Leadership Skills Requirements

| Leadership Strataplex | Mumford et al. (2007) | Developable Leadership Capabilities | Van Velsor & McCauley (2004) |
|---|---|---|---|
| GENERAL SKILLS | SUBSKILLS | GENERAL CAPABILITIES | SUBSKILLS |
| Cognitive | • Speaking<br>• Active listening<br>• Writing<br>• Reading comprehension<br>• Active learning | Self-Management | • Self-awareness<br>• Ability to balance conflicting demands<br>• Ability to learn<br>• Leadership values |
| Interpersonal | • Social perceptiveness<br>• Coordination<br>• Persuasion | Social | • Ability to build and maintain relationships<br>• Ability to build effective work groups<br>• Communication skills<br>• Ability to develop others |
| Business | • Management of material resources<br>• Operations analyses<br>• Management of personnel resources<br>• Management of financial resources | Work Facilitation | • Management skills<br>• Ability to think and act strategically<br>• Ability to think creatively<br>• Ability to initiate and implement change |
| Strategic | • Visioning<br>• Systems perception<br>• Identification of consequences<br>• Identification of key causes<br>• Problem identification<br>• Solution appraisal | | |

A different model has been offered by researchers with regard to individual leadership capabilities that also can be developed (Van Velsor & McCauley, 2004). The three general categories of capabilities or competencies are (1) self-management capabilities, (2) social capabilities, and (3) work facilitation capabilities. Supporting capabilities for each of the general competencies is also provided in Table 14.1. It is interesting that there is relatively little overlap between these two frameworks.

A relevant question to ask is, Which of these models is correct? The answer is that they both could be right, or that one or both could be wrong. Trying to distill leadership into a set of skills or competencies will likely become unwieldy and still omit important things. They are also highly *leader-centric* in assuming that the essence of leadership always rests with the actions of an individual leader.

Nonetheless, understanding leadership as a set of skills or competencies has some advantages. For one thing, a skills-based approach is consistent with the assumption that individual leadership capabilities can be developed (Lord & Hall, 2005). In addition, skills provide a bridge between trait theories and behavioral theories of leadership and help to identify missing components that allow effective leaders to enact the right behaviors at the right time (M. D. Mumford, Zaccaro, Connelly, & Marks, 2000).

A question regarding a skills-based perspective on leadership concerns the expected time frame for complex skills and competencies to develop (Day & Dragoni, 2015). There are recent approaches that have conceptualized leadership skills development in terms of an expert performance model (Day et al., 2009; Lord & Hall, 2005). That is, developing leadership skills and competencies is comparable to developing expertise in other domains such as science, music, chess, and sports (Bloom, 1985; Chi, Glaser, & Farr, 1988; Ericsson, Charness, Feltovich, & Hoffman, 2006). Whereas earlier findings suggest it takes at least 10 years or 10,000 hours of dedicated practice to achieve minimal expert status in a given domain (Ericsson et al., 2006; Ericsson, Krampe, & Tesch-Römer, 1993), more recent meta-analytic findings indicate that practice may account for between 1% to 26% of the variation in performance across a variety of domains (Macnamara, Hambrick, & Oswald, 2014). In other words, the role of practice in developing expertise may be domain specific. But if practice matters in the leadership domain (and we maintain that it does), what would help to motivate the kinds of deliberate practice over such an extended time period to become an expert leader? This was the basis for the integrative approach to leader development proposed by Day et al. (2009).

Other approaches have focused on the development of leaders' strategic thinking skills, arguing that such skills are becoming increasingly important at higher organizational levels. More specifically, strategic thinking competency comprises the knowledge, skills, and abilities leaders need to form "value-creating strategic goals and strategies" (Dragoni et al., 2014, p. 867). Researchers have demonstrated that accumulated work experience positively relates to executives' strategic thinking competency after controlling for individual characteristics and other measures of work experience (Dragoni, Oh, Vankatwyk, & Tesluk, 2011). Additionally, global work experiences—especially those involving greater cultural distance—were shown to develop the strategic thinking of leaders (Dragoni et al., 2014). The role of accumulated work experience (varied levels of roles and responsibilities across a leader's career) extends other research on leadership role occupancy (i.e., having a supervisory role or not). In addition, it flips the focus from whether or not someone occupies a supervisory role as the focal outcome to conceptualizing leaders' portfolio of work experiences as a predictor of their development. This has motivated more recent theorizing on the role of experience as well as time in leader development processes.

In a recent outcome-oriented review of the leader/ship development literature, Day and Dragoni (2015) argue that thinking of programs, experiences, or interventions as directly shaping (causing) leader development is overly simplistic see One reason is that developing leaders start at different points due to their individual capabilities and change in different ways as a function of developmental experiences. As such, experience is a moderator or contingency effect of the relationship between individual capabilities brought to an experience and more immediate developmental outcomes (see Figure 14.1b). Such outcomes include competencies and bundles of knowledge, skills, and abilities as well as what are termed leader self-views in the forms of self-awareness, self-efficacy, and self-concept (i.e., identity). These leader development outcomes are proximal to more distal outcomes related to deeper forms of adult development changes that occur only through extensive, dedicated practice. Such deeper changes can be thought of as altering the internal operating system of a leader and take considerable amounts of time and practice as well as ongoing support. The value of unpacking the outcomes of leader development around a very crude proximal/distal time focus is that the proximal indicators of leader development can suggest that deeper, longer-term development might occur with practice. A similar structure is thought to be in place in developing the longer-term (distal) leadership capacity of groups and organizations.

**Figure 14.1a**    Traditional, Simplistic Thinking on Leader Development

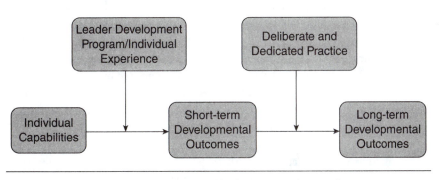

**Figure 14.1b**    Revised, Contemporary Thinking on Leader Development

SOURCE: Adapted from Day, D. V., & Dragoni, L. (2015). Leadership development: An outcome-oriented review based on time and levels of analyses. *Annual Review of Organizational Psychology and Organizational Behavior, 2*, 133-156.

In building on the previous questions of whether leadership development can occur, evaluating the longitudinal evidence that it does develop, and understanding what develops during the process, the next section will examine ways in which leadership development is cultivated in individuals and organizations. Specifically, what are methods for developing leadership skills and competencies and corresponding knowledge structures in individuals?

## How Best to Promote Leader/ship Development?

Most of the attention in the leader/ship development literature has been devoted to proposing ways in which to promote it. This has led to a focus on programs, practices, and other experiences mainly from a practitioner standpoint. An alternative perspective is that more needs to be done to enhance a science of leader/ship development with a greater focus on underlying process issues on which to base various practices. Nonetheless, aspects of how to develop leaders and leadership are important but need to be better integrated with theoretical and empirical concerns. This section will first review different approaches to developmental practices: (1) structured programs, (2) experiences, and (3) relatively recent work on developing organizational cultures in which developmental practices are fostered in an ongoing manner. This is followed by suggestions on how to integrate the practice concerns with those associated with better understanding the leader/ship development process.

**Structured Programs to Develop Leaders and Leadership.** Structured programs typically vary in duration from several hours to several years and provide various types of content. Conger (2010) suggests that leader/ship development initiatives can be classified into four general categories: (1) individual skill development, (2) socialization of organizational vision and values, (3) strategic leadership initiatives to foster large-scale change, and (4) action learning initiatives targeted to address organizational challenges and opportunities.

*Individual skill development* is an extremely popular approach to leader development, with many organizations and consulting firms offering open-enrollment as well as customized programs. Other terms for these kinds of initiatives include assessment for development and feedback-intensive programs (Guthrie & King, 2004). They are so termed because participants complete a number of individual difference measures (e.g., personality, values, leadership skills assessments) and also receive the results of a 360-degree assessment completed by self, subordinates, peers, and superiors (and possibly others). A goal of these kinds of initiatives is to build self-awareness regarding individual strengths and developmental needs, and to enhance an understanding of how one is perceived by others (Day et al., 2014). Especially when linked with coaching and an action-oriented development plan, these initiatives offer a blueprint of sorts for building needed leadership skills while acknowledging and leveraging identified strengths.

Nonetheless, there are a few caveats with regard to the success of skills development programs. In a comprehensive meta-analytic review of the feedback intervention literature, it was found that nearly 40% of the interventions had a negative effect on performance and almost 15% were found to have had no effect (Kluger & DeNisi, 1996). These results suggest that merely providing feedback is no guarantee of positive developmental outcomes. Although research has indicated that working with a coach can help improve 360-degree feedback ratings over time (Smither, London, Flautt, Vargas, & Kuchine, 2003), and that meeting with direct reports to discuss their upward feedback is positively related to subsequent improvement (Walker & Smither, 1999), positive change is not a given. For example, if direct reports are held accountable for their upward feedback in the form of nonanonymous ratings, it is likely to result in inflated ratings of the supervisor's performance (Antonioni, 1994). Improvement is most likely when the following conditions apply: (1) feedback indicates that change is necessary; (2) individuals have a positive feedback orientation (i.e., feedback is viewed positively); (3) change is feasible; (4) appropriate goals are set to regulate behavior; and (5) actions are taken that can lead to skills improvement (Smither, London, & Reilly, 2005).

Leader/ship development programs are also used to *socialize* either new or newly promoted individuals with the *vision and values of the organization*. Along with setting direction and building commitment, researchers have argued that creating alignment is a key leadership process (Drath et al., 2008). An important form of alignment is in developing a shared understanding of organizational priorities and ways of working (Conger, 2010). As compared with leadership skills development programs, these kinds of initiatives tend to be done in-house (i.e., internally developed and delivered), using company leaders as teachers. Although such programs are becoming increasingly popular, their use is still relatively rare compared with other categories of leader/ship development programs. Regardless of its popularity, the approach illustrates how a process designed to socialize leaders on the basic values and operating philosophy of the company has evolved into leader/ship development.

The *active strategic change management* of an organization has also become a driving reason behind leader/ship development in terms of addressing shifts in the requisite leadership capabilities needed to implement widespread change. These kinds of initiatives are typically highly customized to an organization's strategy, with emphases on communicating strategic objectives (especially if they are changing), creating alignment among organizational leaders in terms of the strategy (i.e., building strategic unity), and developing change agents across organizational levels to facilitate change and enhance progress toward strategic priorities. Such programs have potential to be effective for building individual and organizational change-related skills and competencies; however, a key component in their potential success is that the senior leadership team has a clear change agenda and knows what leadership requirements are needed. It almost goes without saying that this is not always a given.

The final category of structured leadership programs involves *action learning initiatives*. As the name implies, such programs involve working together in teams to address problems of strategic importance (action) while simultaneously building self-awareness and learning about leadership through individual and group reflection (learning). The focus of such initiatives is on holistic leader development as compared with *action training* (Frese, Beimel, & Schoenborn, 2003) that focuses on learning by doing through structured practices such as role play with feedback to develop specific skills and competencies (e.g., charisma). Conversely, action learning has roots in the pioneering work of Revans (1980) and is essentially an unstructured or semistructured form of learning by doing.

Action learning can be a powerful tool for leader/ship development; however, there are potential downsides. It is a very intense program that requires a major investment, especially in terms of participants' time, because most participants take on action learning on top of their day-to-day job responsibilities. The value in terms of leader/ship development can be lost or seriously diluted if the focus becomes mainly on getting the project completed (action) with little commensurate attention to development (learning). This is why the use of an independent team coach is recommended. Despite the potential downside to action learning, evidence suggests that such initiatives are widely used—76% of survey respondents reported *extensive use*—for leader/ship development purposes (Conger & Xin, 2000).

In summary, structured programs are a popular method for addressing leader/ship development needs in organizations. Although the variety of programs might be combined into four general categories, there is great diversity within categories in terms of program length, intensity, and focus. There is also the overarching risk of thinking about leader/ship development in programmatic terms, which contributes to the tendency to result in episodic thinking. That is, if development is thought of as occurring only during a designated formal program, then the critical development that must continue when an individual returns to the job is overlooked or downplayed. Individual change and development require an extended period of dedicated practice, as the research from the expert performance domain has demonstrated (e.g., Ericsson et al., 1993). Put differently, if you only try to develop during a formal program, then it is unlikely that you will ever acquire the sophisticated levels of leadership skills and expertise needed to be effective in senior leadership roles.

**Developing Leadership Through Experiences.** Although leader/ship development programs are popular with organizations, when you ask successful senior executives about how they developed as leaders, they tend to claim it was through on-the-job experience. Specifically, it was the lessons of experience that were reported to be the most potent forces for development (McCall, Lombardo, & Morrison, 1988). These findings parallel those from the job performance literature in noting that job experience can have a substantial indirect effect on work performance through its effect on job knowledge (Schmidt, Hunter, & Outerbridge, 1986). This has fostered a 70-20-10 heuristic in that approximately 70% of leader development is thought to come from on-the-job experience, 20% from developmental relationships, and 10% from formal programs. It is important to keep in mind that this is a general heuristic and not a validated formula for developing leader/ship. Nonetheless, it highlights the importance that those involved in leader/ship development design and delivery place on experience for development.

In an attempt to provide some structure to identifying and measuring the developmental components of managerial jobs, McCauley and colleagues developed the Developmental Challenge Profile (McCauley, Ruderman, Ohlott, & Morrow, 1994). Factor analyses of the responses of nearly 700 managers suggested three general underlying categories of developmental job challenges: (1) *job transitions* (e.g., unfamiliar responsibilities, proving yourself); (2) *task-related characteristics* (e.g., creating change, handling external pressure, influencing without authority); and (3) *obstacles* (e.g., lack of top management support, difficult boss). As noted, each of these general categories was multidimensional in nature. Subsequent research on the measure revealed significant gender differences in job challenges, with men reporting greater task-related challenges whereas women managers reported experiencing greater developmental obstacles in their jobs (Ohlott, Ruderman, & McCauley, 1994).

More recent research on developing leaders through experience examined the potential boundary conditions associated with highly challenging experiences. Using the McCauley et al. (1994) Developmental Challenge Profile, researchers linked leadership skills development with the amount of challenge in the experience (DeRue & Wellman, 2009). As hypothesized, the relationship between developmental challenge and leadership skill development showed a pattern of diminishing returns. That is, after a certain point adding more challenge to a developmental experience became less predictive of further skills development. But the researchers also found that aspects of the context in terms of access to feedback (i.e., support) offset the diminishing returns associated with high levels of developmental challenge.

These empirical findings are consistent with a proposed leader development model in which any experience can be made more developmentally powerful to the extent that it includes aspects of assessment, challenge, and support (Van Velsor & McCauley, 2004). It can be argued that having good feedback availability is an important support resource (e.g., reinforcement, knowledge of results) such that even when the developmental challenge is very intense, resources in the form of feedback can help to facilitate further leadership skill development. Without the access to feedback the challenge may become overwhelming, which serves as an obstacle to additional development from the experience.

McCall (2010) has proposed recasting leader/ship development to make better use of experience, while also recognizing that "using experience effectively to develop leadership talent is a lot more complicated and difficult than it appears to be" (p. 3). Part of the issue contributing to this complexity is that experience can be so wide-ranging, including job rotations, strategic job assignments, action learning projects, as well as experientially based development programs. In other words, what is *not* experience? In order to address this challenge, some organizations have developed frameworks that identify and link experiences, competencies, relationships, and learning capabilities that individuals need to develop as they move through job assignments and progress in the organization (Yost & Mannion Plunket, 2010).

Developing this sort of comprehensive taxonomy is a major undertaking. The advantage of having such a framework is that it can be used in identifying the experiences most important for development, redesigning certain jobs to make them more developmental, and evaluating the overall level of leadership capacity in the organization in terms of the breadth and depth of leadership talent. Although potentially very useful, this taxonomy approach appears to ignore the human element in the learning process. Specifically, learning from experience is not always a given because (1) there is not always an awareness that there is something to learn; (2) even if such an awareness exists, it is not always clear what is to be learned; and (3) there is a good deal of ambiguity and uncertainty in determining if or when learning has occurred (Brehmer, 1980; Feldman, 1986).

In summary, experience is often thought of as the most promising and potentially powerful developer of leaders (McCall, 2010). This makes sense at a general level, but when the nature of experience is unpacked it proves more complicated than it sounds. Everything related to leader development could be cast in terms of experience, from the shortest classroom workshop to intense stretch assignments or ongoing work experiences. Experience is also complex and multifaceted, making it difficult to quantify and categorize (Tesluk & Jacobs, 1998). Nonetheless, researchers have demonstrated that it is possible to obtain an estimate of the degree of developmental challenge in work experiences and to link it with relevant outcomes (e.g., DeRue & Wellman, 2009; Dragoni et al., 2011). Because learning from experience is not always easy or straightforward, more attention needs to be given to helping individual learners gain the desired lessons of experience as part of the developmental process rather than merely providing experiences (Day, 2010).

**Deliberately Developmental Organizations (DDO).** The DDO concept is a relatively new addition to the literature on leader/ship development. In particular, it is an innovative approach to simultaneously develop people and organizations (Kegan & Lahey, 2016) by embedding ongoing developmental practices in the culture of an organization.

Kegan and Lahey (2009) assert that developmental initiatives are often undermined due to underlying avoidance pressures. The first of these presses is avoidance of self, which occurs through an inability to acknowledge, share, and openly work on one's weaknesses. The second press is avoidance of others, which occurs through a tendency to speak negatively behind others' backs. Both result in lost productivity due to investment of valuable resources (e.g., time, energy, effort) in "politicking" rather than being authentic. As a result, people waste time looking good, and they waste even more time making others look bad (Kegan & Lahey, 2016). Both of these tendencies present obstacles to leader/ship development.

In response to these problematic dynamics, a DDO is based on three overarching principles: home, edge, and groove. Collectively, these concepts create space for people to be vulnerable with self and others in order to develop human and organizational potential simultaneously. *Home* refers to the need for a community of coworkers built on trust and mutual respect. In this community, rank does not have its usual privileges and everyone actively plays a role in fostering others' development (e.g., through frequent feedback, testing assumptions, and so forth). *Edge* refers to the need to locate one's current self-understanding on a scale of developmental levels that represent increasingly complex ways in which adults understand themselves (Kegan, 1982; Kegan & Lahey, 2009, 2016). While Kegan's full model of adult development contains five developmental levels, he argues that the highest three levels are most relevant to people in contemporary organizations. At level three (*socialized mind*) people internalize and identify with external authorities, which often results in being a loyal and obedient team member. At level four (*self-authoring mind*) socialized expectations lose their grip as the self increasingly identifies with its own unique values and perspectives in prioritizing individual autonomy. At level five (*self-transforming mind*) self-authored perspectives loosen as the self increasingly identifies with the dynamic interdependence between self, others, and the world in prioritizing a more systemic understanding of self. One's edge is typically identified through deep, reflective exercises that require identification of unconscious assumptions that can undermine developmental progress

(Kegan & Lahey, 2009). Whereas Kegan and Lahey (2016) assert that organizations are asking for a major shift in individual mental complexity at all levels, there is somewhat mixed support for a correlation between the developmental level of leaders' self-understanding, their personal effectiveness, and organizational performance (McCauley et al., 2006).

Unlike traditional organizations, which aspire to develop leaders through event-like training programs (Development Dimensions International, 2015), *groove* places the emphasis on development through embedded practice. Practices are short exercises that are deliberately undertaken on a daily (or at least weekly) basis to foster psychological growth along the scale of developmental levels. Practices are tailored to one's current developmental perspective and are deployed during daily tasks with additional support and challenge, and therefore may be more effective than traditional training programs in fostering development (Day, 2010; McCauley et al., 2010).

In practice, implementing the three principles of home, edge, and groove results in a number of distinct departures from traditional organizations. One example is that destabilization can be constructive, in which feelings of inadequacy and incompetence are recognized as resources and are actively promoted (i.e., no pain, no gain; or pain + reflection = growth). A second example is that the interior life is part of what is manageable, in which one's whole self—including values, thoughts, and feelings—are prioritized to the same extent as observable behaviors, thereby closing the arbitrary divide between personal and professional lives.

Preliminary findings suggest that DDO cultures may play an important role in improving various aspects of organizational performance including team effectiveness, financial performance, and market reputation (Kegan & Lahey, 2016). Although DDOs present a potentially exciting new approach to developing people in general and leaders in particular, these conclusions must be interpreted with due caution. Kegan's (1982, 1994) theory has been inferred from relatively small samples, has not been subject to full construct validation, and relatively few psychometric properties are reported on his assessment of developmental levels (Lahey et al., 1988).

Looking ahead to the final section of the chapter, future directions in the science and practice of leader/ship development are considered. Specifically, what remains to be done to further improve and advance the field? Where are the major gaps between what we know and what we need to know?

## How to Improve Leader/ship Development Science and Practice?

**Theory.** There is a recognized need for promoting more integrative theory-building strategies in the general field of leadership (Avolio, 2007), and this certainly also applies to leader/ship development. In moving to the next level of integration, theory could more fully consider the dynamic interplay between leaders and followers, in addition to taking into greater account the context in which these interactions occur (Avolio & Gardner, 2005). Another way of thinking about this proposed integrative strategy is in terms of inclusiveness. Historically, leadership theory mainly has been about leaders in terms of their personal characteristics, mindsets, and behaviors. More integrative theories recognize that the leadership landscape includes leaders, followers, and the situational context as essential ingredients in this dynamic interaction. One of the most appealing aspects of a DDO is the notion of an everyone culture (Kegan & Lahey, 2016) rather than a focus on developing a relatively small percentage of employees (usually no more than 3%–5%) who are considered to be high-potential leaders capable of handling senior leadership roles and responsibilities.

New frameworks of leadership can also help inform leader/ship development. A good example is the theoretical work of Drath and colleagues (2008), who have recast the basic parameters of leadership around the fundamental tasks of direction, alignment, and commitment. As a possible replacement for the traditional leadership "tripod" of leaders, followers, and a shared goal (Bennis, 2007), an alternative ontology for leadership is organized in terms of the leadership outcomes associated with (1) widespread agreement in a collective on the overall goals, aims, and mission (*direction*); (2) the organization and coordination of knowledge and work in a collective (*alignment*); and (3) the willingness of individuals to subsume their own interests and benefit within the collective interest and benefit (*commitment*).

Drath and colleagues (2008) argue that the traditional tripod ontology is too narrow to support emerging leadership theories associated with shared or distributed leadership, applications of complexity science, and relational approaches to leadership. That aside, this new ontology offers fresh ways to conceptualize leader/ship development as well. Anything that can help develop ways to enhance direction, alignment, or commitment at the individual, group, or organizational level would be viable leader/ship development.

Another area of future theoretical interest is in moving toward a more integrative and inclusive leader/ship development of a different kind. Leadership is a dynamic, evolving process. As such, it incorporates behaviors, perceptions, decision making, and a whole host of other constructs. Thus, leadership by nature is an eclectic phenomenon, and attempting to conceptualize and study its development from any one theoretical perspective (e.g., motivational, emotional, behavioral) will yield only limited results. More inclusive and integrative perspectives are needed that cut across a number of theoretical domains. One example is the integrative approach to leader development that links otherwise disparate domains of adult development, identity and self-regulation, and expertise acquisition (Day et al., 2009). Using this as just one example, leader/ship development theory will continue to advance by integrating across multiple domains and disciplines in a more diverse and eclectic manner.

**Research.** The leader/ship development field incorporates several challenging features that need to be considered in moving forward with a research agenda. One such consideration is that of *levels*. Some researchers have commented that leader/ship development is inherently a multilevel process (Avolio, 2004; Day & Dragoni, 2015). Relevant levels to consider include within-person and between-person; higher dyadic levels involving relationships with followers, peers, and subordinates; as well as team and organizational levels. Going forward, researchers will need to be very clear as to the appropriate level(s) at which they are studying leader/ship development and to choose the type of research design, measures, and analyses that are most suitable for the respective focus. In particular, it appears that cross-level approaches (e.g., effects of organizations and teams on individuals) hold great promise for furthering our understanding of developmental processes.

Leader/ship development also is a dynamic and longitudinal process, which inherently involves the consideration of *time* (Day, 2014). As noted at the beginning of this chapter, we need better theory and more research that explicitly address time and the specification of when things occur (Mitchell & James, 2001). There is no area of research where this is truer than leader/ship development. The development of organizational leadership in general and leaders in particular can be conceptualized as a process occurring across the entire adult lifespan (Day et al., 2009). Clearly, there are limits in terms of what any one research study can tackle in terms of time frame; however, it is encouraging to see studies such as the Fullerton Longitudinal Study (Gottfried et al., 2011; Guerin et al., 2011) that are adopting a lifespan development perspective in addressing issues related to leader development. Going forward, acknowledging the longitudinal nature of leader/ship development will ideally challenge researchers to give careful attention to when they measure things, how often they measure, and how many times they measure, and linking these measurement concerns with a theoretical framework that lays out when (and how) developmental changes are thought to unfold. This is indeed a high standard for researchers, but it is one that is likely to reap huge dividends in terms of better understanding leader/ship development and ultimately devising ways to accelerate the underlying processes.

Another research recommendation is more fully to consider the *individualized* nature of development. Leaders do not develop in the same way following identical growth patterns (e.g., Day & Sin, 2011). People often learn different things from the same experience, and some learn the key lessons of experience more readily than others. Methodological and analytical approaches that take a more individualized approach to leader development will likely yield more insight than those that only attempt to model average trends across a given sample.

Raudenbush (2001) has proposed a personal trajectory approach to developmental research. Researchers now have individualized approaches to use, such as group-based modeling of development (Nagin, 2005) and growth mixture modeling (Wang & Bodner, 2007), that can identify and potentially predict different latent trajectory classes (see Day & Sin, 2011). These are powerful techniques that can help researchers better understand the individualized nature of leader development, especially when used in conjunction with informed decisions about time and the timing of key processes, and rigorous theorizing about the appropriate levels on which development is thought to occur.

Related to the individualized nature of development is how motivated or ready (or not) someone is for maximizing developmental opportunities. The general term for this state is *developmental readiness* and, unfortunately, there is not much empirically based research on the topic in the leader development literature. If the focus is on enhancing the likelihood of learning from a developmental experience, then having a relatively strong learning goal orientation (Dweck, 1986) would likely be an important consideration. What is unclear is to what extent a learning goal orientation is a trait (stable across time) or a state (variable to situational demands) phenomenon (DeShon & Gillespie, 2005). Ideally, the factors associated with developmental readiness are things that can be intervened on prior to an individual engaging in a developmental project, which makes genetically based cognitive ability or personality unlikely candidates in practice. But what is needed first is theory-driven research that links various malleable individual differences variables with initial levels (intercepts) and trajectories (slopes) of development over time.

**Practice.** There is a long-standing belief that leaders are ill-prepared to handle future challenges. Drucker (1995) noted some time ago that no more than one-third of executive selection decisions turn out right, about one-third are minimally effective, and fully one-third are outright failures. The distressing aspect of these estimates is that even though leader/ship development is a strategic human capital concern for many organizations, current and past data suggest that it is not being done very effectively.

One issue that has undermined the effectiveness of leader/ship development initiatives is the focus on relatively short-term, episodic-based thinking in terms of how development occurs. Too often the thinking about leader/ship development has viewed it as a series of unconnected, discrete programs with little assistance in integrating across these developmental episodes (Vicere & Fulmer, 1998). Contemporary thinking about leader/ship development views it as a continuous and ongoing process throughout the adult lifespan (Day et al., 2009). In short, just about any experience has the potential to contribute to learning and development, and will likely do so to the extent that it incorporates aspects of assessment, challenge, and support (McCauley et al., 2010).

The primary focus in the field is on developing individual leader skills; however, there is no guarantee that better leadership will result. After all, leadership involves a dynamic social interaction within a given situational context. Thus, effective followers are needed along with effective leaders (Hollander, 2009). In addition, true collective leadership development will likely require intervention at group, team, or organizational levels. Despite the distinction drawn here and in other places between leader development and leadership development, it is not an either/or proposition. Instead, state-of-the-art initiatives seek to find ways to link individual leader development with more collective leadership development to enhance overall leadership capacity in teams and organizations (Day & Dragoni, 2015). Needless to say, significantly more needs to be learned about the nature of leadership and its development before scholars can unequivocally endorse specific developmental policies and practices.

## Conclusions

There are reasons to be hopeful about the future of leader/ship development, especially on the scientific side of the scientist–practitioner equation. Over the past decade there has been increasing attention paid to theorizing about leader/ship development processes, especially in terms of moving beyond any single, bounded theoretical approach to conceptualizing leadership. It is an inherently dynamic, multilevel, and multidisciplinary process, and as such it makes sense to build theoretical frameworks that reflect these features.

Although the absolute number of empirically based publications on the general topic of leader/ship development is still relatively small, it is a growing area that is beginning to contribute to a stronger evidence-based understanding of important aspects of the underlying development process. It is also encouraging to note the increasing attention being paid to using longitudinal designs. But it is a daunting task going forward because of the lengthy time frame involved in the development of leaders and leadership, as well as to the many interrelated issues associated with development. Rather than framing this as a threat, these issues present a wealth of opportunities for researchers. There are countless possible issues to investigate; however, one thing is certain, and that is that single-shot, survey-based research designs are unlikely to add much value to this nascent science of leader/ship development. Research designs that incorporate multiple measurement perspectives, mixed methods, as well as a longitudinal component are more likely to provide scientific insight to the leadership development process (Day, 2011).

Given the evidence that the practice of leader/ship development is slipping in terms of perceived quality and does not add value in organizations (Howard & Wellins, 2008), it may be time to take a step back and rethink what is needed to better support a scientific, evidence-based approach. Specifically, what may be most needed is not only strong, continuing interest in the field theoretically and empirically, but also systematic efforts devoted to translating ideas into action and science into sound practice.

## Discussion Questions

1. Were there any particular experiences that you learned a great deal from in terms of leadership? If so, what were they and what made them so impactful in terms of learning? When have you found it most difficult to learn from experience?

2. What are some of the unanswered questions in the field of leadership development? In other words, what are some things we need to know about leadership development that we do not know at present?

3. In your estimation, what are reasonable estimates on the return on investment for leadership development in financial and nonfinancial terms? What are your reasons for these estimates?

## Recommended Readings

- Day, D. V., & Dragoni, L. (2015). Leadership development: An outcome-oriented review based on time and levels of analyses. *Annual Review of Organizational Psychology and Organizational Behavior, 2*, 133–156.
- McCall, M. W., Jr. (2010). Recasting leadership development. *Industrial and Organizational Psychology: Perspectives on Science and Practice, 3*(1), 3–19.

## Recommended Case Studies

- **Case:** Polzer, J. T., & Gardner, H. K. (2013). *Bridgewater Associates.* Harvard Business School 9-413-702.
- **Case:** Snook, S. A. (2008, June). *Leader(ship) development.* Harvard Business School 9-408-064.

## Recommended Video

- Torres, R. (2013). Roselinde Torres: What it takes to be a great leader (and how to develop one). https://www.ted.com/talks/roselinde_torres_what_it_takes_to_be_a_great_leader

## References

Antonakis, J., Day, D. V., & Schyns, B. (2012). Leadership and individual differences: At the cusp of a renaissance. *The Leadership Quarterly, 23,* 643–650.

Antonioni, D. (1994). The effects of feedback accountability on upward appraisal ratings. *Personnel Psychology, 47,* 349–356.

Arvey, R. D., Rotundo, M., Johnson, W., Zhang, Z., & McGue, M. (2006). The determinants of leadership role occupancy: Genetic and personality factors. *The Leadership Quarterly, 17,* 1–20.

Arvey, R. D., Zhang, Z., Avolio, B. J., & Krueger, R. F. (2007). Developmental and genetic determinants of leadership role occupancy among women. *Journal of Applied Psychology, 92,* 693–706.

Avolio, B. J. (2004). Examining the Full Range Model of leadership: Looking back to transform forward. In D. V. Day, S. J. Zaccaro, & S. M. Halpin (Eds.), *Leader development for transforming organizations: Growing leaders for tomorrow* (pp. 71–98). Mahwah, NJ: Lawrence Erlbaum.

Avolio, B. J. (2007). Promoting more integrative strategies for leadership theory-building. *American Psychologist, 62,* 25–33.

Avolio, B. J., & Gardner, W. L. (2005). Authentic leadership development: Getting to the roots of positive forms of leadership. *The Leadership Quarterly, 16,* 315–338.

Avolio, B. J., Reichard, R. J., Hannah, S. T., Walumbwa, F. O., & Chan, A. (2009). A meta-analytic review of leadership impact research: Experimental and quasi-experimental studies. *The Leadership Quarterly, 20,* 764–784.

Avolio, B. J., Sosik, J. J., Jung, D. I., & Berson, Y. (2003). Leadership models, methods, and applications. In W. C. Borman, D. R. Ilgen, & R. J. Klimoski (Eds.), *Handbook of psychology: Industrial and organizational psychology* (Vol. 12, pp. 277–307). Hoboken, NJ: John Wiley.

Baltes, P. B. (1987). Theoretical propositions of life-span developmental psychology: On the dynamics between growth and decline. *Developmental Psychology, 23,* 611–626.

Baltes, P. B. (1997). On the incomplete architecture of human ontogeny: Selection, optimization, and compensation as foundation of developmental theory. *American Psychologist, 52,* 366–380.

Bennis, W. (2007). The challenges of leadership in the modern world. *American Psychologist, 62,* 2–5.

Bloom, B. S. (Ed.). (1985). *Developing talent in young people.* New York, NY: Ballantine.

Bray, D. W. (1982). The assessment center and the study of lives. *American Psychologist, 37,* 180–189.

Bray, D. W., Campbell, R. J., & Grant, D. L. (1974). *Formative years in business: A long-term AT&T study of managerial lives.* New York, NY: Wiley.

Brehmer, B. (1980). In one word: Not from experience. *Acta Psychologica, 45,* 223–241.

Chan, K.-Y., & Drasgow, F. (2001). Toward a theory of individual differences and leadership: Understanding motivation to lead. *Journal of Applied Psychology, 86,* 481–498.

Chi, M. T. H., Glaser, R., & Farr, M. J. (Eds.). (1988). *The nature of expertise.* Hillsdale, NJ: Lawrence Erlbaum.

Conger, J. A. (2010). Developing leadership talent: Delivering on the promise of structured programs. In R. Silzer & B. E. Dowell (Eds.), *Strategy-driven talent management: A leadership imperative* (pp. 281–311). San Francisco, CA: Jossey-Bass.

Conger, J. A., & Xin, K. (2000). Executive education in the 21st century. *Journal of Management Education, 24,* 73–101.

Cooper, W. H., & Richarson, A. J. (1986). Unfair comparisons. *Journal of Applied Psychology, 71,* 179–184.

Day, D. V. (2000). Leadership development: A review in context. *The Leadership Quarterly, 11,* 581–613.

Day, D. V. (2010). The difficulties of learning from experience and the need for deliberate practice. *Industrial and Organizational Psychology: Perspectives on Science and Practice, 3,* 41–44.

Day, D. V. (2011). Integrative perspectives on longitudinal investigations of leader development: From childhood through adulthood. *The Leadership Quarterly, 22,* 561–571.

Day, D. V. (2014). Time and leadership. In A. J. Shipp & Y. Fried (Eds.), *Time and work* (Vol. 2, pp. 30–52). New York, NY: Psychology Press.

Day, D. V., & Dragoni, L. (2015). Leadership development: An outcome-oriented review based on time and levels of analyses. *Annual Review of Organizational Psychology and Organizational Behavior, 2,* 133–156.

Day, D. V., Fleenor, J. W., Atwater, L. E., Sturm, R. E., & McKee, R. A. (2014). Advances in leader and leadership development: A review of 25 years of research and theory. *The Leadership Quarterly, 25,* 63–82.

Day, D. V., Harrison, M. M., & Halpin, S. M. (2009). *An integrative approach to leader development: Connecting adult development, identity, and expertise.* New York, NY: Routledge.

Day, D. V., & Sin, H.-P. (2011). Longitudinal tests of an integrative model of leader development: Charting and understanding developmental trajectories. *The Leadership Quarterly, 22,* 545–560.

De Neve, J.-E., Mikhaylov, S., Dawes, C. T., Christakis, N. A., & Fowler, J. H. (2013). Born to lead? A twin design and genetic association study of leadership role occupancy. *The Leadership Quarterly, 24,* 45–60.

DeRue, D. S., & Wellman, N. (2009). Developing leaders via experience: The role of developmental challenges, learning orientation, and feedback availability. *Journal of Applied Psychology, 94,* 859–875.

DeShon, R. P., & Gillespie, J. Z. (2005). A motivated action theory account of goal orientation. *Journal of Applied Psychology, 90,* 1096–1127.

Development Dimensions International. (2015). Ready-now leaders: 25 findings to meet tomorrow's business challenges. *Global Leadesrship Forecast 2014–2015.* Pittsburgh, PA: Author.

Dragoni, L., Oh, I.-S., Tesluk, P. E., Moore, O. A., VanKatwyk, P., & Hazucha, J. (2014). Developing leaders' strategic thinking through global work experience: The moderating role of cultural distance. *Journal of Applied Psychology, 99,* 867–882.

Dragoni, L., Oh, I.-S., Vankatwyk, P., & Tesluk, P. E. (2011). Developing executive leaders: The relative contribution of cognitive ability, personality, and the accumulation of work experience in predicting strategic thinking competency. *Personnel Psychology, 64,* 829–864.

Drath, W. H., McCauley, C. D., Palus, C. J., Van Velsor, E., O'Connor, P. M. G., & McGuire, J. B. (2008). Direction, alignment, commitment: Toward a more integrative ontology of leadership. *The Leadership Quarterly, 19,* 635–653.

Drucker, P. F. (1995). *Managing in a time of great change.* New York, NY: Truman Talley Books/Dutton.

Dweck, C. S. (1986). Motivational processes affecting learning. *American Psychologist, 41,* 1040–1048.

Ericsson, K. A., & Charness, N. (1994). Expert performance: Its structure and acquisition. *American Psychologist, 49,* 725–747.

Ericsson, K. A., Charness, N., Feltovich, P. J., & Hoffman, R. R. (Eds.). (2006). *The Cambridge handbook of expertise and expert performance.* New York, NY: Cambridge University Press.

Ericsson, K. A., Krampe, R. T., & Tesch-Römer, C. (1993). The role of deliberate practice in the acquisition of expert performance. *Psychological Review, 100,* 363–406.

Ericsson, K. A., Prietula, M. J., & Cokely, E. T. (2007, July–August). The making of an expert. *Harvard Business Review, 85,* 114–121.

Feldman, J. (1986). On the difficulty of learning from experience. In H. P. Sims Jr., & D. A. Gioia (Eds.), *The thinking organization: Dynamics of organizational social cognition* (pp. 263–292). San Francisco, CA: Jossey-Bass.

Frese, M., Beimel, S., & Schoenborn, S. (2003). Action training for charismatic leadership: Two evaluations of studies of a commercial training module on inspirational communication of a vision. *Personnel Psychology, 56,* 671–697.

Freund, A. M., & Baltes, P. B. (1998). Selection, optimization, and compensation as strategies of life management: Correlations with subjective indicators of successful aging. *Psychology and Aging, 13*, 531–543.

Freund, A. M., & Baltes, P. B. (2002). Life-management strategies of selection, optimization, and compensation: Measurement by self-report and construct validity. *Journal of Personality and Social Psychology, 82*, 642–662.

Gottfried, A. E., Gottfried, A. W., Reichard, R. J., Guerin, D. W., Oliver, P. H., & Riggio, R. E. (2011). Motivational roots of leadership: A longitudinal study from childhood through adulthood. *The Leadership Quarterly, 22*, 510–519.

Guerin, D. W., Oliver, P. H., Gottfried, A. W., Gottfried, A. E., Reichard, R. J., & Riggio, R. E. (2011). Childhood and adolescent antecedents of social skills and leadership potential in adulthood: Temperamental approach/withdrawal and extraversion. *The Leadership Quarterly, 22*, 482–494.

Gully, S., & Chen, G. (2010). Individual differences, attribute-treatment interactions, and training outcomes. In S. W. J. Kozlowski & E. Salas (Eds.), *Learning, training, and development in organizations* (pp. 3–64). New York, NY: Routledge.

Guthrie, V. A., & King, S. N. (2004). Feedback-intensive programs. In C. D. McCauley & E. Van Velsor (Eds.), *The Center for Creative Leadership handbook of leadership development* (2nd ed., pp. 25–57). San Francisco: CA: Jossey-Bass.

Gutiérrez, M., & Tasse, T. (2007). Leading with theory: Using a theory of change approach for leadership development evaluations. In K. M. Hannum & J. W. Martineau (Eds.), *The Center for Creative Leadership handbook of leadership development evaluation* (pp. 48–70). San Francisco, CA: Jossey-Bass.

Hackman, J. R., & Wageman, R. (2007). Asking the right questions about leadership. *American Psychologist, 62*, 43–47.

Hollander, E. P. (2009). *Inclusive leadership: The essential leader–follower relationship*. New York, NY: Routledge.

Hollenbeck, G. P., McCall, M. W., Jr., & Silzer, R. F. (2006). Leadership competency models. *Leadership Quarterly, 17*, 398–413.

Howard, A., & Wellins, R. S. (2008). *Global leadership forecast 2008–2009: Overcoming the shortfalls in developing leaders*. Pittsburgh, PA: Development Dimensions International.

Judge, T. A., Bono, J. E., Ilies, R., & Gerhardt, M. W. (2002). Personality and leadership: A qualitative and quantitative review. *Journal of Applied Psychology, 87*, 765–780.

Kegan, R. (1982). *The evolving self: Problem and process in human development*. Cambridge, MA: Harvard University Press.

Kegan, R. (1994). *In over our heads: The mental demands of modern life*. Cambridge, MA: Harvard University Press.

Kegan, R., & Lahey, L. L. (2009). *Immunity to change: How to overcome it and unlock the potential in yourself and your organisation*. Boston, MA: Harvard Business Press.

Kegan, R., & Lahey, L. L. (2016). *An everyone culture: Becoming a Deliberately Developmental Organization*. Boston, MA: Harvard Business Review Press.

Kluger, A. N., & DeNisi, A. (1996). The effects of feedback on performance: A historical review, a meta-analysis, and a preliminary feedback intervention. *Psychological Bulletin, 119*, 254–284.

Lahey, L., Souvaine, E., Kegan, R., Goodman, R., & Felix, S. (1988). *A guide to the subject-object interview: Its administration and interpretation*. Cambridge, MA: Harvard University Graduate School of Education.

Lamoureux, K. (2007, July). *High-impact leadership development: Best practices, vendor profiles and industry solutions*. Oakland, CA: Bersin & Associates.

Lapour, A. S., & Heppner, M. J. (2009). Social class privilege and adolescent women's perceived career options. *Journal of Counseling Psychology, 56*, 477–494.

Li, W.-D., Arvey, R. D., & Song, Z. (2011). The influence of general mental ability, self-esteem and family socio-economic status on leadership role occupancy and leader advancement: The moderating role of gender. *The Leadership Quarterly, 22*, 520–534.

Lord, R. G., & Hall, R. J. (2005). Identity, deep structure, and the development of leadership skill. *The Leadership Quarterly, 16*, 591–615.

Luthans, F., & Avolio, B. (2003). Authentic leadership development. In K. S. Cameron, J. E. Dutton, & R. E. Quinn (Eds.), *Positive organizational scholarship: Foundations of a new discipline* (pp. 241–258). San Francisco, CA: Berrett-Koehler.

Luthar, S. S. (2003). The culture of affluence: Psychological costs of material wealth. *Child Development, 74,* 1581–1593.

Macnamara, B. N., Hambrick, D. C., & Oswald, F. L. (2014). Deliberate practice and performance in music, games, sports, education, and professions: A meta-analysis. *Psychological Science, 25,* 1608–1618.

Marquardt, M. J., Leonard, H. S., Freedman, A. M., & Hill, C. C. (2009). *Action learning for developing leaders and organizations: Principles, strategies, and cases.* Washington, DC: American Psychological Association.

McArdle, J. J. (2009). Latent variable modeling of differences and changes with longitudinal data. *Annual Review of Psychology, 60,* 577–605.

McCall, M. W., Jr. (2010). Recasting leadership development. *Industrial and Organizational Psychology: Perspectives on Science and Practice, 3,* 3–19.

McCall, M. W., Jr., Lombardo, M. M., & Morrison, A. M. (1988). *The lessons of experience: How successful executives develop on the job.* Lexington, MA: Lexington Books.

McCauley, C. D., Drath, W. H., Palus, C. J., O'Connor, P. M. G., & Baker, B. A. (2006). The use of constructive-developmental theory to advance the understanding of leadership. *The Leadership Quarterly, 17,* 634–653.

McCauley, C. D., Ruderman, M. N., Ohlott, P. J., & Morrow, J. E. (1994). Assessing the developmental components of managerial jobs. *Journal of Applied Psychology, 79,* 544–560.

McCauley, C. D., Van Velsor, E., & Ruderman, M. N. (2010). Introduction: Our view of leadership development. In E. Van Velsor, C. D. McCauley, & M. N. Ruderman (Eds.), *The Center for Creative Leadership handbook of leadership development* (3rd ed., pp. 1–26). San Francisco, CA: Jossey-Bass.

Mitchell, T. R., & James, L. R. (2001). Building better theory: Time and the specification of when things happen. *Academy of Management Review, 26,* 530–547.

Mumford, M. D., & Manley, G. R. (2003). Putting the development in leadership development: Implications for theory and practice. In S. E. Murphy & R. E. Riggio (Eds.), *The future of leadership development* (pp. 237–261). Mahwah, NJ: Lawrence Erlbaum.

Mumford, M. D., Zaccaro, S. J., Connelly, M. S., & Marks, M. A. (2000). Leadership skills: Conclusions and future directions. *The Leadership Quarterly, 11,* 155–170.

Mumford, T. V., Campion, M. A., & Morgeson, F. P. (2007). The leadership skills strataplex: Leadership skill requirements across organizational levels. *The Leadership Quarterly, 18,* 154–166.

Muthén, B. (2004). Latent variable analysis: Growth mixture modeling and related techniques for longitudinal data. In D. Kaplan (Ed.), *Handbook of quantitative methodology for the social sciences* (pp. 345–368). Thousand Oaks, CA: Sage.

Nagin, D. S. (1999). Analyzing developmental trajectories: A semiparametric, group-based approach. *Psychological Methods, 4,* 139–157.

Nagin, D. S. (2005). *Group-based modeling of development.* Cambridge, MA: Harvard University Press.

Ohlott, P. J., Ruderman, M. N., & McCauley, C. D. (1994). Gender differences in managers' developmental job experiences. *Academy of Management Journal, 37,* 46–67.

O'Leonard, K., & Krider, J. (2014, May). *Leadership development factbook 2014: Benchmarks and trends in U.S. leadership development.* Oakland, CA: Bersin by Deloitte.

Plomin, R., DeFries, J. C., & Loehlin, J. C. (1977). Genotype-environment interaction and correlation in the analysis of human behavior. *Psychological Bulletin, 84,* 309–322.

Ployhart, R. E., & Vandenberg, R. J. (2010). Longitudinal research: The theory, design, and analysis of change. *Journal of Management, 36,* 94–120.

Raudenbush, S. W. (2001). Comparing personal trajectories and drawing causal inferences from longitudinal data. *Annual Review of Psychology, 52,* 501–525.

Revans, R. W. (1980). *Action learning.* London, UK: Blond & Briggs.

Schippmann, J. S., Ash, R. A., Battista, M., Carr, L., Eyde, L. D., Hesketh, B., . . . Sanchez, J. I. (2000). The practice of competency modeling. *Personnel Psychology, 53,* 703–740.

Schmidt, F. L., Hunter, J. E., & Outerbridge, A. N. (1986). Impact of job experience and ability on job knowledge, work sample performance, and supervisory ratings of job performance. *Journal of Applied Psychology, 71,* 432–439.

Shadish, W. R., Cook, T. D., & Campbell, D. T. (2002). *Experimental and quasi-experimental designs for generalized causal inference.* Boston, MA: Houghton Mifflin.

Smither, J. W., London, M., Flautt, R., Vargas, Y., & Kuchine, I. (2003). Can working with an executive coach improve multisource feedback ratings over time? A quasi-experimental field study. *Personnel Psychology, 56,* 23–44.

Smither, J. W., London, M., & Reilly, R. R. (2005). Does performance improve following multisource feedback? A theoretical model, meta-analysis, and review of empirical findings. *Personnel Psychology, 58,* 33–66.

Tesluk, P. E., & Jacobs, R. R. (1998). Toward an integrated model of work experience. *Personnel Psychology, 51,* 321–355.

Vicere, A. A., & Fulmer, R. M. (1998). *Leadership by design: How benchmark companies sustain success through investment in continuous learning.* Boston, MA: Harvard Business School Press.

Walker, A. G., & Smither, J. W. (1999). A five-year study of upward feedback: What managers do with their results matters. *Personnel Psychology, 52,* 393–423.

Wang, M., & Bodner, T. E. (2007). Growth mixture modeling: Identifying and predicting unobserved subpopulations with longitudinal data. *Organizational Research Methods, 10,* 635–656.

Yost, P. R., & Mannion Plunket, M. (2010). Developing leadership talent through experiences. In R. Silzer & B. E. Dowell (Eds.), *Strategy-driven talent management: A leadership imperative* (pp. 313–348). San Francisco, CA: Jossey-Bass.

Zaccaro, S. J., & Horn, Z. N. J. (2003). Leadership theory and practice: Fostering an effective symbiosis. *The Leadership Quarterly, 14,* 769–806.

Zhang, Z., Ilies, R., & Arvey, R. D. (2009). Beyond genetic explanations for leadership: The moderating role of the social environment. *Organizational Behavior and Human Decision Processes, 110,* 118–128.

# CHAPTER 15

# Entrepreneurial Leadership

*Maija Renko*

---

## Opening Case: A Day in the Life of a Leader

Pam and Gela could not believe their ears. They had just been told that the spring collection their maternity wear company had designed for the major chain A Pea in the Pod had the highest sell-through of anything they had ever designed for them. It was a major success.

But as they sat across the table from each other in the office of their Los Angeles–based maternity wear business, Pam and Gela were terrified. They felt like the market had just proven to have a horrible taste. The collection they had designed for A Pea in the Pod, including a catsuit, skirt, and jacket, was supposed to be red, white and blue, which had always been one of their favorite color combinations. But A Pea in the Pod had done some market research on its own, and decided to change the color scheme to bright orange, yellow, and lime green. Pam and Gela were appalled and thought this color scheme was for a Hot Dog on a Stick all the way look. They had even tried to pretend the design was not theirs, and they had been absolutely sure the collection was going to bomb. Now that the Hot Dog on a Stick collection was selling, Pam and Gela felt they had no idea what they were doing. They had lost the feel for what was good and bad in the maternity wear market. They could have been making all the money in the world, but if the passion was gone, who cared?

Throughout their careers as business owners, Pam and Gela had always believed they had to be their own customers; unless it was something they would wear, they wouldn't make it. They were always looking for new product extensions. It was a natural part of who they were as business owners and what they did well. They loved their employees and always paid themselves less than anyone who worked for them. They always gave their employees a bonus before giving themselves one. That worked a long way toward keeping early employees motivated and building a feeling of community—even a family—within the company. They said: "We learned early on to make sure the people we were able to employ fit into our culture, and that they understood our speak and believe our dream. Don't just go off a résumé." As the company grew, Pam and Gela continued to design the organization from the bottom up: If they liked a candidate (or their haircut!) for a job, and liked their style and sense of fashion, they had the job.

They called a meeting with the employees and told them that the company's days designing and selling maternity wear were numbered. They were going to start all over, design clothes that were tighter and more fitted, with a vision and style that was forever, not just for 9 months. From this transition, Juicy Couture was born in 1994.

Remaining true to their style of leadership and management, Pam and Gela grew Juicy Couture to $68 million in sales in 2002. They continued to hire people who were passionate about fashion, brought on new ideas, and fit the Juicy Couture family. Leading a group of "believers" was easy, but as the company grew and the operations became more complicated, their product- and fashion-focused entrepreneurial leadership style was not enough anymore. The business was highly profitable: The margins for the products were at 75%, the operating costs of the company were low, and the company had no debt. Yet things were moving fast, and Pam and Gela later wrote that at times they felt like they were in a boxing match; something new was coming at them every day, boom boom boom! In 2003, Pam and Gela sold Juicy Couture for $56 million plus an eventual $200 million earnout. As of 2017, they are again running a small fashion business together: Their new line, Pam & Gela, has taken over where Juicy Couture left off, capturing their personal style in casual luxury.

*NOTE: This description is a mix of information retrieved from the book* The Glitter Plan: How We Started Juicy Couture for $200 and Turned It Into a Global Brand, *which Pam and Gela authored in 2014, is fictional about a hypothetical day that never occurred.*

## References

Skaist-Levy, P., Nash-Taylor, G., & Moore, B. (2014). *The glitter plan: How we started Juicy Couture for $200 and turned it into a global brand.* New York, NY: Penguin Group.

Yahoo Style. (2015, May 22). Studio visit with Pam Skaist-Levy and Gela Nash-Taylor, the designers that invented athleisure. Retrieved from https://www.yahoo.com/style/studio-visit-with-pam-skaist-c1432298294979/photo-inside-design-studio-photo-124130540.html

## Discussion Questions

1. Why would you call Pam and Gela entrepreneurial leaders?

2. Would you have enjoyed working at this company as an employee? Why or why not?

3. Are the skills and behaviors that Pam and Gela demonstrate learnable?

# Chapter Overview

Entrepreneurship is one of the strongest forces shaping the societies of the 21st century. All around the world, people are taking initiative to pursue opportunities for their own financial gain, for their personal development, for the sake of their families, for customers' sake, and for the betterment of their societies.

In developing economies and in the bottom-of-the-pyramid markets around the world, entrepreneurship is flourishing. For many, starting their own business may still be the only way to provide for their family. However, the entrepreneurial energy in developing economies such as India and China is creating real opportunities for entrepreneurs to pursue, and young people are choosing careers as entrepreneurs (Khanna, 2013). Companies such as Alibaba, the world's most popular destination for online shopping that handles more transactions on its online sites than eBay and Amazon combined (*Wall Street Journal*, 2016), have changed the way that the world views Chinese online retail businesses. Even in countries and communities that do not (yet) spawn international entrepreneurship success stories, microentrepreneurs' opportunities to access capital are improved, thanks to microlending organizations and brokers such as Kiva. The Global Entrepreneurship Monitor studies continuously show that a lot of entrepreneurial activity takes place in developing countries (Reynolds, 2015), and leaders around the world are taking notice.

In postindustrialist societies, the taken-for-granted relationship between corporations as "safe" employers and the commitment of their long-term employees has been shattered. There may still be occupations or industries where students graduate to "safe" jobs, but such areas are fewer by the day. Increasingly, people need to be self-starters and act as entrepreneurs even if they work for others. The opportunities to directly match human effort and talent with rewards—both financial and psychological—through entrepreneurship have never been greater. Nimble and small companies can and do compete head to head with corporations that see economies of scale and scope provide fewer advantages than before the age of instant connectivity, social media, millions of user reviews, open source design, 3-D printing, and global outsourcing available to even the smallest players (Anderson, 2012). Corporate scandals and the extreme emphasis on shareholder value have made the customers and the workforce of today wary of highly compensated leaders in large organizations of all types, and the leadership styles need to adapt.

Big questions, then, arise concerning the relationship between leadership and entrepreneurship. How do you lead the entrepreneurial workforce of Millennials and generations after them, who have little trust in formal authorities and want to make meaning through their work (Adkins, 2016; Pew Research Center, 2014)? What is the relationship between entrepreneurship and leadership in informal markets and developing country contexts? How do you lead an emerging organization that is pursuing entrepreneurial opportunities with lots of enthusiasm, but still lacks structure, legitimacy, and any history in "how things are usually done around here"? And what might be the role of leadership in those large corporations that are fighting for their market share in an increasingly transparent environment where stakeholders, including customers, are interested not only in the quality and price of the goods they purchase, but also in the values and practices of the company that stands behind the products? These are some of the questions that research has started to address under the topic of entrepreneurial leadership. In this chapter, you will get an overview of what has been said on this style of leadership, what it means for leadership practice, and what are some of the critical next questions about entrepreneurial leadership that need answering.

## What Is Entrepreneurial Leadership?

**Entrepreneurial Leadership as a Contextual Phenomenon.** Reflecting the variety of relevant research questions at the intersection of leadership and entrepreneurship, researchers have adopted a multitude of perspectives when discussing entrepreneurial leadership. By and large, these perspectives fall into three categories. First, the word *entrepreneurship* typically makes people think about the starting up of a new business. Indeed, this is what entrepreneurship traditionally stands for. With a focus on this type of entrepreneurship, the first strand of entrepreneurial leadership studies adopts an approach where new and/or small-business owners have to assume leadership roles in order for their companies to prosper and grow (e.g., Baum, Locke, & Kirkpatrick, 1998; Ensley, Hmieleski, & Pearce, 2006; Hmieleski & Ensley, 2007; Kang, Solomon, & Choi, 2015; Koryak et al., 2015; Leitch, McMullan, & Harrison, 2013). Related to this line of research, some scholars have expanded the domain of entrepreneurial leadership to cover not only new ventures, but also other "entrepreneurial contexts," such as family businesses (regardless of firm age) and corporations acting entrepreneurially (Simsek, Jansen, Minichilli, & Escriba-Esteve, 2015). Still, the thinking on entrepreneurial leadership in this line of research is focused on the fact that what makes leadership entrepreneurial is the context within which it takes place.

Firms have life cycles: They go from the nascent stage (prefounding) to start-up, consolidation, and growth. The relevant managerial skills needed at each stage differ, and the same is true for leadership, even though this aspect has scarcely been covered in existing literature (Antonakis & Autio, 2006). On the surface, it may seem that leading a new and small organization should be easier than steering a large, old incumbent: In new and small firms, people tend to stay close and know a lot about the business and all stakeholders, while leaders can benefit from informal ways of doing things as well as their greater ability to use personal observation rather than systems for control (Leitch et al., 2013).

In practice, however, many founders of new businesses are consumed by the challenges faced in developing their products or services, bringing them to market, and finding the first customers. The day-to-day management of these product- and customer-focused operations is necessary for making the company profitable, but it may consume all the time and energy that the entrepreneur has, and the "less urgent," leadership-related tasks may fall on the sidelines. Founders, especially those in technology-based ventures, are often great champions of their products or services, which helps in getting the company off the ground and achieving initial product success. However, product development skills rarely benefit these entrepreneurs when it comes to leading a team of employees and motivating them to work for the firm. Often, the early vision that a founder offers to those joining the team reflects a fanatical devotion to the company's specific technology, product, or processes. While such a focus may be helpful in convincing some stakeholders, such as funders or other product/technology enthusiasts, it is not likely to inspire everyone joining the company. Complicating things further, founders are used to being in control of everything, and delegating—giving up even a small amount of control—can be hard for them. It is not a surprise, then, that many founders who excel in building products and companies are not good leaders. There are certainly exceptions, such as Starbucks's Howard Schultz and FedEx's Fred Smith, who have gone on to lead their firms from start to great growth. But more generally, leading people is a challenge for many founders, and this challenge is a moving target as firms make it through the early stages of their life cycles and experience consolidation and growth (Antonakis & Autio, 2006).

Pam and Gela, the entrepreneurs featured in the opening of this chapter, provide a great example of the product focus that is typical of so many new ventures. Fashion enthusiasts Pam and Gela had met in 1988 when working at the same boutique store in Los Angeles. They became very close friends, and soon decided to go into business together taking on the very unglamorous world of maternity wear. Their first company was called Travis Jeans for the Baby in You, after Gela's son Travis, who was born the year they started the business. While pregnant, Gela improvised her husband's pair of Levi's jeans into maternity jeans—probably the first ones that ever saw the light of the day—by sewing in a lycra band where the waistband should be, and this was a huge success. After seeing people's enthusiasm for the jeans, Pam and Gela decided to go in 50–50 and spend $100 each to make some jeans to further test the market. They drove around L.A. showing the jeans to sales staff at fashion and maternity stores who loved them, called their buyers, and placed orders, even if this was a highly unorthodox way of introducing a product to the market. Pam and Gela had a strong belief in their product: "It's all about product. It always has been and it always will be." The team they built at this company, and at Juicy Couture later on, became a reflection of this unwavering focus on their vision of what fashion products should be (Skaist-Levy et al., 2014).

**Entrepreneurial Leadership as a Company Culture.** Besides being a new firm phenomenon, entrepreneurial leadership has also been studied as the culture (value system) of a firm of any size or age that reflects the entrepreneurial values and vision of its leaders (e.g., Covin & Slevin, 2002; Gupta, MacMillan, & Surie, 2004; McGrath & MacMillan, 2000; Thornberry, 2006). Research in this vein comes close to describing entrepreneurial leadership as a company-wide orientation, somewhat similar to entrepreneurial orientation and intrapreneurship, which are widely studied constructs in entrepreneurship research (Antoncic & Hisrich, 2001). For example, Covin and Slevin (2002) argue that companies that have adopted entrepreneurial leadership protect innovations that might even threaten the current business model, question the industry's dominant logic, and link entrepreneurship with their strategic management. Studies in this stream of entrepreneurial leadership research focus less on the leader–follower relationships and interactions and more on the company-level culture, mindset, and strategic orientation. A concept

386 PART III CURRENT TOPICS IN LEADERSHIP

such as 20% time, made famous by Google, or 3M's 15% time is an example of an entrepreneurial leadership practice at a corporate level. Here, the company trusts its creative employees enough to give them completely free hands to do whatever they want with 15% or 20% of their time. Google founders Larry Page and Sergey Brin wrote in the company's 2004 IPO letter: "We encourage our employees, in addition to their regular projects, to spend 20% of their time working on what they think will most benefit Google. . . . This empowers them to be more creative and innovative. Many of our significant advances have happened in this manner." When professional, creative people are trusted and given the permission to self-select and self-organize, they work with passion and can even create blockbuster products, such as Google News or 3M's Post-it note.

**Entrepreneurial Leadership as a Style of Leadership.** Besides being conceptualized as a new firm phenomenon and as an aspect of company culture, recent research has started to examine entrepreneurial leadership as a specific leadership style. Similar to other leadership styles, such as transformational, transactional, or authentic leadership, entrepreneurial leadership in this stream of research is thought of as behaviors, actions, and attributes of leaders that are distinct enough from other styles to warrant a new category of leadership to emerge (Renko et al., 2015). When thought of as a style of leadership, it becomes clear that entrepreneurial leadership can exist in organizations of any age, size, and focus. A manager at Google, as well as a small-business owner in rural Italy, can both exhibit entrepreneurial leadership despite the vastly different contexts as well as organizational and country cultures they are embedded in.

Entrepreneurial leadership style is defined as "influencing and directing the performance of group members toward achieving those organizational goals that involve recognizing and exploiting entrepreneurial opportunities" (Renko et al., 2015). According to this definition, what makes leadership entrepreneurial is determined by the goals of the process, as in specific leadership styles. As an example, creative leadership has been previously defined as "leading others toward the attainment of a creative outcome" (Mainemelis, Kark, & Epitropaki, 2015, p. 393). Here, the creativity is brought about by the very actions and outcomes that are enabled by this leadership style. Similarly, what distinguishes entrepreneurial leadership from other leadership styles, such as transformational leadership (Bass & Avolio, 1995), is its focus on entrepreneurial activities and outcomes: opportunity recognition and exploitation (Shane & Venkataraman, 2000). Entrepreneurial opportunity is the possibility to introduce innovative (rather than imitative) goods/services to a marketplace (Gaglio, 2004; Mueller, 2007). Recognizing an entrepreneurial opportunity entails perceiving this possibility. Because recognition only entails perception, it follows that exploitation of an opportunity is a separate activity, referring to those activities and investments committed to gaining returns from the new opportunity (Choi & Shepherd, 2004). Hence, opportunity recognition is about perception, exploitation is about action, and the goals set by entrepreneurial leaders involve both (Renko et al., 2015).

The notion of opportunity is central to most contemporary definitions of entrepreneurship. Indeed, entrepreneurship relies upon both creative destruction and opportunity recognition (Baron & Ensley, 2006). The entrepreneur may create or may simply discover a potentially disruptive innovative opportunity, and the exploitation of this entrepreneurial opportunity is the central activity of entrepreneurship (Shane & Venkataraman, 2000). Entrepreneurial leadership style, then, is situated at the intersection of opportunity-focused entrepreneurial behaviors and influencing the activities of an organized group—typically, a company of some kind—toward entrepreneurial goal achievement (cf. Rauch & Behling, 1984, p. 46). It concerns the process of influence in an organization that promotes all organizational members to identify and pursue entrepreneurial opportunities. For example, the leadership style of Jeff Bezos, the founder and CEO of Amazon, is not without critics. However, looking at it from a distance, and from an entrepreneurial perspective, one can observe that the leadership at Amazon is highly opportunity focused. Bezos was not the one to invent online retailing, but he did recognize the scope of the opportunity in this industry ahead of many others. More important, Amazon's exploitation of this opportunity has been focused, innovative, and disruptive for a number of industries, making it the retail giant it is today. Bezos would hardly qualify as someone scoring high on individualized consideration, a key aspect of transformational leadership, based on his relationships with followers (Stone, 2014). But one would be hard pressed not to call him an entrepreneurial leader. Not only is he a role model for opportunity recognition and exploitation through his own actions, but he also relentlessly pushes others in the company to do the same. The leadership at Amazon under him strives to, among other things, "expect and require innovation and invention from their teams and always find ways to simplify. They are externally aware, look for new ideas from everywhere, and are not limited by 'not invented here.' As we do new things, we accept that we may be misunderstood for long periods of time."[1]

The three different ways in which entrepreneurial leadership has been presented in the literature are summarized in Table 15.1.

**The Two Pillars of Entrepreneurial Leadership Style.** Entrepreneurial leadership style is built on two pillars: (1) opportunity-focused activities and attributes of the leader himself or herself and (2) the process of influence, whereby the leader motivates

**Table 15.1**   Conceptualizations of Entrepreneurial Leadership in the Literature

| | |
|---|---|
| A leadership style | • A leadership style that has the primary goal of promoting entrepreneurial opportunity recognition and exploitation (e.g., Renko et al., 2015) |
| New firm phenomenon | • Founder of a firm assumes a role as a leader (e.g., Hmieleski & Ensley, 2007) |
| Organizational culture | • The culture of a firm reflects entrepreneurial values and vision (e.g., McGrath & MacMillan, 2000) |

---

1.. From Amazon Jobs, "Leadership Principles," https://www.amazon.jobs/en/principles

and encourages followers to pursue entrepreneurial opportunity recognition and exploitation. The first role, "Entrepreneurial Doer," is largely in line with research that has viewed entrepreneurial leaders themselves as key individuals who, within organizational contexts, identify and develop new business opportunities (Cunningham & Lischeron, 1991; Thornberry, 2006). When asked to think of an entrepreneurial leader, many of us first think about someone who has recognized a significant entrepreneurial opportunity and has built a growing company around it. However, Entrepreneurial Doers also operate on a much smaller scale, and in contexts that do not involve building new companies. For example, the opportunity-focused activities of an entrepreneurial leader may be manifested when taking over a family business and changing its direction based on new market opportunities; when innovating within a business unit of an established corporation (entrepreneurship within existing organizations is called intrapreneurship); when building schools for girls in developing countries, where female education has not been the norm; or when pivoting an established restaurant to match the evolving tastes of customers. Regardless of their scope and context, the opportunity-focused actions of leaders themselves are important for entrepreneurial leadership for two reasons. First, they directly result in recognition and exploitation of new opportunities in an organization, and have a direct bearing on the future offerings, processes, and possibly also the performance of the firm. Second, and more important from a leadership perspective, seeing their leaders behave entrepreneurially creates employees' commitment to do the same; leaders influence and direct their followers by acting as entrepreneurial role models (Kuratko, Ireland, & Hornsby, 2001; McGrath & MacMillan, 2000). Hence, an important part of being an entrepreneurial leader consists of being an Entrepreneurial Doer an actor who himself or herself recognizes new opportunities for the company or the business unit, refines those opportunities, and works within the existing corporate environment to secure resources for the exploitation of the most promising opportunities.

In their second role, as "Entrepreneurial Accelerators," entrepreneurial leaders influence followers by directing followers' attention to entrepreneurial (opportunity-focused) future visions and goals, and by encouraging them to work toward these goals. Rather than getting stuck with "how things have always been done around here," entrepreneurial leaders encourage followers to think boldly about the future. This element of entrepreneurial leadership is aligned with those various definitions of (entrepreneurial) leadership that emphasize leaders' ability to influence others toward a common goal, such as opportunity recognition and exploitation (Gupta et al., 2004; Hunt, 2004; Ireland et al., 2003; Yukl, 2008). Entrepreneurial Accelerators constantly challenge and stimulate their followers to think and act in more innovative ways (Thornberry, 2006). They articulate a compelling and differentiating vision for the future of the company and the business unit, and arouse followers' personal involvement and pride in this vision, thereby motivating them. In their role as accelerators, entrepreneurial leaders also make followers rethink their jobs from the perspective of entrepreneurial opportunities that can be recognized through their specific knowledge and skill areas. While doing this, entrepreneurial leaders also empower and help followers to interpret their identities in the corporation as those who are responsible for its future innovations and success (Renko et al., 2015).

It is worth noting that these two pillars of entrepreneurial leadership map onto the conceptualization of creative leadership described by Mainemelis, Kark, and Epitropaki (2015).[2] According to their extensive review of existing literature, creative leadership involves both fostering the creativity of others in the organization, as well as having the leader himself or herself as the primary source of creative thinking and behavior. These roles are similar to the Entrepreneurial Accelerator and Doer described here, yet the expected outcomes for the two leadership styles differ: novel and useful outcomes for creative leadership and exploitable opportunities in the marketplace for entrepreneurial leadership.

Being led by an entrepreneurial leader is rewarding and empowering at best, but scary and stressful at worst. Not everyone wants the same thing from their workplace and leaders, and some people function much better under the direction of entrepreneurial leaders than others do. Some of the reasons why are cultural, while others are personal. In a large survey of what Millennials want at work, INSEAD's Emerging Markets Institute, Universum, and the HEAD Foundation surveyed over 16,000 people between the ages of 18 and 30 in 43 countries across the world in 2014. Based on the survey responses, there is a lot of variation in what employees in this age range want to see in their leaders. In North America, Western Europe, and Africa, at least 40% of respondents said they wanted managers who "empower their employees," but only about 12% of respondents in Central/Eastern Europe and the Middle East wanted to see that quality in a leader. The study does not provide empirically grounded explanations for why such diverging preferences exist, but they may be associated with the institutional imprint of the autocratic governance structures that were common in Central/Eastern Europe until the 1990s, and are still in place in many parts of the Middle East (Bresman, 2015). Either way, some in the Millennial workforce seem ready to take on the challenges and opportunities offered by entrepreneurial leaders, while others find the prospect of empowerment less appealing.

**Characteristics of Entrepreneurial Leaders.** The domains of Entrepreneurial Doer and Entrepreneurial Accelerator describe what kinds of behaviors entrepreneurial leaders are involved in. As such, to recognize an entrepreneurial leader, one would observe a leadership practice and look for cues of the leader's own recognition and pursuit of entrepreneurial opportunities, as well as cues of his or her facilitation of followers' opportunity recognition and pursuit. These behaviors are reflective of some key attributes that can be used to characterize entrepreneurial leaders: Entrepreneurial leaders are risk takers, creative, passionate, and visionary.

Entrepreneurs are thought of as risk takers when they invest their time, effort, and funds in the development of their business ideas. While it may be that the risks entrepreneurs take are actually not as high as one might first assume (Sarasvathy, 2001), there is certainly truth to the notion that entrepreneurs are less risk averse than corporate managers, for example (Stewart & Roth, 2001). In the context of

---

2. Mainemelis et al. (2015) also identify a third strand of creative leadership research, namely research on leaders in artistic and professional settings, who synthesize their own creative work with the heterogeneous creative contributions of other professionals.

leadership, risk becomes an important element of the entrepreneurial leadership style, since both entrepreneurial leaders' own pursuit as well as their encouragement of followers' pursuit of new opportunities have uncertain payoffs. As well as risks inherent in the new ideas and their introduction in the marketplace, entrepreneurial leaders risk their relationships with those in the company who stand for the status quo. Also, by pushing for resource allocations for innovative projects of their own and of their followers, entrepreneurial leaders risk alienating key organizational resource holders and gatekeepers, should their projects not turn out to be successful.

Besides risk, creativity is another characteristic that entrepreneurial leaders demonstrate. Creativity is characterized as an ability to generate insightful ideas, express unique thoughts, and make breakthrough discoveries (Csikszentmihalyi, 1997). While creativity is an important component of the opportunity recognition and exploitation process, the two are not synonymous. Creativity is required for idea generation, but not all novel and useful ideas qualify as entrepreneurial opportunities. As an example, a creative employee may invent a process that effectively uses social media to source ideas for giving back to the society from a loyal group of company enthusiasts. While this process may prove to be valuable to the organization, it would not qualify as an entrepreneurial opportunity in the sense that we have defined the term for entrepreneurial leadership. Specifically, as defined earlier, entrepreneurial opportunity recognition involves perceiving the possibility to introduce innovative goods/services to a marketplace, while opportunity exploitation refers to those activities and investments committed to gaining returns from the new opportunity. Hence, creative ideas that qualify as entrepreneurial opportunities need to be market-focused, and to be exploitable in the marketplace they have to meet additional criteria regarding customer acceptance and financial feasibility. Furthermore, while creativity is important for most entrepreneurial opportunities to emerge, sometimes these opportunities may be minimally creative in a sense of only being novel to the company but familiar to stakeholders outside of the company. For example, even if the introduction of specialty coffees to menus at McDonald's and Dunkin' Donuts in the United States would qualify as entrepreneurial opportunity recognition and exploitation by these companies, the creativity (specifically, novelty) of such innovations in the eyes of the larger society may be minimal.

Either way, creativity and entrepreneurial opportunities are often closely related, and previous leadership research has demonstrated that followers will be more creative when they perceive their immediate supervisors as being supportive of them and their creative work (Basadur, 2004; Mainemelis et al., 2015; Tierney & Farmer, 2004; Tierney, Farmer, & Graen, 1999). While the focus of leadership that enhances employee creativity is on creating outcomes that are novel and useful for internal or external audiences, the emphasis of entrepreneurial leadership is on promoting behaviors that result in inventing and commercializing products, services, or processes that can result in rent generation for the organization in the market. Creativity is an integrated part of this process, and more often than not, entrepreneurial leaders are described as creative individuals.

Besides risk taking and creativity, passion is another attribute that characterizes entrepreneurial leaders. Research has long recognized that emotions and affective states matter for entrepreneurial behaviors (Goss, 2005), and entrepreneurial passion has emerged as a key area of focus in this line of research (Cardon et al., 2005, 2009). Passion for one's work and business has been described as an intense affective state (X.-P. Chen, Yao, & Kotha, 2009), an intense positive feeling (Cardon et al., 2009), and even love (Baum & Locke, 2004). A strong feeling such as passion can be a driver of both decision making as well as behaviors (Cardon et al., 2009; X.-P. Chen et al., 2009). Intuitively, when people think of entrepreneurial leaders, they often think of individuals who are passionate about their work, their role within the company, and the role of the company in the society. Indeed, experiencing passion is typical of many committed entrepreneurs; it is the "fire of desire" that drives their efforts (Cardon et al., 2009, p. 515) and makes them persist in the face of obstacles (X.-P. Chen et al., 2009). While founders often feel particularly passionate about the problems their company solves for customers or other stakeholders, an entrepreneurial leader's passion does not always need to be driven by the solutions the company offers. For example, a middle-level manager may be passionate about the success of his or her business unit even if other parts of the corporation and its corporate strategy remain distant. Whatever the level of the organization, entrepreneurial leaders' passion is contagious: Through the processes of emotional contagion and goal setting, a leader's passion can influence employees' positive affect at work and their goal clarity, thereby affecting their commitment to the organization (Breugst et al., 2012) as well as their entrepreneurial behaviors. When a passionate entrepreneurial leader pursues opportunity-related goals, it demonstrates to employees that these goals are worthy of excitement, and a priority to the leader. Such communication and clarification of goals help employees better understand their tasks and what is expected of them (Locke & Latham, 1990). When the leader communicates goals and visions with a passion, it demonstrates that the values and entrepreneurial goals the leader preaches are truly shared by them (Haslam & Platow, 2001).

Passion can also facilitate the communication of an entrepreneurial leader's vision for their organization (Baum & Locke, 2004). Indeed, the fourth attribute reflective of entrepreneurial leaders is that they are visionaries; an opportunity-focused vision for the future is a central element in entrepreneurial leadership. Indeed, being a visionary emerges as common to both leaders and entrepreneurs when doing a review of both literatures (Antonakis & Autio, 2006; Cogliser & Brigham, 2004; Fernald et al., 2005; Renko et al., 2015). Reflecting a vision for the future, entrepreneurial leaders possess a strong desire to create, build, or change things (Thornberry, 2006). In sum, a characteristic of entrepreneurial leadership is a vision for the future of the firm based on continuous recognition of new entrepreneurial opportunities, and pursuing this vision through creative, innovative, and sometimes risky tactics.

To be sure, characteristics other than risk taking, creativity, passion, and vision have also been identified as areas of overlap between entrepreneurship and leadership: opportunity focus, influence (both on followers and on a larger constituency), planning, motivating others, achievement orientation, flexibility, patience, persistence, high tolerance for ambiguity, tenacity, self-confidence, power orientation, proactiveness, and internal locus of control (Becherer, Mendenhall, & Eickhoff, 2008; Cogliser & Brigham, 2004; Fernald, Solomon, & Tarabishy, 2005; Renko et al., 2015; Thornberry, 2006). However, the four attributes discussed above emerge as the ones most critical for the understanding of opportunity-focused behaviors of both entrepreneurial leaders and their followers.

**Entrepreneurial Leadership and Transformational Leadership.** Given the wealth of leadership styles already covered in academic research, a student of leadership may question whether we need yet another leadership style, such as entrepreneurial leadership presented here. Would transformational leadership, for example, not do the job? Indeed, the promise of transformational leadership has led to its adoption in the entrepreneurship domain (Baum et al., 1998; Engelen et al., 2015; Ensley, Hmieleski, et al., 2006; Ensley, Pearce, et al., 2006; Ling et al., 2008; Peterson et al., 2009). Transformational leaders employ charismatic role modeling, individualized consideration, inspirational motivation, and intellectual stimulation (Bass & Avolio, 1995), which can also help entrepreneurs achieve their goals. Given the definition of entrepreneurial leadership style provided earlier in this chapter, intellectual stimulation, in particular, seems like an area of overlap between entrepreneurial and transformational leadership as well as entrepreneurial and instrumental leadership in the Antonakis and House (2002, 2014) extended full-range leadership model. Through intellectual stimulation, a leader can stimulate followers to think about old problems in new ways and elicit extra role behaviors, such as creative problem solving (MacKenzie, Podsakoff, & Rich, 2001). This, again, can help the organization accomplish higher-order objectives, such as recognizing novel business opportunities. Intellectual stimulation clearly is an area of overlap between entrepreneurial and transformational leadership (Renko et al., 2015).

However, entrepreneurial and transformational leadership styles have more differences than similarities. Although entrepreneurial leaders lead with clear purpose and goals, they may not be described as charismatic or inspirational by others, as transformational leaders appear to be (Podsakoff et al., 1990). Because entrepreneurial leaders are transparent about the entrepreneurial goals of the organization, the process by which followers internalize their beliefs and values may be based less on inspirational appeals, dramatic presentations, symbolism, or other forms of impression management, and more on the leader's character, personal example, and dedication (Renko et al., 2015). A case in point, Jim Casey, the founder of UPS, who grew the company from modest beginnings to a worldwide phenomenon, did this through continuously challenging all employees to innovate and remain focused on customer needs. He has been described as follows:

> He wasn't the typical corporate cheerleader. Casey's archived gospel is not so much inspiring as preachy and relentless. What Jim lacked in pithy, dramatic oratory, he made up for with unusual and becoming modesty. Unpretentious, he always referred to other people's good examples, never proclaiming his own. . . . Hardly a shining star, Jim Casey was more a steadily burning flame. (Niemann, 2007, p. 29)

Besides the differences placed in the role of charisma in role modeling, entrepreneurial and transformational leadership also differ when it comes to individualized consideration. This is a central component of transformational leadership, but not an integrated element of the more narrowly focused entrepreneurial leadership construct, as mentioned in the Jeff Bezos example given earlier (Stone, 2014). In summary, the key to understanding entrepreneurial leadership is the focus on opportunity-oriented behaviors—by both leaders themselves and those who follow them. While the content and process of transformational leadership contain some elements of such behaviors, they are not as central there as they are in entrepreneurial leadership. The noble requirements of transformational leadership, such as "a leader with vision, self confidence, and inner strength to argue successfully for what he sees is right or good, not for what is popular or is acceptable according to established wisdom of the time" (Bass, 1985, p. 17), describe overall exceptional leadership. However, the mere assessment of what is "right or good" can encompass any variety of domains (from human resource management to product–market strategies, and from new product development decisions to stakeholder management), making transformational leadership a very general construct. One of the benefits of entrepreneurial leadership is that it allows a greater concentration on what truly matters for entrepreneurial action. Entrepreneurial leadership directly contributes to enhanced opportunity recognition and exploitation by an organization through both leaders' and employees' very engagement in opportunity-focused behaviors.

To be sure, entrepreneurial leadership does not exclude other types of leadership. For example, it is possible for an entrepreneurial leader to simultaneously exhibit transformational leadership as well. Furthermore, the components of entrepreneurial leadership are not novel; opportunity recognition, vision, risk, passion, and so forth have been topics of research in entrepreneurship for decades.[3] Yet the combination of aspects that make entrepreneurial leadership unique, as described above, is different from other leadership styles. For example, identifying and articulating a strategic vision for the organization presents an area of overlap between entrepreneurial leadership and both transformational leadership (Podsakoff et al., 1990) as well as charismatic leadership (Conger & Kanungo, 1998). However, these latter leadership styles do not feature the opportunity-focused goals of the leadership process and behaviors of the leader himself or herself that are central to entrepreneurial leadership. In the assessment of any leadership style, including entrepreneurial leadership, one has to adopt a perspective where a single type of behavior, attribute, or goal is not enough to call the leadership style. A holistic assessment of the leader and his or her relationship with followers is needed.

## The Dynamics of Entrepreneurial Leadership

**Antecedents.** It seems feasible to expect that factors that drive individuals to recognize and pursue entrepreneurial opportunities in a variety of contexts also

---

3. For similarities between the components of entrepreneurial leadership style and previous research, see Table 2 in Renko et al. (2015).

facilitate them adopting an entrepreneurial leadership style. For example, entrepreneurial alertness, defined as "an attitude of receptiveness to available (but hitherto overlooked) opportunities" (Kirzner, 1997), is a critical element of an individual's disposition that promotes entrepreneurial opportunity discovery. Put simply, some individuals just have a natural alertness to signals about possible opportunities; Kirzner (1997) described entrepreneurs as being at all times spontaneously on the lookout for hitherto unnoticed features of the environment (present or future) that might inspire new activity. Indeed, entrepreneurial alertness is necessary for people to integrate perceptions about market needs and the means to satisfy those needs and thereby perceive opportunity (Tang et al., 2010). The existence of such alertness helps explain why some individuals become serial or portfolio entrepreneurs, starting multiple companies and running them one after the other (serial) or simultaneously (portfolio). Since being a role model for entrepreneurial opportunity recognition and pursuit is a key part of entrepreneurial leadership, entrepreneurial alertness should be considered a potentially important antecedent of such leadership.

Besides alertness, in order to recognize opportunities, individuals need to have relevant knowledge of the opportunity domain (Kirzner, 1997; Vaghely & Julien, 2010). Indeed, among alert individuals, knowledge of market needs coupled with knowledge of the means to satisfy those needs results in a noticed opportunity (Kirzner, 1997; Shane, 2000). Relevant knowledge is mostly gained through previous experience—either one's own or vicarious experience—and one could assume that the longer one stays in a company or in an industry, the larger his or her knowledge base, and the more likely he or she is to see opportunities for the company. Interestingly, however, longer tenure in an organization hardly makes one more likely to adopt entrepreneurial leadership practices (Zampetakis, Beldekosa, & Moustakis, 2009). While domain-specific knowledge is important for entrepreneurial leadership, so is willingness to step out of line to encourage and pursue opportunities that are out of the ordinary for the firm. The latter may be easier to do if you are new to the company.

Other antecedents that may be relevant for the adoption of an entrepreneurial leadership style include leader demographics, such as their gender (Harrison et al., 2015; Henry et al., 2015), attitudes, values (Gupta et al., 2004), and some aspects of their personality (Nicholson, 1998). As for personality, the Big Five typology has been presented as a potentially fruitful basis for examining the dispositional predictors of leadership. In their extensive review and meta-analysis of previous research, Judge and colleagues (2002) conclude that extraversion, conscientiousness, and openness to experience are the strongest and most consistent personality correlates of leadership. Similarly, a summary of meta-analyses by Brandstätter (2011) concludes that these same three traits consistently characterize more entrepreneurial individuals. Agreeableness is the least relevant Big Five personality characteristic for both entrepreneurship and leadership (Brandstätter, 2011; Judge et al., 2002). Brandstätter's study suggests that entrepreneurs may be low on neuroticism, and the same may be true for leaders, even though the evidence from Judge and colleagues is not as clear. Given these similarities between personality traits that have been linked to both leadership and entrepreneurship, one could expect extraversion, conscientiousness, and openness to experience to be strong correlates for the adoption of an entrepreneurial leadership style. Empirical evidence on these and other possible antecedents of entrepreneurial leadership is yet to be collected.

It is also likely that leaders' positional and organizational context—that is, the position leaders occupy within the organization—may shape their entrepreneurial leadership style. It may be that entrepreneurial leadership occurs more frequently higher in the organizational hierarchy, where leaders may enjoy higher discretion (Shamir & Howell, 1999), enabling them to engage in entrepreneurial leadership. Lower-level leadership has been characterized as being more task focused than higher-level leadership, which is more immediately related to the strategy or vision of an organization (Hunt, 1991).

Can entrepreneurial leadership be developed? It can, but one has to first realize that neither leaders nor entrepreneurs are defined by their personal characteristics. In both entrepreneurship and leadership, there has been a shift of interest away from the personal characteristics of the entrepreneur/leader to the role of entrepreneurship/leadership: that is, from an individualistic and decontextualized conceptualization of heroic individuals to one that emphasizes entrepreneurship/leadership as a role defined by actions and behaviors (Cogliser & Brigham, 2004; Gartner, 1988; Stogdill, 1948). It follows that those interested in developing their entrepreneurial leadership skills should learn to think and act like entrepreneurial leaders, not to look and sound like ones. In this, the focus of programs may be on the enhancement of the relevant creative skills, interpersonal knowledge, trust building with relevant groups, and cognitive abilities—aspects of entrepreneurship- and leadership-specific human capital and social capital (Leitch et al., 2013). Evidence-based research suggests that such human capital can be learned. A recent meta-analysis on the impact of entrepreneurship education and training shows that such education is positively related to the entrepreneurship-related human capital assets as well as entrepreneurship performance, in particular when the education is academically focused (Martin, McNally, & Kay, 2013).

**Outcomes.** Entrepreneurial leaders explicitly strive after the goals of recognizing and exploiting entrepreneurial opportunities through their own actions as well as through the actions of their followers. As such, the most immediate results of entrepreneurial leadership should be seen in the increasing number and quality of ideas for new products or services that the company could offer to the market, ideas for improvements for the current products and services, and both new and improved product/service ideas put into practice. Over time, then, this process of entrepreneurial renewal should benefit company sales and, if managed properly, also the bottom line. Here, when it comes to the ultimate outcomes of entrepreneurial leadership, links to corporate strategy become apparent.

Even if the most direct benefits from entrepreneurial leadership are realized in the form of new business opportunities recognized and exploited, there may be other beneficial outcomes as well. For example, such a leadership style can be helpful in dealing with misunderstandings and conflict, which often arise in growing organizations. To the extent that a focus on entrepreneurial goals can give organizational members a common objective they can all identify with and support, entrepreneurial leadership may have a role in reducing relationship and task conflict (cf. Renko et al., 2012). Consequently, it can lead to improved job satisfaction and performance among those working in the organization (De Dreu & Weingart, 2003). Job satisfaction is also likely to increase as entrepreneurial leadership creates conditions for a meaningful job requiring challenge and providing opportunity for recognition (Herzberg, Mausner, & Snyderman, 1959). Individuals who perceive their jobs to be significant and worthwhile feel higher levels of work satisfaction than those who perceive their jobs as having little value (Hackman & Oldham, 1976). Individuals should derive a sense of satisfaction with the work itself when they are directly involved in outcomes that affect the organization, which is the very case of entrepreneurial leadership (Carsrud et al., in press).

Under entrepreneurial leadership, each member of the organization strives to come up with entrepreneurial solutions to business problems, increasing the number of novel ideas considered by the organization, and hence potentially improving overall decision quality and insight into ideas. In addition, entrepreneurial leadership can provide a unified framework within which all employees are encouraged to achieve and are held accountable for the achievement of entrepreneurial goals. Entrepreneurial leaders may be able to communicate effectively about and offer explanations for the ways in which certain policies and procedures are implemented. This should reduce any bias and favoritism, which may otherwise lead to perceptions of unfair treatment among some (for example, nonfamily employees in a family business; Renko et al., 2012). Finally, if sustained over time, entrepreneurial leadership can help in developing, communicating, and reinforcing desired vision and organizational culture over extended tenures of leaders.

**Moderators and Mediators.** Followers of an entrepreneurial leader are likely to have different levels of susceptibility to the influences of such a leader. Three factors, in particular, are important in explaining follower susceptibility to entrepreneurial leadership: (1) followers' entrepreneurial self-efficacy, (2) their empowerment, and (3) their level of entrepreneurial passion (Renko et al., 2015).

First, with regard to self-efficacy, a growing amount of evidence from entrepreneurship as well as leadership literature points to the power of Bandura's (1986) social cognitive theory in explaining behavior in organizations (Frayne & Latham, 1987) and in entrepreneurial contexts (Baum, Locke, & Smith, 2001). Entrepreneurial self-efficacy is the degree to which an individual believes that he or she is capable of performing the roles and tasks of the entrepreneur (McGee, Peterson, Mueller, & Sequeira, 2009). A follower's belief in their ability to develop a unique idea and identify a business opportunity may be central to their susceptibility to the influence of an entrepreneurial leader (cf. Zhao, Seibert, & Hills, 2005). Followers who believe they actually "have what it takes" to come up with novel solutions and innovations are likely to be encouraged to pursue these paths in the presence of an entrepreneurial leader, whereas followers who are low on such self-efficacy may experience frustration and feelings of inadequacy, making them less susceptible to influences of entrepreneurial leaders (Padilla, Hogan, & Kaiser, 2007). To the extent that women typically have lower levels of entrepreneurial self-efficacy than men do (Wilson et al., 2007), one could also speculate that they may be less susceptible to the influence of entrepreneurial leaders. For now, this remains an empirical question for future research.

Second, closely related to self-efficacy, the topic of employee empowerment has received and continues to receive considerable attention in both the academic and popular press. Empowerment of employees typically involves the delegation of authority from management to employees. Conger and Kanungo (1988) popularized this concept and gave it relational as well as motivational dimensions. In a motivational sense, power refers to one's intrinsic need for self-determination or a belief in personal self-efficacy. Empowerment, then, refers to any managerial strategy or technique that strengthens this self-determination need or self-efficacy belief of employees and makes them feel more powerful. In a relational sense, empowerment is the process by which a leader or manager shares his or her power with subordinates. Here, power is interpreted as the possession of formal authority or control over organizational resources, and the emphasis of empowerment is primarily on the notion of sharing authority. An empowered person or a team has better control over their surroundings and their work. Employee empowerment can be defined as a "process of enhancing feelings of self-efficacy among organizational members through the identification of conditions that foster powerlessness and through their removal both by formal organizational practices and informal techniques of providing efficacy information" (Conger & Kanungo, 1988). However, not all employees on all levels of every organization are equally comfortable with feeling empowered (having shared or distributed leadership; Argyris, 1998). Empowerment comes with responsibility, and for some, feeling responsible for the future of the organization or the business unit may be an overwhelming burden.

Since pursuing entrepreneurial opportunities often falls outside of the employee responsibilities assigned to them by managers, a certain level of employee empowerment may be necessary for the effects of entrepreneurial leadership to materialize. Increasing employees' feelings of self-efficacy and control (e.g., participative decision making) and removing conditions that foster a sense of powerlessness (e.g., bureaucracy) may be necessary steps for managers to take if they wish to see the results of entrepreneurial leadership materialize through employees' opportunity-focused behaviors. Many companies have already eliminated layers of management in order to streamline their organization. The extent to which employees embrace and use the freedoms afforded by empowerment will affect their susceptibility to the influence of an entrepreneurial leader.

Third, research has long recognized that emotions and affective states matter for entrepreneurial behaviors (Baron, 2008). Cardon and colleagues (2009) argue that one's passion for entrepreneurship, defined as intense positive feelings experienced by engagement in entrepreneurial activities, has a particularly strong influence on entrepreneurial pursuits. Simply, individuals who are passionate about certain entrepreneurial tasks, such as identifying and inventing new opportunities, are more likely to engage in these tasks and, hence, achieve associated outcomes (such as opportunity recognition). The idea that followers' emotions and affective states impact the outcomes of leadership processes has proven powerful when other leadership styles have been in focus in previous research. For example, Avolio and colleagues examine how positive emotions impact the relationship between authentic leaders and their followers (Avolio, Gardner, Walumbwa, Luthans, & May, 2004), and it has also been suggested that positive emotions of followers impact the influence of transformational leadership on employee motivation (Ilies, Judge, & Wagner, 2006). In the context of entrepreneurial leadership, the follower's experience of entrepreneurial passion should have a significant, positive effect on their susceptibility to the influence of an entrepreneurial leader.

In addition to follower attributes, contextual factors are likely to influence the strength of association between entrepreneurial leadership and subsequent opportunity-related outcomes (Antonakis & Autio, 2006). As an example, the discovery and pursuit of entrepreneurial opportunities is a process that evolves over time, and a crisis mode in the form of organizational or financial turmoil may distract followers from such long-term endeavors, attenuating the association between entrepreneurial leadership and entrepreneurial opportunity outcomes (Lord & Emrich, 2001). Also, the availability of resources in an organization may influence the entrepreneurial leadership–opportunity exploitation relationship. Entrepreneurs are known to bootstrap their companies for extended periods of time, and resource scarcity does not automatically render new opportunities unreachable. However, especially in a corporate setting, lack of resources dedicated to entrepreneurial initiatives may discourage employee engagement. This is why providing access to resources has been described as an integral part of leaders' creativity-supportive behaviors (Tierney & Farmer, 2004). From the perspective of employees, concrete resources are needed to pursue the recognized opportunities beyond mere ideas. In addition to resources such as time and money to invest in the new opportunities, followers need an innovative climate as well as encouragement, flexibility, and patience from entrepreneurial leaders in order for opportunity-focused behaviors to flourish (Kang et al., 2015). Encouragement, advocacy, and goals specific to entrepreneurship are essential elements of entrepreneurial leadership and necessary for inspiring enterprising followers (Carsrud et al., in press).

The strategic orientation of an organization—particularly, the level of its entrepreneurial orientation—may also influence the extent to which entrepreneurial leadership processes lead to desired outcomes (cf. Dess et al., 2003; Renko et al., 2015). Firm-level strategies and micro-level leadership processes should be aligned, and if internal politics or lack of top management support for entrepreneurial initiatives (that is, lack of entrepreneurial orientation) effectively prevent employees from pursuing entrepreneurial opportunities, entrepreneurial leadership will be of limited value.

Finally, the external environment of the organization may impact the entrepreneurial leadership process, and both markets and culture can play a dominant role. In dynamic and highly competitive markets, the association between entrepreneurial leadership and opportunity recognition/exploitation may be stronger than in less dynamic environments, since such an environment itself may prompt employees to behave entrepreneurially (Renko et al., 2015). Also, in addition to the effects of industrial and professional culture, national culture may alter the enthusiasm with which employees respond to entrepreneurial leadership initiatives. Particularly, effects in low versus high power distance countries may differ. Levels of productive entrepreneurship are also known to vary between countries based on the quality of their institutional environments (Sobel, 2008), and a number of institutional and macroeconomic factors may influence the effectiveness of entrepreneurial leadership. For example, if voids in regulatory institutions make it difficult to protect intellectual property, entrepreneurial opportunity exploitation is likely to suffer (Autio & Acs, 2010).

The dynamics of entrepreneurial leadership, presented above, are illustrated in Figure 15.1. The success of entrepreneurial leadership depends on interrelationships among leaders, followers, and their context. Entrepreneurial leadership is particularly likely to achieve its goals of opportunity recognition and exploitation under circumstances where leaders themselves act as entrepreneurial role models (Entrepreneurial Doers), where empowered followers are guided by leaders' direct encouragement of opportunity-focused behaviors (leaders acting as Entrepreneurial Accelerators), and where organizational and environmental contexts and available resources are favorable. These factors assist entrepreneurial leaders in achieving the goals that distinguish entrepreneurial leadership from other leadership styles: recognizing and exploiting entrepreneurial opportunities.

## Measuring Entrepreneurial Leadership

Given the early stage of research on the topic of entrepreneurial leadership, attempts to directly measure such leadership have been scarce. Gupta, MacMillan, and Surie (2004) used secondary data from the GLOBE study to develop a scale to measure the roles of entrepreneurial leaders. Their scale items ask respondents to

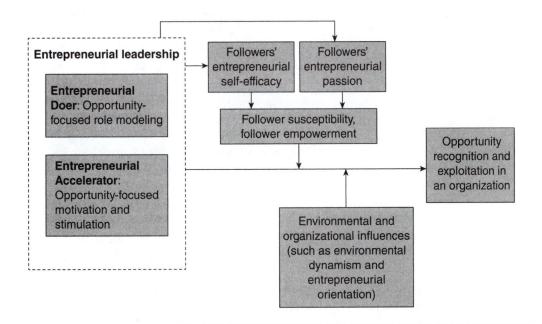

**Figure 15.1**    The Dynamics of Entrepreneurial Leadership Style

rate the degree to which each behavior contributes to "outstanding leadership behavior" in their organizations and societies, in general. Hence, rather than evaluating the leadership style of any one person, as has been common in leadership research, the respondents are giving general evaluations of leadership styles. In another attempt at measuring entrepreneurial leadership, M.-H. Chen (2007) translated the components of organizational entrepreneurial orientation to a measure of individual entrepreneurs' risk taking, proactiveness, and innovativeness. However, it is unclear how strategy characteristics from the firm level can directly translate into leadership dimensions at the individual level.

My colleagues and I (Renko et al., 2015) developed and tested an eight-item ENTRELEAD scale for the measurement of entrepreneurial leadership style. This measurement directly taps into the dimensions of entrepreneurial leadership style presented in this chapter and is suitable for situations where followers (employees) rate the leadership style of their leader. The scale items ask about the leaders' own, direct contributions to entrepreneurial opportunities recognized: Does the leader often come up with radical improvement ideas for the current products/services or ideas of completely new products/services for the company? In addition, the ENTRELEAD scale items ask the respondents to evaluate their leader with regard to the four critical attributes of entrepreneurial leaders presented above: risk taking, creativity, passion, and vision. Finally, the measurement recognizes that entrepreneurial leaders enable followers' entrepreneurial opportunity recognition and exploitation by expecting that followers not only do their job, but also challenge the current ways of doing business. They follow principles such as this one, taken from the leadership principles that Amazon lists on its careers site:[4] "Leaders are obligated to respectfully challenge decisions when they disagree, even when doing so is uncomfortable or exhausting. Leaders have conviction and are tenacious. They do not compromise for the sake of social cohesion. Once a decision is determined, they commit wholly." Table 15.2 summarizes the ENTRELEAD scale and its underlying dimensions.

## Future Research on Entrepreneurial Leadership

The ideas presented in this chapter could be tested in models where more distal attributes (antecedents) will predict the adoption of entrepreneurial leadership, which in turn will be linked to outcomes in certain contexts (contingencies; Antonakis & Autio, 2006). The perspective adopted here and in much of the previous literature on entrepreneurial leadership is that the nature and outcomes of such a leadership style are predominantly positive. However, it is possible and even likely that some of the by-products of entrepreneurial leadership may not be appealing to all. For example, followers who find it hard to believe in their own entrepreneurial skills or who simply do not feel passionate about their organization and its opportunities may find entrepreneurial leaders to be inefficient and even uninspiring. Recent research also suggests that greed and hubris may be

---

4. Retrieved from https://www.amazon.jobs/en/principles.

**Table 15.2**    Measuring Entrepreneurial Leadership With the ENTRELEAD Scale

| Key Roles of an Entrepreneurial Leader | How to Identify an Entrepreneurial Leader | Related Measurement Items From the ENTRLEAD Scale (Renko et al., 2015) |
|---|---|---|
| Doer / Accelerator (upward and downward arrow) | • What does an entrepreneurial leader do in his or her everyday work? | • Often comes up with radical improvement ideas for the products/services we are selling.<br>• Often comes up with ideas of completely new products/services that we could sell. |
| | • How does an entrepreneurial leader make decisions? | • Takes risks.<br>• Has creative solutions to problems. |
| | • How does an entrepreneurial leader feel about his or her organization? | • Demonstrates passion for his or her work.<br>• Has a vision of the future of our business. |
| | • What does an entrepreneurial leader make his or her followers do? | • Challenges and pushes me to act in a more innovative way.<br>• Wants me to challenge the current ways we do business. |

characteristics of entrepreneurial leaders (Haynes, Hitt, & Campbell, 2015). For example, entrepreneurial leaders take significant risks, which means that they must be confident by nature. However, there is a fine line between being highly confident in one's abilities and exhibiting hubris. Similarly, entrepreneurial leaders' pursuit of opportunities is typically, at least to some extent, driven by their interest in seeking financial returns for themselves and their ventures. There is also a fine line between maximizing financial returns and exhibiting greedy behaviors. Also, entrepreneurial leaders' passionate approach to their work and company can be inspiring, but there is a danger that passion can turn into a dogma or an obsession (Vallerand et al., 2003). Observations such as these suggest that research on entrepreneurial leadership should not only focus on the positives, but also explore the negatives of this leadership style for a balanced image to emerge.

A practical challenge for entrepreneurial leaders is to find a balance between the managerial and administrative requirements of their everyday work, on one hand, and the future-oriented and opportunity-focused behaviors of their leadership role, on the other. Firms rely on their leaders for discovery, development, and growth as well as coordination-focused administrative tasks. Future research that can help leaders strike a balance between these two domains will be extremely helpful.

The accumulation of research on entrepreneurial leadership has, in my view, been limited by the wide variety of perspectives that researchers adopt when talking about this topic, as explained in the beginning of this chapter. Moving forward, for a critical body of research to emerge, I encourage others to adopt a perspective where entrepreneurial leadership is truly treated as another leadership style. While it is helpful to study a variety of leadership-related phenomena in new firms, and to link entrepreneurial thinking to firm-level strategies and culture, studies focusing on these topics seldom make contributions that help distinguish entrepreneurial leadership as a construct on its own. Given the importance of both entrepreneurial thinking and effective leadership in today's corporate world, and the popularity of entrepreneurship as a career option among the young and the old, I believe it is very important that academics take on the challenge of studying entrepreneurial leadership style and its implications for people, organizations, and societal development. In doing this, we have to be careful not to deduce core traits of effective entrepreneurial leadership from successful entrepreneurs. Instead, a focus on opportunities as goals of the entrepreneurial leadership process should be helpful. Instead of personality traits of great entrepreneurs and leaders, this chapter has discussed entrepreneurial leaders with regard to what they do in their everyday work, how they make decisions, how they feel about their organization, and what they make their followers do. I encourage researchers to adopt the ideas presented in this chapter as a first step toward understanding entrepreneurial leadership style and to further build on them as they pursue conceptual and empirical research on the topic.

## Discussion Questions

1. Think of your experiences with various leaders you have known (at work, at school, in organizations you have been a member of). Who has been the most entrepreneurial leader you have personally known? What aspects of entrepreneurial leadership did they exemplify? Did they make you behave in a more entrepreneurial way?

2. Even if entrepreneurial leadership is a common topic discussed by practitioners and in the popular press, academic research on the topic has remained underdeveloped and scattered. Why do you think that is? What is needed for research in this area to move forward?

3. Search through articles in the popular press (newspapers, magazines) that describe someone as an "entrepreneurial leader." Find at least three contrasting examples that use the term for a different meaning. Try to find parallels between the examples you find and the way entrepreneurial leadership is defined in this chapter.

## Recommended Readings

- Cogliser, C. C., & Brigham, K. H. (2004). The intersection of leadership and entrepreneurship: Mutual lessons to be learned. *The Leadership Quarterly, 15,* 771–799.
- Leitch, C. M., McMullan, C., & Harrison, R. T. (2013). The development of entrepreneurial leadership: The role of human, social and institutional capital. *British Journal of Management, 24*(3), 347–366.
- McGrath, R. G., & MacMillan, I. C. (2000). *The entrepreneurial mindset.* Boston, MA: Harvard Business School Publishing.
- Renko, M., El Tarabishy, A., Carsrud, A. L., & Brännback, M. (2015). Understanding and measuring entrepreneurial leadership style. *Journal of Small Business Management, 53*(1), 54–74.

- Thornberry, N. (2006). *Lead like an entrepreneur: Keeping the entrepreneurial spirit alive within the corporation.* Boston, MA: McGraw-Hill.

## Recommended Case Studies

- Chakravarthy, B., & Huber, H. (2003, January 1). Internal entrepreneurship at the Dow Chemical Co. IMD.
- Dann, J. (2015, January 12). "Kickboxing" at Adobe Systems. Greif Center for Entrepreneurial Studies–USC Marshall.
- Farhoomand, A., & Lai, R. (2010, July 19). Alibaba's Jack Ma: Rise of the new Chinese entrepreneur. University of Hong Kong.
- Gamble, E., Parker, S., Moroz, P., Baglole, P., & Cassidy, R. (2014, August 19). Entrepreneurial leadership at Maritime Bus. London, UK: Ivey.
- George, W. W., & McLean, A. N. (2006, June 30). Howard Schultz: Building Starbucks community (A). Harvard Business School.

## Recommended Videos

- Branson, R. (2007). Richard Branson: Life at 30,000 feet.
  http://www.ted.com/talks/richard_branson_s_life_at_30_000_feet/transcript?language=en
- Heffernan, M. (2012). Margaret Heffernan: Dare to disagree.
  https://www.ted.com/talks/margaret_heffernan_dare_to_disagree?language=en
- Musk, E. (2013). Elon Musk: The mind behind Tesla, SpaceX, and SolarCity.
  https://www.ted.com/talks/elon_musk_the_mind_behind_tesla_spacex_solarcity?language=en

## References

Adkins, Amy. (2016, May 11). What Millennials want from work and life. *Gallup Business Journal.* Retrieved from http://www.gallup.com/businessjournal/191435/millennials-work-life.aspx

Anderson, C. (2012). *Makers: The new Industrial Revolution.* New York, NY: Crown Business.

Antonakis, J. B. J., & Autio, E. (2006). Entrepreneurship and leadership. In J. R. Baum, M. Frese, & R. A. Baron (Eds.), *The psychology of entrepreneurship* (pp. 189–208). Mahwah, NJ: Lawrence Erlbaum.

Antonakis, J., & House, R. J. (2002). An analysis of the full-range leadership theory: The way forward. In B. J. Avolio & F. J. Yammarino (Eds.), *Transformational and charismatic leadership: The road ahead* (pp. 3–34). Amsterdam, Netherlands: JAI Press.

Antonakis, J., & House, R. J. (2014). Instrumental leadership: Measurement and extension of transformational–transactional leadership theory. *The Leadership Quarterly, 25,* 746–771.

Antoncic, B., & Hisrich, R. D. (2001). Intrapreneurship: Construct refinement and cross-cultural validation. *Journal of Business Venturing, 16*(5), 495–527.

Argyris, C. (1998). Empowerment: the emperor's new clothes. *Harvard Business Review, 76*(3), 98–105.

Autio, E., & Acs, Z. J. (2010). Intellectual property protection and the formation of entrepreneurial growth aspirations. *Strategic Entrepreneurship Journal, 4*(4), 234–251.

Avolio, B. J., Gardner, W. L., Walumbwa, F. O., Luthans, F., & May, D. R. (2004). Unlocking the mask: A look at the process by which authentic leaders impact follower attitudes and behaviors. *The Leadership Quarterly, 15*(6), 801–823.

Bandura, A. (1986). *Social foundations of thought and action: A social cognitive theory.* Englewood Cliffs, NJ: Prentice Hall.

Baron, R. (2008). The role of affect in the entrepreneurial process. *Academy of Management Review, 33*(2), 328–340.

Baron, R. A., & Ensley, M. D. (2006). Opportunity recognition as the detection of meaningful patterns: Evidence from comparisons of novice and experienced entrepreneurs. *Management Science, 52*(9), 1331–1344.

Basadur, M. (2004). Leading others to think innovatively together: Creative leadership. *The Leadership Quarterly, 15*(1), 103–121.

Bass, B. M. (1985). *Leadership and performance beyond expectations.* New York, NY: Free Press.

Bass, B. M., & Avolio, B. J. (1995). *Multifactor Leadership Questionnaire.* Redwood City, CA: Mind Garden.

Baum, J. R., & Locke, E. A. (2004). The relationship of entrepreneurial traits, skill, and motivation to subsequent venture growth. *Journal of Applied Psychology, 89,* 587–598.

Baum, J. R., Locke, E. A., & Kirkpatrick, S. A. (1998). A longitudinal study of the relation of vision and vision communication to venture growth in entrepreneurial firms. *Journal of Applied Psychology, 83*(1), 43–54.

Baum, J. R., Locke, E. A., & Smith, K. G. (2001). A multidimensional model of venture growth. *Academy of Management Journal, 44*(2), 292–304.

Becherer, R. C., Mendenhall, M. E., & Eickhoff, K. F. (2008). Separated at birth: An inquiry on the conceptual independence of the entrepreneurship and the leadership constructs. *New England Journal of Entrepreneurship, 11*(2), 13–27.

Brandstätter, H. (2011). Personality aspects of entrepreneurship: A look at five meta-analyses. *Personality and Individual Differences, 51*(3), 222–230.

Bresman. H. (2015, February 23). What Millennials want from work, charted across the world. *Harvard Business Review.*

Breugst, N., Domurath, A., Patzelt, H., & Klaukien, A. (2012). Perceptions of entrepreneurial passion and employees' commitment to entrepreneurial ventures. *Entrepreneurship Theory and Practice, 36*(1), 171–192.

Cardon, M. S., Wincent, J., Singh, J., & Drnovsek, M. (2009). The nature and experience of entrepreneurial passion. *Academy of Management Review, 34*(3), 511–532.

Cardon, M. S., Zietsma, C., Saparito, P., Matherne, B. P., & Davis, C. (2005). A tale of passion: New insights into entrepreneurship from a parenthood metaphor. *Journal of Business Venturing, 20*(1), 23–45.

Carsrud, A. L., Renko, M., Brännback, M., Sashkin, M., & El Tarabishy, A. (in press). Understanding entrepreneurial leadership: Who leads a venture does matter. In R. T. Harrison & C. M. Leitch (Eds.), *Research handbook on entrepreneurship and leadership.* Northampton, MA: Edward Elgar.

Chen, M.-H. (2007). Entrepreneurial leadership and new ventures: Creativity in entrepreneurial teams. *Creativity and Innovation Management, 16*(3), 239–249.

Chen, X.-P., Yao, X., & Kotha, S. (2009). Entrepreneur passion and preparedness in business plan presentations: A persuasion analysis of venture capitalists' funding decisions. *Academy of Management Journal, 52*(1), 199–214.

Choi, Y. R., & Shepherd, D. A. (2004). Entrepreneurs' decisions to exploit opportunities. *Journal of Management, 30*(3), 377–395.

Cogliser, C. C., & Brigham, K. H. (2004). The intersection of leadership and entrepreneurship: Mutual lessons to be learned. *The Leadership Quarterly, 15,* 771–799.

Conger, J. A., & Kanungo, R. N. (1988). The empowerment process: Integrating theory and practice. *Academy of Management Review, 13*(3), 471–482.

Conger, J. A., & Kanungo, R. N. (1998). *Charismatic leadership in organizations.* Thousand Oaks, CA: Sage.

Covin, J. G., & Slevin, D. P. (2002). The entrepreneurial imperatives of strategic leadership. In M. A. Hitt, R. D. Ireland, S. M. Camp, & D. L. Sexton (Eds.), *Strategic entrepreneurship: Creating a new mindset* (pp. 309–327). Oxford, UK: Blackwell.

Csikszentmihalyi, M. (1997). *Creativity: Flow and the psychology of discovery and invention.* New York, NY: Harper Perennial.

Cunningham, J. B., & Lischeron, J. (1991). Defining entrepreneurship. *Journal of Small Business Management, 29*(1), 45–62.

De Dreu, C. K., & Weingart, L. R. (2003). Task versus relationship conflict, team performance, and team member satisfaction: A meta-analysis. *Journal of Applied Psychology, 88*(4), 741.

Dess, G. G., Ireland, R. D., Zahra, S. A., Floyd, S. W., Janney, J. J., & Lane, P. J. (2003). Emerging issues in corporate entrepreneurship. *Journal of Management, 29,* 351–378.

Engelen, A., Gupta, V., Strenger, L., & Brettel, M. (2015). Entrepreneurial orientation, firm performance, and the moderating role of transformational leadership behaviors. *Journal of Management, 41*(4), 1069–1097.

Ensley, M. D., Hmieleski, K. M., & Pearce, C. L. (2006). The importance of vertical and shared leadership within new venture top management teams: Implications for the performance of startups. *The Leadership Quarterly, 17*(3), 217–231.

Ensley, M. D., Pearce, C. L., & Hmieleski, K. M. (2006). The moderating effect of environmental dynamism on the relationship between entrepreneur leadership behavior and new venture performance. *Journal of Business Venturing, 21*(2), 243–263.

Fernald, L. W. J., Solomon, G. T., & Tarabishy, A. (2005). A new paradigm: Entrepreneurial leadership. *Southern Business Review, 30*(2), 1.

Frayne, C. A., & Latham, G. P. (1987). The application of social learning theory to employee self-management of attendance. *Journal of Applied Psychology, 72,* 387–392.

Gaglio, C. M. (2004). The role of mental simulations and counterfactual thinking in the opportunity identification process. *Entrepreneurship Theory and Practice, 28*(6), 533–552.

Gartner, W. B. (1988). "Who is an entrepreneur?" is the wrong question. *American Journal of Small Business, 12*(4), 11–32.

Goss, D. (2005). Schumpeter's legacy? Interaction and emotions in the sociology of entrepreneurship. *Entrepreneurship: Theory & Practice, 29*(2), 205–218.

Gupta, V., MacMillan, I. C., & Surie, G. (2004). Entrepreneurial leadership: Developing and measuring a cross-cultural construct. *Journal of Business Venturing, 19*(2), 241–260.

Hackman, J. R., & Oldham, G. R. (1976). Motivation through the design of work: Test of a theory. *Organizational Behavior and Human Performance, 16*(2), 250–279.

Harrison, R., Leitch, C., & McAdam, M. (2015). Breaking glass: Toward a gendered analysis of entrepreneurial leadership. *Journal of Small Business Management, 53*(3), 693–713.

Haslam, S., & Platow, M. J. (2001). The link between leadership and followership: How affirming social identity translates vision into action. *Personality and Social Psychology Bulletin, 27*(11), 1469–1479.

Haynes, K. T., Hitt, M. A., & Campbell, J. T. (2015). The dark side of leadership: Towards a mid-range theory of hubris and greed in entrepreneurial contexts. *Journal of Management Studies, 52*(4), 479–505.

Henry, C., Foss, L., Fayolle, A., Walker, E., & Duffy, S. (2015). Entrepreneurial leadership and gender: Exploring theory and practice in global contexts. *Journal of Small Business Management, 53*(3), 581–586.

Herzberg, F., Mausner, B., & Snyderman, B. (1959). *The motivation to work.* New York, NY: Wiley.

Hmieleski, K. M., & Ensley, M. D. (2007). A contextual examination of new venture performance: Entrepreneur leadership behavior, top management team heterogeneity, and environmental dynamism. *Journal of Organizational Behavior, 28*(7), 865–889.

Hunt, J. G. (1991). *The leadership: A new synthesis.* Newbury Park, CA: Sage.

Hunt, J. G. (2004). What is leadership? In J. Antonakis, A. T. Cianciolo, & R. J. Sternberg (Eds.), *The nature of leadership* (pp. 19–47). Thousand Oaks, CA: Sage.

Ilies, R., Judge, T., & Wagner, D. (2006). Making sense of motivational leadership: The trail from transformational leaders to motivated followers. *Journal of Leadership & Organizational Studies, 13*(1), 1–23.

Ireland, R. D., Hitt, M. A., & Sirmon, D. G. (2003). A model of strategic entrepreneurship: The construct and its dimensions. *Journal of Management, 29*(6), 963–989.

Judge, T. A., Bono, J. E., Ilies, R., & Gerhardt, M. W. (2002). Personality and leadership: A qualitative and quantitative review. *Journal of Applied Psychology, 87*(4), 765–780.

Kang, J. H., Solomon, G. T., & Choi, D. Y. (2015). CEOs' leadership styles and managers' innovative behaviour: Investigation of intervening effects in an entrepreneurial context. *Journal of Management Studies, 52*(4), 531–554.

Khanna, T. (2013). *Billions of entrepreneurs: How China and India are reshaping their futures and yours.* Boston, MA: Harvard Business School Publishing.

Kirzner, I. M. (1997). Entrepreneurial discovery and the competitive market process: An Austrian approach. *The Journal of Economic Literature, 35*, 60–85.

Koryak, O., Mole, K. F., Lockett, A., Hayton, J. C., Ucbasaran, D., & Hodgkinson, G. P. (2015). Entrepreneurial leadership, capabilities and firm growth. *International Small Business Journal, 33*(1), 89–105.

Kuratko, D. F., Ireland, R. D., & Hornsby, J. S. (2001). Improving firm performance through entrepreneurial actions: Acordia's corporate entrepreneurship strategy. *Academy of Management Executive, 15*(4), 60–71.

Leitch, C. M., McMullan, C., & Harrison, R. T. (2013). The development of entrepreneurial leadership: The role of human, social and institutional capital. *British Journal of Management, 24*(3), 347–366.

Ling, Y., Simsek, Z., Lubatkin, M. H., & Veiga, J. F. (2008). Transformational leadership's role in promoting corporate entrepreneurship: Examining the CEO-TMT interface. *Academy of Management Journal, 51*(3), 557–576.

Locke, E. A., & Latham, G. P. (1990). *A theory of goal setting and task performance.* Englewood Cliffs, NJ: Prentice Hall.

Lord, R. G., & Emrich, C. G. (2001). Thinking outside the box by looking inside the box: Extending the cognitive revolution in leadership research. *The Leadership Quarterly, 11*, 551–579.

MacKenzie, S. B., Podsakoff, P. M., & Rich, G. A. (2001). Transformational and transactional leadership and salesperson performance. *Journal of the Academy of Marketing Science, 29*(2), 115–134.

Mainemelis, C., Kark, R., & Epitropaki, O. (2015). Creative leadership: A multi-context conceptualization. *Academy of Management Annals, 9*, 393–482.

Martin, B. C., McNally, J. J., & Kay, M. J. (2013). Examining the formation of human capital in entrepreneurship: A meta-analysis of entrepreneurship education outcomes. *Journal of Business Venturing, 28*(2), 211–224.

McGee, J. E., Peterson, M., Mueller, S. L., & Sequeira, J. M. (2009). Entrepreneurial self-efficacy: Refining the measure. *Entrepreneurship Theory and Practice, 33*(4), 965.

McGrath, R. G., & MacMillan, I. C. (2000). *The entrepreneurial mindset.* Boston, MA: Harvard Business School Publishing.

Mueller, P. (2007). Exploiting entrepreneurial opportunities: The impact of entrepreneurship on growth. *Small Business Economics, 28*(4), 355–362.

Nicholson, N. (1998). Personality and entrepreneurial leadership: A study of the heads of the UK's most successful independent companies. *European Management Journal, 16*(5), 529–539.

Niemann, G. (2007). *Big brown. The untold story of UPS.* San Francisco, CA: Jossey-Bass.

Padilla, A., Hogan, R., & Kaiser, R. B. (2007). The toxic triangle: Destructive leaders, susceptible followers, and conducive environments. *The Leadership Quarterly, 18*(3), 176–194.

Peterson, S. J., Walumbwa, F. O., Byron, K., & Myrowitz, J. (2009). CEO positive psychological traits, transformational leadership, and firm performance in high-technology start-up and established firms. *Journal of Management, 35*, 348–368.

Pew Research Center. (2014, March 7). Millennials in adulthood, detached from institutions, networked with friends. Retrieved from http://www.pewsocialtrends.org/2014/03/07/millennials-in-adulthood/

Podsakoff, P. M., MacKenzie, S. B., Moorman, R. H., & Fetter, R. (1990). Transformational leader behaviors and their effects on followers' trust in leader, satisfaction, and organizational citizenship behaviors. *The Leadership Quarterly, 1*(2), 107–142.

Rauch, C. F., & Behling, O. (1984). Functionalism: Basis for an alternate approach to the study of leadership. In J. G. Hunt, D. Hosking, C. Schriesheim, & R. Stewart, (Eds.), *Leaders and managers: International perspectives on managerial behavior and leadership.* Elmsford, NY: Pergamon.

Renko, M., El Tarabishy, A., Carsrud, A., & Brännback, M. (2012). Entrepreneurial leadership in family business. In A. Carsrud & M. Brännback (Eds.), *Understanding family businesses, undiscovered approaches, unique perspectives, and neglected topics* (pp. 169–184). New York, NY: Springer Verlag.

Renko, M., El Tarabishy, A., Carsrud, A. L., & Brännback, M. (2015). Understanding and measuring entrepreneurial leadership style. *Journal of Small Business Management, 53*(1), 54–74.

Reynolds, P. D. (2015). Business creation stability: Why is it so hard to increase entrepreneurship? *Foundations and Trends in Entrepreneurship, 10*(5–6), 321–475.

Sarasvathy, S. D. (2001). Causation and effectuation: Toward a theoretical shift from economic inevitability to entrepreneurial contingency. *Academy of Management Review, 26*(2), 243–263.

Shamir, B., & Howell, J. M. (1999). Organizational and contextual influences on the emergence and effectiveness of charismatic leadership. *The Leadership Quarterly, 10,* 257–283.

Shane, S. (2000). Prior knowledge and the discovery of entrepreneurial opportunities. *Organization Science, 11*(4), 448–469.

Shane, S., & Venkataraman, S. (2000). The promise of entrepreneurship as a field of research. *Academy of Management Review, 25,* 217–226.

Simsek, Z., Jansen, J. J., Minichilli, A., & Escriba-Esteve, A. (2015). Strategic leadership and leaders in entrepreneurial contexts: A nexus for innovation and impact missed? *Journal of Management Studies, 52*(4), 463–478.

Sobel, R. S. (2008). Testing Baumol: Institutional quality and the productivity of entrepreneurship. *Journal of Business Venturing, 23*(6), 641–655.

Stewart, W. H., Jr., & Roth, P. L. (2001). Risk propensity differences between entrepreneurs and managers: A meta-analytic review. *Journal of Applied Psychology, 86*(1), 145.

Stogdill, R. M. (1948). Personal factors associated with leadership: A survey of the literature. *Journal of Psychology, 25,* 35–71.

Stone, B. (2014). *The everything store: Jeff Bezos and the age of Amazon.* New York, NY: Little, Brown.

Tang, J., Kacmar, K. M. M., & Busenitz, L. (2012). Entrepreneurial alertness in the pursuit of new opportunities. *Journal of Business Venturing, 27*(1), 77–94.

Thornberry, N. (2006). *Lead like an entrepreneur: Keeping the entrepreneurial spirit alive within the corporation.* Boston, MA: McGraw-Hill.

Tierney, P., & Farmer, S. M. (2004). The Pygmalion process and employee creativity. *Journal of Management, 30*(3), 413–432.

Tierney, P., Farmer, S. M., & Graen, G. B. (1999). An examination of leadership and employee creativity: The relevance of traits and relationships. *Personnel Psychology, 52,* 591–620.

Vaghely, I. P., & Julien, P.-A. (2010). Are opportunities recognized or constructed? An information perspective on entrepreneurial opportunity identification. *Journal of Business Venturing, 25,* 73–86.

Vallerand, R. J., Blanchard, C., Mageau, G. A., Koestner, R., Ratelle, C., Léonard, M., . . . Marsolais, J. (2003). *Les passions de l'ame:* On obsessive and harmonious passion. *Journal of Personality and Social Psychology, 85*(4), 756–767.

*Wall Street Journal.* (2016). What is Alibaba? Retrieved from http://projects.wsj.com/alibaba/

Wilson, F., Kickul, J., & Marlino, D. (2007). Gender, entrepreneurial self-efficacy, and entrepreneurial career intentions: Implications for entrepreneurship education. *Entrepreneurship Theory and Practice, 31*(3), 387–406.

Yukl, G. (2008). *Leadership in organizations.* Upper Saddle River, NJ: Prentice Hall.

Zampetakis, L. A., Beldekos, P., & Moustakis, V. S. (2009). "Day-to-day" entrepreneurship within organisations: The role of trait emotional intelligence and perceived organisational support. *European Management Journal, 27*(3), 165–175.

Zhao, H., Seibert, S. E., & Hills, G. E. (2005). The mediating role of self-efficacy in the development of entrepreneurial intentions. *Journal of Applied Psychology, 90*(6), 1265–1272.

# PART IV

# Philosophical and Methodological Issues in Leadership

# CHAPTER 16

# Studying Leadership: Research Design and Methods

*Philippe Jacquart*

*Michael S. Cole*

*Allison S. Gabriel*

*Joel Koopman*

*Christopher C. Rosen*

---

## Opening Case: A Day in the Life of a Leader

Susan is a partner at a top consulting firm. Susan rose to fame in the company after her team successfully developed and rolled out a leadership training program that has emerged as one of company's best-selling programs. Over the past few years, top management teams across the country have begun to implement this training program, and the demand is still on the rise. Lately, however, a group of leadership scholars has publicly criticized this program for being nothing more than "fluff wrapped in a beautiful package." Susan has started to consider how she might address these criticisms and, although she strongly believes in the training program, she has begun to question its utility, given the concerns that have been raised by critics.

On a recent morning, Susan was sitting at her desk, reading a popular press article that summarized an academic publication criticizing the training program. The critics argued that her program has no theoretical grounding, that it has never been adequately validated, and that therefore there is no reason to believe it is of any value. "How can they say this?" thought Susan. By now, literally hundreds of teams had gone through this leadership training program, and the feedback from participants was invariably excellent. Furthermore, some companies had even tracked the performance of employees who had attended this training program, and these results showed that, by and large, the participation in the training program was followed by improvement in various performance metrics.

Susan continued reading. The critics argued that whatever effects were observed among managers who had undergone the training provided very little evidence because these effects had not been contrasted against a comparison group of similar managers who had not participated in the program. Thus, according to the critics, any observed effects could result from a self-fulfilling prophecy (i.e., managers selected to attend this reputable training might feel pride and recognition from their employer, and these feelings could, in turn, lead to increased motivation and performance). Furthermore, the critics argued that participants were often selected because they had excelled in their job or were selected as high potentials; thus, managers selected to participate in this training program did not represent the average manager, meaning there might be confounding factors at play. Some of these arguments sounded ridiculous to Susan. Nevertheless, she could understand why more proof was required before these criticisms were put to rest. Susan reflected on what she would need to do in order to make a convincing case that her training program worked and was not just "fluff."

### Discussion Questions

1. Can observed covariation between two variables (e.g., attending a training program and improving in leadership effectiveness) be interpreted as cause and effect?

2. Give three examples of potential confounding variables that could explain the effects observed on participants following training.

3. How could Susan find out, beyond doubt, that her training program is effective?

## Chapter Overview

In our opening example, a consultant is challenged to provide compelling evidence that a leadership training program is indeed effective. Broadening the scope of this example, we could consider the following question: How can we determine whether leadership matters for the effective functioning of institutions? Given the purpose of this chapter, to answer this question we first need to clarify what is meant by the terms *leadership* and *effectiveness*. For example, should we consider leadership to be a stable trait, a formal hierarchical position, an influencing process, or something else? Thus, to begin we need to define and operationalize both leadership and effectiveness, which involves clarifying conceptually what these terms mean and how they are to be measured. Undertaking these steps paves the way for understanding the nature of the relationship between leadership and effectiveness.

Cook and Campbell (1979) suggest that three criteria must be met in order to infer a causal relationship between psychological constructs: (1) there must be covariation between the predictor and the dependent variable; (2) the cause (i.e., predictor variable) must temporally precede the effect (i.e., the dependent variable); and (3) plausible alternative explanations for the assumed cause-and-effect relationship must be ruled out. Whereas the two first criteria are relatively easy to establish, the third usually proves to be a trickier matter. Referring back to our opening example, the purported covariation between the training program and outcomes provides some support for the first and second criteria, but it cannot speak to the third. As the critics suggest, simply attending training may have an effect independently of its content (e.g., it may be simply the recognition associated with being selected for training, and not the content of the training itself yielding the performance improvements). Alternatively, there could exist a third variable that associates with both the likelihood that a manager is selected for the training and the subsequent performance improvements, thus creating a spurious relationship between the two focal variables (James, 1980). As we discuss in this chapter, when testing for a causal relationship, it is critical to have an appropriate design and to collect the needed data in order to justifiably make a causal claim. Indeed, conducting a study on leadership requires a deep knowledge and understanding of research methodology. In this regard, Aguinis and Vandenberg (2014) drew on Ben Franklin's admonishment that an ounce of prevention is worth a pound of cure when they observed that the "investment in theory, design, and measurement issues is likely to yield a much greater return compared with investment in the data analysis stage" (p. 591). Hence, the focus of much of this chapter is on discussing such design conditions and data, because policy can best be informed once causal relations have been uncovered.

The goals of this chapter are threefold. We first provide a succinct overview of quantitative research. We introduce the notion of evidence-based management and clarify what is meant by a theory and the role of quantitative research for theory testing and why measurement and hypothesis testing are key building blocks of quantitative research. We also show how estimates can be obtained from observed data. Second, we explore why observing covariation between two (or more) variables is not necessarily indicative of a causal relationship between variables (this is the notion of endogeneity). Finally, we introduce experimental designs, explaining in detail why the randomization to treatment is so important for experimental research. We also discuss quasi-experimental research designs, which are useful to researchers in cases where experiments are not feasible.

## Part I: The Foundations of Quantitative Research

Over the course of the 20th century, we witnessed a dramatic change in the practice of medicine with the advent of evidence-based practice (see Smith & Rennie, 2014). Evidence-based practice is based on medical practitioners using the most recent evidence available to treat their patients. Similarly, in the context of leadership and management, the validity of theories and practices can be put to the empirical test to "sort the wheat from the chaff" (Pfeffer & Sutton, 2006).[1] This is the notion of evidence-based management (Briner, Denyer, & Rousseau, 2009). The underlying logic is simple: If a claim is true, then one should be able to observe evidence supporting this claim, and our practices and policies should be based on existing evidence. However, determining cause-and-effect relations can prove to be difficult, as we will explore in this chapter, and researchers need to adhere to appropriate procedures and methods in order to make causal inferences from observational data. Doing so is important not only because we are prone to seek information confirming our preconceptions (Nickerson, 1998), but also because the failure to follow adequate procedures can lead to biased results and fallacious conclusions (Antonakis, Bendahan, Jacquart, & Lalive, 2010).

## Theory and Meaningful Contributions

Theory and the development of theoretical frameworks that can explain a practical phenomenon are essential for knowledge accumulation both inside and outside the organizational sciences. According to Lewin (1945), we know that "nothing is as practical as a good theory" (p. 129) and, by extension, a "good" theory provides a framework for proposing what is believed to be true (of note, of course, is the fact that theory should also not be considered an "absolute" law to be abided because theories are only tentatively accepted and thus always open for further inquiry and testing). A theory is about "the connections among phenomena, a story about why acts, events, structure, and thoughts occur. Theory emphasizes the nature of causal relationships, identifying what comes first as well as the timing of such events" (Sutton & Staw, 1995, p. 378). Put differently, theory can be defined as a set of testable assertions that specifies a relationship among two (or more) constructs, for what reasons the relationship is important, how the two constructs interrelate, and under what conditions the relationship is expected to be observed or not (Sutton & Staw, 1995). Having clear theory not only specifies the nature of the relationship between two constructs, but also helps specify why these two constructs should be the focus as opposed to a plethora of alternatives.

Theories can be inductive or deductive in nature. An inductive approach to theory looks to the data to provide meaningful patterns of association. Hence, an inductive approach is commonly characterized as "letting the data speak, such that some forms of analyses result in patterns or concepts, and the researcher's role is to make the connections within those patterns or among those concepts" (Aguinis & Vandenberg, 2014, p. 576). Although such an approach can lead to significant theoretical advancements (Locke, 2007), it is less common to see this type of research in applied psychology and management journals, though some journals are beginning to encourage this type of discovery (see the advent of the new *Academy of Management Discoveries* journal). In contrast, a deductive approach to theory building is grounded in a strong

---

1. It is important to mention here that although it is only through quantitative research that causal claims can unequivocally be made, inroads are being made to more robustly examine possible causal relations in small sample size or case study research (Geddes, 2003; Gerring & McDermott, 2007).

theoretical base. This approach is more common in the organizational sciences, wherein the researcher adopts one (or more) theories to develop and empirically test his or her hypotheses, which, in turn, are empirically evaluated.

## Fundamental Measurement Issues

To be sure, leadership is a complex topic of study; however, the complexity associated with exploring these theoretically and practically important topics does not necessarily limit our ability to study them in a scientific way. Toward this end, when using a deductive approach, leadership scholars must incorporate theory to develop conceptual models that can then be tested via empirical methods. This scientific process must be rigorous (i.e., the methodology used should be systematic, sound, and relatively error free) so that inferences made by the researcher are scientifically valid and robust (Daft, 1984). Moreover, it is particularly important to clarify what is meant by leadership in the context of a given study. Indeed, the construct of leadership is manifold. For example, depending on how the construct is conceptualized, leadership might refer to holding a formal position within organizations, a specific class of behaviors, or a set of individual characteristics. Ultimately, how leadership is conceptualized in a given study will depend on the research question at hand. For instance, a researcher interested in understanding how CEOs are recruited is focused on understanding who is selected to occupy a formal leadership position and in the process could very well examine the role of both individual characteristics (e.g., gender) and certain abilities (e.g., rhetorical skills). Having established what our construct of leadership is, we then focus on how best to measure this construct—that is, how to operationalize leadership. The validity of measures used in a study is a critical aspect of the research design, in that validity gauges a survey instrument's accuracy. In short, validity refers to how well the measures used in a study actually assess what they set out to measure. For example, a measure that claims to measure transformational leadership should not measure "liking" (c.f. Brown & Keeping, 2005).

**Construct Validity.** Perhaps the most fundamental and often overlooked aspect of empirical research is the operationalization of a study's focal construct. Construct validity is the most valuable way of evaluating a survey instrument, as it is a measure of how meaningful a survey instrument or measure is when in practical use (Litwin, 1995). In order to be construed as a valid operationalization of a leadership variable, the researcher must provide a clear and meaningful conceptual definition of the construct under study and use a measure that adequately covers its assumed content domain, is generally free from random error, and is conceptually and empirically distinct from related constructs (Hinkin, 1995).

Unfortunately, recent critiques of the leadership literature suggest that two of the most widely studied leadership styles (viz., transformational leadership and leader–member exchange) fall short in this regard. Van Knippenberg and Sitkin (2013) pointedly commented that "there does not seem to be a conceptually sound and bounded definition of charismatic-transformational leadership" (p. 4). In fact, concerns about the validity of transformational leadership measures are not a recent phenomenon. Yukl (1999), for example, levied many of the same criticisms almost two decades ago. More recently, Antonakis, Bastardoz, Jacquart, and Shamir (2016) similarly outlined conceptual problems with existing definitions of charisma and identified how these issues limit our ability to study this phenomenon in a satisfactory manner.

At the same time that Yukl was criticizing transformational leadership's operationalization and measurement, another camp of leadership scholars (Schriesheim, Castro, & Cogliser, 1999) was similarly criticizing the leader–member exchange (LMX) literature for having "little consistency about the basic definition and content of the LMX construct (even in different works by the same authors)" (p. 77). Perhaps most interesting (at least to us) is that despite repeated criticism of the literature's "gold standard" measures of LMX (see, e.g., Bernerth, Armenakis, Feild, Giles, & Walker, 2007; Colquitt, Baer, Long, & Halvorsen-Ganepola, 2014), the most recently published leadership research carries on using LMX measures that have been meticulously challenged on both conceptual and empirical grounds. Similar critiques exist for other leadership constructs and their associated measures as well (e.g., Cooper, Scandura, & Schriesheim, 2005; Eisenbeiss, 2012).[2]

Fuzzy definitions are problematic and cannot help science advance. To the extent that a leadership measure is not accompanied by a clear conceptual definition and is not shown to be theoretically distinct from other related forms of leadership behavior, one may have difficulty interpreting study findings and providing actionable recommendations to practicing managers. Taken to the extreme, scholars often use the term *construct proliferation* to denote when two (or more) constructs share conceptual content and are difficult to empirically differentiate from one another. According to Shaffer, DeGeest, and Li (2016), construct proliferation reflects "the accumulation of ostensibly different but potentially identical constructs representing organizational phenomena" (p. 80). Moreover, these researchers reported an average correlation of .89 across 13 measures that purportedly assess conceptually unique leadership styles. Such evidence strongly suggests that these widely used leadership measures may not tap into distinct styles of leading. In part, this result is due to the fact that the measures associated with these various leadership constructs contain similar items or may be simply tapping affect-linked outcomes (e.g., Brown & Keeping, 2005).

Thus, researchers must critically evaluate the psychometric properties of existing measures prior to including them in a research study. This step can be easily incorporated into the research design and planning phase. Echoing Locke (2007), who observed that a concept must gradually develop from an accumulating body of evidence in order to have lasting value, we hope to see future studies that focus on improving the psychometric properties of well-known leadership measures and/or research aimed at developing new measures for existing leadership phenomena (see, e.g., Antonakis & House, 2014). To this end, we would expect this research to closely adhere to best practice recommendations to ensure proper measure development (e.g., Hinkin, 1995, 1998). Overall, given the somewhat overwhelming number of leadership theories and constructs that exist in the literature

---

2. There is beyond these critiques a more pernicious problem: Measures akin to LMX as well as most questionnaires gauge observer attitudes, which are endogenous variables (we discuss this problem of *endogeneity* later in the chapter).

(e.g., Dionne et al., 2014), as well as the strong critiques that have been levied against the leadership literature for poor conceptual definition and measurement (e.g., Shaffer et al., 2016; Van Knippenberg & Sitkin, 2013), this is a critical issue for leadership scholars moving forward.

**Assessing Construct Validity**. Ultimately, validity is concerned with the relationship between a construct and the variable purported to measure it (Carmines & Zeller, 1979), in that it assesses the match between the conceptual and operational definitions. To determine whether a measure is valid, several criteria can and should be examined. First, researchers should ensure that their proposed measure has *predictive validity* (i.e., criterion-related validity). In other words, does the measure predict what it theoretically should predict? For example, if theory suggests that the construct of transformational leadership should increase follower trust in the leader, we should be able to observe this relationship empirically. If not, we would have failed to establish the predictive validity of this transformational leadership measure, which casts doubt on the measure's validity. Second, researchers should assess whether a measure has *convergent validity* (i.e., whether the measure positively correlates with other measures of the same construct). For example, if researchers were to propose a new measure of abusive supervision that does not strongly correlate with other established measures of the same construct, this result would signal a validity problem. Third, researchers should demonstrate that a measure has *discriminant validity* (i.e., it does not positively correlate with conceptually distinct variables). That is, the leadership measure used in a research study should be empirically distinguishable from conceptually similar—yet distinct—constructs. Finally, the measure being used should demonstrate *incremental validity* such that the measure needs to explain additional variance in one or more outcomes over and above other meaningful constructs. An example of this can be found in the literature on emotional intelligence and leadership. Indeed, current measures of emotional intelligence have not been shown to predict outcomes above and beyond the effect of general intelligence (Harms & Credé, 2010), suggesting that current operationalizations of emotional intelligence do not tap into anything different than what is already captured by general intelligence. This result may mean that emotional intelligence does not matter for studying leadership, or it may mean that the incremental validity failure is because of measurement issues (Antonakis, Ashkanasy, & Dasborough, 2009).

## Hypothesis Testing

Quantitative research frequently relies on null hypothesis significance testing (NHST) as a means to determine whether observed relationships (or lack thereof) within samples can be considered as indicative of actual relationships in the population. In this approach, the so-called null hypothesis is examined. NHST relies on comparing observed sample data with a theoretical sampling distribution under the assumption that the null hypothesis is true. Rejecting the null, of course, does not mean direct support for the alternative hypothesis that there is necessarily a relationship; also, not rejecting the null hypothesis does not mean the null is true.

For instance, in an experimental setting, using NHST is very useful because a researcher testing a new treatment must test the assumption that the treatment is no different vis-à-vis the control treatment or even an alternative treatment (Murtaugh, 2014); if this assumption were true—that there is no effect of the treatment—NHST simply tells us how likely or probable it is to observe a given result. This probability is quantified in the $p$-value. This $p$-value is a valuable piece of information to have, though it is often misinterpreted (Bettis, Ethiraj, Gambardella, Helfat, & Mitchell, 2016). Because NHST is sometimes misused, some researchers have suggested that NHST be abandoned; however, if correctly used there is nothing wrong with this procedure, per se (Cortina & Dunlap, 1997; García-Pérez, 2016). Note, too, that there are many ways for researchers to test non-nil relations and to use prior information when using classical statistical methods (Antonakis, 2017; Edwards & Berry, 2010).

In terms of interpreting a $p$-value, a $p$-value of, say, .015 (or 1.50%) provides a quantification of the probability that the observed difference (e.g., the difference between the mean of the treated and untreated groups) would happen if the null hypothesis were true. For those of you who will see the recommended video at the end of the chapter (by John Rauser), the analog when using a permutation test is to think of a $p$-value in terms of how often a permutation would indicate a difference as large as that observed in the data if one were to assume the observed values were randomly assigned to the treatments and controls groups (i.e., if the null hypothesis were true). In the above case if $p = .015$, one would then speak of an effect being statistically significant at the $p < .05$ level. By convention, the reported thresholds are 0.1%, 1%, and 5%, though many journals nowadays prefer authors to report the exact $p$-value. Note that the term *significance* does not de facto mean that a relationship is meaningful or important. It is up to the researcher to make the case for the finding's importance, ideally based upon theory and some measure of practical or economic utility.

Another important aspect to bear in mind is errors in hypotheses testing. A small $p$-value indicates that it is unlikely that what is being tested would be true under the null hypothesis—unlikely, but not impossible. That is, a $p$-value of 5% indicates that there is a 5% chance of wrongly rejecting the null hypothesis. To do so is referred to as making a Type I error, or having a false positive (i.e., wrongly concluding there is an effect—akin to convicting an innocent defendant). Conversely, failing to reject the null hypothesis is referred to as making a Type II error, or having a false negative (i.e., wrongly concluding there is no effect). In management and applied psychological research, Type I errors are considered a policy (i.e., set at the alpha level of the significance test, which is typically $\alpha = .05$), whereas Type II errors can vary based on research design factors, particularly sample size (e.g., Cohen, 1992).

To minimize the probability of making such errors and to conduct good research, it is important to follow adequate and rigorous research methods and procedures when designing studies and when collecting and analyzing data (Munafò et al., 2017). For example, a researcher observing an unexpected result might be tempted to revise her original theory, or propose a new theory, to make sense of this finding. However, doing so (i.e., hypothesizing after results are known

[HARKing for short; Kerr, 1998]) can easily lead one to propose an erroneous theory, as the unexpected finding could very well be a false positive. Even in the context of experiments, which are generally viewed as the gold standard for testing causality in the social sciences, one can make a Type I error by engaging in seemingly harmless practices (e.g., focusing only on a subset of measured variables or increasing the sample size post-hoc). These examples fall under the umbrella term of *p-hacking,* and researchers should follow clear guidelines so as not to fall prey to this trap (Simmons, Nelson, & Simonsohn, 2011).

Finally, NHST is not devoid of criticism (see, e.g., Cohen, 1994), in part because of the reliance on arbitrary cut-off *p*-values and because the reliance on statistical significance is sometimes perceived to come at the expense of a study's relevance. Furthermore, critics strongly urge that NHST cannot be blindly followed and that it is the researchers' responsibility to ensure the stage is properly set. For example, sample size is a critical issue for NHST. Indeed, a research study based on a small sample may lack the statistical power to detect effects (Cohen, 1994). Conversely, in an extremely large sample—think "big data"—almost (we do stress *almost*) any relationship would be identified as statistically significant (Lin, Lucas, & Shmueli, 2013), given that the standard errors used to determine *p*-values are a function of sample size (note, though, theoretically, if two variables are orthogonal, they will not correlate significantly as the sample size approaches infinity). This issue underscores the importance of conducting a power analysis prior to running a study to determine what is, and is not, an appropriate sample size based upon anticipated effect sizes.

## Estimating Relationships

We provide here a simple illustration of the workings of the Ordinary Least Squares (OLS) estimator in the context of a simple regression and of the ANOVA estimation. The data used in these examples are presented in Table 16.1.

**Table 16.1**   Data for Empirical Examples

| | A. | B. | C. | D. | E. | F. | G. | H. | I. | J. |
|---|---|---|---|---|---|---|---|---|---|---|
| | $x$ | $y$ | $z$ | $x - \bar{x}$ | $y - \bar{y}$ | $(x - \bar{x})^2$ | $(y - \bar{y})^2$ | $(x - \bar{x}) \times (y - \bar{y})$ | $y - \hat{y}$ | $(y - \hat{y})^2$ |
| 1. | 48 | 21 | 0 | −5.75 | −2.9 | 33.06 | 8.41 | 16.67 | −0.56 | 0.32 |
| 2. | 65 | 25 | 1 | 11.25 | 1.1 | 126.56 | 1.21 | 12.38 | −3.47 | 12.05 |
| 3. | 51 | 12 | 0 | −2.75 | −11.9 | 7.56 | 141.61 | 32.72 | −10.78 | 116.26 |
| 4. | 48 | 24 | 0 | −5.75 | 0.1 | 33.06 | 0.01 | −0.57 | 2.44 | 5.94 |
| 5. | 46 | 21 | 0 | −7.75 | −2.9 | 60.06 | 8.41 | 22.48 | 0.25 | 0.06 |
| 6. | 47 | 18 | 0 | −6.75 | −5.9 | 45.56 | 34.81 | 39.83 | −3.16 | 9.97 |

*(Continued)*

**Table 16.1**   (Continued)

|  | A. | B. | C. | D. | E. | F. | G. | H. | I. | J. |
|---|---|---|---|---|---|---|---|---|---|---|
|  | $x$ | $y$ | $z$ | $x - \bar{x}$ | $y - \bar{y}$ | $(x - \bar{x})^2$ | $(y - \bar{y})^2$ | $(x - \bar{x}) \times (y - \bar{y})$ | $y - \hat{y}$ | $(y - \hat{y})^2$ |
| 7. | 64 | 24 | 1 | 10.25 | 0.1 | 105.06 | 0.01 | 1.02 | −4.06 | 16.52 |
| 8. | 70 | 29 | 1 | 16.25 | 5.1 | 264.06 | 26.01 | 82.88 | −1.50 | 2.26 |
| 9. | 61 | 34 | 1 | 7.25 | 10.1 | 52.56 | 102.01 | 73.22 | 7.15 | 51.18 |
| 10. | 64 | 39 | 1 | 10.25 | 15.1 | 105.06 | 228.01 | 154.77 | 10.94 | 119.58 |
| 11. | 49 | 19 | 0 | −4.75 | −4.9 | 22.56 | 24.01 | 23.27 | −2.97 | 8.82 |
| 12. | 55 | 33 | 1 | 1.25 | 9.1 | 1.56 | 82.81 | 11.38 | 8.59 | 73.82 |
| 13. | 38 | 26 | 0 | −15.75 | 2.1 | 248.06 | 4.41 | −33.08 | 8.50 | 72.24 |
| 14. | 53 | 18 | 0 | −0.75 | −5.9 | 0.56 | 34.81 | 4.43 | −5.60 | 31.31 |
| 15. | 67 | 31 | 1 | 13.25 | 7.1 | 175.56 | 50.41 | 94.07 | 1.72 | 2.95 |
| 16. | 52 | 16 | 0 | −1.75 | −7.9 | 3.06 | 62.41 | 13.82 | −7.19 | 51.68 |
| 17. | 46 | 21 | 0 | −7.75 | −2.9 | 60.06 | 8.41 | 22.48 | 0.25 | 0.06 |
| 18. | 52 | 15 | 0 | −1.75 | −8.9 | 3.06 | 79.21 | 15.57 | −8.19 | 67.06 |
| 19. | 45 | 25 | 0 | −8.75 | 1.1 | 76.56 | 1.21 | −9.63 | 4.66 | 21.67 |
| 20. | 54 | 27 | 0 | 0.25 | 3.1 | 0.06 | 9.61 | 0.77 | 3.00 | 8.99 |
| M = | 53.75 | 23.9 |  | Sum = |  | 1423.75 | 907.80 | 578.50 |  | 672.74 |

**Ordinary Least Squares Estimation.** Let $x$ and $y$ be two continuous and normally distributed variables. Assume we have data on these two variables from a sample of 20 individuals (see Table 16.1) and we are interested in understanding the linear relationship between $x$ and $y$. Thus, we could estimate the following model from our data, using OLS:

$$y = \beta_0 + \beta_1 \cdot x + e_1 \tag{1}$$

where $e_1$ is a disturbance (or error) term. The graphical depiction from the resulting estimation of equation (1) is captured by the regression line in Panel A of Figure 16.1. The intercept $\beta_0$ is the predicted value of $y$ when $x$ is zero and corresponds to the point where the regression line would cut the $y$ axis. The coefficient $\beta_1$ indicates the direction and the strength of $x$ on $y$ (i.e., how an increase in one unit in $x$ affects $y$). The slope of the regression line captures this effect.

The values for $\beta_0$ and $\beta_1$ can be determined under the criterion of minimizing deviations $d = y - \hat{y}$, where $y$ and $\hat{y}$ are, respectively, the observed and predicted values. To cancel out the effect of positive versus negative deviations, we minimize the value of the squared deviation between observed and the predicted values: $\sum d = \sum (y - \hat{y})^2$. This term is the OLS criterion.

How can we compute the values for $\beta_0$ and $\beta_1$ from the observed values of $x$ and $y$ in Table 16.1? The value for $\beta_1$ is simply equal to the covariance of $x$ and $y$ divided by the variance of $x$. The covariance of $x$ and $y$—that is, $cov(x, y)$—is equal to the sum of the cross-deviations of $x$ and $y$ (c.f. column H) divided by $n$, the number of observations, minus one. The variance of $x$ is equal to the sum of the squared deviations of $x$ (c.f. column F) divided by $n - 1$. Thus, we have the following:

$$\beta_1 = \frac{cov(x, y)}{var(x)} = \frac{\sum(x - \hat{x}) \times (y - \hat{y}) \big/ (n-1)}{\sum(x - \hat{x})^2 \big/ (n-1)} = \frac{\sum(x - \hat{x}) \times (y - \hat{y})}{\sum(x - \hat{x})^2} \qquad (2)$$

$$\beta_1 = \frac{578.5}{1423.75} = 0.406$$

The value for $\beta_0$ is simply equal to the mean of $y$ less $\beta_1$ times the mean of $x$. Thus, we have:

$$\beta_0 = \bar{y} - \beta_1 \bar{x} \qquad (3)$$

$$\beta_0 = 23.9 - 0.406 \times 53.75 = 2.06$$

Finally, replacing equations (3) and (2) in (1), we obtain the following estimates for equation (1):

$$y = 2.06 + 0.406 \, x \qquad (4)$$

From equation (4), we can compute the predicted values of $y$ from what we observe on $x$, and with these resulting values, we now have all the information we need to compute the OLS criterion: $\sum d = \sum(y - \hat{y})^2$ (c.f. the sum at the bottom of column J).

From OLS estimation we also obtain a measure of the precision of the estimate $\beta_1$ (i.e., the "standard error" of $\beta_1$), which is computed as follows:

$$SE_{\beta 1} = \frac{\sqrt{\sum(y - \hat{y})^2 \big/ (n-2)}}{\sqrt{\sum(x - \bar{x})^2}} = \frac{\sqrt{672.74 \big/ 18}}{\sqrt{1423.75}} = 0.162 \qquad (5)$$

The standard error is key for hypothesis testing. For instance, for a normally distributed variable, we can infer that there is a 95% chance that the "true" population parameter is contained within the interval defined by $\beta_1 \pm 1.96$ times the standard error of $\beta_1$ (the value of 1.96 comes from the normal distribution; note that there are slight variations to this formula).

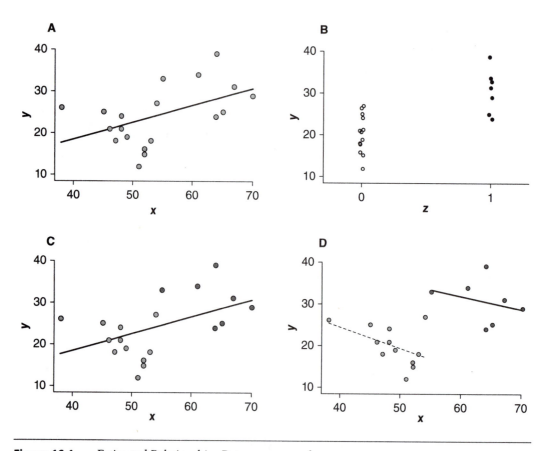

**Figure 16.1**    Estimated Relationships Between $y$, $x$, and $z$

**ANOVA Estimation.** Underlying the ANOVA model is a simple regression with a dichotomous variable (also referred to as a dummy, binary, or indicator variable). In the context of a simple experiment the dichotomous variable would capture whether an observation is part of the treatment group or of the control group. Consequently, the estimate for the dummy variable is referred to as the average treatment effect and measures the difference in mean values between the treated and untreated groups (i.e., the experimental and control groups).

Consider $z$ to be a dummy variable equal to one if participants have been randomly selected to be part of the experimental group and equal to zero if participants are allocated to the control group (see Table 16.1 for the values of $z$). The random variable $y$ is the dependent variable on which the experimental treatment is thought to have an effect. For example, $z$ could capture whether participants attended a leadership training of sorts and $y$ could capture peer ratings of the participants on certain leadership behaviors. These observations are plotted in Panel B, and we can see that on average the treated group scores higher than the control group. Note that the computation of the model estimates follows the same logic as the one outlined above (i.e., in the Ordinary Least Squares Estimation section). Estimating this model gives us the following equation:

$$y = 20.23 + 10.48\,z \tag{6}$$

Thus, replacing the values of $z$ in this equation, we find that the mean for the control group ($z = 0$) is 20.23, whereas the mean for the treatment group ($z = 1$) is 30.71.

# Part II: The Many Flavors of Endogeneity

In brief, nonexperimental field studies, which are the most common quantitative approaches to assessing leadership phenomena, are observational in design and typically use survey instruments to capture data so that inferences about a population can be made. Common approaches used by researchers to gather field data include face-to-face interviews, traditional paper-and-pencil surveys, and web-based surveys incorporated into online platforms (e.g., Qualtrics, SurveyMonkey). Although survey-based research is limited by the instrument or interview format used, it is practical, relatively cheap, and easy to conduct if properly designed (cf. Aguinis & Vandenberg, 2014). Yet unveiling causal relationships using observational data can prove to be a tricky matter. For example, consider a researcher interested in understanding whether, and to what extent, abusive supervision leads to dissatisfaction among employees. This researcher has access to a company and has obtained measures of abusive supervision and employee job satisfaction that she uses to test her model. Let us imagine she finds a negative relationship between these two variables, such that being exposed to higher levels of abusive supervision is associated with lower levels of job satisfaction. Is this enough evidence to conclude that the estimated effect accurately captures a cause-and-effect relationship between abusive supervision and job (dis)satisfaction? The answer is: "Not necessarily." For instance, perhaps employee job satisfaction could be not only predicted by, but also predictive of, abusive supervision (i.e., a simultaneous cause-and-effect relationship could be at play). Consider the following scenarios. Some managers confronted with dissatisfied employees, not knowing how to deal with such employees, might become frustrated and fail to restrain their impulsive tendencies, yielding increases in abusive behavior. Or perhaps the empirical relationship is driven by idiosyncratic aspects of the particular sample of employees being studied. Indeed, dissatisfied employees working under an abusive supervisor might have disproportionality chosen to take part in the study compared to their lesser dissatisfied colleagues working under the same supervisors. Even still, perhaps a third variable could be driving the relationship between abusive supervision and dissatisfaction. For instance, perhaps the reason why a manager is abusive is because of an unmeasured (i.e., third) variable (e.g., working in a high-pressure environment and having limited resources); if this third variable also directly predicts employee dissatisfaction, which it most likely would in this example, then it is not clear to what extent abusive supervision causes employee dissatisfaction because both may be caused by such omitted variables.

These three alternative mechanisms all describe what can be argued to fall under the umbrella term of *endogeneity*. To say that a variable is endogenous is to say that this variable is determined in part by factors at play within the boundaries of a given model. Conversely, an *exogenous* variable is one that cannot be predicted within the confines of a given model. Note that a variable can be endogenous in one model and exogenous in another. For example, if we were to predict leadership effectiveness from personality, we could safely consider personality to be exogenous because personality is generally stable over time, in part because there is a genetic component to it (Caspi, Roberts, & Shiner, 2005). However, in studies that examine the stability of personality over time, personality is endogenous as it would be the dependent variable in this scenario. Endogeneity is a problem (and a serious one) when it affects independent (i.e., predictor) variables. The problem comes from the fact that most estimators (e.g., Ordinary Least Squares, Maximum Likelihood) are based on the assumption that independent variables are exogenous (Kennedy, 2003). When this assumption is violated, the estimates produced by the model are biased and this bias is proportional to the magnitude of the correlation between the endogenous predictor variable and the error term of the model (Antonakis et al., 2010). Note that this problem affects efficient estimators but not consistent ones. The estimates of a *consistent estimator* will converge toward the "true" population estimates as sample size increases toward the population size. An *efficient estimator* produces more precise estimates (i.e., smaller standard errors), but these estimates will be biased in the presence of endogeneity. Thus, when faced with the trade-off between consistency and efficiency, the researcher has a relatively easy choice because precise estimates are of no value if estimates are biased! Therefore, when in doubt, consistency should always be preferred over efficiency.

**An Empirical Example.** Consider Panel A in Figure 16.2. It is the graphical representation of a regression model, which can be written as the following equation: $= \beta_0 + \beta_1 \cdot x + \beta_2 \cdot z + e_1$; where $y$ is a function of $x$ and $z$ and of unobserved factors that are pooled in $e_1$, the error term (or disturbance) of this model. We see from the figure that $x$ and $z$ are exogenous variables (i.e., $\rho(x, e_1) = 0$ and $\rho(z, e_1) = 0$). Thus, the cornerstone assumption of the OLS estimator is met and OLS will provide unbiased estimates. In fact, the Gauss-Markov theorem demonstrates that OLS is the Best Unbiased Linear Estimator (BLUE). That is, OLS will provide estimates that will converge toward the true population estimates as sample size increases.

Consider that we fail to include $z$ in our model. As a result, $z$ will be pooled in the error term of our new (and incorrect) specification depicted in Panel B in Figure 16.2. We now have endogeneity in our model because $x$ correlates with $z$ (i.e., $\rho(x, z) \neq 0$) and therefore with $e_2$ (i.e., $\rho(x, e_2) \neq 0$), the error term of this new specification. Thus, because $x$ is endogenous, $\alpha_1$, the estimated effect of $x$ on $y$ will be biased.

Revert back to the relationship between $y$ and $x$ depicted in Panel A of Figure 16.1. Note, too, that this is the relationship given by equation (4). Imagine that $y$ is a measure of employee compensation of sorts and that $x$ captures employee

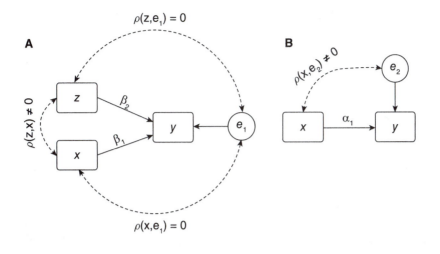

**Figure 16.2**     An Example of Endogeneity

height. These results indicate that taller employees in the observed sample receive a greater compensation. Could there really be a cause-and-effect relationship between height and compensation here?

We may doubt whether height ($x$) is really an exogenous variable. Indeed, it could very well be that a third variable, $z$ (e.g., gender), is driving the relationship we observe between $x$ and $y$ in Panel A of Figure 16.1 (note that the values for $z$ are in Table 16.1). In Panel C of Figure 16.1, we can see how the observations measured along $x$ and $y$ map onto values of $z$. Assuming that observations marked as full black circles indicate men and hollowed-out circles women, we can see that men score higher on both $x$ and $y$. In Panel D, we see two regression lines resulting from estimating the relationship between $y$ and $x$ separately for men and for women. These models are given by the following equations:

$$y = \begin{cases} 43.9 - 0.489 \cdot x, z = 0 \\ 52.15 - 0.336 \cdot x, z = 1 \end{cases} \tag{7}$$

This suggests that equation (4) most likely suffered from omitted variable bias and that the $\beta_1$ estimate of 0.406 is biased. Indeed, if we regress $y$ on $x$, controlling for $z$, we now get:

$$y = 41.07 - 0.43 \cdot x - 17.08 \cdot z \tag{8}$$

And we can see that, once we correctly included the variable $z$ into the model, the coefficient for $x$ changed from *plus* 0.406 (with a standard error = 0.162) to *minus* 0.43 (with a standard error = 0.238). That is, a decrease of over 206% in the coefficient! The effect of $x$ on $y$ is now taking into account the effect of $z$ in the model. If we wanted to test whether this difference is statistically significant, we could apply a Hausman test (Hausman, 1978) for one parameter as follows (this test can accommodate an array of parameters as well):

$$z\ statistic = \frac{\beta_1 - \alpha_1}{\sqrt{(SE_{\beta_1})^2 - (SE_{\alpha_1})^2}} \qquad (9)$$

$$= \frac{-.4308 - .4063}{\sqrt{(.2383)^2 - (.1620)^2}}$$

$$= 4.91$$

The $p$-value associated with this $z$ statistic would tell us how likely it would be to observe these two estimated coefficients under the null hypothesis that $\beta_1$ and $\alpha_1$ do not differ (see also the suggested video case at the end of this chapter). A $p$-value smaller than 5% would be interpreted as a statistically significant difference between $\beta_1$ and $\alpha_1$. This $p$ value is actually 0.00000163, making it rather unlikely that the null, that these two coefficients are not different, is true.

**An All-Pervasive Problem.** Given the inherent goals associated with studying leadership, researchers will be confronted with endogeneity problems. This is because researchers are very much concerned with the idea of process, defined as "the sequence of events from some beginning condition or state to a final outcome" (Spector & Meier, 2014). For example, leadership studies commonly assume that leaders take action to yield positive benefits for their followers and firm. Unfortunately, determining the causal impact of a leader's actions can be difficult with data collected in a nonexperimental setting, due to the lack of control that the researcher or researchers have in eliminating potential study confounds. The interest in process can also be seen in studies involving mediation tests, wherein the event sequence flows from predictor variable to focal outcome variable through one or more intervening mechanisms. Not surprisingly, then, endogeneity problems are ubiquitous to leadership research (Antonakis et al., 2010).

Thus, it is important to raise awareness to issues related to endogeneity, otherwise known as the age-old problem of disentangling causation from correlation (i.e., "correlation does not equal causation"). To be sure, correlation does not initiate causality. And, as the examples above imply, causality issues frequently arise when a researcher has only observational (i.e., nonexperimental) data and finds a statistical relationship between two (e.g., $x$ to $y$) variables. In such instances, it is common to assume that the variance in $x$ is impacting the variance of $y$, but this is not always the case. Given that the data are observational, it is possible that the $x$ variable's variance is not exogenous but endogenous to the model, leading to model misspecification and potential bias in parameter estimates. Endogeneity concerns apply not only to cross-sectional but also to time-lagged research designs (Fischer, Dietz, & Antonakis, 2016). For instance, even when $x$ is measured at time 0 and $y$ is measured at time 1, it is possible that an unobserved third variable ($z$) impacts $x$ at time 0 and $y$ at time 1 and thus explains the covariation that is observed between variable $x$ and variable $y$. To infer that $x$ temporally precedes $y$, the researcher must be able somehow to demonstrate that the variance of $x$ is exogenous in the statistical model.

Thankfully, there are many ways to tackle this endogeneity problem, including empirically testing for it, using instrumental variables, using an experimental design to mitigate it, and/or offering a strong theoretical argument that the expected relationship is indeed from $x$ to $y$ and not the other way around (or, of course, due to an alternative variable). Before examining these methods in the next section, we first provide an overview of the primary sources of endogeneity.

## Sources of Endogeneity

Broadly speaking, sources of endogeneity pertain to either failing to include relevant variables, failing to model sample selection, or failing to model reverse causality. Endogeneity can also be due to including imprecisely measured variables (i.e., failing to model measurement error) or result from gathering independent and dependent measures from the same source (i.e., common method variance).

**Omitted Variables.** Endogeneity can result from model misspecification. A model is said to be misspecified when one (or more) variable that has an effect on both the dependent variable and on one (or more) of the predictors is omitted from the model. For example, a researcher might collect data from subordinates about how "leader-like" they perceive their manager to be and examine whether these ratings can be predicted from social dominance orientation. Failing to control for leader gender would result in endogeneity because men and women differ in their orientation toward social dominance (Sidanius, Pratto, & Bobo, 1994) and gender also influences perceptions of leader prototypicality (Heilman, 2001).

A simple solution to the problem of omitted variable bias could be to include all possible variables in the theoretical model! Given that this is next to impossible in practice, researchers routinely use a statistical approach to control for omitted variable concerns. Despite its assumed advantages, including statistical controls in one's analyses carries consequences for the study's researchers and the findings that are obtained. First, the inclusion of control variables can substantively change the conceptual meaning of the proposed relationship; including statistical controls along with a leadership predictor would inadvertently replace the focal leadership variable with a new and unintended residual predictor (Breaugh, 2006; Edwards, 2008). Second, adding control variables into one's analyses will reduce available degrees of freedom and thus lower statistical power (Becker, 2005; Carlson & Wu, 2012). Third, incorporating control variables can even increase one's chances of finding a spurious (but significant) relationship between exogenous predictors and outcomes (i.e., the product of a suppression effect; MacKinnon, Krull, & Lockwood, 2000). Consequently, the inclusion or exclusion of control variables can lead to ambiguous and even conflicting research findings, hinder replication of results, and in other ways "hamper scientific progress" (Becker et al., 2016, p. 157). Ultimately, there should exist a strong theoretical rationale for including any control variable in the analyses. Moreover, it is in the best interest of researchers to understand the nature of their effects both with *and* without the inclusion of theoretically derived statistical controls (e.g., Spector & Brannick, 2011). For a more detailed discussion of the statistical control of variables in leadership research, see Bernerth, Cole, Taylor, and Walker (2017).

There is a particular situation worth mentioning in regard to omitted variables, which involves working with data that are hierarchical in nature. Indeed, when having observations nested within clusters at different levels (e.g., subordinates working under managers, firms within industries, yearly observations within countries) one cannot assume that observations are independent of this nested structure. Thus, if we assume that there exists a fixed difference between industries (e.g., competitive pressures), firms (e.g., organizational culture), and so on, and that this fixed difference impacts both independent and dependent variables, researchers need to correct for this difference between clusters by including *fixed-effect controls*. A review of leadership studies found that almost two-thirds of studies failed to include such controls when relevant to the study (Antonakis et al., 2010). Time-varying differences that stem from cluster nesting can be estimated using a *random-effects model* (or HLM model) in lieu of a fixed-effect model—if these differences do not correlate with the predictors. However, this assumption must be tested using a Hausman test (Hausman, 1978) to compare estimates obtained from the consistent fixed-effects estimators with those obtained from the efficient random-effects estimator. Differences between the two sets of estimates can be attributed to endogeneity bias in the estimates of the random-effects model.[3]

**Common Method Variance.** Common method variance (CMV) refers to "systematic error variance shared among variables measured with and introduced as a function of the same method and/or source" (Richardson, Simmering, & Sturman, 2009, p. 763). In the organizational sciences CMV is potentially problematic because it serves as an alternative explanation for relationships observed among variables that are assessed using similar methods (e.g., measurement techniques, which include response formats and scale anchors; data sources, such as the self versus other ratings; and time frame; Doty & Glick, 1998). This issue is not uncommon in leadership research, where predictors and outcomes are often assessed using perceptual ratings from a single source (i.e., a single rater) at one point in time. For example, researchers often ask subordinates to provide ratings on leader-related phenomena (e.g., LMX, leader traits, leadership style) and these ratings are examined in relation to self-reported attitudes (e.g., job satisfaction and organizational commitment) and behaviors, such as job performance and organizational citizenship behavior (e.g., Wang, Law, Hackett, Wang, & Chen, 2005). In such situations, CMV may amplify or attenuate relationships among focal constructs (Podsakoff, MacKenzie, Lee, & Podsakoff, 2003; Williams & Brown, 1994), though some methodologists have suggested that problems attributed to CMV may be overstated (Lance, Dawson, Birkelbach, & Hoffman, 2010; Spector, 2006). For

---

3. Note that is also possible both to control for fixed effects and to include time-invariant variables by using the procedure developed by Mundlak (1978).

further information about common method variance and how to eliminate the threats it may pose to research findings, we refer the reader to Podsakoff, MacKenzie, and Podsakoff (2012); Richardson et al. (2009); and Spector et al. (2017).

**Other Sources of Endogeneity.** Endogenous selection to treatment is another source of endogeneity bias—that is, where the units studied sort into the treatment ($x$) and this sorting, or selection, is not correctly modeled when attempting to predict $y$ (see Clougherty, Duso, & Muck, 2016). Yet another source of endogeneity bias is reverse causality, where dependent variable ($y$) is the cause of modeled independent variable ($x$). A more complicated case of this problem is simultaneity, where $x$ and $y$ simultaneously cause each other. In the above cases, the relationship of $x$ to $y$ cannot be interpreted. See Antonakis et al. (2010, 2014) for a more advanced treatment of these topics.

# Part III: Research Designs and Methods

As we saw in the previous section, a key concern with research designs that capture observational data is that the researcher surrenders control over the independent variables and therefore the variance exhibited by the focal outcome(s). Consequently, a study's findings may be attributable to the hypothesized relationship between the two constructs or to statistical biases (e.g., common method, common source, unmeasured third variables) described earlier in this chapter. With nonexperimental data, a researcher making inferences from observed covariation of independent and dependent variables is exposed to the *post hoc, ergo propter hoc* fallacy (i.e., "after this, therefore caused by this")—that is, wrongly interpreting causality by inferring that event A, which temporally precedes event B, is the true cause of B precisely because it occurred before B (Kerlinger & Lee, 2000). In such situations, experimental and quasi-experimental methods and research designs can prove to be invaluable tools.

## Experimental Designs

Experimental research designs manipulate the independent variables in a controlled and isolated manner. Experiments conducted in laboratory settings have been deemed to be "one of the great inventions of all times" (Kerlinger & Lee, 2000) because they allow for the precise study of relationships in uncontaminated research conditions with random assignment of participants to conditions. Random assignment allows researchers to create equivalent groups ensuring that the effect of the treatment (i.e., manipulation) will not be confounded with characteristics of participants (e.g., personality traits or general dispositions), thereby allowing researchers to more confidently rule out a particularly salient threat to the validity of research findings. To take an example, say that $y$ is a measure of leadership effectiveness, that $x$ captures whether supervisors take part in a leadership training or not (i.e., $x = 1$ for the treated group; $x = 0$ otherwise), and that $z$ captures an individual-level predictor of leadership effectiveness (e.g., extraversion). Thus, we would have the following equation:

$$y = \beta_0 + \beta_1 \cdot x + \beta_2 \cdot z + e \tag{10}$$

Imagine that supervisors can freely choose to take part in the leadership training or not (i.e., allocation to conditions is not random). As a result, knowing that the training will involve role playing, extraverted supervisors might be more drawn to taking part in the training (i.e., $x$ will correlate with $z$). In equation (10), $z$ is included as a predictor; thus, the effect of $x$ on $y$ will not be confounded with $z$. However, there could be many other unobserved factors at play that predict both leadership effectiveness and whether supervisors partake in the training (e.g., IQ, work experience, gender)! These factors are pooled in $e$, which reflects the error term of the model. As a result, $x$ will most likely be endogenous. Now imagine that supervisors are instead randomly allocated either to a training condition or to a control (i.e., no leadership training is offered) condition. As a result, the proportion of extraverted supervisors will be about the same in both groups and $x$ and $z$ will not correlate. In fact, both groups ($x$) will now be approximately equivalent not only on $z$, but on all observed and unobserved causes of $y$, which is to say that $\rho(x, e)$, the correlation between $x$ and $e$ will be equal to zero; in other words: $x$ will be exogenous. As a result, we can interpret the estimate of $x$ as the causal effect of the training.

In the organizational sciences, experimental research is typically, but not always, conducted in laboratory settings. Whereas laboratory experiments offer the researcher a high degree of control, which may allow for strong causal inferences, experiments conducted in the field typically sacrifice some experimental control in exchange for conducting the study in real-life conditions. Put differently, a lab experiment will have a high degree of internal validity, but its findings may be criticized for not being generalizable to "real" working conditions with "real" employees (Lykken, 1968), particularly if the study and its manipulations lack psychological fidelity (Highhouse, 2009). Conversely, because a field experiment occurs in a real setting and both the independent variable and participant assignment are controlled by the researcher, they offer the opportunity to tease out valuable insights about behaviors, perceptions, and processes (see Eden, 2016, for a review). Nevertheless, because the experiment is conducted in a field setting, there may exist other, unmeasured variables that are not under the researchers' control but may have an effect on the dependent variables. The decision of which type of experimental design to use when investigating focal phenomena is thus integrally linked to the types of research questions being addressed.

**An Exemplar Study.** Barling, Weber, and Kelloway (1996) conducted a field experiment in a Canadian bank to examine the effects of transformational leadership on organizational performance. In this study, Barling et al. randomly assigned 20 managers from regional branches either to attend a transformational leadership training program or to be part of a control group that did not receive any training whatsoever (a limitation of this particular study). All participants were rated on transformational leadership by their direct reports (or by all employees if direct reports were not available); this measurement would serve to determine whether the training did indeed have an effect on transformational leadership. These same direct reports (or general employees) also provided measures of their own organizational commitment. Finally, branch-level financial performance was measured using two metrics of sales performance (i.e., number of personal loans and credit card sales). All dependent measures were collected 2 weeks prior to the intervention and 5 months after it.

The results of the study show that the number of credit card sales in the experimental group declined by 4.5% from pre- to post-intervention. At first glance this decline seems not to support the hypothesized positive effect of transformational leadership on financial performance. However, this is precisely why comparison with a control group is needed: During the same period, credit card sales dropped by 29.9% in the control group, which is notably different from 4.5%! Thus, we can infer that the transformational leadership training *did* have a positive effect in that it mitigated whatever contextual effects were driving this decrease in sales (e.g., the broader economic context, or increased competition). During this same period, the number of secured personal loans showed an even clearer picture: These increased by 38.5% in the experimental group and declined by 9.3% in the control group.

On one hand, this study makes a strong case for external validity because it is conducted in the field and because the main dependent variables are measured using objective performance measures. On the other hand, one could argue that this study makes a lesser claim to internal validity than would a similar study conducted in a more controlled laboratory setting. Indeed, in the 5.5 months separating the first and the second measurement points a number of factors could have been at play to muddle the results.

## Quasi-Experimental Methods and Designs

Quasi-experiments refer to methods and designs that can be used to draw causal inferences despite not having experimental data—that is, in the absence of randomization to conditions and/or when one does not have exogenously manipulated variables (Shadish, Cook, & Campbell, 2002). Quasi-experimental methods function either by seeking to create valid comparison groups or by correcting for endogeneity through statistical adjustment in regression-based methods. Regression discontinuity design and propensity score matching fall into the former category, whereas difference-in-differences estimation, selection models, and two-stage least squares models would fall in the latter category. Given that these quasi-experimental methods have been thoroughly discussed elsewhere, we quickly introduce them and point interested readers to other available resources. As an aside, quasi-experiments are fairly common in economics but are still scarcely used in leadership research, even though some of these designs were originally developed in psychology.

In a nutshell, the regression discontinuity design (RDD) retrieves causal estimates in the absence of randomization to conditions—if the selection process can be fully observed (and therefore included in the model). We refer readers to Imbens and Lemieux (2008) for a practical review of RDD. Propensity score matching, on the other hand, seeks to create equivalent groups by matching treated and nontreated observations based on the probability of receiving treatment for a given observation. For further information about propensity score matching, we refer the reader to Caliendo and Kopeinig (2008) and to Li (2013).

Difference-in-differences estimation determines the causal effect of a known exogenous event by comparing before and after values of a measured variable in affected and nonaffected groups. We refer interested readers to Angrist and Pischke (2008, Chapter 5) for more information on diff-in-diff estimation. A selection model (also known as a Heckman model) is capable of correcting estimates for sample selection bias when selection to the given sample can be predicted from other exogenous variables. Vella (1998) provides an excellent overview of this method. Finally, a two-stage least squares model (2SLS) is able to estimate the causal effect of an endogenous predictor by leveraging the measurement of other exogenous variables (so-called instruments). In a first step, the endogenous predictor variable is regressed on one (or more) exogenous variables. The predicted values from this first regression are exogenous by design and can be used to test the causal relationship in a second stage. This estimation procedure is also referred to as instrumental variable regression. Bascle (2008) provides a practical step-by-step guide to using 2SLS.

## Conclusion

As noted at the outset of this chapter, leadership studies have much to be proud of in terms of their contributions to our understanding of leadership phenomena. Nevertheless, researchers should always strive to employ state-of-the-art methods and statistical tools that are available to us. By using experimental and quasi-experimental methods, researchers can uncover causal mechanisms in order to better inform practice and policy. Throughout this chapter, we provided references to sources that more fully describe available methods and designs. We therefore hope our brief illustration encourages readers to extend their own research methods competencies by consulting and reading the recommended sources. By doing so, it is our genuine belief that readers will raise their own research to higher methodological levels; secure the validity of their study findings; and, by extension, ensure the advancement of our field.

**Table 16.2**     Research Designs and Methods in a Nutshell

| *The Foundations of Quantitative Research* | |
|---|---|
| Theory | A theory is a framework for understanding phenomena and as such is the ultimate aim of science. Scientific theories are put to the empirical test to examine whether there is any evidence to support them. |
| Validity | Validity is concerned with whether a measured variable adequately captures a theoretical construct. In order to do so, a variable should demonstrate predictive, convergent, discriminant, and incremental validity. |

| *The Foundations of Quantitative Research* | |
|---|---|
| Hypothesis testing | Null hypothesis significance testing is a method to determine how likely a given relationship would be observed if the null were true. |
| Estimating relationships | The Ordinary Least Squares estimator produces estimates by minimizing the overall (squared) differences between observed and predicted values. ANOVA estimation rests on the same mechanism and compares the means of two groups (e.g., in an experiment). |

| *The Many Flavors of Endogeneity* | |
|---|---|
| Variables | A variable is said to be exogenous if its causes lay outside of the boundaries of a given model. Conversely, an endogenous variable is one that can be determined, at least in part, with a given model (e.g., a dependent variable). Most estimators will yield biased estimates if endogenous variables are included as predictors. |
| Sources of endogeneity | Endogeneity can result from omitting relevant variables, from collecting independent and dependent measures from the same source, from sample selection, from simultaneous relationships, or from measuring variables with error. |

| *Research Design and Methods* | |
|---|---|
| Experiments | The gold standard for testing causal relationships. Equivalent groups are created through randomization and exposed to different treatments under the control of the experimenter. As a result of randomization, the treatment effect can be interpreted as causal. |
| Quasi-experiments | Quasi-experiments are methods and designs to test causal relationships either by creating valid comparison groups or by correcting for endogeneity through statistical adjustment in regression-based methods. |

## Discussion Questions

1. Do you agree that "experiments are the gold standard for testing causality"? Explain why.
2. Identify two to three claims pertaining to leadership and answer the following questions:
   a. How would you go about testing their validity using an experiment?
   b. Imagine it is impossible to conduct these experiments (e.g., because of practical or ethical reasons); which quasi-experimental designs and methods might you instead be able to use in the context of your example?

## Recommended Readings

### On Research Design

• Kerlinger, F. N., & Lee, H. B. (2000). *Foundations of behavioral research* (4th ed.). Fort Worth, TX: Harcourt College.

## On Testing for Causality and Quasi-Experiments (With Increasing Amount of Algebra)

- Angrist, J. D., & Pischke, J. S. (2008). *Mostly harmless econometrics: An empiricist's companion.* Princeton, NJ: Princeton University Press.
- Antonakis, J., Bendahan, S., Jacquart, P., & Lalive, R. (2010). On making causal claims: A review and recommendations. *The Leadership Quarterly, 21*(6), 1086–1120.
- Antonakis, J., Bendahan, S., Jacquart, P., & Lalive, R. (2014). Causality and endogeneity: Problems and solutions. In D. Day (Ed.), *The Oxford handbook of leadership and organizations* (pp. 93–117). New York, NY: Oxford University Press.

## On Evidence-Based Management

- Briner, R. B., Denyer, D., & Rousseau, D. M. (2009). Evidence-based management: Concept cleanup time? *The Academy of Management Perspectives, 23*(4), 19–32.
- Pfeffer, J., & Sutton, R. I. (2006). *Hard facts, dangerous half-truths, and total nonsense: Profiting from evidence-based management.* Boston, MA: Harvard Business School Press.

## Recommended Case Study

### On Evidence-Based Management

- Garvin, D. A., Wagonfeld, A. B., & Kind, L. (2013). *Google's project oxygen: Do managers matter?* HBS No. 313–110. Boston: Harvard Business School Publishing.

## Recommended Video

### On Hypothesis Testing

- Rauser, J. (2014). Statistics without the agonizing pain. https://youtu.be/5Dnw46eC-0o

## References

Aguinis, H., & Vandenberg, R. J. (2014). An ounce of prevention is worth a pound of cure: Improving research quality before data collection. *Annual Review of Organizational Psychology and Organizational Behavior, 1*(1), 569–595.

Angrist, J. D., & Pischke, J.-S. (2008). *Mostly harmless econometrics: An empiricist's companion.* Princeton, NJ: Princeton University Press.

Antonakis, J. (2017). On doing better science: From thrill of discovery to policy implications. *The Leadership Quarterly, 28*(1), 5–21.

Antonakis, J., Ashkanasy, N. M., & Dasborough, M. T. (2009). Does leadership need emotional intelligence? *The Leadership Quarterly, 20*(2), 247–261.

Antonakis, J., Bastardoz, N., Jacquart, P., & Shamir, B. (2016). Charisma: An ill-defined and ill-measured gift. *Annual Review of Organizational Psychology and Organizational Behavior, 3*(1), 293–319.

Antonakis, J., Bendahan, S., Jacquart, P., & Lalive, R. (2010). On making causal claims: A review and recommendations. *The Leadership Quarterly, 21*(6), 1086–1120.

Antonakis, J., & House, R. J. (2014). Instrumental leadership: Measurement and extension of transformational–transactional leadership theory. *The Leadership Quarterly, 25*(4), 746–771.

Barling, J., Weber, T., & Kelloway, E. K. (1996). Effects of transformational leadership training on attitudinal and financial outcomes: A field experiment. *Journal of Applied Psychology, 81*(6), 827–832.

Bascle, G. (2008). Controlling for endogeneity with instrumental variables in strategic management research. *Strategic Organization, 6*(3), 285–327.

Becker, T. E. (2005). Potential problems in the statistical control of variables in organizational research: A qualitative analysis with recommendations. *Organizational Research Methods, 8*(3), 274–289.

Becker, T. E., Atinc, G., Breaugh, J. A., Carlson, K. D., Edwards, J. R., & Spector, P. E. (2016). Statistical control in correlational studies: 10 essential recommendations for organizational researchers. *Journal of Organizational Behavior, 37*(2), 157–167.

Bernerth, J. B., Armenakis, A. A., Feild, H. S., Giles, W. F., & Walker, H. J. (2007). Leader–member social exchange (LMSX): Development and validation of a scale. *Journal of Organizational Behavior, 28*(8), 979–1003.

Bernerth, J. B., Cole, M. S., Taylor, E. C., & Walker, H. J. (2017). Control variables in leadership research. *Journal of Management.* Advance online publication. doi:10.1177/0149206317690586

Bettis, R. A., Ethiraj, S., Gambardella, A., Helfat, C., & Mitchell, W. (2016). Creating repeatable cumulative knowledge in strategic management. *Strategic Management Journal, 37*(2), 257–261.

Breaugh, J. A. (2006). Rethinking the control of nuisance variables in theory testing. *Journal of Business and Psychology, 20*(3), 429–443.

Briner, R. B., Denyer, D., & Rousseau, D. M. (2009). Evidence-based management: Concept cleanup time? *The Academy of Management Perspectives, 23*(4), 19–32.

Brown, D. J., & Keeping, L. M. (2005). Elaborating the construct of transformational leadership: The role of affect. *The Leadership Quarterly, 16*(2), 245–272.

Caliendo, M., & Kopeinig, S. (2008). Some practical guidance for the implementation of propensity score matching. *Journal of Economic Surveys, 22*(1), 31–72.

Carlson, K. D., & Wu, J. (2012). The illusion of statistical control: Control variable practice in management research. *Organizational Research Methods, 15*(3), 413–435.

Carmines, E. G., & Zeller, R. A. (1979). *Reliability and validity assessment* (Vol. 17). Thousand Oaks, CA: Sage.

Caspi, A., Roberts, B. W., & Shiner, R. L. (2005). Personality development: Stability and change. *Annual Review of Psychology, 56*, 453–484.

Clougherty, J. A., Duso, T., & Muck, J. (2016). Correcting for self-selection based endogeneity in management research: Review, recommendations and simulations. *Organizational Research Methods, 19*(2), 286–347.

Cohen, J. (1992). A power primer. *Psychological Bulletin, 112*(1), 155–159.

Cohen, J. (1994). The earth is round (p <. 05). *American Psychologist, 49*(12), 997.

Colquitt, J. A., Baer, M. D., Long, D. M., & Halvorsen-Ganepola, M. D. (2014). Scale indicators of social exchange relationships: A comparison of relative content validity. *Journal of Applied Psychology, 99*(4), 599.

Cook, T. D., & Campbell, D. T. (1979). *Quasi-experimentation: Design and analysis issues for field settings.* Boston, MA: Houghton Mifflin.

Cooper, C. D., Scandura, T. A., & Schriesheim, C. A. (2005). Looking forward but learning from our past: Potential challenges to developing authentic leadership theory and authentic leaders. *The Leadership Quarterly, 16*(3), 475–493.

Cortina, J. M., & Dunlap, W. P. (1997). On the logic and purpose of significance testing. *Psychological Methods, 2*(2), 161.

Daft, R. L. (1984). Antecedents of significant and not-so-significant research. In T. Bateman & G. Ferris (Eds.), *Method and analysis in organizational research.* Reston, VA: Reston.

Dionne, S. D., Gupta, A., Sotak, K. L., Shirreffs, K. A., Serban, A., Hao, C., . . . Yammarino, F. J. (2014). A 25-year perspective on levels of analysis in leadership research. *The Leadership Quarterly, 25*(1), 6–35.

Doty, D. H., & Glick, W. H. (1998). Common methods bias: Does common methods variance really bias results? *Organizational Research Methods, 1*(4), 374–406.

Eden, D. (2016). Field experiments in organizations. *Annual Review of Organizational Psychology and Organizational Behavior.* Advance online publication. doi:10.1146/annurev-orgpsych-041015-062400

Edwards, J. R. (2008). To prosper, organizational psychology should . . . overcome methodological barriers to progress. *Journal of Organizational Behavior, 29*(4), 469–491.

Edwards, J. R., & Berry, J. W. (2010). The presence of something or the absence of nothing: Increasing theoretical precision in management research. *Organizational Research Methods, 13*, 668–689.

Eisenbeiss, S. A. (2012). Re-thinking ethical leadership: An interdisciplinary integrative approach. *The Leadership Quarterly, 23*(5), 791–808.

Fischer, T., Dietz, J., & Antonakis, J. (2016). Leadership process model: A review and synthesis. *Journal of Management.* Advance online publication. doi:10.1177/0149206316682830

García-Pérez, M. A. (2016). Thou shalt not bear false witness against null hypothesis significance testing. *Educational and Psychological Measurement.* Advance online publication. doi:10.1177/0013164416668232

Geddes, B. (2003). *Paradigms and sand castles: Theory building and research design in comparative politics.* Ann Arbor: University of Michigan Press.

Gerring, J., & McDermott, R. (2007). An experimental template for case study research. *American Journal of Political Science, 51*(3), 688–701.

Harms, P. D., & Credé, M. (2010). Remaining issues in emotional intelligence research: Construct overlap, method artifacts, and lack of incremental validity. *Industrial and Organizational Psychology, 3*(2), 154–158.

Hausman, J. A. (1978). Specification tests in econometrics. *Econometrica, 46*(6), 1251–1271.

Heckman, J. (1979). Sample selection bias as a specification error. *Econometrica, 47*(1), 153–162.

Highhouse, S. (2009). Designing experiments that generalize. *Organizational Research Methods, 12*(3), 554–566.

Hinkin, T. R. (1995). A review of scale development practices in the study of organizations. *Journal of Management, 21*(5), 967–988.

Hinkin, T. R. (1998). A brief tutorial on the development of measures for use in survey. *Organizational Research Methods, 1*(1), 104–121.

Imbens, G. W., & Lemieux, T. (2008). Regression discontinuity designs: A guide to practice. *Journal of Econometrics, 142*(2), 615–635.

James, L. R. (1980). The unmeasured variables problem in path analysis. *Journal of Applied Psychology, 65*(4), 415.

Kennedy, P. (2003). *A guide to econometrics.* Cambridge, MA: MIT Press.

Kerlinger, F., & Lee, H. B. (2000). *Foundations of behavioral research* (4th ed.). Forth Worth, TX: Harcourt.

Kerr, N. L. (1998). HARKing: Hypothesizing after the results are known. *Personality and Social Psychology Review, 2*(3), 196–217.

Lance, C. E., Dawson, B., Birkelbach, D., & Hoffman, B. J. (2010). Method effects, measurement error, and substantive conclusions. *Organizational Research Methods, 13*(3), 435–455.

Lewin, K. (1945). The research center for group dynamics at Massachusetts Institute of Technology. *Sociometry, 8*(2), 126–136.

Li, M. (2013). Using the propensity score method to estimate causal effects: A review and practical guide. *Organizational Research Methods, 16*(2), 188–226.

Lin, M., Lucas, H. C., Jr., & Shmueli, G. (2013). Research commentary—too big to fail: Large samples and the *p*-value problem. *Information Systems Research, 24*(4), 906–917.

Litwin, M. S. (1995). *How to measure survey reliability and validity.* Thousand Oaks, CA: Sage.

Locke, E. A. (2007). The case for inductive theory building. *Journal of Management, 33*(6), 867–890.

Lykken, D. T. (1968). Statistical significance in psychological research. *Psychological Bulletin, 70*(3), 151–159.

MacKinnon, D. P., Krull, J. L., & Lockwood, C. M. (2000). Equivalence of the mediation, confounding and suppression effect. *Prevention Science, 1*(4), 173–181.

Munafò, M. R., Nosek, B. A., Bishop, D. V., Button, K. S., Chambers, C. D., du Sert, N. P., . . . Ioannidis, J. P. (2017). A manifesto for reproducible science. *Nature Human Behaviour, 1.* Retrieved from https://www.nature.com/articles/s41562-016-002

Mundlak, Y. (1978). On the pooling of time series and cross section data. *Econometrica: Journal of the Econometric Society, 46*(1), 69–85.

Murtaugh, P. A. (2014). In defense of P values. *Ecology, 95*(3), 611–617.

Nickerson, R. S. (1998). Confirmation bias: A ubiquitous phenomenon in many guises. *Review of General Psychology, 2*(2), 175.

Pfeffer, J., & Sutton, R. I. (2006). Evidence-based management. *Harvard Business Review, 84*(1), 62.

Podsakoff, P. M., MacKenzie, S. B., Lee, J.-Y., & Podsakoff, N. P. (2003). Common method biases in behavioral research: A critical review of the literature and recommended remedies. *Journal of Applied Psychology, 89*(5), 879–903.

Podsakoff, P. M., MacKenzie, S. B., & Podsakoff, N. P. (2012). Sources of method bias in social science research and recommendations on how to control it. *Annual Review of Psychology, 63*, 539–569.

Richardson, H. A., Simmering, M. J., & Sturman, M. C. (2009). A tale of three perspectives: Examining post hoc statistical techniques for detection and correction of common method variance. *Organizational Research Methods, 12*(4), 762–800.

Schriesheim, C. A., Castro, S. L., & Cogliser, C. C. (1999). Leader–member exchange (LMX) research: A comprehensive review of theory, measurement, and data-analytic practices. *The Leadership Quarterly, 10*(1), 63–113.

Shadish, W. R., Cook, T. D., & Campbell, D. T. (2002). *Experimental and quasi-experimental designs for generalized causal inference.* Boston, MA: Houghton Mifflin.

Shaffer, J. A., DeGeest, D., & Li, A. (2016). Tackling the problem of construct proliferation: A guide to assessing the discriminant validity of conceptually related constructs. *Organizational Research Methods, 19*(1), 80–110.

Sidanius, J., Pratto, F., & Bobo, L. 1994. Social dominance orientation and the political psychology of gender: A case of invariance? *Journal of Personality and Social Psychology, 67*(6): 998.

Simmons, J. P., Nelson, L. D., & Simonsohn, U. (2011). False-positive psychology: Undisclosed flexibility in data collection and analysis allows presenting anything as significant. *Psychological Science, 22*(11), 1359–1366.

Smith, R., & Rennie, D. (2014). Evidence-based medicine—An oral history. *JAMA, 311*(4), 365–367.

Spector, P. E. (2006). Method variance in organizational research truth or urban legend? *Organizational Research Methods, 9*(2), 221–232.

Spector, P. E., & Brannick, M. T. (2011). Methodological urban legends: The misuse of statistical control variables. *Organizational Research Methods, 14*(2), 287–305.

Spector, P. E., & Meier, L. L. (2014). Methodologies for the study of organizational behavior processes: How to find your keys in the dark. *Journal of Organizational Behavior, 35*(8), 1109–1119.

Spector, P. E., Rosen, C. C., Richardson, H. A., Williams, L. J., & Johnson, R. E. (2017). A new perspective on method variance. *Journal of Management.* Advance online publication. doi:10.1177/0149206316687295

Sutton, R. I., & Staw, B. M. (1995). What theory is not. *Administrative Science Quarterly, 40*(3), 371–384.

Van Knippenberg, D., & Sitkin, S. B. (2013). A critical assessment of charismatic-transformational leadership research: Back to the drawing board? *The Academy of Management Annals, 7*(1), 1–60.

Vella, F. (1998). Estimating models with sample selection bias: A survey. *The Journal of Human Resources, 33*(1), 127–169.

Wang, H., Law, K. S., Hackett, R. D., Wang, D., & Chen, Z. X. (2005). Leader–member exchange as a mediator of the relationship between transformational leadership and followers' performance and organizational citizenship behavior. *Academy of Management Journal, 48*(3), 420–432.

Williams, L. J., & Brown, B. K. (1994). Method variance in organizational behavior and human resources research: Effects on correlations, path coefficients, and hypothesis testing. *Organizational Behavior and Human Decision Processes, 57*(2), 185–209.

Yukl, G. (1999). An evaluation of conceptual weaknesses in transformational and charismatic leadership theories. *The Leadership Quarterly, 10*(2), 285–305.

# CHAPTER 17

# Ethics and Effectiveness: The Nature of Good Leadership

*Joanne B. Ciulla*

---

## Opening Case: A Day in the Life of a Leader

You are the CEO of an investment firm. Your firm is about to open up a new section that caters to high net-worth individuals. You are looking for someone to lead it who has a proven record of success in building and sustaining this exclusive kind of client base. Your team has identified the ideal candidate for the job, Henry Smith. Henry is considered a star performer who works in this area at one of your competitor firms. For the past 6 months you have been recruiting him. Henry strikes you as someone who possesses a quick mind and a good sense of humor. He also has excellent business contacts and a stellar client list. It is likely that many of his clients would follow him to your firm, and this would bring in a substantial amount of income to your business.

After a number of dinners, lunches, meetings, and phone conversations, your team met with Henry today and he finally agreed to jump ship and join your firm. The final meeting ran a bit long, so when you were finished, Henry had to hurry out to catch a flight back to Chicago. As you are walking Henry out of your office, he turns to your administrative assistant, who is on the phone, and says in a very gruff voice, "Hey, you, get off the phone and call me a car—move it or I'll be late!" Your assistant looks surprised and embarrassed but says nothing and makes the call to get a car.

You and your colleagues are surprised and troubled by what you just witnessed. You have met with Henry on several occasions and never saw him behave this way. It makes you wonder: Is this a one-off occurrence because he was excited and in a hurry, or did you get a glimpse of something about the *real* Henry? Is this incident relevant to your assessment of Henry as a leader? Is the Henry you thought would be a leader and a cash cow starting to look like a turkey?

## Discussion Questions

1.  How would you react to this incident if you were the CEO?

2.  Does Henry's behavior raise potential concerns in your mind about his ethics? Why or why not?

3.  If someone in this leadership role produces big profits for the firm, does it matter how he talks to an assistant?

4.  What, if anything, does this behavior have to do with Henry's potential as an effective leader?

5.  After seeing this behavior, would you go ahead as planned and hire Henry?

# Chapter Overview

The moral triumphs and failures of leaders carry a greater weight and volume than those of most other people (Ciulla, 2003b). In leadership, we see morality and immorality magnified, which is why the study of ethics is fundamental to the study of leadership. The study of ethics concentrates on the nature of right and wrong and good and evil, and as discussed in the next section, is interchangeable with the word *morality*. Ethics and morality examine the relationships of people with each other and with other living things. Ethics explores questions related to what we should do and what we should be like as individuals, as members of a group or society, and in the different roles that we play in life. The role of a leader entails a distinctive type of human relationship. Some hallmarks of this relationship are power and/or influence, vision, obligation, and responsibility. By understanding the ethics of this relationship, we gain a better understanding of leadership because some of the central issues in ethics are also the central issues of leadership. They include personal challenges such as self-knowledge, self-interest, and self-discipline, and moral obligations related to justice, duty, competence, and the greatest good.

The challenges of leadership are not new, which is why we find some of the most perceptive work on leadership and ethics in ancient texts. History is filled with wisdom and case studies on the morality of leaders and leadership. Ancient scholars from the East and West offer insights that enable us to understand leadership and formulate contemporary research questions in new ways. History, philosophy, and the humanities in general provide perspective and reveal certain patterns of leadership behavior and themes about leadership and morality that have existed over time. Perhaps the most important benefit of the humanities approach to leadership studies is that it does not allow us to study leader effectiveness without looking at the ethics of what leaders do and how and why they do it. In short, the humanities approach never allows us to forget that the very nature of leadership is inextricably tied to the human condition, which includes the values, needs, and aspirations of human beings who live and work together.

The study of ethics and the history of ideas help us understand two overarching and overlapping questions that drive most leadership research: What is leadership? What is good leadership? The first is about what leadership is, or a descriptive question. The second is about what leadership ought to be, or a normative question. These two questions are sometimes confused in the literature. Progress in leadership studies rests on the ability of scholars to integrate the answers to these questions. In this chapter, I discuss the implications of these two questions for our understanding of leadership. I begin the chapter by looking at how the ethics and effectiveness question plays out in contemporary work on leadership ethics, and I discuss some of the ethical issues distinctive to leadership. Then I show some of the insights gleaned from the ancient literature and how they complement and provide context for contemporary research. In the end, I suggest some directions for research on ethics in the context of leadership studies.

## *Ethikos* and *Morale*

Before I get started, a short note on the words *ethics* and *moral* is in order. Some people like to make a distinction between these two concepts. The problem with it is that everyone seems to distinguish the concepts in a different way. Like most philosophers, I use the terms interchangeably. As a practical matter, courses on moral philosophy cover the same material as courses on ethics. There is a long history of using these terms as synonyms of each other, regardless of their roots in different languages. In *De Fato* (II.i) Cicero substituted the Latin word *morale* for Aristotle's use of the Greek word *ethikos*. We see the two terms defining each other in the *Oxford English Dictionary*. The word *moral* is defined as "of or pertaining to the distinction between right and wrong, or good and evil in relation to the actions, volitions, or character of human beings; ethical," and "concerned with virtue and vice or rules of conduct, ethical praise or blame, habits of life, custom and manners" (*Compact Oxford English Dictionary*, 1991, p. 1114). Similarly, it defines *ethics* as "of or pertaining to morality" and "the science of morals, the moral principles by which a person is guided" (*Compact Oxford English Dictionary*, 1991, p. 534). Perhaps the most compelling evidence for why these terms are not significantly different is that people rarely define the difference between them in the same way. They often tend to define the two terms in ways that best suit their argument or research agenda.

# The Normative Aspects of Definitions

Leadership scholars often concern themselves with the problem of defining leadership. Some believe that if they could only agree on a common definition of leadership, they would be better able to understand it. This does not make sense because scholars in history, biology, and other subjects do not all agree on the definition of their subject, and even if they did, it would not help them to understand it better. Furthermore, scholars do not determine the meaning of a word for the general public. Would it make sense to have an academic definition that did not agree with the way ordinary people understood the word? Social scientists sometimes limit the definition of a term so that they can use it in a study. Generally, the way people in a culture use a word and think about it determines the meaning of a word (Wittgenstein, 1968). The denotation of the word *leadership* stays basically the same in English. Even though people apply the term differently, all English-speaking leadership scholars know what the word means. Yet the meaning of leadership is also a social construction—slight variations in it tell us about the values, practices, and paradigms of leadership in a certain place and at a certain time.

Rost (1991) is among those who think that there has been little progress in leadership studies. He believed that there would be no progress in leadership studies until scholars agree on a common definition of leadership. He collected 221 definitions of leadership, ranging from the 1920s to the 1990s. All of these definitions generally say the same thing—leadership is about a person or persons somehow moving other people to do something. Where the definitions differ is in how leaders motivate their followers, their relationship to followers, who has a say in the goals of the group or organization, and what abilities the leader needs to have to get things done. I chose definitions that were representative of definitions from other sources from the same era. Even today, one can find a strong family resemblance in the ways various leadership scholars define leadership.

Consider the definitions in Table 17.1 (all from American sources), and think about the history of the time and the prominent leaders of that era. What were they like? What were their followers like? What events and values shaped the ideas behind these definitions? What moral assumptions do these representative definitions of leadership make about the relationship between leaders and followers?

**Table 17.1**   Leader–Follower Relationship Through Time

| 1920 | [Leadership is] the ability to impress the will of the leader on those led and induce obedience, respect, loyalty, and cooperation (Moore, 1927, p. 124). |
|---|---|
| 1930 | Leadership is a process in which the activities of many are organized to move in a specific direction by one (Bogardus, 1934, p. 5). |
| 1940 | Leadership is the result of an ability to persuade or direct men, apart from the prestige or power that comes from the office or external circumstance (Reuter, 1941, p. 133). |

*(Continued)*

**Table 17.1**   (Continued)

| | |
|---|---|
| 1950 | [Leadership is what leaders do in groups.] The leader's authority is spontaneously accorded him by his fellow group members (Gibb, 1954, p. 882). |
| 1960 | [Leadership is] acts by a person that influence other persons in a shared direction (Seeman, 1960, p. 127). |
| 1970 | Leadership is defined in terms of discretionary influence. Discretionary influence refers to those leader behaviors under control of the leader, which he may vary from individual to individual (Osborne & Hunt, 1975, p. 28). |
| 1980 | Regardless of the complexities involved in the study of leadership, its meaning is relatively simple. Leadership means to inspire others to undertake some form of purposeful action as determined by the leader (Sarkesian, 1981, p. 243). |
| 1990 | Leadership is an influence relationship between leaders and followers who intend real changes that reflect their mutual purposes (Rost, 1991, p. 102). |
| 2000 | Leadership is shaped by its contextual factors and it occurs when anyone or anything brings forth direction, alignment, and/or commitment (Drath et al., 2008; Hunt & Dodge, 2000, Kort, 2008; Liden & Antonakis, 2009; Uhl-Bien, 2006). |

SOURCE: Created by Joanna B. Ciulla.

Notice that in the 1920s, leaders "impressed" their will on those led. In the 1940s, they "persuaded" followers; in the 1960s, they "influenced" them; whereas in the 1990s, leaders and followers influenced each other: By the 2000s, leadership is a relationship that occurs in a context. Notice how all of these definitions say something about the nature of the leader–follower relationship. The difference between the definitions rests on normative questions: How should leaders treat followers? And how should followers treat leaders? Who decides what goals to pursue? What is and what ought to be the nature of their relationship to each other? The definition debate demonstrates the extent to which the very concept of leadership is a social, historical, and normative construction.

## The Hitler Problem

Some scholars would argue that bullies and tyrants are not leaders, which takes us to what I have called "the Hitler problem" (Ciulla, 1995). The Hitler problem is based on how you answer the question: Was Hitler a leader? According to the morally unattractive definitions, he was a leader, perhaps even a great leader, albeit an immoral one. Heifetz (1994) argues that, under the "great man" and trait theories of leadership, you can put Hitler, Lincoln, and Gandhi in the same category because the underlying idea of the theory is that leadership is a person or group's influence over the course of history. However, when your concept of leadership includes ethical considerations, Hitler was not a leader at all. He was a bully or tyrant—or simply the head of Germany.

We see how ingrained ethical ideas are in the concept of a leader when scholars differentiate between leaders and "real leaders" or "true leaders." Burns (1978) and Bass (1997) suggest that many leaders—transactional ones—are competent in that they promote exchanges among subordinates in their pursuit of collective outcomes, but that only transformational leaders are leaders in a strong moral sense. Extending this distinction, Bass attempts to separate leaders who fit the description of a transformational leader but are not ethical from ethical leaders by distinguishing between transformational and pseudotransformational leaders or authentic transformational leaders (Bass & Steidlmeier, 1999). Brown, Treviño, and Harrison (2005) make this distinction between common leadership and ethical leadership explicit in their concept of ethical leadership: "the demonstration of normatively appropriate conduct through personal actions and interpersonal relations, and the promotion of such conduct to followers through two-way communication, reinforcement, and decision-making" (p. 120). Using Bennis and Nanus's (1985) characterization of leadership—"Managers are people who do things right and leaders are people who do right things" (p. 21)—one could argue that Hitler was neither unethical nor a leader. (Maybe he was a manager?) Bennis and Nanus are among those scholars who sometimes slip into using the term *leader* to mean a morally good leader. However, what appears to be behind this in Bennis and Nanus's comment is the idea that leaders are or should be a head above everyone else morally.

This normative strand exists throughout the leadership literature, most noticeably in the popular literature. Writers will say leaders are participatory, supportive, and so forth, when what they really mean is that leaders should have these qualities. Yet it may not even be clear that we really want is leaders with these qualities. As former presidential spokesman David Gergen (2002) pointed out, leadership scholars all preach and teach that participatory, empowering leadership is best. A president like George W. Bush, however, exercised a top-down style of leadership. Few leadership scholars would prescribe such leadership in their work. Nonetheless, President Bush scored some of the highest ratings for exercising leadership in recent history despite the fact that he also had some of the lowest approval ratings for his actions as a leader (Gergen, 2002). A number of studies help explain this based on the context of Bush's leadership in post-9/11 America. For example, Pillai (1996) found that charismatic leadership is not only about personal characteristics but is also something that emerges in leaders during a crisis. When people feel a loss of control, they look for decisive leaders. In the case of Bush, they may have found his autocratic leadership style comforting. As the crisis subsided later in his presidency, Bush's ratings hit rock bottom. Another explanation for this disparity between what leadership scholars preach and what people want reflects conflicting cultural values. The American ethos of rugged individualism may also help explain Bush's ratings. On one hand, Americans admire leaders who take bold, decisive, and autocratic action, but on the other hand, they do not want to work for them (Ruscio, 2004).

Philosopher Eva Kort (2008) offers a solution to the Hitler problem that goes beyond semantics. She notes that group actions, not relationships, reveal the features that identify what she calls "leadership proper" or "real" leadership from cases of "purported" leadership. Real leadership is ethical and competent leadership. Purported leadership is basically someone in a leadership role, telling people what to do. Kort uses a simple example to illustrate the normative and technical aspects of leadership. A concertmaster holds a formal leadership position. If he conducts the orchestra with instructions that the musicians know are bad, they will follow him because of his position. In this case, Kort says the concertmaster is merely a purported leader, not a leader proper. She writes: "It is only when the concertmaster does lead—participate in the plural action in (generally) the right sort of way—that the concertmaster is the leader in the proper sense" (Kort, 2008, p. 422). Notice how Kort's definition includes unavoidable judgments. Leaders are people whom we choose to follow because they seem competent and, where relevant, ethical. For Kort, leaders are those whose ideas are voluntarily endorsed and acted upon by others in various situations. This is a useful way to understand how ethics and effectiveness are woven together in the concept of leadership. For Kort, the answer to the Hitler problem depends on whether followers freely choose to follow him because they endorse his ethics and think he is competent. This speaks directly to his leadership, but it still does not account for cases where followers are unethical, or morally mistaken, or when they misjudge the competence of their leaders. As philosopher Jacqueline Boaks (2015) argues, ethics is so embedded in the idea of leadership that it has to be grounded in some sense of the good. She argues that this grounding would involve "knowledge of what is needed for the flourishing of both followers and leaders" (Boaks, 2015). In doing so the word *leader* would refer not simply to a person or role but, as Boaks says, to a kind of Aristotelian master virtue that one would attribute to a person. This would resolve the Hitler problem because people who do not promote human flourishing would not possess the virtue that defines them as leaders, but it does not define away the fact that there still are bad leaders.

Hence, the ultimate question about leadership is not "What is the definition of leadership?" We are not confused about what leaders are, but we would like to know what they should be like. The point of studying leadership is to answer the question "What is good leadership?" The use of the word *good* here has two senses: morally good leadership and technically good leadership (i.e., effective at getting the job at hand done). The problem with this view is that when we look at history and the leaders around us, we find some leaders who meet both criteria, some who meet one, and some who meet neither. History confuses the matter further because historians do not write about the leader who was very ethical but did not do anything of significance. They rarely write about a general who was a great human being but never won a battle. Most historians write about leaders who were winners or who changed history for better or for worse.

## Agency and Moral Luck

Historians concern themselves with what leaders do and the consequences of their actions. Biographers are interested in both the actions and the character of leaders. Both must grapple with questions of causation and the agency. Which outcomes are the direct result of a leader's actions and which outcomes come about for other reasons or by chance? Some of our judgments about leaders rest on what philosophers call *moral luck* (Nagel, 1979). Moral luck occurs when we attribute praise or blame to a person for an outcome that was not under their control. In Immanuel Kant's (1783/1993) ethics there is no such thing as moral luck because the morality of an act is based on the agent's intent to do her duty, not on how it turns out. This is because we may try to do what is morally right but things outside of our control may result in disastrous consequences. So for Kant, an act is ethical if it is done with the intent to do one's duty regardless of the outcome, and unethical if it is not based on the intent of doing one's duty and even if it results in a morally good outcome.

In the case of leaders we cannot ignore consequences because they can have a profound impact on the well-being of others. Some leaders may behave recklessly or in self-serving ways, but because of good fortune they can appear to have done morally good things. For example, if a president decided to carpet bomb a terrorist stronghold without regard for innocent civilians and by a twist of fate all of the civilians happened to be out of town that day, then the act may appear to be a good one (especially if the public did not know that the leader took into consideration his or her duty to protect innocent civilians). As Bernard Williams (1982) notes, there are two kinds of moral luck. The first is intrinsic to an action—based on how well a person thinks through a decision and whether his or her inferences are sound and turn out to be right. Careful plans may fail and risky ones may succeed. The second kind of moral luck is extrinsic to a decision. Things like bad weather, accidents, terrorists, malfunctioning machines, and so on may sabotage the best-laid plans or make the worst plans work.

Meindl et al. (1985) found that people tend to think that leaders have more control over outcomes than they actually do. This coincides with one of the most ethically distinctive aspects of being a leader. Leaders are supposed to *take* responsibility for an organization, group, and so on. As a result, they are *held* responsible for things that they did not do or even know about in their organizations. Anything that goes wrong in an organization is their fault and anything that goes right is to their credit. Because the notion of moral agency is sometimes indirect for leaders, especially those operating in complex organizations or systems, luck can play a significant role in our assessment of leaders and their leadership. Some leaders are ethical but unlucky, whereas others are not as ethical but very lucky. Most really difficult moral decisions made by leaders are risky because they have imperfect or incomplete information and lack control over all of the variables that will affect outcomes. Leaders who fail at something are worthy of forgiveness when they act with deliberate care and for the right moral reasons, even though followers do not always forgive them or have confidence in their leadership. Americans did not blame President Jimmy Carter for the botched attempt to free the hostages in Iran, but his bad luck in this case was one more thing that shook their faith in his leadership. The irony of moral luck is that leaders who are reckless and do not base their actions on sound moral and practical arguments are usually condemned when they fail and celebrated as heroes when they succeed. The reckless, lucky leader does not demonstrate moral or technical competency, yet because of the outcome, he or she often gets credit for having both.

## The Relationship Between Ethics and Effectiveness

History often defines successful leaders in terms of their ability to bring about change for better or worse. As a result, for some people, the great leaders in history include everyone from Gandhi to Hitler. Whereas these so-called great leaders usually bring about change or are successful at doing something, the ethical questions waiting in the wings are always these: Was the change itself morally good? How did the leader go about bringing change? What were the leader's intentions? A full analysis of the ethics and effectiveness of any action requires one to ask: Was it the right thing to do? Was it done the right way? Was it done for the right reason? One needs to ask these questions to assess whether leaders who are great in the sense of changing history are also good leaders (see Figure 17.1).

What many scholars mean when they describe a *good* leader is that he or she is an ethical and an effective leader (Ciulla, 1995). Whereas this may seem like stating the obvious, the problem we face is that we do not always find ethics and effectiveness in the same leader. Some leaders are highly ethical but not very effective. Others are very effective at serving the needs of their constituents or organizations but not very ethical. U.S. senator Trent Lott, who was forced to step down

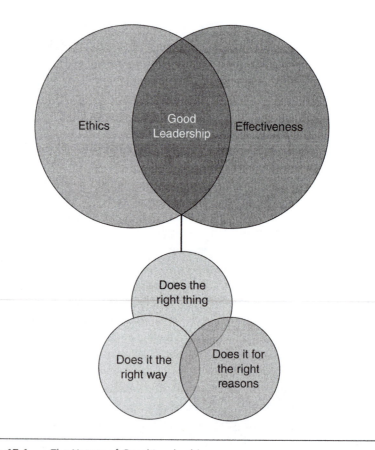

**Figure 17.1**    The Nature of Good Leadership

from his position as Senate majority leader because of his insensitive racial comments, is a compelling example of the latter. Some of his African American constituents said they would vote for him again, regardless of his racist comments, because Lott had used his power and influence in Washington to bring jobs and money to the state. In politics, the old saying "He may be a son-of-a-bitch, but he's our son-of-a-bitch" captures the trade-off between ethics and effectiveness. In other words, as long as Lott gets the job done, we do not care about his ethics.

This distinction between ethics and effectiveness is not always a crisp one. Sometimes being ethical is being effective and sometimes being effective is being ethical. In other words, ethics is effectiveness in certain instances. There are times when simply being regarded as ethical and trustworthy makes a leader effective and other times when being highly effective makes a leader ethical, but as philosopher Onora O'Neill (2013) notes, trustworthiness not only requires people to be honest and competent, it also requires them to be reliable. Given the limited power and resources of the secretary-general of the United Nations, it would be very difficult for someone in this position to be effective in the job if he or she did not behave ethically. The same is true for organizations. In the famous Tylenol case, Johnson & Johnson actually increased sales of Tylenol by pulling Tylenol bottles off their shelves after someone poisoned some of them. The leaders at Johnson & Johnson were effective because they were ethical.

The criteria we use to judge the effectiveness of a leader are also not morally neutral. For a while, Wall Street and the business press lionized Al Dunlap ("Chainsaw Al") as a great business leader. Their admiration was based on his ability to downsize a company and raise the price of its stock. Dunlap apparently knew little about the nuts and bolts of running a business. When he failed to deliver profits at his company, Sunbeam, he tried to cover up his losses and was fired. In this case and in many business cases, the criteria for effectiveness are practically and morally limited. It takes more skill to raise a company's stock price by keeping people employed than it does to raise it by firing them. Also, one of the most striking aspects of professional ethics is that often what seems right in the short run is not right in the long run, or what seems right for a group or organization is not right when placed in a broader context. For example, Mafia families may have very strong internal ethical systems, but they are highly unethical in any larger context of society.

There are also cases when the sheer competence of a leader has a moral impact. For instance, there were numerous examples of heroism in the aftermath of the September 11, 2001, terrorist attack on the World Trade Center. The most inspiring and frequently cited were the altruistic acts of rescue workers. Yet consider the case of Alan S. Weil, whose law firm, Sidley, Austin, Brown, & Wood, occupied five floors of the World Trade Center. Immediately after watching the Trade Center towers fall to the ground and checking to see if his employees got out safely, Weil got on the phone and within 3 hours had rented four floors of another building for his employees. By the end of the day, he had arranged for an immediate delivery of 800 desks and 300 computers. The next day, the firm was open for business with desks for almost every employee (Schwartz, 2001). We do not know if Mr. Weil's motives were altruistic or avaricious, but his focus on doing his job allowed the firm to fulfill its obligations to all of its stakeholders, from clients to employees. Is this an example of good (meaning ethical and effective) leadership?

On the flip side of the ethics effectiveness continuum are situations where it is difficult to tell whether a leader is unethical, incompetent, or stupid. As Price (2000, 2005) has argued, the moral failures of leaders are not always intentional. Sometimes moral failures are cognitive and sometimes they are normative. Leaders may get their facts wrong and think they are acting ethically when, in fact, they are not. For example, in 2000, South African president Thabo Mbeki issued a statement saying it was not clear that HIV caused AIDS. He thought the pharmaceutical industry was just trying to scare people so it could increase its profits (Garrett, 2000). Coming from the leader of a country where about one in five people tests positive for HIV, this was a shocking statement. His stance caused outrage among public health experts and other citizens. It was irresponsible and certainly undercut the efforts to stop the AIDS epidemic. Mbeki understood the scientific literature but chose to put political and philosophical reasons ahead of scientific knowledge. (He later backed away from this position.) When leaders do things like this, we want to know if they are misinformed, or have some other agenda. Mbeki's actions seemed unethical, but he may have thought he was taking an ethical stand. His narrow mindset about this issue made him recklessly disregard his more pressing obligations to stop the AIDS epidemic (Moldoveanu & Langer, 2002).

In some situations, leaders act with moral intentions, but because they are incompetent, they create unethical outcomes. Take, for instance, the unfortunate case of the Swiss charity Christian Solidarity International. Its goal was to free an estimated 200,000 Dinka children who were enslaved in Sudan. The charity paid between $35 and $75 a head to free enslaved children. The unintended consequence of the charity's actions was that it actually encouraged enslavement by creating a market for it. The price of slaves and the demand for them went up. Also, some cunning Sudanese found that it paid to pretend that they were slaves so that they could make money by being liberated. This deception made it difficult for the charity to identify those who really needed help from those who were faking it. Here, the charity's intent and the means it used to achieve its goals were not unethical in relation to alleviating suffering in the short run; however, in the long run, the charity inadvertently created more suffering. This case illustrates the relationship between ethics and effectiveness. One could say the following regarding the charity:

1.  It did the right thing—it intended to free children from slavery—but it ended up increasing the market for child slaves.

2.  It did it the wrong way—taking part in the buying and selling of a human being is unethical.

3.  Yet it did it for the right reason—slavery is immoral because it violates the dignity and human rights of children.

In *The Prince* (1532/1988), Niccolò Machiavelli grappled with the problems that leaders have being ethical and effective. He realized that there are situations where leaders could not be both ethical and effective. Sometimes they need to do the wrong thing for the right reason, or do the right thing the wrong way. Machiavelli says, "If a ruler who wants always to act honorably is surrounded by many unscrupulous men his downfall is inevitable" (Machiavelli, 1988, p. 54). Sometimes we regard a leader who acts honorably when dealing with dishonorable people as naive or incompetent. Machiavelli says that leaders must learn how "not to be good" because there are cases where behaving ethically confers harm on both leaders and followers. We usually dismiss "the ends justifying the means" as a justification for immoral behavior. Nevertheless, leaders frequently face situations where this justification, while morally questionable, characterizes their best course of action. Herein lies the problem: In what kinds of situations do the ends justify the means? For example, does improving the stock price or the bottom line justify cutting employees' wages or downsizing? Sometimes yes, when there is a moral and practical justification for such measures. Moreover, when does the desire to reach a particular end become an excuse for actions that are expedient and generally unethical? How does a leader resist becoming a kind of feckless utilitarian who is willing to do whatever it takes to get the job done? A leader does not have to be a prince in Machiavelli's time to face these challenges.

Echoing Machiavelli, philosopher Michael Walzer (1973) agrees that no leader leads innocently. Leaders often find themselves facing what he calls the "dirty hands problem." The job of most leaders is inherently utilitarian in that they have to look after the greatest good for the whole of their group, organization, country, and so on. Yet we tend to judge the moral character of leaders in terms of their virtues and commitment to moral principles. At some point, most leaders confront tensions between ethical principles and the obligations they have to their followers or organizations. When a leader's moral obligation to prevent harm to followers or their organization can only be fulfilled by doing something unethical, he or she faces a real moral dilemma. Most of the time we face moral problems, which are problems for which we can find satisfactory moral solutions. Moral dilemmas are a distinctive and less common type of moral problem where there is no morally satisfactory solution. No matter what choice you make in a dilemma, you do something wrong. For example, if terrorists take a hostage and threaten to kill him if the president does not release other dangerous terrorists from prison, any choice the president makes leaves him with dirty hands because either the hostage dies or the terrorists are free to commit acts of violence and kill more people.

It is ironic that we select, hire, or elect leaders to make these difficult decisions and get their hands dirty, and then we often reproach them for it when they do. The president would be condemned for the loss of the hostage's life or the subsequent attack by the freed terrorists. While we cannot expect moral purity from leaders (or anyone, for that matter), we hope that when leaders have to do wrong to do right, their conscience makes them feel dirty. Leading is a morally dangerous occupation because leaders have to fight the temptation to become comfortable with the moral compromises they sometimes make to be effective at doing their job.

## Deontological and Teleological Theories

The ethics-and-effectiveness question parallels the perspectives of deontological and teleological theories in ethics. As we saw in the earlier discussion of moral luck, from the deontological point of view, reasons are the morally relevant aspects of an act. As long as the leader acts according to his or her duty or on moral principles, then the leader acts ethically, regardless of the consequences. From a teleological perspective, what really matters is that the leader's actions result in bringing about something morally good or "the greatest good." Deontological theories locate the ethics of an action in the moral intent of the leader and his or her moral justification for the action, whereas teleological theories locate the ethics of the action in its results. We need both deontological and teleological theories to account for the ethics of leaders. Just as a good leader has to be ethical and effective, he or she also has to act according to duty and with some notion of the greatest good in mind.

In modernity, we often separate the inner person from the outer person, and a person from his or her actions. The utilitarian John Stuart Mill (1987) saw this split between the ethics of the person and the ethics of his or her actions clearly. He said the intentions or reasons for an act tell us something about the morality of the person, but the ends of an act tell us about the morality of the action. This solution does not really solve the ethics-and-effectiveness problem. It simply reinforces the split between the personal morality of a leader and what he or she does as a leader. Ancient Greek theories of ethics based on virtue do not have this problem. In virtue theories, you basically are what you do.

Going back to an earlier example, Mr. Weil may have worked quickly to keep his law firm going because he was so greedy he did not want to lose a day of billings, but in doing so, he also produced the greatest good for various stakeholders. We may not like his personal reasons for acting, but in this particular case, the various stakeholders may not care because they also benefited. If the various stakeholders knew that Weil had selfish intentions, they would, as Mill said, think less of him but not less of his actions. This is often the case with business. When a business runs a campaign to raise money for the homeless, it may be doing it to sell more of its goods and improve its public image. Yet it would seem a bit harsh to say that the business should not have the charity drive and deny needed funds for the homeless. One might argue that it is sometimes very unethical to demand perfect moral intentions. Nonetheless, personally unethical leaders who do good things for their constituents are still problematic. Even though they provide for the greatest good, their people can never really trust them.

## Moral Standards

People often say that leaders should be held to "a higher moral standard," but does that make sense? If true, would it then be acceptable for everyone else to live by lower moral standards? The curious thing about morality is that if you set the moral standards for leaders too high, requiring something close to moral perfection, then few people will be qualified to be leaders or will want to be leaders. For example, how many of us could live up to the standard of having never lied, said an unkind word, or reneged on a promise? Ironically, when we set moral standards for leaders too high, we become even more dissatisfied with our leaders because few are able to live up to our expectations. We set moral standards for leaders too low, however, when we reduce them to nothing more than following the law, or worse, simply not being as unethical as their predecessors. A business leader may follow all laws and yet be highly immoral in the way he or she runs a business. Laws are supposed to be either morally neutral or moral minimums about what is right. They do not and cannot capture the scope and complexity of morality. For example, an elected official may be law abiding and, unlike his or her predecessor, live by "strong family values." The official may also have little concern for the disadvantaged. Not caring about the poor and the sick is not against the law, but is such a leader ethical? So where does this leave us? On one hand, it is admirable to aspire to high moral standards, but on the other hand, if the standards are unreachable, then people give up trying to reach them (Ciulla, 1994, pp. 167–183). If the standards are too high, we may become more disillusioned with our leaders for failing to reach them. We might also end up with a shortage of competent people who are willing to take on leadership positions because we expect too much from them ethically. Some highly qualified people stay out of politics because they do not want their private lives aired in public. If the standards are too low, we become cynical about our leaders because we have lost faith in their ability to rise above the moral minimum.

History is littered with leaders who did not think they were subject to the same moral standards of honesty, propriety, and so forth, as the rest of society. One explanation for this is so obvious that it has become a cliché—power corrupts. Winter's (2002) and McClelland's (1975) works on how power motives and on socialized and personalized charisma offer psychological accounts of this kind of leader behavior. Maccoby (2000) and a host of others have written about narcissistic leaders who, on the bright side, are exceptional and, on the dark side, consider themselves exceptions to the rules.

Hollander's (1964) work on social exchange demonstrates how emerging leaders who are loyal to and competent at attaining group goals gain "idiosyncrasy credits" that allow them to deviate from the groups' norms to suit common goals. As Price (2000) has argued, given the fact that we often grant leaders permission to deviate or be an exception to the rules, it is not difficult to see why leaders sometimes make themselves exceptions to moral constraints. This is why I think we should not hold leaders to higher moral standards than ourselves. If anything, we have to make sure that we hold them to the same standards as the rest of society. What we should expect and hope is that our leaders will fail less than most people at meeting ethical standards, while pursuing and achieving the goals of their constituents. The really interesting question for leadership development, organizational, and political theory is "What can we do to keep leaders from the moral failures that stem from being in a leadership role?" Too many heroic models of leadership characterize the leader as a saint or "father-knows-best" archetype who possesses all the right values.

# Altruism

Some leadership scholars use altruism as the moral standard for ethical leadership. In their book *Ethical Dimensions of Leadership,* Kanungo and Mendonca (1996) wrote, "Our thesis is that organizational leaders are truly effective only when they are motivated by a concern for others, when their actions are invariably guided primarily by the criteria of the benefit to others even if it results in some cost to oneself" (p. 35). When people talk about altruism, they usually contrast altruism with selfishness, or behavior that benefits oneself at a cost to others (Ozinga, 1999). Altruism is a very high personal standard and, as such, is problematic for a number of reasons. Both selfishness and altruism refer to extreme types of motivation and behavior. Locke brings out this extreme side of altruism in a dialogue with Avolio (Avolio & Locke, 2002). Locke argued that if altruism is about self-sacrifice, then leaders who want to be truly altruistic will pick a job that they do not like or value, expect no rewards or pleasure from their job or achievements, and give themselves over totally to serving the wants of others. He then asked, "Would anyone want to be a leader under such circumstances?" (Avolio & Locke, 2002, pp. 169–171). One might also ask, "Would we even want such a person as a leader?" Whereas I do not agree with Locke's argument that leaders should act according to their self-interest, he does articulate the practical problem of using altruism as a standard of moral behavior for leaders. Avolio's argument against Locke is based on equally extreme cases. He draws on his work at West Point, where a central moral principle in the military is the willingness to make the ultimate sacrifice for the good of the group. Avolio also used Mother Teresa as one of his examples. In these cases, self-sacrifice may be less about the ethics of leaders in general and more about the jobs of military leaders and missionaries. The Locke and Avolio debate pits the extreme aspects of altruism against its heroic side. Here, as in the extensive philosophic literature on self-interest and altruism, the debate spins round and round and does not get us very far. Ethics is about the relationship of individuals to others, so in a sense both sides are right and wrong.

Altruism is a motive for acting, but it is not in and of itself a normative principle (Nagel, 1970). Requiring leaders to act altruistically is not only a tall order, it does not guarantee that the leader or his or her actions will be moral. For example, stealing from the rich to give to the poor, or *Robinhoodism,* is morally problematic (Ciulla, 2003a). A terrorist leader who becomes a suicide bomber might have purely altruistic intentions, but the means that he uses to carry out his mission—killing innocent people—is not considered ethical even if his cause is a just one. One might also argue, as one does against suicide, that it is unethical for a person to sacrifice his or her life for any reason because of the impact that it has on loved ones. Great leaders such as Martin Luther King Jr. and Mahatma Gandhi behaved altruistically, but what made their leadership ethical was the means they used to achieve their ends and the morality of their causes. We have a particular respect for leaders who are martyred for a cause, but the morality of King and Gandhi goes beyond their motives. Achieving their objectives for social justice while empowering and disciplining followers to use nonviolent resistance is morally good leadership.

People also describe altruism as a way of assessing an act or behavior, regardless of the agent's intention. For example, Worchel, Cooper, and Goethals (1988) defined altruism as acts that "render help to another person" (p. 394). If altruism is nothing more than helping people, then it is a more manageable standard, but simply helping people is not necessarily ethical. It depends on how you help them and what you help them do. It is true that people often help each other without making great sacrifices. If altruism is nothing more than helping people, then we have radically redefined the concept by eliminating the self-sacrificing requirement. Mendonca (2001) offered a further modification of altruism in what he called "mutual altruism." Mutual altruism boils down to utilitarianism and enlightened self-interest. If we follow this line of thought, we should also add other moral principles, such as the golden rule, to this category of altruism.

It is interesting to note that Confucius explicitly called the golden rule altruism. When asked by Tzu-Kung what the guiding principle of life is, Confucius answered, "It is the word altruism (*shu*). Do not do unto others what you do not want them to do to you" (Confucius, 1963, p. 44). The golden rule crops up as a fundamental moral principle in most major cultures because it demonstrates how to transform self-interest into concern for the interests of others. In other words, it provides the bridge between altruism and self-interest (others and the self) and allows for enlightened self-interest. This highlights another reason why altruism is not a useful standard for the moral behavior of leaders. The minute we start to modify altruism, it not only loses its initial meaning but it starts to sound like a wide variety of other ethical terms, which makes it very confusing.

## Why Being a Leader Is Not in a Just Person's Self-Interest

Plato believed that leadership required a person to sacrifice his or her immediate self-interests, but this did not amount to altruism. In Book II of the *Republic,* Plato (1992) wrote:

> In a city of good men, if it came into being, the citizens would fight in order not to rule. . . . There it would be clear that anyone who is really a true ruler doesn't by nature seek his own advantage but that of his subjects. And everyone, knowing this, would rather be benefited by others than take the trouble to benefit them. (p. 347d)

Rather than requiring altruistic motives, Plato was referring to the stress, hard work, and the often thankless task of being a morally good leader. He implied that if you are a just person, leadership will take a toll on you and your life. The only reason a just person will take on a leadership role is out of fear of punishment. He stated further, "Now the greatest punishment, if one isn't willing to rule, is to be ruled by someone worse than oneself. And I think it is fear of this that makes decent people rule when they do" (Plato, 1992, p. 347c). Plato's comment sheds light on why we sometimes feel more comfortable with people who are reluctant to lead than with those who are eager to do so. Today, as in the past, we worry that people who are too eager to lead want the power and position for themselves or that they do not fully understand the enormous responsibilities of leadership. Plato also tells us that whereas leadership is not in the just person's immediate self-interest, it is in his or her long-term interest. He argued that it is in our best interest to be just, because just people are happier and lead better lives than do unjust people (Plato, 1992, p. 353e).

Whereas we admire self-sacrifice, morality sometimes calls upon leaders to do things that are against their self-interest. This is less about altruism than it is about the nature of both morality and leadership. We want leaders to put the interests of followers first, but most leaders do not pay a price for doing that on a daily basis, nor do most circumstances require them to calculate their interests in relation to the interests of their followers. The practice of leadership is to guide and look after the goals, missions, and aspirations of groups, organizations, countries, or causes. When leaders do this, they are doing their job; when they do not do this, they are not doing their job. Ample research demonstrates that self-interested people who are unwilling to put the interests of others first are often not successful as leaders (Avolio & Locke, 2002, pp. 186–188).

Looking after the interests of others is as much about what leaders do in their role as leaders as it is about the moral quality of leadership. Implicit in the idea of leadership effectiveness is the notion that leaders do their job. When a mayor does not look after the interests of a city, she is not only ineffective, she is unethical for not keeping the promise that she made when sworn in as mayor. When she does look after the interests of the city, it is not because she is altruistic, but because she is doing her job. In this way, altruism is built into how we describe what leaders do. Whereas altruism is not the best concept for characterizing the ethics of leadership, scholars' interest in altruism reflects a desire to capture, either implicitly or explicitly, the ethics-and-effectiveness notion of good leadership.

# Transforming Leadership

In the leadership literature, transforming or transformational leadership has become almost synonymous with ethical leadership. Transformational leadership is often contrasted with transactional leadership. There is a parallel between these two theories and the altruism/self-interest dichotomy. Burns's (1978) theory of transforming leadership is compelling because it rests on a set of moral assumptions about the relationship between leaders and followers. Burns's theory is clearly a prescriptive one about the nature of morally good leadership. Drawing from Abraham Maslow's work on needs; Milton Rokeach's research on values development; and research on moral development from Lawrence Kohlberg, Jean Piaget, Erik Erickson, and Alfred Adler, Burns argued that leaders have to operate at higher need and value levels than those of followers, which may entail transcending their self-interests. A leader's role is to exploit tension and conflict within people's value systems and play the role of raising people's consciousness (Burns, 1978).

On Burns's account, transforming leaders have very strong values. They do not water down their values and moral ideals by consensus; rather, they elevate people by using conflict to engage followers and help them reassess their own values and needs. This is an area where Burns's view of ethics is very different from advocates of participatory leadership such as Rost. Burns wrote, "Despite his [Rost's] intense and impressive concern about the role of values, ethics, and morality in transforming leadership, he underestimates the crucial importance of these variables." Burns goes on to say, "Rost leans toward, or at least is tempted by, consensus procedures and goals that I believe erode such leadership" (Burns, 1991, p. xii).

The moral questions that drive Burns's (1978) theory of transforming leadership come from his work as a biographer and historian. When biographers or historians study a leader, they struggle with the question of how to judge or keep from judging their subject. Throughout his book, Burns used examples of a number of incidents where questionable means, such as lying and deception, are used to achieve honorable ends or where the private life of a politician is morally questionable. If you analyze the numerous historical examples in Burns's book, you find that two pressing moral questions shape his leadership theory. The first is the morality of means and ends (and this also includes the moral use of power). The second is the tension between the public and private morality of a leader. His theory of transforming leadership is an attempt to characterize good leadership by accounting for both of these questions.

Burns's distinction between transforming and transactional leadership and modal and end values offers a way to think about the question of what is a good leader in terms of the leader–follower relationship and the means and ends of his or her actions. Transactional leadership rests on the values found in the means or process of leadership. He calls these modal values. These include responsibility, fairness, honesty, and promise keeping. Transactional leadership helps leaders and followers reach their own goals by supplying lower-level wants and needs so that they can move up to higher needs. Transforming leadership is concerned with end values, such as liberty, justice, and equality. Transforming leaders raise their followers up through various stages of morality and need, and they turn their followers into leaders.

As a historian, Burns was very concerned with the ends of actions and the changes that leaders initiate. Consider, for example, Burns's (1978) two answers to the Hitler question. In the first part of the book, he stated quite simply that "Hitler, once he gained power and crushed all opposition, was no longer a leader—he was a tyrant" (pp. 2–3). A tyrant is similar to Kort's (2008) idea of a purported leader. Later in the book, Burns offered three criteria for judging how Hitler would fare before "the bar of history." He stated that Hitler would probably argue that he was a transforming leader who spoke for the true values of the German people and elevated them to a higher destiny. First, he would be tested by modal values of honor and integrity or the extent to which he advanced or thwarted the standards of good conduct in mankind. Second, he would be judged by the end values of equality and justice. Last, he would be judged on the impact that he had on the people whom he touched (Burns, 1978). According to Burns, Hitler would fail all three tests. Burns did not consider Hitler a true leader or a transforming leader because of the means that he used, the ends that he achieved, and the impact he had as a moral agent on his followers during the process of his leadership.

By looking at leadership as a process that is judged by a set of values, Burns's (1978) theory of good leadership is difficult to pigeonhole into one ethical theory. The most attractive part of Burns's theory is the idea that a leader elevates his or her followers and makes them leaders. Near the end of his book, he reintroduces this idea with an anecdote about why President Lyndon Johnson did not run in 1968, stating, "Perhaps he did not comprehend that the people he had led—as a result in part of the impact of his leadership—had created their own fresh leadership, which was now outrunning his" (p. 424). All of the people whom Johnson helped, the sick, the Blacks, and the poor, now had their own leadership. Burns noted, "Leadership begat leadership and hardly recognized its offspring. . . . Followers had become leaders" (p. 424).

Burns and other scholars' use of the word *value* to discuss ethics is problematic because it encompasses so many different kinds of things—economic values, organizational values, personal values, and moral values. Values do not necessarily tie people together the way moral concepts like duty and utility do, because most people subscribe to the view that "I have my values and you have yours." Having values does not mean that a person acts on them. To make values about something that people do rather than just have, Rokeach (1973) offered a very awkward discussion of the "ought" character of values. "A person phenomenologically experiences 'oughtness' to be objectively required by society in somewhat the same way that he perceives an incomplete circle as objectively requiring closure" (p. 9). Whereas Burns provides a provocative moral account of leadership, it would be stronger and clearer if he used the richer and more dynamic concepts found in moral philosophy.[1] This is not philosophic snobbery, but a plea for conceptual clarity and completeness. The implications of concepts such as virtue, duty, rights, and the greatest good have been worked out for hundreds of years and offer helpful tools for dissecting the moral dynamics of leadership and the relationship between leaders and followers.

## Transformational Leadership

Burns's (1978) theory has inspired a number of studies on transformational leadership. For example, Bass's (1985) early work on transformational leadership focused on the impact of leaders on their followers. In sharp contrast to Burns, Bass's transformational leaders did not have to appeal to the higher-order needs and values of their followers. He was more concerned with the psychological relationship between transformational leaders and their followers. Bass originally believed that there could be both good and evil transformational leaders, so he was willing to call Hitler a transformational leader. Bass later made an admirable effort to offer a richer account of ethics. Bass and Steidlmeier (1999) argued that only morally good

---

1. I argued this point with Burns for over 20 years and neither of us ever changed our positions on it.

leaders are authentic transformational leaders; the rest, like Hitler, are pseudotransformational. Bass and Steidlmeier described pseudotransformational leaders as people who seek power and position at the expense of their followers' achievements. The source of their moral shortcomings lies in the fact that they are selfish and pursue their own interests at the expense of their followers. Whereas Bass and Steidlmeier still depend on altruism as a moral concept, they also look at authentic transformational leadership in terms of other ethical concepts, such as virtue and commitment to the greatest good.

Bass (1985) believed that charismatic leadership is a necessary ingredient of transformational leadership. The research on charismatic leadership opens up a wide range of ethical questions because of the powerful emotional and moral impact that charismatic leaders have on followers (House, Spangler, & Woycke, 1991). Charismatic leadership can be the best and the worst kinds of leadership, depending on whether you look at a Gandhi or a Charles Manson (Lindholm, 1990). Bass and Steidlmeier's (1999) recent work runs parallel to research by Howell and Avolio (1992) on charismatic leadership. Howell and Avolio studied charismatic leaders and concluded that unethical charismatic leaders are manipulators who pursue their personal agendas. They argued that only leaders who act on socialized, rather than personalized, bases of power are transformational.

# Critics of Transformational and Charismatic Leadership Theories

There is plenty of empirical research that demonstrates the effectiveness of transformational leaders. Scholars are almost rhapsodic in the ways in which they describe their findings, and with good reason. These findings show that ethics and effectiveness go hand in hand. Shamir, House, and Arthur (1993) stated:

> Charismatic leaders . . . increase followers' self-worth through emphasizing the relationships between efforts and important values. A general sense of self-worth increases general self-efficacy; a sense of moral correctness is a source of strength and confidence. Having complete faith in the moral correctness of one's convictions gives one the strength and confidence to behave accordingly. (p. 582)

The problem with this research is that it raises many, if not more, questions about the ethics. What are the important values? Are the values themselves ethical? What does moral correctness mean? Is what followers believe to be moral correctness really morally correct?

Critics question the ethics of the very idea of transformational leadership. Keeley (1998) argued that transformational leadership is well and good as long as you assume that everyone will eventually come around to the values and goals of the leader. Drawing on Madison's concern for factions in *Federalist* No. 10, Keeley wondered, "What is the likely status of people who would prefer their own goals and visions?" (p. 123). What if followers are confident that the leader's moral convictions are wrong? Keeley observed that the leadership and management literature has not been kind to nonconformists. He noted that Mao was one of Burns's transforming heroes, and Mao certainly did not tolerate dissidents. Whereas Burns's theory tolerated conflict, conflict is only part of the process of reaching agreement on values. Is it ethical for a leader to require everyone to agree on all values?

Price (2000) discussed another problem with the moral view of transformational leadership articulated by Burns (1978) and Bass and Steidlmeier (1999). The leaders they described are subject to making all sorts of moral mistakes, even when they are authentic, altruistic, and committed to common values. The fact that a leader possesses these traits does not necessarily yield moral behavior or good moral decisions. Price further argued that leaders and followers should be judged by adherence to morality, not adherence to their organizations' or society's values. "Leaders must be willing to sacrifice their other-regarding values when generally applicable moral requirements make legitimate demands that they do so" (Price, 2003, p. 80). Sometimes being a charismatic and transformational leader in an organization, in the sense described by some theorists, does not mean that you are ethical when judged against moral concepts that apply in larger contexts.

Solomon (1998) took aim at the focus on charisma in leadership studies. He stated that charisma is the shorthand for certain rare leaders. As a concept, it is without ethical value and without much explanatory value. Charisma is not a distinctive quality of personality or character, and according to Solomon, it is not an essential part of leadership. For example, Solomon stated, "Charisma is not a single quality, nor is it a single emotion or set of emotions. It is a generalized way of pointing to and emptily explaining an emotional relationship that is too readily characterized as fascination" (p. 95). He then went on to argue that research on trust offers more insight into the leader–follower relationship than research into charisma. Solomon specifically discussed the importance of exploring the emotional process of how people give their trust to others.

## Knocking Leaders off Their Pedestals

Keeley's (1998), Price's (2000), and Solomon's (1998) criticisms of transformational and charismatic leadership theories raise two larger questions. First, scholars might be missing something about leadership when they study only exceptional types of leaders. Second, by limiting their study in this way, they fail to take into account the fact that even exceptional leaders get things wrong. Morality is a struggle for everyone, and it contains particular hazards for leaders. As Kant (1785/1983) observed,

From such warped wood as is man made, nothing straight can be fashioned. . . . Man is an animal that, if he lives among other members of his species, has need of a master, for he certainly abuses his freedom in relation to his equals. He requires a master who will break his self-will and force him to obey a universally valid will, whereby everyone can be free. . . . He finds the master among the human species, but even he is an animal who requires a master. (p. 34)

The master for Kant (1785/1983) is morality. No individual or leader has the key to morality, and hence, everyone is responsible for defining and enforcing morality. We need to understand the ethical challenges faced by imperfect humans who take on the responsibilities of leadership, so that we can develop morally better leaders, followers, institutions, and organizations. At issue is not simply what ethical and effective leaders do, but what leaders have to confront and, in some cases, overcome to be ethical and effective. Some of these questions are psychological in nature, and others are concerned with moral reasoning.

Like many leadership scholars, Plato constructed his theory of the ideal leader—the philosopher king who is wise and virtuous. Through firsthand experience, Plato realized the shortcomings of his philosopher king model of leadership. Plato learned about leadership through three disastrous trips to the city-state of Syracuse. Plato visited Syracuse the first time at the invitation of the tyrant Dionysius I, but he soon became disgusted by the decadent and luxurious lifestyle of Dionysius's court. Plato returned to Athens convinced that existing forms of government at home and abroad were corrupt and unstable. He then decided to set up the Academy, where he taught for 40 years and wrote the *Republic.* In the *Republic,* Plato argued that the perfect state could come about only by rationally exploiting the highest qualities in people (although this sounds a bit like a transformational leadership, it is not). Plato firmly believed that the philosopher king could be developed through education. Hence, we might regard Plato's Academy as a leadership school.

About 24 years after his first visit, Dionysius's brother-in-law, Dion, invited Plato back to Syracuse. By this time, Dionysius I was dead. Dion had read the *Republic* and wanted Plato to come and test his theory of leadership education on Dionysius's very promising son Dionysius II. This was an offer that Plato could not refuse, although he had serious reservations about accepting it. Nonetheless, off Plato went to Syracuse. The trip was a disaster. Plato's friend Dion was exiled because of court intrigues. Years later, Plato returned to Syracuse a third time, but the visit was no better than the first two. In Epistle VII, Plato (1971a) reported that these visits changed his view of leadership:

The more I advanced in years, the harder it appeared to me to administer the government correctly. For one thing, nothing could be done without friends and loyal companions, and such men were not easy to find ready at hand. . . . Neither could such men be created afresh with any facility. . . . The result was that I, who had at first been full of eagerness for a public career, as I gazed upon the whirlpool of public life and saw the incessant movement of shifting currents, at last felt dizzy. (p. 1575)

Plato seemed to have lost faith in his conviction that leaders could be perfected. He realized that leaders shared the same human weaknesses of their followers, but he also saw how important trust was in leadership. In the *Republic,* Plato had entertained a pastoral image of the leader as a shepherd to his flock. But in a later work, *Statesman,* he observed that leaders are not at all like shepherds. Shepherds are obviously quite different from their flocks, whereas human leaders are not much different from their followers (Plato, 1971b). He noted that people are not sheep—some are cooperative and some are very stubborn. Plato's revised view of leadership was that leaders were really like weavers. Their main task was to weave together different kinds of people—the meek and the self-controlled, the brave and the impetuous—into the fabric of society (Plato, 1971b).

Plato's ideas on leadership progressed from a profound belief that it is possible for some people to be wise and benevolent philosopher kings to a more modest belief that the real challenge of leadership is working successfully with people who do not always like each other, do not always like the leader, and do not necessarily want to live together. These are some of the key challenges faced by leaders today all over the world. Leadership is more like being a shepherd to a flock of cats or like pushing a wheelbarrow full of frogs (O'Toole, 1995).

Whereas Plato's image of the philosopher king in the *Republic* is idealistic, the *Statesman* and the early books of the *Republic* lay out some of the fundamental ethical issues of leadership; namely, moral imperfection and power. Near the end of the *Statesman,* Plato contended that we cannot always depend on leaders to be good and that is why we need rule of law (Plato, 1971b). Good laws, rules, and regulations protect us from unethical leaders and serve to help leaders be ethical (similar to James Madison's concern for checks on leaders).

Plato, like many of the ancients, realized that the greatest ethical challenge for humans in leadership roles stems from the temptations of power. In Book II of the *Republic,* he provided a thought-provoking experiment about power and accountability. Glaucon, the protagonist in the dialogue, argued that the only reason people are just is because they lack the power to be unjust. He then told the story of the "Ring of Gyges" (Plato, 1992). A young shepherd from Lydia found a ring and discovered that when he turned the ring on his finger, it made him invisible. The shepherd then used the ring to seduce the king's wife, attack the king, and take over the kingdom. Plato asks us to consider what we would do if we had power without accountability. One of our main concerns about leaders is that they will abuse their power because they are accountable to fewer people. In this respect, the "Ring of Gyges" is literally and figuratively a story about transparency. The power that leaders have to do things also entails the power to hide what they do.

Power carries with it a temptation to do evil and an obligation to do good. Philosophers often refer to a point made by Kant (1785/1993, p. 32) as "ought implies can," meaning you have a moral obligation to act when you are able to act effectively. It means that the more power, resources, and ability you have to do good, the more you have a moral obligation to do so. The notion of helpfulness, discussed earlier in conjunction with altruism, is derived from this notion of power and obligation. It is about the moral obligation to help when you can help.

# The Bathsheba Syndrome

The moral foible that people fear most in their leaders is personal immorality accompanied by abuse of power. Usually, it is the most successful leaders who suffer the worst ethical failures. Ludwig and Longenecker (1993) called the moral failure of successful leaders the "Bathsheba syndrome," based on the biblical story of King David and Bathsheba. Ancient texts such as the Bible provide us with wonderful case studies on the moral pitfalls of leaders. King David is portrayed as a successful leader in the Bible. We first meet him as a young shepherd in the story of David and Goliath. This story offers an interesting leadership lesson. In it, God selects the small shepherd David over his brother, a strong soldier, because David "has a good heart." Then, as God's handpicked leader, David goes on to become a great leader, until we come to the story of David and Bathsheba (2 Samuel 11–12).

The story begins with David taking an evening stroll around his palace. From his vantage point on the palace roof, he sees the beautiful Bathsheba bathing. He asks his servants to bring Bathsheba to him. The king beds Bathsheba and she gets pregnant. Bathsheba's husband, Uriah, is one of David's best generals. King David tries to cover up his immoral behavior by calling Uriah home. When Uriah arrives, David attempts to get him drunk so that he will sleep with Bathsheba. Uriah refuses to cooperate, because he said it would be unfair to enjoy such pleasures while his men are on the front. (This is a wonderful sidebar about the moral obligations of leaders to followers.) David then escalates his attempt to cover things up by ordering Uriah to the front of a battle, where he gets killed. In the end, the prophet Nathan blows the whistle on David and God punishes David.

The Bathsheba story has repeated itself again and again in history. Scandals ranging from Watergate to the President Clinton and Monica Lewinsky affair to Enron all follow the general pattern of this story (Winter, 2002, gives an interesting psychological account of the Clinton case). First, we see what happens when successful leaders lose sight of what their jobs are. David should have been focusing on running the war, not watching Bathsheba bathe. He was literally and figuratively looking in the wrong place. This is why we worry about men leaders who are womanizers getting distracted from their jobs. Second, because power leads to privileged access, leaders have more opportunities to indulge themselves and, hence, need more willpower to resist indulging themselves. David could have Bathsheba brought to him by his servants with no questions asked. Third, successful leaders sometimes develop an inflated belief in their ability to control outcomes. David became involved in escalating cover-ups.

The most striking thing about leaders who get themselves in these situations is that the cover-ups are usually worse than the crime. In David's case, adultery was not as bad as murder. Also, it is during the cover-up that leaders abuse their power as leaders the most. In Clinton's case, a majority of Americans found his lying to the public far more immoral than his adultery. Last, leaders learn that their power falls short of the ring of Gyges. It will not keep their actions invisible forever. Whistle-blowers such as Nathan in King David's case or Sherron Watkins in the Enron case call their bluff and demand that their leaders be held to the same moral standards as everyone else. When this happens, in Bible stories and everywhere else, all hell breaks loose. The impact of a leader's moral lapses causes great harm to their constituents.

Read as a leadership case study, the story of David and Bathsheba is about pride and the moral fragility of people when they hold leadership positions. It is also a cautionary tale about success and the lengths to which people will go to keep from losing it. What is most interesting about the Bathsheba syndrome is that it is difficult to predict which leaders will fall prey to it, because people get it after they have become successful. One can never tell how even the most virtuous person will respond to situations in various contexts and circumstances (Doris, 2005). If we are to gain a better understanding of ethics and leadership, we need to examine how leaders resist falling for the ethical temptations that come with power.

## Self-Discipline and Virtue

The moral challenges of power and the nature of the leader's job explain why self-knowledge and self-control are, and have been for centuries, the most important factors in leadership development. Ancient writers, such as Lao tzu, Confucius, Buddha, Plato, and Aristotle, all emphasized good habits, self-knowledge, and self-control in their writing. Eastern philosophers, such as Lao tzu, Confucius, and Buddha, talked not only about virtues but also about the challenges of self-discipline and controlling the ego. Lao tzu warned against egotism when he stated, "He who stands on tiptoe is not steady" (Lao Tzu, 1963, p. 152). He also tells us, "The best rulers are those whose existence is merely known by people" (Lao tzu, 1963, p. 148). Confucius (1963) focused on the importance of duty and self-control. He stated, "If a man (the ruler) can for one day master himself and return to propriety, all under heaven will return to humanity. To practice humanity depends on oneself" (p. 38). Confucius tied a leader's self-mastery and effectiveness together when he wrote, "If a ruler sets himself right, he will be followed without his command. If he does not set himself right, even his commands will not be obeyed" (p. 38).

In the "First Sermon," the Buddha described how people's uncontrolled thirst for things contributes to their own suffering and the suffering of others. Not unlike psychologists today, he realized that getting one's desires under control is the best way to end personal and social misery. This is a particular challenge for leaders, because they often have the means to indulge their material and personal desires. Compassion is the most important virtue in Buddhist ethics because it keeps desires and vices in check. The Dalai Lama (1999) concisely summed up the moral dynamics of compassion in this way:

> When we bring up our children to have knowledge without compassion, their attitude towards others is likely to be a mixture of envy of those in positions

above them, aggressive competitiveness towards their peers, and scorn for these less fortunate. This leads to a propensity toward greed, presumption, excess, and very quickly to loss of happiness. (p. 181)

Virtues are a fundamental part of the landscape of moral philosophy and provide a useful way of thinking about leadership development. What is important about virtues are their dynamics (e.g., how they interact with other virtues and vices) and their contribution to self-knowledge and self-control. The properties of a virtue are very different from the properties of other moral concepts such as values. Virtues are qualities that you have only if you practice them. Values are things that are important to people. Some values are subjective preferences—such as chocolate rather than vanilla ice cream—and others are moral values, like honesty. I may value honesty but not always tell the truth. I cannot possess the virtue of honesty without telling the truth. As Aristotle mentioned, virtues are good habits that we learn from society and our leaders. Aristotle wrote quite a bit about leaders as moral role models, and much of what he said complements observations in research on transformational leadership. He noted, "Legislators make citizens good by forming habits in them" (Aristotle, 1984). Whereas virtues come naturally to those who practice them, they are not mindless habits. People must practice them fully conscious of knowing that what they are doing is morally right.

Perhaps the most striking thing about the Greek notion of virtue (*areté*), which is also translated as "excellence," is that it does not separate an individual's ethics from his or her occupational competence. Both Plato and Aristotle constantly used examples of doctors, musicians, coaches, rulers, and so forth to talk about the relationship between moral and technical or professional excellence. Aristotle (1984) wrote,

Every excellence brings to good the thing to which it is the excellence and makes the work of that thing be done well. . . . Therefore, if this is true in every case, the excellence of man also will be the state which makes man good and which makes him do his work well. (p. 1747)

Excellence is tied to function. The function of a knife is to cut. An excellent knife cuts well. The function of humans, according to Aristotle, is to reason. To be morally virtuous, you must reason well, because reason tells you how to practice and when to practice a virtue. If you reason well, you will know how to practice moral and professional virtues. In other words, reason is the key to practicing moral virtues and the virtues related to one's various occupations in life. Hence, the morally virtuous leader will also be a competent leader because he or she will do what is required in the job the right way. Virtue ethics does not differentiate between the morality of the leader and the morality of his or her leadership. An incompetent leader, like the head of the Swiss charity that tried to free the enslaved children, lacks moral virtue, regardless of his or her good intentions.

# Conclusion

The more we explore how ethics and effectiveness are inextricably intertwined, the better we will understand the nature of good leadership. The philosophic study of ethics provides a critical perspective from which we can examine the assumptions behind leadership and leadership theories. It offers another level of analysis that should be integrated into the growing body of empirical research in the field. The ethics of leadership has to be examined along a variety of dimensions:

1. The ethics of a leader as a person, which includes things like self-knowledge, discipline, intentions, and so forth.

2. The ethics of the leader–follower relationship (i.e., how they treat each other).

3. The ethics of the process of leadership (i.e., respecting followers, command and control, participatory).

4. The ethics of what the leader does or does not do.

These dimensions give us a picture of the ethics of what a leader does and how he or she does it. But even after an interdependent analysis of these dimensions, the picture is not complete. We then have to take one more step and look at all of these interdependent dimensions in larger contexts and time frames. For example, the ethics of organizational leadership would have to be examined in the context of the community and so forth. One of the most striking distinctions between effective leadership and ethical *and* effective leadership is often the time frame of decisions. Ethics is about the impact of behavior and actions in the long and the short run. Leaders can be effective in the short run but unethical and ultimately ineffective in the long run. For example, we have all seen the problem of defining good business leadership based simply on the quarterly profits that a firm makes. Long-term ideas of effectiveness, such as sustainability, tend to be normative.

A richer understanding of the moral challenges that are distinctive to leaders and leadership is particularly important for leadership development. Whereas case studies of ethical leadership are inspiring and case studies of evil leaders are cautionary, we need a practical understanding of why it is morally difficult to be a good leader and a good follower. Leaders do not have to be power-hungry psychopaths to do unethical things, nor do they have to be altruistic saints to do ethical things. Most leaders are neither charismatic nor transformational leaders. They are ordinary men and women in business, government, nonprofits, and communities who sometimes make volitional, emotional, moral, and cognitive mistakes. More work needs to be done on ordinary leaders and followers and how they can help each other be ethical and make better moral decisions.

Aristotle (1984) said that happiness is the end toward which we aim in life. The Greek word that Aristotle uses for happiness is *eudaimonea.* It means happiness, not in terms of pleasure or contentment, but as flourishing. A happy life is one in which we flourish as human beings, in terms of both our material and personal development and our moral development. The concept of *eudaimonea* gives us two umbrella questions that can be used to assess the overall ethics and effectiveness of leadership. Does a leader or a particular kind of leadership contribute to and/or allow people to flourish in terms of their lives as a whole? Does a leader or a particular kind of leadership interfere with the ability of other groups of people or other living beings to flourish? Leaders do not always have to transform people for them to flourish. Their greater responsibility is to create the social and material conditions under which people can and do flourish (Ciulla, 2000). Change is part of leadership, but so is sustainability. Ethical leadership entails the ability of leaders to sustain fundamental notions of morality, such as care and respect for persons, justice, and honesty, in changing organizational, social, and global contexts. Moreover, it requires people who have the competence, knowledge, and will to determine and do the right thing, the right way, and for the right reasons. The humanities offer one source of insight into the nature of right and wrong.

Last, leadership scholars have just begun to scratch the surface of other disciplines. History, philosophy, anthropology, literature, and religion all promise to expand our understanding of leaders and leadership. Ancient writers such as Plato, Aristotle, Lao tzu, and Confucius not only tell us about leadership, they also capture our imaginations. What makes a classic a classic is that its message carries themes and values that are meaningful to people from different cultures and different periods of history. They offer well-grounded ideas about who we are, what we should be like, and how we should live. These ideas offer us a perspective on current empirical research on leadership and help generate new ideas for research. To really understand leadership in terms of ethics and effectiveness, each one of us needs to put our ear to the ground of history and listen carefully to the saga of human hopes, desires, and aspirations, and the follies, disappointments, and triumphs of those who led and those who followed them. As Confucius (1963) once said, "A man who reviews the old as to find out the new is qualified to teach others" (p. 23).

## Discussion Questions

1. Who would you prefer to work for, an effective but ethically questionable leader or an ethical but ineffective leader? How do you weigh the costs and benefits of each type of leader?
2. Why does success have the potential to corrupt leaders? How is corruption from success different from corruption from power?
3. Think of examples where ethical considerations interfere with a leader's ability to be effective. Then think of ways in which a leader's ethics interfere with his or her ability to be effective. Should leaders always pick ethics over effectiveness?
4. How would you redefine effective leadership to take into account normative considerations?
5. Why is it important for leaders to feel like they have dirty hands?

## Recommended Readings

- Ciulla, J. B. (1999). The importance of leadership in shaping business values. *Long Range Planning, 32*, 166–172.
- Heifetz, R. A., & Laurie, D. L. (1997). The work of leadership. *Harvard Business Review, 75*, 124–134.
- Lipman-Blumen, J. (2006). *The allure of toxic leaders: Why we follow destructive bosses and corrupt politicians and how we can survive them.* New York, NY: Oxford University Press.

## Recommended Case Studies

- **Case:** Le Guin, U. (1975/2004). The ones who walk away from Omelas. In *The wind's twelve quarters* (pp. 275–284). New York, NY: Harper Perennial. http://harelbarzilai.org/words/omelas.txt
- **Case:** Orwell, G. (1936). Shooting an elephant. http://www.physics.ohio-state.edu/~wilkins/writing/Resources/essays/elephant.html
- **Case:** Rose, C., & Fisher, N. (2013). Following Lance Armstrong: Excellence corrupted. Harvard Business School Case 314015.

## Recommended Video

- O'Neill, O (2014): What we don't understand about trust, https://www.ted.com/talks/onora_o_neill_what_we_don_t_understand_about_trust

## References

Aristotle. (1984). *Nichomachean ethics* (W. D. Ross, Trans.). In J. Barnes (Ed.), *The complete works of Aristotle: The revised Oxford translation* (Vol. 2, pp. 1729–1867). Princeton, NJ: Princeton University Press.

Avolio, B. J., & Locke, E. E. (2002). Contrasting different philosophies of leader motivation: Altruism verses egoistic. *The Leadership Quarterly, 13*, 169–191.

Bass, B. M. (1985). *Leadership and performance beyond expectations.* New York, NY: Free Press.

Bass, B. M. (1997). Does the transactional–transformational leadership paradigm transcend organizational and national boundaries? *American Psychologist, 52*, 130–139.

Bass, B. M., & Steidlmeier, P. (1999). Ethics, character, and authentic transformational leader behavior. *The Leadership Quarterly, 10*, 181–217.

Bennis, W. (2002). Towards a "truly" scientific management: The concept of organizational health. *Reflections, 4*, 4–13.

Bennis, W., & Nanus, B. (1985). *Leaders: Strategies for taking charge.* New York, NY: HarperCollins.

Boaks, J. (2015). Must leadership be undemocratic? In J. Boaks & M. P. Levine (Eds.), *Leadership and ethics* (pp. 97–127). London, UK: Bloomsbury.

Bogardus, E. S. (1934). *Leaders and leadership.* New York, NY: Appelton-Century.

Brown, M. E., Treviño, L. K., & Harrison, D. A. (2005). Ethical leadership: A social learning perspective for construct development and testing. *Organizational Behavior and Human Decision Processes, 97*, 117–134.

Burns, J. M. (1978). *Leadership.* New York, NY: Harper & Row.

Burns, J. M. (1991). Foreword. In J. C. Rost (Ed.), *Leadership for the twenty-first century* (pp. xi–xii). New York, NY: Praeger.

Ciulla, J. B. (1994). Casuistry and the case for business ethics. In T. Donaldson & R. E. Freeman (Eds.), *Business as a humanity* (pp. 167–183). Oxford, UK: Oxford University Press.

Ciulla, J. B. (1995). Leadership ethics: Mapping the territory. *Business Ethics Quarterly, 5*, 5–24.

Ciulla, J. B. (2000). *The working life: The promise and betrayal of modern work.* New York, NY: Crown Books.

Ciulla, J. B. (2003a). The ethical challenges of nonprofit leaders. In R. E. Riggio & S. S. Orr (Eds.), *Improving leadership in nonprofit organizations* (pp. 63–75). San Francisco, CA: Jossey-Bass.

Ciulla, J. B. (2003b). *The ethics of leadership.* Belmont, CA: Wadsworth.

Ciulla, J. B. (Ed.). (2008a). *Leadership and the humanities.* Westport, CT: Praeger.

Ciulla, J. B. (Ed.). (2008b). Leadership: Views from the humanities [Special issue]. *The Leadership Quarterly, 19*(4).

*Compact Oxford English dictionary.* (1991). Oxford, UK: Clarendon.

Confucius. (1963). Selections from the *Analects.* In W. Chan (Ed. & Trans.), *A source book in Chinese philosophy* (pp. 18–48). Princeton, NJ: Princeton University Press.

Dalai Lama XIV. (1999). *Ancient wisdom, modern world: Ethics for a new millennium* (T. Jinpa, Trans.). New York, NY: Riverhead Books.

Doris, J. (2005). *Lack of character: Personality and moral behavior.* Cambridge, UK: Cambridge University Press.

Drath, W. H., McCauley, C. D., Palus, C. J., Van Velsor, E., O'Connor, P. M. G., & McGuire, J. B. (2008). Direction, alignment, commitment: Toward a more integrative ontology of leadership. *The Leadership Quarterly, 19*(6), 635–653.

Garrett, L. (2000, March 29). Added foe in AIDS war: Skeptics. *Newsday,* p. A6.

Gergen, D. (2002, November). *Keynote address.* Delivered at the meeting of the International Leadership Association, Seattle, WA.

Gibb, C. A. (1954). Leadership. In E. B. Reuter (Ed.), *Handbook of social psychology* (Vol. 2, pp. 877–920). Reading, MA: Addison-Wesley.

Heifetz, R. A. (1994). *Leadership without easy answers.* Cambridge, MA: Harvard University Press.

Hollander, E. P. (1964). *Leaders, groups, and influence.* New York, NY: Oxford University Press.

House, R. J., Spangler, W. D., & Woycke, J. (1991). Personality and charisma in the U.S. presidency: A psychological theory of effectiveness. *Administrative Science Quarterly, 36,* 334–396.

Howell, J. M., & Avolio, B. (1992). The ethics of charismatic leadership. *Academy of Management Executive, 6,* 43–54.

Hunt, J. G. (Ed.). (1991). *Leadership: A new synthesis.* Newbury Park, CA: Sage.

Hunt, J., & Dodge, G. E. (2000). Leadership déjà vu all over again. *The Leadership Quarterly, 11*(4), 435–458.

Kant, I. (1983). The idea for a universal history with a cosmopolitan intent. In T. Humphrey (Ed. & Trans.), *Perpetual peace and other essays on politics, history, and morals* (pp. 29–40). Indianapolis, IN: Hackett. (Original work published 1795)

Kant, I. (1993). *Foundations of the metaphysics of morals* (J. W. Ellington, Trans.). Indianapolis, IN: Hackett. (Original work published 1785)

Kanungo, R., & Mendonca, M. (1996). *Ethical dimensions of leadership.* Thousand Oaks, CA: Sage.

Keeley, M. (1998). The trouble with transformational leadership. In J. B. Ciulla (Ed.), *Ethics, the heart of leadership* (pp. 111–144). Westport, CT: Praeger.

Kort, E. D. (2008). What, after all, is leadership? "Leadership" and plural action. *The Leadership Quarterly, 19,* 409–425.

Lao Tzu. (1963). The *Lao Tzu (Tao-te ching).* In W. Chan (Ed. & Trans.), *A source book in Chinese philosophy* (pp. 139–176). Princeton, NJ: Princeton University Press.

Liden, R. C., & Antonakis, J. (2009). Considering context in psychological leadership research. *Human Relations, 62,* 1587–1605.

Lindholm, C. (1990). *Charisma.* Cambridge, MA: Blackwell.

Ludwig, D., & Longenecker, C. (1993). The Bathsheba syndrome: The ethical failure of successful leaders. *The Journal of Business Ethics, 12,* 265–273.

Maccoby, M. (2000). Narcissistic leaders. *The Harvard Business Review, 78,* 69–75.

Machiavelli, N. (1988). *The prince* (Q. Skinner & R. Price, Ed. & Trans.). Cambridge, UK: Cambridge University Press.

McClelland, D. C. (1975). *Power: The inner experience.* New York, NY: Halsted.

Meindl, J. R., Ehrlich, S. B., & Dukerich, J. M. (1985). The romance of leadership. *Administrative Science Quarterly, 30*(1), 78–102.

Mendonca, M. (2001). Preparing for ethical leadership in organizations. *Canadian Journal of Administrative Sciences, 18,* 266–276.

Mill, J. S. (1987). What utilitarianism is. In A. Ryan (Ed.), *Utilitarianism and other essays* (pp. 272–338). New York, NY: Penguin Books.

Moldoveanu, M., & Langer, E. (2002). When "stupid" is smarter than we are: Mindlessness and the attribution of stupidity. In R. Sternberg (Ed.), *Why smart people can be so stupid* (pp. 212–231). New Haven, CT: Yale University Press.

Moore, B. V. (1927). The May conference on leadership. *Personnel Journal, 6,* 124–128.

Nagel, T. (1970). *The possibility of altruism.* Oxford, UK: Clarendon.

Nagel, T. (1979). *Moral questions.* New York, NY: Cambridge University Press.

O'Neill, Onora (2013). What we don't understand about trust. Retrieved from https://www.ted.com/talks/onora_o_neill_what_we_don_t_understand_about_trust

Osborn, R. N., & Hunt, J. G. (1975). An adaptive-reactive theory of leadership. In J. G. Hunt & L. L. Larson (Eds.), *Leadership frontiers* (pp. 27–44). Kent, OH: Kent State University Press.

O'Toole, J. (1995). *Leading change: Overcoming the ideology of comfort and the tyranny of custom.* San Francisco, CA: Jossey-Bass.

Ozinga, J. R. (1999). *Altruism.* Westport, CT: Praeger.

Pillai, R. (1996). Crisis and the emergence of charismatic leadership in groups: An experimental investigation. *Journal of Applied Social Psychology, 26,* 543–562.

Plato. (1971a). Epistle VII (L. A. Post, Trans.). In E. Hamilton & H. Cairns (Eds.), *The collected dialogues of Plato, including the letters* (pp. 1574–1603). Princeton, NJ: Princeton University Press.

Plato. (1971b). Statesman (J. B. Skemp, Trans.). In E. Hamilton & H. Cairns (Eds.), *The collected dialogues of Plato, including the letters* (pp. 1018–1085). Princeton, NJ: Princeton University Press.

Plato. (1992). *Republic* (G. M. A. Grube, Trans.). Indianapolis, IN: Hackett.

Price, T. L. (2000). Explaining ethical failures of leadership. *The Leadership and Organizational Development Journal, 21,* 177–184.

Price, T. L. (2003). The ethics of authentic transformational leadership. *The Leadership Quarterly, 14,* 67–81.

Price, T. L. (2005). *Understanding ethical failures in leadership.* New York, NY: Cambridge University Press.

Reuter, R. B. (1941). *Handbook of sociology.* New York, NY: Dryden Press.

Rokeach, M. (1973). *The nature of human values.* New York, NY: Free Press.

Rost, J. (1991). *Leadership for the twenty-first century.* New York, NY: Praeger.

Ruscio, K. P. (2004). *The leadership dilemma in modern democracy.* Northampton, MA: Edward Elgar.

Sarkesian, S. C. (1981). A personal perspective. In J. H. Buck & L. J. Korb (Eds.), *Military leadership* (pp. 243–247). Beverly Hills, CA: Sage.

Schwartz, J. (2001, September 16). Up from the ashes, one firm rebuilds. *New York Times,* sec. 3, p. 1.

Seeman, M. (1960). *Social status and leadership.* Columbus: Ohio State University Bureau of Educational Research.

Shamir, B., House, R. J., & Arthur, M. B. (1993). The motivational effects of charismatic leadership: A self-concept based theory. *Organizational Science, 4,* 577–594.

Solomon, R. C. (1998). Ethical leadership, emotions, and trust: Beyond charisma. In J. B. Ciulla (Ed.), *Ethics, the heart of leadership* (pp. 83–102). Westport, CT: Praeger.

Uhl-Bien, M. (2006). Relational leadership theory: Exploring the social processes of leadership and organizing. *The Leadership Quarterly, 17,* 654–676.

Walzer, M. (1973). Political action: The problem of dirty hands. *Philosophy and Public Affairs, 2*(2), 160–168.

Williams, B. A. O. (1982). *Moral luck.* Cambridge, UK: Cambridge University Press.

Winter, D. G. (2002). The motivational dimensions of leadership: Power, achievement, and affiliation. In R. E. Riggio, S. E. Murphy, & F. J. Pirozzolo (Eds.), *Multiple intelligences and leadership* (pp. 118–138). Mahwah, NJ: Lawrence Erlbaum.

Wittgenstein, L. (1968). *Philosophical investigations* (G. E. M. Anscombe, Trans.). New York, NY: Macmillan.

Worchel, S., Cooper, J., & Goethals, G. (1988). *Understanding social psychology.* Chicago, IL: Dorsey.

# CHAPTER 18

# Corporate Social Responsibility and Leadership

*Guido Palazzo*

---

## Opening Case: A Day in the Life of a Leader

On September 23, 2015, Dr. Martin Winterkorn was sitting in his office, shocked and helplessly watching his kingdom collapse due a scandal that soon would be labeled "Dieselgate."

Winterkorn was a brilliant engineer and a highly successful manager. After finishing his PhD at the world-famous Max Planck Institute he started a career that culminated in 2007, when he was appointed CEO of the Volkswagen group. One of the first decisions he made was to set the goal of beating Toyota and becoming the leading car producer in the world. Pursuing an aggressive growth strategy, Winterkorn achieved this ambitious goal within 8 years. Under his leadership the company almost doubled its sales and tripled its profits. In July 2015, Volkswagen surpassed Toyota and became number one. Obviously, this growth was achieved without compromising equally ambitious sustainability goals: Also in 2015, the company proudly announced that the highly influential Dow Jones Sustainability Index had ranked it the world's most sustainable automotive group. Winterkorn was riding the waves of success.

However, he did not have much time to enjoy this seemingly most successful year in his career: On September 18, U.S. authorities revealed that they suspected the company of having manipulated the software of its diesel engines in VW and Audi cars in order to artificially lower toxic nitrogen oxides emissions during obligatory emissions tests in the United States and elsewhere. Volkswagen had to admit the manipulation of at least 11 million vehicles. Nitrogen oxides are responsible for the smog that provokes respiratory diseases in zones with a high traffic density. In the United States, such emissions are thus strictly regulated under the Clean Air Act. Emissions are at the same time the key issue when it comes to the evaluation of corporate responsibility in the automotive industry.

According to the U.S. Environmental Protection Agency, Volkswagen is facing penalties of up to US$ 18 billion in the United States alone. In addition to those penalties, the company will be exposed to class-action lawsuits and criminal charges around the world. It will have to organize costly callbacks and lose sales; the precious Volkswagen brand, the symbol of German engineering art, is severely damaged. The whole corporate social responsibility (CSR) engagement of the company is now perceived as a clever greenwashing exercise. Financial markets understood the risks of the manipulation immediately: "Dieselgate," as the scandal was labeled, wiped out almost US$ 26 billion of Volkswagen's market value within a week. The title of the largest car producer was lost again to Toyota in October as a direct consequence of the scandal.

On September 23, 2015, after some hesitation, Martin Winterkorn resigned as CEO of the Volkswagen group. In a statement published by the company, he stated that he was shocked by this massive misconduct. He announced that he would resign "in the interests of the company even though I am not aware of any wrong doing on my part." Since then, the company has desperately tried to break the wall of silence that surrounds the manipulation. Engineers and line managers refuse to speak about it, and a rising tide of critical voices accuses Winterkorn of having established a culture of pressure and fear.

### Discussion Questions

1. Assuming that Winterkorn was not personally involved in the manipulation, can we still consider him responsible for the scandal?

2. What does the scandal teach us about the link between CSR and leadership?

3. Do corporate leaders have a responsibility to others who are not shareholders in the company? Why, or why not?

# Chapter Overview

Corporations do not exist in a vacuum. They are embedded in a highly complex societal context in which they are confronted with expectations that transcend their economic responsibility in a narrow sense. They have additional social and environmental responsibilities. Scholars in the business and society field disagree about the limits and scope of those responsibilities and even about the terminology they use when describing the role of business in society. Sustainability, corporate social responsibility, and corporate citizenship are some of the labels used—often with overlapping or even identical meaning. We might leave discussions on terminology to the experts who are interested in it. I will make a fuzzy use of those terms and mainly refer to CSR in this chapter and argue that it has become a key pillar of corporate legitimacy.

Corporations have to meet increasing expectations with regard to the social and environmental side effects of their activities in order to be perceived as legitimate actors. Legitimacy can be defined as "a generalized perception or assumption that the actions of an entity are desirable, proper or appropriate within some socially constructed system of norms, values, beliefs, and definitions" (Suchman, 1995, p. 574). Without legitimacy, corporations risk losing the support of their key constituents (Pfeffer & Salancik, 1978). Governments might, for instance, impose stricter regulations, customers might not buy their products anymore, non-governmental organizations (NGOs) might launch campaigns against them and damage their reputational capital, and employees might lose their motivation.

Leadership has been argued to be a key driver of corporate ethics in general (Ciulla, 1999; Paine, 1996; Parry & Proctor-Thomson, 2002; Weaver, Treviño, & Cochran, 1999) and the societal engagement of a company in particular (Mazutis & Zintel, 2015; Ramus, 2001; Treviño, Brown, & Hartman, 2003; Waldman & Siegel, 2005). However, while the debate on CSR has existed for decades, it has been rather silent when it comes to the role of leadership (Doh & Stumpf, 2005; Waldman & Siegel, 2005). Instead, CSR has mainly been discussed along an anthropomorphized understanding of the corporation, similar to how I started this chapter, neglecting the microfoundation of the phenomenon (Morgeson, Aguinis, Waldman, & Siegel, 2013). This silence on leadership is surprising, given the large impact leaders have on the direction corporations take: Research has shown that leaders particularly at the top of the hierarchy have power and discretion (Finkelstein & Hambrick, 1990; Hambrick & Finkelstein, 1987). Decisions that are made in corporations reflect the preferences of the top-level leaders and the interests they represent (Hambrick, 2007; Hambrick & Mason, 1984). The debate on corporate governance is based on the assumption that the alignment of the interest of leaders with those of shareholders is important for the success of corporations (e.g., Rechner & Dalton, 1991). Organizations and their culture are discussed as a reflection of the organization's leadership (Schein, 1992, 1996). The way organizations perform their various responsibilities depends on how leaders perceive and manage them (e.g., Burns & Kedia, 2006; Coles, Daniel, & Naveen, 2006; McWilliams, Siegel, & Wright, 2006). The characteristics (traits, behaviors, preferences, or what have you) of leaders ultimately determine corporate social outcomes (Christensen, Mackey, & Whetten, 2014). If leadership is key for the understanding of corporations, why did the discussion on CSR only recently discover its relevance?

The objective of this chapter is to explain why research on leadership had been more or less absent from the debate on CSR, why this has started to change in recent years, and how the interface of leadership and CSR has to be theorized. I will argue that the high-speed transformation of our society at the beginning of the 21st century is disrupting the established institutional order of the last century. As a consequence of this disruption, the power balance between corporations and governments is changing. Operating along globally stretched value chains, multinational corporations operate in a regulatory vacuum in which they get connected to numerous social and environmental problems—from climate change to modern slavery. Their activities get morally discussed and societal expectations increase. The unprecedented historic change that redefines the role of business in society creates tremendous uncertainties and thus requires disruptive visionary thinking. In stable times, it might be sufficient to *manage* corporations most of the time, but in historic moments of disruptive change, where established practices, values, and beliefs become dysfunctional and the direction of change is unclear, leadership becomes important. Given this distinction between management and leadership, I will use the terms with the connotation of whether decisions can draw from strong routines (*management*) or whether they require imagination and innovation with regard to the societal impact of the corporation (*leadership*).

Decision-making routines of the past become challenged and taken-for-granted beliefs about the responsibilities of a corporation get normatively challenged. New responsibilities for social and environmental problems move center stage and corporations get attacked in a moral language game managers are not used to speaking and barely understand in the context of their previous decision-making routines. I will argue that such a situation requires leaders who can understand and manage CSR-related challenges that emerge along their globally stretched operations. They can do so only by using the language game in which they are approached by their various stakeholders today: moral values. Responsible leaders have to transcend the assumption that it is enough to align their values with those of their followers as it is argued in the context of transformational leadership theory. Rather, they have to integrate three different value-based perspectives: the first-order perspective of value accordance (acting in accordance with their own values), the second-order perspective of value alignment (aligning their own values with those of their followers and the larger circle of stakeholders), and finally the third-order perspective of transnational cosmopolitanism (transcending the local context and taking a universal perspective).

## Corporate Social Responsibility in the 20th Century: No Need for Leadership

For decades, a particular ideology has dominated both management theory and practice: the ideology of shareholder value maximization. In 1970, the economist Milton Friedman published an article in the *New York Times* that became the moral compass for generations of managers. In a nutshell, Friedman argued that managers have fiduciary duties toward the owners of their company and thus must make decisions that are aligned with the interest of those owners. The interest of shareholders is to make as much money as possible. Therefore, according to Friedman, profit maximization is the *only* social responsibility of corporations. How can this be morally justified? Why should society accept such an egoistic behavior? Neoliberal theory offers three answers. First, property rights are a key human right that differentiates the "free" capitalist system from the communist system (after all, in the early 1970s the ideological fight between the two systems was undecided). Property rights of free individuals have to be defended against any arbitrary use of political power by governments. Second, referring to the idea of Adam Smith's invisible hand, neoliberal scholars argue that the self-regulatory forces of the market will transform egoistic individual transactions into welfare for the whole society. Finally, a core assumption of neoliberal theory is that homo sapiens essentially is a homo economicus and thus only interested in his or her own utility maximization. Markets thus mirror the natural predisposition of human actors (Ferraro, Pfeffer, & Sutton, 2005; Gonin, Palazzo, & Hoffrage, 2012). When in 2008 at the climax of the financial crisis, Lloyd Blankfein, the CEO of Goldman Sachs, was attacked for the ruthless greed for which his company had become a symbol, he answered that he was just "doing God's work." This statement reflects very well the deep belief in the idea that profit maximization is good for society.

Of course, Friedman did not advocate a maximization of profit at any price. Limits are set by the rule of law and also, as other scholars have argued, by the values and principles that dominate the society in which the corporations are embedded. As Granovetter (1985) has, for instance, emphasized, "the pursuit of economic self-interest was typically not an uncontrollable 'passion' but a civilized, gentle activity" (p. 488). Friedman's thin definition of corporate responsibility has been contested by scholars in the business and society domain who argued, for instance, that companies do not only have shareholders but also stakeholders (i.e., actors who affect or are affected by the decisions leaders make in corporations such as customers or employees) and thus must manage potentially colliding interests of those different groups instead of maximizing the interests of just one group (Freeman, 1984). These scholars, however, agree with Friedman's key argument that the responsibility of corporations is to comply with the rules of the game (however thin or thick they might be defined). While Milton Friedman (1970, p. 218) argued that companies have to comply with the "basic rules of society," business ethics scholars made very similar claims, arguing that the points of reference for a company are the "broader community values" (Swanson, 1999, p. 517) or that companies must comply with the social expectations "at a given point in time" (Carroll, 1979, p. 500). As a result, the debate on CSR in the 20th century was implicitly based on three basic assumptions: First, corporations are embedded in a more or less functioning and more or less democratic regulatory context. Second, the main responsibility of managers and their companies is to follow the rules of the game. Third, there is a clear division of labor between managers and politicians: Managers pursue private interests and politicians make public rules.

Shareholder value ideology is a child of the Cold War, developed for the capitalist world of Friedman's time: the United States, Europe, and Japan. According to Milton Friedman (1970), if shareholder value maximization leads to negative environmental or social side effects, politicians have the responsibility to deal with it, not managers. Indeed, managers will (and should!) deal with social and environmental issues only if they clearly increase the profits of the company itself (Baron, 2003; Jones, 1995). Such an understanding of responsibility does not require leadership skills. It requires the transactional abilities of managers to fulfill narrowly defined fiduciary duties toward one particular group of actors (shareholders) while complying with the basic rules of their more or less stable and predictable sociopolitical context. It requires no values beyond this feeling of fiduciary duty; no moral aspirations, since such higher-order goals should be separated strictly from the managerial role and can be enacted by the managers in their other roles as parents or churchgoers (M. Friedman, 1970). If the company is just a "nexus of contracts" (Jensen & Meckling, 1976), responsible management requires no deeper understanding of society, no broader horizon, no visionary thinking. It requires no sophisticated concepts of motivation, since objectives can be achieved via the design of corporate governance systems that sufficiently control the managers and set financial incentives that align the potentially deviating interests of the manager with those of the shareholder (Jensen & Meckling, 1976; Sundaram & Inkpen, 2004; Williamson, 1975). Compliance with taken-for-granted rules can be managed more or less on autopilot; it requires no leadership.

Under these conditions, it comes as no surprise that the discussion on leadership entered the debate on corporate social responsibility rather lately and timidly (e.g., Doh & Stumpf, 2005). However, the societal context in which corporations operate is drastically changing, and what were perceived as legitimate routines in the 20th century might lead to legitimacy problems today. Managerial beliefs, values, and practices that shaped decision making in corporations since the late 1960s are becoming dysfunctional. The societies in which managers are making their decisions are going through a paradigm shift—and paradigm shifts create instability and uncertainty, which in turn require leadership qualities.

## "May You Lead in Interesting Times!"

Responsible leaders keep their organizational ship on course in the rough waters of constant societal change. They tenaciously pursue the organizational purpose, aligned with their values and those of their followers (Drath et al., 2008), ideally crafting a vision with an ethical aspiration that points beyond the immediate benefit of the organization itself (Antonakis et al., 2016). Such leaders are transformational in the best sense of the word. There are times in which leaders are highly familiar with the sea and times in which they embark on a journey in uncharted waters. There are times in which the sea is comparably calm and times in which the organizational ship is shaken—and sometimes even drowned—by a tempest. The old Chinese curse "may you live in interesting times" certainly resonates with how leaders experience such a challenging decision-making environment.

While human history is one of constant change, only very rarely does this change take "warp speed" (T. L. Friedman, 2005, p. 46). Drucker (1973) has argued that profound societal transformations occur in moments where sociopolitical changes get leveraged and amplified by new information technologies. When in 1989 the Berlin Wall came down, the bipolar world order that had provided a unique societal stability for almost five decades collapsed. In that same year, the World Wide Web was invented by Tim Berners-Lee at the CERN in Geneva. This new information technology soon started to amplify the sociopolitical changes that the end of the communist system had provoked (Floridi, 2014). Since the 1990s, the consequences of this profound change have been scrutinized. The discussion takes two basic directions: Some have argued that the world becomes flatter (T. L. Friedman, 2005) and more strongly connected (Castells, 1996), with the liberal market economies spreading globally (Fukuyama, 1992). Others have predicted a tribalization of the world, with a return of nationalism (Ignatieff, 1995) and more conflicts along ethnic and religious frontiers (Huntington, 1993).

What those authors agree upon is the overwhelming speed of change, the high complexity and volatility of our time, and the increasing risks connected to decisions made in business and politics (Beck, 2000, 2007; Taleb, 2012). The U.S. Army War College has described the present context as VUCA times, arguing that its key characteristics are volatility (speed and magnitude of change), uncertainty (lack of predictability), complexity (unclear and multiple causalities), and ambiguity (lack of clarity around events; Kinsinger & Walch, 2012; Lawrence, 2013).

VUCA times change the decision-making context of leaders in corporations drastically because they challenge the validity of taken-for-granted practices, values, and beliefs. What is currently changing in particular is the understanding of the responsibility of corporations in society. A lack of understanding for those changes unavoidably leads to legitimacy problems. Our values, beliefs, and practices develop over time and get frozen in routines of world perception and habits of decision making. The longer such routines have been successful, the less they require leadership attention and the more they are change-resistant—a highly risky combination for corporations.

## The Legitimacy Crisis of the Disembedded Corporation

Porter and Kramer (2011, p. 64) observed that "the legitimacy of business has fallen to levels not seen in recent history." Legitimacy describes the overall societal perception that the existence and behavior of a corporation (or any other organization) are appropriate according to the values, norms, and principles that dominate society at a given point in time. Obviously, there are growing concerns about the appropriateness of managerial decision making in corporations. Corporations are discussed as "barbarians at the gate" (Burrough & Helyar, 2004), "cannibals with forks" (Elkington, 1998), or "robber barons" (Burbach, 2001). They become increasingly targeted by NGOs (den Hond & de Bakker, 2007) and are criticized for a lack of engagement for the common good (Barley, 2007).

The fall of the Berlin Wall accelerated the process of globalization (Giddens, 1999; Palazzo, 2015), leading to a new sociopolitical order that has been described as postnational (Habermas, 2001) or post-Westphalian (Kobrin, 2001). Power has shifted from the sovereign of the territory to the masters of speed (Habermas, 2001). The events of 1989 opened up the possibility for corporations to stretch their operations globally. International business as such is not new. However, before the fall of the Berlin Wall, it meant, rather, that corporations produced in places where they wanted to sell their products (Harney, 2009). Constantly falling trade barriers, the establishment of free trade zones, tax incentives, and falling costs for transportation and communication enabled corporations to operate transnationally (Held,

McGrath, Goldblatt, & Perraton, 1999). Therefore, in the late 1980s a different type of internationalization took off: Visionary leaders such as Phil Knight, the founder of Nike, soon realized that they could shift production from the United States and Europe to much cheaper places such as Indonesia, South Korea first, China and Vietnam later in this process. Production was increasingly outsourced to developing countries with low wages (Schrempf-Stirling & Palazzo, 2016). Starting with simple products such as apparel, outsourcing strategies were later applied in the production of complex products such as cars, drugs, and computer hardware as well (Santoro, 2009).

The production in developing countries with weak and corrupt regulatory systems often took place in factories with questionable working conditions including but not limited to the use of child labor, long overtime work, below-minimum-wage salaries, and violation of health and safety standards (Sethi, 2003). These so-called sweatshops not only provoked numerous campaigns of NGOs against multinational corporations (MNCs; Connor, 2002) but also reoriented the debate on CSR where scholars started to discuss whether or not MNCs should be held morally responsible for the worker rights violations committed by their legally independent suppliers (Arnold, 2003; Arnold & Bowie, 2003; Sethi, 2003). While this discussion started as an attack on the apparel industry (Zadek, 2004), it has reached out into numerous other global supply chains, including coffee, cocoa, bananas, computers, mobile phones, cars, sugar, tombstones, gold, diamonds, oil, and many other products (for a historical analysis of the debate, see Schrempf-Sterling & Palazzo, 2016). Furthermore, corporations have been accused of being complicit in human rights violations that occur in the societies where they operate. What started as a debate on the responsibility of Shell for the human rights violations committed by the Abacha regime in Nigeria (Clapham & Jerbi, 2001; Human Rights Watch, 1995) has led to an intensive debate on the responsibility of corporations for promoting human rights (Ruggie, 2007), fighting corruption (Misangyi, Weaver, & Elms, 2008), or maintaining and restoring peace (Fort & Schipani, 2004).

Until the late 1980s, corporations operated in more or less well-regulated, democratic, and stable and predictable societal contexts. With their globally stretched production networks, they suddenly operate in zones of conflict such as the Congo; countries with weak and corrupt governance such as Bangladesh, Nigeria, or India; and repressive contexts such as China or Iran. The taken-for-granted assumption that companies just have to follow the rules of the game makes no sense anymore. The idea that governments provide a reliable regulatory context for the business activities of companies becomes doubtful. What has become increasingly evident since the late 1980s is that the implicit contract between governments and corporations that Milton Friedman assumed is broken. As Barber (2000, p. 275) has argued, "we have removed capitalism from the institutional 'box' that has (quite literally) domesticated it and given its sometimes harsh practices a human face." While companies have gone global, regulation did not follow at the same pace. In the following, I will first describe the changing decision-making context of leaders before I propose a concept of responsible leadership that corresponds to those emerging challenges.

## The New Morally and Politically Enlightened Understanding of Leadership Responsibility

The current legitimacy crisis of the multinational corporation results from a clash between new moral expectations and traditional liability-based managerial decision-making routines. When in the 1990s, NGOs started to target corporations for sweatshop working conditions, the reaction of leaders at companies such as Levi's or Nike was defensive and well aligned with the compliance-oriented understanding of responsibility that had been their point of reference since the 1970s. Basically, they argued that they could not be held responsible for problems that occurred at their legally independent suppliers (Zadek, 2004). However, over time, some leaders understood the legitimacy risks to which they were exposed and started to broaden their idea of responsibility. Under the leadership of Phil Knight, Nike developed a sophisticated audit and certification programs for its business partners. In other companies, codes of conduct for suppliers were developed, third-party auditors were sent to factories, human rights due diligence was done in countries with repressive regimes, and ambitious environmental visions were announced. As Walsh (2005) stated, in some companies, leaders started to implement practices that are not even required by the most demanding normative business ethics theories. Put differently, there was no theory available to make sense of such behavior. In the early 2000s, some scholars started to challenge the taken-for-granted division of labor between corporations and governments and discussed a *politicization* of the corporation (Matten & Crane, 2005; Palazzo & Scherer, 2006; Scherer & Palazzo, 2007; Scherer, Palazzo, & Baumann, 2006; Young, 2004). As those scholars argued, corporate leaders stepped in where governmental decision makers were either not able or not willing to play their regulatory role. They engage in governance without government (Rosenau & Czempiel, 1992).

The rise of the MNC has led to a new phase of capitalism in which the traditional narrow understanding of CSR gets delegitimized. Under the condition of globalization, responsible leadership requires three new decision-making qualities: first, to understand the wickedness of leadership decisions; second, to make morally enlightened decisions; and third, to make politically enlightened decisions. The common good, which was basically perceived as a responsibility of governmental leaders in the past or as a kind of automatic side effect of self-interested profit maximization, moves center stage in corporate decision making (Scherer & Palazzo, 2007).

**Understanding the Wickedness of Leadership Decisions.** The traditional compliance-oriented concept of responsibility assumes problems with low complexity, mainly local impact, and the belief in what Lackoff (2004) has called "direct causation." Direct causation refers to simply cause-effect relations where causalities and responsibilities are obvious and direct action is possible to deal with them: Actor $x$ has caused harm $y$ and must do $z$ to stop or alleviate the harm or else get punished. This is based on the assumption that such causalities can be grasped in a purely scientific language game by advancing or following "facts" that allow for an objective analysis of a particular issue. While in the 20th-century more or less stable context with comparably low complexity and a clear separation of work between governments and business organizations, these assumptions were more or less plausible as a road map for managerial decision making. They become problematic in VUCA times because the character of problems that corporations are confronted with has changed. Problems are increasingly wicked.

If the concept of VUCA times describes the current state of our postnational world, wicked problems might be the appropriate concept when it comes to understanding how managers in organizations perceive their challenges. The concept of wicked problems was introduced by Rittel and Webber (1973). According to these authors, wicked problems share some of the following characteristics: There is no consensus about the problem and its causes, only colliding interpretations. Leaders have incomplete information. Problems are moving targets, they change over time and with a certain probability, and they will probably never be solved completely (e.g., slavery and poverty have been constant phenomena throughout human history). There is no consensus about appropriate solutions, and leaders might even change their own evaluation of a problem as they go about solving it. Solutions might provoke unintended side effects; decisions risk creating path dependencies if they require massive investments. Solutions are difficult to apply across contexts since constellations of wickedness are unique. Wicked problems are nonlinear. They are connected and might reinforce each other. When we look at the social and environmental problems leaders are expected to solve along the supply chains of their corporations, such as global warming, water stress, poverty, slavery, worker rights, or navigating in repressive political structures, we immediately grasp their wickedness. Organizational scholars increasingly acknowledge the need to address such problems that have also been labeled "grand challenges" (Ferraro et al., 2015). Most important, wicked problems are highly moralized, given that normative routines don't apply and the moral neutrality of leadership decisions that Friedman assumed is no longer perceived as legitimate.

**Demonstrating Morally Enlightened Leadership.** While neoliberal ideology has advocated value-free managerial decision-making assigning ethics to the private life (M. Friedman, 1970), today's decisions are unavoidably loaded with normativity that leads to clashes between interpretations and expectations, regardless of the scientific facts behind a particular issue (Palazzo & Scherer, 2006). Recently, Nestlé was attacked for bottling water in California despite the devastating drought the state was facing. Based on the evidence that its tiny water business in California had no impact on the drought, Tim Brown, the CEO of Nestlé Waters, stated that his company had no intention to stop the bottling of water on the West Coast because there was no link between Nestlé's activities and the drought. In a local radio interview, he aggressively stated that he would take even more water there if he could (Neate, 2015). What he completely underestimated in his reaction was the symbolic dimensions of water bottling, a highly disputed business already without the California drought. Nestlé Waters is perceived as *morally* connected to the California drought, whether it wants it or not. Furthermore, it is expected to play an active role in solving the problem, and not just doing business as usual as if it were disconnected from water bottling's sociopolitical context.

While in the past, actors have been held responsible for their own decisions and the consequences thereof (both in a moral and a legal sense), the debate on social and environmental side effects of global production have inspired a historically unprecedented understanding of responsibility. Young (2004) has labeled the traditional understanding a *liability concept of responsibility* and proposed a *social connection concept of responsibility* as an alternative. This, of course, does not replace the idea that actors are responsible for what they do themselves, but it adds a new dimension that is of increasing importance in situations where problems result from the highly complex interaction of numerous different actors and where it is difficult to assign responsibility unequivocally to a particular actor. If harm occurs from the interconnectedness of decisions, a liability concept becomes meaningless. This can be demonstrated, for instance, with the example of the above-mentioned labor rights violations in factories. Workers might work overtime with insufficient wages because the factory owner imposes this on them and might easily replace them, or because the MNCs apply constant pressure on delivery speed and costs. Other factors include corrupt governmental inspectors who do not visit the factory, customers who demand ever cheaper goods at an ever higher volume, or workers who want to work as much as possible to accumulate money to get back home to their provinces as fast as possible. None of these reasons alone explains the sweatshop phenomenon; all of them, however, are relevant. For actors in such interconnected processes, it is easy to shift the blame to someone else and disconnect or rationalize their own behavior (Young, 2004). Leaders are increasingly required to make their decisions based on the social connectedness concept of responsibility that assumes that moral duties derive from the following constellation: (a) an actor is causally connected to a harm, (b) they profit from the harm, and (c) they have the resources to reduce or alleviate the harm (Young, 2004).

Corporate leaders have not been elected to fulfill a public responsibility. However, in contexts where governments are absent or corrupt, they increasingly decide (or are pushed) to step in. How can their political engagement be evaluated? Corporations that make decisions on behalf of the common good have to be evaluated along two different aspects (Habermas, 1996; Scherer, Rasche, Palazzo, & Spicer, 2016; Young, 2004). First, the democratic understanding of political decision making requires that binding decisions result from a process of collective decision making in which those affected or their representatives participate. Second, it requires a process of public deliberations in which participants exchange arguments and ideally make decisions based on the convincing power of the better argument instead of following the decisions of those who have the power to manipulate the deliberation. This normally manifests in processes of collaboration between corporations and civil society in so-called multistakeholder initiatives such as the Fair Labor Association or the Forest Stewardship Council. Politically enlightened leadership requires the willingness and ability to engage in a democratically organized regulatory process that (a) includes the suppliers, workers, government representatives, and others who are connected to the problem and (b) follows deliberative standards that give voice to marginalized stakeholders (Mena & Palazzo, 2012).

## Irresponsible Leadership and Corporate Greenwashing

Before outlining my proposal for responsible leadership under the above-described conditions, I would like to investigate inappropriate reactions of leaders to the changing conditions of legitimacy. What worked well in the 20th century—a politically disconnected management style that focused on the moral minimalism of legal compliance—doesn't work anymore in the 21st century, where CSR-related expectations have changed drastically. Corporations face an unprecedented legitimacy crisis due to the social and environmental harm that results from their business activities. Corporations have been increasingly criticized for violating human rights, collaborating with dictators, and polluting the environment. However, to assume that they do so because managers are greedy and evil is too simplistic. Decision-making routines of leaders are only the surface of deeply rooted beliefs and values, and changing what we believe about the world or what we consider important is difficult and tedious. As Diamond (2004) has argued, civilizations often collapse because of fundamental changes that occur and are misinterpreted or poorly understood. In such situations, some societies tend to reinforce exactly those routines that created the problems in the first place. Obviously, corporations are exposed to the same kinds of vulnerability as civilizations. When beliefs about the world are no longer aligned with the direction the world has taken, we would assume that reasonable leaders would adapt their beliefs to the facts. In reality, however, those beliefs are so strong, and their understanding of the changing societal context is so poor, that they ignore the facts (Festinger, Riecken, & Schachter, 1956).

Managers are caught in their institutional routines and often do not see the harm they co-create. They do not see the causal link to their decisions or have no expertise in solving sociopolitical problems. The philosopher Hannah Arendt (1963) once argued that bad things are not necessarily done by bad people but could result from the cooperation of average or even good people who lack the moral imagination to see the harm that results from their decisions. In such a case, leaders might make decisions that are perceived as irresponsible not because they are immoral persons, but because their strong routines blind them for the moral dimension of their decision (Palazzo, Krings, & Hoffrage, 2012) and because their role never required a high moral attentiveness and visionary thinking for social and environmental issues in the past (Reynolds, 2008). On the contrary, in the past, organizations tended to impose moral muteness on their leaders, since talking about values and principles was considered a weakness (Bird & Waters, 1989).

In the past, when the responsibility of companies was narrowly defined, leaders could argue that they were acting responsibly because they followed the rules of the game, created jobs, paid taxes, provided useful products, and sometimes used their discretionary power to give something back to society. The 20th century had established decision-making routines that did not require much attention for societal challenges such as global warming or slavery. Leaders tend to make decisions in accordance with their values and beliefs (Hambrick, 2007). If those values and beliefs circulate around shareholders, it is less probable that the company invests extensively in sustainability (Godos-Dietz et al., 2011). Therefore, the first response leaders—who are still driven by their traditional values and beliefs about responsibility—typically show when they are challenged about their social and environmental responsibility is to engage in philanthropy. They donate money to good causes and sell this engagement as proof of their responsible behavior. When Walmart was attacked on numerous issues—from how it treats its own employees to working conditions at its suppliers—it launched a PR campaign that emphasized the local philanthropic engagement of the company (Beaver, 2005).

While the ethical blindness of leaders might explain some of the current legitimacy problems of corporations, there are obviously also cases of conscious rule breaking for the sake of profit maximization. In such a case, the refusal to adapt to changing societal expectations typically manifests in greenwashing activities: Managers sometimes react to public legitimacy pressure by creating a façade of societal engagement for their corporation, using the expected sustainability vocabulary in their communication while trying to keep their business operations unchanged behind this PR façade (Laufer, 2003). Why do they do so? In transition times, it is often much easier to understand that change is occurring than to understand which direction it will take—the U of uncertainty in VUCA. Making a bet on one possible future is risky; sticking to routines that feel familiar is easier. Furthermore, managers in corporations receive mixed signals: Their shareholders tell them and incentivize them to continue with business as usual, while NGOs confront them with a new type of expectation they never faced before in a (moral) language they didn't have to understand and speak in their role as corporate leaders before. Greenwashing could be considered an easy way out by some managers under such conditions. The quests for profits can induce cheating on stakeholders, and given that such leaders are socialized with a much thinner idea of corporate responsibility, they might perceive their cheating as harmless or even appropriate (Ariely & Jones, 2012; Mazar, Amir, & Ariely, 2008; Mazar & Ariely, 2006).

Whether the Dieselgate scandal of Volkswagen results from the ethical blindness of the company leaders or, rather, represents a case of conscious immoral and illegal behavior remains an open question. The currently available information seems to signal a mix of both effects. As the opening case illustrates, the recent Volkswagen scandal demonstrates that whereas the automotive industry feels pressure to become more sustainable, the direction of such an engagement is difficult to determine. There are various technologies they can choose from ranging from hydro to electric energy solutions and each technology requires tremendous financial investments. Given the speed of change, companies sometimes risk betting on the wrong technology. Furthermore, customers hesitate to buy cars with alternative technologies that are better for the environment and continue to ask for big polluting cars, especially as fuel prices plummet. As a result, car producers hesitate to invest significantly in new technologies and innovations rather come from outside: Tesla innovates the battery; Google experiments with self-driving vehicles. Companies like Volkswagen do not have an ambitious strategy of green mobility. Instead of disrupting old technologies, they try to optimize them in a way that they comply with growing sustainability expectations without changing their business strategy itself. Volkswagen was betting on diesel technology and tried to reduce emissions. It was under pressure to comply with ever more demanding emissions standards, in particular in the U.S. market. This pressure created trade-offs between sustainability and profits. The higher the performance of an engine with regard to emissions reduction, the higher the overall vehicle costs. For small cars, this sooner or later leads to a point where shrinking margins make it difficult to comply with the laws while still making a profit. Volkswagen pursued an aggressive strategy of market growth and profit maximization as if the world had not changed and tried to hide this behind face-saving greenwashing communication. While most companies in the automotive industry followed the same approach, few of them went as far as Volkswagen and even broke the law. Volkswagen not only lacked leadership with regard to sustainability, it was known for having a culture of fear in which engineers would not dare admit that it could not achieve the reduction of emissions within the limits of the cost planning it was facing. Informing the CEO about such problems would have been a career-terminating move. Volkswagen was recently described as a kind of "North Korea without concentration camps," a label that was used to describe the culture of pressure and fear that had been created by the CEO Winterkorn and his mentor, the former CEO Piech (Hawranek & Kurbjuweit, 2013). The fear inside the company and the awareness of the fact that most companies in the industry manipulate their emissions with borderline immoral and sometimes even outright illegal methods might have created the impression among the engineers that their behavior was appropriate. The engineers, who did not dare to admit that the target publicly set by their CEO was impossible to achieve, started to cheat and probably perceived their cheating as harmless, as argued above, given that their competitors had demonstrated doubtful practices with regard to diesel emissions as well.

While Volkswagen might be an extreme case, the lack of insight in the need for a radically new understanding of responsible leadership is widespread in the board room. The human tendency to search for simple solutions for complex problems manifests in the assumption that sustainability does not challenge the basic ideological assumptions but can be enacted in small adaptations of the established practices, values, and beliefs. Business as usual. A key example of this mindset can be found in the recent work of Michael Porter, one of the most influential management scholars of our time. Together with Mark Kramer, he argued that managers can transform social and environmental problems into win–win solutions for both society and the company. Put differently: They can comply with rising societal expectations without giving up the ideology of profit maximization (Porter & Kramer, 2011). Crane, Palazzo, Matten, and Spence (2014) have recently deconstructed Porter and Kramer's claims as another example of the naive interpretation of wicked problems, and indeed, the many companies that have started to apply the concept of Creating Shared Value point to the small win–win philanthropic projects they have started, such as financing a school here and there. As an answer to the profound change of societal expectation and the complexity of wicked problems companies face along their supply chains, it is obviously inappropriate. One of the key aspects of wickedness is the fact that ideal solutions and win–win options are rare, while most of the time, painful trade-offs are more probable. The purely instrumental vision of making more money with societal problems is a transactional response to a transformational challenge.

If leaders pursue a traditional and narrow understanding of responsible leadership, they will continue to focus on the economic performance of the company and tend to ignore issues they perceive as not relevant to their business (Hahn, Preuss, Pinkse, & Figge, 2014; Pless, Maak, & Waldman, 2012). Such a leadership style, however, is perceived as less inspirational and motivational by followers (Waldman et al., 2011), it tends to be reactive instead of proactive (Basu & Palazzo, 2008; Hahn et al., 2014), and it is obviously not appropriate to deal with wicked problems in a morally and politically enlightened way.

## Toward a New Theory of Responsible Leadership

At the beginning of the 21st century, the ideological narrative that determined managerial decision making since the late 1960s is eroding. As I have argued, VUCA conditions have replaced the relative stability of the 20th century. In stable times, with clear rules and a limited scope and impact of their decisions, managers can decide on CSR-related issues more or less on autopilot. They don't have to be leaders. In unstable times, where they face grand challenges with high levels of environmental uncertainty and accelerated speed of change and where decisions get moralized, managers have to virtually reinvent their organizations and inspire their followers to disrupt their routine beliefs and practices. As Colquitt and George (2011, p. 432) recently pointed out, "the fundamental principles underlying a grand challenge are the pursuit of bold ideas and the adoption of less conventional approaches to tackling large, unresolved problems." Times of high-speed change trigger moral questions because the established regulatory and normative mechanisms used to solve societal problems become inefficient. Under the conditions of the emerging postnational constellation, leadership becomes a key aspect of the CSR discourse.

Responsible leadership with regard to CSR challenges is increasingly being discussed with reference to the concept of transformational and charismatic leadership. As transformational leaders, managers develop a new vision and re-embed their organization in (the globalizing) society by aligning the organizational strategy and purpose to higher-order ideals and values (Antonakis, 2012; Antonakis & House, 2002). As charismatic leaders, they build strong emotional connections to their followers, show contagious passion for their vision, and move it center stage in their communication in order to raise the motivation and ethical aspiration of the followers (Antonakis, Bastardoz, Jacquart, & Shamir, 2016; Jacquart & Antonakis, 2015). These characteristics of transformational and charismatic leadership seem to be well aligned with the above-described need for responsible leadership in a globalizing decision-making context. The concept thus has already been applied to the CSR debate in general and the above-outlined concept of political CSR in particular. Pless and colleagues (2012) have argued that transformational leaders who are inspired by their new political role in geopolitical contexts, where governments are either not able or not willing to sufficiently regulate corporations, understand that the challenges they face with this enlarged responsibility require collective action. Maak, Pless, and Voegtlin (2016) have recently argued that transformational leaders show a social welfare orientation and feel moral obligations toward many stakeholders.

Overall, one gets the impression that responsible leadership is somehow equalized with transformational leadership. I find this application of transformational leadership to CSR not totally convincing. The idea of transformational leadership might build around important elements of responsibility such as values, value alignment, and the common good; however, the concept has been discussed basically along the relationship of leaders and followers. Transformational leadership has not been theorized yet beyond that relationship, since this is what leadership scholars examine in their research. Transformational leadership is about transformative effects inside organizations, promoting the interests of leaders and followers—ideally with good effects for society at large as well, but focused more on the good for the inside group itself (Bass, 1985).

It is possible that the values a transformational leader uses to align and motivate followers around a common goal might be the wrong values or motivate for the wrong goals from a CSR perspective. In addition, I would assume that proponents of transformational leadership have not sufficiently acknowledged the consequences of globalization and, rather, build on the above-criticized 20th-century idea of a neat and clear division of labor between corporations and governments and a stable normative context, manifesting in the rule of law and shared morality. A de-centered concept of responsibility might well resonate with the idea of transformational leadership, but it has not been sufficiently theorized. Furthermore, a purely transformational leadership style might lack the transactional efficiency that leaders need when managing highly complex problems such as working conditions up and down their supply chains, and transactional leadership qualities might be required to implement new social and environmental corporate practices. The idea of authentic leadership (Avolio & Gardner, 2005; Bass & Steidlmeier, 1999) is not sufficient either, since leaders can indeed be authentic and believe in the values they preach, but nonetheless do great harm to society. While the concept of servant leadership does create a reference point for the normative evaluation of leaders, it is still too much centered around the direct relations of leaders and followers, neglecting the universal impact of leadership on a globalizing society (Greenleaf & Spears, 1977).

All these approaches, however, explicitly or implicitly make the assumption that responsible leadership has to do with communicating and performing values and inspiring others to perform those values as well. Responsible leadership thus is by definition value-based leadership (House, 1996), and if it is value-based, it cannot find firm ground in thin instrumental calculations such as the fear to lose reputation. The importance of moral values becomes obvious in the discussion on corporate legitimacy. The current legitimacy crisis creates a situation in which the two basic methods to keep or repair legitimacy do not work anymore: When leaders make decisions that are perceived as inappropriate, they can either manipulate their key stakeholders in a way that they change their evaluation, or they change their behavior and comply with the rules (Suchman, 1995). However, in a globalizing context, with absent or contradictory normative expectations and increased transparency on corporate practices, the impact of those two methods is very limited (Palazzo & Scherer, 2006) or even counterproductive (Scherer, Palazzo, & Seidl, 2013). Instead, corporations have to join the public moral debates in order to redefine the appropriate rules of the game with their leaders as visible and credible voices in the debate (Suchman, 1995).

Values have been defined as "desirable, trans-situational goals, varying in importance, that serve as guiding principles in people's lives" (Schwartz, 1996, p. 2). The leadership debate is not the only debate that highlights the importance and performative power of values. Values are at the core of the individual sense of identity (Hitlin, 2003; Shamir, House, & Arthur, 1993) and simultaneously shared by groups of individuals (Parson, 1991). They are important for the creation of institutions and thereby guide the behavior of large groups (Rao, Monin, & Durand, 2003) and individual actors at the same time (Hitlin & Piliavin, 2004; Maio, Pakizeh, Cheung, & Rees, 2009). As Gecas (2000, p. 95) has argued, "people feel pride and satisfaction at the affirmation of their values, guilt and shame if not living up to their values, and anger or fear when their values are threatened." Values motivate action (Bansal & Roth, 2000; Gehman, Treviño, & Garud, 2013) and provide meaning (Rokeach, 1973). While normally, values are in a "dormant state" (Maurer, Bansal, & Crossan, 2011, p. 438), they can be activated for driving change (Verplanken & Holland, 2002). As House (1996) has argued, "value-based leadership gives meaning to efforts and goals by connecting them to the deeply held values of [stakeholders]." Recently, Hoffman (2015) has argued that the failure to transform the behavior of people toward a more sustainable lifestyle might be caused by the wrong approach of convincing them: Instead of advancing cold, scientific arguments against global warming, for instance, using tailored narratives that resonate with the values of particular individuals or groups would be much more effective.

Values can be approached from three different perspectives. They are called first-, second-, and third-person perspectives (Keane, 2015; see Figure 18.1). The first-person perspective refers to the values held by individual actors and their ability to act in accordance with those values. From a second-person perspective, we try to act in accordance with the expectations, values, and norms of the communities in which we are embedded. Finally, from a third-person perspective, we try to universalize the application of values and principles independent of space and time, keeping in mind the impact of decisions on humanity in general—both today and in the future. While leadership theories have focused on the first two perspectives (following one's values and aligning personal values with those of followers and stakeholders), the third perspective is largely neglected on the interface of leadership and CSR. My key argument is that responsible leadership in global contexts requires leaders to make careful and balanced decisions along all three dimensions. A decision that is authentic but does not go beyond the first perspective might be good for the individual leader and promote self-perfection, but can turn out to be harmful for stakeholders or unacceptable from a universal perspective. A decision that aligns leaders' and followers' values might not necessarily be appropriate from a universal perspective that transcends the particular community of the leader. And finally, a universally appropriate decision might result in harmful consequences for the leader's immediate stakeholders. The integration of all three dimensions is thus important for the understanding of (global) responsible leadership. This does not, of course, mean that trade-offs between perspectives disappear. It only means that such trade-offs result from a careful moral evaluation instead of a disregard for one or the other perspective.

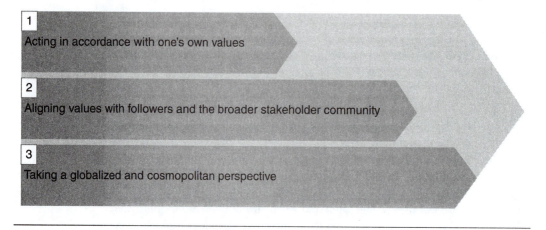

1

Acting in accordance with one's own values

2

Aligning values with followers and the broader stakeholder community

3

Taking a globalized and cosmopolitan perspective

**Figure 18.1**    Three Perspectives of Responsible Leadership

The third perspective can be imagined as a social contract between the organization and society (Donaldson & Dunfee, 1999) by which a leader commits to some universal higher-order values while pursuing the interests of the corporation and his and her own interests. This perspective points to the fact that grand and wicked challenges "extend beyond the boundaries of a single organization or community" (Ferraro et al., 2015, p. 3). Since the 1960s, the global character of modern technology, and in particular the global scope of technological risks, has been discussed (Carson, 1962). Humanmade disasters, resulting from scientific progress, expose humankind to new types of risks. The explosion at Chernobyl demonstrated the potential impact of those new technological risks and spread the awareness of the fact that we live in a risk society (Beck, 1992). The philosopher Hans Jonas (1984) has pointed to the fact that we not only connect across space but also do so across time, influencing the living conditions of future generations through our decisions today. The irreversible character of technological risks imposes a new ethical imperative on us. According to Jonas, we have to consider the consequences of our decisions for people living in remote spatiotemporal context. Today, most human challenges follow a transnational logic. They cannot be solved inside individual nation-states but require transnational and transgenerational mindsets and collaboration (Beck, 2007). The third moral perspective provides such a mindset. It resonates with Immanuel Kant's idea of a cosmopolitan world order that he developed in his essay on perpetual peace in 1795. While Kant was hoping for a globalized rule of law to end war, philosophers today interpret cosmopolitanism as a cultural process of developing transnational values and a transnationally shared indignation for the violation of such values (Appiah, 2007; Benhabib, 2008; Held, 2010). Today, responsible leaders have to critically evaluate whether the values in which they believe are aligned with their followers' values, resonate with the larger community of stakeholders in which their organization is embedded, and promote transcendental moral objectives beyond such communities and independent from time and space.

**Table 18.1**   Corporate Responsibility in the 20th and 21st Centuries

| Corporate Responsibility in the 20th Century | Corporate Responsibility in the 21st Century |
| --- | --- |
| Shareholder value maximization | Embedded and enlightened pursuit of profit |
| Clear division of labor between corporations and governments, governance by governments | Corporations as political actors, governance without governments |
| Focus on first- and second-person value perspective in a mainly local and national context | Additional focus on third-person value perspective in a mainly global context |
| Liability concept of responsibility (mainly manifesting in following legal rules) | Social-connectedness concept of responsibility (mainly manifesting in the global co-creation and interpretation of moral rules) |
| Nationally embedded business operations | Globally stretched supply chains |
| Relative stable and predictable sociopolitical context | Transnational context, VUCA times |
| Moral evaluations are more or less static and more or less homogeneous | Moral evaluations change at high speed and are heterogeneous and contradictory |
| Responsibility could be "managed" with a minimal investment in moral reflections (compliance-orientation) | Responsibility requires the systematic analysis of moral issues and visionary thinking |
| No need for multistakeholder collaboration | Main activities occur in multistakeholder networks |
| Responsibility is voluntary/discretionary | Responsibility is strategic |

In contrast to the above-discussed example of Volkswagen, some leaders have already started to redirect their companies in such a direction. The founder of Patagonia, Yvon Chouinard, is an example of a visionary leader who challenges the prevailing economic paradigm of growth and consumption. He acknowledges the limits of our growth-driven economy and invites consumers to buy less stuff. Patagonia created a system of reuse and repair to reduce the environmental impact of the company's products. Chouinard understood early on that only in the interface of production conditions and consumer habits can sustainable practices be established. He has developed a vision of an economy that "cultivates healthy communities, creates meaningful work, and takes from the earth only what it can replenish." The vision of Patagonia—discussed as the "New American Dream" on its website—is initiated on the basis of the founder's moral convictions, based on broadly shared values, and simultaneously takes a broader and global perspective by developing an alternative concept of the economy (degrowth), alternative consumption practices, and this vision is enacted in numerous partnerships and multistakeholder initiatives.

Paul Polman, the CEO of Unilever, is another example of a leader who has demonstrated powerful moral skills already with regard to the third moral perspective.

Under his leadership, Unilever has drafted the "Sustainability Living Plan" (Unilever, 2015, cited in Maak et al., 2016), which pursues the ambitious goal of decoupling growth from a negative environmental and social impact. Explicitly building on the insights of the VUCA concept, the company pledged to reduce its environmental footprint and increase its social impact while doubling its business in the next 10 years (Lawrence, 2013). As Polman (cited in Maak et al., 2016) has argued, "We firmly believe that if we focus our company on improving the lives of the world's citizens and come up with genuine solutions, we are more in sync with consumers and society and ultimately this will result in good shareholder returns." He confronts grand challenges with "humility" and the insight that Unilever needs "to invite other people in," since it "cannot do it alone" (cited in Ferraro, Etzion, & Gehman, 2015).

As these examples show, responsible leadership does not require giving up the profit motive. However, leaders who are able to make a systematic moral evaluation have understood that sustainable profits cannot be made in rotten societies and thus, promoting a healthy business environment is important. In both cases, bold visions of sustainable business were translated into deep organizational changes that also require transactional leadership skills.

Leaders in corporations can no longer assume that someone else (e.g., politicians) will take care of the problems around them. The postnational constellation has disrupted the cozy business environment of the last decades, the golden age of comparably low complexity. As a result, the role of business in society and the conditions of corporate legitimacy are renegotiated globally. Therefore, it comes as no surprise that leadership enters the debate on corporate responsibility. Without responsible, value-based leadership, corporations will hardly learn to navigate safely in the rough waters of the emerging global world order.

## Discussion Questions

1. Why does the management of CSR require value-based leadership?
2. What are the key differences between corporate responsibility in the 20th and 21st centuries?
3. Why do corporations become political actors?
4. What is greenwashing, and what does it have to do with leadership?

## Recommended Readings

- Crane, A., Palazzo, G., Matten, D., & Spence, L. (2014). Contesting the value of the shared value concept. *California Management Review, 56*(2), 130–153.
- Pless, N. M., Maak, T., & Waldman, D. A. (2012). Different approaches toward doing the right thing: Mapping the responsibility orientations of leaders. *Academy of Management Perspectives, 26*, 51–65.
- Scherer, A. G., & Palazzo, G. (2011). The new political role of business in a globalized world: A review of a new perspective on CSR and its implications for the firm, governance, and democracy. *Journal of Management Studies, 48*, 899–931.

## Recommended Case Studies

- **Case:** Carroll, G., Schifrin, D., & Brady, D. (2013). Nike: Sustainability and labor practices 2008–2013. Harvard Business Publishing. https://cb.hbsp.harvard.edu/cbmp/product/IB106-PDF-ENG
- **Case:** Paine, L. S., Hsieh, N., & Adamsons, L. (2013). Governance and sustainability at Nike. Harvard Business Publishing. https://cb.hbsp.harvard.edu/cbmp/product/313146-PDF-ENG

## Recommended Videos

- Chouinard, Y. (2014). Yvon Chouinard: The company as activist. https://www.youtube.com/watch?v=sbsLeXldDrg
- Palazzo, G. (2014). Guido Palazzo: TEDx Responsible consumption—the soft power of story-telling. https://www.youtube.com/watch?v=j7c9b9A2AHc
- van Heerden, A. (2010). Auret van Heerden: TEDx Making global labor fair. https://www.ted.com/talks/auret_van_heerden_making_global_labor_fair

## References

Antonakis, J. (2012). Transformational and charismatic leadership. In D. V. Day & J. Antonakis (Eds.), *The nature of leadership* (pp. 256–288). Thousand Oaks, CA: Sage.

Antonakis, J., Bastardoz, N., Jacquart, P., & Shamir, B. (2016). Charisma: An ill-defined and ill-measured gift. *Annual Review of Organizational Psychology and Organizational Behavior, 3,* 293–319.

Antonakis, J., & House, R. J. (2002). The full-range leadership theory: The way forward. In B. J. Avolio & F. J. Yammarino (Eds.), *Transformational and charismatic leadership: The road ahead* (pp. 3–33). Amsterdam, Netherlands: JAI.

Appiah, K. A. (2007). *Cosmopolitanism: Ethics in a world of strangers.* New York, NY: W. W. Norton.

Arendt, H. (1963). *Eichman in Jerusalem: A report on the banality of evil.* New York, NY: Viking Press.

Ariely, D., & Jones, S. (2012). *The (honest) truth about dishonesty.* New York, NY: HarperAudio.

Arnold, D. G. (2003). Exploitation and the sweatshops quandary. *Business Ethics Quarterly, 13*(2), 243–256.

Arnold, D. G., & Bowie, N. E. (2003). Sweatshops and respect for persons. *Business Ethics Quarterly, 13*(2), 221–242.

Avolio, B. J., & Gardner, W. L. (2005). Authentic leadership development: Getting to the root of positive forms of leadership. *The Leadership Quarterly, 16,* 315–338.

Bansal, P., & Roth, K. (2000). Why companies go green: A model of ecological responsiveness. *Academy of Management Journal, 43,* 717–736.

Barber, B. (2000). Can democracy survive globalization? *Government and Opposition, 3,* 275–301.

Barley, S. R. (2007). Corporations, democracy, and the public good. *Journal of Management Inquiry, 16,* 201–215.

Baron, D. P. (2003). Private politics. *Journal of Economics & Management Strategy, 12,* 31–66.

Bass, B. M., & Steidlmeier, P. (1999). Ethics, character, and authentic transformational leadership behavior. *Leadership Quarterly, 10*(2), 181–217.

Basu, K., & Palazzo, G. (2008). Corporate social responsibility: A process model of sensemaking. *Academy of Management Review, 33*(1), 122–136.

Beaver, W. (2005). Battling Wal-Mart: How communities can respond. *Business and Society Review, 110*(2), 159–169.

Beck, U. (1992). Risk society. *Towards a new modernity.* Thousand Oaks, CA: Sage.

Beck, U. (2000). *What is globalization?* Cambridge, UK: Polity Press.

Beck, U. (2007). *World at risk.* Cambridge, UK: Polity Press.

Benhabib, S. (2008). *Another cosmopolitanism*. Oxford, UK: Oxford University Press.

Bird, F. B., & Waters, J. A. (1989). The moral muteness of managers. *California Management Review, 32*, 73–88.

Burbach, R. (2001). *Globalization and postmodern politics: From Zapatistas to high-tech robber barons*. London, UK: Pluto Press.

Burns, N., & Kedia, S. (2006). The impact of performance-based compensation on misreporting. *Journal of Financial Economics, 79*(1), 35–67.

Burrough, B., & Helyar, J. (2004). *Barbarians at the gate*. Lancashire, UK: Arrow.

Carroll, A. B. (1979). A three-dimensional conceptual model of corporate performance. *Academy of Management Review, 4*, 497–505.

Carson, R. (1962). *The silent spring*. Boston, MA: Houghton Mifflin.

Castells, M. (1996). *The rise of the network society*. Oxford, UK: Blackwell.

Christensen, L. J., Mackey, A., & Whetten, D. (2014). Taking responsibility for corporate social responsibility: The role of leaders in creating, implementing, sustaining, or avoiding socially responsible firm behaviors. *Academy of Management Perspectives, 28*(2), 164–178.

Ciulla, J. B. (1999). The importance of leadership in shaping business values. *Long Range Planning, 32*(2), 166–172.

Clapham, A., & Jerbi, S. (2001). Categories of corporate complicity in human rights abuses. *Hastings International and Comparative Law Review, 24*, 339–349.

Coles, J. L., Daniel, N. D., & Naveen, L. 2006. Managerial incentives and risk-taking. *Journal of Financial Economics, 79*(2): 431–468.

Colquitt, J. A., & George, G. (2011). Publishing in AMJ—Part 1: Topic choice. *Academy of Management Journal, 54*, 432–435.

Connor, T. (2002). *We are not machines: Clean clothes campaign*. Ottawa, ON, Canada: Oxfam Community Aid Abroad.

Crane, A., Palazzo, G., Matten, D., & Spence, L. (2014). Contesting the value of the shared value concept. *California Management Review, 56*(2), 130–153.

den Hond, F., & de Bakker, F. G. A. (2007). Ideologically motivated activism: How activist groups influence corporate social change activities. *Academy of Management Review, 32*, 901–924.

Diamond, J. (2004). *Collapse: How societies choose to fail or succeed*. London, UK: Penguin.

Doh, J. P., & Stumpf, S. A. (2005). Towards a framework of responsible leadership and governance. In J. P. Doh & S. A. Stumpf (Eds.), *Handbook on responsible leadership and governance in global business* (pp. 3–18). Cheltenham, UK: Edward Elgar.

Donaldson, T., & Dunfee, T. W. (1999). *Ties that bind: A social contracts approach to business ethics*. Boston, MA: Harvard Business Press.

Drath, W. H., McCauley, C. D., Palus, C. J., Van Velsor, E., O'Connor, P. M. G., & McGuire, J. B. (2008). Direction, alignment, commitment: Toward a more integrative ontology of leadership. *The Leadership Quarterly, 19*(6), 635–653.

Drucker, P. (1973). *Management: Tasks, responsibilities, practices*. New York, NY: Harper & Row.

Elkington, J. (1998). *Cannibals with forks: The triple bottom line of 21st century business*. Gabriola Island, BC, Canada: New Society.

Ferraro, F., Etzion, D., & Gehman, J. (2015). Tackling grand challenges pragmatically: Robust action revisited. *Organization Studies, 36*, 363–390.

Ferraro, F., Pfeffer, J., & Sutton, R. I. (2005). Economics language and assumptions: How theories can become self-fulfilling. *Academy of Management Review, (30)*1, 8–24.

Festinger, L., Riecken, H., & Schachter, S. (1956). *When prophecy fails*. Minneapolis: University of Minnesota Press.

Finkelstein, S., & Hambrick, D. C. (1990). Top-management-team tenure and organizational outcomes—The moderating role of managerial discretion. *Administrative Science Quarterly, 35*(3), 484–503.

Floridi, L. (2014). *The fourth revolution: How the infosphere is reshaping human reality*. Oxford, UK: Oxford University Press.

Fort, T. L., & Schipani, C. A. (2004). *The role of business in fostering peaceful societies.* Cambridge, UK: Cambridge University Press.

Freeman, R. E. (1984). *Strategic management: A stakeholder approach.* Boston, MA: Pitman.

Friedman, M. (1970, September 13). The social responsibility of business is to increase its profit. In T. Donaldson & P. H. Werhane (Eds.), *Ethical issues in business: A philosophical approach* (pp. 217–223). Englewood Cliffs, N.J.: Prentice Hall. (Reprinted from *New York Times Magazine*)

Friedman, T. L. (2005). *The world is flat: A brief history of the twenty-first century.* New York, NY: Farrar, Straus & Giroux.

Fukuyama, F. (1992). *The end of history and the last man.* London, UK: Penguin.

Gecas, V. (2000). Value identities, self-motives, and social movements. In S. Stryker, T. J. Owens, & R. W. White (Eds.), *Self, identity, and social movements* (pp. 93–109). Minneapolis: University of Minnesota Press.

Gehman, J., Treviño, L. K., & Garud, R. (2013). Values work: A process study of the emergence and performance of organizational value practices. *Academy of Management Journal, 56,* 84–112.

Giddens, A. (1990). *Consequences of modernity.* Cambridge, UK: Polity Press.

Godos-Diez, J.-L., Fernandez-Gago, R., & Martinez-Campillo, A. (2011). How important are CEOs to CSR practices? An analysis of the mediating effect of the perceived role of ethics and social responsibility. *Journal of Business Ethics, 98,* 531–548.

Gonin, M., Palazzo, G., & Hoffrage, U. (2012). Neither bad apple nor bad barrel—How the societal context impacts unethical behaviour in organizations. *Business Ethics: A European Review, 21*(1), 31–46.

Granovetter, M. (1985). Economic action and social structure: The problem of embeddedness. *The American Journal of Sociology, 91*(3), 481–510.

Greenleaf, R. K., & Spears, L. C. (1977). *Servant leadership: A journey into the nature of legitimate power and greatness.* Mahwah, NJ: Paulist Press.

Habermas, J. (1996). *Between facts and norms: Contributions to a discourse theory of law and democracy.* Cambridge, MA: MIT Press.

Habermas, J. (2001). *The postnational constellation.* Cambridge, MA: MIT Press.

Hahn, T., Preuss, L., Pinkse, J., & Figge, F. (2014). Cognitive frames in corporate sustainability: Managerial sensemaking with paradoxical and business case frames. *Academy of Management Review, 39,* 463–487.

Hambrick, D. C. (2007). Upper echelons theory: An update. *Academy of Management Review, 32,* 334–343.

Hambrick, D. C., & Finkelstein, S. (1987). Managerial discretion—A bridge between polar views of organizational outcomes. *Research in Organizational Behavior, 9,* 369–406.

Hambrick, D. C., & Mason, P. A. (1984). Upper echelons—The organization as a reflection of its top managers. *Academy of Management Review, 9*(2), 193–206.

Harney, A. (2009). *The China price: The true cost of Chinese competitive advantage.* London, UK: Penguin Books.

Hawranek, D., & Kurbjuweit, D. (2013, August 19). Wolfsburger Weltreich. *Der Spiegel.* Retrieved from http://www.spiegel.de/spiegel/print/d-107728908.html

Held, D. (2010). *Cosmopolitanism: Ideals and realities.* Cambridge, UK: Polity Press.

Held, D., McGrath, A., Goldblatt, D., & Perraton, J. (1999). *Global transformations: Politics, economics and culture.* Stanford, CA: Stanford University Press.

Hitlin, S. (2003). Values as the core of personal identity: Drawing links between two theories of self. *Social Psychology Quarterly, 66,* 118–137.

Hitlin, S., & Piliavin, J. A. (2004). Values: Reviving a dormant concept. *Annual Review of Sociology, 30,* 359–393.

Hoffman, A. (2015). *How culture shapes the climate change debate.* Stanford, CA: Stanford University Press.

House, R. J. (1996). Path-goal theory of leadership: Lessons, legacy, and a reformulated theory. *The Leadership Quarterly, 7*(3), 323–352.

Huntington, S. P. (1993). The clash of civilizations. *Foreign Affairs, 72*(3), 22–49.

Ignatieff, M. A. (1995). *Blood and belonging: Journeys into the new nationalism.* New York, NY: Farrar, Straus and Giroux.

Jacquart, P., & Antonakis, J. (2016). When does charisma matter for top-level leaders? Effect of attributional ambiguity. *Academy of Management Journal, 58,* 1051–1074.

Jensen, M. C., & Meckling, W. H. (1976). Theory of the firm: Managerial behavior, agency costs and ownership structure. *Journal of Financial Economics, 3*(4), 305–360.

Jonas, H. (1984). *The imperative of responsibility: In search of ethics for the technological age.* Chicago, IL: University of Chicago Press.

Jones, T. M. (1995). Instrumental stakeholder theory: A synthesis of ethics and economics. *Academy of Management Review, 20,* 404–437.

Keane, W. (2015). *Ethical life: Its natural and social history.* Princeton, NJ: Princeton University Press.

Kinsinger, P., & Walch, K. (2012). *Living and leading in a VUCA world* (White paper). Glendale, AZ: Thunderbird University.

Kobrin, S. J. (2001). Globalization, multinational enterprise, and the international political system. In A. M. Rugman & T. L. Brewer (Eds.), *The Oxford handbook of international business* (pp. 181–205). New York, NY: Oxford University Press.

Lakoff, G. (2004). *Don't think of an elephant!* White River Junction, VT: Chelsea Green.

Laufer, W. S. (2003). Social accountability and corporate greenwashing. *Journal of Business Ethics, 43,* 253–261.

Lawrence, K. (2013). *Developing leaders in a VUCA environment* (White paper). Chapel Hill, NC: Kenan-Flagler Business School.

Maak, T., Pless, N. M., & Voegtlin, C. (2016). Business statesman or shareholder value advocate? CEO responsible leadership styles and the micro-foundations of political CSR. *Journal of Management Studies, 53,* 463–493.

Maio, G. R., Pakizeh, A., Cheung, W.- Y., & Rees, K. J. (2009). Changing, priming, and acting on values: Effects via motivational relations in a circular model. *Journal of Personality and Social Psychology, 97,* 699–715.

Matten, D., & Crane, A. (2005). Corporate citizenship: Towards an extended theoretical conceptualization. *Academy of Management Review, 30,* 166–179.

Maurer, C., Bansal, P., & Crossan, M. M. (2011). Creating economic value through social values: Introducing a culturally informed resource-based view. *Organization Science, 22,* 432–448.

Mazar, N., Amir, O., & Ariely, D. (2008). The dishonesty of honest people: A theory of self-concept maintenance. *Journal of Marketing Research, 45*(6), 633–644.

Mazar, N., & Ariely, D. (2006). Dishonesty in everyday life and its policy implications. *Journal of Public Policy & Marketing, 25*(1), 117–126.

Mazutis, D., & Zintel, C. (2015). Leadership and corporate responsibility: A review of the empirical evidence. *Annals in Social Responsibility, 1,* 76–107.

McWilliams, A., Siegel, D. S., & Wright, P. M. (2006). Corporate social responsibility: Strategic implications. *Journal of Management Studies, 43*(1), 1–18.

Mena, S., & Palazzo, G. (2012). Input and output legitimacy of multi-stakeholder initiatives. *Business Ethics Quarterly, 22,* 527–556.

Misangyi, V. F., Weaver, G. R., & Elms, H. (2008). Ending corruption: The interplay among institutional logics, resources, and institutional entrepreneurs. *Academy of Management Executive Review, 33*(3), 750–770.

Morgeson, F. P., Aguinis, H., Waldman, D. A., & Siegel, D. S. (2013). Extending corporate social responsibility research to the human resource management and organizational behavior domains: A look to the future. *Personnel Psychology, 66*(4), 805–824.

Neate, R. (2015). Nestlé boss says he wants to bottle more water in California despite drought. *The Guardian.* Retrieved from http://www.theguardian.com/us-news/2015/may/14/nestle-boss-wants-bottle-more-water-california-drought

Paine, L. S. (1996). Moral thinking in management: An essential capability. *Business Ethics Quarterly, 6,* 477–492.

Palazzo, G. (2015). Globalization and the rise of the multinational corporation. In M. Raza, H. Willmott, & M. Greenwood (Eds.), *The Routledge companion to philosophy in organization studies* (pp. 395–402). New York, NY: Routledge.

Palazzo, G., Krings, F., & Hoffrage, U. (2012). Ethical blindness. *Journal of Business Ethics, 109,* 323–338.

Palazzo, G., & Scherer, A. G. (2006). Corporate legitimacy as deliberation: A communicative framework. *Journal of Business Ethics, 66,* 71–88.

Parry, K. W., & Proctor-Thomson, S. B. (2002). Perceived integrity of transformational leaders in organisational settings. *Journal of Business Ethics, 35,* 75–96.

Parsons, T. (1991). *The social system.* London, UK: Routledge.

Pfeffer, J., & Salancik, G. (1978). *The external control of organizations: A resource dependence perspective.* New York, NY: Harper and Row.

Pless, N. M., Maak, T., & Waldman, D. A. (2012). Different approaches toward doing the right thing: Mapping the responsibility orientations of leaders. *Academy of Management Perspectives, 26,* 51–65.

Porter, M. E., & Kramer, M. R. (2011, January/February). Creating shared value. *Harvard Business Review, 89,* 62–77.

Ramus, C. A. (2001). Organizational support for employees: Encouraging creative ideas for environmental sustainability. *California Management Review, 43*(3), 85–105.

Rao, H., Monin, P., & Durand, R. (2003). Institutional change in Toque Ville: Nouvelle cuisine as an identity movement in French gastronomy. *American Journal of Sociology, 108*(4), 795–843.

Rechner, P. L., & Dalton, D. R. (1991). CEO duality and organizational performance: A longitudinal analysis. *Strategic Management Journal, 12*(2), 155–160.

Reynolds, S. J. (2008). Moral attentiveness: Who pays attention to the moral aspects of life? *Journal of Applied Psychology, 93,* 1027–1041.

Rittel, H. W. J., & Webber, M. M. (1973). Dilemmas in a general theory of planning. *Policy Science, 4,* 155–169.

Rokeach, M. (1973). *The nature of human values.* New York, NY: John Wiley.

Rosenau, J. N., & Czempiel, E. O. (1992). *Governance without government: Order and change in world politics.* Cambridge, UK: Cambridge University Press.

Ruggie, J. (2007). Business and human rights: The evolving international agenda. *American Journal of International Law, 101*(4), 819–840.

Santoro, M. A. (2009). *China 2020: How Western business can and should influence social and political change in the coming decade.* Ithaca, NY: Cornell University Press.

Schein, E. H. (1992). *Organizational culture and leadership* (2nd ed.). San Francisco, CA: Jossey-Bass.

Schein, E. H. (1996). Culture: The missing concept in organization studies. *Administrative Science Quarterly, 41*(2), 229–240.

Scherer, A. G., & Palazzo, G. (2007). Toward a political conception of corporate responsibility: Business and society seen from a Habermasian perspective. *Academy of Management Review, 32,* 1096–1120.

Scherer, A. G., Palazzo, G., & Baumann, D. (2006). Global rules and private actors—Towards a new role of the TNC in global governance. *Business Ethics Quarterly, 16*(4), 505–532.

Scherer, A. G., Palazzo, G., & Seidl, D. (2013). Legitimacy strategies in a globalized world: Organizing for complex and heterogeneous environments. *Journal of Management Studies, 50,* 259–284.

Scherer, A. G., Rasche, A., Palazzo, G., & Spicer, A. (2016). Managing for political corporate social responsibility—New challenges and directions for PCSR 2.0. *Journal of Management Studies, 53,* 273–298.

Schrempf-Stirling, J., & Palazzo, G. (2016). Upstream corporate social responsibility: From contract responsibility to full producer responsibility. *Business & Society, 55*(4), 491–527.

Schwartz, S. H. (1996). Value priorities and behavior: Applying a theory of integrated value systems. In J. O. C. Selilgman & M. Zanna (Eds.), *The psychology of values. The Ontario Symposium* (Vol. 8, pp. 1–24). Mahwah, NJ: Lawrence Earlbaum.

Sethi, S. P. (2002). Standards for corporate conduct in the international arena: Challenges and opportunities for multinational corporations. *Business & Society Review, 107*(1), 20.

Shamir, B., House, R. J., & Arthur, M. B. (1993). The motivational effects of charismatic leadership: A self-concept based theory. *Organizational Science, 4,* 577–594.

Suchman, M. C. (1995). Managing legitimacy: Strategic and institutional approaches. *Academy of Management Review, 20,* 571–610.

Sundaram, A. K., & Inkpen, A. C. (2004). The corporate objective revisited. *Organization Science, 15,* 350–363.

Swanson, D. L. (1999). Toward an integrative theory of business and society: A research strategy for corporate social performance. *Academy of Management Review, 24,* 506–521.

Taleb, N. N. (2012). *Antifragile: Things that gain from disorder.* London, UK: Penguin Books.

Treviño, L. K., Brown, M., & Hartman, L. P. (2003). A qualitative investigation of perceived executive leadership: Perceptions from inside and outside the executive suite. *Human Relations, 56*(1), 5–37.

Verplanken, B., & Holland, R. W. (2002). Motivated decision-making: Effects of activating and self-centrality of values on choices and behavior. *Journal of Personality and Social Psychology, 82,* 434–447.

Waldman, D. A. (2011). Moving forward with the concept of responsible leadership: Three caveats to guide theory and research. *Journal of Business Ethics, 98*(Suppl. 1), 75–83.

Waldman, D. A., & Siegel, D. (2008). Defining the socially responsible leader. *The Leadership Quarterly, 19*(1), 117–131.

Walsh, J. P. (2005). Taking stock of stakeholder management. *Academy of Management Review, 30,* 426–452.

Weaver, G. R., Treviño, L. K., & Cochran, P. L. (1999). Integrated and decoupled corporate social performance: Management commitments, external pressure, and corporate ethics practices. *Academy of Management Journal, 42*(5), 539–552.

Williamson, O. E. (1975). *Markets and hierarchies: Analysis and antitrust organization.* New York, NY: Free Press.

Young, I. M. (2004). Responsibility and global labor justice. *Journal of Political Philosophy, 12,* 365–388.

Zadek, S. (2004). The path to corporate responsibility. *Harvard Business Review, 82*(12), 125–132.

# CHAPTER 19

# The Chronicles of Leadership

*Foreword*

*David V. Day*

*John Antonakis*

Tribute to Warren Bennis

**Professor Warren Gamaliel Bennis** (March 8, 1925–July 31, 2014) was an American scholar, organizational consultant, and author; he is widely regarded as a pioneer of the contemporary field of leadership studies.

Warren was our colleague, collaborator, and friend. It was with great sadness that we learned of his death in 2014. We, as well as the broader leadership community, miss him. Our brief essay is a tribute to this thought leader wherein we reflect on work he contributed to the first two volumes of this book. It is a testimony to his character that he would be so generous with his time given his lofty status in the leadership field. We hope that you enjoy his essay and get as much from it as we have. As preface and tribute to his chapter, which we have lightly edited to better align with contemporary issues, the following paragraphs attempt to summarize what we have learned from his essay and broader work in general.

In an essay published in the first edition of this book, subsequently revised for the second edition, and reprinted with edits in this third edition, the leadership scholar Warren Bennis made several compelling and even prescient points. Perhaps the most insightful of these points is that it is important to remember that the quality of all our lives is dependent on the quality of our leadership. These words ring especially true in the political landscape of the current times circa 2017. In particular, what can we learn from his essay about living and leading in a divided nation (not just the United States) and a divided world? To a large degree, Bennis attributes much to the role of effective leadership in ensuring a safe and prosperous planet—or not. For these reasons, leadership studies are vitally important, given that a lot hinges on our collective, scientific understanding of leadership.

A related point is that scholars should study leadership scientifically, just as life-threatening diseases are studied. Thus, understanding leadership will likely occur only if scientists from various disciplines collaborate—what has been called in a general sense "consilience" by Wilson (1998). Why? In many ways it goes to the nature of leadership, which is multidisciplinary. Leadership is a complex and even elusive phenomenon that cannot be explained through the lens of any single discipline. We are beginning to see this more clearly as various chapters in this book attest in terms of biological, evolutionary, social cognitive, philosophical, and other seemingly "fringe" approaches to understanding the nature of leadership.

Bennis shows amazing foresight in terms of the role of the media and digital technology in shaping our perceptions of leaders. Initially written well before the phenomenal rise of the Internet, not to mention the so-called Internet of things, he points out that "leadership is and always has been a performance art." Leadership as performance plays out not just in mainstream movies and television, but what is available to virtually every person on the planet who has access to a computer, tablet, or smartphone. Not only are we subjected to words, images, and videos reflecting various perspectives and understandings of leadership, it also appears to be the case that media can be willfully distorted for the purposes of people and organizations who have potentially destructive ulterior motives. Perhaps the most insidious form of media bias is a form of self-censorship pertaining to confirmation bias: attending to messages that confirm what is already believed.

Bennis also highlights the need for greater innovation on the part of leaders to co-create "faster, smarter, more inventive solutions . . . that can be achieved only collaboratively." Indeed, an influential movement within the field of leadership over the last few decades is going from understanding leadership in the singular (i.e., leader-centric approaches) to leadership in the plural (i.e., shared, distributed, and networked perspectives). No doubt, part of this movement can be attributed to the increasing complexities of challenges facing humanity (e.g., climate change, terrorism, population migration, to name just a few) such that no single leader has the requisite complexity to solve such challenges individually, despite what some leaders naively promise. Instead, leaders need to work with others, including other leaders, perhaps as teams of teams to try first to understand the underlying nature of the respective challenge or problem before attempting to understand the nature of leadership that is needed in response. As Bennis notes, context always counts when it comes to leadership. The contexts at issue presently are those complex adaptive challenges that require effective leadership if they are to be addressed successfully.

Other insights from Bennis's essay stem from the perennial questions concerning how leaders use both formal and informal aspects of power. High-profile ethical failures of leaders have not waned since Enron and the *Challenger* disaster discussed by Bennis. Indeed, it seems almost a daily litany of ethical failures chronicled in the news, from Wall Street to politics to journalism to car companies to sport. Specific names need not be mentioned because everyone can think of examples from these and other domains where leaders have come up short in handling the ethical dilemmas they faced. It raises an important question: Why do our leaders seem to fail us so often? Is it that those who tend to seek out power are also prone to misuse and abuse it? Perhaps it is institutions that are not correctly structured, or is it that power corrupts? These issues are another important piece of the leadership puzzle to understand because it is disheartening to consider that the nature of leadership may be rotten at its core.

Bennis also chronicles what has become the rise of tribalism, a powerful force throughout the world that undermines globalization. Tribalism is almost the antithesis of what researchers investigated in the GLOBE project, which Bennis references. That is, there appears to be the need now more than ever to understand each other, our respective values, symbols, and mindsets; yet we see nationalism and even xenophobia raise their ugly heads in myriad forms. But in the backlash against adopting a global mindset, such as resisting efforts to help refugees fleeing from the ravages of terrorism and war in their respective countries, there is a trend toward pulling in one's borders and resisting efforts that reflect what should be universal character virtues such as compassion and benevolence. The problems of tribalism raise another important question in terms of understanding the moral character of leadership and how it can reflect or even shape the moral identity of a country: Is there a universal moral character of leadership?

And what about the followers, Bennis asks? They are important co-creators of leadership. Researchers, even those who put the leader in the middle of a theory, now see that leadership is not just what the leader says and does: How followers legitimize leaders matters, too. We have seen relatively recent theory and research devoted to understanding follower-oriented perspectives on leadership. Of course, this line of research is not a completely new undertaking—Ed Hollander has discussed for decades the importance of followers in building inclusive leadership (e.g., Hollander, 2009). But his was often a voice in the wilderness that was lost amid all of the various leader-centric perspectives on leadership. Without followers, or at least others who are engaged in participating in the process of leadership, there can be no leadership; leadership resides in the minds of those whom the leader affects. Understanding their perceptions and why they willingly follow a leader (or not) is vital for understanding leadership.

One of the most powerful lessons we, and all leaders, can learn in these divisive and sometimes alienating times is this: Leadership cannot happen unless those portrayed as followers come along. Without those who agree to play followership roles, any leader is potentially a solitary voice in the wilderness. Even the most charismatic, inspiring, and visionary leaders cannot lead if stranded alone on a desert island. They must be in touch with the values of the collective but not to the point that they pander and please just to ensure that they are accepted. Nelson Mandela did not fully reflect what his people wanted when they were freed from the shackles of apartheid. Instead of revenge and retribution against the oppressors, Mandela convinced his people to engage in reconciliation and respect.

Leadership is a process and, it is worth saying again, not a position. This process involves engaging with others, building toward a common vision, and ideally, making life better and more meaningful for everyone—not just those who occupy societal or organizational roles that might be construed as more central to those leadership processes.

In closing, an overarching message conveyed by Warren Bennis through his life and his writing is that with leadership comes great responsibility. Bennis embraced responsibility as a young lieutenant during World War II. He demonstrated responsibility and other positive values as a writer, chronicler, and even as the moral conscience of leaders. Those who strive to lead must understand that it is not all glory. It is often hard work that challenges—and tempts, ethically—even the most talented people in our societies. But the reward in terms of contributing to the effectiveness and success of the human race and our planet in small and large ways is responsibility unparalleled in our existence.

# References

Hollander, E. P. (2009). *Inclusive leadership: The essential leader–follower relationship.* New York, NY: Routledge.

Wilson, E. O. (1998). *Consilience: The unity of knowledge.* New York, NY: Knopf.

## Warren Bennis (deceased)

It was the practice of Ralph Waldo Emerson to ask old friends he had not seen in a while: "What's become clear to you since we last met?" As this revamped volume makes clear, those engaged in the study of leadership have learned an enormous amount in the century or so since the enterprise began to evolve from the study of "great" men. It would have been unthinkable a couple of decades ago that evolutionary theorists and biologists would have contributed to such a volume. Yet, as I make it clear later, truly understanding this mystical phenomenon called leadership will occur only if scientists from various disciplines work in collaboration.

The 20th century was marked by the emergence of some of the most powerful and disturbing leaders in human history. Millions died as a direct result of failed or evil leadership—in the death camps of the Third Reich but also in the Soviet Union and in famine-ravished China. The misery inflicted by malicious leaders continues into the 21st century. Millions today face a similar fate in dictatorships like North Korea. The open tab in the form of a "butcher's bill" is a reminder of why we study leadership in the first place. Our very lives depend on it. That has never been truer than it is today, because one consequence of the extraordinary leadership of Franklin Delano Roosevelt was the creation of genuine weapons of mass destruction. I bring these matters up, not because any of you need a capsule history lesson, but because it is important to remember that the quality of all our lives is dependent on the quality of our leadership. The context in which we study leadership is very different from the context in which we study, say, astronomy. By definition, leaders wield power, and so we study them with the same self-interested intensity with which we study diabetes and other life-threatening diseases. Only when we understand leaders will we be able to control them. Today, studying leadership is still an important scientific imperative; scandal after scandal, economic crisis after crisis, ecological disaster after disaster, and the anticipated but unrealized flowering of democracy in Arab countries can be partly traced back to failed leadership. It is through effective leadership that our human race and planet will prosper.

I would argue that context always counts when it comes to leadership, and in the next few pages, I want to examine certain enduring issues and questions related to leadership in today's milieu. I want to look at how recent events and trends are reshaping contemporary ideas about leadership.

In the United States, at least, leadership studies changed in some basic way on September 11, 2001. As the nation watched, in horror, the television footage of people fleeing the World Trade Center and, in even greater horror, the collapse of the Twin Towers, I realized as so many others did that this was one of the transformational events of our time. One immediate consequence of the terrorist assaults on New York and the Pentagon was to make leadership a matter for public discussion in the United States in a way it has not been since World War II. Leadership became central to the public conversation—displacing the endless background noise about celebrity and pushing aside even worried talk about the sorry state of the economy. People in other parts of the world have been dealing with the ugly realities of international terrorism for decades, and to them, the stunned horror of Americans must have seemed more than a little naive. But the United States has long had the luxury of studying leadership with the leisurely detachment that only those in peaceful, prosperous nations can afford.

The assault on a nonmilitary target in the paradigmatic American city was more stunning, in many ways, than Pearl Harbor. Not since the Civil War had ideologically motivated violence occurred on such a scale in a city in the United States. Americans are still sorting out the consequences of the attacks of 9/11 and will continue to do so for decades. But with the collapse of the Twin Towers came a new awareness that leadership is more than a matter of who looks best on television. Since 9/11, government officials have been scrutinized for evidence of leadership ability with an intensity usually seen only in wartime. And indeed, in describing how then New York City mayor Rudolph Giuliani and others responded to al Qaeda's assault, the media referred repeatedly to the larger-than-life leaders of World War II. The iconic leader du jour was unquestionably Winston Churchill. It was noted, for instance, that Karen Hughes, then special assistant to President George W. Bush, kept a plaque on her desk that bore Churchill's stirring line: "I was not the lion but it fell to me to give the lion's roar."

The invocation of Churchill was a secular prayer for help, but it was also evidence of a shift in the very idea of leadership—a return to a more heroic, more inspirational definition than had been the fashion for decades. In the rubble of Ground Zero, people did not want a leader who could organize cross-functional teams; they longed for a leader for the ages, a sage and savior to lead them out of hell. It is human nature to look for strong leadership in times of crisis, however misguided. No solitary leader, no matter how smart or accomplished, has the wherewithal to solve our most pressing societal problems. It is leaders that we need—not a leader.

Whatever else 9/11 meant, it was a vivid reminder that one of the sweeter uses of adversity continues to be its ability to bring leadership to the fore. What Abigail Adams wrote to son John Quincy Adams in the tumult of 1780 is still true today: "These are the times in which a genius would wish to live. It is not in the still calm of life, or in the repose of a pacific station, that great challenges are formed. . . . Great necessities call out great virtues." When Robert Thomas and I were doing the research for *Geeks & Geezers* (Bennis & Thomas, 2002), we interviewed almost 50 leaders—some aged 75 and older, the rest 35 and younger. In every case, we found that their leadership had emerged after some defining experience, or crucible, as we called it. These were often ordeals, and among the older leaders, they often occurred in wartime. The crucibles of our leaders included such personal tragedies as television journalist Mike Wallace's discovery of the body of his son after an accident in Greece, and global business pioneer Sidney Rittenberg's harrowing 16 years in Chinese prisons—much of them in solitary confinement, often in the dark. Most people realize how crucibles can be transforming events. Political leaders have instrumentalized their "crucible" experiences and vie to take advantage of the media to communicate them in vivid ways. They know that voters are more likely to trust those who have known suffering, yet voters are becoming wary of such efforts that smack of inauthenticity.

In a foreword to our book, David Gergen, head of the Center for Public Leadership at Harvard's John F. Kennedy School of Government, describes the crucible in which Harry Truman discovered that he was a leader. We tend to think of Truman as the one-time haberdasher whose leadership emerged only after the death of Roosevelt. But as Gergen recounts, Truman was tested during the Great War on the battlefields of France. The head of an artillery battery, he was in the Vosges Mountains when his position was shelled by the Germans. His men panicked, and Truman's horse panicked as well, falling on him and almost killing him. But as historian David McCullough wrote in his prize-winning biography of Truman, the future president crawled out from under his horse and overcame his own fear, screaming profanities at his men until most of them returned to their posts. Truman's men never forgot that his courage under fire had saved their lives, and Truman discovered that he had a taste for leadership as well as a gift for it.

Again and again, we found that something magical happens in the crucible—an alchemy whereby fear and suffering are transformed into something glorious and redemptive. This process reveals, if it does not create, leadership, the ability to inspire and move others to action. We found intelligence, optimism, and other traits traditionally associated with leadership present in all our subjects, but those traits are no guarantee that the alchemy of leadership will take place. Countless gifted people are broken by suffering. But our leaders discovered themselves in their crucibles, for reasons we still do not fully understand. However searing the experience, our leaders were able to make sense of it or organize meaning around it—meaning that subsequently attracted followers. Instead of being defeated by his or her ordeal, each of our leaders saw it as a heroic journey. Whatever their age, these men and women created their own legends. Without being untruthful, they constructed new, improved versions of themselves. In many cases—as in Truman's— the ordeal and the leader's interpretation of it led others to follow the newly revealed leader.

In the model of leadership development that grew out of that research, success- ful individuals all evidenced four essential competencies—adaptive capacity, the ability to engage others through shared meaning, a distinctive voice, and integrity. Often these abilities were evident to some degree before their ordeals, but they were intensified by the crucible experience. Of all these abilities, the most important was adaptive capacity. All our leaders had an extraordinary gift for coping with what- ever life threw at them. I believe that adaptive capacity is essentially creativity—the ability to take disparate things and turn them into something new and useful. Indeed, it is no accident that there is a convergence between leadership studies and studies of creativity—a convergence that dates back to the first studies of Darwin, Einstein, and other geniuses or thought leaders. When we speak of exemplary leadership, we are often talking about exemplary, creative problem solving—the discovery of new solutions to unprecedented problems.

But let's return to the lessons of 9/11. During the 1950s, no one who heard Marshall McLuhan speak so confidently of the global village or the extent to which the medium is the message had any idea how truly prescient he was. But the terror- ist attacks of 2001 underscored that ours is indeed one world, albeit a profoundly splintered one, and that television and more recent technologies are its primary mediators. Here were multinational terrorists dispatched by an individual holed up in an apartment, or a cave, in Afghanistan or elsewhere in the Middle East. Digital technology was used to advance a medieval ideology, with orders and money trans- ferred in a nanosecond halfway across the planet. Globalization has created a host of new dangers that require a new kind of leadership—one that is, above all, collaborative. It was the inability of security agencies in the United States to work effectively together that allowed the 9/11 terrorists to enter and remain in the country and to learn how to fly a jet into a skyscraper at American flight schools.

And global terrorism is only one contemporary threat that requires a multina- tional, collaborative response. Disease, poverty, and the oppression of minorities, women, and political dissidents are urgent international concerns. As the outbreak in 2003 of severe acute respiratory syndrome (SARS) or the much-hyped but rela- tively anodyne 2009 swine flu illustrated, the ability of almost anyone to jump on a plane and fly to some distant city has created the real possibility that future flights will spread deadly plagues with unprecedented ease and rapidity.

In the months that led up to the toppling of the regime of Iraq's Saddam Hussein in 2003, much was made in the media, and rightfully so, of President George W. Bush's failure to build a global coalition. His "either you're with us or against us" attitude and his decision to enter Iraq with support from only a handful of nations (Great Britain, Australia, and Poland, among them) was widely seen as a leadership failure, despite the defeat of Hussein in record time. Hussein's defeat turned out to be just the beginning in Iraq. The critique of the president reflected more than political differences on whether American military action was appropriate only if legitimized by the United Nations. The criticism reflected an understanding that coalition building is one of the essential competencies of all leaders—in some ways, the defining one. And again, leadership came to the fore long after the war was over: Securing the peace in Iraq has proven very difficult, and some of the disastrous consequences have been blamed on precipitous policies, bad planning, and lack of shared leadership. Iraqis were rid of their dictator only to be replaced by al Qaeda.

Among the committed coalition builders President Bush might have emulated was his father. Before the first Gulf War, President George Herbert Walker Bush doggedly wooed world leaders. When the president was not smiling over banquet tables himself, he dispatched his secretary of state, James Baker, on eight consensus-building trips abroad, trips that took Baker to 18 European capitals. The result was that the United States went to war as part of a genuine "coalition of the willing." We cannot know what father said to son in private conversation before the Iraqi conflict. But we do know what the older Bush counseled in a speech at Tufts University in February 2003. "You've got to reach out to the other person," he said, describing what leaders in an interconnected world must do. "You've got to convince them that long-term friendship should trump short-term adversity." The senior Bush was articulating what democratic leaders have always known. In a society in which power must be given freely, not coerced, leaders make alliances by persuading others that their interests and fates are intertwined. Today, it is clear that the United States needs allies more than ever, as disorder continues in post-Hussein Iraq and the Persian Gulf region in general, where some perceive the forces of the United States and her handful of allies as occupiers rather than liberators.

Coalition building is also an essential element of corporate leadership. Until American business was roiled by recent corporate scandals, we had long been guilty of treating chief executive officers (CEOs) and other business leaders as demigods whose success was a unilateral achievement resulting from their special genius. This tradition dates back at least as far as our deification of such business titans as Thomas Edison and Henry Ford, and it resurged during the late 1970s when Lee Iacocca was hailed as the savior of the American auto industry. In retrospect, the lionization of anyone connected with the battered U.S. auto industry seems like a cruel joke. But we forget, now that so many corporate heads have rolled, how recently CEOs were treated both as celebrities and as thought leaders whose public comments were scrutinized for hidden wisdom like tea leaves.

In many ways, the rise of the celebrity CEO was a regression to the era when great institutions were thought to be the lengthened shadows of great men. The late-20th-century version of that durable myth differed only in conceding that a few great institutions—such as the Martha Stewart empire—were lengthened shadows of great women. But as Patricia Ward Biederman and I wrote in *Organizing Genius* (Bennis & Biederman, 1997), one has almost always been too small a number for greatness. Whatever their sphere, authentic leaders know, even if they do not bruit it around, that their power is a consequence of their ability to recruit the talent of others to the collective enterprise. The Lone Ranger has never been as dead as he is today. In all but the simplest undertaking, great things are done by alliances, not by larger-than-life individuals, however powerful they may seem.

I doubt that the world was ever so simple that a single heroic leader, however capable, could solve its problems unilaterally. Today's world requires unprecedented coalition building. The European Union may be the paradigmatic response to this changed reality. For those of us who experienced World War II firsthand, it is heartening to see such a high level of economic and political cooperation among nations that were so recently at one another's throats. And more and more coalitions, created and maintained by collaborative leaders, will be required in the years ahead. That this volume now includes a chapter on shared leadership gives me hope that business schools and political science departments will pay more attention to leadership as a collaborative endeavor.

The pace of change is not slowing. It is accelerating as never before. Ever-changing problems require faster, smarter, more inventive solutions, solutions that can be achieved only collaboratively. In recent years, even the way leaders make decisions has changed. The day is all but over when a leader has the leisure to digest all the facts and then to act. As psychologist Karl Weick has pointed out, today's leaders are more often required to act first, assess the results of their actions, and then act again. Thanks to digital technology, facts can be collected and numbers crunched with unprecedented ease. In this new climate, information is always flooding in, and there is no final analysis, only constant evaluation and reevaluation. Action becomes one more way to gather information, which becomes the basis for further action. As Weick so eloquently put it, in such a world, leaders cannot depend on maps. They need compasses. And as never before, they need allies.

The ability to form and maintain alliances is not just a political tool. The successful older leaders that Robert Thomas and I interviewed made it a point to seek out and befriend talented younger people. Forming these social alliances was a strategy the older leaders used to stay in touch with a rapidly changing world. These social alliances helped keep the older leaders vital in a way their less successful, more isolated peers were not. The younger leaders also benefited from relationships with more seasoned, older friends. And this strategy of forming alliances is not limited to humans. Stanford neurobiologist Robert Sapolsky, who lived for a time as part of a group of Serengeti baboons, found that the older males most likely to survive were those who were able to form strong bonds with younger males. Teamed with youthful allies, the senior males were able to compensate for the losses brought about by age. Mentoring is a variation on this primal theme, a way for the young and the old to pool their wisdom and energy to their mutual benefit.

Because leaders have power, the question of whether they use it for good or ill continues to be desperately important. We could argue forever over whether Hitler was an authentic leader or whether leadership, by definition, implies a kind of virtue. Certainly, Hitler had many of the competencies of leadership—a vision, the ability to recruit others to it, insight into what his followers needed, if only in the most demonic parts of themselves. He had the unquenchable self-confidence that is associated with leadership, the ambition, the obsessive sense of purpose, the need to communicate it, and the oratorical gifts to do so. He even had a kind of twisted integrity, in that he was always what his followers knew him to be. My fear is that our concern over this question is a dead end. Like the problem, the solution may be a matter of semantics. Perhaps we should reserve the word *leader* for those whose leadership is morally neutral (if that is possible) or tilted toward the good. We might simply stop calling Hitler an evil leader and refer to him as a despot or simply as a *Führer,* the straightforward German word for leader until Hitler poisoned it.

To say that the problem of how to label bad leaders distracts us from more pressing concerns is not to say that morality and leadership are trivial matters. They are of the utmost importance, now and forever. As Harvard Business School scholar Lynn Sharp Paine says of morality and business, ethics may not always pay, but it always counts. Far more urgent than the issue of what to call bad leaders is the question of how to create a culture in which despots or even plain-vanilla corporate tyrants of the "Chainsaw" Al Dunlap sort cannot flourish. In truth, I think we do that by creating the same kind of climate in which talented people blossom and the very best work can be done. Fertile, liberating environments almost always have two components: able leaders who listen and capable followers who speak out. There is a memorable story about Nikita Khrushchev on this point. After the death of Joseph Stalin, the Soviet premier was at a public meeting at which he denounced Stalin's reign of terror. After Khrushchev spoke, someone in the audience confronted him. "You were a confidant of Stalin's," a voice called out from the crowd. "What were you doing when Stalin was slaughtering his own people?" "Who said that?" Khrushchev demanded to know. There was no answer. "Who said that?" he asked again, pounding the podium. And then Khrushchev explained: "*That's* what I was doing!"

By his silence, Khrushchev proved himself a bad follower (albeit a live one). This is one of those areas in which the lessons of leadership cry out for application in the workplace. The corporate scandals of the past few years (not to mention the 2008 economic crisis triggered by liquidity problems in U.S. banks) have caused unprecedented havoc in the American economy and tumult that has rocked the linked economies of the world. And in nearly every case, those scandals resulted not simply from crooked accounting and other crimes but from the failure of corporate leadership to create a culture of candor and transparency. Enron is a perfect example. Long before the energy giant crashed and burned, key employees knew that the books were being manipulated in ways that were deceptive, if not illegal. Enron executive Sherron S. Watkins did the right thing and warned her bosses that "Enron could implode in a wave of accounting scandals." Naive but admirably concerned about the good of the organization, Watkins expected to be heard, if not rewarded. Instead, company chief financial officer (CFO) Andrew Fastow buried the evidence and immediately set out to get rid of Watkins. The problem at Enron, she said later, was that few were willing to speak truth to power. Employees, including management, knew better than to point out the increasingly obvious ethical lapses in the company's business practices. Critical talk was taboo at Enron. "You simply didn't want to discuss it in front of the water cooler," Watkins said.

It is one thing to remain silent when your life or that of your family is in danger. It is quite another to remain silent when other people's lives are at risk and the worst thing that can happen to you is losing your job. And yet many organizations implicitly demand silence and denial on the part of their employees, even at the cost of human lives. When the space shuttle *Challenger* exploded shortly after takeoff in 1986, killing all seven on board, the blame was ultimately put on the space shuttle's O-rings, which failed in the unseasonable cold the morning of the launch. Tragically, the potential flaw in the O-rings had been repeatedly noted by Roger Boisjoly, an engineer with NASA supplier Morton Thiokol. Only the day before, Boisjoly had made one more desperate attempt to warn his superiors that the crew was in danger. But the company suppressed the information. As for Boisjoly, the whistleblower got the reward that annoying truth tellers so often receive. He lost his job, and indeed never worked again as an engineer; he did, however, receive the Scientific Freedom and Responsibility Award from the American Association for the Advancement of Science. He now makes his living giving talks on organizational ethics.

To an outsider, it is almost impossible to imagine that any organization would prefer silence to honest criticism that saves lives. But such deadly organizational quietism happens all the time. And one tragedy is often not enough to bring about change. In a report prepared after the shuttle *Columbia*'s deadly failure in 2003, investigators put part of the blame on "a flawed institutional culture that plays down problems," according to the *New York Times*. Just as Boisjoly had been ignored when he raised his concerns in 1986, a new generation of space-program managers had chosen to ignore signs of potential problems, including e-mails from employees warning of flaws in the system. The fiery failure of the *Columbia* killed seven astronauts, whose deaths are attributable, at least in part, to managers who closed their minds to vital but unwanted news. NASA created a system that rewarded silence before safety, and that is what it got.

Corporate enthusiasm for collective ignorance has launched a thousand "Dilbert" cartoons. Movie mogul Samuel Goldwyn, famous for his malapropisms as well as his autocratic rule, is said to have snarled at his underlings after a string of box-office flops, "I want you to tell me what's the matter with MGM even if it means losing your jobs." Too often, that is exactly what happens. More recently, Compaq CEO Eckhard Pfeiffer lost dominance of the computer market to Gateway and Dell, not because he lacked talent but because he surrounded himself with an A-list of yes men (or yes people, these days) and closed his office door to anyone who had the courage to tell him what he did not want to hear.

In the 2003 scandal at the *New York Times* that led to the resignations of Executive Editor Howell Raines and Managing Editor Gerald Boyd, insiders repeatedly told other media that the real problem was not the pathological behavior of rogue reporter Jayson Blair but a newsroom culture that rewarded a handful of favorites of questionable merit and marginalized everyone else. It was also a place where control was concentrated in the hands of a few, and dissent was unwelcome. Neither Raines nor Boyd listened when another editor warned that Blair must stop reporting for the *New York Times* immediately. Much has been made of Raines's role in the scandal, but the *Wall Street Journal* reported a disturbing example of Boyd's arrogant resistance to the truth as well. When the paper's national editor suggested a story to Boyd on the *Columbia* disaster, Boyd nixed it, saying it had already run that morning in *USA Today.* Investigations Editor Douglas Frantz subsequently brought Boyd a copy of *USA Today* to prove that the story had not appeared. Boyd, of course, should have acknowledged his mistake and ordered up the story. Instead, he told Frantz he should not embarrass his managing editor and handed Frantz a quarter to call his friend Dean Baquet, a former *Times* editor who had gone to the *Los Angeles Times.* In essence, Boyd told Frantz to hit the road. And like a number of other unhappy veterans of the *New York Times,* Frantz quit to go to Los Angeles.

Linda Greenhouse, who covers the Supreme Court for the *New York Times,* told *Journal* reporters Matthew Rose and Laurie Cohen: "There is an endemic cultural issue at the *Times* that is not a Howell creation, although it plays into his vulnerabilities as a manager, which is a top-down hierarchical structure. And it's a culture where speaking truth to power has never been particularly welcomed."

You would hope that leaders in any organization would have the ego strength to accept well-intentioned criticism from talented underlings. You would hope that leaders would be wise enough to know that what you do not want to hear is often the most valuable information you can get. This makes me wonder why organizations do not go out of their way to use findings from differential psychology. Although far from perfect, sophisticated psychometric tests can identify leaders who will be smart and relatively open-minded, honest, and assertive enough to lead in an effective way. You would also think that czar-like executive compensation packages would more than make up for any embarrassment corporate leaders feel when subordinates choose candor over ego massage. But such is rarely the case. Executive arrogance poisons the atmosphere in far too many organizations. It is especially deadly in idea-driven organizations (as more and more are) in which subordinates are often as talented as their leaders, or more so. In hard economic times, autocratic leaders may be able to retain talent. But as soon as the economy rebounds, talented people who do not respect the people they work for head for the door. At the height of the now battered New Economy, employers knew that talent was their treasure, and they treated their employees with respect. In hard times, employers often become arrogant again, forgetting that good times will return and that the talent will again take flight.

The change that New York Times Company chair Arthur Sulzberger Jr. undertook to address the paper's leadership problem was to name former executive editor Joseph Lelyveld, whom Raines had succeeded, as his interim replacement. Well-liked by reporters and editors, Lelyveld seemed to understand, as Raines did not, that the *New York Times* was about the work, not about the executive editor. Lelyveld had decentralized control, giving editors and reporters more autonomy and more discretion to work on longer, thoughtful stories appropriate to journalists at the top of their game (in contrast, Raines liked to dispatch masses of reporters to cover a breaking news story, a process he called "flooding the zone"). And, unlike Raines, who assigned reporters to execute his story ideas for the front page, Lelyveld joked that he had trouble getting his story ideas into the paper—an offhand reminder to his staff that he did not confuse himself with god. Interestingly, Lelyveld was repeatedly described by those who worked with him as "aloof." He was not a charismatic leader, nor a warm, fuzzy one—just an able one whom people respected. Lelyveld understood that smart, capable people should be treated with respect—not just because it is the right thing to do but because it is good business. Lelyveld was also a reminder that leadership abilities are ultimately more important than leadership styles.

# Future of Leadership Research

In reading the earlier chapters in this book, I was struck by how rich and varied the study of leadership has become over the past 20 or so years. My sense is that the field is now on the brink of the kind of major breakthroughs that revolutionized social psychology in the 1950s and 1960s. Inspired by the earlier chapters, I will focus on three topics, among others, that seem to demand further study.

## Leadership and Globalization

The Global Leadership and Organizational Behavior Effectiveness (GLOBE) Project, in which social scientists from approximately 60 countries look at leadership from a cross-cultural perspective, is an important start. In a world made smaller by technology, it is more urgent than ever that we understand each other's symbols, values, and mindsets. Only then can we hope to reach consensus on common goals, including how to ensure global peace and prosperity. In the past few years, Westerners have become acutely aware of how little they know about Islamic cultures, including how to speak their languages. One subject that cries out for more scrutiny is tribalism, a powerful force throughout the world that undermines globalization at every turn. The private sector has long been aware of the importance of understanding its audiences and markets. Advertising agencies regularly recruit new PhDs in cultural anthropology to study the customs and values of consumers. We need to turn even more experts loose on comparing cultures on such fundamental problems as what we mean when we use certain terms. This is essential, not just to understand those who oppose us but to ensure the forging of effective alliances.

As recounted in an issue of *Smithsonian,* British and American military had so much trouble communicating during World War II that the Allies asked anthropologist Margaret Mead to try to find out what the problem was. Writer Patrick Cooke explains: "Mead discovered that the two cultures possessed fundamentally different world views. One simple way to demonstrate this was to ask an English person and an American a single question: What's your favorite color?" The American would answer immediately with the color of his or her choice. The English person would answer with a question: "Favorite color for what? A flower? A necktie?" Cooke explains: "Mead concluded that Americans, raised in a melting pot, learned to seek a simple common denominator. To the British, this came across as unsophisticated. Conversely, the class-conscious British insisted on complex categories, each with its own set of values. Americans interpreted this tendency to subdivide as furtive." How right Churchill was that the English and the Americans were great nations separated by a common language!

From our vantage point, Mead's conclusions seem a little simplistic. But you cannot help admiring the unidentified leader who recognized the Allies' communication problem as cultural and, instead of assigning blame, chose an expert to study the problem dispassionately. Effective leadership will increasingly depend on being able to decipher what people really mean when they do and say things that baffle us.

## Leadership and the Media

Leadership is and always has been a performance art. Rhetoric first developed as a tool of leadership, and leadership continues to involve both artifice and the perception of authenticity. There is a tendency to think of image consciousness on the part of leaders as a modern phenomenon. But as historian Leo Braudy tells us, Alexander the Great facilitated the spread of his power by putting his image on the coins of his empire. We take as a given that television gave JFK an edge over Nixon during their debates because of the latter's five o'clock shadow and sour scowl. But do we yet know the real extent to which our public figures are created or undone by the media, and the nature of these processes? To understand leadership today, it is essential to see how the competitive pressures of the media affect the reputations and the behavior of public officials. And you cannot get a handle on modern leaders without at least trying to gauge where spin begins and reality ends. When President George W. Bush made his famous tailgate landing on the carrier *Abraham Lincoln,* associating himself with both the Great Emancipator and the pop-culture warriors of the movie *Top Gun,* did he do something qualitatively different than Alexander the Great, who associated his exploits with those of the deities of his time? What impact does the public's knowledge that reality is being manipulated have on its trust in its leaders? And how does the Internet affect modern leadership, given its ability to create buzz about an individual or vilify him or her with a keystroke? The mastery of Internet-based media by Obama's team apparently helped play a role in his victories over McCain in 2008 and Romney in 2012. These are things we need to know in an age when television cameras can create seeming character and instant polling allows leaders to change their positions in midspeech.

## Multidisciplinary Approaches to Leadership

It may be possible in the near future to develop a true science of leadership (it will always be an art as well). Obviously, this scientific understanding has been a dream since the first postmortem examination of a leader's brain. But the technology now exists to make real strides. It sometimes seems as if every department in every university wants PET (positron emission tomography) and fMRI (functional magnetic resonance imaging) technology of its own, however many millions the machines cost. But there may be real gains to having leaders, nonleaders, and followers submit to brain scans in hopes of discovering more about the neuroscience of leadership. What happens in a follower's brain as the person hears a rousing speech? Do the brains of autocratic leaders show different patterns of activity than those of collaborative ones? What about their respective followers? There is also new work to be done on how hormones affect leadership and, too, how dominance and subordination affect hormones, mood, health, and other outcomes. Does bad management literally make people sick? One immediate benefit of a rigorous science of leadership would be better management, now too often based on tradition and clumsy improvisation. Integrating basic biological sciences in the study of management and leadership, as *The Economist* suggested in an article published in September 2010, may provide the next major paradigm shift in the organizational sciences.

# Conclusion

Having studied leadership for the past six decades, I still find it remarkable how often leaders in talent-driven organizations (e.g., the *New York Times*) forget what scholarship tells us about how to manage genius. They encourage competition among colleagues, instead of the more productive competition with outside organizations. They forget that most talented people chafe at bureaucracy and hierarchy. They forget that intrinsic rewards are the best motivators. They refuse to believe that work should feel like fun, or better than fun.

In the gifted groups that Biederman and I studied, the most successful leaders were those who saw themselves not as top guns but as facilitators. Although many had healthy egos, they were far more concerned with the project than with shows of deference on the part of their subordinates. Indeed, they did not regard the others as subordinates; they saw them as colleagues or as fellow crusaders on a holy mission (whether that mission was creating the first personal computer or the first animated feature film). These leaders saw their primary responsibility as unleashing the talent of others so the collective vision could be realized. These leaders prided themselves on their ability to discover and cultivate talent and to recognize the best ideas that came across their desks. They concerned themselves with such issues as keeping the project moving forward, making sure everyone had the tools and information they needed, and protecting the group from outside interference. A spirited collegiality is the usual mood of these great groups. As head of the Manhattan Project, J. Robert Oppenheimer successfully fought the government's initial insistence on secrecy within the group. Oppenheimer understood that the free exchange of ideas was essential to the project's success because ideas ignite each other and create more ideas. At Los Alamos, candor within the group was so valued that no one was shocked when cheeky young Richard Feynman disagreed with legendary Nobelist Niels Bohr. If Los Alamos was not a genuine republic of ideas, Oppenheimer did all he could to make it feel like one. Inside the fence, he rewarded frankness and transparency as well as utter dedication to the urgent task at hand. The result was that the atomic bomb was built more quickly than anyone believed possible. The first mushroom cloud still hung in the air when some of the scientists realized that they had unleashed a terrible force on the world. But most spoke admiringly of Oppenheimer's leadership for the rest of their lives.

Even though Oppenheimer's scientists were part of the Allied war effort, he treated them as if they were free agents. Oppenheimer realized that the most heroic effort is given freely; it cannot be coerced. He did not order. He inspired.

Perhaps the best exchange on the limits of power is from Shakespeare's *Henry IV, Pt. I.* Glendower boasts to Hotspur: "I can call spirits from the vasty deep." And Hotspur responds: "Why, so can I, or so can any [person]; But will they come when you do call them?" Whatever the arena, genuine leaders find ways to make others want to come when they are called.

## Discussion Questions

1. With respect to some of the core themes in this chapter, what are the major contrasts regarding the presidential styles of Donald Trump and Barack Obama?
2. Discuss a current situation, whether political, economic, or even one you know firsthand, that parallels what Bennis says with respect to people not wanting "a leader who could organize cross-functional teams; they longed for a leader for the ages, a sage and savior to lead them out of hell." Did that particular leader do a good job? Why or why not?
3. What crucible events have you or someone you know well experienced? Discuss.

## Recommended Readings

- Bennis, W. G., & Biederman, P. W. (1997). *Organizing genius: The secrets of creative collaboration.* Reading, MA: Addison-Wesley.
- Bennis, W. G., & Biederman, P. W. (2010). *Still surprised: A memoir of a life in leadership.* San Francisco, CA: Jossey-Bass.
- Bennis, W. G., & Thomas, R. J. (2002). *Geeks and geezers: How era, values, and defining moments shape leaders.* Boston, MA: Harvard Business School Press.

## Recommended Case Studies

- **Case:** Gruber, D. A., Smerek, R. E., Thomas-Hunt, M., & James, E. H. (2015, March). The real-time power of Twitter: Crisis management and leadership in an age of social media. Harvard Business School Case BH658-PDF-ENG.
- **Case:** Koehn, N. F., Helms, E., & Mead, P. (2003, April). (Revised 2010, December). Leadership in crisis: Ernest Shackleton and the epic voyage of the endurance. Harvard Business School Case 803-127.

## Recommended Video

- Varoufakis, Y. (2011). A modest proposal for transforming Europe. https://youtu.be/CRRWaEPRlb4

# Name Index

Armenakis, A. A., 114, 416
Armstrong, J. S., 232
Arnold, A. P., 287
Arnold, D. G., 476
Arthur, M. B., 65, 191, 236, 301, 457, 485
Arvey, R. D., 13, 191, 202, 203, 255, 358, 359, 360
Ashford, S. J., 86, 112 (table), 129, 175, 290, 319
Ashforth, B. E., 129, 303
Ashkanasy, N. M., 115, 128, 129, 234, 417
Atwater, L. E., 66, 71, 90, 147, 148, 152, 158, 177, 210
Auerbach, J., 203
Aumann, K., 257
Aung, San Suu Kyi, 332
Autio, E., 384, 385, 391, 398, 399, 400
Avolio, B. J., 10, 12, 15, 48, 59, 66, 67, 69, 72, 85, 97, 98, 140, 146, 150, 152, 154, 155, 159, 170, 176, 177, 178, 203, 204, 234, 236, 251, 289, 331, 332, 355, 356, 358, 359, 371, 372, 392, 397, 398, 452, 454, 457, 484
Awamleh, R., 72
Aycan, Z., 340–341
Ayman, Roya, 17, 138, 139, 140, 142, 143, 148, 153, 154, 155
Ayoko, O. B., 48

Babiak, P., 209
Bacharach, S. B., 10, 13
Bachrach, D. G., 152
Back, M. D., 227
Backert, S. G., 95
Bader, P., 31, 71, 139
Baer, M. D., 416
Baglole, P., 403
Bahiense, E., 150
Bailey-Werner, B., 259
Baker, James, 502
Bakhtin, M. M., 124
Bakker-Pieper, A., 37
Baldwin, M. W., 127
Balkundi, P., 12, 111, 128, 279
Ballew, C. C., 231, 232
Balliet, D., 255
Baltes, P. B., 355, 361
Balthazard, P. A., 13, 177
Banaji, M. R., 202, 232
Bandura, A., 86, 91, 177, 316, 320, 396
Banks, G. C., 67, 69, 70
Bansal, P., 485
Baquet, Dean, 505

Barber, B., 476
Barbey, A., 98
Bargh, J. A., 282
Barley, S. R., 475
Barling, J., 72, 290, 430
Barnard, C. I., 172 (table)
Baron, D. P., 473
Baron, R. A., 225, 225 (table), 226, 387, 397
Barraza, J. A., 288
Barrett, H. C., 194
Barrick, M. R., 11, 43, 281n
Barron, R. A., 179
Barsalou, L. W., 95, 98
Barsh, J., 261
Barsoux, J. L., 330
Bartels, A., 291
Bartol, K. M., 171
Basadur, M., 390
Bascle, G., 14, 432
Bass, B. M., 5, 6, 8, 12–13, 32, 46, 59, 62–63, 65–67, 75, 76, 84, 89, 97, 98, 169, 170, 178, 191, 192, 234, 236, 237, 329, 331–332, 347, 392, 393, 443, 456–457, 458, 484
Bass, R., 5, 6, 8, 169, 329, 332, 347
Bastardoz, N., 7, 9, 10, 11, 13, 58, 59, 70, 277, 415, 483
Basu, K., 483
Bauer, T. N., 112 (table), 113, 114, 115, 119, 121, 122, 131
Baum, J. R., 384, 391, 392, 396
Baumann, Beate, 244
Baumann, D., 477
Baumeister, R. F., 87, 195, 205
Baumgarten, P., 252
Baumgartner, T., 288
Bealer, D., 330
Beaver, W., 481
Bebb, M., 12, 66, 178
Becherer, R. C., 392
Beck, U., 475, 486
Becker, J., 151, 155
Becker, T. E., 427
Bedeian, A. G., 115
Bedell-Avers, K. E., 87
Beer, J., 288
Behling, O., 387
Beimel, S., 70, 367
Beldekosa, P., 394
Benard, S., 257
Bendahan, S., 11, 13, 14, 16, 60, 68, 70, 117, 204, 252, 275, 285, 289, 414, 434
Benenson, J. F., 209

Brehmer, B., 369
Brennan, T. C., 169
Brescoll, V. L., 259
Bresman, H., 389
Breugst, N., 391
Brewer, M. B., 129, 224
Brigham, K. H., 391, 392, 395, 402
Brin, Sergey, 386
Briner, R. B., 414, 434
Brion, S., 279, 280, 281, 284
Brodbeck, F. C., 319, 332, 342
Brooks, D., 238
Brosnan, S. F., 195, 203
Brouer, R. L., 113
Brower, H. H., 111
Brown, D. J., 10, 17, 82, 84, 87, 95, 99, 205, 207, 224, 226, 228, 229, 231, 234, 236, 301, 313, 415, 416, 428
Brown, E., 223
Brown, E. R., 245n, 255
Brown, M., 470
Brown, M. E., 69, 443
Brown, T., 212
Brown, Tim, 478
Brown, V., 91
Bruce, V., 222, 224
Bruggerman, P., 247
Brunell, A. B., 209
Brunswik, E., 225 (table), 227
Bryman, A., 6, 12, 58, 276
Bu, N., 330, 338
Buchanan, D., 260
Buckley, M. R., 235
Buddha, 462
Bullmore, E., 286
Bundick, M. J., 227
Burbach, R., 475
Burgmer, P., 284
Burke, D. M., 233
Burke, M. J., 143
Burke, P. J., 318
Burns, J. M., 12, 59, 62, 65–66, 314, 443, 454–456, 458, 470
Burrough, B., 475
Burt, R. S., 261, 279
Bush, George Herbert Walker, 502
Bush, George W., 443, 499, 501, 508
Buss, D. M., 192, 194, 253, 254
Butler, C., 349
Butler, M., 13, 91, 150, 201
Buunk, A. P., 281
Byrne, D., 114
Byron, K., 253

Cable, D. M., 96, 98, 208, 314
Cacioppo, J. T., 92, 128
Caesar, A., 255
Calder, B. J., 11, 64, 88
Caliendo, M., 432
Call, J., 223
Callan, V. J., 247
Camerer, C., 4, 201
Cameron, A. C., 71
Cameron, K. S., 277–278, 279, 281, 292
Campbell, A., 286
Campbell, B. C., 13, 15
Campbell, D. T., 431
Campbell, J. T., 401
Campbell, R. J., 209, 356, 359
Campion, M. A., 234, 362
Canato, A., 76
Cannon, J. P., 335
Cannon-Bowers, J., 173 (table)
Cantor, N. W., 92
Caporael, L. R., 223
Cardon, M. S., 391, 397
Carli, L. L., 17, 209, 224, 244, 247, 251, 258, 259, 264
Carlson, K. D., 427
Carlyle, T., 31, 169
Carmines, E. G., 417
Carnes, M., 263
Carney, D. R., 236, 282
Carroll, B., 112 (table)
Carré, J. M., 230
Carroll, A. B., 473
Carroll, G., 489
Carson, J. B., 43, 123, 176
Carson, K. P., 12
Carson, R., 486
Carsrud, A. L., 396, 398, 402
Carter, D. R., 111, 112 (table), 123
Carter, Jimmy, 445
Cartwright, E., 201
Case, B., 146
Casey, Jim, 392
Caspi, A., 424
Cassidy, R., 403
Castaño, N., 329, 330
Castells, M., 475
Castro, S. L., 127, 334, 416
Catano, V. M., 38
Cavarretta, F. L., 159
Cavazotte, F., 38, 150
Ceranic, T. L., 289
Certo, S. T., 14
Cha, J., 150, 152

Epitropaki, O., 12, 17, 92–95, 97, 109, 112 (table), 113, 114, 116, 122, 127, 128, 129, 202, 204, 231, 386, 389
Epley, N., 92
Erber, R., 284
Erdogan, B., 112 (table), 113, 119, 121, 122, 131
Erez, M., 42, 46, 173 (table)
Erickson, D. J., 64
Erickson, Erik, 454
Ericsson, K. A., 364, 368
Eriksen, M., 112 (table), 124, 125
Eriksson, P., 170
Escriba-Esteve, A., 384
Etcheverry, P. E., 120
Etgen, A. M., 287
Ethiraj, S., 418
Etzion, D., 488
Etzioni, A., 6, 61–62, 275, 277
Eubanks, D. L., 13, 60
Evans, M. G., 145

Fahrbach, S. E., 287
Fairhurst, G., 112 (table), 124, 125
Farb, A. F., 248
Farh, J. L., 150, 330
Farhoomand, A., 403
Farmer, S. M., 390, 398
Farr, M. J., 364
Fast, N. J., 284
Fastow, Andrew, 504
Fausing, M. S., 175, 177
Fehr, E., 278, 288
Fehr, R., 120, 201
Feild, H. S., 416
Feinberg, B. J., 158
Feldman, D. C., 261
Feldman, J., 369
Fellous, J. M., 227
Feltovich, P. J., 364
Fenley, M., 59, 72, 75, 234
Fenters, V., 201
Fernald, L. W. J., 391, 392
Fernandez, C. F., 146
Ferraro, F., 473, 478, 486, 488
Ferreira, D., 252
Ferrin, D. L., 174
Ferris, G. R., 39, 113, 115, 119, 205, 235
Festinger, L., 122, 173 (table), 480
Fetscherin, M., 238
Fetter, R., 67
Feyerherm, A. E., 112 (table)
Feynman, Richard, 509

Fiedler, Fred E., 5, 10, 85, 139, 140, 142, 143, 144, 156, 158, 191
Field, H. S., 114
Field, R. H. G., 8, 15
Fielding, K. S., 304, 306, 311
Figge, F., 483
Figueira, T. J., 169
Fincher, C., 206
Finkelstein, S., 33, 470
Fischbacher, U., 288
Fischer, T., 15, 70, 71, 426
Fischer, W. A., 349
Fisher, B. M., 145
Fisher, N., 466
Fiske, S. T., 86, 222, 223, 284, 292
Fitzsimmons, T. W., 247
Flautt, R., 366
Fleener, B., 153, 158
Fleishman, E. A., 7, 65
Fletcher, G. J. O., 120
Floor, L. G., 9
Floridi, L., 474
Flynn, F. J., 9, 252, 280
Foa, E. B., 113
Foa, U. G., 113
Foley, R. A., 195
Follett, Mary Parker, 121, 171, 172 (table)
Fonda, Henry, 76
Ford, Henry, 272–273, 502
Forrier, A., 249
Fort, T. L., 476
Foster, C., 34n
Foster, E. M., 14
Foti, R. J., 12, 36, 39, 40, 42, 43, 88, 95, 100, 140, 228, 229
Fowler, J. H., 13
Fox, R. L., 248
Frame, M. C., 158
France, J. T., 13
Francis, Pope, 281
Frank, G. H., 173 (table)
Franklin, Benjamin, 413
Franks, N., 196n
Franz, Douglas, 505
Fraser, S. L., 97
Frayne, C. A., 396
Freeman, J. B., 223, 224, 225, 226 (table), 228, 237
Freeman, R. E., 473
Freiberg, S. J., 84, 301
French, J., 6, 143, 275, 277, 279, 281, 287
Frese, M., 70, 72, 367
Frey, D., 177

# Subject Index

Abacha regime (Nigeria), 476

Abusive leaders, 94

*Academy of Management Discoveries* journal, 414

Achievement motivation, 33, 35, 42

Acquaintance phase, in LMX development, 118

Active strategic change management, 367

Adaptive computational rule, 194

*Advancing Relational Leadership Research* (Uhl-Bien and Ospina), 125

Affect, in relational leadership, 128–129

Affect changes to leaders, 283 (table), 284–285

Affective-identity component of motivation, 38

Agent-based models, 200, 203

Age-related changes in leader attributes, 48

Agreeableness, as leadership attribute, 33–35, 44

Alcoholics Anonymous, shared leadership in, 182

Alibaba, 383

Alliance formation, leadership for, 197

Altruism, 452–453. *See also* Ethics

Amazon, Inc., 383, 387

American Association for the Advancement of Science, 505

American Student Government Association, 248

Ancestral and modern environment mismatches, 195, 208

Ancient Greece, charismatic leadership in, 59–61

ANOVA estimation, for research design, 422–423

Antecedents:

entrepreneurial leadership, 393–395

leader behavioral contingency approaches, 146, 149

LMX research, 113–117, 126

power, 278

shared leadership, 174–177

Apple, Inc., 308

Aristotelian triad, 60 (figure)

Assertiveness, gender differences in, 255

*Atlantic, The,* 260

Attachment theory, 120–121

AT&T Management Progress Study, 359

Attributes. *See* Traits and attributes

Attribution theory of charismatic leadership (Conger and Kanungo), 64

Authentic leadership, 68–69, 281

Authentic Leadership Questionnaire, 69

Authoritarian leadership style, 201, 206

Autocratic leaders, democratic leaders *versus,* 9

Autonomy, shared leadership and, 178

Basic leader category, 92

Bass' transformational-transactional leadership model, 66–67

Bathsheba syndrome, 461–462

Behavioral changes to leaders, 283 (table), 285–286

Behavioral contingency models of leadership, 144–146

Behavioral flexibility in leaders, 48

Behavioral leadership instruments, 97

Behavioral maintenance strategies for relationships, 120

Behavioral school of leadership, 8 (figure), 9–10

# About the Editors

**John Antonakis** is professor of organizational behavior in the Faculty of Business and Economics of the University of Lausanne, in Switzerland. Professor Antonakis's research is currently focused on predictors and outcomes of leadership, leadership development, psychometrics, and research methods. He has published articles in prestigious journals including *Science, Psychological Science, Academy of Management Journal, Journal of Applied Psychology, Journal of Management,* and *Harvard Business Review,* among many others. He has been awarded or directed research funds totaling over $2.45 million. Professor Antonakis is editor in chief of *The Leadership Quarterly* and also serves on the editorial boards of many top journals in management and applied psychology. He has twice won *The Leadership Quarterly* award for best article of the year. He is a fellow of the Society of Industrial and Organizational Psychology as well as of the Association for Psychological Science.

**David V. Day** is professor of psychology, Steven L. Eggert '82 P'15 Professor of Leadership, and George R. Roberts Fellow at Claremont McKenna College, in the United States, where he also serves as the academic director of the Kravis Leadership Institute. He is the lead author on *An Integrative Approach to Leader Development* (Routledge, 2009) and the editor of *The Oxford Handbook of Leadership and Organizations* (Oxford University Press, 2014). He served as an associate editor for the *Journal of Applied Psychology* from 2008 to 2014 and is currently the editor of *The Leadership Quarterly Yearly Review.* Day is a fellow of the American Psychological Association, Association for Psychological Science, Society for Industrial and Organizational Psychology, and International Association of Applied Psychology. He is the 2010 recipient of the Walter F. Ulmer Research Award from the Center for Creative Leadership for outstanding, career-long contributions to applied leadership research.

# About the Contributors

**Roya Ayman**, PhD, is professor and the director of the Industrial and Organizational Psychology program, Department of Psychology, of the Lewis College of Human Science, and Illinois Institute of Technology (IIT). She has received awards and honorary positions such as faculty fellow of the leadership Academy at IIT; fellow at Leadership Trust Foundation; and the Dean's leadership award. Among her scholarship, she was the coeditor of books titled *Leadership Theory and Research: Perspectives and Directions* and *The Work-Family Interface in Global Context*. Her main areas of research are leadership and work-family interface considering gender and cultural impact. She is on the editorial boards of *The Leadership Quarterly, Journal of Management and Organization*, and *Journal of Cross-Cultural Management*. As a practitioner, she has served on executive and advisory boards of nonprofit organizations and conducted training on diversity, cross-cultural interaction, leadership development, and leadership in diverse and multicultural settings.

**Warren Bennis** (deceased) was University Professor and Distinguished Professor of Business Administration at the Marshall School and founding chairman of the Leadership Institute at the University of Southern California. He was considered one of the world's leading experts on leadership. A lecturer, consultant, and writer, Professor Bennis was an adviser to four U.S. presidents, including John F. Kennedy and Ronald Reagan. He was the author of numerous books, including the classic *On Becoming a Leader* and *Leaders*, both translated into 21 languages. He cochaired the advisory board of the Center for Public Leadership at Harvard University's Kennedy School of Government. Professor Bennis was a former distinguished research fellow at Harvard Business School, former president of the University of Cincinnati, as well as former provost and executive vice president of SUNY-Buffalo.

**Douglas J. Brown** is a professor of psychology at the University of Waterloo. He received his PhD from the University of Akron. He is coauthor of the book *Leadership Processes and Follower Self-Identity*, and his research has appeared in such outlets as *Organizational Behavior and Human Decision Processes, Academy of Management Journal, Journal of Applied Psychology, Journal of Management, The Leadership Quarterly*, and *The Academy of Management Annals*. He currently serves on various editorial boards, including those for *Academy of Management Journal, Journal of Applied Psychology, Journal of Organizational Behavior*, and *The Leadership Quarterly*. In addition, he is currently an associate editor for *Organizational Behavior* and *Human Decision Processes,* as well as *Organizational Psychology Review*. He is a fellow of the Association for Psychological Science and the Society for Industrial and Organizational Psychology. His current research interests include leadership, self-control, employee well-being, and workplace deviance.

**Linda L. Carli** holds a PhD in social psychology from the University of Massachusetts at Amherst. She taught at the College of the Holy Cross and Mount Holyoke College before joining Wellesley, where she teaches courses in organizational and applied psychology. An authority on social influence, gender discrimination, and the challenges faced by professional women, she coauthored (with Alice Eagly) *Through the Labyrinth: The Truth About How Women Become Leaders* (2007). The book received the 2008 Distinguished Publication Award from the Association of Women in Psychology, and an article based on the book received a McKinsey Award as the second most significant article published in the *Harvard Business Review* in 2007. She has developed and conducted diversity training workshops and negotiation and conflict resolution workshops for women leaders and has lectured widely on gender and diversity for business, academic, and other organizations.

**Joanne B. Ciulla** is professor of leadership ethics and academic director of the Institute for Ethical Leadership at Rutgers Business School. She is also a founding faculty member and Professor Emerita of the Jepson School of Leadership Studies. A philosopher by training, Ciulla has published extensively on business ethics and has dedicated most of her scholarly work to developing the field of leadership ethics. Some of her books include *The Ethics of Leadership; Leadership Ethics, Honest Work: A Business Ethics Reader;* and *Ethics, The Heart of Leadership*. She is on the editorial boards of *The Leadership Quarterly, Leadership, Leadership and the Humanities,* and *The Business Ethics Quarterly,* and she edits the New Horizons in Leadership Studies series. Ciulla is former president of the International Society for Business, Economics, and Ethics and the Society for Business Ethics.

**Michael S. Cole** is associate professor in the Department of Management, Entrepreneurship, and Leadership at Texas Christian University. His professional interests focus on multilevel theories, research, and methodologies as they relate to behavior in organizations. His research has appeared in the *Academy of Management Journal, Journal of Applied Psychology, Journal of Management,* and *Organizational Research Methods,* among others. Michael is also a member of the editorial review boards for *Journal of Applied Psychology* and *Journal of Organizational Behavior,* and he has served as senior associate editor for *The Leadership Quarterly*. He is also a member of the executive leadership team for RM division (2016–2020).

**Deanne N. Den Hartog** is full professor of organizational behavior, head of the Leadership and Management Section, and director of the Amsterdam Business School Research Institute at the University of Amsterdam, in the Netherlands.

Deanne earned her PhD (1997) from the Vrije Universiteit Amsterdam, in the Netherlands. She has held a number of visiting positions in the United States and the United Kingdom, and is currently visiting research professor at the University of Southern Australia. Her research interests include cross-cultural, (un)ethical, and charismatic leadership; dark traits; proactive and innovative work behavior; human resource management; and trust. She has published widely on these topics and serves on several editorial boards.

**Marcus W. Dickson** is professor of organizational psychology and director of both the terminal master's program in I/O and applied research and consulting training in the doctoral program in the Department of Psychology at Wayne State University, in Detroit, Michigan. Marcus's research has focused on issues of cross-cultural leadership (including serving as coprincipal investigator for Project GLOBE for several years) and on organizational climate and culture. A fellow of SIOP, his work has appeared in *The Leadership Quarterly, Journal of Applied Psychology,* and other leading peer-reviewed outlets in the field, as well as in books such as *The Handbook of Organizational Culture and Climate.* He has served or is serving on the editorial boards of several journals, including *The Leadership Quarterly, Journal of Organizational Behavior,* and *Academy of Management: Learning and Education.*

**Samantha Dubrow** received her Bachelor of Arts degree in psychology from The George Washington University in 2014. Since then, she has held positions in marketing and human resources at a Washington, D.C., tech startup, Aquicore. At Aquicore, Samantha has been responsible for sourcing, screening, interviewing, hiring, and onboarding new team members, including several entry-level employees and interns. Currently, Samantha is a second-year doctoral student at George Mason University, studying industrial/organizational psychology under Stephen Zaccaro. She is involved with projects regarding multiteam systems, creativity and innovation, decision making, and social network analysis in science team and emergency response contexts. Samantha has taught undergraduate Statistics and Research Methods in Psychology at George Mason University.

**Alice H. Eagly** is a social psychologist with research interests in many topics, including gender, feminism, attitudes, prejudice, stereotyping, and leadership. She has written more than 200 articles and chapters in edited books. Her books include *Psychology of Attitudes,* written with Shelly Chaiken, and *Through the Labyrinth: The Truth About How Women Become Leaders,* written with Linda Carli. Eagly is professor of psychology and of management and organizations, James Padilla Chair of Arts and Sciences, and faculty fellow in the Institute for Policy Research, all at Northwestern University. She has received several awards, including the Distinguished Scientific Contribution Award from the American Psychological Association, the Gold Medal Award for Life Achievement in the Science of Psychology, and the Eminent Leadership Scholar Award from the Network of Leadership Scholars of the Academy of Management. She is also a member of the American Academy of Arts and Sciences.

**Olga Epitropaki** is professor of management at Durham University Business School, in the United Kingdom. She has research interests in the areas of implicit leadership theories, leader–member exchange (LMX), creative leadership, identity, as well as psychological contracts and employability. Her research has been published in top-refereed journals, such as the *Academy of Management Annals, Journal of Applied Psychology, The Leadership Quarterly, Personnel Psychology, Journal of Organizational Behavior, Journal of Occupational and Organizational Psychology,* and *Personality and Social Psychology Bulletin,* among others. She is senior associate editor of *The Leadership Quarterly,* associate editor of the *British Journal of Management,* and member of several editorial boards. She is also the founder and organizer of the annual Interdisciplinary Perspectives on Leadership Symposium (www.leadership-symposium.com).

**Allison S. Gabriel** is an assistant professor of management and organizations in the Eller College of Management at the University of Arizona. She received her PhD in industrial-organizational psychology from the University of Akron. Her research spans topics related to emotions, motivation, job demands and worker resources, and employee well-being, and she is particularly interested in understanding these phenomena from a within-person perspective with an emphasis on event-level processes. Allison's research has been published in leading outlets such as *Academy of Management Journal, Journal of Applied Psychology, Journal of Organizational Behavior, Organizational Research Methods,* and *Personnel Psychology.*

**Philippe Jacquart** is an associate professor of leadership at EMLYON Business School, in France. He received his doctorate in management from the Faculty of Business and Economics of the University of Lausanne, in Switzerland, and was a postdoctoral researcher at the Wharton School at the University of Pennsylvania. His research focuses on leadership at the upper echelons of organizations. He has published research in academic journals such as *Academy of Management Journal* and *The Leadership Quarterly.* His research has been featured in the press, including the *Financial Times, Forbes, Fox News, The New Yorker, Psychology Today,* and *Al Jazeera America.*

**MaryJo (MJ) Kolze** is a second-year doctoral student in the Industrial-Organizational Psychology program at George Mason University. She received her bachelor's degree with distinction in psychology, with a minor in analytical chemistry, from the Honors College at Missouri State University (MSU), and attended the master's program in I-O psychology at MSU, while completing a 5-year NCAA Division 1 volleyball career. She holds a graduate certificate in research design and analysis, also from MSU. During her graduate studies, MJ worked as an intern at Skyfactor Mapworks, where she analyzed national benchmarking data for various colleges and universities. She has taught courses in cross-cultural psychology, and is involved in research projects regarding leadership, leader development, and systems thinking.

**Joel Koopman** is an assistant professor of management in the Mays Business School at Texas A&M University. He earned his PhD in 2014 from Michigan State

University. His research interests include organizational justice, daily studies of employee well-being, and research methodology. His research has been published in a number of top-tier journals, including *Academy of Management Journal, Journal of Applied Psychology, Journal of Organizational Behavior, Organizational Behavior and Human Decision Processes,* and *Organizational Research Methods.* He serves on the editorial boards of *Journal of Applied Psychology, Journal of Organizational Behavior, Organizational Behavior and Human Decision Processes,* and *Journal of Business and Psychology.*

**Matthew Lauritsen** is currently a doctoral student in industrial and organizational psychology at the Illinois Institute of Technology, where he earned his MS in personnel and human resources development. He is currently employed as the associate director for research at the Center for Corporate Performance at the Stuart School of Business at Illinois Institute of Technology. His current research interests include strategic leadership and diversity in leadership. He is also interested in studying quantitative methods in general and psychometrics in particular. An avid violinist, Matthew regularly performs around the Chicago area as well as with a community orchestra, where he serves as concertmaster.

**Robin Martin** is professor of organisational psychology at Alliance Manchester Business School, University of Manchester, in the United Kingdom. He was previously on the faculties of the Universities of Aston, Queensland, Cardiff, Swansea, Sheffield, and Open. He has held numerous senior roles in these institutions, including executive education co-ordinator (Manchester); Faculty Research Programme director (Aston); director, Centre for Organisational Psychology (Queensland); and assistant director, Applied Behavioural Unit (Swansea). His main research areas are in leadership (especially relationship-based approaches), leadership training and development, team working, and social influence strategies. He has over 120 publications in book chapters and scientific articles. He has extensive experience of designing and delivering leadership training programs to many organizations in various parts of the world.

**Lucas Monzani** is assistant professor in organizational behavior at Ivey Business School in Western Ontario University (Canada). Previously, he was a lecturer in leadership at the Postgraduate School of Management of Plymouth University (United Kingdom). Also, he is an associate researcher at the Institute for Organizational Development and Quality of Work Life of the University of Valencia (Spain) and the Center for Leadership and Behavior in Organizations at Goethe University (Germany). Monzani holds a PhD in psychology of human resources by the University of Valencia and is an Erasmus Mundus Master in Work, Organizational, and Personnel Psychology. After obtaining his PhD, Monzani completed a postdoctoral fellowship at the Ian O. Ihnatowycz Institute for Leadership at the Ivey Business School of Western Ontario University. His research interests involve positive forms of leadership, leaders' commitment, and bridging findings between neuropsychology and organizational behavior.

**Guido Palazzo** is professor of business ethics at the Faculty of Business and Economics at the University of Lausanne. He studied business administration and philosophy at the University of Bamberg (Germany) and received his PhD in political philosophy from the University of Marburg. His current research interests include corporate social responsibility, (un)ethical decision making, organized crime, and social change. His work has been published in the *Academy of Management Review, Academy of Management Journal, Journal of Management Studies, Business Ethics Quarterly,* and other research outlets. He has worked with numerous multinational corporations on ethics-related projects.

**Craig L. Pearce**, PhD (University of Maryland, College Park), is the Ben May Distinguished Professor in the Mitchell College of Business at the University of South Alabama. He is an international management consultant and keynote speaker specializing in executive leadership development; he is also an entrepreneur, having cofounded an agricultural biotechnology company and a real-estate development firm. He pioneered the development of shared leadership theory. His work has appeared in top journals and has spawned scores of doctoral dissertations. He has received widespread acclaim in the practitioner community—including a feature article in the *Wall Street Journal.* He has received many awards for his work, including the Pennsylvania State University Alumni Fellow Award, the Ascendant Scholar Award, the Asia Pacific HR Leadership Award, and an award from the Center for Creative Leadership for his work on shared leadership. His research has been cited more than 9,000 times in scholarly outlets.

**Maija Renko** is an associate professor of entrepreneurship at the University of Illinois at Chicago. She received her DSc. in business administration degree from Turku School of Economics (Finland) in 2006, and a PhD in business administration from Florida International University (United States) in 2008. Maija's research and teaching interests are focused on the early stages of the entrepreneurial process (entrepreneurial motivation, opportunities and nascent entrepreneurship), social entrepreneurship, and technology entrepreneurship. Her research has been published in leading management and entrepreneurship journals, including *Journal of Management, Journal of Business Venturing, Entrepreneurship Theory and Practice, Journal of Small Business Management, International Small Business Journal, Small Business Economics,* and *Academy of Management Discoveries.*

**Christopher C. Rosen** is professor of management in the Sam M. Walton College of Business at the University of Arkansas. Rosen received BA degrees in psychology and economics from Washington and Lee University, his MA degree in industrial/organizational psychology and human resource management from Appalachian State University, and his PhD in industrial/organizational psychology from the University of Akron. His research covers a broad range of topics, including workplace politics, motivation, citizenship behavior, and employee well-being. His research has also focused on methodological questions pertaining to the measurement and modeling of higher-order multidimensional constructs. His research on these topics has appeared in journals such as *Academy of Management Journal, Academy of Management Review, Journal of Applied Psychology, Journal of Management, Organization Science, Organizational Behavior and Human Decision Processes,* and *Personnel Psychology.*

**Nicholas O. Rule** received an AB from Dartmouth College in 2004 and a PhD in psychology from Tufts University in 2010. He was appointed assistant professor and Canada Research Chair in Social Perception and Cognition in the Department of Psychology at the University of Toronto in 2010, and promoted to associate professor with tenure in 2015. His research explores the accuracy and consequences of how people perceive and form impressions of each other and has been supported by various private and public funding sources in the United States and Canada. He has received awards from the Association for Psychological Science, International Social Cognition Network, Foundation for Personality and Social Psychology, International Academy for Intercultural Research, and Ontario Ministry of Research and Innovation, and he presently serves as an associate editor at the *Journal of Experimental Social Psychology* and *Journal of Nonverbal Behavior.*

**Rachel E. Sturm**, PhD, is a tenure-track assistant professor of management and international business at the Raj Soin College of Business, Wright State University. She was awarded the 2016 university-wide Presidential Award for Early Career Achievement for her excellence in research, teaching, and service. Her research interests include leadership, power, virtuousness, self-other agreement, and international management. She teaches leadership development, organizational behavior, and international management, and regularly publishes her research in peer-reviewed journals, such as *Journal of Management, The Leadership Quarterly, Journal of Organizational Behavior,* and *Journal of Business Ethics.* She has also presented numerous papers at professional organizations, including the Academy of Management and the Society for Industrial and Organizational Psychology. She earned her PhD degree in business administration from the University of Houston.

**Geoff Thomas** is professor of organizational psychology at Surrey Business School at the University of Surrey. He served previously on the faculties of the Universities of Aston and Cardiff. His research focus includes leadership (especially leader–member exchange theory) as well as relationship science (relationship cognition, development and maintenance) and judgment accuracy/biases. His research has been published in top-refereed journals, such as *Personnel Psychology, The Leadership Quarterly, Journal of Organizational Behavior, Journal of Occupational and Organizational Psychology, Journal of Personality and Social Psychology, Personality and Social Psychology Review,* and *Personality and Social Psychology Bulletin,* among others.

**Aiden M. A. Thornton** (PhD candidate) is a scholar-practitioner with over 20 years of global experience in leader(ship) development. As a practitioner, he has held multiple senior management roles in which he has been accountable for the strategic direction, design, implementation, and measurement of leader(ship) development initiatives. As a scholar, he is undertaking an interdisciplinary PhD that lies in the intersection of leadership, complex adaptive systems, and cognitive developmental psychology. He is passionate about contributing to the emergence of integrative leadership, which strives to coordinate multiple perspectives on the nature of leadership. All of Aiden's work is focused on the goal of constructing knowledge that may foster requisite levels of leadership to thrive in complex 21st-century conditions.

**Konstantin O. Tskhay** holds a doctoral degree from the University of Toronto (2016); a Master of Arts degree from the University of Toronto (2012); and a Bachelor of Arts degree from the University of California, Riverside (2011). Konstantin's research focuses on how people process information about others and how this information informs their judgments, touching and focusing on person perception, nonverbal behavior, intergroup relations, charisma, and charismatic leadership. He has published in a variety of peer-reviewed research outlets and has received funding from the government of Ontario and the Society for Personality and Social Psychology to conduct research focused on leadership and charisma.

**Daan van Knippenberg** is professor of organizational behavior at the Rotterdam School of Management. His main research interests are in leadership, diversity, teams, and creativity. Daan is editor in chief of *Academy of Management Annals,* was founding editor of *Organizational Psychology Review*, and is associate editor of *Academy of Management Journal, Organizational Behavior and Human Decision Processes,* and *Journal of Organizational Behavior.* He is a fellow of the Society for Industrial and Organizational Psychology and of the American Psychological Association.

**Mark van Vugt** is professor of evolutionary psychology, work, and organizational psychology at the VU Amsterdam, and a research associate at the University of Oxford. He is the author of more than 150 scientific articles, books, and book chapters in which he applies evolutionary perspectives to understand human organizational behavior. He is interested in themes such as leadership, power, status, altruism, cooperation, and intergroup relations. Insights from his research have been applied to various societal challenges involving leadership development, financial risk taking, environmental sustainability, philanthropy, and intergroup conflict. He is author or coauthor of several books, including a trade book (Harper Business) on the evolution of leadership. Mark is on the editorial boards of various journals in psychology. His research has been awarded with multiple grants and prizes.

**Christina L. Wassenaar** is an instructor in the Mitchell College of Business at the University of South Alabama. She is also an international management consultant with expertise in leadership development, corporate strategy, and educational planning. She has taught in the United States and internationally at the undergraduate, graduate, and executive levels in academic and corporate settings. Prior to transitioning to academia and consulting, she spent 11 years in research, marketing, and development for companies including Johnson & Johnson, MGM, ACNielsen, and Verizon. Her primary areas of research focus on shared leadership theory, corporate social responsibility (including questions of irresponsibility), and corruption.

**Stephen J. Zaccaro** is a professor of psychology at George Mason University, in Fairfax, Virginia. He is also an experienced leadership development consultant and a member of the Mason Institute for Leadership Excellence. He has written over 140 journal articles, book chapters, and technical reports on leadership, group dynamics, and work attitudes. He has authored a book titled *The Nature of Executive Leadership: A Conceptual and Empirical Analysis of Success,* and coedited five other books on organizational leadership, leadership development, multiteam systems, psychosocial aspects of cybersecurity, and occupational stress. He serves on the editorial board of *The Leadership Quarterly,* and he is an associate editor for *Journal of Business and Psychology* and *Military Psychology.* He is a fellow of the American Psychological Association, Divisions 14 (Society for Industrial and Organizational Psychology) and 19 (Military Psychology), and the Association for Psychological Science.